P9-DGM-731

The Publisher gratefully acknowledges
the generous contribution provided by the Director's Circle
of the Associates of the University of California Press,
whose members are

JOLA AND JOHN ANDERSON

ELAINE MITCHELL ATTIAS

JUNE AND EARL CHEIT

MARGIT AND LLOYD COTSEN

PHYLLIS K. FRIEDMAN

SUSAN AND AUGUST FRUGÉ

HARRIETT AND RICHARD GOLD

ELLINA AND ORVILLE GOLUB

JANIE AND JEFFREY GREEN

FLORENCE AND LEO HELZEL

JEANNIE AND EDMUND KAUFMAN

LISA SEE AND RICHARD KENDALL

NANCY AND MEAD KIBBEY

YVONNE LENART

LISA SAWYER AND JOHN T. LESCROART

SUSAN AND JAMES MCCLATCHY

HANNAH AND THORMUND A. MILLER

MR. AND MRS. RICHARD C. OTTER

JOAN PALEVSKY

SHIRLEY AND RALPH SHAPIRO

JUDY AND DONALD SIMON

SHARON AND BARCLAY SIMPSON

MAGDA AND FRED WAINGROW

MELINDA MCCARRY WULFF

WALT WHITMAN

Concord, Mass'tts. 21 July
1855.

Dear Sir:

I am not blind to the worth of the wonderful gift of "Leaves of Grass". I find it the most extraordinary piece of wit and wisdom that America has yet contributed. I am very happy in reading it as great power makes us happy. It meets the demand I am always making of what seemed the sterile and stingy Nature, as if too much handiwork or too much lymph in the temperament were making our western wits fat and mean.

I give you joy of your free & brave thought. I have great joy in it. I find incomparable things said incomparably well, as they must be. I find the courage of treatment which so delights us, and which large perception only can inspire.

I greet you at the beginning of a great career, which yet must have had a large foreground somewhere, for such a start. I rubbed my eyes a little to see if this sunbeam were no illusion; but the solid sense of the book is a sober certainty. It has the best merits, namely, of fortifying & encouraging.

I did not know until I last night saw the book advertised in a newspaper that I could trust the name as real & available for a post office. I wish to see my benefactor & have felt much like striking my tasks, & visiting New York to pay you my respects.

Walt Whitman } R. W. Emerson.

The famous Emerson letter in Whitman's hand. Columbia University Library.

WALT WHITMAN

THE SONG OF HIMSELF

Jerome Loving

UNIVERSITY OF CALIFORNIA PRESS

BERKELEY LOS ANGELES LONDON

University of California Press
Berkeley and Los Angeles, California

University of California Press, Ltd.
London, England

Library of Congress Cataloging-in-Publication Data

Loving, Jerome, 1941–
Walt Whitman : the song of himself / Jerome Loving.
p. cm.
Includes bibliographical references (p.) and index.
ISBN 0-520-21427-7 (alk. paper)
1. Whitman, Walt, 1819–1892. 2. Poets, American—19th century—Biography. I. Title.
PS3231.L68 1999
811′.3—dc21
[B] 98-29647
CIP

Printed in the United States of America
9 8 7 6 5 4 3 2 1

The paper used in this publication meets the minimum requirements of American National Standards for Information Sciences—Permanence of Paper for Printed Library Materials, ANSI Z39.48-1984.

To My Family
and
To the Memory
of
Charles Gordône

❧ ❧ ❧

Whitman
is so hard to grasp,
to put in a statement.
One cannot get to the bottom of him . . .
he is bottomed in Nature,
in democracy, in science,
in personality.

JOHN BURROUGHS

❋ ❋ ❋

Whitman
is so hard to grasp,
to put in a statement.
One cannot get to the bottom of him . . .
he is bottomed in Nature,
in democracy, in science,
in personality.

JOHN BURROUGHS

CONTENTS

Illustrations follow pages 208 and 368.

PREFACE

During Walt Whitman's lifetime, his poetry was generally reviled, condemned by reviewers as obscene in content, deficient in diction, irregular in rhythm, and absent of rhyme. In a final review of *Leaves of Grass* published on March 28, 1892, in the same issue that carried the poet's obituary, the *New York Times* declared that Whitman could not be called "a great poet unless we deny poetry to be an art." Today the *Times*—reflecting the opinion of literate America and the rest of the world—would probably consider Whitman the inventor of modern American poetry. The author of six ever-expanding editions of *Leaves of Grass,* he is now known as the "Poet of Democracy," who introduced freer, speechlike rhythms into the poetry of fixed verse and replaced its themes of New England villages and sentimental love with songs about occupations and sexuality.

Between the first (1855) edition of *Leaves of Grass* and the last in 1881, and in the poems that made up the two Annexes in 1888 and 1891, Whitman experimented with the American vernacular as it enclosed and showcased the American experience directly before, during, and after the Civil War. Having written conventional poetry in the 1840s, he finally broke into free verse to celebrate not merely "Mother Nature" but his own nature as representative of all humankind in its endless variety. In doing so, he put on record a personality that has enthralled readers and influenced almost every major poet of the twentieth century—from Ezra Pound to Galway Kinnell. From the very beginning, William Carlos Williams observed in the centenary year of the first *Leaves,* Whitman's book "enunciated a shocking truth, that the common ground is of itself a poetic source." Or as Whitman wrote in "Song of Myself" (capitalizing the pronoun to invoke a spiritual identity): "What is commonest, cheapest, nearest, easiest, is Me."

Since 1883 there have been approximately fifteen formal biographies of America's most comprehensive poet. The first Whitman practically wrote himself when he "critiqued" Richard Maurice Bucke's draft of *Walt Whitman.* Three were written by Frenchmen, another three by Englishmen, and one by a Canadian. Another, by Emory Holloway, won the Pulitzer Prize in 1926. The standard biography, no longer in print, is *The Solitary Singer: A Critical Biography of Walt Whitman* by Gay Wilson Allen. Published more than forty years ago, it has become out of date because of manuscript discoveries and recent scholarship. In fact, the current post–New Critical approaches suggest that when Whitman created the body of poetry that so dramatically and irrevocably changed the American literary landscape, he was not so "solitary" (culturally speaking) as had been assumed. Three important biographies have appeared since Allen's: Justin Kaplan's *Walt Whitman: A Life* (1980); Paul Zweig's *Walt Whitman: The Making of a Poet* (1984); and David S. Reynolds's *Walt Whitman's America: A Cultural Biography* (1995). All three make unique contributions to our appreciation of the poet, yet none of them goes significantly beyond the basic facts of the life as established in *The Solitary Singer.*

Inspired by Whitman centennial celebrations around the world in 1992, I set out to build on my own Whitman studies of the previous twenty years by writing a new critical biography based in part on previously unknown archival evidence and informed by the last forty years of scholarship. One of Whitman's earlier biographers wrote that the chronicler of the life of this poet had to be wealthy because of all the travel necessary for consulting manuscripts in private hands, but today, with most of Whitman's papers gathered in the Library of Congress and other major university archives, that biographer has now only to be rich in friends who know Whitman biography and its vast scholarship intimately. I was fortunate to have several of these benefactors. Ed Folsom, editor of the

Walt Whitman Quarterly Review and author of several books on Whitman, read my chapters as they were turned out and offered invaluable advice. Reading along with Folsom was Roger Asselineau of the Sorbonne, the author of *The Evolution of Walt Whitman,* published more than thirty years ago, as well as countless articles on the poet. I am deeply indebted to Professors Folsom and Asselineau for their generosity in this and other projects. A third giant of Whitman studies who assisted me is Edwin Haviland Miller, who—among many other impressive scholarly achievements—has impeccably edited the *Correspondence of Walt Whitman.* Professor Miller, always helpful with advice, also read my manuscript and made available several rare Whitman volumes from his library. And one other person loomed large in my first circle of advisors: Robert D. Richardson, Jr., who has written celebrated biographies about two of Whitman's closest compatriots in making literature fit for a democracy, Ralph Waldo Emerson and Henry David Thoreau.

Many others known for their work on Whitman also helped. Martin G. Murray and M. Wynn Thomas critiqued the chapters on the Civil War. I am in debt to Joel Myerson, not only for loaning me his microfilm collection of the Whitman papers at the Library of Congress but for his excellent descriptive bibliography of the poet. Alice Lotvin Birney of the Manuscript Division helped me get to the Whitman collections at the Library of Congress that were not available on microfilm. This biography probably could not have been written in Texas without the primary textual and manuscript resources of the Harry Ransom Humanities Research Center at the University of Texas at Austin. For years of friendly assistance there I thank Jake Baxter, Ken Craven, and Pat Fox as well as its director, Thomas F. Staley, and curator John Kirkpatrick. Virginia L. Close of the Dartmouth College Library helped me find new evidence about Whitman's visit to the college in 1872. Others who assisted in one way or another are Dennis Berthold, Louis J. Budd, Jennifer Chenoweth, William Bedford Clark, James M. and Marguerite Cox, Sonja Geerling, M.D., Claude Gibson, Sally Wofford Girand, Arthur Golden, Terence Hoagwood, William Innes Homer, Young Min Hyun, Justin Kaplan, M. Jimmie Killingsworth, Joann P. Krieg, Clinton Machann, John J. McDermott, Kathleen McGinn, the late DeWolfe Miller, J. Lawrence Mitchell, Dan Osterman, Geneva Phillips,

Angel Price, Kenneth M. Price, David S. Reynolds, Paul Salveson, Emily Sturgess, Joan Templeton, Paul Van Riper, Marion Alcaro Walker, and James L. W. West III. Much more "long-distance" research was conducted through the office of Inter-Library Services of the Sterling C. Evans Library at Texas A&M University, where I would like to thank Cathy Jackson and Margaret Hassel. I was also assisted at my university with a College of Liberal Arts faculty development leave in 1995 and English Department support in the way of supplies and clerical support. I would also like to thank the Henry E. Huntington Library for a Mayer Fund Fellowship in the summer of 1994.

At the University of California Press, I would like to thank Stanley Holwitz, associate director and acquisitions editor, and my editors Scott Norton and Betsey Scheiner.

One special person to thank is the late Charles Gordône, author of the play *No Place to Be Somebody* (to whose memory this book is partly dedicated). He occupied the office next to mine during most of the research and writing of this book, and I shared with him many of my discoveries and tried out many passages on him. It was the closest thing to having Whitman himself at my side as I read and wrote. Two others not to be forgotten are the late Clarence Gohdes, who formally introduced me to Whitman almost thirty years ago at Duke University, and the late Gay Wilson Allen, the "dean" of Whitman studies and an early mentor of mine, who was always generous with his knowledge of the poet. I am also grateful to Elaine E. Warner of the Texaco-Metropolitan Opera for making available the text of Father Owen Lee's stirring Radio Intermission paper on Whitman and opera.

Working on a New York poet while living in the great state of Texas can be expensive, but my sister Mary Loving always had room for me at her West Side apartment when I required a week or so at the New York Public Library. Thanks, too, are certainly in order to my grown children, my son, David, and my daughter, Cameron, who "grew up" on Whitman—and to their spouses, Patricia Sandoval and Donald House, Jr., who I hope will now share that legacy with my grandchildren (represented to date only by Amanda). The first one to thank, always last in such exercises, is my lifelong inspirer and wife, Cathleen Creighton Loving.

I

CARESSER OF LIFE

❋ ❋ ❋

> These Hospitals, so different from all others—these thousands, and tens and twenties of thousands of American young men, badly wounded . . . open a new world somehow to me, giving closer insights, new things, exploring deeper mines than any yet.
>
> WALT WHITMAN
>
> *to Nathaniel Bloom and John F. S. Gray, March 19, 1863*

Toward the end of 1862 Walt Whitman traveled to war-torn Virginia in search of his brother, George. The poet stepped off the train at Falmouth Station, near Fredericksburg, and climbed a hill overlooking the Rappahannock River and the previous week's battle site. One of the first scenes that grimly welcomed him, he told his mother on December 29, "was a heap of feet, arms, legs, &c. under a tree in front of a hospital."[1] After finding George at his encampment and spending the next day with him and his regimental comrades ("Capt. Sims, Lieut. Frank Butler, Orderly McReady . . . all used me well"), he began to visit the wounded of the Army of the Potomac. In his notebook he wrote of seeing "the hard accommodations and experiences of campaign life—the shelter tents—the improvised fireplaces in holes in the ground, with small subterranean passages and small mud chimneys, lengthened out by a barrel with both ends knocked out." Near the Lacy House, the major hospital receiving the worst cases (he recalled in 1875 in *Memoranda During the War*), several bodies lay covered only by a "brown woolen blanket. In the door-yard, towards the river, are fresh graves, mostly of officers, their names on pieces of barrel-staves or broken boards, stuck in the dirt." In the subsequent week, such sights wore even harder on the poet:

> The results of the late battle are exhibited everywhere about here in thousands of cases, (hundreds die every day,) in the camp, brigade, and division hospitals. These are merely tents, and sometimes very poor ones, the wounded lying on the ground, lucky if their blankets are spread on layers of pine or hemlock twigs, or small leaves. . . . The ground is frozen hard, and there is occasional snow. I go around from one case to another. I do not see that I do much good to these wounded and dying; but I cannot leave them. Once in a while some youngster holds on to me convulsively, and I do what I can for him.

One day Whitman followed a burial party down to the river under a flag of truce. He made friends not only among the Fifty-First and the wounded in the other Union regiments but also with Confederate soldiers who had been taken prisoner. One of the Fifty-First from Brooklyn, where Whitman had known him as a lad, was lying on the cold ground, "all bloody, just after the arm was taken off." Another was a nineteen-year-old captain from Mississippi, whom he found at the Lacy House shortly after the young officer's leg was amputated. He was subsequently transferred to Emory Hospital in Washington, where Whitman visited him frequently. "Poor boy," he told friends back in Brooklyn. "He has suffered a great deal, and still suffers—has eyes as bright as a hawk, but face pale—our affection is quite an affair, quite romantic—sometimes when I lean over to say I am going, he puts his arm round my neck, draws my face down, &c."[2]

Although Whitman was slow to engage emotionally in the war effort, these kinds of experiences made it impossible for him ever to retreat from it again. For the poet the Civil War became a marriage ceremony of sorts—between him and his country—and his poignant wartime poems in *Drum-Taps* (1865) a betrothal and a spiritual renewal. Earlier—in "Song of Myself"—Whitman had portrayed himself as a bachelor before the American democracy, "of Manhattan the son, / Turbulent, fleshy, sensual, eating, drinking and breeding." This prewar self was representative of the American people, in the best tradition of Ralph Waldo Emerson (where the artist descends into the minds of everyone when he thinks for himself), but it also represented the egotist that found "no sweeter fat than sticks to my own bones."

With the war the self-styled "caresser of life" became more of a democrat and less of a "kosmos."

In 1861 the war began, as southern state after state seceded. These actions and their blow to democracy no doubt suggested the idea of a private secession to the Poet of Democracy. The man who would come to be known as the "wound dresser" stayed away from the conflict for almost two years. He had written some poems about loneliness and the need for companions in "Out of the Cradle Endlessly Rocking" and the "Calamus" series, and this mood prevailed amid the hubbub of the war. Shortly after the firing on Fort Sumter, he wrote a few upbeat poems about the war—recruiting poems, it seemed, that may have inspired enlistments when they appeared in the newspapers. In fact, exactly a week after the firing on Fort Sumter on April 12, 1861, George Washington Whitman—one of the poet's five brothers—enlisted as a hundred-days' soldier in the Thirteenth Regiment of the New York State Militia. In September of that year he reenlisted, this time in the Fifty-First Regiment of New York Volunteers. Shortly afterward, on May 28, 1862, another brother, Andrew Jackson Whitman, became a three-months' soldier in the Union cause, which seemed to worsen by the battle.[3]

The first two years of the Civil War are among the most obscure in the record of Whitman's life, second only to large patches of the famous "foreground" Emerson suspected when he first read *Leaves of Grass* in 1855. Whitman fairly disappears from all biographies between May 24, 1860, when he took the new Shore Line Railroad back from Boston after seeing the third edition of *Leaves of Grass* through the press, to December 16, 1862, when the Whitman household at 122 Portland Street, near Myrtle Avenue in Brooklyn, got its first indication that brother George had been wounded at the Battle of Fredericksburg.[4] At thirty-six, when Walt Whitman published the first *Leaves of Grass,* he looked his age. Seven years later, at forty-three, he looked fifty-three. Yet the same liquid eyes look out from Matthew Brady's photograph of 1863 as they do from the frontispiece in the first edition, their stare penetrating, as if to say—as Whitman does in "Song of Myself"—"I see through the broadcloth and gingham whether or no." His X-ray vision in poetry had gotten him in a lot of trouble in the interim, especially after the third edition and the "Children of Adam" poems, which bluntly describe the sexual magnetism between a man and a woman. A phrenological exam made in 1849—when the pseudoscience of gauging character by measuring cranial bumps was popular—had declared this six-foot, two-hundred-pound, still somewhat firmly apportioned male to be "voluptuous." By 1860 he was fulfilling the prophecy—if perhaps only vicariously and in the poems.

Whitman's disappearance may have been part of a pattern, begun in 1848 after the initial failure of his Free-Soil newspaper, *The Freeman,* and repeated in 1855, when he spent the summer in the fishing and whaling village of Greenport, at the northeastern end of Long Island, after publishing his first book of poetry.[5] With the third edition of *Leaves of Grass,* instead of getting out of town to watch the literary fireworks, he dropped out of sight—at least as far as his future biographers were concerned. The disappearance may have been as much personal as political. The poems of the 1860 edition—"Children of Adam," "Calamus," "Out of the Cradle Endlessly Rocking," "As I Ebb'd with the Ocean of Life"—suggest that the late 1850s were "the darkest years of his life."[6] And the celebrative "Starting from Paumanok," written earlier than these poems, seems to force its optimism upon the matter, even in its final revision.

> Starting from fish-shape Paumanok where I was born,
> Well-begotten, and rais'd by a perfect mother,
> After roaming many lands, lover of populous pavements,
> . . . .
> . . . I strike up for a New World.

"Take my leaves America," he said in the poem, and in the context of his controversial literary career after 1855, the phrase seems almost a supplication. Here he resembles his mentor Emerson. At the close of "The Poet" (published in 1844)—the very essay that inspired Whitman as a young journalist when he heard it delivered as a lecture in 1842 in New York City—Emerson exhorted American poets to "doubt not . . . but persist. . . . Stand there, balked and dumb, stuttering and stammering, hissed and hooted."[7] Emerson himself may have felt "balked and dumb" by 1842—recently stunned by the sudden death of his five-year-old son and soon to pen his essay "Experience," which tempered the optimism of his earlier work. Certainly, Whitman was "hissed and hooted" for the latest expansion of his poetic vision. In the *Saturday Press,* perhaps the forerunner of *The New Yorker, Leaves of Grass* received a thrashing review that advised its author to commit suicide.[8] By June of 1861, when he returned to newspaper work with the "Brooklyniana" series, his third edition was already lost in the steadily increasing mayhem of the war. Unable to collect revenues from their Southern clients, his publishers had gone bankrupt. Better to secede himself for a time.

"Brooklyniana," a series of twenty-five pieces in the *Brooklyn Standard* between June 1861 and November 1862, turned back the clock, looking journalistically at the history of Long Island. The island, which stretched out 120 miles from Brooklyn to Montauk, was once the home of the "royal tribe" of old Wyandanch. "This chief," Whitman had written in the *Brooklyn Daily Eagle* of September 20, 1847, "held a position not unlike our American president." Long Island had been originally the home of thirteen distinct Indian tribes, where "the Indian inhabitants . . . numbered a million and a half." Realizing this figure might be an exaggeration, he nevertheless insisted that the "red race" had been very numerous, "as evidenced by many tokens." Taking up perhaps for the first time a theme that would become the title of his lifelong book, Whitman quoted an "ancient Indian" who "declared to one of the earliest inhabitants of Easthampton, that within his recollection the natives were *as many as the spears of grass.*"[9]

In the series Whitman quickly established the original superiority of Brooklyn to Manhattan. Manhattan, he wrote in No. 1, had been selected by Dutch settlers mainly "as an outpost or place for a trading station, a store and fort—and not for residences." Because of its sand and rock foundation, the employees of the West Indian Company had settled instead "on the aboriginal island of Paumanock" (or *Paumanake,* as it sometimes appeared in old Indian deeds).[10] Also spelled "Paumanack," the American Indian name for Long Island meant "fish-shaped." In No. 13 of the series, Whitman half in jest suggested changing the island's name back to Paumanok, as it might "be a kind of poetic justice to the departed tribes of the great nation of Lenni-Lapape, or Delawares, of which stock the aborigines of this region were a part." By the Civil War, this Indian nation had largely disappeared from the island and, indeed, from most of the East as a result of the American Policy of Removal. In Brooklyn and King's County the native residents had been the Canarsees, who—Whitman correctly guessed—had been extinct since 1800. "Now that they have all forever departed," he told a readership then preoccupied with war, "it seems as if their shades deserve at least the poor recompense of the compliment connected in preserving the old name by which they themselves designated and knew this territory."[11]

Although the poet is today identified as much with Manhattan and Broadway as he is with Brooklyn and Long Island, his loyalty in 1861 was to the east—to the whole of Long Island and "The *State of* PAUMANOK!" Yet as recently as 1857, in "Broadway, the Magnificent!" Whitman had sung of Manhattan with the brilliance he'd put into the first two editions of *Leaves of Grass.* "Broadway!" he exclaimed in *Life Illustrated,* an upscale literary magazine published by his phrenologist friends Fowler and Wells, "that ever-flowing land-river, pouring down through the center of Manhattan Island!" The implicit comparison of New York's most famous avenue with the mighty Mississippi, which he celebrated in writings connected with his visit to New Orleans in 1848, was well won: the river that ran through the heart of America had exchanged its muddy banks for "granite blocks,—its side-banks of marble, iron, plate-glass, brick, and wood." In 1857 Whitman was still upbeat about his chances as a poet and about the nation with poetry in its veins that he celebrated. Manhattan, or "Mannahatta" as he called it, borrowing another Indian name, was the greatest city in the great nation, and Broadway was the city's most brilliant symbol, its delights perfect filler for the poet's long catalogs.

This land-river ran continually between its banks, "ebbing and flowing with American men, women, and with strangers. There they pass, a hundred thousand a day,—sometimes two hundred thousand." In pointing out the historic spots from the Battery upward, Whitman mentioned the "Negro Plot" of 1741 in which "eighty-three persons, mostly blacks, were either burnt at the stake, hanged, transported, or sold into slavery for a conspiracy to destroy the city." One of the stakes where blacks were burnt, he noted, was at the intersection of Wall Street: "You who come down town to business in the morning! you little think of the horrid spectacle that corner more than once exhibited! the iron pillar—the chains—the fagots of dry wood and straw—the African negro in the middle—the pile touched off—the yells and howls and agonized shrieks—the crowd around stolid and indifferent."[12] Whitman was writing after the bloody incidents in Kansas over the proposed extension of slavery into the new territories, and like his fellow New Yorker Herman Melville (in "Benito Cereno," published in 1856), he was warning of the coming national storm over the old question of slavery in the New World.

❊ ❊ ❊

At the time when Whitman was writing the "Brooklyniana" series, he had returned to the tranquillity of Greenport. The last stop on the Long Island Railroad, the old whaling village was the home of the poet's sister, Mary Elizabeth, who, more than twenty years before, had at the age of eighteen married Ansel Van Nostrand. The couple's five children are the only source of the Whitman family's descendants today. Like many of the men in his wife's family, Van Nostrand was a shipyard worker; he was also an alcoholic, whose regular binges gave Walt another reason to visit the elder of his two sisters. Since 1855, when his father died at age sixty-five, Whitman had been the family "patriarch," although "troubleshooter" is perhaps a more accurate characterization. He also attended to the problems of his other married sister, a hypochondriac caught up in a bad marriage to a New England landscape artist, as well as those of an older brother with mental deterioration, resulting from a shipboard accident, and a probable case of syphilis, another brother beset by alcoholism and tuberculosis, and a third mentally and physically handicapped.

Whitman made his latest visit to Greenport and vicinity, as he recalled in "Brooklyniana" Nos. 37–39, during the fall of 1861. While the poet fished off the town dock, a party of lively girls, "conveyed by a clerical looking personage, and one or two younger fellows," invited him to join them on a pleasure cruise out to Montauk Point. "It was a very pleasant and sensible party," he told his Brooklyn readers; "the girls were unaffected . . . and the minister laughed and told stories and ate luncheons, just like a common man, which is quite remarkable for a country clergyman." The poet who had in the 1860 edition of *Leaves of Grass* confessed to the "need of comrades" here reveled in the company of young ladies. He enjoyed the group's merry stories and riddles as it sailed out of Greenport "at a stiff rate," passing Gardiner's Island ("the first English settlement ever made in the present limits of the state of New York") on its way to the Montauk peninsula and the reserved home of what relatively few American Indians still remained on the tip of Long Island.

"Montauk Point!" he exclaimed in No. 38. "How few Americans there are who have not heard of thee—although there are equally few who have seen thee with their bodily eyes, or trodden on thy greensward." Once ashore, the party "took a long ramble to and fro," declaiming what they remembered to be lines from Shakespeare's *Richard III.* Intoxicated with the wilds of Long Island's easternmost tip, they "pranced forth" and threw their hats in the air, "aimed stones at the shrieking sea-gulls, mocked the wind, and imitated the cries of various animals in a style that beat nature all out!" After cooking dinner aboard their moored sloop, they found that nightfall prevented their safe return and spent the night onboard, returning to Greenport the next morning. In recalling the trip, Whitman blessed his "lucky star," he said, "merely to sail—to bend over and look at the ripples as the prow divided the water—to lie on my back and *to breathe and live* in that sweet air and clear sunlight—to hear the musical chatter of the girls, as they pursued their own glee—was happiness enough for one day."

It may bother some to think that this poet of the people was enjoying himself while his country—as well as his own brothers—was engaged in a bloody civil war. The Montauk outing, in fact, was a solitary voyage of the imagination—a verbatim account for the most part of an essay published under the pen-name of "Paumanok," in 1849.[13] Nevertheless, Whitman appears at this point almost untouched by the conflict. He had, of course, already written those recruiting poems—"First O Songs for a Prelude," "Eighteen Sixty-One," and "Beat! Beat! Drums!"—which he would collect in *Drum-Taps.* But they reflected the North's initial excitement about the war, which was expected to be over after one or two decisive northern victories. By the time he wrote of "loafing" out at Greenport and Montauk, the national mood had changed to bewilderment and impatience, many protesting that President Lincoln was too rigid with the seceding states. It was becoming more likely that a long and deadly conflict lay ahead.

Even Lincoln's Preliminary Proclamation to the emancipation of African slaves, which gave the rebellious states until New Year's Day 1863 to return to the Union or lose their slaves, failed to deter the South from its course of action. Brother George, who had just survived the Battle of Antietam (September 17, 1862), wondered why "Uncle Abe has issued a proclamation declaring the slaves free in all the States that are in rebellion." At the same time, southern or border states that had not rebelled could keep their slaves, as Lincoln, in the Emancipation Proclamation of January 1, 1863, was to free slaves in every place except where he had the actual authority to do so. "I don't know what effect it is going to have on the war," George told Walt, "but one thing is certain, he has got to lick the south before he can free the niggers, and unless he drives ahead and convinces the south, before the first of January, that we are bound to lick them, and it would be better for them to behave themselves and keep their slaves, than to get licked and lose them. I don't think the proclamation will do much good."[14]

George's disregard for the slavery question may reflect the "New York feeling" that had kept the Empire State politically "neutral" on the issue ever since the signing of the Declaration of Independence, but the North as a whole—as Lincoln's presidential ploy suggests—was more committed to the integrity of the nation than it was to the abolition of slavery. Even when the Emancipation Proclamation was signed, it did not include slaves in the loyal slave states—Tennessee and those parts of Virginia and Louisiana under northern control.[15] Whitman, himself a pronounced anti-slavery person (though "free-soil" rather than the more radical "abolitionist"), was at least ambivalent about the place of black Americans in a society of snow-white "divine average," and it would take something more direct and dramatic to take his attention away from long-ago Paumanok or present-day Manhattan. In addition to writing the "Brooklyniana" series, between March and May 1862 he also contributed seven pieces entitled "City Photographs" to the *New York Leader.* The "Brooklyniana" pieces were anonymous, and the poet continued to keep his identity quiet in "City Photographs" by using the pseudonym "Velsor Brush," joining the maiden surnames of his maternal and paternal grandmothers.[16] Whitman has been called a "hack writer" as a journalist, a label that is probably unfair when we compare his work to what was passing for journalism (and "hack" journalism) in the era of two-penny political presses. But "Brooklyniana"—with a few startling exceptions—tends to reinforce the label with its cribbing from local histories.

The same is true of "City Photographs." It is as if Whitman were somewhere else, back in the 1840s as editor of the *New York Aurora* or the *Brooklyn Daily Eagle,* as he mixed statistics about the Broadway Hospital and its administrators with observations of the humanity that thrived and faltered in spite of the status quo. His descriptions of the hospital, and of the Bowery in other articles as well, come alive when he talks directly about the people involved, and we can understand how readily Whitman took up his famous hospital work once he moved to Washington, D.C., in 1863. Seeing (and listing for his readers, just as he had cataloged humanity in *Leaves of Grass*) every patient from the amputee to the sufferer of delirium tremens, "Velsor Brush" exclaimed in the editorial of March 15: "What a volume of meaning, what a tragic poem there is in every one of those sick wards! Yes, in every individual cot, with its little card-rack nailed at the head."[17] The future "wound dresser" and "good gray nurse" was already ministering to the sick and wounded—among them relatively few soldiers and mainly stage drivers recuperating from broken collarbones, arms, or legs acquired in collisions on the cobblestoned and congested Broadway. These teamsters were the poet's first "soldiers" and his introduction to hospital work. In "Broadway, the Magnificent!" he had described the avenue as alive with omnibuses: "The drivers, on their boxes, sharply look out for passengers, interrogating all with crooked thumb." In the first *Leaves* he wrote: "The heavy omnibus, the driver with his interrogating thumb, the clank of the shod horses on the granite floor."

"I have spent," he wrote in the *Leader* of April 12, "two or three Sunday afternoons, of late in going around among these sick soldiers, just to help cheer and change a little the monotony of their sickness and confinement." Although Whitman took an active part in assisting physicians in the war (his narrator in *Drum-Taps* assists in amputations), much of his talent as "nurse" probably lay in the area of psychology, in engaging the former farmboys and city laborers as "dear friends" instead of patients. In a mood that anticipated the positive "joy" of the intense comradeship of his Washington nursing experiences, he remembered, on the first anniversary of Fort Sumter, one Sunday evening in a veterans' ward of the Broadway Hospital. It was "one of the most agreeable evenings of my life amid such a group of seven convalescent young soldiers from a Maine regiment. We drew around together, on our chairs, in the dimly-lighted room, and after interchanging the few magnetic remarks that show people it is well for them to be together, they told me stories of country life and adventures, &c., away up there in the Northeast."[18]

Whitman was still biding his time, now in the company of real rather than imaginary friends, but he was also edging closer to the war. Or the war was getting closer to him. From Newbern, North Carolina, George, recently promoted from the ranks to second lieutenant, reported on confiscated Confederate stationery that General Ambrose E. Burnside's Ninth Army had "given the Secesshers another thundering, thrashing, and have gained a splendid victory."[19] Andrew, too, was getting closer to the war. Plagued by a tubercular cough, which finally took his life in 1863, and by an emotionally unstable wife, who joined the ranks of Brooklyn's wartime streetwalkers after her husband's death, Andrew probably sought out military life because he could not get steady work at the Brooklyn shipyard. When Lincoln called for more troops after Stonewall Jackson's successful Shenandoah Valley Campaign, George's old state militia reappeared with a fresh lot of recruits, Andrew among them. Walt Whitman may have started to hear the drums and bugles that he reproduced in "Beat! Beat! Drums!"

and "First O Songs for a Prelude." In the latter, the drums produce "a shock electric" that prompts the mechanic, the lawyer, the wagon driver, and the salesman to enlist ("Squads gather everywhere by common consent and arm").

But still the poet was slow to commit himself. Near the end of Whitman's life, Thomas Wentworth Higginson, himself a wounded veteran, accused the poet of purposely avoiding military service in the war.[20] At forty-three, however, Whitman was already too old for the rigors of combat and campside living (he recalled after the war that his brother George had traveled over 20,000 miles, marched across fifteen states, and "taken a hand in nearly all the historic campaigns of the war"). And even though he is alleged to have thrown a pro-slavery Democrat down the stairs of the *Brooklyn Eagle* office in the 1840s, Whitman was probably not inclined to combat, although in a wartime publication he hinted otherwise.[21] If Whitman was to participate in the war, he needed to find another role.

The poet's lack of focus on wartime matters also reflected the North's confusion during the first eighteen months of the war. In spite of major battles at Bull Run, the North Carolina peninsula, Cedar Mountain, and Antietam, nothing was getting settled. In this respect, the Union experience resembled the American one in Vietnam little more than a century later, where villages captured or hills successfully defended at the cost of many lives lost their relevance as quickly as the newspaper headlines that publicized them. In both cases, it was the superior force that had to invade the enemy's territory. At the outset of the American civil war (as throughout the Vietnam conflict), the morale of that enemy was higher because it believed it was fighting a war for independence. In addition, Whitman's inattention may have reflected a widespread support for Confederate sentiment—as George's comment about the impending Emancipation Proclamation documents—which was strong in the state and city of New York as well as in the North generally.[22] Whitman was more pro-Union than he was anti-slavery and favored with Lincoln the recolonization of Africans—though for Whitman the "colony" could have been located in the United States. The poet began to shift his thoughts from Montauk and Broadway to Washington and Richmond only after repeated losses by Union troops made it clear that the war would be long and indeed even suggested that the Union might well be cut in two.

Closer to home and the more immediate reason for Whitman's interest in the war was a report in the *New York Herald* of December 16, 1862, that a "First Lieutenant G. W. Whitmore" was among the 13,000 Federal troops either killed or wounded under the misguided efforts of Burnside, Lincoln's latest supreme commander, to engage Confederate forces at Fredericksburg, Virginia. George, meticulously considerate throughout the war of his family's fears back in Brooklyn, had been careful not to report himself among the wounded, but when his regimental commander, Colonel Robert B. Potter, noticed the "scratch" on George's cheek, he added Whitman's name to the list. From George's letters the family knew the names of all the officers in the Fifty-First and guessed correctly that "Whitmore" was a misprint for "Whitman," confirmed the next day in the *New York Times* ("Lieut. Whitman, Co. E, 51st New York—cheek"). To defuse the panicky state of his Brooklyn household, Walt left New York the same day, but not before securing letters of introduction from the former and current mayors of Brooklyn in the event he might have to relocate in order to nurse George in one of Washington's more than forty hospitals, where he expected to find him.[23] Whitman went by ferry to New Jersey and by train to Philadelphia, where he had his pocket picked while changing trains for Washington. After arriving in the capital penniless and spending a day searching the hospitals for his wounded brother, he met Charles W. Eldridge, who had been one of the Boston publishers of the third edition of *Leaves of Grass* in 1860 and was now employed in the Army Paymaster's Office. He also found William Douglas O'Connor, another new government employee, in the Office of the Light-House Board of the Treasury Department. O'Connor's antislavery novel *Harrington* had been published by the same Boston house in 1860, and the two first met in its offices. With Eldridge's and possibly O'Connor's help Whitman secured a military pass and went by barge down the Potomac River to Aquia Creek and then by train to Falmouth, arriving on December 19. There the Ninth Army, under the command of

Orlando B. Willcox following Burnside's promotion to commander of the Union forces, was encamped after the battle.

For all the Whitmans back on Portland Avenue knew, George was seriously wounded or even dead by this time. Living with the widowed Louisa Van Velsor Whitman were, along with Walt, his brother Jeff and his wife, Martha Mitchell Whitman ("Mattie"), their young daughter, Mannahatta ("Hattie"), and the poet's disabled brother, Edward ("Tobias"). Since Mrs. Whitman was also renting half the house to the family of John Brown, a tailor with two children, it is doubtful that other family members lived with her—though several must have been frequent visitors.[24] From a camp near the Antietam battlefields in September, George had imagined the family back in Brooklyn: "ile bet now, that Mother is makeing pies. I think Mat is putting up shirt bosoms like the deuce so as to get through before dinner. I guess Sis [Hattie] is downstairs helping Mother mix the dough, Walt is upstairs writing, Jeff is down at the Office, Jess is pealing Potatoes for dinner, and Tobias has gone down cellar for a scuttle of coal. Bunkum I guess is around somewhere looking for a good chance to go sogering." Jesse Whitman, the poet's older brother, was sustained by temporary jobs at the Brooklyn shipyard not far from the Whitman residence, but his unstable and increasingly worsening mental condition, which culminated in a physical attack on family members, eventually forced Walt to have him committed to an insane asylum.[25] "Bunkum" was the family nickname for Andrew Whitman, who had by then found his "chance to go sogering" and had returned home after three months' service. When news of George's probable wounding reached Brooklyn, Mattie threatened to go to Washington to nurse George herself. Mattie had taken the place of the two married Whitman daughters and was a constant comfort to the Whitman family, especially Walt and his mother.[26] No doubt her excitable husband had insisted that *somebody* travel to Washington, or wherever they might find George. Mattie's threat that she might be the one (Jeff in those days often talked a bigger game than he carried out) probably convinced Walt to act at once.

Needless to say, the entire Whitman family was frantic about George. Walt even sought out his congressman, but Moses Fowler Odell could not see the poet on such short notice. By Friday afternoon, December 19, Whitman found George's regiment encamped outside Falmouth about a mile downriver from the Lacy House, which had served as the headquarters of the Right Grand Division of Burnside's reorganized army until the battle and afterward as a hospital for Union wounded.[27] He described the ordeal to his mother as "about three days of the greatest suffering I ever experienced in my life." "When I found dear brother George, and found that he was alive and well," he told her, "O you may imagine how trifling all my little cares and difficulties seemed—they vanished into nothing."[28]

This was Walt Whitman's first visit to the front, and he could not have come upon more death and misery, the result of an ill-conceived and botched campaign. Historians agree that Burnside was foolish to go through with his planned attack on Fredericksburg (which constituted the straightest line to the Confederate capital in Richmond). Even his own generals, including Joseph Hooker, who would succeed Burnside as head of the Union troops in January, protested beforehand that the task was impossible unless the Union force outnumbered the Confederate armies two to one, which it did not.[29] Arriving in Falmouth almost a month before the day of the main battle, Union troops under the command of Edwin V. Sumner (the Right Grand Division under which the Fifty-First New York Volunteers fought) could have taken Fredericksburg almost without a fight. But Burnside, under pressure to prevail where Lincoln's first top general, George B. McClellan, had delayed, delayed himself by ordering Sumner to wait for the delivery of pontoon bridges from Washington to ford the Rappahannock; thus, the Union crossing of the Rappahannock to occupy Fredericksburg was postponed until December 11, long after the combined forces of James Longstreet and Stonewall Jackson had reached the city to join with Robert E. Lee's forces behind a fortified stone wall atop Marye's Heights, just west of the city. Once the Union troops crossed the river under sharpshooters' fire and engaged the enemy in street fighting in Fredericksburg on December 13, they had to fight across a wide plain, exposing themselves to enemy artillery and percussion shells. As Union regiment after regiment attempted to cross, their ranks were scattered and thousands were killed and wounded, leaving the battlefield with bodies three-deep in some places.

George told Jeff on January 8, 1863, as Burnside prepared to renew his ill-fated attack on Lee's fortifications with the notorious "Mud March" above Fredericksburg, "It was a mighty warm place we were into when I was hit as the Rebs had a battery planted right in front of us and not more than 1000 yards distance, and they poured grape and cannister into us like the very devil. . . . the range was so short, that they threw percussion shells into our ranks. . . . they would drop at our feet and explode killing and wounding three or four every pop. It was a piece of one of that kind of varmints that struck me in the jaw." The "spent slug" made a hole completely through George's cheek and rattled around in his mouth.[30] As part of the Ninth Army, George's regiment—and its second brigade, under General Edward Ferrero—made the final, suicidal assault late in the day on the Confederates, who enjoyed a superior position on the terraced slopes of Marye's Heights. In his official report, General Willcox recorded that George's brigade "encountered the full weight of the enemy's metal. . . . and marched under a heavy fire across the broken plain, pressed up to the field at the foot of the enemy's sloping crest, and maintained every inch of their ground with great obstinacy until after nightfall, but the position could not be carried." Although the architect of the Union assault was despondent over the legions of dead and wounded, Burnside insisted that he had come painfully close to succeeding and wanted (incredibly) to renew the attack the next day.[31]

Following the fighting on the afternoon and evening of the 13th, Burnside's army pulled back to Fredericksburg and then across the Rappahannock to Falmouth, unable in many cases to retrieve its wounded. One witness in George's division recalled, "That night was bitter cold and a fearful one for the front line hugging the hollows in the ground [to avoid enemy fire on the battle plain], and for the wounded who could not be reached. It was a night of dreadful suffering. Many died of wounds and exposure, and as fast as men died they stiffened in the wintry air, and on the front line were rolled forward for protection to the living. Frozen men were placed for dumb sentries." The Fifty-First New York alone lost sixty-nine men killed and wounded, including six of its officers. After hardly a year of combat, its number stood at three hundred out of an original total of a thousand soldiers.[32] By the end of the war, George Whitman was the only member of his regiment who had started out with it back in the fall of 1861; the rest were either killed, wounded, sent home at the end of their three-year enlistments, or—in relatively few cases—transferred to other military units.

❋ ❋ ❋

On December 28 Whitman accompanied a government transport of wounded (and dying) back to Washington, where he was met by O'Connor and his wife, Nelly. The reunion was the beginning of a close friendship with the O'Connors, who were instrumental in Whitman's success in the Washington hospitals by providing the samaritan with a circle of friends sympathetic both to his current activity as "wound dresser" and to the controversial *Leaves of Grass.* To the very end of his life, the loyal O'Connor remembered the poet as he first arrived: "narrow at the flanks: the beard, the red in his face—not bloat . . . but a sort of sun-fish flush."[33] It is not completely clear just when Whitman decided to remain in Washington, find a job, and continue the hospital work he had begun in New York City. "Since I have laid my eyes on dear brother George, and saw him alive and well—and since I have spent a week in camp . . . and seen what well men and sick men, and mangled men endure—it seems to me," he told Mattie, "I can be satisfied and happy henceforth if I can get one meal a day." He added from the third-floor apartments rented by the O'Connors at 394 L Street, where he first lived in Washington, that he hoped soon to be back in Brooklyn with his family and "have some little steady paying occupation." This wish faded rapidly after seeing the broader results of the Fredericksburg massacre and in particular the wounded of the Fifty-First in Campbell Hospital: "O my dear sister, how your heart would ache to go through the rows of wounded young men, as I did—and stopt to speak a comforting word to them. There were 100 men in one long room, just a long shed neatly whitewashed inside. One young man was very much prostrated, and groaning with pain." This was John A. Holmes, about whom Whitman eventually wrote a touching report in the *New York Times* of February 26.[34] There were so many "Brooklyn boys" in need of attention—"John Lowery, shot at Fredericksburg, and lost his left forearm, and Amos H. Vliet . . . has his feet frozen." These and others he had first seen at Falmouth, and their condition had worsened almost to a man.

By the middle of January, he decided to remain. From Brooklyn Jeff sent $6 for the soldiers, and throughout the war he forwarded contributions collected from his friends and fellow engineers at the Brooklyn Water Works.[35] Needing a job to sustain himself, Walt asked Emerson, who had been the first to recognize the genius of *Leaves of Grass,* for letters of introduction to William H. Seward, secretary of state, and Salmon P. Chase, secretary of the treasury. Although Emerson had suddenly become mute after Whitman published his private letter of praise without permission in 1855, he broke his silence in 1863 by promptly sending the two letters of introduction. Apparently, neither thought it strange that a job-seeker might start so high in the bureaucracy to find what turned out to be a rather lowly position. In both letters, Emerson described Whitman "as a man of strong original genius, combining, with marked eccentricities, great powers & valuable traits of character." As it turned out, neither cabinet member helped Whitman. He never used his letter to Seward, and Chase, a presidential hopeful for 1864 bothered by the sexual aspects of *Leaves of Grass,* failed to assist—though he kept Emerson's letter as a souvenir. Senator Charles Sumner—whom Whitman saw on the matter three times—promised (albeit vaguely) to help.[36] It was his former Boston publisher, Charlie Eldridge, who came to the rescue by finding the poet his job as a copyist in the Army Paymaster's Office.

Whitman's descriptions in letters, newspaper articles, and *Specimen Days* (based directly on journal entries written during the war) show that he was already becoming conscious of a new subject. Earlier he had thrown himself into the lifejoys of Brooklyn, Manhattan, New Orleans, and—by vicarious extension—the rest of the United States; now he immersed himself in the pathos of America's terrible quarrel with itself. At this point in the *Drum-Taps* poems, the tone shifts from the excitement of going to war to the recognition of the war's frightening toll on the American "camerado." Those wounded and dying young soldiers, of whom Whitman was to see more than 100,000 (by his count) during the next three years, stirred the poet's avuncular impulses, which had previously been reserved mainly for his own family members.

In *Drum-Taps* Whitman revived the old "Calamus" idea of male friendship, now lacing the poems with expressions of empathy instead of the earlier romantic longing that is today viewed as homoerotic. Because of the ongoing debate over the place of homosexuality in America today, the discussion of Whitman's sexual orientation will probably continue in spite of whatever evidence emerges. One fact is clear: he required from his earliest adult years the company of young men, working men, and "roughs." What may have changed with the war was the nature of that need. Just as the theme of the self in the early editions of *Leaves of Grass* gives way in *Drum-Taps* to the theme of altruism, where the self is celebrated in the selfless action of others and ultimately in the self of the assassinated Lincoln, the poet's desire for male friendship (or lovers) may have shifted to a desire for sons. The "Calamus" feeling was becoming sweetly solemnized (if never completely anesthetized) by death.[37]

The poignant *Drum-Taps* poems were born at Fredericksburg, where he first saw "*war-life,* the real article." The scenes along the Rappahannock and subsequently in the military hospitals in Washington had opened up new horizons for him. "To these," he asked, "what are your dramas and poems, even the oldest and the tearfulest? Not old Greek mighty ones, where man contends with fate (and always yields)—not Virgil showing Dante on and on among the agonized & damned, approach what here I see and take a part in." What most impressed him so was the "American man—how he holds himself cool and unquestioned master above all pains and bodily mutilations."[38]

Some of the greatest poems of *Drum-Taps* were conceived near the very battlefield they effectively describe. "Vigil Strange I Kept on the Field One Night," generally regarded as a vicarious military experience, reflects directly on the solemn Christmas Whitman spent at Fredericksburg.

> Vigil strange I kept on the field one night;
> When you my son and my comrade dropt at my side that day,

> One look I but gave which your dear eyes return'd with a look
> I shall never forget,
> One touch of your hand to mine O boy, reach'd up as you lay on
> the ground

The next line has the poet speeding into battle, a surrogate experience for his hospital work both in Fredericksburg and later in Washington. He returns to find his comrade and son—as he doubtless had with so many of his hospital charges—"in death so cold."

Also directly traceable to the Fredericksburg experience is "A Sight in Camp in the Daybreak Gray and Dim." Not only was the weather brutally cold that December, but the area around the river was thick with fog, delaying the building of the pontoon bridges used to cross over into Fredericksburg:

> A sight in camp in the daybreak gray and dim,
> As from my tent I emerge so early sleepless,
> As slow I walk in the cool fresh air the path near by the
> hospital tent,
> Three forms I see on stretchers lying, brought out there
> untended lying,
> Over each the blanket spread, ample brownish woolen blanket,
> Gray and heavy blanket, folding, covering all.

In "Down at the Front" (an essay penned in Falmouth on December 21), the same "brownish woolen blanket" is mentioned, and in another, "After First Fredericksburg" (December 23 to 31), the same wounded are lying on the ground outside the tent hospitals.[39] Furthermore, two days before his departure for Washington, he walked in the early morning to find soldiers digging graves for the dead of George's regiment and another. "Death is nothing here," he recorded. "As you step out in the morning from your tent to wash your face you see before you on a stretcher a shapeless extended object, and over it is thrown a dark gray blanket—it is the corpse of some wounded or sick soldier of the reg't who died in the hospital tent during the night."[40]

Similarly, the second stanza of "A Sight in Camp" :

> Curious I halt and silent stand,
> Then with light fingers I from the face of the nearest the first
> just lift the blanket;
> Who are you elderly man so gaunt and grim, with well-gray'd
> hair, and flesh all sunken about the eyes?
> Who are you my dear comrade?
> Then to the second I step—and who are you my child and
> darling?
> Who are you sweet boy with cheeks yet blooming?

In the third and final stanza, poetic transubstantiation takes place, creating a symbolic trinity of which the third soldier is a part:

> . . . a face nor child nor old, very calm, as of beautiful yellow-white
> ivory;
> Young man I think I know you—I think this face is the face of the
> Christ himself,
> Dead and divine and brother of all, and here he again lies.

We know that Whitman wrote the trial lines for the poem in his notebook while still at the place of inspiration: "*Sight in daybreak* (in camp in front of hospital tent) on a stretcher, three dead men lying, each with a blanket spread over him—I lift up one and look at the young man's face, calm and yellow. 'Tis strange! (Young man: I think this face of yours the face of my dead Christ)."[41] Like most of *Drum-Taps,* this poem remained unchanged through all editions.[42] These solemn poems were the poet's monument to immediate experience and as a result could never be revised. In one sense (emotionally, not politically) the war froze him in time. Even the earlier "Song of Myself," Whitman's greatest poem, underwent significant changes, but the Falmouth experience was personal, not poetic, history.

In 1855 Whitman had generally foresworn the poetic tradition of singing of wars and conquests. But in "To Thee Old Cause" (1871), which makes up part of the "Inscriptions" section of the definitive 1881 arrangement of *Leaves of Grass* (in a line that strikes readers as odd since the first three editions were written before the war), he announces, "my book and the war are one." In thanking Emerson for his letters of introduction, Whitman told him he intended "to write a little book about this phase of America, her masculine young manhood, its conduct under most trying of and highest of all exigency, which she, as by lifting a corner in a curtain, has vouchsafed me to see America, already brought to Hospital in her fair youth—brought and deposited here in this great, whited sepulchre of Washington itself."[43] This was to be *Drum-Taps* and later *Memoranda During the War* and finally a significant part of *Specimen Days. Drum-Taps* and the poems that follow it—such as "Proud Music of the Storm" and "Passage to India"—show us a poet as one of the folk. The poet of "Passage to India," for example, swiftly shrivels "at the thought of God," while the poet of "Song of Myself" was the *son* of God, or at least a close relative. This mystical claim in Whitman probably ceased with the 1855 edition. In the finest poem of the 1856 edition, "Crossing Brooklyn Ferry," the poet can master space and time but is no more (or less) eternal than those who will follow him a hundred years hence. By "Calamus" and the great seashore poems of the late 1850s, his mystical feeling about himself was gone, replaced by the "need of comrades." In the war he found "divinity" in the crucified sons of God instead of the resurrected self of "Song of Myself."

Beginning as we have, *in medias res,* Whitman has first come on stage after his best work. This may be the best place to begin, however, because he never fully appreciated his own poetic achievement until he saw Americans literally die for the democracy he had celebrated in the earlier editions of *Leaves of Grass.* We will have to return to the actual beginning of his life to see what he saw, not only from the perspective of the war and the personality of the poet, but also from the political history that led up to the national crisis and so influenced this poetic genius. To his soldiers, his poetry did not exist. In fact, nothing he ever wrote would have competed with the great compassion he showed them. He read poetry to the soldiers but never his own. Yet it was his capacity to love that was the grand dynamo in *Leaves of Grass.* First he learned to love himself, overcoming the degradation of a poverty school in Brooklyn run by supercilious, ferruling teachers; then avoiding the use of the rod as a teacher himself; and finally learning from Emerson and the transcendentalists to see himself and every other human being as an emblem of God because all were part of nature. Nature, as Emerson had said, was the last thing of God. This idea Whitman never forsook, even after his own remarkably healthy body began to desert him with his first paralytic stroke in 1873.

Despite his experiences as a teacher, a journalist, and a printer-poet, Whitman did not think he knew America until he knew the country's wounded and sick soldiers—mechanics from the city, farmers from the country, young men from the West. He was wrong, for early editions of *Leaves of Grass* show a keen and penetrating understanding of working-class America and its middle class. The war simply gave shape to this career, serving as the midpoint but not the centerpiece of a life in poetry and politics. It began and ended in politics, in the early journalistic pieces and short fiction, in the old-age essays and conversations with his "Boswell," Horace Traubel. In the middle, his "great career" began almost by accident, in the early compositions of *Leaves of Grass.* A former printer, he set up part of the first edition himself, as he discovered the transformative power of the printed page. The printer's term for such experimental writing was "grass," the job to be put up during idle times.

This second eldest son of a family that today might be defined as "dysfunctional" transformed American poetry and set the agenda for poets in the twentieth century. He rescued its themes from New England graveyards and snowy country lanes, took its style from England, and gave it a rhythm that required a new meter and a new reader, fashioned not merely out of "pure" nature but from the raw essence of emerging cities and family farms. He went beyond Emerson's emblematic nature to celebrate nature for its own sake. Its mettle "tested" by the Civil War, *Leaves of Grass*—first under the former journalist's shrewd maneuvering and then on its own poetic (and political) steam—reshaped the canon of American literature and remains today its central document. After the war Whitman went on to write many more poems, more than 400 during his lifetime. As a former journalist, he developed into a poet of occasion, marking such events as Grant's death, the completion of the Washington Monument, Custer's defeat, the Johnstown Flood, and, most touchingly, a gentle New Jersey breeze that brought him relief shortly before his death in 1892. Whitman, himself tested by life, led a life that has been told before but needs to be told again, this time updated by new facts drawn from newspapers and recently discovered manuscripts as well as our perspective at the end of the twentieth century.

What, for example, is the basis for claims today for the poet's homosexuality? What of his alleged racism? What is the true value of Whitman's earlier, conventional poetry? What was the extent of his romantic affiliations during his stay in New Orleans in 1848 and what did he actually write there? Was he truly the racist, misogynous editor of the *Brooklyn Daily Times* in the late 1850s? Who was the mysterious "Ellen Eyre" who wrote the poet a most intriguing love letter in 1862? What was the actual nature of his close relationship with the ex-Confederate soldier Peter Doyle, and later the farmer's son and printer's apprentice Harry Stafford? What are the facts of the Whitman-Wilde meetings in 1882? Who exactly was Horace Traubel, and does his now discovered bisexuality cast any light on the Whitman biography? What indeed is the relevance of *Leaves of Grass* today (and yesterday) and the nature of its poet, who defied literary decorum, stoically withstood condemnation, and pursued his own way in stubborn Quaker-like fashion? In "Crossing Brooklyn Ferry" and elsewhere the poet identifies with the reader then "and centuries hence," saying, "Just as any of you is one of the living crowd, I was one of the crowd." Though there have been new insights, we have continued to take our basic facts from a critical biography written more than forty years ago.[44] Otherwise, the facts of Whitman's life have been Freudianized and historicized to fit current political and literary ideologies. Whether Whitman himself would have fully accepted these various classifications and affiliations, he never would have rejected them outright. "I am large, I contain multitudes," he said at the close of his greatest poem, "Song of Myself," and his political conversations with

Traubel, a budding socialist, bear him out. The job of the critical biographer, however, is to reconfirm or correct the facts of the life, discover new ones, and reconsider the biographical evidence so that we can continue to study and appreciate this great poet as accurately as possible in the twenty-first century.

2

A THOUSAND SINGERS, A THOUSAND SONGS

❋ ❋ ❋

No one can ever really get at Whitman's poems,
and their finest lights and shades, until he has visited
and familiarized himself with the freshness, scope, wildness
and sea-beauty of [Long Island].

WILLIAM DOUGLAS O'CONNOR
(quoted in Richard Maurice Bucke, Walt Whitman*)*

Walt Whitman was essentially an island poet, whether of Long Island, Manhattan, or the "island" of American democracy in a world where other revolutions, especially the European ones of 1848, had failed. He was a seashore poet, the poet of "Paumanok" who envisioned some of his greatest themes in terms of the land and the sea, between life and death. In "Brooklyniana" Whitman dwelled at length on the beauties of his native island, which he apparently knew intimately from Brooklyn to Montauk. When he prepared his autobiography, *Specimen Days,* he titled one of the earliest sections "Paumanok, and My Life on It as Child and Young Man." The title reveals the symbiotic relationship between the first impressions of youth and the poetic ones of Whitman's maturity. We see this relationship most clearly in the poem "Out of the Cradle Endlessly Rocking," where he describes the island's lock on his imagination as the man-child wakes up to the call of "a thousand singers, a thousand songs." Similarly, he wrote in *Specimen Days* of the eastern edges of the Hempstead Plains: "Here, and all along the island and its shores, I spent intervals many years, all seasons, sometimes riding, sometimes boating, but generally afoot, . . . absorbing fields, shores, marine incidents, characters, the bay-men, farmers, pilots—always had a plentiful acquaintance with the latter, and with fishermen—went every summer on sailing trips—always liked the bare sea-beach, south side, and have some of my happiest hours on it to this day."[1]

Long Island was part of Whitman's consciousness, the foundation of his aesthetic appreciation of nature. In "The Sleepers," an 1855 poem and still today about one of the most famous dreams in American literature, he alludes directly to "the loss of the ship 'Mexico' in 1840" off the shores of Paumanok.[2] As this poem suggests, much of *Leaves of Grass* stems from the poet's identity with Long Island, or Paumanok:

> I wander all night in my vision,
> Stepping with light feet, swiftly and noiselessly stepping and stopping,
> Bending with open eyes over the shut eyes of sleepers,
> Wandering and confused, lost to myself, ill-assorted, contradictory,
> Pausing, gazing, bending, and stopping.

Whitman, who witnessed many sunrises and sunsets on the island, seems to have anticipated the French surrealists a century later. Magritte's simultaneous evocation of night and day in the painting "L'empire des lumières" is similar to what Whitman achieves in "The Sleepers." Magritte's darkened mansion, illumined only by a street lamp on a tree-lined street and contrasted brilliantly with one of his famous skies, is reminiscent of the house of "The Sleepers" that Whitman entered through his daydreams. There, in the daytime of Whitman's poem, the "married couple" sleeps, the "sisters sleep lovingly side by side in their bed," the "men sleep lovingly side by side in theirs / And the mother sleeps with her little child carefully wrapt." Even in his old age, Long Island evoked those "carefully wrapt" memories of childhood. "As I write," Whitman recalled in *Specimen Days,* "the whole experience comes back to me after the lapse of forty and more years—the soothing rustle of the waves, and the saline smell—boyhood's times, the clam-digging, barefoot, and with trowsers roll'd up—hauling down the creek—the perfume of the sedge-meadows—the hay-boat, and the chowder and fishing excursions;—or, of later years, little voyages down and out New York bay, in the pilot boats."[3] Even after he had moved permanently from the island's isolated hamlets to the expanding city of Brooklyn and the other island of Manhattan, he returned at regular intervals during the 1840s and 1850s.

Late in the summer of 1881, Whitman came back once again to Paumanok. In the company of his Canadian disciple Richard Maurice Bucke, he paid a visit to the farming community of West Hills near Huntington. The two "put up at the Huntington House" and spent the first part of their three-day visit "in calls and explorations" in the general Hempstead area.[4] They visited the burial places of the poet's mother and father, which were located on opposite sides of the Nassau/Suffolk county line. Whitman's ancestry is essentially Dutch and English, like the post-Columbian settlement of Long Island. The Dutch developed the western end of the island, the English the eastern. Appropriately, Louisa Van Velsor Whitman rested to the west of the county line, while her husband of thirty-nine years lay to the east, both in the immediate vicinity of their birthplaces.

Whitman described the visit to his father's gravesite, writing "these lines seated on an old grave (doubtless of a century since at least) on the burial hill of the Whitmans of many generations." He surveyed more than fifty Whitman graves, which constituted his entire family history in America, "with its succession of links, from the first settlement down to date, told here—three centuries concentrate on this sterile acre."[5] The next day Bucke, his gait only slightly revealing a partially amputated foot, and Whitman, limping himself from a series of paralytic strokes, traveled across the county line to the birthplace and grave of the poet's mother near Cold Spring Harbor. At the cemetery Whitman wrote up a summary of his maternal ancestry as he had for his father. "I went down," he recorded, "from this ancient grave place eighty or ninety rods to the site of the Van Velsor homestead, where my mother was born (1795,) and where every spot had been familiar to me as a child and youth." He found, however, not a "vestige left" of what he had remembered of the Van Velsor homestead. "Only a big hole from the cellar, with some little heaps of broken stone, green with grass and weeds, identified the place."

Like many of the families in the eastern seaboard and middle-Atlantic states, the Whitman line in America had begun in New England. John Whitman, an Englishman born in 1602, arrived on the

True Love in 1635, settling in Weymouth, Massachusetts. His brother, a clergyman named Zechariah Whitman, came over on the same ship, either at the same time or a year or two later. He lived in Milford, Connecticut. In 1657 his son Joseph migrated across Long Island Sound to Huntington, New York. The fertile land and clear springs of the Hempstead Plains provided the next three generations with prosperity, which was enhanced by the labor of slaves. Yet by the time Whitman's father was born in 1789, the family fortunes had dwindled, and most of the rich lands and property had been sold off. The family of Whitman's maternal grandmother consisted mostly of Quakers and sailors. Naomi Williams Van Velsor, whose dress evinced the Quaker faith and lifestyle, lost her father and only brother at sea. Whitman's maternal grandfather, Cornelius Van Velsor, carried the title of "Major," a rank Walt's brother George attained in the Civil War. The family had been horse breeders, and Whitman's mother was "a daily and daring rider" of horses.[6]

After an apprenticeship under his cousin Jacob Whitman, a carpenter in New York City, Walter Whitman, Sr., worked in the city for three years and then returned to Long Island and married Louisa Van Velsor in 1816. The couple had the first of nine children, Jesse, in 1818. The next year on May 31 "Walt" was born, so called from the very beginning (by everyone except his mother) to distinguish him from his father. A common practice for naming male children then was to use patriotic namesakes—no doubt reflecting the rise of nationalism following the War of 1812. Walt was named after his father, but Jesse was named after his paternal grandfather, a militiaman during the Revolutionary War. As Justin Kaplan astutely puts it, "Walter Whitman, Sr. was born on July 14, 1789, the day the Parisians stormed the Bastille, and he believed in resisting much, obeying little. He named three of his six sons after heroes of the Republic . . . and he trained them as radical Democrats, on the side of the farmer, the laborer, the small tradesman, and the 'people.'"[7] After the births of two daughters and one unnamed male child who died after six months, the boys were named after national fathers—Andrew Jackson, George Washington, and Thomas Jefferson. The final child was born to Louisa when she was forty, probably with Down's syndrome; he was named simply Edward.

When Whitman was four, his father sold what little was left of the family homestead in West Hills and moved to Brooklyn—"in Front, Cranberry and Johnson streets," the poet recalled in *Specimen Days.* "In the latter my father built a nice house for a home, and afterwards another in Tillary street. We occupied them, one after another, but they were mortgaged and we lost them." Whitman's fixation with the Brooklyn Ferry stretched back to his earliest memories. Even as a small child, he "tramp'd freely around the neighborhood; was often on the aforesaid ferry; remember how I was petted and deadheaded by the gatekeepers and deckhands . . . and remember the horses of the boats making the water-power."[8] With steam-powered ferry boats coming into use, Brooklyn was booming in housing starts in the mid-1820s, and Walter Whitman should have prospered. Yet just as his ancestors on Long Island had lost farm land generation by generation, he lost business and residential investments one after another. Walt no doubt inherited his impracticality from his father. His brother George remembered Walt's "stubborn reserve, patience. He got offers of literary [journalistic] work—good offers: and we thought he had chances to make money. Yet he would refuse to do anything except at his own notion."[9]

Walter Whitman may have had—even at that early date—a problem with alcoholism, which had doubtless run through the Whitman family line from the time of America's alcoholic eighteenth century. His oldest son, Jesse, may have been a sot, and his third-eldest son, Andrew, was definitely an alcoholic, plagued throughout his brief adulthood with unemployment. Whitman's temperance tale, *Franklin Evans; or The Inebriate* (1842), suggests that the poet may have had—or feared—a drinking problem himself in his twenties; afterward he imbibed infrequently until his final years, when he developed a fondness for champagne and brandy.

One of his earliest memories of Brooklyn was of Independence Day 1825, when the Marquis de Lafayette held him in his arms at the dedication of the Apprentices Library. General Lafayette had donated some $200,000 in personal funds to the Revolution and served alongside George Washington. Whitman later recalled slightly different versions of this event, but he never forgot that he had been in the very presence of one of the heroes his father taught him to cherish.[10]

Thomas Paine was another one of Whitman's patriotic heroes. Walter Whitman, Sr., once met the famous pamphleteer for the Revolution in New York City, when Paine was down on his luck and perhaps an alcoholic. The poet later wrote an affectionate essay in his defense.

Because of the family's low income and increasing numbers, Walt did not attend private schools. He was admitted to District School No. 1, Brooklyn's only public school, perhaps as an impoverished student. "District" schools were generally considered "charity" schools—though parents with means were required to pay an annual tuition of four dollars a child.[11] In New England and parts of New York, these schools were seen as the foundation of a democratic society, but in Brooklyn with its proud Dutch ancestry they carried the social stigma of the poor. Brooklyn had been slow to embrace the idea of free education, a reluctance so pervasive that many parents unable to afford private schools for their children preferred no school at all. In 1828, when the poet was in the third grade, a school census reported that at least 240 of more than 2,000 Brooklyn children between the ages of five and fifteen were being allowed to grow up in ignorance.[12]

The school at the corner of Adams and Concord streets, where the young Whitman received his instruction, had only recently been constructed—the school board trustees having been "thrust from office" in 1816 by citizens incensed at the notion of "a *tax for building a school house!*" It held hundreds of students, with the eldest white children being taught in the basement, the youngest taught on the first floor, and the black children segregated on the top floor (this order was subsequently reversed).[13] The curriculum, which discouraged individuality, consisted of an endless repetition of lessons: the school day began with Bible reading, followed by grammar dictation, spelling, vocabulary, arithmetic, geography, and penmanship. Pupils learned by the Lancastrian method, an economical and quasi-military way to educate the poor that employed a strictly rote approach, in which the district teacher could instruct up to a thousand pupils with the help of student monitors.[14]

For all that Whitman had to say as a journalist about education, he never mentioned his own experience as a student. Nor did he ever mention any of his teachers in his memoirs,[15] although he suggested their frequent use of corporal punishment in the short story "Death in the School-Room (A Fact)" and in several newspaper editorials. Like many of his early fictions that present cruel or apathetic paternal figures and forlorn sons, "Death in the School-Room," published in the *Democratic Review* in 1841, features a stern, sadistic schoolmaster and a frail, fatherless youth. The boy, suffering an unknown malady, dies in school. The ferruling teacher thinks he is sleeping in class and ends up flogging a corpse. In "The Whip in Schools," Whitman suggests that "there are better traits in a child's character than that of animal fear."[16]

Although Whitman's teacher at District School No. 1, B. B. Halleck, favored corporal punishment, the pattern in Whitman's writing may reflect more than the young boy's schoolroom experiences. In "There Was a Child Went Forth," a poem in Whitman's first edition of *Leaves of Grass,* the father is described as "strong, self-sufficient, manly, mean, anger'd, unjust." The next line suggests paternal violence as well: "The blow, the quick loud word, the tight bargain, the crafty lure." In the short story, Whitman's very first, the schoolteacher looks at his victim "with a frown which plainly told that he felt in no very pleasant mood."[17] On the other hand, Whitman here may be in fact thinking of Halleck, who considered his student "clumsy and slovenly" and who may have whipped him. In Whitman's biography by Bucke, which the poet himself heavily revised, Walter Whitman, Sr., is described as a "large, quiet, serious man, very kind to children and animals, and a good citizen, neighbor, and parent."[18]

❋ ❋ ❋

At the tender age of eleven, which was not so tender in the nineteenth century, Whitman concluded his formal schooling and became an office boy for James B. Clarke and his son Edward, two prominent Brooklyn attorneys on Fulton Street. The Clarkes were also members of Saint Ann's church, where the future poet had attended Sunday school (much preferred to regular school) for the last two years. The younger Clarke instructed Whitman in composition and also bought him a membership in a Brooklyn circulating library. Whitman recalled the latter in *Specimen Days* as "the signal event of my life up to that time." Among the many literary discoveries he made were *Arabian Nights, Robinson Crusoe,* and all the novels of Sir Walter Scott.

Whitman had already begun to learn from life as well as from school and books. While still in school, he went to hear the Quaker preacher Elias Hicks speak "in a ball-room on Brooklyn Heights," a memory he cherished to the end of his life. Whitman also met the ex–vice president Aaron Burr, to whom he took messages in Manhattan for the Clarke attorneys. He later thought the Revolutionary traitor "was [one] damned and damned again in history and yet who had his parts." He kept his first job for about a year and then went to work briefly for a Brooklyn physician by the name of Hunt, nearby at the corner of Concord and Fulton streets. Soon afterward, the next phase of his education began when he became employed in the printing office of Samuel E. Clements, editor of the *Long Island Patriot.*[19]

Shortly before the Civil War, Whitman remembered Clements as a hail-fellow-well-met, of southern heritage and Quaker beliefs, who frequently strode down the village streets in a "long-tailed blue coat with gilt buttons, and on his head in summer an enormous broad-brimmed, low-crowned loghorn hat." "Imagine him promenading the streets (then lanes, with trees,) of Brooklyn—or riding out in his skeleton sulky," he urged his readers of the *Brooklyn Daily Times.* "He always kept a horse, generally a pretty fast one; to his country subscribers out in Bushwick, New Lots, Flatlands, &c., carrying round his papers himself."[20] Besides running one of Brooklyn's two weekly newspapers dedicated to a particular political view (the other was Alden Spooner's more established and respected *Long Island Star,* a Whig publication), Clements was Brooklyn's postmaster, no doubt a reward for his paper's support of the populist ideas of President Jackson's administration.

Whitman learned to write among politicians, local "politicos" and officeholders such as Clements, whose newspaper was more than loosely connected with Tammany Hall; one of the *Patriot*'s themes was "the right of the people to rule in every case."[21] Like Mark Twain, Walt Whitman probably learned to "parse and spell" at the composing table. From time to time, Clements allowed the young Whitman to print juvenile features in the *Patriot,* constituting, though now lost, the poet's earliest published writings. Whitman was not the only great American writer to meet his craft and art in a printing office and the editorial parlors of a newspaper. Benjamin Franklin preceded him in his brother's print shop and newspaper, and along with Mark Twain the list includes William Dean Howells, Theodore Dreiser, and Ernest Hemingway.[22] It was in the printing office too that Whitman developed an appreciation for the aesthetics of the page so evident in *Leaves of Grass* with its innovational use of long lines and blank spaces. When this printer became the printer-poet in 1855, he set up the first part of his famous book himself.[23]

Clements's association with Whitman lasted only six months. As Whitman told the story in 1857, the part-time postmaster and editor became involved in a scheme to disinter the body of the Quaker preacher Hicks, who had died on February 27, 1830, at Jericho, Long Island. Although there existed "a good portrait of Hicks," the venerated old Quaker had never permitted a figure of himself to be taken for a bust. "Immediately coincident with the death of Elias," Whitman recalled, Clements and local sculptor Henry Kirke Brown (in the early 1850s a friend of Walt's) recovered the corpse to make a mold from "the face and head!" A quarrel between the two ensued ("in reference to the division of the anticipated profits from the sale of the bust"), and the incident became public. Whether the publicity led to Clements's removal from his editorship, his postmastership, and his residence in Brooklyn, Whitman does not say—only that "after a short reign" Clements "got into difficulties [probably with the local Democratic Party] and disappeared west."[24]

After Clements fled to New Jersey (he settled ultimately in Camden, the city of the poet's last residence), the young Walt stayed on with the *Patriot*, or more precisely its print shop. The first newspapers in Brooklyn (and America) had been single-editor shows in which reporter and printer were one (frequently with the additional chores of running the press's lending library and lottery), but by the two-penny press days, when Whitman entered the profession, the operations had expanded to a separate editor and printer. Whitman actually saw less of Clements than he did of William Hartshorne, who ran Clements's print shop on Fulton Street near Nassau and seems to have been the teacher to the boy that the austere Mr. Halleck had not been. Hartshorne gave Whitman a lifelong love of the "printing craft." Later, as a mature poet, he could never "finish" a poem without first having it set up in print. "What compositor, running his eye over these lines, but will easily realize the whole modus of that initiation?" he asked. That beginning in the world of cold type and "book-words" found the young Whitman "half eager, half bashful . . . the awkward holding of the stick—the type-box, or perhaps two or three old cases, put under his feet for the novice to stand on, to raise him high enough . . . the thumb in the stick—the compositor's rule—the upper case [of type] almost out of reach—the lower case spread out handier before him . . . the pleasing mystery of the different letters." In "Song of the Exposition," read at the opening of the fortieth annual exhibit of the American Institute in 1871, he wrote, "You shall watch how the printer sets type, and learn what a composing stick is, / You shall mark in amazement the Hoe press whirling its cylinders, shedding the printed leaves steady and fast."

Whitman long remembered Hartshorne, who lived some fifteen years beyond his retirement—from "a trade considered unhealthy." As he noted in "Brooklyniana" No. 6, written two years after the printer's death, he had often encountered the old man "walking slowly in pleasant weather, through Fulton street, or some neighboring thoroughfare, with broad-brim hat, his cane, and chewing his quid of tobacco."[25] When the aged printer finally died at the age of eighty-four in 1859, Whitman wrote his obituary in the *Brooklyn Daily Eagle* of December 31 (from which he later borrowed phrases for "Brooklyniana" No. 6). Whenever the poet met the old man on Brooklyn's streets, he said, "I used always to stop and salute him, with good-will and reverence."[26] We do not know, of course, what Hartshorne thought of *Leaves of Grass*—or its printing job.

His next "teacher" was another printer, by the name of Erastus Worthington, who ran the bookstore and lottery for Alden Spooner's *Star.* It is not clear why Whitman changed newspapers and printers, but by the fall of 1832 he had worked directly for Worthington since the summer and was then employed by Spooner himself. That the *Long Island Star* was a Whig newspaper made little difference to Whitman at his young age. Even though he had been influenced by his father's love for the workingman's rights and apparent dedication to the socialist ideals of the Scotswoman and political activist Frances Wright, Walt now focused primarily on learning the trade of a printer. Looking back on the education he received at the printing press, he told Traubel: "there you get your culture direct: not through borrowed sources—no, a century of college training could not confer such results on anyone."[27]

In either 1833 or 1834, the future poet's father evidently decided he had had enough of the cutthroat competition in Brooklyn and took his rapidly expanding family (Thomas Jefferson Whitman, eighth of nine born to Louisa Whitman, arrived that summer) back to the country. It is not known for sure whether Whitman worked steadily for Spooner after the Whitman family returned to the Hempstead region, but he doubtless made frequent visits there, often on the back of his grandfather Van Velsor's farm-to-market wagon. He may have earned his journeyman printer's credentials at sixteen, and before that he had written occasionally for several newspapers, including the fashionable *New York Mirror*.[28] For a time he also ventured across the river to work as a compositor in New York City, but the move was ill-timed. His career there was cut short by a huge fire that destroyed much of the printing and press district and threw thousands out of work. If this catastrophe were not enough, an even more disastrous fire broke out in the financial district on Wall Street, sending many uninsured businesses into bankruptcy. The local crisis was further exacerbated by the death throes of the National Bank, which lost its federal deposits as the culmination of President Jackson's four-year assault on an institution he believed was undemocratic. This helped to produce the infamous Panic of 1837. In the midst of the ensuing financial chaos, the seventeen-year-old Whitman returned to the Long Island countryside to teach school.

❋ ❋ ❋

It was not yet time for Whitman to make any permanent crossing on the Brooklyn Ferry. Like Melville—also born in 1819—he was driven to teaching for the want of a better job. This, it seems, was a crucial turn in Whitman's life and career, not so much because of the teaching, which he apparently liked no better than Melville, but because he returned to Long Island and the countryside of his first memories. Now his experience as a young adult reinforced the childhood wonder of the island and its seashores; eventually these experiences found their way into some of the most memorable poems in *Leaves of Grass.*

Between June 1836 and spring 1841 Whitman taught at eight "district" schools on Long Island.[29] It would not have been strange to start teaching in June because the country schools, such as they were, operated year round in sessions of thirteen weeks, with holidays only on Sunday and every other Saturday; no others were recognized—not Independence Day, Christmas, or New Year's Day, and especially not Thanksgiving, which did not become a national holiday in the United States until the Civil War. Schoolhouses were primitive one-room affairs, heated with a stove. Because matches had yet to be invented, the teacher sent students "next door" for "a brand of fire to kindle with." Teachers used large, 13-inch by 16-inch sheets of paper, which they had to fold and line themselves, and pens were made of goose quills, which they had to sharpen and split. It is no wonder that Whitman, like Melville and others such as Emerson and Thoreau, who also taught when no other employment was available, did not make teaching his career and in fact taught only intermittently. It was not enviable employment and depended on "chance teachers," as Whitman would remember them in the *Long Island Star* of October 2, 1845: "young men during college vacations, poor students, tolerably intelligent farmers, who have some months of leisure in the winter."[30] Teachers like these often moved abruptly to new districts when they were found unsatisfactory by school boards making unscheduled inspections. Whitman's salary at Smithtown for the five months of the 1837–38 fall and winter terms was $72.20, in addition to room and board at various homes in the school district.[31]

Whitman changed jobs frequently, perhaps indicating his ineptitude or dissatisfaction as a teacher. Between 1836 and 1841 he taught in East Norwich (summer 1836), Babylon (winter 1836–37), Long Swamp (spring 1837), Smithtown (fall and winter 1837–38), Little Bay Side (winter 1839–40), Trimming Square (spring 1840), Woodbury (summer 1840), and Whitestone (winter and spring 1841).[32] It appears that he kept fairly close to wherever his parents were living, first in

West Hills, then in Babylon to the south, and finally back near West Hills in a community called Dix Hills. He may have even thought to help his father and brothers at farming—though brother George recalled that during this period Walt would rarely do farm work.[33] Whitman's lifelong pattern of "laziness" was probably already set. One of his students remembered his teacher as "careless of time and the world, of money and of toil"; another thought the future poet somewhat out of his element even as a teacher—"always musin', and writin'." A third, however, remembered Whitman as something of a role model, who never smoked or drank, was clean-shaven, and eschewed the use of corporal punishment.[34]

These were restless years for Whitman, teaching, "loafing" at his parents' various Long Island dwellings, or "boarding round" at the homes of his students' parents, and separated from his only other way of making a living, printing. After a second stint of teaching at Smithtown (where he also joined a debating society),[35] he moved back to Huntington in the spring of 1838 and started his own newspaper. Misremembering the year as 1839 in *Specimen Days,* he makes it clear that his principal motivation, initially at least, came as much from the printer in him as from the journalist. "I had been teaching country school for two or three years . . . , but liked printing; had been at it while a lad, learn'd the trade of compositor, and was encouraged to start a paper in the region where I was born."

It was a bold move for someone so young, not even twenty at the time, but apparently the experiment was something of a success—or at least it was remembered that way. "Everything seem'd turning out well; (only my restlessness prevented me gradually establishing a permanent property there)." Having satisfied his yearning for a return to the country (reinforced by the New York City fire) and the places of his youth, he very likely wanted to get back to the city, to join the ranks of those people with whom he identified as an adult. With no printer's or journalist's job available, establishing the *Long-Islander* represented a way of creating his own work experience.

No copies exist of the *Long-Islander* during Whitman's control of the paper, when it was supposed to be a weekly but probably came out intermittently (the paper existed until the 1980s). Whitman recalled not his editorial duties but the joy of delivering his papers on horseback (following the example of his former employer Samuel Clements) and the thrill of his jaunts to the various hamlets around Huntington: "the dear old-fashion'd farmers and their wives, the stops by the hay-fields, the hospitality, nice dinners, occasional evenings, the girls, the rides through the brush."[36] Otherwise, the only evidence of his editorship consists, possibly, of two short prose pieces and a poem, which were reprinted by the poet's next employer, James J. Brenton, editor of the weekly *Long Island Democrat,* in the fledgling community of Jamaica.

The *Long-Islander* experiment also represented Whitman's first attempt to escape from teaching. Once the enterprise fizzled in the summer of 1839, he continued to resist the call of the classroom and worked for Brenton, at whose residence he also boarded. Although the young man may have captured the affection of Brenton, he incurred the dislike of Brenton's wife, who—as her daughter-in-law later recounted—thought the twenty-one-year-old "dreamy" and inconsiderate of his responsibilities. Whenever Whitman came home from the printing office for mid-day dinner, she recalled, "he would go out into the garden, lie on his back under the apple tree, and forget everything about going back to work as he gazed up at the blossoms and the sky. Frequently, at such times, Mr. Brenner [Brenton] would wait for him at the office for an hour or two and then send the 'printer's devil' up to the house to see what had become of him. . . . When spoken to, he would get up reluctantly and go slowly back to the shop."[37] Whitman lasted with the *Democrat* only through the fall, before he was forced to accept another teaching position, this time in nearby Little Bayside.

Until recently, not much has been known about Whitman's life during this period, or the span of years between 1836 and 1841 in general. In an effort to imagine his situation, or at least how the future poet viewed his situation, biographers have generally fallen back on the "fact-romance" or short story Whitman published in the *Union Magazine* of June 1848—"The Shadow and the Light of a Young Man's

Soul." Early letters recently discovered confirm the story's autobiographical significance. Indeed, Whitman states in italics that "the foregoing incident is a fact."

The plot concerns Archibald Dean, who like Whitman is forced from the city because of the "destructive New-York fire of '35" to teach in "a little district school" in the country. A morbid youth, Archie looks "on the dark side of his life entirely too often." From his country school he writes a self-pitying letter to his mother, in which he admits that she might be tiring of such "outpourings of spleen" but that he will feel better for unburdening himself. "I am in that mood," he tells her, "when sweet music would confer on me no pleasure. Pent up and cribbed here among a set of beings to whom grace and refinement are unknown, with no sunshine ahead, have I not reason to feel the gloom over me? Ah poverty, what a devil thou art! How many high desires, . . . how many aspirations after goodness and truth thou hast crushed under thy iron heel!" He ends the letter by complaining bitterly that his "throat chokes, and my blood almost stops, when I see around me so many people who appear to be born into the world merely to eat and sleep, and run the same dull monotonous round—and think that I too must fall in this current, and live and die in vain!"[38]

Whitman was almost thirty when this story was published, but its first draft was probably written much earlier—closer to the time when he felt like Archie Dean. This mood may not have colored all his teaching stints—at least not the last at Whitestone, overlooking Long Island Sound—but the narrator's attitude matches well with the Walter Whitman who taught at Woodbury during the summer of 1840. The letters he wrote there to his friend Abraham Paul Leech indicate someone as frustrated and bored as the autobiographical Archie. Calling Woodbury ("*would*-bury me") variously "Devil's den" and "Purgatory Fields," Whitman told Leech on July 30, 1840, that he was "but little in the humour for writing any thing that will have the stamp of cheerfulness" because "Life is a dreary road, at the best; and I am just at this time in one of the most stony, rough, desert, hilly, and heart-sickening parts of the journey." By August 11 Whitman was more direct about his "Woodbury" condition: "how tired and sick I am of this wretched, wretched hole!—I wander about like an evil spirit, over hills and dales, and through woods, fields, and swamps. . . . O, damnation, damnation! thy other name is school-teaching and thy residence Woodbury." He continued, much in Dean's vein, saying that not "a refined or generous idea was ever born in this place. . . . Never before have I entertained so low an idea of the beauty and perfection of man's nature, never have I seen humanity in so degraded a shape, as here.—Ignorance, vulgarity, rudeness, conceit, and dulness are the reigning gods of this deuced sink of despair."[39] Matching as they do the moroseness found in "The Shadow and the Light," these letters show us a Whitman diametrically opposed to the optimist who in *Leaves of Grass* would find divinity in the lowest order of social existence.

Since we do not have letters written during his other teaching stints, we cannot be sure that Woodbury was an unusual experience for Whitman, though student testimony from other places suggests he had been a little happier. He may have found Whitestone, his last teaching stint, as greedy and "gold-scraping" a place as Woodbury, but he was certainly happier with the physical surroundings, especially the Long Island Sound with its "vessels, sometimes a hundred or more, all in sight at once, and moving so gracefully on the water." What began to change, in addition to the school district or the physical surroundings, was Whitman's basic attitude—about himself and the world. That is to say, around 1841 he began to come out of a post-adolescent "slough"—something linked to his relative poverty and uncertainty about finding a satisfying profession. Although he probably had not yet heard about Emerson's ideas on self-reliance, he shared the transcendentalist's attitudes. He may in fact have taken the cure of his protagonist in the story, whose title suggests the lifting veil of shadowy despondency to let in the light. "Poor youth," Whitman wrote, "how many, like you, have looked on man and life in the same ungracious light! Has God's all-wise providence ordered things wrongly, then? Is there discord in the machinery which moves systems of worlds, and keeps them in their harmonious orbits? O, no: there is discord in your own heart; in that lies the darkness and the tangle. . . . Is *this* the place for a failing soul? Is *youth* the time to yield, when the race is just begun?" From Whitestone, Whitman sounded much like the improved Archie. He told Leech (who apparently received Whitman's screeds on a "semi-weekly" basis during the summer of 1840), "Do not think I am going to fall into the splenetic, fault-finding current, on which those Woodbury documents were set afloat."[40]

Two letters from Leech for this period, or fragments from them, survive. They suggest that the correspondent, a genial and educated person but also a religious person with a keen interest in the temperance movement then rekindling itself in America, was an effective sounding board for the poet. Indeed, he may have influenced Whitman to write his temperance tract in 1842. He and Whitman were debaters together in Jamaica (Leech reports that the last debate topic was on the use of manual labor in schools), and Leech, who was familiar with Woodbury, may have been a native of the place. His letters suggest that Whitman's derisive comments about the town were somewhat sarcastic, though with an unmistakable undertone of unhappiness. In response to a letter that most certainly predates those most recently discovered, Leech writes: "What shall I send you in return for all the news of Woodbury? Oh! Billy Sealy has been put in the cells two or three times for getting drunk. The cars ran over a cow a week or two ago. . . . Aunt Sally's Uncle Jonathan's son's daughter's child has had the measles very bad but is quite smart now."[41] Seeming to mock Whitman and himself for their gossiping, Leech also matches the future poet's condescending attitude toward country folk and his humorous way of dispatching them.

Yet such banter was all Whitman had or knew at this point in his life. Only twenty-one, he had been back in the country for five years, with little prospect of becoming anything but a country schoolmaster. Nevertheless, his experiment with the *Long-Islander* had stimulated not only his journalistic interest but also his desire to become a poet or professional writer. His first extant poem, which was reprinted in Brenton's *Long Island Democrat* of October 31, 1838, first appeared in the *Long-Islander.* His earliest extant prose, a piece of journalism, has allegedly been traced to the *Long-Islander* as well. "Summer Produce and Fall Crops" and "Effects of Lightning" were reprinted from the *Long-Islander* in Brenton's newspaper on August 8, 1838. Yet aside from the statement about their source in the *Long-Islander,* neither piece shows any evidence of having come from Whitman's pen.[42] As noted,

Whitman showed little interest in farming. And in "Effects of Lightning," the author seems to think that thunder precedes lightning.

Whitman's earliest known poem is "Our Future Lot," its authorship documented by the fact that it appeared as "Time to Come" in the *New York Aurora* in 1842 when Whitman was its editor. In its focus on death and the mysteries beyond the grave, it resembles William Cullen Bryant's "Thanatopsis." Yet Whitman's "view of death" never goes so far as to find in nature the pre-transcendentalist notion of "a still voice." Instead, the narrator is left with his questions completely unanswered:

O, powerless is this struggling brain
    To pierce this mighty mystery;
In dark, uncertain awe it waits
    The common doom—to die![43]

The 1842 revision of "Our Future Lot" appeared in the *Aurora* only a month after Emerson delivered his lecture on "The Poet" in New York City. In his debut lecture in Manhattan, Emerson invited his audience "to a consideration of the nature and offices of the Poet: to the power he exerts and the means and materials he employs; to the part he plays in these times, and is likely to play."[44] Whitman was there and described it for the *Aurora* as "one of the richest and most beautiful compositions, both for its matter and style, we have ever heard anywhere, at any time." In his tribute to Emerson's performance, he added that "it would do the lecturer great injustice to attempt anything like a sketch of his ideas." It is doubtful that the twenty-two-year-old editor fully grasped the concept of Transcendentalism or glimpsed his future role as its democratizer.[45] Even in its 1842 revision, "Our Future Lot" gives no clue of the poet who would envision death in "Song of Myself" as a recycling of the spirit: "And as to you Death, and you bitter hug of mortality, it is idle to try to alarm me." In "Our Future Lot" (actually in "Time to Come"), the body after death may remain "bloomless," whereas in "Song of Myself" it becomes the compost of life:

I smell the white roses sweet-scented and growing,
I reach to the leafy lips, I reach to the polish'd breasts of melons.

By 1855 Whitman had read Emerson and was familiar with the transcendentalist doctrine of nature as the emblem of God.

Whitman was still adjusting to the world of journalism as he recirculated his early poems in the *Aurora* and elsewhere. In "Fame's Vanity," published in the *Long Island Democrat* of October 23, 1839, and revised and reprinted as "Ambition" in *Brother Jonathan* of January 29, 1842, he also took up the subject of death, this time modeling his theme after Thomas Gray's "Elegy Written in a Country Churchyard." His not altogether original meditation on the foolishness of earthly fame conjures up Gray's statement, "The paths of glory lead but to the grave."

For mighty one and lowly wretch,
Dull, idiot mind, or teeming sense
Must sleep on the same earthy couch,
A hundred seasons hence.

In its 1842 revision, Whitman dropped this stanza and framed the others with stanzas in blank verse. He also distanced himself by treating its subject in the third person as "an obscure youth, a wanderer," and fame as a coal "burning and glowing" in "that youth's heart." This pattern of revisiting earlier poems became lifelong, as evidenced by the successive editions of *Leaves of Grass.* More important, however, here the poet linked together the "lowly" and the "rich" in the democracy of death. Later, in the democracy of *life,* he joined together the prostitute and the president in a catalog that included everybody.

The city sleeps and the country sleeps,
The living sleep for their time, the dead sleep for their time,
The old husband sleeps by his wife and the young husband sleeps
by his wife;

And these tend inward to me, and I tend outward to them,
And such as it is to be of these more or less I am,
And of these one and all I weave the song of myself.

When Whitman first wrote "Fame's Vanity" and was trying his hand at journalism with the *Long-Islander* and Brenton's *Long Island Democrat,* he was, of course, far from representing "every hue and caste" in his writing. He continued in the pre-romantic vein of Bryant and Gray with "My Departure," published in the *Democrat* of November 27, 1839, and as "The Death of the Nature Lover" in *Brother Jonathan* of March 11, 1843. As with the revision of "Fame's Vanity" into "Ambition," the major difference between "My Departure" and "Death of the Nature Lover" is the shift from the first to the third person—as the older poet takes clearer account of his original emotions as well as his situation when the poems were first drafted and published. Otherwise, the protagonist still belittles fame and prefers to bid "adieu to earth, and [step] / Down to the World Unknown."

His subdued hopes for the future in this poem are perhaps counterbalanced by the willed optimism of "Young Grimes," published in the *Democrat* on January 1, 1840. It may have been Whitman's New Year's resolution to become "A chip of the old block," as he writes of Young Grimes, working hard and achieving success, but the fact was that he was then out of work and faced with the dreary prospect of school teaching again. The poem is mostly hack work, inspired by Brenton's fondness for the long popular "Old Grimes" by Albert Gorton Greene. It has been called a "verse biography"—accurate all the way down to the fact that Whitman never used tobacco.[46] We learn that "Young Grimes" disliked school but never smoked, swore, or gave his mother "much pain," and "ne'er went to see the girls / Before he was fourteen." Whitman was eighteen when this was published, and at the time he was already involved with "the girls," though mainly as an observer of their interaction with other young men. "Tim Hewitt," he told Leech that summer, "vowed he ought to have a buss from Patty Strong; Patty modestly declined the honour.—A struggle was the result, in which Tim's face received permanent marks of the length of Patty's fingernails."[47] The rhetoric here, with its overarching stiffness, suggests his position on the margins of life. In "Song of Myself," he was "both in and out of the game" of life when he observed the same woman, or her social equal, as a sexually frustrated voyeur. Then he knew her poetically, if not physically.

> She owns the fine house by the rise of the bank,
> She hides handsome and richly drest aft the blinds of the window.
> Which of the young men does she like the best?
> Ah the homeliest is beautiful to her.

Not long after Whitman lost or left his job on the *Long Island Democrat* in the late fall of 1839, he returned to Hempstead, in the general vicinity of his parents' latest lodging (Dix Hills, near West Hills). His next teaching stint—that winter in Little Bay Side—took him back to the general area of Jamaica, but before he resumed teaching he must have made another journalistic connection, this time with the *Hempstead Inquirer.* Here he published the first three installments of the "Sun-Down Papers, From the Desk of a Schoolmaster." The schoolmaster connection is not particularly evident in the subjects taken up in the series, which does not talk about pedagogical matters; Whitman probably felt the need for some sort of professional identity, a basis for authorship and authority, just as he avers in the preface to the first edition of *Leaves of Grass,* where the poet is said to replace the priest.

The ten essays—published between February 29, 1840, and July 20, 1841, in three different newspapers[48]—are often didactic, warning against the ills of smoking, fashion, low self-esteem, materialism, religious dogma, and the futility of quarreling. They also tell us something about Whitman at the time. In "Sun-Down Papers" No. 1, the subject is retrospection and its joys. Yet in young Whitman's case memories of childhood lead to the fear that he is wasting his life. "I was thinking, the other night, as I sat in mine elbow chair, of the manner in which the past few years of my life had been passed." "As the reveries I have been describing passed off; and as I realized the actual life around me," he told his *Hempstead Inquirer* readers, "a saddening influence fell upon my soul. I considered with pain that the golden hours of youth were swiftly gliding; and that my cherished hopes of pleasure had never yet been attained." Here Whitman may not be lamenting simply the passing of time and his unfulfilled ambition but also—in well-veiled language—his lack of intimacy. "Silently and surely are the months stealing along.—A few more revolutions of the old earth will find me treading the paths of advanced manhood." Sounding again like Archie Dean and the teacher of Woodbury, he confesses: "This is what I dread: for I have not enjoyed my young time. I have been cheated of the bloom and nectar of life.—Lonesome and unthought of as I am, I have no one to care for, or to care for me." The essay ends on the high note: the writer snaps out of his Sunday depression and visits one Kitty Denton. But the conclusion may be a cover-up. If indeed Whitman was a homosexual, this may represent his first consciousness of the fact. As we shall see in Chapter 5, he later changed the sex of a lover in a poem from male to female.

The third essay in the series speaks of "the empty heartlessness of the fashionable female." Its proper subject is the error of the workingman to "live genteelly," that "the ambition to be fashionable is in itself without counting the consequences, one of the greatest torments that a mechanic can be subject to." Even though Whitman was something of a dandy himself (as suggested by his 1840 daguerreotype), he was already beginning to rally the worker, the "divine average" he would come to celebrate. Here, though, he uses gentle criticism. He chides the worker about seeking "to hide what he is" by aping the manners "of those whom he foolishly supposes to be his superiors, merely because they are of no use in the world, have small and soft hands, and never bend themselves down to the practice of vulgar industry or labor."

Whitman was beginning to sort out internal social problems, not just spiritual ones. His exploitation of his personal life came to a boil in the summer of 1840 when he railed about the sterility of the working people in the village of Woodbury, and specifically about the self that might have become one of them. Under the guise of another journalistic sermon that summer, he lamented—in "Sun-Down" No. 6—the death of a teenaged friend only a few years younger than himself. "The last time I saw him," he wrote in the *Long Island Democrat* of August 11, 1840, "we walked a mile or two together. It was in the country, and the season was Autumn. How little did I think that ere the grain or fruits would ripen again he would be blighted!—that *his* Autumn would arrive ere the Spring had passed."

Death was the subject of his poems that spring, summer, and fall of 1840 as well—in "The Inca's Daughter," "The Love That Is Hereafter," "We Shall All Rest at Last," "The Spanish Lady," and "The End of All" (all published in the *Democrat*). These poems and the "Sun-Down Papers" suggest that though Whitman was working at cross purposes with himself (his poetry praising the relief of the next life, his prose urging mechanics to take pride in their austere and earthly existence), he was also working his way out of what seems to have been a delayed adolescence. After having gone through the conventional exercises with the opposite sex, he receded from all females but mother-women, proto-feminists perhaps, who may well have become his exclusive female friends in adult life. From the series Whitman learned also—as he already had with his poems—to see himself from the outside, or in the third person. *Leaves of Grass* is conspicuous, of course, for its first- and second-person points of view, but Whitman as both a poet and a journalist had to take himself out of the first person in order to find his originality as an American poet, to discover the "I" that could celebrate *itself* with the assurance of another's point of view.

In the fall of 1840 he made the prophetic announcement that he was thinking of writing a book. "And who shall say that it might not be a very pretty book? Who knows but that I might do something very respectable?" He was already thinking as an author and entertaining what he called in "Sun-Down" No. 7 the "pretensions to be a philosopher." The "purgatory" of Woodbury had burned away any youthful illusions that he was "normal," not only in his orientation toward the work-a-day world but perhaps in sexual orientation as well. By 1840, a former student named Charles A. Roe recalled, "The girls did not seem to attract him. . . . Young as I was, I was aware of that fact."[49] One of the problems with thinking Whitman a homosexual, however, is that we are more than a century removed from a period in which close male friendship was taken at face value (and there is no indication in the Leech letters that the two were more than friends in that tradition). "The love that dare not speak its name" wasn't phrased until the 1895 sodomy trials of Oscar Wilde, leading to the twentieth-century construct of "homophobia."

By fall 1840, after Woodbury, Whitman got himself appointed—probably with Brenton's help—as the Democratic electioneer in Queens County.[50] The occasion was Van Buren's unsuccessful attempt to win a second term in the White House. Even Leech had decided to vote for William Henry Harrison, telling Whitman from Jamaica that "people hereabouts are turning from Martin to Harris like lost sheep from the wilderness to their shepherd's peaceful fold."[51] Whitman remained with the cause of the "people"; like most of white America, he was probably not troubled by the fact that Van Buren's administration had been responsible for driving the Cherokee Nation west along the infamous "Trail of Tears."

Whitman remained politically with the cause of the "people" because, paradoxically, he was no longer directly involved as a (first) person. "The soul knows no persons," Emerson had declared in his Harvard Divinity School Address of 1838. There is no evidence that Whitman was directly familiar with the address, which was available then only in pamphlet form, but he had apparently imbibed its spirit. In perhaps the first—and certainly almost the last—political speech of his career, he told his fellow Democrats in New York City on July 29, 1841, to treat the individuality of the candidate as an afterthought. "I beseech you," he told them, "to entertain a noble and more elevated idea of our aim and struggles as a party than to suppose that we are striving [to raise] this or that man to power." It was his conviction, he said, that the next Democratic officeholder would be carried into power by the "guardian spirit" of Thomas Jefferson. "It is our creed—our doctrine, not a man or set of men, that we seek to build up."[52]

It took him another fifteen years to comprehend the dynamic of character and issues poetically. After the election, he returned to teaching briefly. But perhaps he already sensed that it was time to cross the Brooklyn Ferry again, this time more profitably.

3

SOME LITERARY PERSON

⁂

New York is a great place. . . . Here are people of all classes and stages of rank—from all countries on the globe—engaged in all the varieties of avocations—of every grade, every hue of ignorance and learning, morality and vice, wealth and want, fashion and coarseness, breeding and brutality, elevation and degradation, impudence and modesty.

WALT WHITMAN
*"Our City" (*New York Aurora, *March 8, 1842)*

According to his own records, the man from Paumanok returned to Manhattan in May 1841. He worked first as a printer at Park Benjamin's *New World,* a new but already highly successful and influential semiliterary weekly to which he also gradually contributed. On one occasion the young writer had both a poem and a short story on its front page.[1] He also wrote for its literary rival, *Brother Jonathan,* and provided news articles and editorial essays to the *Aurora,* where after several months of freelancing he was finally hired for a brief stint as editor in late March 1842. Whitman was never destined for success as a newspaper reporter or editorial writer; the poetically rambling *Democratic Vistas* (1871) provides overwhelming evidence of that. His forte, like Theodore Dreiser after him, was the feature article usually found in the supplements to today's Sunday newspapers: short essays that accommodated wide-ranging observation, which he later poeticized into his famous catalogs of American life instead of direct statement of fact or opinion.

Whitman entered a colorful publishing world in New York. Besides Benjamin's *New World,* there were James G. Wilson's *Evening Tattler* and *Brother Jonathan,* James Gordon Bennett's *Herald,* Horace Greeley's *Herald-Tribune,* William Cullen Bryant's *Post,* Moses Y. Beach's

Sun, William L. Stone's *Commercial Advertiser,* James Watson Webb's *Courier and Enquirer,* and an array of less successful one-, two-, and six-penny presses, all aligned with a particular political view. This was an era of journalism as "yellow" as the 1890s, when the term first came into use to describe sensationalism and bias in the press. Editors during Whitman's tenure regularly accused and abused their counterparts in print, and from time to time physically accosted each other on the street. The now stately and established Bryant had once resorted to physical force by thrashing his rival Stone with a horsewhip. As late as 1839 the city's more traditional editors had fought a "Moral War" against Bennett's exploitative journalism, especially hated for its disrespect for organized religion. In the same year James Fenimore Cooper sued several newspaper editors for libelous remarks; Benjamin, who was one of the defendants, was ordered to pay Cooper $375. Back home after years abroad, the author of the Leatherstocking Saga and more recently of *Home as Found* (1838), a trenchant critique of American society under Jacksonian democracy, was appalled at the slovenly manners of his countrymen. Years later Whitman expressed admiration for Cooper's work but regretted that he shared Thomas Carlyle's cynicism about the common man.[2]

As the New York papers grew exponentially and circulation widened, Whitman could always find work as a printer when no editorial position or payments for stories and poems were coming in. Yet within no time he went ahead as a penny-a-line journalist as well as a fiction writer, jumping in with better-known writers on the *New World* and elsewhere. He also established himself as a frequent contributor of fiction to the *Democratic Review,* the premier literary magazine of its day, where he may have received as much as $2 a page.[3] The *Democratic Review* was founded and edited by John L. O'Sullivan, who is also credited with the earliest use of the term "Manifest Destiny." His authors included Nathaniel Hawthorne, Edgar Allan Poe, John Greenleaf Whittier, James Russell Lowell, and Whitman's favorite poet, William Cullen Bryant. Whitman's first contribution—"Death in the School-Room"—appeared in August 1841. By the time he was editing the *Aurora,* he had already published five of the eight short stories he ultimately placed in O'Sullivan's prestigious magazine within the span of a year.

The tone of Whitman's early writings is overwhelmingly moralistic, continuing the didacticism of his "Sun-Down Papers" and generally reflecting the implicit mission of the nineteenth-century American press, when it wasn't sensationalizing the new, to instruct as well as to inform. It was the era of the Lyceum Movement, America's first "night school," which provided forums for ambitious young men to educate themselves by teaching—giving lectures to one another on topics only recently researched and not necessarily mastered. Emerson, among others, began his career as a lecturer as a lyceum speaker.

In "Each Has His Grief," published in the *New World* of November 20, Whitman again echoed Bryant's theme in "Thanatopsis" and also anticipated Longfellow's "Nature," which allegorized death as bedtime to a cranky child. Here the focus is on the burdensome cares that punctuate life.

> But like unto a wearied child,
>   That over field and wood all day
> Has ranged and struggled, and at last,
>   Worn out with toil and play,
>
> Goes up at evening to his home,
>   And throws him, sleepy, tired, and sore,
> Upon his bed, and rest him there,
>   His pain and trouble o'er.

The next month the *New World* published "The Punishment of Pride" (December 18), a poem about an angel sent down to earth only to be recalled by God through death because he lacked sympathy for human frailty and suffering. The poem resembles Poe's "Israfel" slightly for the idea that it is the pain of this world that makes for the stuff of poetry. Both Whitman poems were first drafted when he taught at Little Bay Side during the winter of 1840. "Each Has His Grief" had appeared as "We Shall All Rest at Last" in Brenton's *Long Island Democrat* of July 14. One of Whitman's students at Little Bay Side testified that "The Punishment of Pride" was a poem—then called "The Fallen Angel"—his teacher had required them to memorize.[4]

In the stories, the two main elements are unloving fathers and preferred older brothers. Here family relationships tend to become dysfunctional—with alcoholism as the primary cause. Whitman's physical settings are largely undefined, reflecting the fact that he grew up in both Brooklyn and West Hills. The quasi-religious theme of psychological redemption from the difficulties of this life as well as from the sin that threatens our status in the next is to be expected from a member of a farm family relocated to the city of contradictory values and aims. In "Wild Frank's Return," published in the *Democratic Review* of November 1841, a runaway returns home after many years to find that his father still favors his older brother. The plot must in some way reflect the situation of the poet's older brother, Jesse. Thought to have "the best mind of any of the children" until suffering an accident, involving either a blow to the head or a fall from a mast, while serving in the Merchant Marine around 1848, Jesse became an alcoholic whose mental instability finally landed him in the King's County Lunatic Asylum in 1864 (and in a potter's field a few years after that).[5] For all that is known (almost nothing before the Civil War), the poet's older brother may have outshone the awkward and prematurely large Walt as a youngster and may have prospered as either a farmer on Long Island or a carpenter in Brooklyn while Walt was shifting from job to job. On the other hand, Jesse may have been an alcoholic. In "The Child's Champion," appearing the same month in the *New World,* the child is harassed by a drunken sailor, who could have been modeled on Jesse. Both "Wild Frank" and "The Child's Champion" are clumsy in plot and stiff in narrative, the second so moralistic as to serve—with Walt's added introduction—as a temperance tale in the *Columbian Magazine* in 1844 and the *Brooklyn Daily Eagle* three years later.

The neglected son also appears again in "Bervance; or Father and Son" (*Democratic Review,* December 1841), and here he is decidedly an alcoholic. Whitman himself may not have realized what he was revealing when he created this particular uncaring father, who prefers the older son and neglects the younger, called Luke. When Luke is forbidden to join the rest of his family in his father's theater box, he shows up to embarrass the entire family and taunt his father. "There he sat, indeed," recalls the father in what is a retrospective, confessional narrative. "He looked over to where I was seated, and while my sight was riveted upon him in unbounded astonishment, he deliberately rose—raised his hand to his head—lifted his hat, and bowed long and low—a cool sarcastic smile playing on his features all the time,—and finally breaking into an actual laugh, which even reached my ears."[6] In a tipsy condition, Luke physically attacks his father at home and is committed to an insane asylum. "Bervance" is clearly an improvement over Whitman's previous fiction. In choosing to tell the story from the father's point of view, the poet who would see and celebrate life from all angles of democratic vision perhaps turns the tables on himself, the son who is so angry at his father's neglect that he becomes an alcoholic.

Doubtless, Whitman had written many of these stories before recrossing the East River; "Death in the School-Room," for example, was written while he was teaching in Little Bay Side, near Jamaica, in the winter of 1840.[7] Their wellspring appears to have been his continued association, on and off as his teaching positions placed him around Long Island, with his parents and their large family. He must also have been privy to such scenes in other farming families with whom he boarded while teaching. Probably, in an area where tippling was not unusual, some of his students emerged from such troubling homes, and as their teacher he was placed in a unique situation from which to view father-son relationships similar to his own.

In January 1842 Whitman returned to his musings about the mysteries of the grave by revising the poem "Fame's Vanity" for *Brother Jonathan* under the title of "Ambition." The same month he placed "The Tomb Blossoms" in the *Democratic Review.* Internal evidence suggests that he was still teaching in Whitestone—or at least thinking of that place—when he composed it.[8] The tale bears a faint resemblance to Washington Irving's "The Broken Heart" in *The Sketch-Book,* where a melancholy woman has been abandoned by her lover. In "The Tomb Blossoms," the object of pity is an indigent country wife who places flowers at two different graves in a potter's field because she is not sure which one holds her husband, the authorities having buried the man while she was ill. "What a wondrous thing is woman's love!"

exclaims the narrator. The author was possibly thinking of his own mother, whose husband may have been emotionally distant because of his drinking.

Whitman obviously saw his mother as a heroine. But he also admired his father, whose sturdy admiration for the Revolutionary heroes had been inscribed in his imagination. "The Last of the Sacred Army" contains a dream sequence in which the Revolutionary heroes are honored for the last time. The occasion is joyous because they have performed so well as role models for the new and emerging national power. "Do you suppose, young man," the narrator is asked by "a learned philosopher," "that it is by sermons and oft-repeated precepts we form a disposition great or good? The model of one pure, upright character, living as a beacon in history, does more benefit than the lumbering tomes of a thousand theorists." Later, in *Franklin Evans,* this story was adapted into a reformed drinker's dream of universal temperance in America. In that celebration, the figure of "a fair female, robed in pure white" conducts the celebration. Her eyes "beamed benevolence and purity of heart; and in her hand she held a goblet of clear water."[9] "The Last of the Sacred Army" appeared in the *Democratic Review* of March 1842, and Whitman's very next story—"The Child-Ghost; a Story of the Last Loyalist"—appeared there in May. These two tales played to O'Sullivan's nationalism, the first eulogizing the Revolutionary heroes, and the second dramatizing the departure of British troops from a New World governed by common people instead of kings.

After freelancing news pieces for the *Aurora* for several months, Whitman became its official editor during the last week of March 1842.[10] The *Aurora* had been started the previous fall by two feisty entrepreneurs, Anson Herrick and John F. Ropes, who also ran a successful Sunday paper called the *Atlas* and would soon capitalize on the renewed interest in temperance with a paper called the *Washingtonian.* After three months in existence, the *Aurora*—established as a six-day-a-week daily—had reached the respectable circulation of 5,000, perhaps mainly because of the efforts of its first editor, Thomas Low Nichols. Nichols had left the paper in late February, having been dismissed for printing libelous claims.[11] Actually, the libel was probably the fault of Herrick, and after Nichols's sudden departure (and during Whitman's editorship) the *Aurora* readership started on a downward spiral. By May 3—with Whitman already gone from the paper—Herrick and Ropes, who were editing it themselves—announced under the leader "Libels, Bails!" that they were under warrant "in six different suits brought by one individual in a pretty little sum of $19,000." They tried to put the best face on their problems, exclaiming that "we feel as lively as ever, and grow fat" under the pressure of the litigation. "We must be of considerable importance in the community or we shouldn't be troubled to this extent." The newspaper folded after another year of publication.

Evidence found in the actual pages of the *Aurora* suggests that Whitman left under his own steam. When work from the *Aurora* assumed to be Whitman's was reprinted in 1950, however, its editors concluded that the poet had been fired from the daily. They quote William Cauldwell, writing in the *New York Times* of January 26, 1901. Cauldwell, who worked as a printer in the building that housed the *Aurora* at 162 Nassau Street, not far from Tammany Hall, described Whitman's routine as editor, mentioning in particular Whitman's retort to his bosses that "if you want such stuff in the *Aurora,* write it yourself."[12] Cauldwell was alluding to the effects of the political climate under John Tyler, who had occupied the White House since April 1841 when the newly elected Whig president Benjamin Harrison died of pneumonia after only four weeks in office. Herrick, the ruling partner in the ownership of the *Aurora,* had profited from the vice president's ascension by securing the position of custom house weigher, under the Collector of the Port of New York. According to Cauldwell, Herrick got his political inspiration "for the conduct of the paper" from the Collector, "and Herrick, in turn, sought to 'inspire' Whitman, but in this he had a tough job; for often, after a heated discussion, the conference between the two grinders of the party 'organ' ended in Whitman picking up his hat and cane and marching out of the office in high dudgeon." Missing from these accounts of Cauldwell's remarks (which were later printed in full in Horace Traubel's *Conservator*)[13] is the information that soon thereafter Whitman's "good nature got the better of his temper, and he would return to take his medicine with as few wry faces as possible." Cauldwell added that Whitman "sundered his relations with The Aurora" only "after the expiration of the term for which [he] had engaged."

The theory that Whitman was not dismissed from his post finds support from a co-worker, James Robinson Newhall, who "occupied chairs at the same table" with Whitman at the Nassau Street offices "and of course saw much" of the future poet. Newhall recalled that although the proprietors of the *Aurora* were occasionally annoyed at Whitman's absences on Broadway and the Battery, it was commonly understood that these rambles produced useful copy for their newspaper. Once when Whitman asked Newhall to fill in for him (Newhall probably edited the *Atlas,* which was housed with the *Aurora*), Herrick called Whitman a "lazy ___ !" Yet he added that if Newhall chose to do Whitman's work "and your own, too, and make an accommodating turn-about, I have no objection." Newhall mentioned nothing about Whitman's being fired, and it appears that while the poet was uncomfortable with some of the paper's political stances, or more precisely Herrick's high-handed ways, he nevertheless completed his "term," which was probably offered for no more than a month because of the paper's financial problems. The departure may not have been wholly congenial, perhaps explaining the *Aurora*'s editorial quip of May 3, "There is a man about our office so lazy that it takes two men to open his jaws when he speaks. If you kick him he's too idle to cry, for then he'd have to wipe his eyes. *What* can be done with him?"[14] But Whitman was probably out of his editorship by the end of April, or before (his last identifiable editorial appeared on April 23), and so the comment might not have been directed exclusively at him. When the generic leader, "Laziness is a disease," is restored to the quote, it certainly appears possible that the criticism had a wider target. Furthermore, the publication of Whitman's "Reuben's Last Wish" in Herrick and Ropes's *Washingtonian* of May 21 suggests that the parting was amicable.

If the proprietors had been as angry with Whitman as the previous readings of this point in his biography suggest, they wouldn't have printed the following statement on May 16, which betrays no animosity toward their former employee: "Mr. Walter Whitman desires us to state that he has been for three or four weeks past, and now is, entirely disconnected with the editorial department of the Aurora." Whitman probably asked for the announcement because he was getting ready—as a writer for the *Evening Tattler*—to avenge himself for those many times he had been forced to give in to Herrick's authority. He had already attacked another former employer, Park Benjamin, but then Benjamin had made many enemies in the newspaper business. So had Herrick and Ropes. The editor of the *Hartford Review* condemned the two *Aurora* owners as "a couple of renegade English cut-throats, who had to leave the dog-kennels of their own country to save their necks from the gallows."[15] Whitman may have been simply joining the fray when he denounced the *Aurora* in the *Tattler* as "a trashy, scurrilous, and obscene daily paper, under charge of two as dirty fellows, as ever were able by the force of brass, ignorance of their own ignorance, and a coarse manner of familiarity, to push themselves among gentlemen." He said that he had been duped into being their editorial patsy because they were incapable of "constructing two lines of grammar or meaning" and had to engage "some literary person" to "do" their paper. But he remained in their employ, he added, only a "few weeks."[16]

This attack, not any less serious quarrel during his employment at the *Aurora,* concluded for the moment Whitman's association with Messrs. Herrick and Ropes. Otherwise, he would most likely have serialized *Franklin Evans; or the Inebriate* in the *Washingtonian* instead of the *New World.* Whitman had quarreled with the editor of that paper, too, but the dispute was probably less heated. In any case, profit took precedence over such squabbles, allowing Whitman to print the first two chapters of his second temperance novel, *The Madman* (1843), in the *Washingtonian.* Whitman, of course, had gotten along best with Herrick and Ropes when he was writing nonpolitical editorials such as those describing his walks on Broadway and in the Battery. They had been the original basis of his freelance and later editorial relationship with the owners of the *Aurora.* Cauldwell recalled that "according to agreement, Whitman was to have full swing to write just what he chose in any other part of the paper (of course not antagonistic to its politics), but the senior proprietor, Herrick, who ran the political crank, was to have the toning of its leaders."[17]

Whitman's best writing for the *Aurora* appeared before he became ensconced in the editorship, when he was freelancing. He thrived on idleness. It was his custom as editor of the *Aurora* to spend at least two hours every day walking in Battery Park or up and down Broadway. "He usually wore a frock coat and a high hat," recalled Cauldwell, "carried a small cane, and the lapel of his coat was almost invariably ornamented with a boutonniere."[18]

His catalogs of the city's diversity, not only early in his career at the *Aurora* but also later in *Leaves of Grass,* found a sympathetic echo in the writing of Lydia Maria Child, then best known for *Hobomok* (1824), one of the earliest uses of the Indian in American fiction. Child wrote in the *Boston Courier* that nothing was more observable in New York City "than the infinite varieties of character. Almost without effort, one may happen to find himself in the course of a few days beside the Catholic kneeling before the Cross, the Mohammedan bowing to the East, the Jew veiled before the ark of the testimony, the Baptist walking into the water, the Quaker keeping his head covered in the presence of dignitaries and solemnities of all sorts, and the Mormon quoting from the Golden Book which he has never seen."[19] Child, however, was a New England reformer, who not only demanded full legal rights for Negroes long before the Civil War but also made a living with books of advice aimed at women. Her catalog of New York City is finally judgmental. "Life is a reckless game, and death is a business transaction," she wrote on October 21, 1841. "Warehouses of ready-made coffins stand beside warehouses of ready-made clothing." She was as fascinated as Whitman by the thriving mixture of good and evil, the city's "mercantile familiarity with death," she calls it, but she lacked his love of the average, his Emersonian trust in the divine goodness of the lowest common denominator of society. "Whoever does not know that 'our city' is the great place of the western continent, the heart, the brain, the focus, the main spring, the pinnacle, the extremity, the no more beyond, of the New World?" he asked in the *Aurora* of March 14.[20] By this time Whitman had heard Emerson deliver an early version of "The Poet" in the Society Library in Manhattan during the first week of March. Here he was first introduced to the transcendentalist idea that the "meaner the type by which a spiritual law is expressed, the more pungent it is, and the more lasting in the memories of men."[21] Whitman continued to dabble in the reform effort in his temperance pieces, but this doctrine probably saved him from a career in it.

⁂ ⁂ ⁂

The year 1842 was pivotal in Whitman's development as a poet. Not only did he first hear (and probably read) Emerson then, but he had the opportunity to expand his fiction and poetry skills into the essay form, which in the *Aurora* was allowed to run to two columns, each twenty-one inches long. His subject expands almost exponentially from a moralism focused on death and family relationships to a world stage upon which all nationalities and types interact. It is from the essay, more than anywhere else perhaps, that Whitman's use of free verse came into being. He democratized the Emersonian essay by giving the "emblem of nature" a viable (and virile) body. "How the crowd rolls along!" he wrote of New York's markets on March 18. "There comes a journeyman mason (we know him by his *limy* dress) and his wife—she bearing a little white basket on her arm. With what an independent air the mason looks around upon the fleshy wares; the secret of the matter is, that he has his past week's wages in his pocket, and therefore puts he on that devil-may-care countenance." In his journalistic voyeurism Whitman looked inside his subjects as well: "Notice that prim, red cheeked damsel, for whom is being weighed a small pork steak. . . . How the young fellow who serves her, at the same time casts saucy, lovable glances at her pretty face; and she is nothing loth, but pleased enough at the chance for a little coquetry."[22]

Later in "Song of Myself," in Section 11 where the "twenty-ninth bather" exercises her erotic fantasies by spying on naked men swimming, Whitman poeticized the deep structure of pre-Freudian America. In 1842 he merely verged on that yawning inner sanctum of the world's first modern democracy, content to show his readers how

Americans lived day-to-day. It may have been in "New York Boarding Houses" that the future poet first came upon the method of his famous catalog to celebrate the strength of American democracy and diversity. By 1842 the wealthier merchants, the middle class and above, had moved north of the noisy Wall Street area to the still sylvan environs of Washington Square Park, originally a potter's field whose "compost" produced the first upper-class neighborhood in New York City. Generally, only the working classes and the poor remained and lived in rooming houses among the buildings devoted to commerce. In the *Aurora* of March 18, Whitman wrote: "Married men and single men; old women and pretty girls; milliners and masons; cobblers and colonels, and counter jumpers; tailors and teachers; lieutenants, loafers, ladies, lackbrains, and lawyers; printers and parsons—'black spirits and white, blue spirits and gray'—all 'go out to board.'"[23]

Whitman himself boarded, of course, but at one of the better establishments, he said, run by a Mrs. Chipman at the corner of Chambers and Centre, in the northwest shadow of City Hall.[24] The experience of living among the city's 200,000 inhabitants contrasted sharply with country life on Long Island. In "The Clerk from the Country" (*Aurora* of March 24), he wrote of the exploitation of one boarder, a youth like the one he would write about in *Franklin Evans.* The subject of his essay, a young man who had been caught pilfering from his landlady, "had come to New York, without a home, and ignorant of all the arts and tricks of city life." Indebted to "designing sharpers" who had loaned him money, he became "a mere catspaw to further their schemes of villainy."[25]

But mainly the New York boarders were strong-willed and hard-working Americans who did not, in Whitman's opinion, deserve the abuse they received from foreign observers such as the supercilious Frances Trollope in her *Domestic Manners of the Americans* (1832) or Charles Dickens in his *American Notes* (1842). Although Whitman never met Dickens, he was one of the many journalists who flocked to cover Boz's first and famous visit to New York City in February 1842.[26] Within months of his return to England, Dickens was falsely accused of printing a letter with sentiments "so derogatory to our country," in the words of Philip Hone, the city's one-time mayor and influential friend of Whig politicians, "that nothing is left for Mr. Dickens but to deny its authenticity."[27] Dickens did indeed deny authorship but undermined his claims of innocence later that summer in *American Notes.* The U.S. press (which Dickens had criticized) denounced the book as much from its own paranoia as for the author's perceived British condescension toward Americans. The quarrel between England and America, smoldering ever since the wars of Independence and 1812, had rekindled itself by the time Dickens visited the city, and the American press, almost to a person, became nationalistic (and neurotic) whenever the British culture police spoke. The many British accounts and caricatures in the British press (one cartoon in *Punch* depicted a Yankee holding a pistol to an English visitor, exclaiming "Pass the mustard!") no doubt contributed to the defensive pride with which Whitman characterized his countrymen in his newspaper articles.

Whitman was also anxious to defend his countrymen against attacks at home. He did not hesitate to censure American authorities when it appeared that the poor were being exploited, when for example prostitutes were rounded up on Broadway or ragged children were brutally routed from Battery Park by police using physical force. His editorial on behalf of the prostitutes was so strenuously critical of the police that he had to qualify it the next day by saying that his language "denouncing the kidnapping of women" did not apply to the police "as citizens." His follow-up column was a waffling act in which he barely apologized—the conciliation no doubt urged upon him by his boss, Herrick. As for the urchins in the park, this "poverty-school" dropout remarked, "On the Battery, and in other public grounds, any quantity of the offspring of the rich and fashionable may be daily seen playing and no objections made."[28]

Given Whitman's inbred sympathy for the average person, for the working poor who would be included among the "divine average" in *Leaves of Grass,* it is difficult to believe that he participated comfortably in the xenophobic, "Native American" campaign the *Aurora* launched in March and April against the (Irish) Roman Catholic demand for public support of its parochial schools in the city. Led by Bishop John Hughes, himself an Irish émigré, the Catholics got the backing of Tammany Hall by threatening to withhold—or even to redirect toward Whig candidates—their 70,000-strong voting bloc. The *Aurora* was one of three newspapers (the others were Bennett's *Herald* and Stone's *Advertiser*) that so heated up the controversy that an Irish mob took to the streets on election night armed with loaded revolvers and brickbats, clashing with "Americans" disgusted with "foreigners" as well as with the way the Tammany establishment had given in to political blackmail. In one of its earliest editorials, the *Aurora* described the Irish as of "the lowest class of foreigners," "bands of filthy wretches, whose very touch was offensive to a decent man, drunken loafers; scoundrels whom the police and criminal courts would be ashamed to receive in their walls," and generally "disgusting objects bearing the form human."[29]

It should be remembered that Anson Herrick "ran the political crank"[30] at the *Aurora* and probably did more than simply "inspire" its opinions. The general invective of the anti-Irish editorials matches more with the language of Herrick and Ropes's denunciation of Whitman in August, after he copied gossip from the *Hartford Review* into the *Tattler*. There is a clear sense of ownership—more than the mere rhetoric of the editorial "we"—in the statement the next day that the *Aurora* "needs no certificate of its character for courage. We do *not* fear, either the attacks of those whom, by exposing their wickedness, we have made enemies of—nor any 'tempest' that our conduct may bring down upon our head." The allusion here is to other political squabbles the *Aurora* had engaged in before Whitman's association with the paper. No doubt Whitman's Jeffersonian allegiance to the separation of church and state made him somewhat receptive to the *Aurora*'s complaints about and perhaps even its abuse of Bishop Hughes and his followers. Nevertheless, it is beyond even the power of the miraculous transformation of what Emerson called the poet's "long foreground" to think that the spouter of these xenophobic editorials is the same person who not only wrote *Leaves of Grass* but praised the working folk in the *Aurora* editorials on the New York boardinghouses and markets. And by the end of March even readers sympathetic with the *Aurora*'s position on the "School Question" had begun to complain about the vindictiveness and general lack of charity in the paper's otherwise legitimate position in terms of the Constitution's insistence on the separation of church and state. "You have loaded those whom you dislike" one reader wrote, "with abuse and opprobrium to a degree that I do not recollect ever to have seen equalled before; the fiercest invective, and the hottest hate can hardly lead you farther than you have already gone" in the *Aurora*'s stand "against FOREIGNERS."

The controversy was actually begun by Governor William Seward, later Lincoln's secretary of war, as he looked for a way to reduce the Irish resentment at the "Native American" stance adopted by the Whig party in New York City after the election of Mayor Aaron Clark in 1837.[31] Seward defended the School Bill in terms of what we would call today "cultural diversity," arguing in the state legislature for "the establishment of schools in which [the children of New York] may be instructed by teachers speaking the same language with themselves and professing the same faith."[32] He thought that many of the children of foreigners were being denied equal education because of religious and racial bias, a problem that had been recognized ever since the founding of the city's Public School Society in 1805. By the 1840s it was clear that the guiding members of the Society, which already gave public funds to private schools, were Protestant and tended to give in the direction of their religious preferences.

Hence, the main issue was not so much the separation of church and state as the "Native American" hatred of foreigners, especially the Irish, who in the nineteenth century before the Emancipation Proclamation occupied the lowest rung of American society. Although one of Whitman's sisters-in-law, Nancy McClure, was Irish, there is, in fact, brief evidence of anti-Irish sentiment in Whitman's family. Following the draft riots of July 1863, Jeff Whitman told Walt that he was "perfectly rabid on an Irishman. I hate them worse than I thought I could hate anything."[33] Yet this was following one of the worst civil disturbances in the history of New York City, in which more than 500 people were killed—including children in a Negro orphanage that was set afire—by Irish mobs ransacking the city in protest of the military draft. The Irish feared that the emancipation of slaves (for which they as draftees would be fighting) would introduce workers into the labor market place who would undercut their own already pitiable wages.

Even Jeff (who bought himself out of military duty the next year)[34] felt uncomfortable in venting such ethnic hatred; he added in his letter that the Irish "conduct for the past week has made me do it." Walt stayed above the controversy. After describing the angry feeling in Washington, where he was then living ("savage & hot as fire against New York," or its "*copperhead mob*"), he told his mother: "I do not feel it in my heart to abuse the poor people, or call for rope or bullets for them, but that is all the talk here, even in the hospitals."[35]

The editors of the 1950 edition of Whitman's writing for the *Aurora* included the anti-Irish editorials that appeared in the paper, noting that "this phase of Whitman's career" cannot be "admired or defended," only "explained." They point out that a number of prominent political leaders and literary men (e.g., James Harper and Seba Smith) were Nativists, and that Whitman was simply doing the politically expedient thing.[36] Yet the pattern of Whitman's career, in both journalism and poetry, implies that he was rarely expedient. As we shall see, he lost his best newspaper job—with the *Brooklyn Daily Eagle*—in 1848 by finally refusing to support the Democratic paper's position on the Free-Soil issue in Texas. And when Emerson urged him to tone down or excise the sexual "Enfans d'Adam" poems in the 1860 edition of *Leaves of Grass* (to give the book a "chance to be popularly seen, apprehended"), Whitman politely refused, saying that it would seriously compromise his literary message.[37] If Whitman had been "politically" astute, he could have become a successful journalist like Bryant, whom he admired for his poetry, if not always his editorship of the *Post.*[38] But even in 1842, as a young journalist establishing himself as an author in the popular *New World* and *Democratic Review,* Whitman followed a zigzag course wherein he responded, Quaker-like, to his inner impulses.

It seems out of character, therefore, for him to have locked himself into the rigid positions of the *Aurora* on the question of the Irish, who are also included in the "divine average" of 1855. In fact, Whitman's attempt to soften the *Aurora*'s position—in an anti-Nativist editorial that more resembles his literary style—may have led him to the voluntary conclusion of his duties there (probably as well to take the job on the *Evening Tattler,* a much more successful paper). Lamenting the undue influence of things foreign, though from more powerful European countries than Ireland, he wrote that he "could see no man disfranchised, because he happened to be born three thousand miles off." "Through me many long dumb voices," the poet would write in "Song of Myself,"

> Voices of the interminable generations of prisoners and slaves,
> Voices of the diseas'd and despairing, and of thieves and dwarfs,
> Voices of cycles of preparation and accretion.

Whitman was already assuming as journalist the role he would take up as Emerson's poet—the representative singer of *all* the voices. These clearly included the Irish, whose immigration Whitman heartily welcomed as editor of the *Brooklyn Daily Eagle.* Later on, he told Traubel that he stood in awe of the Irish people, but he noted that their "temperament is their glory and their danger at the same time."[39]

❋ ❋ ❋

Ever since his political speech of July 29, 1841—which was even criticized by his former employer at the *Brooklyn Evening Star*[40]—Whitman preferred literary writing to political reporting. For even though he would again become actively involved in politics (and not merely as a journalist) throughout the 1840s, he had initially come to New York City to make his fortune as a literary person. Armed with a batch of short stories and poems, he had already succeeded in getting his name around town. On April 9, he republished "Our Future Lot" (his earliest known poem) as "Time to Come" in the *Aurora* with the notation "From the Democratic Review."

This poem has not previously been identified as having appeared in the *Democratic Review,* but it would not have been unusual to see something in two (or more) different papers. American literary sheets (such as the *New World* and *Brother Jonathan*) regularly reprinted English novels, and in the era before the International Copyright Agreement (not adopted until 1891) both English and American authors had to rationalize thefts by viewing their victimization as a badge of success. Whitman, who later wrote his own press releases and reviews of his work, took advantage of the situation and stole from himself (just as he later anonymously reviewed himself, or *Leaves of Grass*).

The other identifiable poem he placed in the *Aurora* is "The Death and Burial of McDonald Clarke. A Parody," published on March 18, 1842. Clarke, whose poetry Whitman admired for its "bold, startling images, and strange pictures," had just died in a lunatic asylum shortly after being released from the Tombs Prison on lower Broadway; there he had been held for alleged drunkenness, though his condition was no doubt the result of mental derangement. Clarke's outlandishness and unorthodox behavior may have suggested to Whitman for the first time that an American poet did not have to be a "gentleman" like Bryant, Longfellow, or Holmes.

Born in New England, Clarke had come to the city via Philadelphia in the year of Whitman's birth and fallen in love with an actress, who briefly deserted her promising career to elope with him. After some months of relative poverty with Clarke, she returned to her mother and a successful theatrical career, which took her to the London stage. Her former husband never got over the loss. His mental instability gradually increased with subsequent disappointments in love so that he eventually came to be called the "Mad Poet"—"A poet comfortably crazy," he described himself in one of his verses. Although he had some family money, he gave away his possessions and lived in the streets.

Clarke's fame had gone well beyond the city when Whitman arrived there. Mirabeau Buonaparte Lamar, the second president of Texas, once met Clarke and left this record:

Say have you seen Macdonald Clarke,
  The Poet of the Moon?
He is a damned eccentric lark,
  As famous as Zip Coon.
He talks of Love and dreams of Fame,
  And lauds his minstrel art;
He has a kind of zig-zag brain—
  But yet a straight-line heart.

Upon Clarke's death he became the subject of newspaper columns around the country, including Lydia Maria Child's in the *Boston Courier* of March 17. After mentioning Whitman's obituary of Clarke in the *Aurora* of March 8, she wrote: "Often, when [Macdonald] had nothing to give, he would snatch up a ragged, shivering child in the street, carry it to the door of some princely mansion, and demand to see the lady of the house. When she appeared, he would say, 'Madam, God has made you one of the trustees of his wealth. It is His, not yours. Take this poor child, wash it, feed it, clothe it, comfort it—in God's name.'"[41]

Whitman, whose 1855 Preface to *Leaves of Grass* advised its readers to "despise riches" and "give alms to every one that asks," must have been attracted to Clarke. Though the poem he wrote for him in the *Aurora* of March 18, 1842, is sentimental ("No friend stood near him / . . . / To weep o'er the poet's sacred bier"), the obituary of March 12 was more effective: "It is a dreary thought—the likelihood that, through the chillness of destitution, this man, his soul swelling with gorgeous and gentle things, was prevented the chance of becoming an ornament to the world, instead of its scoff and laughing stock." Four years later, as editor of the *Brooklyn Daily Eagle,* Whitman once again praised the unappreciated Clarke, "whose grave is now verdant in Greenwood."[42]

Human interest stories were more in line with Whitman's literary and journalistic talent, rather than the political harangues that characterized the editorial complaints of not only Herrick but also the other papers of the day. The short stories expressed his compassion for those that even the "good cause" of democracy had somehow overlooked. By the time he left the *Aurora* in the spring of 1842, he had seen a good deal of New York life—what he called "a mighty world in itself." That world included prostitutes, unwed mothers, orphans, alcoholics, thieves, and muggers.

One day he visited a reform school in the city. "We saw about two hundred lads," he wrote on April 13 in the *Aurora,* "some of whom had been incipient thieves, and all, perhaps, more or less steeped in that vice, which runs through the Atlantic cities—loaferism—reduced to a state of the most perfect discipline." Though he praised the penal institution, Whitman also asked, on April 16 in the *Aurora,* for sympathy from the public, for understanding of the criminal poor as well as the working poor—and especially their children. "We love children," he wrote in the paper three days later. Here the children included a disguised and only partial reference to his youngest brother, Edward, now seven years old, lame, and "deaf and dumb from his birth."

> During a call we made at his parents', a few days ago, he came running in with a picture he had just found in ransacking a portfolio, and which baffled him to comprehend. It was the crucifixion of Christ and the thieves. His head bound with thorns and leaning from the weight of his awful misery—large drops of blood mixing with the sweat that poured down upon his breast—the Man of Grief still bore upon his features the impress of a mighty and unconquerable, and benevolent mind. A thief was upon either side.

Whitman noted how "very singular" it was that "the mind of this dumb youth seemed at once to respond to the idea of a God."[43] The retarded Eddy (who was not deaf) may resurface in "Song of Myself" as the "lunatic [who] is carried at last to the asylum a confirm'd case / He will never sleep any more as he did in the cot in his mother's bedroom." In 1864, long after these lines were first composed, Whitman's older brother, Jesse, was in fact so confined.

Whitman was playing around the edges of the sentimental, but the image of Christ as the epitome of compassion would find its way into *Leaves of Grass.* Emerson once said that *Leaves of Grass* was a blend of the *Bhagavad Gita* and the *New York Herald*—or the high sentiment of the Bible and the low sensationalism of William Gordon Bennett's newspaper, devout but also profane. In the middle, Whitman found his "divine average." Yet he had a long way to go, through many newspaper jobs, poems, and stories before he discovered—as Emerson had said in his March lecture—that "small and mean things serve just as well as great symbols."[44] He would continue to edit and write for newspapers and keep in his hand at fiction. Now, however, the fiction embraced family problems as social instead of personal problems.

❈ ❈ ❈

Franklin Evans, published in 1842 exclusively in the service of alcohol reform, was by no means Whitman's only temperance tale. In this phase of Whitman's literary development, the subject of alcoholism, construed in the 1840s as a threat to democracy and the rights of workers, is almost ever-present. Before the 1840s, America thought it had successfully put the alcoholic eighteenth century behind itself. Then alcohol had been part of everyday (and family) life, and even thought to be a health benefit. When Benjamin Franklin, for example, worked in a print shop in London in 1724, he disapproved of but was in no way surprised by the quantities his companions drank. He recalls in his *Autobiography* that at least one of his fellow workers drank "every day a Pint before Breakfast, a Pint at Breakfast with his Bread and Cheese; a Pint between Breakfast and Dinner; a Pint at Dinner; a Pint in the Afternoon about Six o'clock, and another when he had done his Day's Work." The "Water-American," as Franklin was called by his British co-workers, found the custom detestable, but the British acceptance of this kind of fare was almost wholly transplanted to America, beginning with the American Puritans whose ship, the *Arbella,* reached the New World with 10,000 gallons of beer and 12 gallons of distilled spirits.[45]

Virtually everyone consumed alcohol at meals. Water—in the era of polluted ground water and no urban waterworks—was considered unsafe, and coffee and tea were expensive because of heavy tariffs. This was the America into which Whitman's father was born in 1789. As one historian describes it, "Most alcohol consumption probably took place within the family. . . . Both beer and cider were drunk with meals as well as on social occasions; heavy drinking to the point of drunkenness seems to have been expected, or at least tolerated."[46] Although several temperance efforts were begun in New England by the end of the eighteenth century, the American Temperance Society was not formed until 1826, when Walter Whitman, Sr., was almost forty. Its popularity, if not its success, is indicated by the fact that by 1833 there were more than 4,000 local temperance societies in the country; however, the Society's prohibition banned only spirits and permitted the drinking of wine, beer, and cider, creating a partial pledge that Whitman assails in *Franklin Evans.*

Just when Whitman decided to write his temperance novel for Benjamin's *New World* is not known for sure. The poet may have simply seized the opportunity when Benjamin was trying to capitalize on the growing interest in the movement. By 1851 the "Maine Law" had established the first statewide prohibition of the sale of alcoholic beverages, which spread to many other states by the time of the Civil War. Whitman probably saw the spectacle of the sot in his family members, if not perhaps on occasion in himself. We know definitely that there was excessive drinking in his family (by Andrew Whitman and very possibly by his oldest brother, Jesse, and his father). Furthermore, the theme of intemperance runs through many of his plots. And as I have (most tentatively) suggested, the poet may have had a passing bout with intemperance. Although he later claimed that he did not taste "strong liquor" until he was thirty,[47] he may have experimented with the devil's brew while still living on Long Island and teaching school. In a draft of his letter of June 27, 1840, his friend from Jamaica, Abraham Leech, wrote: "You talk of smacking your lips over a *decoction of Dogwood* or engulphing a bottle of *sham pain.* Fie upon you boy, you are out of your sences [*sic*]. 'Much learning (no, not learning but wine) hath made you mad.' But I do not intend to preach a temp[erance] discourse on this occasion. I dare say friend Abel will favor you with one. All that I have to say more is in the language of a wiser than many of us: 'Wine is a mouth; strong drink is saying, whoever is deceived thereby is not wise.'"

Leech, it will be recalled, was Whitman's correspondent when he was carrying on so about the social disadvantages of teaching in Woodbury. He was four years Whitman's senior, having made his acquaintance in Jamaica in 1838, and an avid member of the temperance movements on Long Island and in New York City. His diary records attendance at various rallies between 1838 and 1844, including the "Great Mass Temperance Meeting" at Tompkins Square, New York, on November 13, 1841. As Leech kept up with Whitman's address through 1844, there is every reason to think that the two remained friends after Whitman moved back to New York in 1841, and he may even have been persuaded to join his friend at that temperance meeting or another. Whitman's familiarity with the movement, as he made clear in *Franklin Evans* and with at least the title of *The Madman*, was by no means hastily acquired, distant, or secondhand. Leech was a fanatic about his beliefs, which in addition to temperance included fasting for Christ. For one year, as he recorded in his diary, he "lived on bread & water."[48] Given Leech's penchant for reform, it would have been difficult, if not impossible, for Whitman to have this acquaintance on any but his friend's terms.

Leech spoke at temperance meetings and was no doubt a supporter of the Washingtonian movement, the clearest predecessor to today's Alcoholics Anonymous. Drawing almost exclusively on reformed drunks as speakers for the cause, it began in the early 1840s when six blue-collar men from Baltimore sobered up to sign a temperance pledge that banned the consumption of all alcohol, not simply hard liquor but also wine and beer. This particular temperance effort became a labor movement in which workers were encouraged to abstain from the use of alcohol so as not to be exploited by their bosses. Whitman, whose journalistic writings in the late 1840s took up the cause of the worker, would have been naturally drawn to the movement. Even the young politician Abraham Lincoln made a speech that year in support of the movement. He noted that its success depended on the example and exhortation of the average man previously held down by alcoholism, not the clergy, lawyers, or paid agents of temperance who spoke down to the masses and shamed them for their behavior.[49] To make matters worse for the working-class drinkers Lincoln addressed, they could afford only strong, home-manufactured whiskey because less addictive, middle-class drinks of wine and other fermented beverages were usually imported and thus too expensive. By the time Whitman sat down to write *Franklin Evans*, the temperance movement in the New York area was in full swing.

Responding to the interest in temperance, Herrick and Ropes established the *Washingtonian* in March, and two months later this weekly publication dedicated exclusively to the movement featured "Reuben's Last Wish," which was actually Whitman's first full-fledged temperance tale, not *Franklin Evans*. No doubt the new paper suggested the idea of writing in such a genre, but Whitman seems remarkably well prepared in terms of plot lines. The drunkard here is Franklin Slade, who drives his first son to sea and his second, Reuben, to an early grave, his last wish being that his father sign "the Temperance Pledge." The theme of brothers returns in "A Legend of Life and Love" and "The Angel of Tears," both published in the *Democratic Review* of July and September 1842, and the second also features alcoholism as one of the causes of fratricide ("minds maddened by intoxication").[50]

Franklin Evans, of course, is clear evidence that Whitman thought at the time that "the demon rum" would be the ruination of young America. Reporting on a temperance parade for the *Aurora* in March, he admired the young firemen ("fine, stalwart, handsome young men") who participated. In his first "song for occupations," he noted the other trades represented by banners declaring "Beware of the first glass!" or depicting a sheaf of grain with the motto "If you eat me, I am life; if you drink me, I am death."[51]

In the opening chapter of *Franklin Evans,* when Whitman shifts from the third to the first person ("Reader, I was that youth"), the admission comes as a shock because it sounds so sincere. The story begins where Whitman began, on Long Island, and takes the hero, at about the same age, to New York City. Although the tale warns country youths of the dangers of the city with its "musical saloons," it also reflects the problems of alcoholism in rural areas such as West Hills. We learn that the "sickly-looking, red-nosed" owner of the tavern, where Evans boards the stagecoach on the Long Island turnpike to New York, was a hale and hearty farmer "previous to his keeping the tavern." Once addicted, everything seems to go wrong: crops fail, business deals go sour, and the general health of not only the drunk but his family declines. "The truth is," Whitman writes with perhaps more insight than he would admit to his Camden disciples in his old age, "that habits of drunkeness [*sic*] in the head of a family, are like an evil influence—a great dark cloud, overhanging all, and spreading its gloom around every department of the business of that family, and poisoning their peace, at the same time that it debars them from any chance of rising in the world."[52]

The only beverage Whitman mentioned in the *Aurora* as having imbibed was lemonade, but a contemporary of Whitman's in those days testified that he drank "gin cocktails" at the Pewter Mug, around the corner from Tammany Hall on Spruce Street.[53] Years later, while contributing to the *Brooklyn Daily Times,* the poet spoke of the New York barroom and its "foaming ale in the cool tankard" as "wonderfully attractive."[54] Possibly embarrassed when his Camden disciples discovered he had written *Franklin Evans,* he claimed he had done the work "with the help of a bottle of port or what not."[55] And Charles Eldridge recalled that Whitman said he wrote the novel under the "stimulus . . . of relays of strong whisky cocktails, in order to keep the printer's devil, who was waiting, supplied with copy."[56] The question, of course, is whether Whitman was covering up his embarrassment by suggesting he was under the influence while writing the now disclaimed temperance tale (he, or the printer, did misnumber chapters 20 and 21), or he was admitting to some alcohol abuse himself. Whitman was—as *Franklin Evans* attests—acutely aware of the dangers of intoxicating drinks, but he was never a teetotaler. Also not an abuser, at least after the early 1840s, he drank beer at Pfaff's in New York in the 1850s, preferred ale in the 1860s while living in Washington, D.C., and later adopted a fondness for other alcoholic beverages, supplied by his Camden supporters.[57]

Franklin Evans; or The Inebriate. A Tale of the Times appeared in a special issue of the *New World* on November 23, 1842. Perhaps 20,000 copies of the pamphlet-sized novel were sold, a figure not unusual for cheaply priced works of a sensational nature distributed by newspapers. Also, temperance novels were usually bought up in large quantities by temperance organizations, and *Franklin Evans,* which sold individually for twelve and a half cents, could be had at $1 for ten copies or $8 for one hundred. Whitman received $75 initially for the work, and another $50 a few weeks later. The book was advertised as having been written "By a Popular American Author," who was not named in the promotion but was identified as "Walter Whitman" on the title page. Whitman claimed to have written the tale of approximately 50,000 words in three days, but even a maudlin and superficial drama like this one probably would have taken longer. The poet later called it "damned rot," but he put much of his own experience in the book as well as in his other shorter fiction.[58]

The tale concerns a young man who falls in with the "wrong sort," frequents bars and whorehouses, and marries one "good woman," only to drive her to an early grave because of his alcoholism. He goes south to Virginia, where he marries a Creole woman recently released from slavery; he falls out of love with her to love a white woman who is finally murdered through the agency of the spurned Creole. Franklin Evans then returns north, where people whom he had helped earlier now help him. In the end he is left a small fortune by a former employer and lives happily ever after. After his first wife died, he had taken the "Old Pledge," but finally he takes the "New Pledge" and abstains from all alcoholic beverages. Whitman argues that frequent inebriation affects the individual not only when drunk but during sober periods, tearing down the "energy of character."[59] Although the tale is farfetched in places, the homilies on intemperance were probably effective, and perhaps still are today.

Evans's interactions with women are also farfetched and stereotypical. The women are mannequins, and Margaret, the Creole wife he spurns, is hardly imaginable, except in her hatred of the other woman and in her ex-slave status. Foreshadowing Mark Twain's hot-blooded and ravishing Roxy in *Pudd'nhead Wilson* more than fifty years later, Margaret is "luscious and fascinating" with "large, soft voluptuous eyes and beautifully cut lips." Yet once this stock character, the same type of olive-skinned woman Melville exploited in his early novels, is set down, she fades into the stereotype of the uneducated and miscegenated Negro reflecting the state of freed slaves Whitman may have known in New York when he was growing up. She also becomes the cause of great guilt for the white Evans, who deeply regrets his hasty marriage to her—as if he has just awakened from a dream and a drunken binge. Again like Twain, Whitman shows his black antiheroine little sympathy. Just as Roxy is held in contempt at the end of *Pudd'nhead Wilson* for switching the "black" and white babies, Margaret's stage exit requires her incarceration and suicide. And the other woman, Margaret's white victim, is described as "wonderfully fair, not dark and swarthy, which I detest!"[60]

Whitman's racial attitudes and education were fairly typical of nineteenth-century America, though here he may have been playing to current prejudices to ensure the success of this tale. He never became an abolitionist (neither did Hawthorne and Melville) except in the metafiction of "Song of Myself," where, for example, the narrator in Section 10 assists a runaway slave. Margaret, however, is merely a stock character in a drama about the dangers of freedom in a new democracy. Just as Whitman's political tract *The Eighteenth Presidency!* (1854–56), emphasizing the aims of "free soil" in the West over "abolition" in the South, is more concerned about the rights of white workingmen than those of black slaves, this temperance tract, reflecting the aims of the Washingtonian movement, fears for the same white worker pulled down by the evils of the demon rum.

Without becoming a reformer himself, Whitman kept company with progressives throughout his life, not only temperance advocates but strivers for women's rights, workers' rights, freelovers' rights, and even moderate movers and shakers against slavery. He believed in temperance at this point in his life (indeed throughout the 1840s), and *Franklin Evans* was not written only for the money, or even on the spur of the moment, since Whitman had been rehearsing this theme in his shorter fiction. He himself—like the hero in his novel—may have been caught between the "Old" and "New" temperance pledges. In the conclusion, he reflects on the movement: "A great revolution has come to pass within the last eight or ten years. The dominion of the Liquor Fiend has been assaulted and battered." Perhaps speaking of the newest temperance people, the Washingtonians, as Lincoln had, he said: "The Reformers have one great advantage . . . which makes up for any want of polish, or grace. They are sincere, and speak with the convictions of their own experience." Whitman spoke here with the conviction of his own experience as well—as he would more famously thirteen years later in the first edition of *Leaves of Grass.* In the preface to his first great book of poems he reveals his anxiety that his personal experience would not be seen somehow as universal. "The proof of the poet," he insists, "is that his country absorbs him as affectionately as he has absorbed it." *Franklin Evans* concludes with a similar remark: "if my story meets with that favor which writers are perhaps too fond of relying upon, my readers may hear from me again."[61]

❋ ❋ ❋

Hear from him they did—in the very paper of the movement he was heralding in *Franklin Evans.* Hardly three months after the appearance of *Franklin Evans,* the first installment—one chapter and the beginning of a second, halted by the parenthetical "to be continued"—of *The Madman* appeared in the *Washingtonian* on January 28, 1843. Thus far no further chapters have been discovered,[62] and the only evidence that *The Madman* was intended as a temperance tract (besides the obvious significance of the title) is the fact that it appeared in a temperance publication. Despite its awkward phrasings and use of the passive voice in the initial paragraph, this tale promised to be the best of Whitman's fiction thus far. Whereas in *Franklin Evans* the plot features a single character who is clearly heterosexual, *The Madman* introduces two male characters in its first two chapters, Arden and Barcoure, whose sexual orientation, at least to today's reader, is at best unclear. They may be, of course, simply presented in the convention of nineteenth-century America where men could touch one another—even sleep in the same bed with each other—and not be thought homosexual.

There is in *The Madman,* however, a definite same-sex theme. The shift perhaps foreshadows the shift from heterosexuality to male "Adhesiveness" that Whitman made between "Children of Adam" and "Calamus." The complementary nature of the protagonists is reminiscent of Poe's use of the *doppelganger* in such stories as "William Wilson" and "The Man in the Crowd." Whitman's use of two main characters instead of one perhaps signals his emerging interest, in fiction at least, in the neutral territory of bisexuality, because he says, somewhat awkwardly, that "it may be found before the end of my story, that the right of main personage may lie between the two."

Barcoure turns out to be an accurate projection of the all-embracing author of *Leaves of Grass.* This character is described as not quite an infidel: he maintains a vague sense of conventional "morality and virtue," but he "rejected all of what he called the *superstitions* of mankind. He held that each code of religion contained more or less excellence—and more or less fanaticism. A strange and dreamy creature was Pierre Barcoure." The description also rather accurately reflects Whitman as a reformer of the 1840s, when he upheld accepted beliefs about social conduct and responsibility while also pleading the case of the poor, the prostitute, the abandoned or mentally retarded child—in a phrase, the notable and bothersome exceptions to a supposedly model society energized by its belief in "Manifest Destiny." In "Song of Myself," of course, Whitman's "religion" would include all religions:

> I do not despise you priests, all time, the world over,
> My faith is the greatest of faiths and the least of faiths,
> Enclosing worship ancient and modern and all between ancient
>   and modern.
>
> (Section 43)

Barcoure is Whitman, down to the dreaminess and the possible vulnerability in his early twenties to alcohol abuse. Franklin Evans has drinking partners, too, but the relationships are vaguely described, the other characters mere stage scenery to the drama of Evans's alcoholism and debauchery. The existing chapters of *The Madman* suggest that the noble Barcoure will be tempted by the distinctly lower-middle-class Arden, whose appearance opens the novel at "one of the large eating houses in the upper part of Fulton street."

Arden and Barcoure first meet at the restaurant. The following day they bow to each other. "The next day, each gave the other his name. The next week, they were on the footing of intimacy and familiarity." In *The Madman,* Whitman remarks at the rather miraculous, certainly inexplicable, nature of male friendships: "How strangely we form acquaintances! How strange, indeed, and how complete a matter of chance, are many of those incidents and occurrences which have a lasting influence on a future destiny—trivial, as they seem at first, but potent for good or evil, in the future." In "Calamus" the poet allegedly revealed "the secrets of [his] nights and days"—with "comrades." In No. 18 of the 1860 series, he addresses Manhattan as the "City of my walks and joys!" And after surveying the sights of the city—its pageants, its "interminable rows of your houses," its "ships at the wharves"—he says that the only thing that finally repays him is its stream of "continual lovers." Unmarried throughout his life, Whitman had several longstanding female friends as well as male ones. Yet it may have been the passing male relationships that offered him the freedom of the city, the run of its haunts as the *flaneur* in him looked into many possible situations. Unfortunately, we cannot follow Arden and Barcoure into the secrets of their "nights and days."

We can, however, follow—or glimpse—another pair of Whitman's bachelors, in another of his unfinished tales. As with *The Madman,* only the first two chapters of *The Fireman's Dream: With a Story of His Strange Companion* were completed. Subtitled "A Tale of Fantasie," the fragment—which also ends in midair with the bracketed "to be continued"—was published in the *Sunday Times & Noah's Weekly Messenger* of March 31, 1844.[63] It concerns a fireman and a Native American and is as dreamlike as the poem "The Sleepers" that went into the first edition of *Leaves of Grass.* Chapter 1 describes a part-time New York fireman and apprentice cabinetmaker, George Willis, who is almost killed in the line of duty. On a summer outing to Hoboken before he is injured, he notices an Indian, "a man of about twenty three or four, that attracted more than ordinary attention." After his injury, he falls into delirium and imagines "himself a trackless Indian." He wanders into the wilderness and meets his "companion, not much beyond his own age, but of the hue of the sons of the forest." As the Native American tells his story, "mourning the decay of his ancient race," Willis "drank in his narrative with delight." Chapter 2 is told from the first-person point of view of apparently the same Indian, an unnamed "white man by education and an Indian by birth." As a child he was found "far in the outskirts of one of the western states," wounded and abandoned, and taken in by Sampsom Boanes and his wife, a pioneer couple. "That Indian boy," Whitman writes with the same intensity as in his first-person identification with Franklin Evans, "was *myself.*" He learns the white language and in time becomes an outstanding student, second in achievement only to Anthony Clark, a distant relative of the people who adopted the Indian boy. Clark comes to live with the Boanes. The narrator asks rhetorically, "Why should I not have mentioned this before, when the name of the person is burnt in welcome characters of fire upon my soul?" Just where Whitman was going with either this tale or *The Madman* is impossible to tell, but the subject in both cases is male comradeship—long before the "Calamus" tale.

4

HEART-SONGS IN BROOKLYN

❧ ❧ ❧

I will not have a single person slighted or left away,
The kept woman, sponger, thief, are hereby invited,
The heavy-lipp'd slave is invited, the venerealee is invited;
There shall be no difference between them and the rest.

WALT WHITMAN
"Song of Myself"

Whitman resided in Manhattan until 1845 and worked for several newspapers in the city. These included the *New York Sun,* the *Subterranean,* the *Sunday Times & Noah's Weekly Messenger,* the *New-York Democrat,* the *Statesman,* and the *Daily Plebeian* (where he was once visited by James Russell Lowell) during the late fall or early winter of 1843.[1] On October 14, 1842, the *Plebeian* carried what may have been Whitman's first effort at self-promotion in the press, a practice that crested with his three anonymous reviews of the 1855 *Leaves* but continued steadily throughout his life. An article about the Queens County Democratic campaign, in which he had taken an active part, noted that it was "a pity the people of Queens have not some one to stir them up in the columns of the 'Democrat,' as in the fall of 1840, by a certain young fellow from the eastern part of the island, who 'fluttered the Volsces,' at no small rate, and contributed materially to the unexpected triumph of the party at that period."[2] Whitman promoted himself anonymously again in the *New York Sun* of December 1, in a piece entitled "Dangers to Country Youth in the City." Warning young men awash in urban temptations, he puffed his own work by referring to the "author of the lately-published novel of 'Franklin Evans,'" whose central character "was led onward to the very verge of ruin by his weak and unmanly desire to ape the habits and manners of the town."[3]

On December 10, 1842, two weeks after the publication of *Franklin Evans,* Park Benjamin published the poem "A Sketch" in his *New World.* Even in its poetic orthodoxy, it is our first important literary preview of the private poet who would make public his boundless affection for the one in the many, the representative lover. Here, of course, the private thoughts of the public poet are subdued by the general nineteenth-century fear of the body. Still much more the journalist and the fiction writer, throughout the decade he continued giving out conventional advice to working men and women, apprentices and youths, and public servants. It is clear from Whitman's early writings that the poet's famous foreground imbibed the spirit of the times—a reform mentality whose intensity Emerson once characterized as so thoroughgoing that even "the insect world was to be defended."[4] Yet Whitman was no New England reformer. His idea of utopia was no agrarian retreat—no transcendentalist Brook Farm or Fruitlands—but the American city, which must allow the democratic spirit of the Revolution to flourish, engendering a true citizenry of energetic equals.

"A Sketch" was signed only "W." and has not until recently been known or identified as yet another of Whitman's early poems.[5] Benjamin, a poetaster like the young Whitman and a glad-hander who seemed to know everyone in journalism and politics, was a fierce literary nationalist who had strenuously objected to the lavish reception given Charles Dickens earlier that year. When he started the *New World* on January 6, 1840, its motto claimed that the "whole unbounded continent is ours." The literary organ outlasted its chief competitor, *Brother Jonathan,* by two years, though Benjamin's name does not appear on the title page after 1843. Benjamin, like his fellow journalists, was outspoken and quarreled with just about everybody in the business in and around Nassau Street. This included Whitman at one point, but apparently Benjamin thought enough of Whitman's literary skills to publish his first (and perhaps only) novel. Athough the two had at least one other spat, while Whitman was editor of the *Eagle,* Benjamin became an admirer of *Leaves of Grass,* most probably for its claim as homegrown literature.[6]

The *New World* years were apparently Benjamin's most successful, for his final decades were spent somewhat listlessly as a literary agent, lecturer, and finally obsequious jobseeker in government during the Civil War. The closest he came to a government sinecure was securing Lincoln's authorization to write a biography, which he never even began. His last attempt at organizing a newspaper was also apparently a failure. In advertising a paper to be called the *Constellation* in January 1859, he described it as "A Perfect Family Newspaper! never to contain a line either in its reading or advertising columns to give offence to any one. THE SLAVERY QUESTION WILL BE WHOLLY IGNORED IN ITS COLUMNS. . . ." He died during the war—of natural, not military, causes—and left behind a wife and six adolescent children.[7]

"A Sketch" resembles in theme and metrics "Each Has His Grief" and "The Punishment of Pride," which Benjamin had published in 1841. The old idea that the next life awaits to erase the burdens of this one is cadenced out in iambic tetrameter, the favored rhythm of the 1830s and 1840s and one of Emerson's frequent meters. The poem also bears a strong kinship to Whitman's earliest known poem, "Our Future Lot" (later "Time to Come").[8]

Because of Emerson's fondness for iambic tetrameter, it would be nice to think we have here an Emersonian influence on Whitman earlier than what has been thought, but he probably had not read any of Emerson's poems by 1842, which—with the exception of the few in one of Rufus Wilmot Griswold's poetry collections published in the early 1840s—did not officially make their debut until 1847 with Emerson's first volume of verse. Whitman's primary models were more probably the poets of the day published in both the *New World* and *Brother Jonathan,* poets like Benjamin himself or Nathaniel P. Willis, both of whom hammered out their verse in tetrameters. Perhaps his main model, for this poem at least, was Poe, whose "To Helen" had been published in 1831. Although Whitman had not yet met Poe, he was undoubtedly familiar with his works, even though his most popular poem, "The Raven," had not yet appeared. In its own fashion "To Helen" is, like "A Sketch," a seashore poem in which the subject's beauty brings the "weary, way-worn wanderer" home to "his own native shore."

"A Sketch" is Whitman's first seashore poem, anticipating, though vaguely and in the convention of the times, the painful separation of lovers as contemplated on the shores of what later would be identified as Paumanok, or Long Island. In "Out of the Cradle Endlessly Rocking" in 1860 and "Out of the Rolling Ocean, the Crowd" in 1865, the poet stands on the shore before the "irresistible sea" and essentially asks for "a clew." In "A Sketch," however, the narrator seems more confident about life's denouement. The poem uses the same consonants suggesting fatigue and melancholy ("wave-worn shore") that Poe employed in "To Helen." The future "Solitary Singer," as he is called in Gay Wilson Allen's biography, looks upon a "solitary form," pining over his dead lover. This loss of a beautiful woman, in Poe fashion, prompts the forlorn lover to ask her spirit to help him understand the "chastening hand of heaven" that took her away. The poem's last two stanzas (of five) conclude with the narrator's plea:

> Could I this sacred solace share,
>   'Twould still my struggling bosom's moan;
> And the deep peacefulness of prayer,
>   Might for thy heavy loss atone!
> Earth, in its wreath of summer flowers,
>   And all its varied scenes of joy,
> Its festal halls and echoing bowers,
>   No more my darkened thoughts employ.
>
> But here, the billow's heaving breast,
>   And the low thunder's knelling tone,
> Speak of the wearied soul's unrest,
>   Its murmurings, and conflicts lone!
> And yon sweet star, whose golden gleam,
>   Pierces the tempest's gathering gloom,
> In the rich radiance of its beam,
>   Tells me of light beyond the tomb!

The object of the speaker's loss is a woman—the opposite gender of what an early biographer discovered, albeit reluctantly, in a draft of

"Once I Pass'd Through a Populous City" (1860).[9] It has been argued elsewhere that such a late poem as "Out of the Rolling Ocean, the Crowd" is also about the loss of a beautiful woman, or at least a mysterious woman Whitman is supposed to have known.[10] And in the case of "Out of the Cradle," the separation is also between opposite sexes, a "he-bird" and a "she-bird." Had Whitman fallen in love with a woman in 1842—as other biographers have argued that he did in 1848, during his New Orleans period—or a man?

There is no clear documentary evidence for either claim. In his biography of Whitman, Justin Kaplan suggests that Whitman may have visited prostitutes during the 1840s,[11] yet the known circumstantial evidence about his movements then does not support this speculation very steadily. Furthermore, the heterosexual exchanges in *Franklin Evans* ring hollow and superficial, whereas same-sex possibilities hinted at in the opening chapters of *The Madman* may be more persuasive. "A Sketch," nevertheless, is conventionally heterosexual and conventionally poetic, expressing in public acceptable sentiments for its day. Whitman was still sacrificing at what he would call in the *Brooklyn Eagle* of November 5, 1847, "the shrine of formal construction." The poem shows no hint of following Emerson's exhortation in "Nature and the Powers of the Poet," the lecture Whitman had heard in March of 1842—"New topics, new powers, a new spirit arise, which threaten to abolish all that was called poetry"—an appeal that became a call for a "meter-making argument" in the printed version of the lecture in 1844.[12] Yet neither did Emerson follow his own advice in his *Poems,* where many of the poems employ the same poetical conventions found in "A Sketch." What is remarkable about "A Sketch" in its claim as part of the poet's early canon is not its rhyme and meter but the fact that in addition to its early use of the seashore it reveals—perhaps for the first time in the poetry—the loneliness found in parts of "Song of Myself," the "Calamus" poems, and of course the "Sea-Drift" series, not only "Out of the Cradle," but "As I Ebb'd with the Ocean of Life." Whitman's narrator seems lonely even in the midst of lovers.

Twenty-three when he published "A Sketch," Whitman stood just under six feet and weighed then about 180 pounds, though his full adult weight reached 200. Although he was remembered as dressing like a farmer when he was editor of the *Eagle* at the age of twenty-seven and twenty-eight in the late 1840s, at the beginning of the decade he still dressed like the other writers and journalists—generally in black from head to toe. In his earliest-known photograph, Whitman is depicted in the conventional pose of that era. Holding a walking stick or bent-handled cane to his right shoulder, the hatted figure stares into the camera's eye. Indeed, Whitman looks almost eyeless, the result no doubt of a poor daguerreotype exposure. His hair, which was auburn, is slightly wavy, covering the ears and blending with his rather Mennonite-like beard (no mustache), already splotched with gray about the chin. His collar is loosely starched and adorned with a neckerchief. The daguerreotype, the first of many for this poet who loved the body too much for the nineteenth century, suggests someone looking (and dressing) for conventional love. "Who goes there?" we might ask in echo of the Self who would sing so boldly in 1855 and beyond. Then—as shown in the 1855 frontispiece—he stood coatless, right hand mounted on his hip, the other in his pocket, putting the stamp of his personality on record. The photograph that greets the reader of the 1855 and 1856 editions of *Leaves of Grass* seems more to suggest a man with a carnal appetite already whetted by experience.

❋ ❋ ❋

But in those early years, only the fiction, which ran until 1848, touched occasionally on the underside of the public writer. And here we have to wait another year, for the March 1843 issue of the *Columbian Magazine,* which carried his "Eris: A Spirit Record." The plot, whose theme also anticipates Poe's in "Annabel Lee" (1849), concerns the angel Dai, who is commanded to watch over the dying Eris as her lover remains by her side. Instead, Dai—like the angels in Poe's poem—envies the earthly lovers and promptly falls in love with Eris, who is then swept away to heaven. Dai is blinded by God and sentenced to hover over the abandoned earthly lover till he dies and joins Eris in heaven. The moral, rather standard for the fiction of the time, a decade in which spiritualism and its "table-rappers" attracted a great deal of attention, is that "the pure love of two human beings is a sacred thing, which the immortal themselves must not dare to cross."[13] Like the "bad angel" in "The Punishment of Pride," Dai has little sympathy with the common man. This idea may have fed into Whitman's lifelong distrust of organized religion, whose churches in the nineteenth century not only recognized the different economic and social levels within their congregations but condescended to the poorer members.

He returned to the seduction theme in "Dumb Kate," which appeared in the *Columbian* of May 1844. The newspapers of the era were full of stories about women who were cast off by their families after succumbing sexually to a promise of marriage. Here the "bad angel" is a mortal, a villainous young man who seduces a "deaf and dumb" young woman, who dies in shame. In the September issue of the same magazine, Whitman also published "The Little Sleighers: A Sketch of a Winter Morning on the Battery," which is preoccupied as well with the loss of innocence. Yet he may have sensed, aside from the real social problems he was airing, how sentimentally bloated and conventional his treatments were—finally exclaiming at the end of this sketch, "what a sombre moralist I have become!"[14]

His fiction had been reduced, more and more it seemed, to a sketchy didacticism. Even the autobiographical "My Boys and Girls," published in the short-lived *Rover* on April 20, 1844, concludes melodramatically. In the similarly titled "Boys and Girls," published in the *Plebeian* on March 1, 1843, he had imagined children as miniature adults, "reflecting the wisdom of the incipient man of the world, as if they knew sorrow."[15] In "My Boys and Girls," youthful innocence is related to the adulthood of the new nation and its hallowed leaders: "What would you say, dear reader, were I to claim nearest relationship to George Washington, Thomas Jefferson, and Andrew Jackson? . . . Several times has the immortal Washington sat on my shoulders. . . . Around the waist of the sagacious Jefferson have I circled one arm, while the fingers of the other have pointed him out words to spell. And though Jackson is (strange paradox!) considerably older than the other two, many a race and tumble have I had with him." These, of course, were references to three of his brothers, with whom he would soon be living again in his parents' home in Brooklyn. But rather than develop this clever allegory in which the Whitman family becomes the national family—as the poet Walt Whitman would become representative of America—he allows the sketch to devolve into the hackneyed sentimentality of the kind found in the fiction of Lydia Sigourney and others popular in the literary press of the 1840s. "It is a dreary thought to imagine what may happen, in the future years, to a handsome, merry child," Whitman wrote in tandem with the moralists of his day, "to gaze far down the vista, and see the dim phantoms of Evil standing about with nets and temptations—to witness, in the perspective, purity gone, and the freshness of youthful innocence rubbed off, like the wasted bloom of flowers."[16]

Whitman needed a fresh subject if he was to stay alive as a writer and not merely contribute to the melodramatic musings that made up the theme of that era's fiction and poetry in America. He found it, or at least shifted the focus of his sentimentality, by returning his thoughts to Paumanok, to the theme of the American Indian. "Arrow-Tip," published in the *Aristidean* in March, may contain the seeds of the powerful lines that open Section 39 of "Song of Myself":

> The friendly and flowing savage, who is he?
> Is he waiting for civilization, or past it and mastering it?

Basing their interpretations on the subsequent lines, which find the "savage" embodied in the American frontiersman and settler, several critics have tended to see this figure as the new American Superman who brushes aside the old gods of European society in order to return to nature's laws—and of course its innocence.[17] Although in *Leaves of Grass* Whitman probably also intended the cultural ambiguity of the Indian (in a country that dwelled more and more on its difference from Europe as it destroyed its indigenous population), in this story he is probably invoking the tradition of the "Noble Savage," a concept that was occasionally celebrated (e.g., in Longfellow's *Hiawatha* in 1855) in the Indian-hating century of American history. As Roy Harvey Pearce notes of the success of Longfellow's poem, which sold 38,000 copies during its first year of publication, "the noble savage lived on in spirit precisely because he no longer lived on in the flesh."[18]

In "Arrow-Tip" the American Indian is viewed generally as a victim of the kind of frontier prejudice that Melville examined in "The Metaphysics of Indian-Hating" chapter of *The Confidence-Man* in 1856. Whitman would again turn to the subject in his "Brooklyniana" series. Yet Arrow-Tip is no angel; he is simply a "noble bystander" betrayed not by the white man but by another "Indian," a half-breed named Boddo. Boddo, as the name suggests, is a latter-day Caliban, a hunchbacked creature whose "face was the index to many bad passions." Like the spurned Margaret in *Franklin Evans,* he is the product of racial interbreeding and consequently has few redeemable features. When Whitman republished the tale in the *Eagle* the next year as an "Original Novelette," he called it "The Half-Breed: A Tale of the Western Frontier."[19]

Prejudice against the American Indian was at its height at the time Whitman published his tale. As Melville wrote in *The Confidence-Man,* the Indian was in the view of the backwoodsman automatically guilty of lying, theft, and double-dealing. He was thought to be—like an animal—almost completely without a (white) conscience.[20] When Boddo steals from the settlers, for example, the Indian, Arrow-Tip, is their natural suspect. Boddo is caught because of Arrow-Tip's honesty, but Boddo gets his revenge by withholding evidence when Arrow-Tip is wrongfully convicted and executed for killing a white settler.

In the nineteenth century as in most of the twentieth, the term "half-breed" was pejorative. (The word "miscegenation" would not be invented until the 1860s—by David G. Croly, a future acquaintance of the poet's—with the simultaneous rise of pseudoscience and the recycled idea of recolonizing blacks back to Africa.)[21] Its negative connotation in this century has hinged on the lack of white purity, but in the nineteenth century "half-breed" alluded almost exclusively to ethnically mixed Americans whose native identity was tainted with European blood: Boddo is evil not because he is half Irish but because he is not entirely Indian. This story condemns the half-breed and laments the passing of the full-blooded Indian. Whitman's tendency was to find redeeming features in the national enemy—the Mexican peasants over their corrupt leaders during the Mexican War, southern farmers over aristocratically bred politicians, and high-ranking officers over enlisted men during the Civil War. A reformer but almost never a radical on social questions, he believed that America was losing something by pursuing its Policy of Indian Removal. Yet at the same time he accepted with Darwinian confidence the Indians' fated extinction—as he would the fate of the giant Sequoias in "Song of the Redwood-Tree" in 1874. After Arrow-Tip's execution, his brother Deer "led his tribe still further into the west, to grounds where they never would be annoyed, in their generation at least, by the presence of the white intruders."[22]

Whitman had mixed feelings about American Indians throughout his life—as he had about African Americans. In his youth and early manhood he had encountered the lingering remnants of the Iroquois at Montauk and the frequently unemployed free blacks of Brooklyn—both groups ignored and scorned by the dominant white culture. Basically, he wanted both minorities to evolve out of their own identities, to be given that opportunity in the dominantly white, European-sourced America. Whitman returned to the subject of the Indian from time to time in his writings and acquired an increased sensitivity regarding black slavery while editing the *Eagle,* but generally he was more concerned with the problems of whites in a growing democracy. These included the state of public education, the tariff question, the National Bank (a problem, like the tariff, still lingering from the previous decade), internal improvements, and—by 1846—conflicts with England over the Oregon territory and with Mexico over the new state of Texas and the California territory (which included New Mexico and Arizona).

Whitman studied problems closer to home as a freelance reporter and editorialist for the *Brooklyn Evening Star* and as a frequent contributor of social fiction to the *Democratic Review* and Thomas Dunn English's short-lived *Aristidean.* He had worked, it will be recalled, for Alden Spooner's *Star* in the 1830s (then called the *Long Island Star*) as a printer's devil. Now the colonel's son, Edwin B. Spooner, was the editor, and Whitman enjoyed a regular connection with the Whig newspaper between August 1845 and March 1846, when he assumed the editorship of the *Eagle*—one of the most enjoyable "sits" of his working life. The commencement of his work with the *Star* coincided with his family's move back to Brooklyn from Dix Hills; he probably boarded with his parents and siblings first on Gold Street and afterward at 71 Prince Street.[23]

He had published in the *Star* as early as February 18, 1845—printing "Shirval: A Tale of Jerusalem" possibly before it appeared in the March issue of the *Aristidean.* (No mention of the story's journal publication appears in the *Star* printing.) Echoing the story of Christ's restoring the life of a twenty-four-year-old man (Luke vii: 11–18), the biblical allusion underscores the romantic concept behind Whitman's reform efforts at both the *Star* and the *Eagle.* For students of Whitman, however, "Shirval" is particularly interesting for its introductory matter, which contains the first hint of the reformer of American literature as found in *Leaves of Grass.* There is, for example, a foreshadowing of the poet's marvelous apostrophe to earth in "Song of Myself," though in "Shirval" the earth is addressed as a "huge tomb-yard of humanity!" Whitman's later pantheistic celebration of the body is also reflected here in the idea that when death comes we do not disappear from the earth but become part of it: the earth contains "the mixed remains, of myriads of human forms that were once as we are now." "These buried men and women," Whitman speculated in anticipation of another great poem, "lived and loved—wrought and grieved like us;—had their crimes and agonies, as the living now have."[24] In his early fiction, Whitman spoke about the afterlife; in 1845 it took a "miracle" to erase the distance between life and death. Eleven years later, he spoke in "Crossing Brooklyn Ferry" as if from the grave, believing then that the afterlife was simply another part of our existence:

I am with you, you men and women of a generation, or ever so
  many generations hence,
Just as you feel when you look on the river and sky, so I felt,
Just as any of you is one of the living crowd, I was one of the crowd,
Just as you are refresh'd by the gladness of the river and the bright flow,
  I was refresh'd.
Just as you stand and lean on the rail, yet hurry with the swift current, I
  stood yet was hurried,
Just as you look on the numberless masts of ships and the thick-
  stemm'd pipes of steamboats, I look'd.

In 1856 the poet could proclaim that neither time nor space makes any difference in the mind of the living reader. "It avails not, time nor place—distance avails not." In the transcendentalist scheme, the human mind reflected the mind of God.

⁂ ⁂ ⁂

Still essentially immersed in the mediums of journalism and sentimental fiction, Whitman had a long way to go on the road to this kind of psychic liberation. He was busy and would remain so, protesting any and all threats to democracy: whipping in schools, lack of Christian charity among church leaders, the death penalty, lazy apprentices, alcoholism in the working class, street crime, copycat drama, and even classical music—though he had yet to discover or fully appreciate opera. In April the *Aristidean* published his "Richard Parker's Widow," a tale based on the mutiny at the Nore—the infamous takeover of a British military vessel in the late eighteenth century, which, the author noted in sympathy for the mutineers, "shook with terror the foundations of the throne itself!" As Whitman wrote in the *Eagle* almost exactly a year after the publication of his story, he thought the navy with its emphatic distinctions of rank a "most aristocratic, unwholesome institution."[25] "The Boy-Lover" (*American Review,* May) contains strong temperance overtones,[26] and "Revenge and Requital; A Tale of a Murderer Escaped" (*Democratic Review,* July–August) argues indirectly against capital punishment. At the same time, in a speech before the Eighteenth Annual Fair of the American Institute in September 1845 entitled "Tear Down and Build Over Again," he warned against the kind of "progress" that threatened to obliterate the history of George Washington and his noble compatriots. Otherwise, however, "No friend are we to the rotten structures of the past, either of architecture or government." So optimistic was Whitman about America's future that he saw evidence of democratic change even in the new British queen, Victoria, who showed "fewer faults, and more estimable qualities thus far, than any of the long line of monarchs who have sat upon the British throne, and so generally oppressed the British people."[27] The democrat would admire the queen, born in the same year as the poet, until the end of his days. To Traubel's socialist dismay, he wrote a poem to Victoria on her seventy-second birthday, although he did not include it in *Leaves of Grass.*

When he was not calling for reform in the *Star,* he was contributing heavily didactic and sentimental material to the *Aristidean.* "Some Fact-Romances," published in December 1845, is a medley of "true-life" incidents on Long Island, maudlin and romanticized by their remoteness in time. The sketches recount personal failure and personal triumph. In the first, a man impulsively saves his sweetheart from drowning at the cost of the life of his sister in need of the same help; he marries the girl but pines away in Hawthornian gloom. The second concerns an aged black "widow-woman" who aids the deaf daughter of "intemperate parents." Whitman's wonderment over the black woman's "disinterested love" may anticipate his bewilderment over the patience of the "dusky" ex-slave in "Ethiopia Saluting the Colors" in 1871. The other pieces consist of mere observations (one only a paragraph). Whitman later published three of them as fillers in the *Eagle.* It appears that the *Star* provided him with his final journalistic apprenticeship for the *Eagle* editorship, while the *Aristidean* served as the final resting place for most of his new fiction.

Besides the cause of temperance, another issue that seems to have encapsulated his democratic fears and hopes was capital punishment. Until the nineteenth century, the death penalty was accepted with little ambivalence as simply a means of retribution. Beginning with the Jacksonian era, arguments about deterrence became necessary. As early as 1842 Whitman had spoken out against the death penalty—in the *New York Sun* of November 2, 22, and 24—calling it the cruel and irrevocable means by which society shirked its responsibility to provide an environment that cultivated good citizenship instead of criminality. Whitman thought that the death penalty was no deterrent to the crimes it punished, pointing to the good effects of its abolition in other countries and to the fact that less serious offenses no longer punished by death in America had not increased. Moreover, if hanging was truly a deterrent, why were executions not carried out publicly as they had been until the previous century? If one execution worked to that effect, why not execute all of New York's estimated twenty condemned or the nation's estimated two hundred on death row? Finally, he opposed the death penalty because, as he said in 1845 in "A Dialogue," it destroyed "that cunning principle of vitality which no human agency can replace." He was appalled by that human agency's attempt to play God by "founding the whole breadth and strength of the hanging system . . . on the Holy Scriptures." Later, in the *Eagle,* he adjusted his view of the death penalty slightly by conceding that juries tended to acquit in order not to be associated with the morally doubtful act of taking another person's life, and near the end of his life, he still opposed capital punishment, but only moderately so.[28] But in 1845—publishing with "A Dialogue" his most developed argument in both the *Democratic Review* and the *Star*[29]—Whitman opposed it not merely on moral grounds but on the political grounds that it symbolized society's frequent unfairness to the common man gone astray mainly because of social and economic inequities.

In "A Dialogue" Whitman used the Socratic method to produce an eerie exchange between society and a criminal—"the imposing majesty of the people speaking on the one side, a pallid, shivering convict on the other." Most likely, he got his method from "Dialogue Between a Master and a Slave" in Caleb Bingham's *The Columbian Orator* (1797), the standard manual on oratory in the early nineteenth century. Possibly, Whitman was directed there by reading *Narrative of the Life of Frederick Douglass,* published earlier in 1845. Douglass refers to the master-slave dialogue in his discussion of "voluntary emancipation."[30] Whitman too appealed to conscience, thinking—just as he later would about slavery—that once the whole argument against capital punishment was laid out, the public would abolish the practice. The condemned man in Whitman's dialogue, guilty of murder in a frenzied moment, is perhaps a "slave" to a flawed democracy. He asks whether there is not an alternative punishment that might save him for the possible good of society. When he is told that he should never have committed the crime in the first place, he asks whether society itself is not guilty of crimes. The answer is "none which the law can touch." "True," it admits, "one of us had a mother, a weak-souled creature, that pined away . . . , and at last died, because her son was intemperate, and treated her ill. Another, who is the owner of many houses, thrusts a sick family into the street because they did not pay the rent. . . . And another—that particularly well-dressed man—effected the ruin of a young girl, a silly thing who afterward became demented, and drowned herself in the river. One has gained much wealth by cheating his neighbors—but cheating so as not to come within the clutches of any statute."

Clearly, Whitman saw capital punishment in the broader context of the haves and the have-nots. In the *Eagle* of March 23, 1846, he railed against the hanging of an ex-slave who—hardened after a long term of possibly false imprisonment—was condemned for murder. "What remains then [after the corruption brought on by prison life]? *Hang him!* In the work of death, let the law keep up with the murderer."[31] Later that year, he sympathetically followed the events leading to the execution of a man called Wyatt, whose full or real name was never identified by the newspapers or police. Nor was his unstable background, on which Whitman shrewdly speculated. When Wyatt attempted suicide in his cell, Whitman mocked on August 18 that it was thought Wyatt "would survive long enough to be strangled according to law." When that day came—forty-eight hours later—Whitman reported the condemned man's last words and actions as dignified, while the rival Whig paper, the *Star*, wrote that Wyatt "acted perfectly frantic, remarking that it was hard to be hanged for killing such a poor miserable creature as [the victim], and was sorry he had not killed two or three of the keepers; then he would be satisfied."[32] Wyatt's last words sound like those of the condemned man sentimentalized in "A Dialogue," so there is the possibility that the *Star* had the more accurate report.

Whitman was no "bleeding heart"—even in the 1840s—who pitied criminals while ignoring their crimes. Much of his humanity was informed by the Bible, a major influence on his later poetry, and its Christian doctrine of inclusiveness. In "Song of Myself," he would include the prisoner—if not the condemned man—in the "hue and caste" of the America he absorbed—"farmer, mechanic, artist, gentleman, sailor, quaker, / Prisoner, fancy-man, rowdy, lawyer, physician, priest." Time and again, Whitman was primarily interested in the "crimes," or inequities, of the society that helped to produce a murderer. When he found whipping in the schools and alcoholism in its students' homes, he looked to the sources of the social malady, arguing that society ought to provide before it punishes. From this wellspring came editorials with such titles as "Some Hints to Apprentices," "Living Too High," "Educating the Young—Manners," "The Lash in Schools," and "Something About Children."[33] In one voice he sounds like a haughty schoolmaster, but in the other—when social instruction and opportunity are absent—he sounds the democratic alarm.

It was probably Whitman's concern for the schools that got this former teacher interested in music, and ultimately opera, another major influence on *Leaves of Grass.* Following the spirit of Horace Mann's call for school reform, Whitman visited Brooklyn's schools frequently and reported on almost every aspect of the classroom in nineteenth-century America. Besides the need for more professional teachers and better ventilation, less rote learning and harsh discipline, he thought every child's education ought to include music. Just as in today's schools music education is usually the first item to disappear from a shrinking budget, in the mid-1800s it was not highly regarded or even seen as an essential part of a sound curriculum. Whitman advocated in the *Star* of January 7, 1845, the teaching of music as another branch of the pupil's education, as important as reading or arithmetic. We must not imagine, he added, "that the most potential influence exerted over children is that which shows itself the quickest and most vividly. On the contrary, many things that are unthought of, and frequently unseen sway the movements and mould the characters of the young, with wonderful power."[34]

In a century when the masses heard instrumental music only at events like Fourth of July celebrations, the other "music" they heard was the sound of the human voice. This is important to a full appreciation of *Leaves of Grass,* where one of the dominant distinctions is its orality. Although opera, not only Italian but French and German, was available on a limited basis in New York City in the early 1840s, Whitman had probably not—as late as 1845—developed a full appreciation for what he initially viewed as a "foreign" form of entertainment. On November 3, a Monday evening, at Niblo's Saloon he heard for the first time a performance of the Cheney Family, a quartet of three brothers and a sister from New Hampshire who occasionally performed at abolitionist rallies. The experience overpowered him "with delightful amazement." Writing in the *Star* two days later he continued: "They certainly, to our taste, excel all the much vaunted foreign artists. . . . Simple, fresh, and beautiful, we hope no spirit of imitation will ever induce them to engraft any foreignness upon their native graces." Promising to say more on the subject, he hoped that the example of the Cheneys and the Hutchinsons, a similar group, would serve as a "starting point from which to mould something new and pure in American music."

He said more on the subject of music in the November 29 issue of the *Broadway Journal,* then edited by Poe, who met with his contributor in the *Journal*'s editorial offices. In "Art-Singing and Heart-Singing" Whitman, in Emersonian fashion, protested that America had "listened too long" to European influences in music. (In his Phi Beta Kappa Address of 1837, Emerson had written—and Whitman had probably later read—"We have listened too long to the courtly muses of Europe.") Acknowledging the cultural power of music, Whitman wrote:

> As for us of America, we have long enough followed obedient and child-like in the track of the Old World. We have received her tenors and her buffos [buffas]; her operatic troupes and her vocalists, of all grades and complexions; listened to and applauded the songs made for a different state of society—made, perhaps, by royal genius, but made to please royal ears likewise; and it is time that such listening and receiving should cease. The subtlest spirit of a nation is expressed through its music—and the music acts reciprocally on the nation's very soul.[35]

Whitman had argued in a similar vein when he called for music education in the schools. But here the language and style of his defense of music resemble that of the Preface to the 1855 edition of *Leaves of Grass:* "The Americans of all nations at any time upon the earth have probably the fullest poetic nature. The United States themselves are essentially the greatest poem." In both instances, we glimpse the orator Whitman once hoped to become and the debater he was during his school teaching days.

But this editorial, Robert D. Faner observes, is the work of a writer "whose own experience has by no means been limited to concerts by singers of heart songs."[36] Free tickets to opera and drama had been available to Whitman since his days at the *Aurora.* Nevertheless, he had yet to embrace the beauty and drama of the voice as it was exalted in opera, and especially Italian opera, where instrumentation was minimized. Around 1845 and 1846—perhaps as late as 1850—he saw music, the "heart-songs" of the Cheneys instead of the "art-songs" of opera, as one of the important agencies of democracy. Its effects, he wrote, "enter into religious feelings—they tinge the manners and morals—they are active even in the choice of legislators and high magistrates." Bad laws might be changed and new ones enacted, he thought, but "no human power can thoroughly suppress the spirit which lives in national lyrics, and sounds in the favorite melodies sung by high and low." Poe, whose contribution to the lyric in poetry was already secure, wholeheartedly agreed. In an editorial postscript to Whitman's essay, he wrote that the author desired him to say that "he pretends to no scientific knowledge of music. He merely claims to appreciate so much of it (a sadly disdained department, just now) as affects, in the language of the deacons, 'the natural heart of man.' It is scarcely necessary to add that we agree with our correspondent throughout."[37]

It would be fascinating to know more about the meeting, apparently the first and only one, of Walt Whitman and Edgar Allan Poe. Poe's postscript is his only known comment on Whitman, who remembered Poe that day as "dark, quiet, handsome—Southern from top to toe: languid, tired out . . . but altogether ingratiating." He thought Poe was "curiously a victim of history—like Paine." In *Specimen Days,* Whitman remembered that his meeting with Poe was held "in his office, second story of a corner building, (Duane or Pearl Street)" and praised the poet for his "intense faculty for technical and abstract beauty, [but] with the rhyming art to excess." By then, Whitman had long abandoned the "rhyming art," although in recalling the embryonic period for *Leaves of Grass* in "A Backward Glance O'er Travel'd Roads" (1889), he admitted looking over Poe's poems.[38]

❖ ❖ ❖

Whitman continued his contributions to the *Star* during the first months of 1846, but he also moved closer to regular employment on the *Eagle,* reprinting "Shirval" on its pages for January 22 (again, as with its *Star* publication, without any allusion to the tale's initial publication in the *Aristidean*). This means that he was acquainted with William B. Marsh, the editor of the paper since 1841. Marsh fell ill during the first week of February and died, aged thirty-three, of cancer of the liver before the end of the month. The poet probably attended his funeral at the Brooklyn Tabernacle at the corner of Fulton and Pineapple streets. Either days before or following Marsh's death, Whitman became editor of the *Eagle.* "The Funeral of Mr. Marsh," published in the *Eagle* of March 2, may have marked Whitman's first day on the job as editor. Whoever wrote the account remarked, "After a fervent and eloquent prayer, the friends of the deceased were invited to view the body; and nearly all present crowded up to take a last farewell look. But how strangely altered by the ravages and sufferings of disease was that countenance, so recently beaming in the midst of us with life and intellect." Compared with the other accounts, this one is written more in Whitman's prose style. And it may have been Whitman who continued the theme of changed countenances in "Change," a poem published in the *Eagle* of March 5:

Rolling, rolling, ever rolling!
　　So the Ages sweep along;
Time his bell is ever tolling,
　　O'er the beautiful and strong!

Roll the seasons, fades the Summer,
　　Melting soon in Autumn's gloom;
The wild tempests—sons of Winter,
　　Hurry Nature to her tomb.

Comes the spring-time—breezes softest
　　Re-awake Earth's dormant pow'rs;
Brighter verdure clothes the forest;
　　Song re[-]wakes in rosy bow'rs.

Man, too, changes! his joys fleeting,
Oft they're whelm'd by sorrow[']s wave;
Now he's singing—now he's weeping;—
Thus he hastens to his grave.

Golden visions—Hopes the sweetest,
Gild his life with one soft ray:
Baseless rainbows!—Night-fires fleetest!
Dim they shine, then fade away.

In deep sadness, grief and sorrow,
Peace I seek; I pray for rest:
"Holy Father! may the morrow
Tranquillize my anxious breast."

Look I upward through life's portal;
Deathless flow'rs bloom there for me;
Loves unbroken! Joys eternal!
Hope, up-springing endlessly!

Since this poem is not signed "W," as "A Sketch" was, there is no way of concluding with the same assurance that "Change" came from the pen of the new editor. Though the lines are four feet in length, its trochaic rhythm is not found in Whitman's other early poems. On the other hand, the circumstantial evidence suggests that "Change" may have been Whitman's first elegy. The fact that the poem is not signed may be due to its solemn occasion, where identity of authorship would take attention away from the specific reason for the verse. Marsh is also not named, but neither is Lincoln in "When Lilacs Last in the Dooryard Bloom'd"; and traditionally elegies do not mention the name of the deceased in order to allow the lament to have universal application. "Lilacs" undergoes the same turmoil as "Change" (its anguish about the tides of time) before finding resolution. The opening cadence of "Change" also bears a striking resemblance to the rolling tone of another poem, "Beat! Beat! Drums!" in *Drum-Taps:*

Beat! beat! drums!—blow! bugles! blow!
Through the windows—through doors—burst like a ruthless
force,
Into the solemn church, and scatter the congregation,
Into the school where the scholar is studying;
Leave not the bridegroom quiet—no happiness must he have
now with his bride,
Nor the peaceful farmer any peace, ploughing his field or
gathering his grain,
So fierce you whirr and pound you drums—so shrill you bugles
blow.

Like change, "Rolling, rolling, ever rolling!" hurrying "Nature to her tomb" without regard for the human desire for life, the drums of war in this early *Drum-Taps* chant (which has two more stanzas) invade the lives of everyone. Indeed, "Change," with its observation of life finally phased out by the pathos of death, outlines the thematic development of *Drum-Taps,* which opens with the excitement of war and concludes in the confusion and final clarity of death. The war poems also conclude, however, with the hope that death, as Whitman wrote in "Song of Myself," is only the latest of nature's "perpetual transfers and promotions." "Change," like the other early poems including "A Sketch," concludes with the announcement of nature's unbroken chain of love, which promises "Joys eternal." It was appropriate for Whitman to print such a poem in the first days of his editorship not only to mourn the passing of a popular editor but, more important, to signal his own interest in giving readers something more than mere "news." Within three months he added a literary section to the paper.

His move from a Whig paper to this organ of the Democratic-Republican Party (as it was formally called) is not as mystifying as it would be today when the opposing viewpoints of the Republicans and Democrats seem to be set in ideological concrete. Whitman had worked for newspapers of different political stripes in the 1830s, and it should be borne in mind that both the *Star* and the *Eagle* were homegrown, local concerns—one agrarian and the other urban, both imbued with a sense of pride in Brooklyn and Long Island pitted against New York City. It was not surprising to find little difference in their editorial opinions except around election time. Furthermore, Whitman, as we have noted, had campaigned for Van Buren in Jamaica during the election of 1840 and had made political speeches both there and in New York City. He was not perhaps as much of a "party man" as Marsh, but his politics meshed well during most of his tenure at the *Eagle* with those of Isaac Van Anden, a prominent member of the Democratic Party of Kings County and owner of the newspaper since 1842. Under Marsh, the *Eagle* had come out against capital punishment, and generally it supported the territorial expansionist politics of President Polk. According to William Henry Sutton, a printer's devil with the *Eagle* during Whitman's time as editor, Van Anden seldom saw Whitman. Unlike Herrick and Ropes of the *Aurora,* Van Anden kept to the business end of the paper's operation and allowed Whitman complete editorial control as long, of course, as he did not wander too far afield of the owner's politics.[39] And this was—until the party split in late 1847 over the Wilmot Proviso—generally in keeping with Whitman's political point of view.

As editor of the *Brooklyn Eagle* between 1846 and 1848 Whitman analyzed foreign policy questions as a moderate on the Oregon dispute and an expansionist Democrat on the challenges of America's southwestern and western frontiers, reflecting perhaps the common wisdom of the day, articulated by Senator Thomas Hart Benton of Missouri, that "Great Britain is powerful and Mexico is weak." Because Whitman's subjects were mostly dictated by the run of political and social events, his journalism that has been ferreted out and published in scholarly editions has been organized topically instead of chronologically. A chronological examination of these items, including several that have yet to be republished in scholarly editions, however, gives us perhaps a more coherent picture of Whitman's life during this period. As the poet's *Star* editorials have suggested, this picture restores the immediacy and character of Whitman's revelations and pronouncements as he applied the ideals of both Jefferson and Jackson to the important political and cultural developments of the 1840s. If a whaling ship was Melville's Harvard and his Yale, Brooklyn and newspaper work were this poet's university.

For the first time in four years—since his brief stay at the *Aurora*—Whitman enjoyed a regular editorship. Situated at the foot of Fulton

Street and a focal point in Brooklyn (because the Fulton Street Ferry was by far the busiest), Whitman's editorial office afforded him a view of the comings and goings of Brooklyn, as clerks, housekeepers, and the majority of Brooklynites commuted to and from the metropolis of Manhattan for their work. From his office window as well as from the pilot house of the ferries he rode daily, he recalled in *Specimen Days,* "I could get a full sweep, absorbing shows, accompaniments, surroundings."[40] Brooklyn at the time he assumed his editorial post was a thriving city of 40,000 residents and would approach 70,000 by the time he left the *Eagle* in early 1848. House lots went for about 100 dollars apiece as the city stretched down Fulton Street to populate the general areas of Myrtle and Flatbush avenues, pushing in the direction of Fort Greene. At least two ferry crossings were added during his tenure on the *Eagle* as the traffic on Fulton Street increased.

Whitman, well-traveled in both New York and Brooklyn as well as Long Island, was perhaps the perfect editor for the city's leading paper at such a time of growth. The affairs of the city were much more than "news" to him, for he was sincerely interested in how his city would contribute to the democracy franchised by the founding fathers. Always "on duty" as editor, he reported back to his readers the results of his travels via Brooklyn's omnibuses, its stages, its ferries, the Long Island Railroad (where one could buy a round-trip ticket to Greenport for a dollar), and—of course—his own shoe leather as he sauntered and rambled throughout the city and the countryside of western Long Island. "This is the city and I am one of its citizens," he would write in "Song of Myself," and there is little doubt that the *Eagle* editorship was his first important step to becoming a citizen of the world that Emerson had beckoned him to enter during his lecture on "The Poet" in 1842.

Whitman's daily schedule was pretty much the same as with the *Aurora:* he wrote his editorials in the morning and—sending copy to the composing room—took a turn around the city, this time mainly Brooklyn instead of Broadway. After lunch he returned to read proof and then took a twenty-minute dip at the Fulton Ferry Salt Baths, adjacent to the *Eagle* offices. (Earlier biographers have perhaps overemphasized the importance of the phrase "exactly twenty minutes" in a contemporary description—as if Whitman were something of an eccentric in his use of the baths. But twenty minutes, as the owner Edward Gray's advertisements in the *Eagle* suggest, was the allowable maximum for the price of one admission.) Whitman occasionally mentioned Gray's bath in his editorial column. In "A Plea for Bathing" (March 23, 1846), he advised that "a good bath" was the best thing for "slight attacks of illness, and quite all fits of hypochondria, and such nervous diseases." In the evening he frequently either traveled by ferry to Manhattan to attend a play or opera or took in a lecture at his "university" in Brooklyn, where during the months of February and March 1846 he could choose from the "Institute course; Dr Baird's lectures on Europe at the Church of the Pilgrims in Henry street; and Professor Fowler's on Phrenology at Hall's Buildings"—all quite popular, especially the phrenology lectures, with Brooklynites.[41]

On March 7 he reported on Orson S. Fowler's lecture of the night before, calling it "the most curious that we have ever attended," an assessment in sharp contrast to his characterization of the lecture he heard by Emerson in 1842 as "one of the richest and most beautiful compositions we have ever heard anywhere, at any time."[42] Rather, in 1846 the poet who would have his head phrenologically examined three years later and then, even later, use such phrenological terms as "Adhesiveness" and "Amativeness" to classify the "Calamus" and "Children of Adam" poems thought the system an intellectual fraud. "In good truth," he wrote, "the lectures of Mr. Fowler present the greatest conglomeration of pretension and absurdity it has ever been our lot to listen to." Yet Whitman was attracted to the pseudoscience's assertion that certain human faculties could be modified for the good of both the individual and society. Hence he concluded his review, entitled "A Chance for Men of Bad Character," by saying, "We do not mean to assert that there is no truth whatever in phrenology, but we do say that its claims to confidence, as set forth by Mr Fowler, are preposterous to the last degree."

In "The Wrongs of Women" (March 17), Whitman displayed a conventional regard toward the opposite sex as representing the "moral affections," his central concern here being marriage and the husband's proper treatment of his spouse. Generally, women were loyal to a fault. "And in the phase of motherly love—the crowning glory of the human attributes—what similitude to the immortal kindness of our Saviour himself!" "Rais'd by a perfect mother," as he would declare in *Leaves of Grass*, Whitman was doubtless thinking of his own beloved mother, Louisa, who, despite her occasional illnesses and the domestic grumbling brought about by her husband's possible intemperance, had held the family of eight children together. Her sense of humanity is probably what drew him to Christianity, whose true teachings he found useful to society, though like the fictional Barcoure he did not consider them truer than those of other religions. In a pair of essays a few days later on "Splendid Churches," he deplored the showy architecture of Grace Church and others, which were so imposing that Christ Himself might not enter.

For Whitman, everything went back to the good order and diversity of the urban unit as it confronted the challenges of democracy and capitalism—good ferries, reasonably priced fares, trains to the Greenwood cemetery or as far away as Greenport, the development of a park and Revolution memorial at Fort Greene, fair pay for sewing women, instruction on the dangers of alcohol consumption (but no prohibition laws; here he parted company with a much more famous reformer, Horace Mann), the doings of the local churches, respect for firemen, and (even) the unfortunate, if not yet completely "evil," aspects of slavery. Yet at the same time that he looked for social order and morality, he was opposed to laws to enforce it—the Seduction Law, for example, which would have held men liable for "breach of marriage promise" in the cases of unwed mothers. The proposed law never passed—neither did one giving a wife full ownership of her personal property after marriage, which he did support[43]—but Whitman continued to report on female misfortunes from time to time, always lamenting the woman's treatment. In "One More Unfortunate" (January 4, 1847), he told of a young woman left pregnant and homeless in New York City in the dead of winter. After reporting her problem to a police officer, she was conveyed "to the Lying-in Asylum," where she was ultimately rejected—"that institution being only for the respectable and the virtuous poor."

❖ ❖ ❖

In "The Little Minstrel Girl—A Tale of Truth," a story Whitman could have written, the themes of temperance and patriotism are combined to tell a moralistic tale about a little street singer who charms the patrons of a tavern in Philadelphia.[44] He may have been thinking of those six drunks in Baltimore who sent one of their number abroad to hear a temperance lecture and ended up founding the Washingtonian temperance movement described in Chapter 3. In the story, the inebriated patrons take up a collection for the girl, and upon her return the following evening her medley of songs inspires a rich man from Pittsburgh to take in both the girl and her mother ("Tears of delight coursed down his sunburnt cheeks as he listened to the patriotic strain—for he was heart and soul an American"). Eventually, the girl marries the man's son. The tale, the author noted, was intended "as a new incentive for the young to be good and virtuous."

Whitman felt sorry for the victims of capitalism, but he was also losing sympathy for those who had gone astray of the law. During his second year on the *Eagle,* his opposition to the death penalty was strained by the mugging of a Brooklyn jeweler who sustained permanent brain damage. Outraged, Whitman followed the stages of his miserable decline for months. In July of the same year, he complained of the lack of discipline in the Kings County Jail. As to its hard labor, Whitman quipped after a visit: "We never happened to see the convicts doing anything harder than masticating wholesome victuals, lolling on comfortable straw mattresses and staring stone walls out of countenance."[45]

By the summer of 1847 Whitman had moved out of his father's house on Prince Street and was boarding with a family on Adams Street, off Myrtle. We can merely speculate on the move, but probably Whitman's steady income allowed him his own rented room—no doubt to the relief of the Whitman family, which crowded into its own rented rooms on Myrtle. He warned his readers about rabid dogs loose in the streets. After several persons were fatally bitten, the city sent out armed men at $2 a day to shoot all dogs without "rattraps over their mouths." "Up to yesterday only *four* dogs have slipped their mortal coils under official sanction," he complained on July 7, 1847. "There ought to have been at least four hundred." A month later, Whitman himself was nearly poisoned when a druggist on Myrtle Avenue mistakenly sent his household "a prodigious dose of *oxalic acid* instead of tartaric acid [baking powder], (which was wanted to put in some batter cakes)"—apparently not an altogether uncommon problem.[46]

Whitman's high-pitched indignation over the short-circuiting of the social routine suggests a return of the Woodbury whining, a fussiness that he now usually overcame. He could be particularly petty when quarreling with another newspaper, such as the *Brooklyn Advertizer,* or jousting with a literary rival, like his old boss and publisher Park Benjamin. There may have been a somewhat nasty exchange in the summer of 1846 when Benjamin's return to New York City was publicized as having exercised the "spleen and ire of his contemporaries in the press." "The only safety for a writer in New York now," observed the *Star* of July 14, "is in joining the 'Mutual Admiration Society of the Literati.' That is the only covenant of peace—the only ark of safety. Once you wear the insignia of the order, an oiled feather, and use it in *tickling* the ears of your brother members—you are safe." A few months earlier Whitman noted that Benjamin, "well known as a writer of perhaps third rate ability," was quarreling with another writer, whose private letters Benjamin had made public. "The action of betraying a confidence this way," wrote the man who would publish Emerson's famous letter of 1855 without permission, "whatever the provocation, is about as despicable and cowardly, as a man can possibly be guilty of. Indeed we would think more and better of the bold bluff villain that presents his pistol to the breast in a by road, and asks for one's pocket book, than of these sneaking stabbers, who violate every dictate of honor and gentlemanly feeling, by the publication of private letters."[47]

Whitman was free to say whatever he thought in the *Eagle* as long as he steered clear of Van Anden, and that was relatively easy until the Democratic-Republican Party split over the question of slavery in the new western states and territories, especially Texas. All other humanitarian questions fell within the tolerance of what was essentially a workingman's and people's party. An editorial of July 29, 1847, for example, chastised the early English governors in New York (and indirectly New York City developed by the English) for their shameful exploitation of American Indians. With the English rule on Manhattan and Long Island in the wake of the Dutch came, he wrote, "the beginning of foul play, of driving the Indians off either by force or fraud, of quarrels, of taking property unjustly. . . . they violated 'vested rights' with a daring hand; and the Indians, being without either power, active friends in the government, or knowledge, were the victims of these wicked governors."

The Indians were simply another class of victims, and Whitman—who would advise his readers in his 1855 Preface to love the earth, stand up for the stupid and crazy, and hate tyrants—made no exceptions. Though he may have been ambivalent about the role of blacks in a white society (as most white people in the nineteenth century were), he opposed slavery. Yet it must be remembered that the mainstream presses of New York and elsewhere paid the anti-slavery movement scant attention, despite the publication of the *Narrative of the Life of Frederick Douglass* in 1845 and its accompanying increase in the activities of the supporters of William Lloyd Garrison, whose newspaper *The Liberator* had been operating since 1831. The question of slavery had been more or less "settled" since the Missouri Compromise of 1820. It was only with the advent of the Mexican War (which Whitman vigorously supported) and the proposal of the Wilmot Proviso, which would have banned slavery in new territories of the West, that slavery assumed the proportions of a new issue. Not only was Whitman free in his *Eagle* editorials to oppose the continuing but illegal slave trade—as he did as early as March 18, 1846, in "Slavers—and the Slave Trade"[48]—but he frequently ran poems by Longfellow (such as "The Quadroon Girl" and "The Slave's Dream") sympathetic to the slave's degradations as well as items from other papers about barbarity to slaves and free blacks in the South. He carried the story from the *New Orleans Picayune* of the legal whipping of five Negroes convicted of exhuming the body of a white man in Mobile, Alabama, and cutting out his tongue for a charm; two were given fifty lashes, the other three sentenced to receive only thirty-nine of the dreaded stripes. On another occasion, referring to a case of runaway slaves apprehended in Mt. Holly, Pennsylvania—which could have served as a basis for his poem "A Boston Ballad" in 1854 as well as the Anthony Burns case that is most often cited as the poem's inspiration—Whitman pointed out that in the rush of citizens to prevent the slaves from being returned, the blacks were "badly used" by the military.[49]

One account, which Whitman paraphrased from the *Picayune* on April 8, 1846, is particularly revealing of the editor's developing view of slavery. In "A Beautiful and Instructive 'Moral Lesson,'" he reported the hanging of the slave Pauline for "cruelty to her mistress."

> As near as we remember, the master had a licentious passion for the slave, and shamelessly placed her in her mistress's position, in his own house! And Pauline improved her power to degrade and abuse the unhappy wife! If any one deserved severity, it seems to us to have been the *husband,* not the miserable, ignorant, contemptible negress.

What followed was a graphic description of her execution, reflecting Whitman's general opposition to capital punishment. He sought to whip up sympathy for both the condemned and the slave by making the hanging "public" in the minds of his readers (Pauline's hanging was in fact public). Brought out in a "long white robe, her arms bound with a black cord, the white cap placed upon her head," "she was perfectly firm, and apparently indifferent to her fate." After describing the "fearful struggles" of the woman who—because of a short drop to prevent the rope from snapping—dangled helplessly for twenty minutes instead of dying instantly, Whitman shifted from the oppression of the slave to concerns affecting the rest of white society, lamenting the fate of "a duplicate of the humanity which we share in common." In this "moral lesson" the horrors of capital punishment and the marital abuse of a (white, slaveholding) spouse received as much attention as the actual murder. Clearly, Whitman pitied Pauline, but he also lamented her "ignorant, contemptible" situation, which rendered her in his mind almost subhuman and only a "duplicate" of the humanity he stood up for in his editorials. In 1872 this concern led him to quarrel bitterly with his best friend and an adamant champion of *Leaves of Grass,* William O'Connor, over the wisdom of the Fifteenth Amendment, which enfranchised freedmen politically before educating them.[50]

In his attention to the evils of slavery Whitman uncannily anticipates—from a decidedly white perspective—W. E. B. Du Bois's "double-consciousness," his feeling of "twoness,—an American, a Negro."[51] Slavery was a social evil that he wanted erased from the Constitution that his hero Jefferson had helped to author. Calling the Wilmot Proviso the "Jeffersonian proviso," he wrote near the end of his editorship of the *Eagle:* "*We must plant ourselves firmly on the side of freedom, and openly espouse it.*"[52] Yet he meant first of all the freedom for America to develop without the burden of slavery. And just as he used the pathos of a black woman's hanging to rail against capital punishment and abusive marriages, he later echoed another black writer in his support of American workingmen. Frederick Douglass wrote in *My Bondage and My Freedom* (1855) that the "white man is robbed by the slave system, of the just results of his labor, because he is flung into competition with a class of laborers who work without wages."[53] In *The Eighteenth Presidency!* (1854–56) Whitman argued that slavery was most evil because it degraded the work of the (white) laborer in the North.

As late as 1846 Whitman thought the abolitionists were doing more harm than good. On November 7 he wrote that if the "ultraism and officiousness of the Abolitionists had *not* been, the slave states at the south would have advanced much farther in the 'cause of freedom' to their slaves than they have advanced." Six weeks later (December 29), he wondered why the 2,700,000 black slaves in America got all the abolitionist sympathy "while the fate of fifty millions of white men [in Russia and Austria], physically as good as their owners, don't seem to attract the slightest attention." It took in part the Wilmot Proviso to push him over the line with regard to his passivity about slavery. Yet even when Pennsylvania congressman David Wilmot's rider to an appropriations bill was voted down by the U.S. Senate in 1847, Whitman still called for a peaceful resolution of the slavery question. "We, too, desired the enactment of that proviso," he said in the *Eagle* of March 1, "but it is by no means vitally important." Noting that the issue had created "too much angry excitement in congress," he looked to the calming effect of public opinion, which, he said, was "ahead of law in this matter."

Yet by the fall of 1847, as the "people" in the anti–Wilmot Proviso wing of his—and Van Anden's—party gained control, Whitman's time as editor and fence straddler on the slavery issue quickly approached its end. On November 8 he defended himself against the *Star's* accusation that he was either a "Barnburner" or a "Hunker" (radical or conservative) by claiming neutrality. But politics finally brought an end to Whitman's editorship of the *Eagle.* And in fact, by the end of the 1840s all the Whitmans, including George and Jeff, had turned away from the Democratic Party and become "what orthodox Democrats would call—deep-dyed heretics."[54] The Democratic-dominated House of Representatives was persuaded to drop its support for the Wilmot Proviso by General Lewis Cass, who became the Democratic-Republican candidate for the presidency in 1848 and ultimately lost to Zachary Taylor. Van Anden, who was treasurer of the local Democratic-Republican Committee that election year, had already shifted to the Hunker position, opposing the Proviso. Whitman's editorial opposing Cass on January 3, therefore, was probably the occasion for his dismissal, which took effect a couple of weeks later. On January 19 the *Brooklyn Evening Star* reported that "Mr. Whitman has had to give way." Two days later this news was confirmed in the *New-York Daily Globe.*[55]

Interestingly, Van Anden, Cass, and the House of Representatives were not exactly pro-slavery. Instead, they were closer to Whitman in their apathy about the situation of the Negro. They held that prohibiting slavery in the new territories would create civil unrest there (which in fact it did in Kansas in 1856) and that the question of slavery ought to be decided on a local, or statewide, basis. Whitman argued, questionably, that since these future states were still territories, they fell under the "local" authority of Congress—just as states came under the power of their legislatures, but his tacit argument was that slavery was bad for the future of the United States and especially demeaning for the majority of white workers.

As his steady employment came to an end, Whitman began to see slavery fully in human terms. At the Brooklyn Institute on December 10, 1847, he appears to have heard—and listened seriously to—his first abolitionist lecture, which he described as "one of the most powerfully written and warmly delivered speeches we ever heard." He noted that "rarely, if ever, has the accursed nature of tyranny and slavery, in all their influences and results, been pourtrayed [*sic*] in words more effective and clear, or in a manner more enthusiastic!" He was impressed by how the speaker brought home the inhumanity of slavery: "The lecturer's picture of a slave, the *thing* without the feelings of a man—*not* a husband, *not* a parent, *not* a wife, *not* a patriot." Whitman, it seems, had suddenly broken away from the nineteenth-century stereotypes about the slave as less than human to see blacks in the context of citizenry and the social roles he had championed for whites in his editorials throughout the 1840s. African Americans too, it seemed, were part of the democratic catalog to be celebrated in *Leaves of Grass.* He thanked the speaker, the Irish-born Unitarian minister Henry Giles, in "the name of all who love freedom and hate oppression" for expressing principles "that lie at the foundation of our republican government and the rights of all human beings."[56]

Whitman would never become an "abolitionist" in the formal or political sense. Yet he now went beyond the position of many abolitionists—Garrison included, as evidenced by his condescending manner toward Douglass[57]—who thought Africans inferior but not deserving of slavery. Whereas Whitman had voiced the opinion that most abolitionists were the *cause* of national unrest over slavery, he was more receptive to the Reverend Mr. Giles, who though an outspoken anti-slavery man was not considered an "agitator." Giles succeeded where other abolitionists failed—by focusing on the slave's humanity instead of the slaveholder's immorality and cruelty. "This is the meal equally set," Whitman would proclaim of American democracy in "Song of Myself."

At almost the same time he heard the anti-slavery lecture, he rediscovered Emerson. It is difficult to believe that Whitman had not read Emerson's essays after hearing him speak in 1842, except that the tone of his writings up till 1848 is more politically or socially oriented than reflective of a new, transcendental way of thinking about America. After a long period of avoidance, Emerson himself had faced up to the slavery issue in his 1844 speech on the tenth anniversary of the emancipation of the slaves in the British West Indies.[58] At any rate, five days after Whitman's political conversion by the Reverend Mr. Giles, the poet referred to "Spiritual Laws," a piece that had appeared in Emerson's first volume of essays in 1841. He called it a lecture, and of course most of the *Essays,* the First Series as well as the Second of 1844, were developed directly from lectures of the same titles, but there is no way Whitman could have heard Emerson deliver it. In the *Eagle* he quoted a "striking paragraph" that sums up the transcendentalist doctrine more succinctly than anything else in the writings of Emerson:

> When the act of reflection takes place in the mind, when we look at ourselves in the light of thought, we discover that our life is embosomed in beauty. Behind us, as we go, all things assume pleasing forms, as clouds do afar off. Not only things familiar and stale, but even the tragic and the terrible, are lures of memory. . . . Even the corpse that has lain in the chambers, has added a solemn ornament to the house.—The soul will not know either deformity or pain.[59]

If there is a historical moment for the nexus of Body and Soul celebrated in *Leaves of Grass,* it may have been in December 1847. One of the duties of a great poet, its author later wrote, was "to cheer up slaves and horrify despots." Seen transcendentally, everything—and everybody—was beautiful and deserved liberation, poetically and politically, from the old contexts. "America . . . perceives that the corpse is slowly borne from the eating and sleeping rooms of the house," he wrote at the opening of *Leaves of Grass,* placing Emerson's "solemn ornament" at the center of American development.

5

CRESCENT CITY SOJOURN

❋ ❋ ❋

I am very warmly disposed towards the South:
I must admit that my instinct of friendship
towards the South is almost more than I like to confess:
I have very dear friends there: sacred, precious memories.

WALT WHITMAN
to Horace L. Traubel, 1888

Whitman lost his job at the *Eagle* in January 1848; in the middle of February he found himself traveling down the Mississippi on the steamboat *St. Cloud,* on his way to a new position at the *New Orleans Crescent.* Throughout his life, Whitman considered his southern sojourn crucial to his development as a poet; but consciously cloaking it in personal myth, he has provoked considerable speculation about what actually happened there. In the final version of the poem "When I Read the Book" (1871), he challenged future biographers to explain his paradoxes, saying that even he himself knew little of his "real life." He was speaking of the life of the mind and soul as well as that of the nineteenth-century physical person, but biographers have embellished this particular three-month chapter of his life with rumors of lost love and abandoned children.[1]

It may seem strange that Whitman, after being so moved by an anti-slavery speaker in December 1847, should turn around and accept a position on a newspaper deep in the heart of the slaveholding South. "Being out of a job," he recalled in *Specimen Days,* "I was offer'd impromptu, (it happened between acts one night in the lobby of the old Broadway theatre near Pearl street, New York City,) a good chance to go down to New Orleans on the staff of the 'Crescent,' a daily to be started there with plenty of capital behind it. One of the owners, who was north buying material, met me walking in the lobby, and though that was our first acquaintance, after fifteen minutes' talk (and a drink) we made a formal bargain, and he paid me two hundred dollars down to bind the contract and bear my expenses to New Orleans."[2]

In actuality, Whitman probably found this job in the following manner. Two newspapermen, J. E. ("Sam") McClure and A. A. Hayes, had recently bolted from the *New Orleans Delta* to start a paper of their own.[3] McClure, the "owner" in Whitman's account, was a native of Vermont[4] who, like tens of thousands of other Americans, had flocked to the "Crescent City" (named for its position on one of the tightest bends in the Mississippi River) in the decades following the Louisiana Purchase and the opening of that territory to Americans. New Orleans already had at least six daily newspapers—the *Picayune,* the *Bee,* the *Commercial Times,* the *Courier,* and the *Bulletin,* in addition to the *Delta.* Yet there was easily room for another newspaper in this city teeming with planters traveling up and down the Mississippi and with soldiers under the commands of Generals Winfield Scott ("Old Fuss and Feathers") and Zachary Taylor ("Old Rough and Ready") who were either leaving for the war in Texas and Mexico or returning triumphantly from the front.

Before the age of wire services such as Associated Press and United Press International, newspapers exchanged information to supply local readers with news from around the country. In order to compete with the excellent national and international coverage already available to New Orleans's 125,000 residents, the owners of the *Crescent* needed someone with connections to northern newspapers. As a veteran New York City newspaperman and the recent editor of the *Brooklyn Daily Eagle,* Whitman was a perfect fit. His position, as he noted, was not that of "chief editor" but a member of the "staff"—an "exchange editor" whose specific task, he recorded in another memorandum, consisted of "overhauling the papers rec'd by mail, and 'making up the news,' as it is called, both with pen and scissors."[5] Whitman probably heard about the new journalistic venture through the grapevine of exchange papers and, needing employment, sought out McClure when he came north to buy equipment and supplies.

Because of New Orleans's position as the principal staging area for the Mexican War, it was an appropriate place for the ex-editor of the *Eagle.* The excitement Whitman had followed closely for the last two years was far from over. As he noted years later, the best war correspondents were working out of the city, bringing the news first to New Orleans, sometimes even before official military dispatches reached Washington. "Probably the influence most deeply pervading everything at that time . . . ," he told the *New Orleans Picayune* in 1887, "was the Mexican War just ended. Following a brilliant campaign (in which our troops had march'd to the capital city, Mexico, and taken full possession), we were now returning after our victory. From the situation of the country, the city of New Orleans had been our channel and *entrepot* for everything, going and returning."[6] General Scott, in one of the American navy's first amphibious invasions, had recently completed Taylor's work in the semi-deserts of northern Mexico by capturing Mexico City, and the Treaty of Guadalupe-Hildalgo had been signed (but not yet approved by the U.S. Congress) on February 2.

One of Whitman's first tasks on the *Crescent* was to set up exchanges with New York newspapers, including the *Eagle,* where his successor, S. G. Arnold, readily complied with his request. He also brought his own expertise as a former printer to the operation of the new paper, as well as the skills of his fourteen-year-old brother, Jeff, then a printer's apprentice, who came with him. Jeff also assisted in sorting through the exchange papers at a salary of $5 per week.[7]

Whitman was useful as an experienced editorial and feature writer as well, and his initial contribution appeared in the first issue of the *Crescent* on March 5. "Crossing the Alleghenies," the first of three essays under the heading "Excerpts from a Traveller's Note Book," recounted the first leg of his journey to New Orleans, which took him first by rail to Baltimore and Cumberland, then by stagecoach over the Allegheny Mountains, and finally on the steamboat *St. Cloud* from Wheeling down the Ohio River to the Mississippi and New Orleans. Whitman first met McClure in New York on February 9. He left for the South with Jeff two days later, arriving in New Orleans on February 25 after a torturously slow and sometimes boring steamboat journey that involved frequent stops to pick up and deposit cargo. "In poetry and romance," he wrote in the *Crescent* of March 10, "these rivers are talked of as though they were cleanly streams; but it is astonishing what a difference is made by the simple fact that they are always and altogether excessively muddy. . . . There is no romance in a mass of yellowish brown liquid."[8]

Steamboats at that time were primarily engaged in transporting machinery and supplies to bustling New Orleans and along the mighty Mississippi, but as Jeff noted in one of the many unanswered letters home (the two brothers did not hear from their mother until a month after their arrival), the passenger accommodations were far from meager. "You have no idea," the teenager informed his mother, "of the splendor and comfort of these western river steam-boats. The cabin is on the deck, and state rooms on each side of it, their [*sic*] are two beds in each room. . . . Every thing you would find in the Astor House in New York, You find on these boats."[9] The steamboat's luxurious accommodations (not affordable to Jeff and his brother, who secured at best second-class berths) and the high living of those passengers who could afford them prepared the Whitman brothers for the dandies, actors, "model artists," politicians, prostitutes, and planters they would see in New Orleans, swelling the city to its highest occupancy during the winter months when cholera and typhoid fever were in abeyance. (In a news item "overhaul'd" from the *New Orleans Medical Review* on March 17, Whitman spoke of the latter as "Ship Fever," caused by the crowding together of thousands of "half-starved" Irish immigrants from Europe who, unhappy with economic conditions at home, poured into the port of New Orleans, usually packed in the steerage of cargo vessels.)

It was dusk when the *St. Cloud* reached New Orleans and docked at the busy levee at the foot of Conti Street in the French Quarter. As the two ship-weary brothers looked out at the city, the St. Charles Hotel was off to their left, its Greek Revivalist architecture capped by a huge glittering dome. Taking up an entire block on St. Charles between Gravier and Common streets, this imposing structure had been built as the first major hotel in New Orleans in 1837 and was considered one of the finest hotels in America. It stood just outside the *Vieux Carré,* on the other side of Canal Street, in what is today downtown New Orleans. In Whitman's day, this was the "American" section of the city, and the construction of the St. Charles outside the Quarter, primarily occupied by French-speaking occupants, had stirred Creole business leaders to construct the St. Louis Hotel on Royal Street.

Slightly to the right, from the vantage point of the people on the deck, lay Jackson Square and the St. Louis Cathedral, its central spire flanked by bell-capped hexagonal towers. This edifice—the second of the St. Louis Cathedral structures and until 1829 the church of the city's beloved Père Antoine—was already in rapid decay after more than half a century of service. It would be replaced in 1851 by the present-day church. In this plaza, formerly the Place d'Armes, Whitman's political hero Andrew Jackson had been honored for his victory at the Battle of New Orleans in 1815 and again celebrated by the citizens of New Orleans during his visit as a former president of the United States in 1840. Another hero of Whitman's, General Lafayette, had been mourned at the cathedral in 1834, in the most imposing funeral service there since the death of Napoleon. And just months before the arrival of Walt and Jeff, more than 40,000 people had crowded into Jackson Square and its surrounding neighborhood and rooftops to welcome the hero of the Mexican War, Zachary Taylor, as his steamboat docked.

⁂ ⁂ ⁂

After remaining onboard the *St. Cloud* Friday night, Walt and Jeff made their way the next morning through the Old Quarter to find their first lodgings in the "American" section on Poydras Street, at the corner of St. Charles Avenue. It was only a block or two from the magnificent St. Charles Theatre, which seated 1,100 persons, and the new offices of the *Crescent,* directly across the street at 95 St. Charles Avenue. This boardinghouse proved to be too dirty for the New Yorkers, however, and by the middle of March they were living at the Tremont House, "next door to the Theatre and directly opposite the [*Crescent*] office." Whitman may have moved a third time at the beginning of May, no doubt to placate his teenaged brother, who was homesick ("I never wanted your cleanliness so much," he told his mother) and also occasionally weakened by dysentery.[10] Wherever they lived in the "American" quarter, they could not escape the hustle and bustle of St. Charles Avenue, which provided besides the elegant bar in the St. Charles Hotel approximately forty-five barrooms, restaurants, and "eating-houses" between Canal Street and Lafayette, a stretch of only six blocks. Whitman described the street noise as "incessant, day and night."[11] Then as today, there were frequent parades in the city, and Jeff noted at least "two or three" that came down St. Charles during the first month of their stay. On their first Sunday they walked back into the French Quarter and visited the cathedral, known then, to Americans at least, as the "French Church" to distinguish it from the "English-speaking" Catholic Church of St. Patrick's, constructed in 1833 on Camp Street in the "American" section. Observing the congregation, Jeff remarked in a letter home to the parents of the "free-soil" editor that "every one would go and dip their fingers in the holy water and then go home and *whip* their *slaves.*"[12]

Just around the corner from the Whitmans' first residence on St. Charles were the offices of "Pierson & Bonneval, Auctioneers," at 67 Gravier Street, who bid off land, machinery, and sawmills along with human lives, usually at the Bank's Arcade Hotel and Dining Saloon, a nearby gathering place of businessmen and journalists. Possibly, Jeff and Walt were on hand for more than one of these auctions at New Orleans's "acre-large" barrooms—scenes of which resurfaced in "I Sing the Body Electric" (1855).

> A man's body at auction,
> (For before the war I often go to the slave-mart and watch the sale,)
> I help the auctioneer, the sloven does not half know his business.

The "sloven" Whitman's narrator helps was possibly based on the auctioneer J. O. Pierson. The *New Orleans Delta* reported on September 10, 1848, that Pierson, known for his "business talent," had become, along with John C. Larue, a business partner of Hayes and McClure in the ownership of the *Crescent.* After Whitman's departure and Larue's elevation to co-owner, the quartet of owners hired as their editor

William Walker, later the fiery-speeched, self-proclaimed "Commander-in-Chief of the Republic of Nicaragua," finally executed in Honduras in 1860 (with the help of the Americans and British) for his adventurism.

Walker, of course, was the politician Whitman was not. Walt's contributions to the *Crescent* were mainly literary, although he was not—in this biographer's opinion—the author of the "Sidewalks and Levees" sketches that have been attributed to him. This is not to say that the background they provide for the New Orleans Whitman knew is not useful. Through profiles of Peter Funk, Miss Dusky Grisette, Daggerdraw Bowieknife, John J. Jinglebrain, Timothy Goujon, Patrick McDray, and Samuel Sensitive, we get the color of the city's lower life that Whitman would have experienced—its barrooms, its confidence games at auctions, its Creole flower vendors, its gentlemanly duels, its oyster hawkers, its Irish deliverymen, and its southern gallants. But the style of the sketches more resembles an irreverent Charles Dickens than that of the former editorial writer of the *Brooklyn Eagle.* Their treatment of the "average" with its strained literary allusions is also more than slightly condescending. Nowhere, for example, can we find anything in the known writing of Whitman to match the following paragraph, which opens the essay on Peter Funk:

> To illustrate the "life, fortune, and sacred honor" of the distinguished individual whose name heads off our present sketch of noted characters, is a task as tasteful as it is agreeable. The duty of the faithful chronologist and biographer is particularly a cheerful one when the subject of such notice is calculated to heighten the interest we feel in the dignity and delicate sensibilities of human nature.[13]

There is little or nothing in the two-volume collection of Whitman's *Eagle* editorials to compare with the stiffness of this language, its sense of distance between writer and reader. In "Ten Minutes in the Engine Room of a Brooklyn Ferry Boat," for example, published in the *Eagle* only two months earlier, Whitman wrote: "Crossing the Fulton Ferry the other evening we were invited by a friend, of engineering accomplishments, to walk down in the engine room. This is a place, doubtless, which very few of the thousands of passengers who cross the ferry ever visit. But it is an almost sublime sight that one beholds there."[14] Here we have the almost effortless irony of the high and low as it is filtered through a banal discussion of a ferryboat engine room.

The "Sidewalks and Levees" sketches are done in the antebellum tradition of the Humor of the Old Southwest, before the era of Mark Twain, before literary language—even the literary frame employed by the likes of Thomas Bangs Thorpe—was dropped for the vernacular and its malapropisms. Their tone is like that of George W. Harris's Sut Lovingood or Johnson J. Hooper's Simon Suggs, whose motto is "It is good to be shifty in a new country." Furthermore, the jaundiced view of woman in "Miss Dusky Grisette" is uncharacteristic of Whitman's sympathetic depiction of fallen women in his *Eagle* editorials, not to mention the portrait found in "To a Common Prostitute" in 1860. He would never have delighted, as the author of "Miss Dusky Grisette" does, in the young woman who "has a smile and a wink for every one of the passers-by." This piece as well as the others were probably written by a local humorist, or perhaps by "Mr. Reeder," who was in charge of the "city" news.[15] Reeder, whom Whitman remembered as "an amiable-hearted young man, but excessively intemperate," probably frequented the "watering hole" in the St. Charles Hotel (directly opposite the *Crescent* offices), one of the many pubs along St. Charles Avenue where Miss Grisette hawked her flowers and her body.

When Emory Holloway later published this sketch, he—to his credit—admitted that the description of "Miss Dusky Grisette" does not agree with Whitman's description of the mulatto woman at the French market he often visited,[16] but he nevertheless included the piece in a collection of writings that future biographers have taken as authentic Whitman. Holloway also missed—or omitted—a "Sidewalks and Levees" sketch that does what Whitman does nowhere in his writings—rebuke a woman for her vanity and inattention to her children.[17] In "Mrs. Giddy Gay Butterfly" (April 12), we read of an aged "Butterfly" who ignores the fact that "time had laid the very tips of his fingers gently upon her," who "loves her children vastly . . . , but whether her love for them is of a practical, serviceable nature, we shall see presently." The writer's central point is that "there is a fashion in the world, of praising, rather say idolizing women, whether they deserve it or not. A sort of blind, Pagan idolatry of woman, because she is a woman: that is, while youth and beauty blooms about her—for when 'declined into the vale of tears,' the worship becomes more rational and very often the meed of well-deserved approval is then withheld." The writer here is not Whitman but a misogynist who perhaps in his intemperance has seduced many young women and now condemns them as middle-aged human beings, the same one who in depicting Miss Grisette the day after her performance in front of the St. Charles, when she is serving coffee on the street corners, notes, "Hard-working men like draymen, want coffee and not glances—they need the stomach and not the appetite to be feasted."[18] Whitman seems to have loved motherhood more than womanhood, but he praised both in his poetry.

More Whitmanesque, certainly, is "Honored Be Woman," which Whitman extracted in his job of exchange editor. "The following extract is familiar, but what it says is so correct and beautiful," he wrote on March 15, "that it cannot be too often repeated." Reflecting exactly his *Eagle* sentiments on the subject of women, he said: "We know of nothing which more certainly marks the true *man* than an appreciation of the worth of women, and of his duty on all occasions to honor, protect, and love them." Such chivalry was indeed American: "One of our greatest prides, as an American, is, that our countrymen are peculiarly distinguished for their devotion and kindness to the sex." And in defining such "real" gentlemen, the democratic journalist noted that such character was "not confined to the rich and educated only."

Whitman never married and, as far as we know, never fell in love with a woman, but a number of biographers have suggested that he did. The matter was of no concern to his first biographer and disciple, Richard Maurice Bucke, but it was to his first objective biographer, Henry Bryan Binns. Binns speculated in 1905 that while in New Orleans Whitman fell in love with "some woman of higher social rank than his own—a lady of the South where social rank is of the first consideration—that she became the mother of his child, . . . and that he was prevented by some obstacle, presumably of family prejudice, from marriage or the acknowledgment of his paternity."[19] Binns had absolutely no evidence to support his theory except the uncorroborated statement of the poet in a letter written to John Addington Symonds on August 21, 1890, to wit: "Tho' always unmarried I have had six children—two are dead—One living southern grandchild, fine boy, who writes to me occasionally. Circumstances connected with their benefit and fortune have separated me from intimate relations."[20] Twenty years after Binns blazed this new trail in Whitman biography, Emory Holloway pursued it in a slightly different direction, encouraged perhaps by the 1908 biography by Leon Bazalgette, where the range of lovers is imagined as extending across the socioeconomic spectrum.[21] With no more evidence than either Binns or Bazalgette, Holloway speculated that the mystery woman was a Creole octoroon. His suspicion that Whitman was even attracted to the New Orleans beauties is based on a piece in the *Crescent* of May 18 entitled "A Night at the Terpsichore Ball." It is a satirical sketch, highly artificial and unoriginal, about a man who unknowingly falls in love with another man's wife. As another biographer wisely observed, it is hardly evidence of the author's seriousness about the love he describes.[22] Nor, it should be added, is there any stylistic evidence to suggest it came from Whitman's pen.

Whitman, of course, had many opportunities to become involved with women in this exotic city, far from the vestiges of puritanism in New York and New England—even though he had his young brother in tow. But as during the *Brooklyn Eagle* years, there is no indication of such activity in New Orleans. If he indulged himself in any way, it may have been in the plush surroundings of the St. Charles Hotel and Theatre with their stately barrooms, or in those less pretentious institutions along St. Charles Avenue. Jeff noted the intemperance of some of his brother's acquaintances and newspaper associates (Reeder died later that year, no doubt of typhoid complicated by his alcoholism and loose living). He told his family that "they never meet a friend but you have to go drink and such loose habits." In a contemporary assessment of the city and its low morals, one witness wrote: "Probably no city of equal size in christendom receives into its bosom every year a greater proportion of vicious people than New Orleans." In sharing his view of the city with the folks back in Brooklyn, Jeff added, perhaps significantly, "You know that Walter is averse to such habits, so you need not be afraid of our taking it."[23]

Although Whitman had supported temperance movements in Brooklyn and New York, he was probably not averse to moderate imbibing when he lived in New Orleans. Its climate, both social and meteorological, offered that "hail-fellow-well-met" society that encouraged drinking. Like Frederick Douglass in Baltimore, city slaves in New Orleans had more freedom than their country compatriots, and the lower variety of grog shops enticed even them into riotous inebriation. The St. Charles Hotel, also known as the "St. Charles Exchange," offered a Grand Salon—a great circular hall with white walls and red carpets—where journalists went to pick up the commercial news, reports of troop movements in Mexico, and perhaps a mint julep or two. Its well-dressed visitors were enchanted by their reflections in the room's endless mirrors, which also reflected crystal chandeliers and gold-framed wall coverings. In such an ambiance, Whitman no doubt indulged on occasion his life-long appreciation of beer and spirits.

"The Inhabitants of Hotels," whose allusions to New York City writers and places suggests it is Whitman's, observes that "There is no actual need of a man's traveling around the globe in order to find out a few of the principles of human nature." It was not necessary to attend "a college or a primary school"; merely let him "visit the precincts of some of our 'first-rate, tip-[top]' bar-rooms on Saturday or Sunday night." Later, in the late 1850s, Whitman observed tavern life in Pfaff's cellar bar on Broadway. The New Orleans experiences were less literary than those in the Pfaffian days, when the young William Dean Howells and other writers claimed to have seen Whitman with a glass of beer, sitting alone against the back wall. Instead of literary bohemians in New Orleans, Whitman found idle young men in shiny black coats, inevitably smoking "Havana segars"—or older fops who twirled the seals at the end of their pocket-watch chains and signaled the bartender "twice in every half hour" to mix them a brandy toddy.[24] The author of *Franklin Evans* was already "in and out of the game," and at least one memory may have made its way into *Leaves of Grass* intact. On April 4 the *Crescent* reported that the grandson of the famous orator and statesman Henry Clay had blown out his brains "with a pistol, in his lodging, at the St. Charles Hotel." In "Song of Myself," Whitman would write:

> The suicide sprawls on the bloody floor of the bedroom,
> I witness the corpse with its dabbled hair, I note where the pistol
> has fallen.

❋ ❋ ❋

In addition to frequenting the St. Charles Hotel, walking the Quarter, and having coffee or fruit at the French Market, on the site of an Indian trading ground, Whitman attended performances at the St. Charles Theatre, where the actress Julia Dean performed for more than a week in April. In March Dr. Collyer's "Model Artists" played to a mostly male audience. Horace Greeley's *Tribune* had already complained that such performances were vulgar and lewd when given in New York City,[25] and in anticipation of the troupe's arrival in New Orleans either Whitman or Reeder responded: "They say the sight of such things is *indecent;* if that be so, the sight of nearly all the great works of painting and sculpture—pronounced by the united voice of critics of all nations to be master-pieces of genius—is likewise, indecent."[26] (Eighteen years later William Douglas O'Connor made the same argument in defense of *Leaves of Grass* in his spirited pamphlet *The Good Gray Poet.*) Prior to the first performance of the "Model Artists" on March 21, the *Crescent* advised its more than 2,000 subscribers: "These are *true* Artistes, and will of course not be confounded with those vulgar charlatans who have caused so much disturbance at the North." Either partially nude under dimmed house lights or in flesh-colored tights, the performers adopted the classical poses found in paintings by Titian and Rubens, in sculptures of Greek gods, in depictions of Eve when first seen by Adam, or at the Last Supper.[27] By the second or third performance, the *Crescent* reported that the theater "was crowded almost to suffocation," yet its female complement totaled only "*one lady and a half*—that is to say a lady and her young sister." It had been feared that the questionable performances would culminate in "an outbreak of indignation," resembling the riot that occurred over a similar production in New York City in March, but the performances went off "with the greatest enthusiasm and the most splendid *eclat.*" The next night the *Crescent* reporter counted four women in the packed audience—to whom Dr. Collyer appeared on stage after the performance for a bow, shoeless in a black coat and a vest of a "pea-green hue."[28] Whitman may have witnessed multiple performances of the Collyer actors, for he was on hand on May 9 to record the appearance of Zachary Taylor. "In the dim light, the gas being turned off to give effect to the performances, the General's entrance was not noticed," the *Crescent* said. "When the lights shone out again, however, the most vociferous cheering announced that the people recognized him." This was followed by the spontaneous playing of the "The Star Spangled Banner" and a tableau "purposely complimentary to General Taylor."[29]

By late March the *Crescent* began to be held accountable for its lack of neutrality in political matters. The first issue of the newspaper had attacked the highly controversial "*Triste* Affair," as the treaty ending the Mexican War was known because of the unhappy and drawn-out negotiations of President Polk's chief clerk of the State Department, Nicholas B. Trist. An editorial condemned the agreement for not going far enough in demanding territorial concessions from Mexico. All of Texas, New Mexico, Arizona, and the vast territory of California was apparently not enough; the editorial argued that the boundary between the United States and Mexico should be the Sierra Madre instead of the Rio Grande. This position reflected the consensus among the New Orleans and southern press. Whitman had entertained the same idea ("new states for the Spangled Banner") the previous year in the *Eagle*,[30] but he was probably not the writer of this editorial. Most of the *Crescent* editorials were written by John C. Larue, a lawyer who also collected debts for northern creditors.[31] Larue's northern affiliations and expansionist enthusiasms have led scholars to attribute much of his editorial work to Whitman, but the poet himself states in an 1848 notebook that Larue, "(a good writer,) generally prepared the leading editorials."[32]

Responding to the *Washington Union*'s accusations that it was being "political" in opposing the Trist Treaty, which was about to be ratified by Congress, the *Crescent* maintained that it was standing up for political principle and not any party ideology. Yet the paper *was* partisan and took a strong "Manifest Destiny" position on the outcome of war with Mexico, thinking that American leadership could turn the neighboring country in the right direction. In extracting an account from *Hunt's Magazine,* the editors commented, "Surely no person can read over the following account of the resources possessed by Mexico at the commencement of the present century—and know that she has made no advance upon them—without feeling convinced that so lethargic a people is unworthy of so rich a country."[33] This feeling of Yankee superiority was similar to the attitude of Whitman's successor, William Walker, toward Nicaragua in the 1850s.

The paper was also "southern" in its support of slavery and began during Whitman's tenure to worry about runaway slaves not returned from the north, anticipating the call for a stronger fugitive slave law in 1850.[34] Although biographers have speculated that Whitman lost his job over his anti-slavery views, he apparently kept silent about them for most of his stay. Certainly, they could have never been directly aired in a New Orleans newspaper of the day. Even the politically moderate *Crescent,* which vowed in its opening editorial to divest itself of "party politics," was carrying slave auction advertisements like the following by the middle of April—perhaps an indication that Pierson was already edging closer to the newspaper's founders, Hayes and McClure.

Negroes—Negroes.
By Pierson & Bonneval, Auctioneers,
Office, No. 67 Gravier street.
Will be sold at AUCTION, on Saturday, April 15, at 12 o'clock—at Bank's Arcade—

TEMPE—Negress, aged 35 years—French and American cook; speaks French and English; honest and sober, title guarantied only.

JANE—Likely Negress—plain cook, washer and ironer, and No. 1 field hand; fully guarantied.

LOUISA—Negro girl, about 15 years old; child's nurse and house servant, well recommended, of fine character; fully guarantied.

BRICE—Negro man, about 25 years old; a good warehouse man, hostler, and rough cooper, title only guarantied.

Terms—Cash[35]

During Whitman's tenure the *Crescent* published an account of a female slave who voluntarily returned from Ohio, asking her former master "to dispose of her as he thought proper." On other occasions, it published complaints about "Unruly Negroes" in grog shops and a piece on the disastrous economic effects of the liberation of slaves in the British West Indies.[36]

Because Whitman was a "free-soiler" instead of an abolitionist, his attitudes toward slavery and toward blacks were still (and remained throughout his life) two different subjects. Whereas he was appalled by the concept of slavery, he was described by friends during and after the Civil War as less than enthusiastic about freed slaves' chances of contributing to America's progress.[37] Whitman is more positive on the subject of black Americans in his poetry, where he vicariously assists a fugitive slave and celebrates the American free black along with the other (white) workers in "Song of Myself." His personal attitude generally reflected the common northern attitude in the nineteenth century (when, following the Civil War, many former abolitionists considered their cause fulfilled with the Emancipation Proclamation), while the poetic vision adumbrated concerns and attitudes of the late twentieth century. Nevertheless, even though Whitman's "free-soil" position was not as alien to the pro-slavery, southern view as the anti-slavery, New England view, he must have felt uneasy in the face of the South's solid growing resistance to *any* type of slavery reform.

There was, however, one area of human rights where his allegiance matched that of his employers and associates—the European revolutions that erupted in late March. In the *Eagle* Whitman had given some attention to the social and economic inequities that would lead to the European disturbances of 1848.[38] In the *Crescent,* however, it is difficult to identify most of the items on the subject as the poet's because Whitman was not the editorial writer, not even the editor for foreign news (who was, according to Whitman's records, a man named Da Poute).[39] At least two literary historians have credited Whitman with an unsigned article in which the author writes, "One's blood rushes and grows hot within him, the more he learns or thinks of this news from the continent of Europe! Is it not glorious?" The March 31 piece, printed without a leader, is introduced by lines from William Cullen Bryant, Whitman's favorite poet—possibly evidence that Whitman wrote the article—and it voices Whitman's sentiment, long on record, that bids "farewell to the monarchies and aristocracies of the old world."[40] Whitman may also have been the author of at least one article, on May 20, dealing with Alphonse Marie de Lamartine's study of the French Revolution of 1789. Lamartine became France's foreign minister after King Louis Philippe abdicated during the Revolution of 1848, an upheaval that sent shock waves through Europe, igniting similar, if less successful, uprisings in Germany, Poland, Austria, Ireland, and elsewhere.

The *Crescent*'s response to the revolutions ("France and Liberty!" was the leader for March 27, just days after news of the eruptions reached New Orleans) matched the American response in newspapers generally, sparking liberty celebrations in both New York City and New Orleans. It also reflected, ironically, the imperialist sentiment of the *Crescent* (and the pro-slavery South in general) with regard to Mexico. The editors of the *Crescent,* who welcomed the European revolutions, were otherwise delighted to think the revolutions rendered "it certain that Mexico cannot receive any assistance from England or any of them, by word or deed. She would then be entirely at our mercy—or rather our sense of justice—were it not for this wretched Trist treaty."[41]

Because the taking of even part of Mexico threatened to open the door to the expansion of slavery in the United States, Whitman found that his association with the *Crescent* entangled him with pro-slavery, anti-Wilmot politics in general. He had favored the annexation of Mexico while editor of the *Eagle,* saying the "scope of our government, (like the most sublime principles of Nature), is such that it can readily fit itself, and extend itself, to almost any extent," and he was probably prepared to accept even the extension of American slavery in Texas (where it already existed before statehood anyway) in order to realize the inevitable growth of what he called in *Leaves of Grass* his "teeming nation of nations."[42] In *The Eighteenth Presidency!* he would declare that fugitive slaves ought to be returned under the provisions of the Compromise of 1850. He could think so because he firmly believed that slavery was only temporary—that the American people would eventually rise up and abolish it in accordance with the destiny of American democracy.

When the French revolutionary government began to look socialist, the *Crescent* voiced its concern on April 18: "A dynasty may be overthrown in an hour—the form of government changed in a day—but the reconstruction of the social system, and the emancipation of a people from the habits, prejudices, modes of life and of business which have characterized their past existence, is the work of generations." Its main fear that France or other revolutionary governments would spread their revolution to countries such as Mexico was alleviated when Lamartine refused to aid the Irish. The *Crescent* of May 3 praised him, saying, "God seems to have raised up this man as Washington was raised for us in our great struggle." Yet the editorial hedged its bet on Lamartine—and the revolutions—by adding, "It is, perhaps, too early to speak decidedly of his character." The comparison to George Washington, whose memory Whitman (along with the rest of nineteenth-century America) cherished, could be reason enough to say that Whitman is the author here, too, but the evidence regarding editorial assignments on the paper weighs against the possibility.

More likely, he was responsible as exchange editor for the *Crescent*'s printing on April 7 of the "Marseilles Hymn," whose translation was copied from the *New York Daily Tribune*. This spirited call to arms in the struggle for peace and liberty may have inspired Whitman to write "The Old World," which appeared in the *Crescent* on April 28.

> Italia! Italia! See! See!
> The day star of Liberty shines;
> The tyrants of earth in their places quake,
> The pillars of priestcraft and policy shake,
> The despot his sceptre resigns—
> Italia! Italia! awake!
>
> Hispania! Hispania! *a ello!*
> The Gaul his oppressor has crush'd;
> The slaves of the Bourbon presented the chain,
> With one mighty struggle he snapp'd it in twain,
> And forth to his freedom he rush'd.
> Hispania! Hispania! arise!

Germania! Germania! *auf! auf!*
The blood of the Frank has been shed;
The nations of earth are arous'd from their sleep;
The slave must rejoice, the enslaver must weep,
The living must follow the dead.
Germania! Germania! up! up!

Britannia! Britannia! beware!
Nor trust in thy nobles or gold,
Thou art proud in thy wealth, and mighty in war,
But the voice of mankind shall be mightier far,
When the banner of freedom's unroll'd.
Britannia! Britannia! beware!

Fellow mortals! thanksgiving to God!
His spirit is stirring on earth;
He has heard the loud cry of the poor and the slave;
He has shivered the strength of the statesman and the knave;
He has given young liberty birth.
Fellow mortals! Thanksgiving to God!

Earth! Earth! cry out and rejoice!
Truth, freedom, religion are thine;
In one mighty bond let the nations unite,
To win and guard their freedom and right,
The "holiest right divine."
Earth! Earth! cry out and rejoice!

The alliance of kings is destroyed,
The union of people remains;
The Briton unites with the Spaniard and Gaul;
The Italian and German are brothers, and all
Fling back to the tyrants their chains.
The alliance of kings is destroyed!

But Gaul! keep thy hand on thy sword!
Be fixed in the right to the death;
The voice and the heart of mankind are with thee,
And if tyrants should dare, our hands too, shall be

Thine, thine, to the last dying breath.
But Gaul! keep thy hand on thy sword!

It is remarkable that the owners of the *Crescent,* or even Larue, would have printed a poem envisioning a situation in which "The slave must rejoice, the enslaver must weep." Or one in which God "has heard the loud cry of the poor and the slave." It was one thing to rail against economic slavery, but these sentiments referred directly to human slavery, which the European empires had already relegated to their colonies, where it was now threatened because of the revolutions. If this poem came from Whitman's pen, and it is difficult to imagine who else on the *Crescent* staff or elsewhere in New Orleans might have composed such a poem, it may have effected his eventual dismissal the way his editorial about Cass and the Wilmot Proviso prepared the way for his departure from the *Eagle.*

Yet by the time of the publication of "The Old World," there were already signs that the revolutions were losing some of their steam. They appeared to be failing utterly in the campaigns of the English Chartists and the Irish Repealers. And in early April Pope Pius IX withdrew his troops from the Italian army fighting for its country's independence from Austria. The message of "The Old World" is that revolution is now well underway but be ever vigilant lest the resistance fall apart ("But Gaul! keep thy hand on thy sword!"). Two years later, when the revolutions *had* failed, Whitman published what may be viewed as an updated version of "The Old World," a poem that ultimately carried the title of "Europe" in the definitive edition of *Leaves of Grass* in 1881. It was also included among the untitled poems of the first edition of *Leaves of Grass* and was called "Resurgemus" when Whitman first published it in Greeley's *Tribune* of June 21, 1850. (Curiously, William Douglas O'Connor, an abolitionist, published a poem entitled "Resurgamus" in 1853, which lamented the fall of a benevolent ruling class.)[43] "Frightened rulers come back," Whitman's poem observed, yet

Those corpses of young men,
Those martyrs that hang from the gibbets,
Those hearts pierced by the grey lead,
Cold and motionless as they seem,

> Live elsewhere with undying vitality;
> . . . .
> Not a grave of those slaughtered ones,
> But is growing its seed of freedom,
> In its turn to bear seed,
> Which the winds shall carry afar and resow,
> And the rain nourish.

The long mid-stanza lines of "The Old World" are shortened somewhat in "Resurgemus," but they point to the longer ones of *Leaves of Grass,* where the originally short lines of "Resurgemus," or "Europe," are doubled up to make long lines. The *Crescent* poem employs the repetition of later Whitman poems—as well as foreign terms, whose use Whitman renewed after 1860. It also contains those Whitman words of excitement and exhilaration employed in *Drum-Taps* (1865). In "First O Songs for a Prelude," everyone's step is quickened by the upbeat rhythm (later to become the "shock electric") of war. And in "The Old World" we have the use of the elided vowel in the past tense as well, which Whitman also returned to in 1860 in his quest to capture the sound of the American vernacular (e.g., "The nations of earth are *arous'd* [instead of the more genteelly poetic *arous-ed*] from their sleep"). In "The Wound-Dresser," before the narrator faces up to the slaughter of innocent youth, he is "Arous'd and angry" in his anticipation of a Union victory. Finally, the line in the first stanza about "The pillars of priestcraft" that fail anticipates Whitman's prediction about organized religion in the 1855 Preface—reflecting a Quaker prejudice that ran deep in the Whitman family—that "There will soon be no more priests. Their work is done."

Probably because of Whitman's reputation as a political moderate—or even conservative—in old age, biographers have noted that he was silent on the slavery question during his stay in New Orleans. But this poem with its references to individual as well as economic slavery suggests that he was not quite mute on the subject. Jeff's comment about the parishioners of the St. Louis Cathedral blessing themselves in holy water and then going home to whip their slaves suggests that neither Whitman was comfortable with that hypocritical segment of southern life (whose memories the poet otherwise savored throughout his days).[44] Cheering the European revolutions while calling for harsher and more effective ways to maintain slavery in their own land was about the same as blessing oneself and whipping one's slave.

In his memorandum on the New Orleans period, Whitman wrote: "Through some unaccountable means . . . both H. and M'C [Hayes and McClure], after a while, exhibited a singular sort of coldness, toward me . . . I had been accustomed to having frequent conferences, in my former situations with the proprietors of newspapers, on the subject of management, etc.—But when the coldness above alluded to broke out, H. seemed to be studiously silent upon all these matters." Hayes, as has been noted, was the senior partner in the ownership of the *Crescent* and probably the business associate who invited the slave auctioneer Pierson to buy into the newspaper; McClure was from Vermont, and probably closer to Whitman on the slavery question. It was he who had hired Whitman in New York and may have assured the poet of the paper's promised moderation in editorial positions. (McClure eventually outlived the other original partners, opening "Sam's Saloon," probably in the "American" section of the city.)[45] Hence, Whitman's fate at the *Crescent* may have come about from the not unusual situation of having been liked (and hired) by one partner and not by the other, who in this case probably had the final say. It was left nevertheless to the junior partner to do the dirty work of discouraging Whitman at the *Crescent.* On May 24 Whitman requested "a small sum of money." Whether this was for an advance or for money already owed is not clear, but Jeff records that Walt had been saving a good deal of money, or hoped to be doing so;[46] therefore, it was probably for wages earned. McClure refused, and in the ensuing exchange of office memoranda with the two partners, Whitman reminded "them of certain points which appeared to have been forgotten, making me *not* their debtor, and told them in my reply I thought it would be better to dissolve the connection." Whitman recorded that his "pride was touched—and I met their conduct with equal haughtiness on my part."[47] The day he had words with Hayes and McClure, *The Pride of the West* arrived from the Illinois River, suggesting an alternate and immediate route back to Brooklyn.

Most biographers accept the proposition that Whitman lost his job on the *Brooklyn Eagle* because of his support for the Wilmot Proviso, and that he joined the staff of the *Crescent* as a secret abolitionist, eventually losing that job as well because he could not contain his anti-slavery sentiments. Whitman was indeed fired from the *Eagle* because of his free-soil politics, but the decision to let him go may not have been shared by all, possibly not by S. G. Arnold, who kept up friendly relations with Whitman. His separation from the *Crescent* may not have been a clear-cut case of dismissal but instead may have come about by mutual agreement, however compelled on Whitman's part. In his attitude toward slavery Whitman was less an abolitionist than a free-soil proponent (less anti-slavery, more pro-white), concerned mainly with the expansion of white labor into the new territories unfettered by the shame slave labor cast on the capitalistic ethic of honest work in a democracy. Despite Whitman's new-found sympathy for slaves as human beings, the focus of his politics remained the good of the country as a whole, just as it had been during his days at the *Eagle*—and just as, during the Civil War, he considered the integrity of the Union more important than the abolition of slavery.[48]

As Whitman looked out from the main deck of *The Pride of the West* while the steamboat cleared port on Saturday afternoon, May 27,[49] he could take some satisfaction with his literary writing over the last three months, if not his progress as a journalist. Besides "The Old World," which may well be his work, he had also published "The Mississippi at Midnight" on March 6, a poem he would exclude from *Leaves of Grass* but include (in a more didactic version) in *Specimen Days*. The daytime Mississippi River with its endless carpet of muddy water and marshy banks became for the poet in the moonless night the "tireless waters" of "Life's quick dream."

How solemn! the river a trailing pall,
    Which takes, but never again gives back;
And moonless and starless the heavens' arch'd wall,
    Responding an equal black!

Oh, tireless waters! like Life's quick dream,
Onward and onward ever hurrying—
Like Death in this midnight hour you seem,
Life in your chill drops greedily burying!

For the poet who had not ventured far beyond New York and Long Island before his long journey south, the miracles of a larger landscape seemed to unlock the imagination. While crossing the Alleghenies, he saw things, he said, that afforded "first rate scenes for the *American* painter—one who, not continually straining to be merely second or third best, in *imitation,* seizes original and really picturesque occasions of this sort for his pieces." He saw evidence of Creation that, as he proclaimed in "Song of Myself," would "stagger sextillions of infidels." He had written in the *Crescent* of March 5, "Faith! If I had an infidel to convert, I would take him on the mountains, of a clear and beautiful night, when the stars were shining."[50] Stars overhead or not, the night seemed to embrace the earth and the life it nourished like a mother's love or—as he put it in Section 21 of "Song of Myself"—a lover's nearness:

I am he that walks with the tender and growing night,
I call to the earth and sea half-held by the night.
Press close bare-bosom'd night—press close magnetic nourishing night!
Night of south winds—night of the large few stars!
Still nodding night—mad naked summer night.

Like "The Old World," "The Mississippi at Midnight" appears to have opened the way, more than slightly, to new linguistic horizons, abysses that no longer faded out as they did in "A Sketch" with conventional sentiments such as "the chastening hand of Heaven" or "The Soul's high culture." A real world with real people in it existed in a visible culture beyond the pale of conventional literature with its human stereotypes, yet well within the grasp of the "*American* painter," who "imitated" only *eye-witness* impressions.

In "Night," a prose piece published the day after "The Mississippi at Midnight," he symbolized night as the alter-ego of existence:

> beautiful in itself, but still more beautiful in its associations: it is not linked, as day is, with our cares and our toils, the business and the littleness of life. The sunshine brings with it its action: we rise in the morning, and our task is before us; but night comes, and with it, rest. If we leave sleep, and ask not of dream forgetfulness, our waking is in solitude, and our employment is thought. Imagination has thrown her glory around the midnight—the orbs of Heaven, the silence, the shadows are steeped in poetry. Even in the heart of a crowded city, where the moonlight fell but upon the pavement and roof, the heart would be softened and the mind elevated, amid the loneliness of night's deepest and stillest hours.
>
> (*Crescent,* March 7, 1846)

We can see here, in our own moonlit view of the poet's foreground, the writer of "The Sleepers," who would "wander all night in my vision." We can also see how those dreams invested the day, "the heart of the crowded city," to make the first few editions of *Leaves of Grass* sparkle so with originality.

In his journalism, Whitman looked at the underside of the Mexican War; he also turned to the artisan now employed in its business of death. "How he toils!" he wrote of "The Cabinet Maker" on April Fools' Day in New Orleans. "He saws out unearthly looking pieces of board, and makes them into coffins! Oh, humanity is strange! it is a riddle to the wise, and a mere joke to those whose souls are full of sarcasm." Writing about a war that was a dress rehearsal for the Civil War, he continued, in a rehearsal for the later emotions of *Drum-Taps* and his poignant essays about the war in *Memoranda During the War* and *Specimen Days:*

> It was but yesterday that our business called us to visit the shop of a cabinet maker. There, in solemn array, stood lines of coffins, and they almost seemed to say "takes us away—bury us—for we do not wish to make mankind forget that life is life." In the middle of the room were five deal boxes, common deal boxes, and yet each one contained the body of a hero! One had fallen at the siege of Vera Cruz, another at the National Bridge, another at Jalapa, and two others at the gates of Mexico [City]. The bullet, the sabre, the cannon and the lance, had done

> their cruel work, and the aspirations of valor—the yearnings after glory, and all that makes a warrior, were lost in the annals of the past.
>
> (*Crescent,* April 1, 1848)

Just as during the Civil War Whitman would place the common soldier above the general with his haughty "shoulder-straps," he felt during the Mexican War that there was more than one "Hero of Buena Vista," Vera Cruz, Mexico City, and elsewhere among the monuments of the American victory. "Other states indicate themselves in their deputies," he would write in the 1855 Preface, "but the genius of the United States is not best or most in executives or legislatures, nor in its ambassadors or inventors. . . . but always most in the common people."[51] It was only shortly after the appearance of Whitman's piece on the coffin maker that he was on hand at the St. Charles Theatre to see the people thrill over the sight of General Taylor.

The photograph of Whitman that we now know was taken in New Orleans may have been done at Maguire's Daguerreotype at 6 Camp Street, just a block over from the *Crescent* offices on St. Charles. James Maguire, considered one of the city's finest daguerreotypists, had photographed Zachary Taylor in January.[52] Looking only slightly older than the hatted image of the *Aurora* days, Whitman gazes more alertly into the camera obscura now. He had perhaps learned more about the human and social condition in the last three months than in the last three or four years. He still lacks a mustache, but his hair has a streak of light across the front. The look is less trustful than before—suggesting a wariness about his future. Doubtless, it must have occurred to Whitman by now that he was fast wearing out his options in journalism—having gone off and afar to one job after ending another under less than wholly agreeable circumstances. Now after only three months he was about to return to Brooklyn with no steady job. Not long before he and Jeff left New Orleans, a destructive fire burned down many shops on Magazine Street, near their lodgings at St. Charles and Lafayette, not a good omen, Whitman might have concluded. The fire prefigured one of even greater proportions in Brooklyn later that year, which would cut short his next foray into journalism the way the 1835 Wall Street fire had cut short his first try at New

York City. One poem in the *Crescent* we know for sure Whitman did not write was "Brother! Come Home!" signed "W.H.U." on May 24, but it may have echoed his determination on that crucial day to "dissolve the connection" with New Orleans. Jeff, suffering again from dysentery that had affected him when they first entered the city, was hankering for home, and Walt may have feared the outbreak of disease in New Orleans with the coming of summer (Sam McClure almost died of cholera in the fall of 1848).[53]

Thanks to the *New Orleans Picayune,* which on its fiftieth anniversary in 1887 queried him about his stay in New Orleans ("when you were younger and less famous than now"), we have the fullest account of his itinerary back to New York, which also can be found, but only partially, in an 1848 notebook entry. Before quoting directly from his notebook in his response to the *Picayune,* he remembered once more the stately barrooms of the St. Charles and St. Louis hotels, though in reprinting the piece in *November Boughs* in 1889 he failed to list among their many activities—"Bargains, appointments, business conferences, &c."—the slave "auctions," which are mentioned in the *Picayune* text. Whitman may have wanted—as the "Poet of Democracy"—to distance himself ever so slightly from his beloved South, or at least its history of race relations, which in 1889 was about to enter its Jim Crow chapter. And when lamenting in the *November Boughs* copy his failure to gain a "better knowledge of French and Spanish Creole New Orleans people" (and writing parenthetically, "I have an idea that there is much and of importance about the Latin race [*sic*] contributions to American nationality in the South and Southwest that will never be put on record"), he inserted before the final prepositional phrase: "with sympathetic understanding and tact." Since *November Boughs* was finalized for the press during one of the poet's most serious illnesses, these minor but interesting changes may have been effected or influenced by Horace Traubel, then on the scene and a champion of progressive causes.[54]

Whitman found the shores of the Mississippi as "monotonous and dull" as before, and it took an entire week to reach St. Louis, which he and Jeff explored "a little." (As a married man and civil engineer, Jeff would make his home there after the Civil War, where this former victim of dysentery would help to supervise the construction of the city's waterworks.) From St. Louis they took the steamer *Prairie Bird* up the Illinois River to LaSalle, from where they traveled by canal to Chicago. The brothers got to see more cities than before—as well as farmlands that compared favorably with those they knew on Long Island. In Chicago, "I rambled with my brother over a large portion of the town, searched after a refectory, and after much trouble, succeeded in getting some dinner." Illinois he thought "the most splendid agricultural country I ever saw." After a night in Chicago, they sailed Lake Michigan on the *Griffith,* delighting in the towns they saw on the Wisconsin side. They briefly visited Milwaukee before entering Lake Huron, also stopping at Mackinaw. During the Lake Michigan leg, "a crazy lady" jumped overboard. Whitman remembered, "It was horrible, and made me feel the most distressing sensations!"[55] While on Lake Erie headed for Buffalo, they spent the night of June 11 in Cleveland. There, though it was already dark, Whitman rambled "about the place; went up in the heart of the city and back to what appear'd to be the court house." The next day, halfway across the lake, the water ("rougher than on Michigan or Huron") made the poet seasick.[56] Upon reaching Buffalo, the two explored that city and visited Niagara Falls. The next day, June 14, Walt and Jeff traveled by rail to Albany, arriving late on June 15. "There was a political meeting (Hunker)," Whitman noted, "but I pass'd it by." After a day's journey down the Hudson River, they arrived back in Manhattan and probably reached their parents' house on Adams Street near Myrtle Avenue late that evening.

Throughout his life, Whitman considered the New Orleans sojourn crucial to his development as a poet. In an eleventh-hour attempt at autobiography (May 1891), he romanticized this period only slightly as "two years on a working and journeying tour, through nearly every one of the Middle, Southern, and Western states, and to Louisiana and Texas (during the Mexican War of 1848 and '49)."[57] With the exception of Texas, whose territory was still in dispute in 1848, Whitman's passage south had touched "nearly every one of the Middle, Southern, and Western states" as they stood that year. The experience would help to release the vicarious traveler of *Leaves of Grass* in the 1850s.

6

SIMMERING, SIMMERING, SIMMERING

Growing its seed of freedom,
In its turn to bear seed,
Which the winds shall carry afar and re-sow
And the rain nourish.

WALT WHITMAN
"Resurgemus"

As Whitman returned from New Orleans and set about looking for another living, he began to internalize all that had whirled about him in the last decade and especially in the last three months. The suicide of Henry Clay's grandson in New Orleans and the slave auctions he had witnessed in that city, for example, would come to mean more than the sum of a journalistic conclusion. The democracy he had so studiously attended to during his *Eagle* days began to take on aspects of divinity. Beginning in the summer and fall of 1848, the immediate "foreground" of the first *Leaves of Grass,* the poet began to dive below the surface meanings of life and beneath his own superficialities.

Whitman had saved a sum of money while in New Orleans (enough eventually to get him into the real estate and building speculation business in Brooklyn), but in the summer of 1848 he faced a bleak economic future with no steady job in hand. Even though he had been gone from the city only three and a half months, no one in the newspaper business seemed to notice him publicly or want him on the staff. Even the often quoted but misdated *Eagle* piece—originally cited as appearing in 1848—that depicted Whitman as too lazy to kick a politician downstairs did not appear until the summer of 1849. He wrote no more fiction as far as we know, but to help support himself he recycled some old pieces during the first years of his return from New Orleans. One of these, "The Shadow and the Light of a Young Man's Soul," published in the *Union Magazine of Literature and Art* in June of 1848, had never actually appeared before, but it is fairly certain that Whitman wrote it when he was still teaching school on Long Island.[1]

A year later, he republished "A Legend of Life and Love" in James J. Brenton's *Long Island Democrat.* This was one of his temperance tales, which had first appeared in the *Democratic Review* in 1842. Brenton had employed Whitman in Jamaica in the fall of 1839. Even though the young typesetter and occasional contributor to the *Democrat* had not altogether worked out at the position, Brenton took a lifelong interest in Whitman and noticed him favorably in his newspaper whenever Whitman took a new post.[2] Brenton (Whitman called him "Dr. Franklin") not only shared Whitman's interest in temperance movements but agreed with the poet that the working class deserved more respect in their fledgling democracy. He also recycled Whitman's third piece of fiction, "The Tomb-Blossoms," in *Voices from the Press* in 1850. In his introduction to the book, which included contributions from many former and current journalists who had emerged from humble backgrounds like Whitman's (Horace Greeley, Nathaniel P. Willis, Bayard Taylor, B. P. Shillaber), Brenton wrote: "The chief merit of this volume consists not so much in its literary excellence, as in the evidence it exhibits of what industry and application, unaided by wealth and patronage, can accomplish." Many of the pieces, he added, had been "written by those who were born under the most unfavorable auspices—cast in early life destitute upon the world." Brenton hoped it would inspire "even the poor printer's devil" that the path to honor and usefulness was "as open and free to him as to the most highly favored son of affluence and birth."[3]

These would have been Whitman's exact sentiments. From our twentieth-century perspective, we tend to forget that Whitman, the product of "charity" schooling in Brooklyn, was socially and economically different from Emerson and many of the New England writers of his day, different even from his fellow New Yorker Melville, who though he never went to Harvard or Yale came closer in his formal education to the "New England Brahmin" than Whitman ever did. When Emerson went abroad for the first time in 1832, his career was still undistinguished. Yet all the important doors were open to this aspiring writer as he traveled through Europe, and in England he was received by celebrities such as Wordsworth, Coleridge, and John Stuart Mill.

Indeed, Whitman's interest in keeping slavery out of the new territories sprang from this "voice from the press" and its "practical" printers and editors, who did not want to see free labor degraded because they so depended upon its spirit to lift them out of their impoverished beginnings. Just after his return from New Orleans, he was appointed as one of fourteen delegates to represent the radical Democrats of Kings County at the state Free-Soil presidential convention in Buffalo on August 9. The Barnburners (so called because they were like farmers who would burn down their barns to rid them of rats) had formed a third party because they were opposed to the Democratic presidential candidate, Lewis Cass, whose Hunker platform allowed new states and territories to determine for themselves whether they would be slave or free. They were also opposed to the Whig candidate, Zachary Taylor, a southerner who owned many hundreds of slaves.

As early as January 1848, before he went down to New Orleans, Whitman had been mentioned as a possible editor of the *Brooklyn Freeman,* to be founded because the *Eagle* refused to carry free-soil viewpoints, but it was probably his political involvement in Brooklyn and the Buffalo meeting of New York free-soilers that clinched his decision to take the helm of the *Freeman.*[4] Frederick Douglass had already shown the way by successfully founding his own anti-slavery paper, the *North Star,* in Rochester. Later Whitman recalled that he had heard Douglass (and Emerson) speak at the Tabernacle and Athenaeum theaters in New York City, and he may have met America's most famous ex-slave before that at the Buffalo convocation during the second week of August.[5] The *Freeman* was the conception of a group of Brooklyn free-soilers. Spearheaded by Judge Samuel B. Johnston, known for his aid to fugitive slaves in the city, it was originally to be called the *Banner of Freedom* (perhaps laying the seed for Whitman's planned *Banner at Daybreak* in 1860). When Whitman received the list of financial backers, he changed the name to the *Freeman.*[6]

He found office space for the newspaper in the basement of the Franklin Building at 110 Orange Street near Fulton. The building housed the *Brooklyn Evening Star*, whose editor, Alden Spooner, had employed Whitman as an apprentice in the late 1830s and who was a fellow delegate with him at the Buffalo meeting. Also sharing office space at 110 Orange was Henry A. Lees, editor of the Whig paper, the *Brooklyn Advertizer.* He too was friendly to Whitman, though mainly to antagonize the *Eagle* after the poet's departure as editor.

"Free Soilers! Radicals! Liberty Men!" Whitman's first number announced, "all whose throats are not quite tough enough to swallow Taylor or Cass! come up and subscribe for the '*Daily Freeman.*'" The *Freeman* was established to follow up on the convention in Buffalo, where Martin Van Buren, a former president, and Charles Francis Adams, the son of a former president, were nominated for the third-party ticket. Ironically, none of the three presidential candidates was truly anti-slavery. Indeed, Whitman's position was part-abolitionist, part free-soiler, and the paper's name probably referred to white workingmen, or "freemen," rather than blacks, who were known as "freedmen." Generally, if not always consistently, his editorial position on the paper was that slaves were to be freed (or at least the institution of slavery kept out of the new territories) in order that white labor not be demeaned by having the slaves do for nothing what the whites did for wages. The first issue used the term "abolitionist" freely and literally in its evocation of Jefferson, described as an abolitionist who made "five or six" attempts to abolish slavery in Virginia while serving in its legislature. In concluding his article on Jefferson, full of quotations from the third president, Whitman lamented "how much better would it have proved for us all now, had slavery been abolished by the southern states" in Jefferson's day. "The reflection," he concluded, "unavoidably follows: How important that we should not saddle future generations in new states with this wicked and most dangerous curse!"[7]

Elsewhere in the first issue Whitman's tone tried to soften the anti-slavery message so as to offend as few as possible. In "Our Enmity to the South," he adopted the same approach he had taken toward Mexico during the war and envisioned the enemy as an "aristocratical minority—some fifteenth, or at the utmost some tenth, of the white inhabitants of the South, who hold bondsmen." He even counted among his southern friends "a very respectable body of slave owners, who, the same as we, condemn slavery." Just who these individuals were is hard to know, but Whitman no doubt imagined southern slaveowners who were converted to free-soil if not genuine anti-slavery positions by the development in certain southern states during the last five years "of manufacturing energy, . . . and a consciousness awakened to the great natural riches . . . so long unimproved under the lethargic influence of slave institutions."

Whitman got out his first (and only known extant) issue of the two-penny weekly on September 9. The very next night a fire broke out at a nearby furniture and upholstery store. Because most of the adjacent buildings were made of wood and a recent drought had made water scarce, the flames quickly spread over eight blocks in the densest part of Brooklyn. More than two hundred buildings were destroyed, including the one that housed the *Freeman.* To stop the fire, marines were called in from the Brooklyn navy shipyard to blow up key buildings in the fire's path.[8] Once again a terrifying conflagration had rudely changed Whitman's plans.

After the fire, it took Whitman another two months to get out the second issue. There had been no insurance, and he lost what little equipment the paper had owned or borrowed. On November 1 he set up facilities at 96 Myrtle Street and announced in the *Brooklyn Evening Star* that he was "determined to go ahead. Smiles or frowns, thick or thin, we shall establish a Radical Newspaper in Kings County." It may have succeeded because on April 25, 1849, the *Freeman* became a daily. By then he had moved the paper to 106 Myrtle, where he purchased a corner lot and built a house; it was at this time that Whitman also became a bookseller and set up shop at his residence.[9] Yet the effort to keep the new territories free of slaves was clearly fading after the election of a slaveholder as president. Also part of Whitman's ultimate failure, after he resumed publication of the *Freeman,* may have been because his anti-slavery opposition sometimes exceeded the limits of the free-soil position of the paper. He recalled in his autobiography that he had once been something of a radical on the subject before the Civil War.[10]

By the summer the Brooklyn radicals' solidarity began to weaken, and "compromise" was heard from both sides—though not from Whitman, who by September 11 had announced his resignation, which was copied in the *Eagle.* "After the present date," he wrote somewhat bitterly, "I withdraw entirely from the Brooklyn *Daily Freeman.* To those who have been my friends, I take occasion to proffer the warmest thanks of a grateful heart. My enemies—and old Hunkers generally—I disdain and defy the same as ever."[11]

Since only the first issue of the *Freeman* is known to exist, we do not know the details of Whitman's editorship. During the summer of 1849 the *Eagle* added to Whitman's distractions about the crumbling of the radical front—and the accompanying reduction in advertising and circulation—by lashing out at him for his past performance as editor of the *Eagle.* Stirred by Lees's comment in the *Advertizer* of July 18 that Whitman had been fired for resisting "Old Hunkerism," even to the point of kicking down a flight of stairs "a certain prominent politician" from the conservative wing of the Democratic Party, the *Eagle* described its former editor as "slow, indolent, heavy, discourteous and without steady principles . . . [and] a clog upon our success." Stating again that Whitman was totally without "political principles," the editorial concluded: "Whoever knows him will laugh at the idea of his *kicking any body,* much less a prominent politician. He is too indolent to kick a musketo."[12] Not long after his resignation from the *Freeman,* Whitman must have puffed himself in one of the Sunday papers, for the *Eagle* struck at him again, claiming on September 24 not only that he had been "thrust out" of his place at the *Eagle* and the *Crescent* but also "kicked out of his own paper." On September 28 it followed up: "So Mr. Whitman took the barnburners flag, principles, and party away with him."

Whitman was definitely fired or pushed out of this newspaper editorship as the paper gradually adopted a softer (and more anti-Wilmot) political tone. By November Samuel F. Coggswell, a former *Eagle* reporter, had taken over, and the *Eagle* referred to a *Freeman* editorial of November 12 indicating that the paper was expected to "cut loose from party politics and to be devoted entirely to the current news of the day." Thus ended forever Whitman's full-time career in journalism. His only other stab at running a newspaper was the weekly *Salesman and Traveller's Directory for Long Island,* an advertising sheet. Whitman, who throughout his life never showed much interest in material success, launched the strictly money-making venture on June 4, 1851, but the paper lasted less than a month.[13]

❋ ❋ ❋

Not that Whitman didn't attempt to stay on the editorial side of journalism. He resorted to freelancing—something he hadn't done on a steady basis since his *Star* days. Between October and January 1850, he published ten casual essays under the general heading of "Letters from a Travelling Bachelor" in the *New York Sunday Dispatch.* Perhaps to avoid the evil eye of the *Eagle* (Whitman's September "puff" may have appeared in the *Sunday Dispatch*), he signed these letters "Paumanok." His use of the Indian name for Long Island had the effect of a double entendre—evoking the place and its poet. It never became Whitman's nickname (as "The Raven" became Poe's for a time), but the spirit of the word is embedded in *Leaves of Grass* and, of course, "Starting from Paumanok."

Whitman had learned the art of the journalistic essay largely at the *Eagle,* which lost much of its literary quality after he departed. His work for the *Sunday Dispatch* consisted of travel pieces on the same order as his longer essays in the *Eagle*—for example, the three-part essay about his railroad journey to Greenport in the *Eagle* in 1847. He used Greenport again more than a decade later, borrowing from the "Travelling Bachelor" letters for his "Brooklyniana" series.[14]

Shortly after resigning from the *Freeman,* Whitman apparently retreated to Greenport. The old whaling village often served him as a retreat from the city, especially in the summer of 1855 following the publication of the first *Leaves of Grass.* In his first "letter" on the alleged joys of the country, the "Travelling Bachelor" quickly established that he preferred the city for the construction of the complete individual, or "whole man," as he had no doubt read in Emerson. Whitman thought for all the freedom the countryside offered, it also led to a "kind of lazy pride." The air was more wholesome, of course, but "that advantage," he said, was generally counterbalanced by certain evils not so common in the city. He who had shirked his chores on the farm now noted that "the country child is put to hard work at an early age; he soon loses the elasticity of youth, and becomes round-shouldered and clumsy. He learns to smoke [a practice Whitman eschewed], chew, and drink, about as soon as his town prototype."[15] The opening poem of the first *Leaves* would be more about the city than the country. The Brooklynite in this Long Islander prevailed, yet he united city and country in the way he united so many other entities, especially those of body and soul in *Leaves of Grass.* To Whitman the city was the body, the country the soul. "Lack one lacks both" is what he finally said in "Song of Myself."

The first five "letters" take the reader on the railway from the South Ferry in Brooklyn to Greenport, and then by other means as far out as Montauk Point. Beginning with Number 6, the essays become anecdotal, commencing with a tale about a hunter some ten years earlier who became lost on the island and was invited to spend the night with a newly wedded couple—not in a guest room but in their very bed. The story may be true and perhaps provides the autobiographical spark to Whitman's pronouncement in "Song of Myself"—"I turn the bridegroom out of bed and stay with the bride myself." Indeed, there are several aspects of this collection of essays that reveal the foreground to the poetry of 1855 and 1856. In Number 7 Whitman tours the Croton Reservoir (today the site of the New York Public Library) and projects the scene forward a century, as he will in "Crossing Brooklyn Ferry." "You and I, reader, and quite all the people who are now alive, won't be much thought of then; but the world will be just as jolly, and the sun will shine as bright, and the rivers off there—the Hudson on one side and the East on the other—will slap along their green waves, precisely as now; and other eyes will look upon them about the same as we do." (Whitman turns out to have been prescient about everything except the "green waves" of the Hudson and East rivers.) Number 10 suggests that he was already thinking of his "Sun-Down Poem" (as "Crossing Brooklyn Ferry" was originally called). Here he wrote: "Many books have been written, to describe journeys between the Old and New World. . . . But we know of no work—at least we feel sure none has yet been issued by the Harpers, Appletons, or any of our great publishers—describing a voyage across the Fulton Ferry." During his days on the *Eagle,* he frequently took a ferry across and back again just "to get," as he wrote in "Travelling Bachelor" Number 10, "the pure air, at the economical price of a penny trip." He wrote about ferries then and would again, not only in his great poem but in *Specimen Days.*[16]

The "open road" pattern of the series is much like that of "Song of Myself." Whitman takes his reader first to the countryside and hamlets of Long Island and then through Manhattan, strolling by Union Square, past Grace Church, down Broadway and into the museum of the American Art Union ("Never before has any art exhibition in America contained pieces or work of such high order as this"). He testified later that *Leaves of Grass* "began to take a sort of unconscious shape in his mind" in the early 1850s.[17] But these essays give us even a better fix, not only on just when *Leaves of Grass* first took "unconscious shape," but on when the great poem of the second edition first came into the poet's imagination. "Who has crossed the East River and not looked with admiration on the beautiful view afforded from the middle of the stream? [he wrote in Number 10.] The forests of the New York shipping, lining the shores as far as one can see them—the tall spire of Trinity looming far up over all the other objects—various other spires—the tops of the trees on the Battery and in the Parks—these we have left behind us. In front stands Brooklyn—Brooklyn the beautiful! The Heights stretch along in front. . . ."[18] In "Crossing Brooklyn Ferry" he wrote,

> Others will enter the gates of the ferry and cross from shore to shore,
> Others will watch the run of the flood-tide,
> Others will see the shipping of Manhattan north and west, and
> the heights of Brooklyn to the south and east.

One of Whitman's notebooks ("[T]albot Wilson") suggests that "Song of Myself" may have been in the poet's imagination as early as the lines anticipating "Crossing Brooklyn Ferry." The poet's practice of mixing in entries from later years, however, has severely hampered the effort to date the earliest lines of Whitman's greatest poem.[19]

Another clue to the early development of *Leaves of Grass* is Whitman's phrenological exam, performed either in the spring or the summer of 1849.[20] Although in the *Eagle* of 1846 he had criticized Orson S. Fowler's lecture on the pseudoscience as a "conglomeration of pretension and absurdity," he revised his opinion the next year, saying in the same newspaper, "there can be no harm, but probably much good, in pursuing" its study.[21] Phrenology assigned numbers between 1 and 7 (6 being the safest high; 7 excessive or disproportionate) to the size of cranial bumps. The readings measured the growth of individual parts of the brain and their corresponding traits on the phrenological map of the head. Whitman scored a "6" in both "Amativeness" (sexual passion) and "Adhesiveness" (friendship). The report, by Orson Fowler's brother Lorenzo, said in part: "Leading traits of character appear to be Friendship, Sympathy, Sublimity and Self-Esteem, and markedly among his combinations the dangerous faults of Indolence, a tendency to the pleasure of Voluptuousness and Alimentiveness, and a certain reckless swing of animal will, too unmindful, probably, of the conviction of others."[22] This description, which was remarkably accurate, would have been a serious influence on Whitman's view of himself, since phrenology enjoyed so much respect (much more than its twentieth-century counterpart, astrology).

Phrenology in the hands of this budding transcendentalist suggested that a sound body was the signature of a healthy soul—and thus a sound character, however unusual it was.[23] Shortly after his return from New Orleans, Whitman had rediscovered the phrenological cabinet of Fowler & Wells in Manhattan, and he subsequently published one of his anonymous reviews of the first *Leaves of Grass* in their *American Phrenological Journal.* The phrenological firm also published or distributed the second edition of *Leaves of Grass,* in which one of the new poems includes part of his 1849 phrenological reading. As Whitman approached the authorship of *Leaves of Grass,* he became increasingly interested in any and all clues to the mystery of life. Furthermore, his particular phrenological analysis—as he could tell from reading the Fowler brothers' *Phrenology Proved, Illustrated and Applied* (1837)—scored higher marks than those recorded for such literary worthies as N. P. Willis and William Cullen Bryant. At a time when the *Freeman* was slipping away from him and unemployment threatened, the phrenological report card was certainly encouraging, or at least flattering to an ego that proclaimed in "Song of Myself," "I wear my hat as I please indoors or out."[24] Whitman never totally embraced the claims of phrenology, but the report may have emboldened him to publish his first poem in a long time.

On January 15, 1850, the *Eagle* reported that nearly all the buildings destroyed "by the great fire of 1848" had been rebuilt. Yet as Whitman looked at the new year, he was again down on his luck. Though he still had the bookstore on Myrtle, his newspaper was gone, and with it the cause of the Wilmot Proviso. Recently, a North Carolina congressman had been one of the first to publicly suggest secession, an idea also favored by New England abolitionists, including William Lloyd Garrison. On January 29 Henry Clay of Kentucky, the grandfather of the New Orleans suicide Whitman had reported and a senator from a slave state who thought slavery immoral, rose in the Senate to propose a compromise to ease the growing tension between North and South. California had already voted to enter the Union as a free state. Thinking it unlikely that slavery would be successfully introduced in any of the new territories, Clay suggested that the other territorial governments should be established without any restrictions on the practice. He proposed a ban on bringing slaves into the District of Columbia, where there had been anti-slavery agitation since 1848, but he balked at abolishing slavery in the nation's capital without the consent of Maryland (which had donated most of the land for Washington to the country) and the people of the federal district. Finally, he advocated a stronger fugitive slave law.[25]

A speech by John Calhoun followed and then, on March 7, one by Daniel Webster. In their attempts to keep the Union together, the famous and now aged triumvirate of American statesmen—Clay, Calhoun, and Webster—set it irrevocably on the path to war a decade later, after all three had died. In the meantime they set northern liberals and radicals to seething in the press. The response was especially heated in Bryant's *Evening Post* and Greeley's *Tribune,* where Whitman's anti-slavery poems were published.

❋ ❋ ❋

Whitman entered the political fray with "Song for Certain Congressmen," published in the *Evening Post* on March 2. Later called "Dough-Face Song" (when he printed it in *Specimen Days* under the misleading title "Pieces in Early Youth. 1834–'42"), it castigated "dough-faced" politicians whose political countenances could be shaped and reshaped according to current political fashion. Following his practice with the *Sunday Dispatch* essays, he signed himself "Paumanok." Written from the point of view of congressmen (or senators) Whitman considered corrupt, the poem began,

We are all docile dough-faces,
  They knead us with the fist,
They, the dashing southern lords,
  We labor as they list;
For them we speak—or hold our tongues,
  For them we turn and twist.

We join them in their howl against
  Free soil and "abolition,"
That firebrand—that assassin knife—
  Which risk our land's condition,
And leave no peace of life to any
  Dough-faced politician.

. . . .

And what if children, growing up,
  In future seasons read
The thing we do? and heart and tongue
  Accurse us for the deed?
The future cannot touch us;
  The present gain we heed.

Then, all together, dough-faces!
  Let's stop the exciting clatter,
And pacify slave-breeding wrath
  By yielding all the matter;
For otherwise, as sure as guns,
  The Union it will shatter.

The twelve-stanza poem, sarcastic in tone and somewhat crude in rhythm (Whitman's last poem in conventional meter and rhyme), concluded with four more stanzas, attacking by name, among others, General Lewis Cass, the unsuccessful Democratic candidate for president in 1848. With historical hindsight in the poem's printing in *Collect,* Whitman added the name of Daniel Webster.[26]

It was probably Webster's notorious "Seventh of March Speech," supporting the compromise, that elicited Whitman's next political poem. Whittier castigated Webster in the poem "Ichabod" that year, and "Blood-Money" was essentially a modern rendering of Judas's betrayal of Christ. When first published, in a special supplement to Greeley's *Tribune* of March 22, the poem was signed "Walter Whitman"; in its reprinting in Bryant's *Evening Post* of April 30, it appeared under the name of "Paumanok." Although there is ample testimony from Whitman about his opinion of Bryant's poetry, we don't know what the poet-turned-editor thought of Whitman—then or later—though Bryant must have thought Whitman had talent since he published two of his poems. Greeley definitely favored Whitman's poetical talents (at least before the sexually graphic poems of *Leaves of Grass*). Soon after the initial publication of "Blood-Money," he spoke in a lecture of Whitman's "rare poetic genius."[27]

"Blood-Money" is probably Whitman's first free-verse poem. Just what brought about this auspicious change is hard to know. Gay Wilson Allen notes that the poet was already "fumbling" after the parallelism that characterizes his later verse structure as he paraphrased the thought and imitated the prose rhythm of Matthew 26–27. Whitman's lines, however, still run on without pause—an enjambment that would cease with the poetry of 1855.[28]

> Of olden time when it came to pass
> That the beautiful god, Jesus, should finish his work on earth,
> Then went Judas, and sold the Divine youth,
> And took pay for his body.

The image of Iscariot's thirty pieces of silver obtains again in 1850:

The cycles with their long shadows have stalked silently forward
Since those ancient days, many a pouch enwrapping meanwhile
Its fee, like that paid for the Son of Mary.

Addressing Christ in the second and final stanza ("thou bear'st man's form again") and describing his martyred condition ("Bruised, bloody, and pinioned"), Whitman anticipates his first-person Christ identification with the downtrodden and the slave in "Song of Myself," not only in Section 10, where the fugitive slave's "sweated body and bruis'd feet" are bathed, but in the following lines from Section 33:

I am the hounded slave. . . . I wince at the bite of the dogs,
Hell and despair are upon me. . . . crack and again crack the marksmen,
I clutch the rails of the fence. . . . my gore dribs, thinned with the
 ooze of my skin,
I fall on the weeds and stones,
The riders spur their unwilling horses and haul close,
They taunt my dizzy ears. . . . they beat me violently over the head with
 their whip-stocks.

Whitman returned to the theme of betrayal in "House of Friends," published in the *Tribune* of June 14. (Greeley also published "Resurgemus" a week later, further evidence of his enthusiasm for Whitman's political poetry.) Like Christ, who was betrayed by a friend, the free-soil movement was being betrayed by those who were supposedly in support of it, not merely its formal foes in the South. This poem, too, was written in something approaching the free verse of *Leaves of Grass.* This time Whitman took his biblical cue from the Old Testament (Zechariah 13: 6), perhaps in part because the name of the prophet was also the Christian name of one of his earliest American ancestors. In the beginning of the poem he seems to use the text ("And one shall say unto him, What are those wounds in thy hands? Then he shall answer, Those with which I was wounded in the house of my friends") to anticipate Christ's betrayal:

If thou art balked, O Freedom,
The victory is not to thy manlier foes;
From the house of thy friends comes the death stab.

Perhaps taking another cue from Quaker poet John Greenleaf Whittier, this time his scolding apostrophe to the state of Virginia (in "Massachusetts to Virginia," 1843), the Long Island poet with "Friends" in his bloodline addressed Virginia as the "mother of greatness." This time, however, the Old Dominion wasn't to be shamed for betraying the heritage of Jefferson and the spirit of the Revolution (Whitman would turn to that theme in "A Boston Ballad" in 1854). Instead, the cause of liberty was undermined by northern "Dough-faces, Crawlers, Lures of Humanity." He called on the "Young North" to arise because "Our elder blood flows in the veins of cowards."

The poem was viciously descriptive of its foes, Whitman pulling no punches with his degrading adjectives and analogies. Henry Lees viewed it as a direct attack on Whitman's political enemies in Brooklyn and took advantage of both sides with the following observation in the *Advertizer* of June 22: "When our friends the locofocos fall out, they occasionally amuse themselves by drawing portraits of each other. The schism of Hunkers and Barnburners has been especially prolific of these interesting specimens of descriptive literature." Adding that much of what each side said of the other was true, he wrote: "Here, now, is a specimen of the way one of the young democracy, Master Walter Whitman, lays it on to members of 'the party' whom he has had the pleasure of knowing." Lees was referring, of course, to the fact that Whitman had served the Brooklyn Democratic Party, or the pre-Hunkers, as editor of the *Eagle.* Emory Holloway speculates that Whitman may have been attacking the Brooklyn Hunkers because they had somehow turned the *Freeman* into a Hunker paper and that Lees suspected this motive, but Whitman's target was clearly the politicians in Washington who would crush the hopes of the Wilmot Proviso with the Fugitive Slave Law of 1850. The fact that the *Eagle* did not retaliate seems to indicate Van Anden and his compatriots did not consider the poem an attack upon them personally.[29]

By the time "House of Friends" was published, the cause of freedom in the territories seemed to be quickly slipping away. That month a convention of slave states met in Nashville and passed a resolution stating that the South was willing to restrict slavery in the new territories to the latitude of the Missouri Compromise of 1820. The "concession," as it was called, had no legal standing even in the South, where only some of the states sent delegates to the convention. Yet the proceedings were nationally reported, adding to northern tension, which had begun to abate somewhat after the speeches of Clay, Calhoun, and Webster.[30]

This climate brought forth not only "House of Friends" but also "Resurgemus" (discussed in Chapter 5). "Resurgemus" appeared in the *Tribune* of June 21 and again in the *Sunday Dispatch* of August 28, when the hated "compromise" with its stiffened fugitive slave law was finally passed by Congress. "Resurgemus" laments the defeat of democracy, the "good cause" that Whitman would celebrate in *Leaves of Grass.* "When liberty goes," he wrote in its 1855 Preface, "it is not the first to go nor the second or third to go. . . . it waits for all the rest to go. . . . it is the last." "Resurgemus" was the only anti-slavery poem, besides "A Boston Ballad," to be included in the first or subsequent editions of *Leaves of Grass.* In 1850 its author, here signed "Walter Whitman," concluded:

> Liberty, let others despair of thee,
> But I will never despair of thee:
> Is the house shut? Is the master away?
> Nevertheless, be ready, be not weary of watching,
> He will surely return; his messengers come anon.

Again, as in "Blood-Money" and "House of Friends," we can hear biblical echoes. The absent "master" of the house is the God of Genesis or the Christ of the New Testament, probably the latter. Whitman was again making, albeit vaguely, the Christ identification. The central figure in this drama of the lost cause was both a victim and a hero. Agonies were merely one of his "changes of garments," as he would write in "Song of Myself."

Coinciding with the publication of Whitman's poems in March was Emerson's second speaking engagement in New York City, including his first opportunity to deliver three lectures at the Female Academy in Brooklyn. Whitman's involvement with Emerson goes back at least to 1842, when he first heard him speak in Manhattan. Later, as has been noted, Whitman alluded to "Spiritual Laws" in the *Eagle*. When *Leaves of Grass* first came out, it was thought by some to be a "transcendental" poem and in part an effort to revive a literary movement already considered passé by 1855.

Parallels abound between Emerson's first two volumes of essays and Whitman's first three editions of *Leaves*.[31] *Leaves of Grass* was a transcendental book salted down with an actual body instead of the emblem of one. But Emerson also may have given Whitman the inspiration for the Christ identification. In his sermons the Unitarian minister Emerson had dealt with the Unitarian removal of Christ from the Godhead by gradually developing a sense of Christ rediscovering the pure spirit of the Gospel. Christian revelation and Romantic inspiration became indistinguishable as Emerson moved from speaking *about* to speaking *as* Christ, and this identification with and appropriation of the role of Christ led to the concept of the Central Man in his lectures and essays.[32]

Emerson arrived in New York City and checked into the Astor House on March 13; he concluded his lectures in Manhattan, Brooklyn, Newark, and Paterson on April 2 and traveled to Philadelphia the next day to give another series of lectures.[33] Therefore, it is safe to assume that he first read Walt Whitman in 1850, not 1855. Although he gave his lecture on "Natural Aristocracy" in Newark the day Whitman's "Blood-Money" appeared in the *Tribune,* Emerson was in his Astor House room as late as 4:30 P.M. that day and would have seen the Friday morning free supplement to Greeley's paper carrying Whitman's poem prominently on its front page.[34] Just what Emerson thought of the poem we will never know since there is no extant letter greeting this Paumanok at the beginning of a great career. Perhaps, however, he mentioned the poem to Washington Irving, who joined him for dinner at the home of the historian George Bancroft two days later.

More important for our purposes is what Whitman thought of Emerson and the lectures he gave that month. Whitman had ample time and opportunity to hear him at least once. The New Englander had come principally to give a series of seven lectures at Hope Chapel in New York City, arranged by Henry James, Sr. Emerson had given these lectures many times during his second visit to England in 1847–48, and they were delivered in New York City in the following order: "Natural Aristocracy," "The Superlative in Literature, Manners, and Races," "Eloquence," "Books," "England," "The Spirit of the Age," and "Instinct and Inspiration." Out of the seven, he delivered three in Brooklyn at a gathering arranged by the Quaker reformer and abolitionist Marcus Spring: "Natural Aristocracy," "Books," and "England." The lectures were advertised in Bryant's and Greeley's newspapers as well as in the *Eagle* for the Brooklyn engagements.

Even without going to either Newark or Paterson, Whitman thus had opportunities in both New York and Brooklyn to hear "Natural Aristocracy," a lecture that alarmed at least one member of the British aristocracy when Emerson first gave it in England in 1848 because it expressed sympathy for the peasant driven to barnburning.[35] Whitman may not have heard Emerson's first delivery at Hope Chapel on March 14. The *Evening Post* described it as having "one of the most crowded audiences" thus far that season. It added that the audience responded with several rounds of applause when Emerson treated his subject "with all that originality, insight, varied learning, quaint and racy expression, and thorough absence of logic, for which he is famous."[36] It is almost beyond belief that Whitman, with his interests in the problems of democracy and the origin of genius, would have missed this lecturer and this lecture when Emerson crossed the Brooklyn Ferry four days later. In the poem "Pictures," Whitman wrote directly after his "picture" of Jefferson, "And there, tall and slender, stands Ralph Waldo Emerson, of New England, at the lecturer's desk lecturing." Years later he recalled hearing Emerson often in New York City, including his reading of "his essay on Slavery."[37]

Emerson's literary executor, James Eliot Cabot, was redundant when he later entitled "Natural Aristocracy" simply "Aristocracy": Emerson says in the lecture that the only viable aristocracy is the one that has been ordained by nature. Whitman, whose once proud line of Dutch and English ancestors had fizzled down to a landless family of ten, probably heard Emerson refer to the capriciousness of nature as a reason to scoff at the "prejudice men have in favor of hereditary transmission of qualities." "The English government and people, or the

French government," he said, "may easily make mistakes; but Nature makes none." He appealed to the conservative side of Whitman's nature when he noted that the existence of an upper class is "not injurious, as long as it is dependent on merit." Such distinctions exist, he said, and "are deep, not to be talked or voted away." Then Emerson turned to a truth the Brooklynite had recently seen reinforced in phrenological terms. "Since the body is the pipe through which we tap all the succors and virtues of the material world," Emerson said, "it is certain, that a sound body must be at the root of any excellence in manners & actions: a strong & supple frame which yields a stock of strength & spirits for all the needs of the day."

Emerson must have especially pleased the author of "Blood-Money" with the observation, "Whoever wants more power than is the legitimate attraction of his faculty, is a politician." And he noted that the one good thing to come out of slavery was the pricing of men. He said he would like to see such an appraisal published somewhere for every man, but in the "absence of such anthropometer I have perfect confidence in natural laws." Emerson's respect for the body (at least as a conduit for the world's virtues) and his desire to arrive at an assessment of each person's value may have helped to lay the foundation for Whitman's similar thoughts in "I Sing the Body Electric."

Generally, the lecture was a version of "Self-Reliance" aimed at the artist—or a postscript to "The Poet," which Whitman had heard in 1842 and doubtless read in 1844 when it appeared as an essay. "Genius," Emerson said in "Natural Aristocracy," "what is so called in strictness,—the power to affect the Imagination, as possessed by the orator, the poet, the novelist, or the artist,—has a royal right in all possessions and privileges, being itself representative and accepted by all men as their delegate." In other words, genius was not only a matter of power but one of representation. "What I assume you shall assume" is the way Whitman phrased the proposition in 1855.[38]

He may also have heard Emerson give his talk on "Eloquence" at Hope Chapel the next evening. The *Evening Post* of the following day (March 20) pronounced it possibly one of the most successful discourses that Emerson had yet given—"His description of a New England anti-slavery orator was full of fine points, and elicited several rounds of plaudits." Whitman's brother George testified that around the time of the early 1850s, Walt "had an idea he could lecture. He wrote what Mother called 'barrels' of lectures."[39] It is hard to believe someone thinking of oratory as a career would miss a lecture on eloquence by one of the foremost lecturers of the day. Several commentators have noted Whitman's lack of oratorical talent,[40] but what Emerson said that evening in "Eloquence" would have been particularly encouraging even to someone without obvious oratory skills. Eloquence consisted, Emerson said, not of "a particular skill in telling a story, or neatly summing up evidence, or arguing logically, or dexterously addressing the prejudice of the company." Rather, it was "a taking sovereign possession of the audience" by force of personality. "The orator must be, to a certain extent, a poet." Whitman had probably been most prompted to take to the speaker's platform in the cause of the Wilmot Proviso, whose downfall pushed him as far to the left politically as he would ever go. Emerson noted in his speech that the "resistance to slavery in this country has been a fruitful nursery of orators."[41] Whitman would also have appreciated Emerson's argument that the power of personality was the key to eloquence, just as it was—as he said in "Natural Aristocracy"—for nature's favorites. "From the opening of the Oration & on through, the great thing is to be inspired as one divinely possessed," Whitman wrote in a notebook about this time. He already possessed an intriguing personality. George remembered that both family members and neighbors—even strangers—"saw that there was something in him out of the ordinary."[42]

❋ ❋ ❋

Whitman's schooling with Emerson was much more than a brief encounter. In "Books," which Emerson delivered in Brooklyn on March 25, Whitman could have heard more about natural aristocracy, this time in the context of books and their authors: "Nature is always clarifying her water and her wine. . . . She does the same thing by books as by her gases and plants. There is always a selection in writers, and then a selection from the selection." Again, Emerson was expressing the power of personality. (In his later years Whitman—who then tried to downplay Emerson's influence on the making of *Leaves of Grass*—wrote an essay entitled "Personalism.") In "England," given in Brooklyn on March 29, Emerson bemoaned the loss of personality (or magnanimity in its treatment of the poor) that he saw in the mother country. He would later develop the case fully in *English Traits.* In the meantime, he continued the theme of nature's selection of the strong in "Power" and "Wealth," in lectures delivered in New York City two years later and ultimately in essays collected in *The Conduct of Life* (1860). In addition, Whitman may have heard Emerson deliver "Fate" in Manhattan on February 18, 1852, though its message about divine boundaries for the imagination would not be of direct use to Whitman until the third edition of his book.

In "Books" Emerson advised his auditors to "read no mean books. Shun the spawn of the press and the gossip of the hour." He praised George Sand's novels, including *Consuelo,* one of Whitman's favorites, but at the same time he noted how "far off from life and manners and motives the novel still is!" Emerson generally disliked fiction as an art form and thought that his former Concord neighbor, Nathaniel Hawthorne, was wasting his time and talent in the manufacture of romances. "This passion for romance, and this disappointment," he said, "show how much we need real elevations and pure poetry."[43]

Whitman owned few books and was never (aside from his brief stint as a bookseller) much of a book collector, but he did—as his *Brooklyn Eagle* reviews and clippings show—read a great many novels and romances.[44] For him, the work of Sand, or Madame Dudevant, was a staple. Not only had he read a translation of *Consuelo* (1842–44), but also its sequel, *The Countess of Rudolstadt* (1843–45), and the novels *The Journeyman Joiner* (1840) and *The Devil's Pool* (1848).[45] He reviewed *The Journeyman Joiner* in a brief notice in the *Eagle* on September 27, 1847. In fact Esther Shephard asserts, in a study now generally ignored, that Whitman shamelessly stole the ideas for his persona as a bohemian carpenter from *The Countess of Rudolstadt* and *The Journeyman Joiner* and that *Leaves of Grass* as a result is a fraud.[46] In *The Countess,* a *rhapsode vagabond* dressed as a peasant composes "a most magnificent poem" during a mystical experience. In *The Journeyman Joiner* a Christlike carpenter, a philosopher in plain clothes, also dresses like a worker or a mechanic. Probably the most conclusive dismissal of Shephard's charges comes from Sand's own countryman Roger Asselineau, who argues that although the comparisons are "striking," there is no reason to assume that Whitman owed anything more to the French writer. "As for the philosophical and social ideas of these heroes whom Esther Shephard accuses him of copying," writes Asselineau, "he could equally well have found them in the works of Carlyle and Emerson."[47]

Indeed, the notebooks leading up to *Leaves of Grass* strongly imply that Whitman was awash in romantic ideas about art and the artist and that he owed his vision to nothing in particular, but rather to a broad confluence of ideas and events. Certainly, Sand stimulated his sense of romance. The book of hers that did it best was *Consuelo,* which Whitman read at least twice. His mother, thought to be semi-illiterate, also read it—or at least read in it at the suggestion of her dearest son. Later, he told Horace Traubel that he never tired of reading in the book,[48] especially the beginning where Consuelo, a contralto, sings when challenged by her teacher in front of the singing class: "Then Consuelo, with unaffected simplicity and ease, raised her clear and thrilling voice, and filled the lofty room with the sweetest and purest notes with which it had ever echoed."

The novel reads like a Hawthornian romance, though with too much abundance (*Consuelo* is some 800 pages long). Its heroine would probably reappear to Whitman every time he witnessed a performance of the great contralto Marietta Alboni. As might be expected, the romance has a sleepy, dreamy aspect, which especially appealed to Whitman at the time of the first edition of *Leaves of Grass.* (His notebooks for the period suggest a retreat into the imagination, indeed a rather reckless one.) Consuelo's opposite in the novel, Count Albert Rudolstadt, was probably as interesting to Whitman as Consuelo. Something of a psychic and a mystic, he suffers strange fits of sleeping sickness and melts with sorrow in front of the impoverished.[49]

Whitman thought Sand's romances superior to those of Victor Hugo (although we don't know what, if anything, he thought of her earlier work attacking the institution of marriage).[50] His preference is perhaps understandable when we learn that he was also a fan of the impenetrable romances of Bernhard S. Ingemann—or at least one of them (almost as long as *Consuelo*). Four days before "Resurgemus" appeared in the *Tribune,* Whitman wrote a remarkable letter to the editors of the *New York Sun,* where he had been an occasional reporter in the mid-1840s. Not only does it show how desperate he was financially; it shows his willingness to steal from another writer's work for profit. Although Ingemann was still living, Whitman wanted to sell the *Sun* a much shortened version of the 1846 English translation of *The Childhood of King Eric Menved* (1828) for serialization. Ingemann is generally noted for having given poetic life to Denmark's middle ages, but he also wrote historical novels along the line of Sir Walter Scott's novels, though Ingemann was more concerned with history than he was with fiction. The Danish novelist was deeply religious, and his historical objectivity is occasionally lacking. All this makes for a dense and confusing story in the novel Whitman chose to promote in the American press. Today that novel, even in Denmark, is considered naive by leading critics and fit only for adolescents.[51]

The Childhood of King Eric opens in 1285 with the king's father, Erik Glypping, still on the throne. Glypping is assassinated, and Prince Waldemar, a probable successor, is suspected and thrown into prison because he had opposed Glypping earlier. During his incarceration, he falls into trances, much like Sand's Count Rudolstadt. The sleep induces fits of democratic sentiment—much in the way a dream led Rudolstadt to sympathy for the poor. Waldemar's dreams lead him to realize that "a crown could not be won, like a castle or a piece of land, by daring heroism and foreign armies. . . . The souls of the people—their hearts—had to be won first."[52] This is precisely the kind of political message Whitman had been preaching since before the 1848 national election.

Whitman wanted to entitle his version of the novel "The Sleeptalker." "The romance is a stirring and lively one, and it seems to me, fitted to become very popular," he told the Beach brothers, co-editors of the *Sun.* "I desire but a moderate price.—After running through the Sun, it seems to me it would pay handsomely to print it in a neat 25 cent book form."[53] Possibly "The Sleeptalker" was an improvement on the original story (which Whitman nevertheless considered "the most interesting, romantic, . . . of any I have ever come across"), but we will probably never know because the *Sun,* which featured mainly poems and stories, apparently did not accept Whitman's offer—nor has such a tale been located in any of the other New York or Brooklyn newspapers.[54]

In a letter written a year later, Whitman urged the Free-Soil presidential candidate of 1852, Senator John Parker Hale of New Hampshire, to support "an American Democracy with thews and sinews worthy this sublime age." "Out of the [third-party] Pittsburgh movement and 'platform,'" Whitman said of the Free-Soil convention that had nominated Hale, "it may be that a real live Democratic party is destined to come forth, which . . . will gradually win the hearts of the people."[55] If Whitman had read on in Ingemann, as his enthusiasm for the Dane's works in his letter to the Beaches suggests he did, he would have come upon a similar theme in the novel's three-volume sequel, *King Eric and the Outlaws.* Possibly, Whitman encountered the volumes as the owner of a bookstore, and at this particular time his only employment was to sit in his store and read. "In the early stages of Denmark," Ingemann states, "the people bore an important part in the affairs of government. . . . The people at large decided on war or peace, nor was any royal decree considered valid until it had obtained their consent."[56] This idea is expressed throughout Ingemann's novels, reminding his readers of how great Denmark once was and could be again. Indeed, the following statement—from the lips of the "Sleeptalker"—in *The Childhood of King Eric*—would fit comfortably, in sentiment if not in style, into the prose of Whitman's 1855 Preface: "The mere external dominion, which has not its roots in the deepest heart of the people, and is not bound up with the popular mind and the true renown, is worthless and despicable, did it even extend over the whole universe."[57]

Except for his corner bookstore, Whitman probably spent the summer of 1850 unemployed. To make ends meet, he undertook a series of sixteen flattering sketches of prominent Brooklynites for the *Brooklyn Daily Advertizer* between April 30 and June 6, including a piece on the Rev. Henry Ward Beecher, future admirer of *Leaves of Grass* and brother of the future author of *Uncle Tom's Cabin* (1852). On October 10 Whitman inquired of Carlos D. Stuart, who was establishing a penny paper in the city, about "any sort of 'opening' in your new enterprise. . . . I am out of regular employment, and fond of the press—and, if you would be disposed to 'try it on,' I should like to have an interview with you."[58]

The gloom of his unemployment may have been broken temporarily by the wave of "Lindiana" that hit New York City on September 1. On that day, with all the hoopla P. T. Barnum could organize, the famed Swedish soprano Jenny Lind arrived on the steamship *Atlantic.* Hundreds gathered at the landing, eager to get their first glimpse of the person whose arrival, her promoters claimed, ushered in The Age of Music in America. "On the top of a light deck-house, erected over the forward companion-way," the *Tribune* of the next day reported, "sat the subject of the day's excitement—the veritable Jenny Lind—as fresh and rosy as if the sea had spared her its usual discomforts." The twenty-nine-year-old singer, considered the most popular vocalist in Europe, carried a lapdog given her by Queen Victoria, and she and her pet were almost mobbed by excited fans when Barnum, after greeting her with a choice bouquet carefully stuck in the bosom of his white vest, drove her away in his carriage. The *Tribune* estimated that more than 200 bouquets were thrown at her departing figure.[59]

Lind owed her American engagement to Barnum, who had agreed to pay her $1,000 per concert, which he further hyped by auctioning off the choice seats for each performance. Even though she was popular in Europe, her reception wouldn't have been quite the same without the public relations effort of Barnum, who was as high on America as Whitman was—and would be later on *Leaves of Grass.* Whitman had interviewed Barnum for the *Eagle* in 1846, when the carnivalist and entrepreneur had just returned from Europe, having exhibited the tiny General Tom Thumb. When Whitman asked him whether he had seen anything in the Old World that made "him love Yankeedom less," Barnum replied, his eyes flashing: "My God! . . . no! not a bit of it! Why, sir, you can't imagine the difference.—There every thing is frozen—kings and *things*—formal, but absolutely *frozen:* here it is *life.* Here it is freedom, and here are *men.*" Whitman added prophetically that "a whole book might be written on that little speech of Barnum's."[60]

We don't know what Whitman thought of all the excitement attending Lind's reception, but the *Eagle,* after publishing a poem welcoming her, complained of "the leatherheaded *elite* of New York" who continued "to make themselves look ridiculous, and degrade the character of their country, by their disgusting adulations of Miss Lind."[61] Whitman didn't think that highly of Lind's singing, compared to that of Marietta Alboni and the tenor Alessandro Bettini. "The Swedish Swan," he wrote the following summer as Paumanok, "with all her blandishments, never touched my heart in the least." Whitman heard her sing at Castle Garden (also called The Battery, where it was located) and admired her technical skill as a singer, for which she is recognized today. For the poet, however, she may have been less appealing because, unlike Alboni or Bettini, she never performed in an opera. Lind gave only concerts.[62] Whitman summed up the difference between this singer and the opera greats in *Good-Bye My Fancy* by saying that Lind had "the most brilliant, captivating, popular musical style and expression of any one known; (the canary, and several other sweet birds are wondrous fine—but there is something in song that goes deeper—isn't there?)."[63]

❋ ❋ ❋

That something was Italian opera. Whitman's favorite composers and operas were Rossini (*William Tell, Gazza Ladra*), Donizetti (*Lucrezia Borgia, La Favorita, Lucia di Lammermoor*), Bellini (*Norma*), and Verdi (*Ernani, Rigoletto, Trovatore*). He had been exposed to English and French opera in the 1840s, but it was Italian opera with its emphasis on the human voice over orchestration that won him over musically in the late 1840s and early 1850s.[64] It is because of Italian opera that *Leaves of Grass* must be read aloud to appreciate its full power. Its musical influence is not merely a matter of "sound-and-sense" such as William Wordsworth created in "The Solitary Reaper," where we can hear the strokes of the scythe through the repeated "s" sounds. Rather, the Solitary Singer—or Paumanok—sought an effect deeper and earthier (than even that of Wordsworth's peasants). His revolutionary verse pursued not merely description, but emotion. Opera awoke in

Whitman the beauty of life. As one recent commentator has noted, its "wonderful melodies, astonishing cadenzas, and sustained high notes were paradigms at once of the beauty and power within us and of the hurtling and orbiting planets of creation beyond us." As Whitman himself is alleged to have put it, "But for the opera, I could not have written Leaves of Grass."[65]

Bel canto (literally, "beautiful song") sent Whitman into moments of rapture. Here was the human voice—the noblest of all musical instruments—at its apex in the aria. Clearly, it was the most moving and symbolic dramatization of the human condition, expressing sadness, helplessness, and suffering in the face of the unknown.[66] In June 1852 the great Alboni began her only operatic tour of America, and Whitman swore that he attended her every performance in New York City. Later he wondered "if the lady will ever know that her singing, her method, gave the foundation, the start, thirty years ago, to all my poetic literary effort since."[67] Shortly after his second edition of *Leaves of Grass,* he described Alboni as the "best songstress ever in America. . . . We used to go in the upper tiers of the theatre, (the Broadway,) on the nights of her performance, and remember seeing that part of the auditorium packed full of New York young men, mechanics, 'roughs,' &c., entirely oblivious of all except Alboni, from the time the great songstress came on the stage, till she left it again."[68] Marietta Alboni, who performed through the spring of 1853, was as different from Jenny Lind as night from day. She came to America at her own financial risk, almost completely unheralded and without a publicist such as Barnum. Although her face was as pretty as Lind's, Alboni was fat, her figure some said composed of "a connected system of globes and ellipses." To Whitman, though, Alboni was a "fully developed woman, with perfect-shaped feet, arms, and hands.—Some thought her fat—*we* always thought her beautiful."[69]

It was not only the pure tone of the *bel canto* or the robustness of the tenor's voice that excited Whitman; it was the opera's rhythm, particularly in the recitative, which got its start with opera itself in John Dryden and Sir William D'Avenant's play *The Siege of Rhodes* in 1662, which launched the literature of the English Restoration. This kind of accompanied declamation, in which the actors sing the words in irregular rhythms simulating speech, suggested to Whitman that words in a poem needed to sound the human rhythm of speech rather than the cadenced rhythm of traditional poetry. Thus was born *vers libre* in English—speech or verse free to play its own music, which in turn sounded its own deep emotion. Possibly, for Whitman the spirit of speech and its body were joined in the character of Consuelo, who may have shown him for the first time the true value of opera. "Here," writes Robert Faner, "in what was to him a powerful and absorbing story about the career of a great singer, he found the appeal of lofty music explained and analyzed." And in Sand's novel he would have read that "Music expresses all that the mind dreams and foresees of mystery and grandeur."[70] Poetry, far above politics or oratory, talked about the inexplicable and the beautiful. Its "faint clews and indirections" were the music of the mind—and the imagination.

Whitman's indebtedness to Alboni and opera at the time of her visit suggests that the penultimate stage of the foreground of *Leaves of Grass* occurred between 1850 and 1852, beginning when the poet heard Emerson lecture. He allegedly told his friend John Townsend Trowbridge (who also recorded his statement about the importance of opera for *Leaves of Grass*) of his indebtedness to Emerson. "I was simmering, simmering, simmering," Whitman declared. "Emerson brought me to a boil."[71]

His publications in 1850 and 1851 show him still involved in free-soil politics and public questions but also seriously branching out his interests into the world of art, first opera and then the graphic arts. He started freelancing again at the end of the summer. Curiously, he chose a very political publication to explore his interest in art and culture in general—Gamaliel Bailey's *National Era.* Bailey was a nationally known abolitionist who was also recognized for his objectivity and fairness. The *National Era,* founded in 1847 by the American and Foreign Anti-Slavery Society, was a national periodical based in Washington, D.C. While Whitman was in New Orleans, it had stirred up debate and potential violence over the question of whether the District of Columbia should be slave or free.[72]

Whitman contributed three letters to the *National Era* in the fall of 1850 under the heading of "Letters from New York" and, once again, under the sign of "Paumanok." No doubt he got into the paper because of the political commentary in the letter of October 25, complaining of the Hunker, or conservative, Whigs as well as the Hunker Democrats. He also returned Greeley's favors of earlier that year by praising his efforts in support of Governor Seward's Wilmot efforts. This letter and the other two soon turned to the subject of art, beginning with a mild criticism of Jenny Lind (prompting the *National Era* editors to say that "the writer does well to preserve his *incog*"). Whitman had gone to hear her final American concert at Castle Garden and been disappointed. He also spoke of attending a recent exhibit at the American Art Union in Manhattan, where he found that most of the paintings lacked proper emotion ("all spack [*sic*] and span, and shining, in their handsome frames"), but he did admire a painting by Richard Caton Woodville called "Old '76, and Young '48"—probably because its juxtaposition of a Revolutionary veteran with one from the Mexican War reminded him of his similar themes in "The Last of the Sacred Army" and "The Child-Ghost; A Story of the Last Loyalist."

He was developing his own theory of art, an *American* theory, which insisted on true life in art and expressed in its gospel of beauty the life of the average. "It is a distressing fault of our painters," he said of the exhibit, ". . . that they strain so hard to make every material thing so clean-lined and clear, lest a body may fail to understand what they mean."[73] Nature was never so obvious. Too many of the artists, he thought, got lost on the "minutest" details, instead of aiming to produce "a beautiful resemblance" of the subject. Like Poe, he sought beauty as the object of art, not exclusively, however, Poe's "supernal beauty" but the beauty of life in the here and now, in nature, which was also Emerson's emblem of the supernal. Whitman sought the democratic in art, not merely the desire of "the moth for the star." The problem with European art, he said in the *Post* a few months later, was that it bore the "stamp of class" on all its otherwise great works. On the other hand, in his fellow Brooklynite painter Walter Libby's "Boy with a Flute," there was "nothing to prevent [the boy's] becoming a President, or even an editor of a leading newspaper."[74]

Whitman's second letter to the *National Era* was another rehearsal of the poet of the "open road." On November 14, he took the reader by the arm and escorted him up Broadway, beginning at the Battery. He noted in particular the many daguerreotypists who occupied the top floors of the buildings to take advantage of the skylights. New York daguerreotypists were the finest in the world, he said, and one of the best of them was Gabriel Harrison, the photographer whose engraving would become the frontispiece for the first edition of *Leaves of Grass.* Whitman was excited about the emergence of photography, seeing it possibly as part of the democratization of art because it now brought the "portrait," among other pictures, down to the financial level of the average consumer. Later, the photograph would also "de-center" art, influencing the work of the French impressionists and their unposed takes of reality. "Whatever artistical objections may be brought against this sort of picture," he said, "it is not the less true, that some of the Broadway operators [especially Harrison] do produce the form and spirit of the face to a degree that defies criticism."[75]

Whitman's future brother-in-law Charles L. Heyde was among the artists he associated with in Brooklyn and New York during the early 1850s, after the two men met through Bryant. Most likely born in France and brought up in Philadelphia (his father perished at sea en route from Philadelphia to France), Heyde became a good friend of Whitman's—good enough not only to become one of the poet's "family" boarders at 106 Myrtle in 1851, where he may have had his *atelier,* but also to marry the poet's younger sister. Heyde would be one of those painters put out of work by photography in the 1880s. By that time his repeated paintings of Mt. Mansfield and Shelburne Bay in Vermont, where he and Hannah Louisa, Whitman's favorite sister, moved in 1852, had become monotonous and uninspired—no longer sustained by wealthy patrons devoted to nostalgic settings. The fact that he drank excessively by middle age also did not steady his painter's eye.[76] Heyde became Whitman's lifelong nemesis ("the bed-buggiest of men," the poet told Traubel), but he may also have been one of the poet's few "relatives" to appreciate (to the point of jealousy) Whitman's accomplishments in *Leaves of Grass.* At the time he met Whitman, Heyde had exhibited his work at the National Academy of Design, and in 1863 he was commissioned to redesign and paint Vermont's coat-of-arms.[77]

Whitman's friendships with artists even such as Heyde strengthened, in the words of one recent art critic, "his already keen visual acuity and provided him with important philosophical and procedural tools for challenging the ideas of his contemporaries."[78] The poem "Pictures," which imagines a picture gallery in one's head, could have been written about this time. He began in 1851 and 1852 to see a difference between the technical and the spiritual dimensions of art. In his third letter to the *National Era* (November 21), he wrote: "Music, in the legitimate sense of that term, exists independently of technical music [Whitman could not read music], as much as language exists independently of grammar—or, perhaps I might say, just as poetry exists independently of rhyme." He may have already been thinking of Emerson's "metre-making" arguments in "The Poet" (or their spirit in "Natural Aristocracy" and "Books"). In the spring of 1851, Whitman was nominated to be the Brooklyn Art Union's next president (the organization ceased operations the following fall for lack of funds), mainly because of a speech he gave to the organization on March 31. His polished pronouncement on the value of art in a busy world was itself poetic, the fourth paragraph almost a free-verse poem. Put into poetic lines (already separated by Whitman by dashes), it looks and sounds like something belonging to the first *Leaves of Grass:*

> When God, according to the myth, finished Heaven and Earth,
> When the lustre of His effulgent light pierced the cold and terrible
>   darkness that had for cycles of ages covered the face of
>   the deep,
> When the waters gathered themselves together into one place
>   and made the sea,
> . . . .
> Then God looked forth and saw everything that he had made, and
>   pronounced it good.

"To the artist," Whitman insisted, "I say, has been given the command to go forth into all the world and preach the gospel of beauty."

He quoted lines from Bryant's "A Forest Hymn" to the effect that youth and beauty of the earth ever push the same energy through nature as previous generations: "These lofty trees / Wave not less proudly than their ancestors / Moulder beneath them." Then he did a remarkable thing. Not only did he end his talk on art with excerpted lines from "Resurgemus," but he now used those lines, which had only recently mourned the dead of the 1848 revolutions, as a metaphor for the beauty of the earth, which also would always rise again—now through the medium of art. Art, he said in the poem, was "growing its seed of freedom, / In its turn to bear seed, / Which the winds shall carry afar and resow, / And the rain nourish."[79] Whitman employed organic images similar to Emerson's analogy in "The Poet," where he compares creativity to the botanical process in which a fungus produces countless spores. Most are subject to decay and oblivion, as are most human acts in history, but one "atom of seed is thrown into a new place, not subject to the accidents, which destroyed its parent two rods off. . . . So when the soul of the poet has come to ripeness of thought, [nature] detaches and sends away from it its poems or songs,—a fearless, sleepless, deathless progeny, which is not exposed to the accidents of the weary kingdom of time."[80]

❋ ❋ ❋

Whitman spoke out frequently for the painters and sculptors of Brooklyn and New York—as not only the Brooklyn Art Institute disappeared but also the American Art Institute in Manhattan, the first of its kind in the United States. He also returned to Greenport and to the use of his "Paumanok" penname that summer. "Having neither the funds nor disposition to pass my little term of ruralizing at the fashionable baths, or watering places," he wrote in the *New York Post* of June 25, 1851, "I am staying awhile down here at Greenport, the eastern point of the Long Island Railroad. That is, my lodging is at Greenport; but in truth, I 'circulate' in all directions around." The three essays he contributed to the *Post* were mainly filler, though in the third, published on August 14, he spoke of the power of opera, especially the "delicious music" of Donizetti's *La Favorita.* He also spoke out in "A Plea for Water" about the desperate need for an aqueduct in Brooklyn similar to the one in New York, a sign that Americans had begun to think more seriously about cleaner drinking water, worrying about the impurities of well water in urban locations increasing in density. Brooklyn, however, would have to wait until after the Civil War for safer water.[81]

On July 4, 1853, the World's Fair opened for a year in the newly constructed Crystal Palace at the foot of Manhattan, where Whitman continued his education in the graphic arts. "I went a long time (nearly a year)," he recalled in *Specimen Days,* "days and nights—especially the latter—as it was finely lighted, and had a very large and copious exhibition gallery of paintings, . . . hundreds of pictures from Europe, many masterpieces—all an exhaustless study."[82] It might seem that Whitman was fading into the world of art, and out of the world of politics, but in fact he was taking politics with him as he thought more about art instead of journalism as a medium of urban expression. Over the years he had been reading and clipping articles from various journals on British poetry and on the subject of poetry in general, and commenting in the margins of the magazines he had purchased, probably as owner of his bookstore. Here, too, he was forming his own opinion—not only on poetry but on poets' lives. He read a review of Wordsworth's *Prelude* in the *Whig Review* of May 1851 but was more interested in the author's life. When he read how Wordsworth had benefited financially from his political connections, receiving a sinecure as distributor of stamps as well as various pensions from patrons, Whitman responded sarcastically in the margin, "So it seems Wordsworth made a 'good thing,' from the start, out of his poetry: legacies! a fat office! pensions from the crown!"[83]

Whitman's ideal was an American poet who had none of these trappings but rather sprang from people with backgrounds similar to the contributors to Brenton's *Voices from the Press.* Such a poet must not become corrupted, or too conservative (as Wordsworth did as poet laureate) by overly close ties to the power structure. Whitman would have three government jobs during the war years, but they were not sinecures, as the many official documents in the poet's hand from the Attorney General's Office, now buried in the National Archives, attest. He was always self-identified as one of the people, even when he became politically moderate in the 1870s and 1880s.

At least two of Whitman's biographers have suggested that he essentially deserted politics for poetry in the 1850s to write *Leaves of Grass.*

More recent speculations have favored a political poet—even in the early editions of the book.[84] Yet neither conclusion is persuasive, because Whitman never gave up the body for the soul, or politics for poetry. As Daniel Hoffman suggests, Whitman's conception was all-inclusive, with the Self (the Soul) "flowing into the Not-Me" (the Body), and the Body flowing likewise into the Soul.[85] As much as the poet was disgusted with the triumph of Hunkerism in the Democratic Party in the late 1840s, he in fact introduced politics into poetry in *Leaves of Grass* by invoking the concerns of middle America—its occupations and need for jobs, its confusion about slavery, its need for spiritual leaders other than conventional religionists, its democracy and hatred of kings and aristocracies as well as its enthusiasm for the European revolutions of 1848. Part of the originality of *Leaves of Grass,* of course, is its use of material objects as objects and not merely as vehicles for poetical flight. Yet there is definitely something spiritual in Whitman's material catalogs of everyday life.

Whitman has testified that he began writing *Leaves of Grass* in 1854,[86] but if we count "Resurgemus," included in the first *Leaves,* he actually began the book in 1850. The inclusion of this poem brought the more ostensible parts of the political poet into the book. Another poem to do so was "A Boston Ballad," dated 1854, the year the fugitive slave Anthony Burns was returned to his southern owner by federal marshals in Boston. Burns's trial in June—right on the heels of the passage of the Kansas-Nebraska Act—became so well known that when Whitman wrote his poem based on the incident, he did not feel it necessary to describe completely the occasion for the poem (confusing to readers today). In fact, there is no mention of Anthony Burns or his trial and return, merely a dramatic description of the failure of the kind of political ethic that had fueled the American Revolution. As the "President's marshal" does his dirty work, the ghosts of the founding fathers look on helplessly:

> What troubles you, Yankee phantoms? what is all this chattering of bare gums?
> Does the ague convulse your limbs? Do you mistake your crutches for firelocks, and level them?

If you blind your eyes with tears you will not see the President's
 marshal,
If you groan such groans you might balk the government cannon.

For shame old maniacs! . . . Bring down those tossed arms, and let your
 white hair be;
Here gape your great grandsons. . . . their wives gaze at them from
 the windows,
See how well-dressed. . . . see how orderly they conduct themselves.

Poetry, for this poet, would also serve the social cause.

Yet these poems came from the surface of the mind that wrote the best of the first edition of *Leaves of Grass.* In *Cosmic Consciousness* (1901), Richard Maurice Bucke speculates—either upon Whitman's implication or by inference from what became Section 5 of "Song of Myself"—that Whitman experienced a mystical awakening on a June day in either 1853 or 1854. "It would seem that he was at first in doubt what it meant, then became satisfied," Bucke wrote. After the poet's death, Charles W. Eldridge told John Burroughs that the first *Leaves of Grass,* according to Whitman, "was produced in a mood, or condition of mind, that he had never been able to resume, and that he had felt utterly incompetent to produce anything equal to it since.—That in contemplating it he felt in regard to his own agency in it like a somnambulist who is shown during his waking hours the giddy heights and impossible situations over which he has passed safely in his sleep."[87] In the first edition Whitman wrote of what is generally thought to be a sexual union of Body and Soul—with the body speaking:

I mind how we lay in June, such a transparent summer morning;
You settled your head athwart my hips and gently turned over
 upon me,
And parted the shirt from my bosom-bone, and plunged your tongue
 to my barestript heart,
And reached till you felt my beard, and reached till you held my feet.

> Swiftly arose and spread around me the peace and joy and knowledge
> that pass all the art and argument of the earth.

There is, of course, no way of verifying Whitman's mysticism; it is as elusive as that claimed by Bucke and others for such well-known figures as Christ, St. Paul, Plotinus, Mohammed, and Dante. What does suggest such an occurrence, however, is the remarkable material in the early notebooks, those immediately predating (by as many as eight and as few as two years) the first edition of *Leaves of Grass.*

We have easily recognizable trial lines. For example, Whitman wrote in his notebook, "I never yet knew how it felt to think I stood in the presence of my superior.—*If the presence of* God were made visible immediately before me, I could not abase myself."[88] In the first poem of his first edition, Whitman would write:

> I believe in you my soul. . . . the other I am must not abase itself to
> you,
> And you must not be abased to the other.

These lines and the notebook version suggest that Whitman felt he had somehow become one with everything around him (suggesting as well, of course, the theme of "There Was a Child Went Forth"). In the same notebook he wrote: "The soul or spirit transmutes itself into all matter—into rocks, and can live the life of a rock—into the sea, and can feel itself the sea—into the oak, or other tree—into an animal, and feel itself a horse, a fish, or a bird—into the earth—into the motions of the suns and stars." (This spirit of transubstantiation would lead the poet in his postwar years to the philosophy of stoicism, especially the first-century work of Epictetus.) Trial lines abound in the notebooks. He wrote, for example, whereas "the ignorant man is demented with the madness of owning things, the wisest soul knows that no object can really be owned by one man or woman any more than another."[89] In the poem, the poet would declare that he "could turn and live awhile with animals":

They do not sweat and whine about their condition,
They do not lie awake in the dark and weep for their sins,
They do not make me sick discussing their duty to God,
Not one is dissatisfied. . . . not one is demented with the mania of
owning things.

Sometimes what he wrote was more error than trial, as in these lines, which seem to anticipate the satires of *Leaves of Grass* that began as early as the 1860s:

I am the poet of little things and of babes
Of each gnat in the air, and of beetles rolling balls of dung.[90]

Some of these lines would make it into the final version, such as "The scent of these arm-pits aroma finer than prayer," but mostly Whitman took the wheat from the chaff.

Whitman appears to have rediscovered not only the spiritual but the physical: he wrote in his notebook, "A touch now reads me a library of knowledge in an instant" and would admit in "Song of Myself" to being overwhelmed by the power of touch. It is as if he—in his late twenties—had discovered masturbation. With the abundance of pseudoscientific literature against sexual acts (the inventor of the graham cracker, for example, equated the male's loss of semen during one sexual act to the loss of forty ounces of blood),[91] it would not have been out of the range of possibility that he discovered the practice after adolescence. What seems clear is that he had no heterosexual romance in New Orleans—as Jean Catel and other biographers have suggested. The ecstasy expressed in the notebooks and in what became Section 28 of "Song of Myself" about the delights of touch is probably autoerotic. This poet who rushed into the crowd, yet kept to himself, delighted more in *seeing* than he did in interacting. In this sense, *Leaves of Grass* itself is a solitary act, all the way down to the poet's printing part of the first edition himself.[92] Yet its narrator claimed to speak for everybody in this most self-reliant flight of poesy.

7

THE BEGINNING OF A GREAT CAREER

Quit house-building in the spring of 1855
to print and publish the first edition.

WALT WHITMAN
quoted in Richard Maurice Bucke, Walt Whitman

The central literary event of the nineteenth century began rather haphazardly in 1855, either a day before or a day after America's Independence Day, when Walt Whitman published *Leaves of Grass.* Nothing he wrote afterward compared to his accomplishment in the early editions of this book, and especially in the first. There, he said, he had fulfilled "an impervious conviction, and the commands of my nature as total and irresistible as those which make the sea flow, or the globe revolve." Whitman practically walked away from his life to write his book. "After continued personal ambition and effort, as a young fellow, to enter with the rest into competition for the usual rewards . . . ," he recalled, "I found myself remaining possess'd, at the age of thirty-one to thirty-two, with a special desire and conviction . . . that had been flitting through my previous life, or hovering on the flanks, [which] finally dominated everything else."[1]

Whitman had taken his manuscript to Andrew and James Rome's print shop at Cranberry and Fulton streets, where he and the Rome brothers set it into type during idle periods between commercial jobs. The poet would soon develop a lifelong fondness for seeing his poems in print before he gave public readings or revised them for publication. The practice of making the writing process part of the printing process had probably begun long before 1855, when as a printer he had the opportunity to experiment with the printed page, seeing how his handwritten creations "translated." Such casual amusement, common among printers when there wasn't any other business, produced what was known in the jargon of their trade as "grass"—compositions of dubious value. The "leaves" were the pages, but in printer's lingo they were also "leaves" in the sense of bundles of paper.[2] This explanation of Whitman's title is not as neat as the conventional one, which sees the grass as a transcendentalist symbol for nature, but as we shall see the first *Leaves* was anything but neat and structured.

A green folio of ninety-five pages (described by Malcolm Cowley as "about the size and shape of a [thin] block of typewriting paper"), gold-stamped in lush leaf-and-vine letters, introduced twelve unrhymed poems.[3] If we forget what literary greatness the cover embraced, it looks rather clumsy and homemade. The title "Leaves of Grass" is weighted down with sprouts and uprooted roots, leaves pointing this way and that. Apparently, not much thought was given to the book's external presentation—its design is a close copy of the cover of Sara Payson Parton's *Fern Leaves from Fanny's Portfolio, First Series,* a book of feminine witticisms published in 1853. In the same year that Whitman's book appeared, Parton (also known as "Fanny Fern") published *Ruth Hall,* a tale of female independence in which a struggling writer wins success in the popular press. Yet Parton and her *Portfolio* probably had no particular influence on Whitman's choice of design. The use of similar cover designs and the word "leaves" in book titles was common in the 1840s and 1850s with such works as *Gathered Leaves, Fresh Leaves from Western Woods, Autumn Leaves,* and *Stray Leaves from the Book of Nature.*[4]

Whitman first gave the book to a regular bookseller on Nassau Street, but that merchant apparently found it offensive and ordered its removal the very next day. The organization that had performed his phrenological reading, Fowler & Wells in Manhattan, ultimately became the distributor of the first edition. Fowler & Wells, whose other books explored health fads along with phrenology, put the book up for sale not only at its establishment in New York City but at its cabinet on Washington Street in Boston. The book was also available at the

Old Corner Bookstore in Boston. In addition, about sixty copies were left on consignment at Swayne's Book Shop on Fulton Street in Brooklyn, which may have had a close association with the nearby print shop of Andrew and James Rome.

The first *Leaves* was a blend of dream-vision and autobiography. Its "Yankee transcendentalism" came right out of Concord, and its "New York rowdyism" had the brag of Brooklyn. "We knew he was printing the book," George Whitman recalled, adding that Walt slept late every morning, "and after getting up would write a few hours." This suggests that Whitman was still revising the poems of the first edition as he began to print them. The Whitman clan, now on Ryerson Street in Brooklyn, knew little else about the book, which was in all likelihood formally begun in the late fall of 1854.[5]

In writing the first *Leaves,* Whitman turned away from good opportunities to make money, as his brother remembered. In those days, Brooklyn housing construction was booming, and Whitman after 1852 was fairly involved in the profitable business, having sold a number of houses he had built, perhaps with the labor of his brothers, if not his carpenter father, whose health began to fail a few years before the publication of *Leaves of Grass.* He sold the Myrtle Street house, where his printing business and bookstore had been, in May 1852. He bought lots on Cumberland Street and built two three-story houses there, which he sold in March 1853. The same year, on April 21, he bought and occupied a two-story house on Cumberland and lived "there one year exactly." In May 1854 he built a house on Skillman Street and lived in it for a year before selling it. By May 1855, just six weeks before the publication of his book (and the death of his father on July 11), he moved himself and his family to Ryerson Street, where he purchased a house in his mother's name for $1,840 cash.[6]

For all his spending and getting (this was probably the family's first unmortgaged purchase of a home), there were elements of the vagabond in Whitman. In his day, poets were usually a respectable part of the "establishment." They were "gentlemen" like James Russell Lowell, Oliver Wendell Holmes, and Thomas Wentworth Higginson—trinomials whose names, a novelist has recently suggested, were too long for their works. Only later, in the twentieth century, was Whitman's way of life institutionalized by the Beat poets of the 1950s and the protest poets of the 1960s—social dropouts like Jack Kerouac and Allen Ginsberg, anti-war poets like Adrienne Rich and Gary Snyder, whose work and lifestyle spoke their unhappiness about American society and whose views and use of literature set the agenda for many American poets to follow. Whitman was angry at his government, too, but that anger is not "political" in *Leaves of Grass.* By this time he had turned into a transcendentalist, an idealist instead of a materialist. He viewed the social crisis of the day, the year, or the decade indirectly, as merely the growing pains of a good society. While the materialist thought empirical experience was real, the idealist knew, Emerson wrote, "how easy it is to show him that he also is a phantom walking and working amid phantoms, and that he need only ask a question or two beyond his daily questions to find his solid universe growing dim and impalpable before his sense."[7]

This idealism, newly acquired and combined with Whitman's long-standing interest in dreams, accounts for the somnambulistic aspect of his first book. The fourth poem, which became "The Sleepers," is a daydream about midnight, where realist and idealist meet on neutral ground. This poem is very likely an out-take from the larger dream-poem that opened the book—a cutting from the main shoot in the first *Leaves.* Whitman told Traubel in 1891 that "before the 'Leaves' had ever been to the printer, I had them in half a dozen forms—larger, smaller, recast, outcast, taken apart, put together."

The main shoot—"Song of Myself," as the opening poem was ultimately called—bursts forth upon the page in the first edition, immediately introducing the poet and his transcendental motif of the grass.

> I CELEBRATE myself,
> And what I assume you shall assume,
> For every atom belonging to me as good belongs to you.
>
> I loafe and invite my soul,
> I lean and loafe at my ease. . . . observing a spear of summer grass.

Originally, the poem was not divided into sections, but Whitman had a division in mind when he first prepared the manuscript for printing.

In estimating how many pages his book would require, he compared the number of lines and letters in a page of Shakespeare's poems and figured *Leaves of Grass* would run to "about 127 pages." He envisioned "I CELEBRATE myself" as consisting of five sections instead of fifty-two.[8]

The poem came right out of what Whitman's mother described as his "barrels of lectures," and the punctuation in the last line of verse quoted above serves not as an editorial ellipsis but as an oratorical mark intended to pace its spoken delivery. Actually, there *were* no lectures, or at least none surviving in the poet's personal papers—only notes relating to lectures, opening and closing paragraphs for speeches, tentative titles for a collection of his speeches, even homemade advertisements for public addresses.[9] But oratory was the main art form of nineteenth-century America, and as Whitman wrote the poems, he read them aloud in a "palpable voice" to get a "new angle" on what he had just written.

Even the ten-paged, double-columned, closely printed Preface was an appendage to the great poem at the beginning—"written hastily," he told an admirer in 1870, "while the first edition was being printed in 1855." He added, "I do not consider it of permanent value." It never appeared in subsequent editions of *Leaves of Grass,* except as fodder for other poems, mainly "By Blue Ontario's Shores" and "Song of Prudence."[10] The Preface served as the equivalent to Emerson's exhortation in "The Poet." The compelling orator from Concord had said, "our stumps and their politics, our fisheries, our Negroes and Indians, our boats and our repudiations, the wrath of rogues and the pusillanimity of honest men, the northern trade, the southern planting, the western clearing, Oregon and Texas, are yet unsung." In 1841, when Emerson first delivered "The Poet," the Oregon territory was not yet a potentially explosive issue with Great Britain, and the twenty-eighth state of the Union was only a glimmer in its parents' eyes—still a "lone star." But Emerson saw the potential, declaring that "America is a poem in our eyes; its ample geography dazzles the imagination, and it will not wait long for metres." In the Preface Whitman responded with the pronouncement, "The United States themselves are essentially the greatest poem."

❋ ❋ ❋

An odd feature of the first edition of *Leaves* is the fact that its 795 copies included a "second issue," appearing at the end of 1855, which came equipped with its own reviews. They were initially put in to boost sales, which for the first issue were poor to nonexistent, but Whitman came to see this issue as the "fullest version of the original edition."[11] Since three items of this supplementary material were reprintings of anonymous self-reviews, the issue constitutes an addendum to the Preface.

In the Preface Whitman speaks in detail about "the greatest poet." A reader with any doubts about whom he had in mind needed only read one of the three anonymous self-reviews. In "Walt Whitman, A Brooklyn Boy," initially published in the *Brooklyn Daily Times* on September 29, he was more personal and direct than in the Preface, describing himself as of "pure American breed, of reckless health, his body perfect, free from taint from top to toe, free forever from headache and dyspepsia, full-blooded, six feet high, a good feeder, never once using medicine, drinking water only—a swimmer in the river or bay or by the sea-shore."[12] To complete the portrait, he included his phrenological analysis from 1849.

Not usually pointed out is that some of the added material was not exclusively concerned with *Leaves of Grass*. The first extract, for example, came from an 1844 review by E. P. Whipple of Rufus Wilmot Griswold's *Poets and Poetry of America*, published in 1842. The extract could also have come from Whitman's Preface. Whipple (who later found in *Leaves of Grass* no fig leaf) wrote, "The man whose heart is capable of any patriotic emotion, who feels his pulse quicken when the idea of his country is brought home to him, must desire that country to possess a voice more majestic than the roar of the party, and more potent than the whine of sects." The poet's voice in the 1855 Preface must also be "transcendent and new." We know from Whitman's editorials in the 1840s, especially in the *Brooklyn Star* and *Eagle*, that he never forgot his underprivileged background. His interest in opposing capital punishment or supporting the temperance movement, for example, was based primarily on the belief that the common person, even in America, was the underdog in law and commerce. When he put aside party politics, he elevated the ideals of democracy, whose responsibility at mid-century was in any case shifting from the Democratic Party to the Whigs, or Republicans. "Other states indicate themselves in their deputies . . . but the genius of the United States is not best or most in its executives or legislatures, nor in its ambassadors or authors or colleges or churches or parlors, nor even in its newspapers or inventors. . . . but always most in the common people." Later Whitman maintained that *Leaves of Grass* was a "cathedral," the result of a well-considered plan, but the evidence does not support this claim. Roy Harvey Pearce sums up the matter best by saying that Whitman may have wanted to build a cathedral but instead kept constructing antinomian chapels. Whipple, whose interest in romantic poetry stopped with Coleridge (finally too "foreign" and aristocratic for democratic America), would not have worshiped there.[13] In the second issue, Whitman exploited Whipple's desire for a national poetry that "shall make us more in love with our native land by converting its ennobling scenery into the images of lofty thought." Like Coleridge and Whipple, Whitman found spiritual meaning in the material. He located it, however, not merely in the American landscape but in the American average.

Using Whipple to advance his book was doubly hypocritical because the essay was a review of Griswold's anthology of American poets, which would never have admitted Whitman to its canon. And perhaps to make sure his book was never included, to ensure that he was never seen as anything but uniquely beyond the conventional, Whitman included something by Griswold in his supplements to *Leaves of Grass*—a review of *Leaves of Grass* from the *Criterion* of November 10, 1855. Upset about the letter from Emerson that Whitman had published in the *Tribune* exactly a month earlier, Griswold denounced the poetry as "a mass of stupid filth." "There was a time," he said indignantly, "when licentiousness laughed at reproval; now it writes essays and delivers lectures." He also hinted, though in Latin, at the possibility—and it is important to note that Whitman included this in his use of Griswold's review—that the licentiousness included unconventional sex: *Peccatum illud horribile, inter Christianos non nominandum*" (That horrible sin not to be mentioned among Christians). We can only wonder why Whitman included this potentially damaging charge from the self-appointed arbiter of American poetry. We might also wonder which of the twelve poems in the first edition he was referring to—since the "Calamus" poems did not appear until the third edition.

As Poe's literary executor, Griswold had already maligned the Raven in his "memoir"; he was now doing battle with the "latest form of infidelity." The phrase belongs to Harvard Divinity Professor Emeritus Andrews Norton (whose poetry appeared in Griswold's anthology) to describe Emerson's "Divinity School Address," but the battlefield had now become secular. The battle was not for religion, in this nation codified by deists such as Jefferson and Adams, but for the national literature, and Whitman's version of it surely smacked of infidelity to current standards of decency. *Leaves of Grass* was also the latest and most threatening attempt to revive Transcendentalism—what another reviewer, more favorable to Whitman's book, described as "the speculations of that school of thought which culminated at Boston fifteen or eighteen years ago."[14]

Despite its unprecedented mention of the body, *Leaves of Grass* was decidedly a spiritual—or "transcendental"—poem. The original transcendentalists had shocked their elders by demanding that Unitarianism, or Christianity with its social emphasis, recover the spiritual balance lost in the eighteenth-century retreat from the hellfire-and-brimstone harshness of Puritanism. This movement of mainly Unitarian clergymen wanted to inject more "life," or emotion, into the dry bones of latter-day deism. "Why should not we have a poetry and philosophy of insight and not of tradition, and a religion by revelation to us, and not the history of theirs?" Emerson had asked in *Nature.* They were called "transcendentalists" initially as a pejorative to suggest their position as beyond reason and sanity. They seemed to be beyond rational argument. After the "Divinity School Address" in 1838, Henry Ware, Jr., another of Griswold's poets and Emerson's predecessor as minister of the Second Unitarian Church of Boston, asked Emerson to provide something more than intuition, or transcendentalist reason, in support of his attack on the priority of scripture over nature as God's word. "I do not know what arguments mean, in reference to any expression of a thought," Emerson mockingly responded to his former colleague.[15] Obviously, when Emerson wrote his famous letter on July 21, greeting Whitman "at the beginning of a great career," he viewed *Leaves of Grass* as a means of reviving Transcendentalism. Yet Whitman's brand of Transcendentalism, with its equality of Soul *and* Body, violated the decency standards of the "evening lamp," which wrote "women and children" as one word. Natural facts were evidence of a spiritual fact, or God's love, Emerson had written in *Nature,* but Whitman's natural facts emphasized the human body and even its private parts.

Whitman's attention to nature and sexuality has perhaps been overemphasized itself in the twentieth century, first with its existential focus on nature as the only spirit in the age of modernism and then with its collapse of meaning, or "truth," altogether in the era of postmodernism. And the poets of this century who retreat behind nature, or the body, instead of the soul are equally but differently evasive of reason. "So much depends," William Carlos Williams's now familiar line reads, "upon a red wheel / barrow / glazed with rain / water / beside the white / chickens." And so much depends, in the mind of the postmodernist, on the subjective "construction" of things. But to attribute this contemporary ideology (either modernism or postmodernism) to Whitman is to remove him from his times. The body, overclothed and understated in the nineteenth century, was merely one of his priorities. He was, as he announced, the poet of the body and the poet of the soul—half New York journalist, half New England transcendentalist. The body was God's emblem, but it also embraced the workingman and -woman, the "divine average" who had been perhaps overlooked in Emerson's deification of the American scholar, the divinity school student, or the poet who in spite of Emerson's advice still wrote in iambic tetrameter.

Whitman was ambitious about his poetic program and planned rather carefully the debut of *Leaves of Grass,* if not the design of its green cover. He made sure, for example, that it got the most favorable review possible in Greeley's *Tribune,* then edited by Charles A. Dana. In fact, Whitman may have written this review himself or given Dana, whom he no doubt knew from his previous publications in the *Tribune,* notes from which to work it up. The sentence in the review, for example, asserting that the poems were shaped on "no preexistent model" is similar to a statement in one of Whitman's three self-reviews, published in the *Democratic Review* and included with the material sewn into the second issue of *Leaves of Grass,* to wit: "The style of these poems . . . is simply their own style, just born and red."[16] Add to that the fact that Dana's review employs liberal doses of quotations from Whitman's poetry and throws in just enough negative criticism to make it sound less like a puff (something Whitman did with aplomb in the selection of reviews he put into the second issue), and the probability of Whitman's authorship increases.

The clincher, however, was the evocation of Emerson's name (as well as Alcott's *Orphic Sayings*) to describe the oratorical style of the poetry. "Of the nature of poetry the writer discourses in a somewhat too oracular strain, especially as he has been anticipated in his 'utterances' by Emerson," the reviewer complained ever so faintly. Whitman or his distributors, Fowler & Wells, had sent Emerson a paperbound copy of the first *Leaves,* and the poet must have hoped for a response from the Concord poet and philosopher. Indeed, Emerson had responded two days earlier, and Whitman, had he been in town, could have received the letter by the time the *Tribune* review appeared.

If Whitman was not the author of this review, which amounted to a two-column puff in which the poet is likened to Emerson's "Central Man," he had lighted upon the perfect press agent in Dana. A veteran of the utopian community of Brook Farm outside Boston and a contributor to the *Dial* and the *Harbinger,* Dana was particularly qualified to recognize a "transcendental" poem. A poor boy from Buffalo who had made it big in journalism (he had been Greeley's city editor for almost a decade and became as famous as Joseph Pulitzer by the 1890s), he was also qualified to recognize the "rowdyness" in Whitman's transcendental vision—with or without the poet's private tutoring. "We may infer," the review stated, that the author "belongs to that exemplary class of society irreverently styled 'loafers.'" It spoke of the Whitman who appeared in Gabriel Harrison's 1854 daguerreotype, as rendered in a steel engraving by Samuel Hollyer—"in a garb, half sailor's, half workingman's, with no superfluous appendage of coat or waistcoat, a 'wideawake' perched jauntily on his head, one hand in his pocket and the other on his hip, with a certain air of mild defiance, and an expression of pensive insolence in his face which seems to betoken a consciousness of his mission as the 'coming man.'"[17] It is strange that Whitman did not include this review with those appended to the second issue of *Leaves of Grass.*

❋ ❋ ❋

The only eyewitness sighting of Whitman late that summer comes from Moncure Conway, a Calvinist minister from Virginia who converted to Unitarianism, New England, and Emerson. After visiting Emerson one evening in Concord in September and hearing him praise *Leaves of Grass,* Conway purchased a copy in Boston and read it on a steamer to New York City the next day. He then set out for Brooklyn and the author of the book he had been reading. It wasn't easy to find Whitman, especially for a "gentleman" who had to take the horse trolley from the Brooklyn Ferry all the way out Myrtle Avenue ("out of Brooklyn nearly," he complained to Emerson in his report of the excursion on September 17). When he finally arrived at the Ryerson Street residence, "one of a row of small wooden houses with porches, which all seem occupied by mechanics," Conway learned to his frustration that the poet was not at home but at Rome's print shop, all the way back down Myrtle to Fulton and Cranberry streets. He found the poet there sitting on a stool setting type, possibly for the second issue of his (1855) book. In spite of the unconventional nature of *Leaves of Grass* and the working-class environment of Ryerson Street, Conway probably still expected to find Emerson's new poet dressed like a gentleman, but instead he found Whitman in "a blue striped shirt" with its open collar revealing a red flannel undergarment. He thought Whitman's manner "blunt" but not disagreeable.

Conway was a name dropper and a sycophant, and his testimony, later contradicted slightly in his memoirs, has to be read with care. One item, however, is particularly significant and revealing. "I told him that I had spent the evening before with you," Conway told Emerson, "and that what you had said of him, and the perusal of his book had resulted in my call. He seems very eager to hear from you and about you, and what you thought of his book."[18] There was no reason for Whitman to lie about not already having heard from Emerson; as noted, he had probably not seen the letter by that time. In his letter to Whitman, Emerson expressed doubt about the poet's correct address. He did not know Whitman's home address, of course, and had sent his letter to the Broadway offices of Fowler & Wells, who had advertised the book in both the New York and Boston newspapers. Whitman therefore probably did not see the letter, one of the most famous in American literary history, until early October, when he promptly either persuaded Dana or acceded to his request (Greeley was in Europe at the time) to publish it.

Not one to beat around the bush with any kind of preamble, Emerson got right to the point.

> Dear Sir,
>
> I am not blind to the worth of the wonderful gift of "Leaves of Grass." I find it the most extraordinary piece of wit & wisdom that America has yet contributed. I am very happy in reading it, as great power makes us happy. It meets the demand I am always making of what seemed the sterile & stingy nature, as if too much handiwork or too much lymph in the temperament were making our western wits fat & mean. I give you joy of your free & brave thought. I have great joy in it. I find incomparable things said incomparably well, as they must be. I find the courage of *treatment,* which so delights us, & which large perception only can inspire. I greet you at the beginning of a great career, which yet must have had a long foreground somewhere for such a start. I rubbed my eyes a little to see if this sunbeam were no illusion; but the solid sense of the book is a sober certainty. It has the best merits, namely, of fortifying & encouraging.
>
> I did not know until I, last night, saw the book advertised in a newspaper, that I could trust the name as real & available for a post-office. I wish to see my benefactor, & have felt much like striking my tasks, & visiting New York to pay you my respects.

Some said that Whitman carried the letter around Brooklyn in his pocket the rest of the summer, but he more likely did not see it until after his return from Greenport. George remembered his brother as being "set up" by the Emerson letter, but he does not say when he received it. George's description no doubt understates the excitement on Ryerson Street when the most important man of American letters greeted the obscure poet "at the beginning of a great career."[19]

Whitman did not include Emerson's "review" in his second issue. Instead, he did worse: after what he claimed were repeated requests from Dana, he published the letter in the *Tribune* of October 10, 1855.[20] Later he did paste a copy of what had appeared in the *Tribune* into a few volumes of the second issue, but he may have considered the letter simply too valuable to be lumped among the other reviews. He ultimately selected the second edition of *Leaves of Grass* for its showcasing. And despite the fact that Whitman published this letter in the *Tribune* without the author's permission, Emerson kept his promise and dined with Whitman in New York on December 10, 1855.[21]

What was it in *Leaves of Grass* that compelled the busiest man of American letters first to write this remarkable (some of his Boston friends thought "hasty") letter of high praise and second to "strike [his] tasks" to visit the self-described poet-mechanic? After announcing in "The Poet" that he looked "in vain" for the person described there, Emerson had greeted other poets at the beginning of promising careers, but not with the same level of pointed enthusiasm he offered Whitman.[22] What did Whitman's "great career" offer? Today, in an age of computerized identity, Emersonianism seems almost anachronistic with its emphasis on individual freedom. But we must remember the Emerson of the "Divinity School Address," who advised the graduates of 1838 to "go alone"; in so doing, he risked his livelihood as a public lecturer after he was branded as a religious heretic. This was the Emerson of "Self-Reliance," who was even prepared to put his creative freedom before family responsibility if necessary. He found the same risk-taker in Whitman, who announced in his Preface, "There will soon be no more priests. Their work is done. . . . every man shall be his own priest" (my ellipses).

By 1855 Emerson was prepared to recognize nature as something more than a mere emblem of the soul. Now the materialist and the idealist were on a more even footing. Like body and soul, poet (in effect, the secular clergyman of the nineteenth century) and priest were one in *Leaves of Grass.* Emerson was never prepared to go as far as Whitman. Rather, like the Unitarians from whom he sprang, who recognized Christ without embracing the concept of a Holy Trinity, Emerson "recognized" nature after reading *Leaves of Grass.* And this is what he found.

> I believe in you my soul. . . . the other I am must not abase itself to you,
> And you must not be abased to the other.
>
> Loafe with me on the grass. . . . loose the stop from your throat,
> Not words, not music or rhyme I want. . . . not custom or lecture, not
> even the best,
> Only the lull I like, the hum of your valved voice.

[There was no secondary accent marker on "valvèd" in the crudely printed first edition.]

> I mind how we lay in June, such a transparent summer morning;
> You settled your head athwart my hips and gently turned over
> upon me,
> And parted the shirt from my bosom-bone, and plunged your tongue
> to my barestript heart,
> And reached till you felt my beard, and reached till you held my feet.
>
> Swiftly arose and spread around me the peace and joy and knowledge
> that pass all the art and argument of the earth;
> And I know that the hand of God is the elderhand of my own,
> And I know that the spirit of God is the eldest brother of my own.

This poem, the first in the book—pages 13 to 56, more than half the volume—must have seemed to Emerson a most original description of the second coming of the spirit, or a second Sermon on the Mount. Beckoned earthward, the soul embraces and legitimizes the body, underscoring the idea that the "origin of all poems" is, as Emerson said, the spirit as emblemized through nature. Now, however, nature and spirit are equal—each as good as the other. What is so modern—or postmodern—about this edition of *Leaves of Grass* is that it threatens at times to throw off the spirit altogether in its mesmerizing catalogs of nature. Both Whitman and Emerson realized this possibility later, after the third edition of 1860—but for now Emerson apparently was not distracted by the catalogs. Whitman's poem lived up to Emerson's definition of poetry in "The Poet," which was restated in the Preface: "Of all nations the United States with veins full of poetical stuff most need poets and will doubtless have the greatest and use them the greatest."

From all of nature Whitman selected the grass as his principal emblem of God's love. It was God's calling card and attention getter.

> A child said, What is the grass? fetching it to me with full hands;
> How could I answer the child?. . . . I do not know what it is any more than he.
>
> I guess it must be the flag of my disposition, out of hopeful green stuff woven.
>
> Or I guess it is the handkerchief of the Lord,
> A scented gift and remembrancer designedly dropped,
> Bearing the owner's name someway in the corners, that we may see and remark, and say Whose?

The grass, its meaning both secret and sacred, was the "uniform hieroglyphic"—"Sprouting alike in broad zones and narrow zones, / Growing among black folks as among white." It was perhaps strange that this city poet should select something more common to the country. But then the country was still within the city in the 1850s. In "Letters from a Travelling Bachelor," published in 1849, Whitman described how he often went up to the rim of the Croton Reservoir at 40th Street and Fifth Avenue, where forty-five feet above the pavement there was a broad walkway from which to view the city. To the north were mainly trees, spotted with clearings for houses that had sometimes been blocked out but generally not yet constructed.[23] Indeed, in the poem he may have had in mind the grass of cemeteries in the city, often the use of land immediately before it was occupied by dwellings for the living ("And now it seems to me the beautiful uncut hair of graves").

The grass said that all the dead were "alive and well somewhere." It assured us that "All goes onward and outward." And that it was "lucky" to die.

> I pass death with the dying, and birth with the new-washed babe. . . .
> and am not contained between my hat and boots.

Nothing escaped divinity or notice in this poem.

> The blab of the pave. . . . the tires of carts and sluff of bootsoles and talk of the promenaders,
> The heavy omnibus, the driver with his interrogating thumb, the clank of the shod horses on the granite floor,
> The carnival of sleighs, the clinking and shouted jokes and pelts of snowballs;
> The hurrahs for popular favorites. . . . the fury of roused mobs,
> The flap of the curtained litter—-the sick man inside, borne to the hospital,

Everyone is included here, even the runaway slave, to whose neck and ankles the poet applies medicinal plasters.

It is probably true that Whitman would not have participated in the Underground Railroad, as Thoreau did at Walden Pond. (New York City was a notoriously unsafe stop on the Underground Railroad.) Whitman was more concerned about the question of slavery's extension to the territories, possibly content to let slavery wear itself out in a South increasingly isolated and outvoted by the territorial expansion. He also believed in law and order and the Constitution, which unfortunately allowed for slavery in certain states of the Union. In the proofs to *The Eighteenth Presidency!*—a political pamphlet never published during his lifetime—Whitman insisted that as long as the Constitution permitted slavery, the Compromise of 1850 required fugitive slaves to be returned.[24] Yet about the same time he wrote "A

Boston Ballad" (the ninth poem in the first *Leaves*), which harshly satirized the use of the slave law. But both the satire and the melodrama in the poem are uncharacteristic of Whitman's poetry.

Of course, in *Leaves of Grass* the speaker was Walt, not Walter—the one vicarious, the other more political and practical. Whereas the unemployed journalist and housebuilder had to cling to a certain decorum, the poet could talk about or relate to anything, even a sexually aroused (or frustrated) woman:

> Twenty-eight young men bathe by the shore,
> Twenty-eight young men, and all so friendly,
> Twenty-eight years of womanly life, and all so lonesome.
>
> She owns the fine house by the rise of the bank,
> She hides handsome and richly drest aft the blinds of the window.
>
> Which of the young men does she like the best?
> Ah the homeliest of them is beautiful to her.
>
> Where are you off to, lady? for I see you,
> You splash in the water there, yet stay stock still in your room.
>
> Dancing and laughing along the beach came the twenty-ninth bather,
> The rest did not see her, but she saw them and loved them.
>
> The beards of the young men glistened with wet, it ran from their long hair,
> Little streams passed all over their bodies.
>
> An unseen hand also passed over their bodies,
> It descended tremblingly from their temples and ribs.
>
> The young men float on their backs, their white bellies swell to the sun.
> . . . they do not ask who seizes fast to them,

> They do not know who puffs and declines with pendant and bending
> arch,
> They do not think whom they souse with spray.

The *Brooklyn Eagle* of September 15 wondered whether the "lady" fell in love with the twenty-ninth bather—a question clearly based on a misreading of the poem, possibly intended to ignore the woman's sexual behavior, however vicarious. Modern-day readings, on the other hand, have made the passage racier than it probably was in 1855. The "pendant and bending arch" today suggests oral sex, but that was probably out of the question in the nineteenth century—at least with such middle-class women as the "twenty-ninth bather." The idea of sex in general was bold enough. For such a woman to even *think* about it was shocking in an age that would cultivate censors like Anthony Comstock. Whitman addressed the question more formally and directly in his open letter to Emerson in the 1856 edition and in "Children of Adam" (then called "Enfans d'Adam") in the 1860 edition. In the 1855 edition he said, "What is commonest and cheapest and nearest and easiest is Me."

Whitman said he was "afoot" with his vision, but "aloft" is more accurate.

> Divine am I inside and out, and I make holy whatever I touch or am
> touched from;
> The scent of these arm-pits is aroma finer than prayer,
> This head is more than churches or bibles or creeds.

We can hear in this last line an echo of the blasphemy of Tom Paine in *The Age of Reason,* but it is partly muffled by the Transcendentalism of the first line; the result, here and in the first *Leaves* generally, is to give the baseness of the body a new holiness, best suggested in the middle line about "arm-pits" and "prayer." Transcendence is curiously "inverted" because the soul now "transcends" to the body, or meets it halfway.[25] Not only are the priests gone from the temple; the temple is gone as well. It now resides in individual bodies, which are—in a democracy—the most suitable places of worship.

Along with blurring the distinction between the material and the spiritual, Whitman blurred the difference between poetry and prose. Emerson had as well, but from the other direction, with essays often thought to be more rhythmical than logical. And in fact, since all good writing is rhythmical, we should say that when Whitman presented his prose-looking, unrhymed, unmetered, unenjambed lines as "poetry," he was blurring the distinction between prose and conventional verse, not between prose and poetry. Most American poets before Whitman, from Longfellow to Bryant, took as their models such English versifiers as Wordsworth and Coleridge or Byron and Shelley. But the battle over form had already been initiated under the influence of William Blake, an ardent sympathizer with the French Revolution, a man caught in the Age of Reason who abhorred rationalistic philosophy, and a poet who urged the young artists of his day to trust their own imaginations over the classical models in art.[26] Like Blake, Whitman was concerned about the political fetters of his time, which eventually lead him to cast off the fetters of literary language—the use of recurrent patterns of sounds or meters—which by the nineteenth century generally meant the iambic unit.

In "The Poet" Emerson had called for a "metre-making argument," but Whitman made the argument without the conventional meter. Emerson called for "a thought so passionate and alive that like the spirit of a plant or an animal it has an architecture of its own, and adorns nature with a new thing." Whitman's thought had no architecture, or structure as it was commonly understood in a poetical composition. The fact that so many divergent theories today vie for the last word on the structure of "Song of Myself" underscores its overall lack of a conventional structure.[27] Not a problem today as it was yesterday, however, is the poem's lack of fixed versification. Whitman had shown the first signs of free verse five years earlier in "Blood-Money," and the fact that he made the change in a political poem is significant. Part of the poet's abandonment of versification (which he could handle as well as most poets of his day) was the abandonment of a structure that had served a higher class, when poetry was the pastime of the "gentleman" who enjoyed economic privilege and iambic tetrameter. The failure of the Wilmot Proviso showed that the current political structure had betrayed democratic principles, and betrayal was the subject of "Blood-Money" and "House of Friends," where Whitman also adopted a form relatively free of conventional versification.

Whitman needed a freer form for his message, but there were nevertheless poetic principles behind his "barbaric yawp." Primarily, they came from Emerson's insistence that form reflect meaning. In the first edition of *Leaves of Grass,* more than in subsequent editions, the meaning expressed is a freedom to realize God's purpose in nature.

> Urge and urge and urge,
> Always the procreant urge of the world.

This urge in nature is not merely sexual; it includes the need to procreate the self's vision of democracy.

Whitman took the single line as the rhythmical unit in his new "metre-making" argument. In a construction that Gay Wilson Allen and others have termed the poet's "parallelism" or his "thought-rhythms," each line generally "sounds" its own idea, which is merely "parallel" to the next idea, not dependent on it for coherence. Probably Bliss Perry, like Allen a biographer of Whitman, was right when he determined that Whitman's main model for his new "prosody" was the English Bible. "Here," Perry wrote, "was precisely that natural stylistic variation between the 'terrific,' the 'gentle,' and the 'inferior' parts, so desired by William Blake. . . . The parallelism which constituted the peculiar structural device of Hebrew poetry gave the English of the King James version a heightened rhythm without destroying the flexibility and freedom natural to prose. In this strong, rolling music, this intense feeling, these concrete words expressing primal emotions in daring terms of bodily sensation, Whitman found the charter for the book he wished to write."[28] As Whitman himself states in the Preface, "The profit of rhyme is that it drops seeds of a sweeter and more luxuriant rhyme, and of uniformity that it conveys itself into its own roots in the ground out of sight. The rhyme and uniformity of perfect poems show the free growth of metrical laws." In "Walt Whitman and His Poems,"

Whitman paraphrased himself more transcendentally, saying, "His rhymth [*sic*] and uniformity he will conceal in the roots of his verses, not to be seen of themselves, but to break forth loosely as lilacs on a bush."

Like T. S. Eliot's *The Waste Land,* "Song of Myself"—the final title of the longest and most important poem of the 1855 edition—was probably once a much longer poem. In the same anonymous self-review, Whitman said that the eleven other poems had each distinct purposes, "curiously veiled." This may have been true with regard to the poet's experience of writing them, for some were probably begun more than a year earlier and one—originally called "Resurgemus"—was five years old. But many also betray their origin in "Song of Myself." The order of the eleven untitled poems following "Song of Myself" was "A Song for Occupations," "To Think of Time," "The Sleepers," "I Sing the Body Electric," "Faces," "Song of the Answerer," "Resurgemus" ("Europe"), "A Boston Ballad," "There Was a Child Went Forth," "Who Learns My Lesson Complete?" and "Great Are the Myths." It was a poet's potpourri—some great poems, some good ones, and some bad enough to be pushed to the far corners of the definitive edition of *Leaves of Grass* in 1881. Indeed, one poem, "Great Are the Myths," was ultimately excluded from the book.

Shortly before the printing of the first edition, when he first brought the manuscript to the printing shop, Whitman actually had a different order for his poems. "Song of Myself" still opened the book, but "Song of the Answerer" (a poem of dubious quality that Whitman expanded in the next edition) was second. It was somehow to be fused with "There Was a Child Went Forth," giving the book a total of only eleven poems. "Faces" followed in the fourth position. "Great Are the Myths" was next, followed by "The Sleepers," "A Song for Occupations," "Who Learns My Lesson Complete?" "Resurgemus," "To Think of Time," and "I Sing the Body Electric." This last poem was tentatively called "Slaves," suggesting that the auctioneer's survey of the human body—something Whitman witnessed in his New Orleans days—may have begun the original poem.[29]

"A Song for Occupations" was not one of Whitman's best certainly, but it is noted today because of its democratic subject. Whitman revised the poem repeatedly between 1855 and 1881, but he never got it right.

Even in its final version, it has poor coherence and unity, probably because it was not originally about occupations at all: the focus—if it has one—in its initial version is on the tools of work. It may continue the occupation theme of Section 15 of "Song of Myself," but the first lines, which Whitman subsequently dropped, anticipate the "Calamus" poems.

> Come closer to me,
> Push close my lovers and take the best I possess,
> Yield closer and closer and give me the best you possess.

Here "A Song for Occupations" continues the colloquy between poet and reader begun in "Song of Myself." In "A Song for Occupations" the poet supports and encourages the reader as Whitman had the worker in his *Eagle* editorials. "I bring what you much need, yet always have," he says in the 1855 "Occupations," "I bring not money or amours or dress or eating. . . . but I bring as good." In the "Sun-Down Papers" he had warned his ideal reader/worker not to "live genteelly" or follow fashion; he had sought to raise his reader's self-esteem (as he then sought to raise his own). Now the schoolteacher-turned-poet is not satisfied to keep his distance and complains of the "cold types and cylinder and wet paper between us." "I pass so poorly with paper and types. . . . I must pass with the contact of bodies and souls."

Whitman lost his composure in this poem and perhaps should have omitted it from the cuttings. In the Preface and "Song of Myself," he had kept a loving distance as he instructed and inspired the reader. He regained that position in "To Think of Time," the third poem in the book. The poem deserves more attention than it has received, ignored probably because Whitman took up a theme already common to great poets, the ravages of time. Even its first line, which became its final title, is hackneyed. But almost immediately he personalizes the subject and addresses the reader the way he did in "Song of Myself."

> Have you guessed you yourself would not continue? Have you dreaded those earth-beetles?
> Have you feared the future would be nothing to you?
> . . . .

When the dull nights are over, and the dull days also,
When the soreness of lying so much in bed is over,
When the physician, after long putting off, gives the silent and terrible
look for an answer,
When the children come hurried and weeping, and the brothers and
sisters have been sent for,
When medicines stand unused on the shelf, and the camphor-smell has
pervaded the rooms,
When the faithful hand of the living does not desert the hand of the
dying,
When the twitching lips press lightly on the forehead of the dying,
When the breath ceases and the pulse of the heart ceases,
Then the corpse-limbs stretch on the bed, and the living look upon
them,
They are palpable as the living are palpable.

"You are not thrown to the winds," the poem continues. "You gather certainly and safely around yourself, / Yourself! Yourself! Yourself forever and ever!" In "Song of Myself," he raises the same issue.

What do you think has become of the young and old men?
And what do you think has become of the women and children?

They are alive and well somewhere;
The smallest sprout shows there is really no death,
And if ever there was it led forward life, and does not wait at the end to
arrest it,
And ceased the moment life appeared.

All goes onward and outward. . . . and nothing collapses,
And to die is different from what any one supposed, and luckier.

"To Think of Time" introduces "an old stagedriver" whose death is not terminal, for he lives in the memory of the mourners.

He was a goodfellow,
Freemouthed, quicktempered, not badlooking, able to take his own
part,

Witty, sensitive to a slight, ready with life or death for a friend,
Fond of women . . . played some . . eat hearty and drank hearty,
Had known what it was to be flush . . grew lowspirited toward the
last . . sickened . . was helped by a contribution,
Died aged forty-one years . . and that was his funeral.

Whitman is not slumming here. He knew this "goodfellow" and his class firsthand. Doubtless, he knew many who needed a "contribution" in both sickness *and* health. The passage describing the funeral of the "old" stage driver came from life—from one of those mechanics' "wooden houses with porches" on Ryerson Street at which Conway had looked askance, where residents probably pronounced "eat" as "et" and meant "ate." (Whitman later changed "eat" to "ate" in this description of the stage driver.)

The next poem in the first *Leaves,* "The Sleepers," has puzzled a number of readers. John Burroughs, Whitman's close friend and the author of the first critical study of the poet (which Whitman helped write), claimed after the poet's death that he had never understood the poem. Richard Maurice Bucke seemed to satisfy the critics most by observing that the poem was "a representation of the mind during sleep—of connected, half-connected, and disconnected thoughts and feelings as they occur in dreams, some commonplace, some weird, some voluptuous, and all given with the true and strange emotional accompaniments that belong to them." This exegesis is worth quoting because it appeared in the Bucke biography, not only authorized by Whitman but like Burroughs's book "proofed" by the poet. It is probably Whitman's statement as much as it is Bucke's, even though the language is that of an alienist, or psychiatrist, which was Bucke's profession as the director of an insane asylum in Canada.

Poetry, like music, is about emotion, which words (and psychiatrists) can only approach. "Sometimes," Bucke added, "(and these are the most astonishing parts of the poem) the vague emotions, without thought, that occasionally arise in sleep, are given as they actually occur, apart from any idea—the words having in the intellectual sense no meaning, but arousing, as music does, the state of feeling intended. It is a poem that with most people requires a great deal of study to make anything of it, but to certain minds it would, no doubt, be plain at once."[30] Such "vague emotions, without thought" work as music does upon the mind. Dreams are full of words and usually devoid of logic as the mind wanders.

> I WANDER all night in my vision,
> Stepping with light feet. . . . swiftly and noiselessly stepping and
> stopping,
> Bending with open eyes over the shut eyes of sleepers;
> Wandering and confused. . . . lost to myself. . . . ill-assorted. . . .
> contradictory,
> Pausing and gazing and bending and stopping.

This sleepwalker is also Whitman's "sleeptalker," whom he wrote about in 1850 in his truncated version of Ingemann's novel. The sleeper tells stories. One, describing his mother taking in a "red squaw," is similar to Whitman's taking in the fugitive slave in Section 10 of "Song of Myself," suggesting again that "The Sleepers"—like "A Song for Occupations"—originated in "Song of Myself." Whitman never completely satisfied himself with this poem either and finally after much revision (and excision) placed it in the back part of his definitive edition.

❋ ❋ ❋

The fifth poem, "I Sing the Body Electric," attained and held onto a prominent place in the Whitman canon, and for good reason. In 1855, of course, it had no title, and the ultimate title line was not even part of the original poem until 1867. Nor were "electric" and "electricity" household words at that time. "I Sing the Body Electric" was Whitman's first installment in his intention, as he told Emerson a year later, to express "the body of a man or woman" in poetry. *Leaves of Grass,* it is seldom noted, was hardly ever, if at all, assailed in the nineteenth century for its suggestions of homosexuality; the exception is Griswold's Latin adage, cited earlier, which anticipated the phrase in the 1890s "the love which dare not speak its name." The problem with *Leaves of Grass* was always and simply sexuality.

Like "To Think of Time" and the other cuttings, "I Sing the Body Electric" came right out of the poet's Brooklyn and Long Island experience. The clue here is similar to the one in "To Think of Time." Both poems contain a portrait drawn from the poet's lower-middle-class, working man's background. In "To Think of Time" we have the funeral of the stage driver; in "I Sing the Body Electric," it is an octogenarian farmer, whom Whitman doubtless knew while growing up or teaching in the country. Possibly, the figure here is modeled after his maternal grandfather, Cornelius Van Velsor, whom the poet adored.

> I knew a man. . . . he was a common farmer. . . . he was the father of five sons . . . and in them were the fathers of sons . . . and in them were the fathers of sons.
> This man was of wonderful vigor and calmness and beauty of person;
> The shape of his head, the richness and breadth of his manners, the pale yellow and white of his hair and beard, the immeasurable meaning of his black eyes,
> These I used to go and visit him to see. . . . He was wise also,
> He was six feet tall. . . . he was over eighty years old. . . . his sons were massive clean bearded tanfaced and handsome,
> They and his daughters loved him . . . all who saw him loved him . . . they did not love him by allowance . . . they loved him with personal love;
> He drank water only. . . . the blood showed like scarlet through the clear brown skin of his face;
> He was a frequent gunner and fisher . . . he sailed his boat himself . . . he had a fine one presented to him by a shipjoiner. . . . he had fowling-pieces, presented to him by men that loved him;
> When he went with his five sons and many grandsons to hunt or fish you would pick him out as the most beautiful and vigorous of the gang,
> You would wish long and long to be with him. . . . you would wish to sit by him in the boat that you and he might touch each other.

The "electricity" of the body described here is more than skin deep. Whitman is describing the "body" of his experience, and this body—like the one the phrenologists, the century's health-fitness experts, knew—is ideal in its warmth, look, and general appeal. It is ideal as well in its earthiness, its "average" divinity. Just as the stage driver was fond of women, "played some," and drank heartily (no doubt bringing about his early death at forty-one), the venerable, water-drinking farmer had the sexual appetite of a man virile enough to have sired five sons and probably as many daughters. (It is alleged that Whitman's maternal grandfather took a second wife and sired a son after Naomi died.)[31] He was a man who liked to sail his boat, go hunting, and generally be in the company of men.

This is a man, Whitman says, "You would wish long and long to be with." In Section 32 of "Song of Myself," though not in the first edition, he used the same phrase ("long and long") to describe how he pondered the contentment of lower nature—like sex, part of the Emersonian emblem left unmentioned in *Nature.* Whitman was trying to get through to a particular something in his poetry at this time. Not only did "cold types and cylinder and wet paper" separate him from the object of desire; so too did society's implicit condemnation of the body and thus its spiritual essence. "There should not be infidelism about sex, but perfect faith," he told Emerson.[32] Emerson had asked rhetorically in *Nature,* "To what end is nature?" Whitman narrowed the question to the meaning of the body and its sexual needs.

In "Faces" he continues to look for nature's secrets. He explores not only the faces of healthy people, like the octogenarian in "I Sing the Body Electric" whose "blood showed like scarlet through the clear brown skin of his face," but also the faces of the broken and deformed, like the poet's youngest brother, Eddy, and his eldest brother, Jesse ("I knew of the agents that emptied and broke my brother"). Like the potential he would find in the corrupted body of the woman in "To a Common Prostitute," he found even in the "face of the most smeared and slobbering idiot they had at the asylum" "the real landlord perfect and unharmed, every inch as good as myself." It was the poet's job to identify these faces—to reclaim the body as part of the soul.

In "Song of the Answerer," this poet finds his power by identifying with everybody else.

> Then the mechanics take him for a mechanic,
> And the soldiers suppose him to be a captain. . . . and the sailors that he has followed the sea,
> And the authors take him for an author. . . . and the artists for an artist,
> And the laborers perceive he could labor with them and love them;
> No matter what the work is, that he is one to follow it or has followed it,
> No matter what the nation, that he might find his brothers and sisters there.

Not only does Whitman anticipate his own experience as the "Good Gray Poet" who ministered successfully to sick and wounded Civil War soldiers in Washington because he could identify with their often humble and hard-working backgrounds; he asserts here that the poet is representative because he is at ease with all men and women, who accept him as a friend and a brother.[33]

The other poems—the last five of the first edition—don't maintain the same level of originality found in the first six—possibly seven—poems in the volume. What became "Europe" in the definitive edition was a slight reworking of the 1850 "Resurgemus." The next poem, ultimately entitled "A Boston Ballad," was also political and alluded, cryptically, to the controversial enforcement of the Fugitive Slave Law. Then, true to the "native" origin of the 1855 *Leaves,* Whitman returned to the Self in what became "There Was a Child Went Forth." Like "To Think of Time," this poem tackles an old subject, the Wordsworthian absorption of nature. But in his treatment, Whitman was in harmony with the change in American poetry from neo-classical to romantic—from treating the objects of nature externally to internalizing nature or emphasizing not nature alone but the impact of nature upon the imagination.

THERE was a child went forth every day,
And the first object he looked upon and received with wonder or pity
or love or dread, that object he became,
And that object became part of him for the day or a certain part of the
day. . . . or for many years or stretching cycles of years.

Biographers have used the poem to argue that Whitman's father was stern or worse ("The father, strong, selfsufficient, manly, mean, angered, unjust"), but *Leaves of Grass* in 1855 is about the underprivileged working class for whom democracy is a good thing and the gateway to divinity. There is strong evidence from personal rather than literary sources that Walt Whitman, Sr., was much loved by his son.[34] Whitman speaks equally of "His own parents" in "There Was a Child Went Forth"—"he that had propelled the fatherstuff at night, and fathered him. . and she that conceived him in her womb and birthed him . . . . they gave this child more of themselves than that, / They gave him afterward every day. . . . they and of them became part of him."

Whitman's unprecedented inclusion of these intimate details of life rather than giving an ideal picture of the family contentedly gathered around sexless parents (and a passive mother) probably encouraged the incomparable Fanny Fern to write one of the first favorable reviews of *Leaves of Grass,* certainly the first by a woman. In the *New York Ledger* of May 10, 1856 (and reprinted in *Life Illustrated* a week later), the feminist writer found Whitman's book "unspeakably delicious, after the forced, stiff, Parnassian exotics" that then passed as poetry. "Walt Whitman," she exclaimed, "the effeminate world needed thee." It needed such a poet who was "enamored of *women,* not *ladies—men,* not *gentlemen.* . . . It needed a man who dared speak out his strong, honest thoughts in the face of pusillanimous, toadying, republican aristocracy; dictionary-men, hypocrites, cliques, and creeds." She concluded that her "moral constitution" might be "hopelessly tainted," "but I confess that I extract no poison from these 'Leaves'—to me they have brought only healing."[35]

The final two poems—ultimately "Who Learns My Lesson Complete?" and "Great Are the Myths"—support the transcendentalist ideas that the human mind or soul is immortal and that everything in nature, the symbol of our harmony with the Oversoul, is equally "great." Nature is a "myth" because nature is—in the rhetoric of Emerson and Kant—the Not-me. It is "great" because it stands for the soul. Besides the personal reference to the poet's growing "six feet high" and becoming "thirty-six years old in 1855" in "Who Learns My Lesson Complete?" (information subsequently removed), the two poems lack the "body" of Whitman's new poetic. That body had already announced itself in what became Section 24 of "Song of Myself."

> Walt Whitman, an American, one of the roughs, a kosmos,
> Disorderly fleshy and sensual. . . . eating drinking and breeding,
> No sentimentalist. . . . no stander above men and women or apart from them. . . . no more modest than immodest.

After the saltiness and sweat of the earlier poems, where the stench of armpits "is aroma finer than prayer," the last two poems have the effect of a benediction. Yet in "Song of Myself" and most of its cuttings, he spoke the "password primeval," which was "the sign of democracy." "By God!" averred the poet who had grown up and lived among the economic average and below-average, "I will accept nothing which all cannot have their counterpart of on the same terms."

Leaves of Grass came out of the Ryerson Streets and the Myrtle Avenues of Brooklyn, which was then a fairly reliable microcosm of the United States. It also originated in Transcendentalism, the American filter for English and German romanticism and orientalism, which suggested the mysticism in religious and poetic acts. Whitman's adaptation essentially rerouted the path of Emerson's spiritual amelioration with its journey motif and its image of an impeded return to Ithaca. In Whitman there is only an "open road," where the scenes passed are more important than the destination. Likewise, there is no crossing over, or movement from A to Z, in the soul's migration. In his final explanation of the meaning of life, in the future Section 44 of "Song of Myself," he says that "Cycles ferried my cradle." Ferrying across an expanse is much like a "crossing," as in the great poem he wrote for his second edition, "Crossing Brooklyn Ferry." The motion is back and forth rather than forward. The journey of the soul is therefore relative—with time and distance availing for nothing. The imagery also reflects a real, physical journey, for Whitman, as we have said, often took the ferry for the fresh air, spending a few pennies for health and vigor, especially when he resided at the foot of the Brooklyn Ferry in the offices of the *Brooklyn Eagle.* Indeed, his adult and professional life had been a series of to-ing and fro-ing, not only between Brooklyn and Manhattan, but between professions and vocations. Now the poet had finally arrived. "All forces have been steadily employ'd to complete and delight me," Whitman states in "Song of Myself." "Now on this spot I stand with my robust soul."

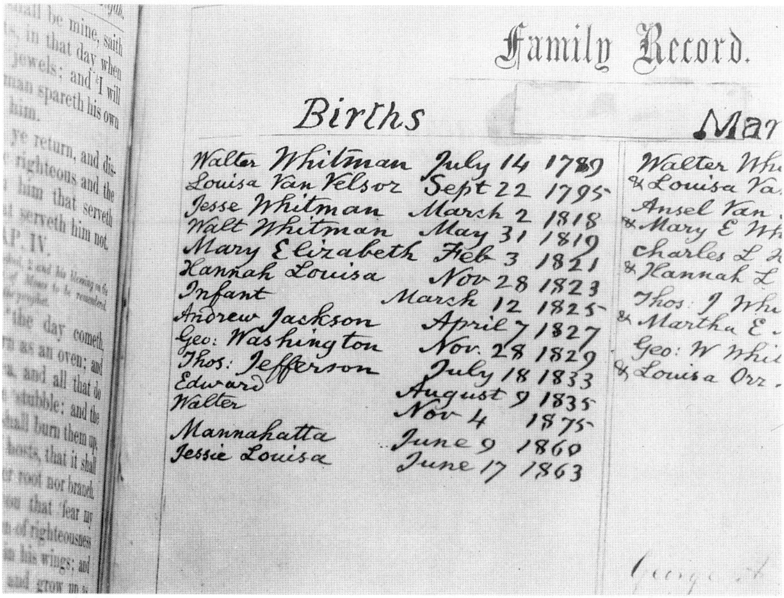

Whitman family Bible. Library of Congress.

Horace Traubel and other members of the "Walt Whitman Fellowship" before the offices of the *Long-Islander,* founded by Whitman in 1838. Library of Congress.

Above: Whitman's earliest daguerreotype, taken in 1840. Ed Folsom Collection.

Left: Park Benjamin, editor of the *New World.* Columbia University.

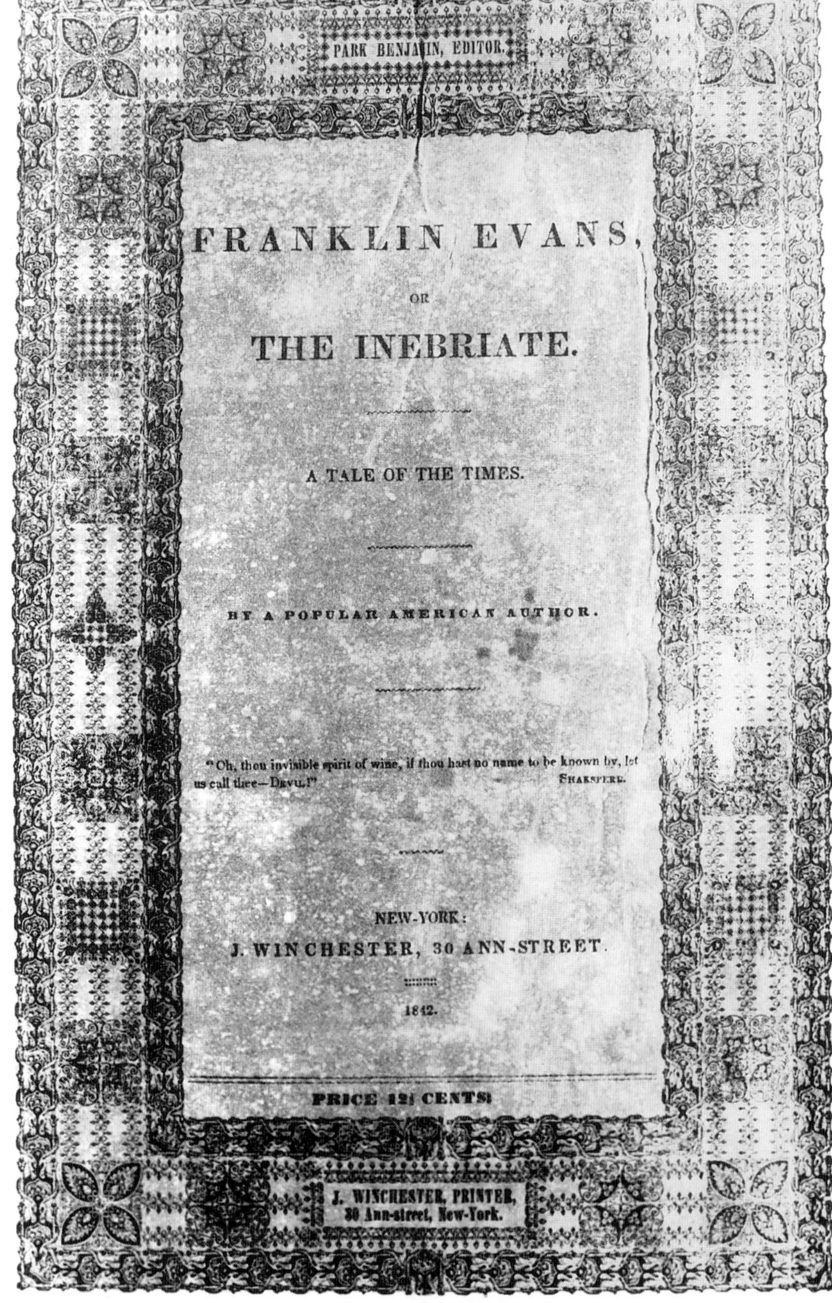

PARK BENJAMIN, EDITOR.

FRANKLIN EVANS,

OR

THE INEBRIATE.

A TALE OF THE TIMES.

BY A POPULAR AMERICAN AUTHOR.

"Oh, thou invisible spirit of wine, if thou hast no name to be known by, let us call thee—Devil!"
SHAKSPERE.

NEW-YORK:

J. WINCHESTER, 30 ANN-STREET.

1842.

PRICE 12½ CENTS.

J. WINCHESTER, PRINTER,
30 Ann-street, New-York.

Title page of *Franklin Evans.* University of Texas at Austin.

The St. Charles Theater in New Orleans, where Whitman saw the "Model Artists" and General Zachary Taylor. Courtesy of The Historic New Orleans Collection, Museum/Research Center.

ST. CHARLES EXCHANGE HOTEL, NEW ORLEANS, La
LESSEES – MUDGE & WILSON – 1846.

Above: The St. Charles Hotel in New Orleans, where Whitman frequented its lavish bars. Courtesy of The Historic New Orleans Collection, Museum/Research Center.

Right: Whitman in New Orleans in 1848. Walt Whitman House, Camden, N.J.

Opposite, top: Croton Reservoir. New-York Historical Society.

Opposite, bottom: Whitman in 1854. Engraving by Samuel Hollyer, used as the frontispiece for the 1855 and 1856 editions of *Leaves of Grass.*

Walt Whitman
from life
1855

Leaves of Grass.

I CELEBRATE myself,
And what I assume you shall assume,
For every atom belonging to me as good belongs to you.

I loafe and invite my soul,
I lean and loafe at my ease .... observing a spear of summer grass.

Houses and rooms are full of perfumes....the shelves are crowded with perfumes,
I breathe the fragrance myself, and know it and like it,
The distillation would intoxicate me also, but I shall not let it.

The atmosphere is not a perfume.... it has no taste of the distillation .... it is odorless,
It is for my mouth forever .... I am in love with it,
I will go to the bank by the wood and become undisguised and naked,
I am mad for it to be in contact with me.

The smoke of my own breath,
Echos, ripples, and buzzed whispers .... loveroot, silkthread, crotch and vine,
My respiration and inspiration .... the beating of my heart .... the passing of blood and air through my lungs,
The sniff of green leaves and dry leaves, and of the shore and darkcolored sea-rocks, and of hay in the barn,
The sound of the belched words of my voice .... words loosed to the eddies of the wind,
A few light kisses .... a few embraces .... a reaching around of arms,
The play of shine and shade on the trees as the supple boughs wag,
The delight alone or in the rush of the streets, or along the fields and hillsides,
The feeling of health .... the full-noon trill .... the song of me rising from bed and meeting the sun.

Facsimile from the 1855 *Leaves of Grass;* a page set in type by the poet himself.

99 Ryerson Street today: where the first *Leaves of Grass* was completed. *New Yorker,* June 12, 1995, p. 99. Courtesy of Ken Schles.

Above: Louisa Van Velsor Whitman, the poet's mother, in 1855. Ohio Wesleyan University.

Right: Ralph Waldo Emerson, about the time he greeted Whitman "at the beginning of a great career."

☞ The Poems of

LEAVES OF GRASS,

PUBLISHED BY THE AUTHOR,

May be ordered at any Book-Store or Newspaper Depot, or especially of

FOWLER & WELLS, 308 Broadway, New York.

Their place of business is the principal Agency for the Work, wholesale and retail. A note written to them, giving the writer's address, and enclosing $1 00, will procure a bound copy, post-paid, by return mail.

They supply Booksellers at a liberal discount.

'LEAVES OF GRASS' may also be purchased or ordered by mail, or the country-trade supplied, from the following *Agencies:*

BOSTON, . . . Fowler, Wells & Co., 142 Washington St.
PHILADELPHIA, Fowler, Wells & Co., 231 Arch street.
BALTIMORE, . . J. W. Bond & Co.
TORONTO, (Ca.,) Maclear & Co.
BUFFALO, . . . T. S. Hawks.
" . . . A. Burke, Jr.
CINCINNATI, . . F. Bly.
CHICAGO, . . . R. Blanchard.
ST. LOUIS . . . E. K. Woodward.
NEW ORLEANS, J. C. Morgan.
SAN FRANCISCO, George M. Bourne, M.D.

FOREIGN AGENCIES.

LONDON, . . . Horsell & Co., Oxford St.
PARIS, ... H. Bailliere & Co.
BRUSSELS, . . . William Good, Antwerp.

☞ Any communication by mail, for the author of Leaves of Grass, can be directed to him, namely,

WALT WHITMAN, care of

FOWLER & WELLS, 308 Broadway, New York.

Advertisement for the 1856 edition of *Leaves of Grass.* University of Texas at Austin.

Opposite, top: Henry David Thoreau in 1856. Concord Free Public Library.

Opposite, bottom: Ada Clare, the Queen of Bohemia, at Pfaff's. From Albert Parry, *Garrets and Pretenders: A History of Bohemianism in America* (New York: Dover, 1933), 15.

Above: Whitman in 1860, used as the frontispiece for the 1860 edition of *Leaves of Grass.* Ohio Wesleyan University.

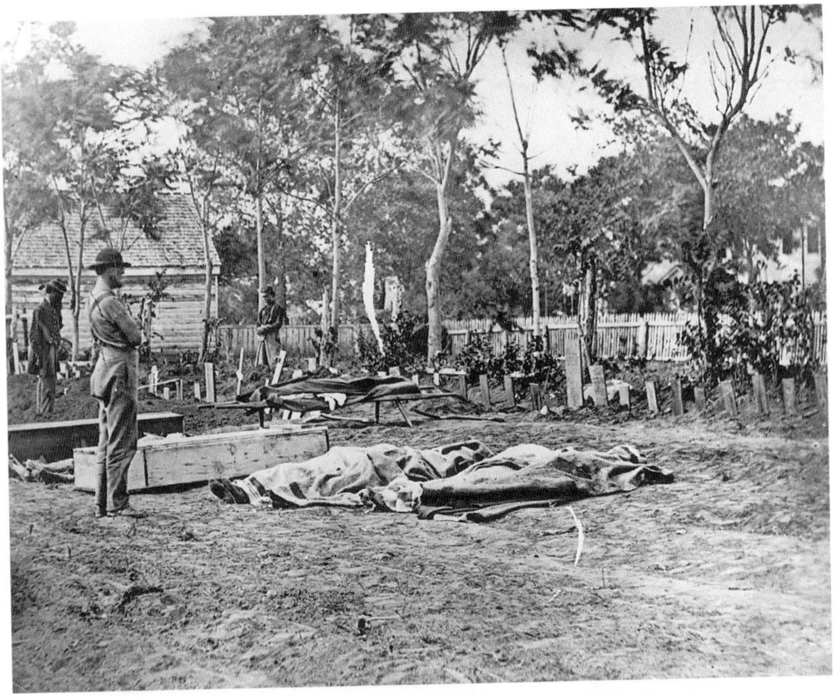

Opposite, top: The dead ready for burial at Fredericksburg. National Archives.

Opposite, bottom: The interior of Carver Hospital, now the site of Howard University. National Archives.

Above: George Washington Whitman after the New Bern campaign in 1862. Duke University.

General Ferraro's staff, including George Whitman, far right on the steps. National Archives.

Antietam Battleground, where George Washington Whitman fought in 1862. Library of Congress.

Opposite: Whitman in 1863 in Washington, D.C. Photograph by Matthew Brady. Ohio Wesleyan University.

Above: Tobacco warehouse, Danville, Virginia, where George Whitman was imprisoned during the Civil War. Library of Congress.

The United States Patent-Office Department, Washington, D.C., which housed the Bureau of Indian Affairs.

Lincoln's funeral cortege in Manhattan, on Broadway passing City Hall, April 24, 1865. New-York Historical Society.

The Hon. James Harlan, who fired Whitman from his clerkship in the Bureau of Indian Affairs in 1865 for being a "dirty poet." National Archives.

The Hon. James Speed, attorney general at the time of Whitman's dismissal from the Department of the Interior. National Archives.

The Grand Review of May 23, 1865. Painting by Frank Wright, 1990–91.

8

THE NEW AMERICAN BIBLE

❋ ❋ ❋

One book, last summer, came out in New York,
a nondescript monster which yet had terrible eyes and buffalo strength,
and was indisputably American.

RALPH WALDO EMERSON
to Thomas Carlyle, May 6, 1856

In the spring of 1856 Whitman was getting ready to put the second edition of *Leaves of Grass* to press. He was now committed to writing a literature fit for "These States." "It seems to me quite clear and determined," he told himself in a diary entry, "that I should concentrate my powers [on] 'Leaves of Grass'—not diverting any of my means, strength, interest to the construction of anything else." Whitman had crossed the Rubicon and was undeterred by hostile critics, whose attacks he almost relished. He included a cranky review from the *London Critic* in the "Opinions" section of "Leaves-Droppings," an appendix to the 1856 edition, published in September. "Is it possible," asked the *Critic,* "that the most prudish nation in the world will adopt a poet whose indecencies stink in the nostrils?"[1] Whitman had already managed to generate a good many reviews for the first edition, and it became his lifelong habit to get his book featured in the press, either anonymously or through the work of others, such as John Burroughs and William O'Connor. Among the authors to whom he sent copies of *Leaves of Grass,* however, only Emerson had responded, and it was the Concord transcendentalist's letter that rekindled his ambition and encouraged him, in the face of ridicule and contempt to continue his new literary program.[2]

True to the promise in his letter to the poet of July 21, Emerson had struck his tasks and visited Whitman in Brooklyn on December 11, 1855.[3] Thirty-three years later Whitman vividly remembered the event for Horace Traubel: "I shall never forget the first visit he paid me—the call, the first call." The Whitman family was then still living on Ryerson Street. "I can hear his gentle knock still," Whitman said, simulating the sound by faintly rapping on the arm of his chair. "My mother stood by the door: and the words, 'I came to see Mr. Whitman.'" Emerson was back in New York City to give another lecture, possibly in Brooklyn again. He invited Whitman to dinner and suggested they return to the Astor House, where Emerson usually stayed when he visited New York. Instead of taking the horse cars back down Myrtle from Ryerson Street to the ferry, the two authors made the three-mile trip by foot—"the long stroll," Whitman noted, "being very happy, memorable."

The Astor House was an ironic place for Emerson and Whitman to meet. On the one hand, it afforded all the Victorian comforts expected by a person of Emerson's social stature. On the other, the two were surrounded by the American working class that Whitman (and Emerson, after his fashion) had celebrated. At the hotel there was an embarrassing moment when the clerk—one of the "roughs" Whitman had been encouraging since the "Sun-Down Papers"—refused to admit the casually dressed Whitman to Emerson's hotel room while Emerson was rechecking his travel plans. Afterward, Emerson found Whitman still waiting in the lobby. He seemed put out with the clerk's refusal, but Whitman defended the man's position, easily persuading Emerson to let the matter pass. "Did Emerson see it? I should say so—like a flash. . . . saw everything, literally everything, in right perspective—things personal, things general." It has been claimed that Whitman may have been loud, or acting the part of his "noisy fire-engine society," and this may be partly true. Whitman remembered that they "got into some discussion at dinner. . . . sometimes things would get hot, stormy (for us): we differed sharply in some things—never hesitated to express our differences—doing so this day rather loudly."

One subject was the national character of the British Isles. Emerson tended to favor the English average over the Scots-Irish. Whitman disagreed, thinking not merely of the feats of the Scots but also of the power and humanity of the Irish, whom he had defended as editor of the *Eagle.* Emerson retorted, "I like the English—I do not like the Scotch so well: and as for the Irish . . ." Here he stopped and glanced awkwardly at Whitman because the waiter, standing near their table, was Irish, then only one economic level above black freedmen. Today, we might scoff at Emerson for his class prejudice, but Whitman (perhaps giving himself the better image here) appreciated the consideration Emerson showed the man. Their frank talk extended to Emerson's asking Whitman whether his intimacy "with anybody in any crowd" was ever misunderstood, but Emerson probably did not refer to Whitman's unauthorized publication of Emerson's letter in the *Tribune.*[4] There would have been no constructive reason for Emerson to bring up the matter, and he could not have known (could he?) that Whitman was already thinking of reprinting the letter again and more prominently, linking Emerson forever to *Leaves of Grass,* in the 1856 edition.

Emerson's approval had persuaded Whitman to exploit the situation. On the bottom of the spine of the second edition, a smaller but much thicker volume of 384 pages and twenty new poems, he crowded in the words in gold lettering, "I Greet You at the / Beginning of A / Great Career / R W Emerson." This stunning announcement to a literary world that cherished rhyme and reasonable behavior glittered beneath the name of the poet and his book—from each of which hung a leaf or clover that looked (or looks to the Freudian imagination) mildly phallic. Whitman's little-known holograph of the Emerson letter (see frontispiece) follows the same reparagraphing the poet used in the text reprinted in "Leaves-Droppings," accompanied by an open letter to Emerson. In copying the frontispiece version (which he sent to Moncure Conway in England on July 21, 1870—the fifteenth anniversary of the date of Emerson's original letter), he wrote "long foreground" as "large foreground."

Curiously, no record exists of either Whitman's sending Emerson a personal copy of the 1856 edition, whose spinal comment implicitly credited the New Englander with championing twenty new poems he had never read, or Emerson's receiving such a copy. Apparently, Whitman thought the open letter would get to Emerson on its own (which it did through several outraged Bostonians).[5] Moreover, he never sent Emerson a personal letter in response to the one he so liberally quoted in support of his second edition. "Here are thirty-two Poems, which I send you, dear Friend and Master," he told the possibly astonished Emerson in his open letter, "not having found how I could satisfy myself with sending any usual acknowledgment of your letter."

Missing from this edition was the Preface, which had been prominent in the first edition. Whitman debated with himself again and again over the need for a preface as he prepared new editions of his book, ultimately rejecting the use of anything more than a prefatory remark in the subsequent editions of *Leaves of Grass*.[6] It was unusual anyway, if not unprecedented, for a book of poetry to have an introduction, as if the poet were formally introducing himself. He had already reviewed himself, and the second edition carried his three self-reviews among the nine of the first edition. He slightly altered the one from the *Brooklyn Daily Times* of September 29, 1855, to read that the author of *Leaves of Grass* "is not prejudiced one mite against the Irish" and "talks regularly with niggers."

Whitman did not abandon politics to write *Leaves of Grass*. In the surviving printer's proofs to *The Eighteenth Presidency!* he talks of "dough-faces" (recalling his 1850 poem "Song for Certain Congressmen"); the attempted renewal of slave trade, or the importation of slaves from other countries, particularly Cuba; and the fact that the founding fathers were "declared abolitionists" (echoing his assertion in the first issue of the *Freeman* that the slave-holding Jefferson had been an abolitionist). He announces that his call for freedom would be heard as far away as "the archipelagoes, Australia,"[7] (anticipating the 1856 title of "To a Foil'd European Revolutionaire," originally called "Liberty Poem for Asia, Africa, Europe, America, Australia, Cuba, and the Archipelagoes of The Sea"). Add to these facts that the original title of "I Sing the Body Electric" was "Slaves," and we can see that at this juncture Whitman was introducing into poetry more than unconventional verse.

The poet's hardy family, having moved once again and now residing on Classon Street, didn't know what to think of yet another edition of poems from Brother Walt. When the first edition appeared, Whitman's mother guessed "that if [Longfellow's] Hiawatha was poetry, perhaps Walt's was." "No one of my people," Whitman recalled, though only partly correct, "—the people near to me—ever had any time for Leaves of Grass." He was not alone, however, in his excitement over the book. The distributors and de facto publishers of the first edition, the phrenologists Fowler & Wells, were almost as enthusiastic about the second edition. Yet before they put their full weight behind it, they insisted that Whitman cleanse it of "certain objectionable passages." (Whitman later told John Burroughs, who put the information in his 1867 book on the poet, that the objectional piece was "Poem of Procreation," retitled "A Woman Waits for Me" in 1867.) Otherwise, they said they would not "publish" his new edition. Since they did sponsor it, we have to assume that Whitman made the required changes, marking the first time he bowed to censors—long before he agreed to expurgation in the English edition of 1868.[8]

On August 16 Fowler & Wells placed a wordy advertisement in *Life Illustrated,* their weekly magazine, announcing the new poet as a "fixed fact" in the American literary spectrum. Conceding, curiously, that the first "volume was clumsy and uninviting, the style most peculiar, the matter (some of it at least) calculated to repel the class whose favorable verdict is supposed to be necessary for literary success," these first agents of Whitman's lifelong literary campaign bragged falsely, as Whitman did in his open letter to Emerson, that the first edition had sold a thousand copies (when in fact only 795 had been printed and few had actually been sold).[9] They also joined Whitman in exploiting Emerson's letter, saying the first *Leaves* had received the "emphatic commendation of America's greatest critic." Once the second edition was actually published in September, they ran another advertisement in the *Tribune* for almost the entire month of September—this one containing a slightly erroneous physical description of the book:

A small, thick, & col. green and gold, 400 pp., 24 mo.,
handy for pocket, table or shelf:
WALT WHITMAN'S "LEAVES OF GRASS" New. Vol.
(Thirty-two poems)

This was no ineffective sales effort. Greeley's *Tribune* boasted the largest daily circulation in America, and *Life Illustrated* had at the time a distribution of more than 75,000 copies.[10]

Few others could have brought off such a literary or public relations coup. Whitman's success reflected his experience as a veteran of the press and his renown as a feature writer. He had been appearing regularly in the pages of *Life Illustrated* since November 1855 with a piece entitled "The Opera." The next issue carried his essay on Dr. Henry Abbott's Broadway Museum of Egyptian Antiquities. In January 1856 he returned to admonish his readers about the middle-class showiness of Grace Church in Manhattan, which he had criticized in the *Eagle.* In April he appeared with two articles, "America's Mightiest Inheritance [the English language]," and "Decent Homes for Working-Men." He dusted off the summer with a series of articles under the general heading of "New York Dissected," which covered everything from the illegal slave trade to giving "Advice to Strangers."

These essays have been known to students of Whitman since the 1930s, when they were collected by Emory Holloway, but Whitman's relationship with *Life Illustrated* and its phrenologist editors did not end with the publication of the second edition in September. It continued that fall with two of the poet's most interesting prose pieces. "Greenwood Cemetery," which appeared in September, describes one of the sylvan showcases of Brooklyn in Whitman's day.[11] For more than a century, this "metropolis of the dead" with its "forest flourishes" would continue to acquire occupants, including not only the poet's father but Horace Greeley, Henry Ward Beecher, and a host of other nineteenth-century dignitaries. Seemingly everyone in New York, or at least Brooklyn, wanted a plot there. One "old gentleman," Whitman wrote, "brought with him from Italy a piece of marble and an artist." Upon arriving home, he bought a plot in Greenwood for ten dollars, "had a suitable pedestal made, and placed his marble self upon it." "He frequently visits his grave," Whitman quipped, "and is fond of exhibiting the statue to his friends." Critics have often complained, not entirely incorrectly, that Whitman was without humor, but this passage is clearly an example of his wit. Generally, however, the relentless democrat in Whitman overwhelms other concerns. In making fun of the pretentious and vulgar monuments in Greenwood, he also takes pride in "the *best* monuments . . . erected by admiring comrades and a grateful public to the memory of firemen, pilots, and captains, who lost their lives in rescuing infants and women from the fire or from the flood."

In November Whitman crossed over to Manhattan to devote an essay to Broadway. He had already included a short piece on the avenue in *Life Illustrated* under the general heading of "New York Dissected," and here he developed the topic into a full-blown analogy with the Mississippi River. Whitman had not yet written his many short poems in salute to Broadway, but the grand pathway had always interested, and fascinated, him as much as the Brooklyn Ferry. "Broadway," he wrote in "Broadway, the Magnificent!" "will never fail in riches, arts, men, women, histories, stately shows, morals, warnings, wrecks, triumphs—the profoundest indices of mortality and immortality."[12] It was, like the United States it mirrored, "essentially the greatest poem."

❋ ❋ ❋

Whereas the first edition of *Leaves of Grass* is mainly about freedom, the second edition introduces the idea of unity of all things, all humankind. This unity included women. Directly after "Poem of Walt Whitman, an American" ("Song of Myself") the poet placed "Poem of Women," later entitled "Unfolded Out of the Folds." Its theme is that nothing is possible without women and their procreative and nurturing gifts. Whitman has long been celebrated for his equal treatment of women and especially his delight in recognizing their potential, particularly when they become mothers ("there is nothing greater than the mother of men," he says in "Song of Myself"). But it has been overlooked that this attitude, not prominent in the first edition, was shaped mainly in 1856 after the poet fell in with the company of protofeminists and utopianists. Clearly, "Poem of Women" reflects their impact on the poet's imagination. A man, even a poet, "is a great thing upon the earth, and through eternity," Whitman wrote in No. 2 of his second edition, "—but every jot of the greatness of man is unfolded of women."

The most intimate of these women was Abby Price, who lived in Brooklyn beginning in 1856. She had come from the Raritan Bay Union, a Fourierist or socialist conclave near Perth Amboy, New Jersey, founded by Marcus Spring, the wealthy Quaker abolitionist who had arranged Emerson's Brooklyn lectures in 1850. Before that she had spent eleven years at the Hopedale Community in Massachusetts, a Christian socialist community active since the 1840s in challenging the status quo of American social, political, and economic structures. Whitman may have heard of Price or first seen her name listed in Greeley's *Tribune* in 1851 when she was a speaker at the second national women's rights convention in New York City. Her home in what is now the Brooklyn Heights area became a salon of sorts for social idealists and reformers. Whitman, as Abby's daughter Helen remembered, spent many hours in this company.

"Although he talked of music and books with me," Helen remembered, "and of politics, patriotism, and the news of the day with Mr. A. [George B. Arnold, a local Unitarian minister and believer in spiritualism], it was in talking with my mother on the spiritual nature of man, and on the reforms of the age and kindred themes, that he took special delight." She remembered that her mother and Whitman had "similar sympathies and tastes."[13] Whitman also took an interest in Abby's home sewing business, if not in her husband's pickle factory. No doubt, he saw her frequently in the company of her former women's rights conventioneers, Paulina Wright Davis, Ernestine L. Rose, Lucretia Mott, Anna Q. T. Parsons, and Sarah Tyndale, the last an abolitionist from Philadelphia. Whitman's praise of Tyndale in a letter the next year suggests his affection for this group of reformers. "I often recall your visits to me," he told her, "and your goodness. I think profoundly of my friends—though I cannot write to them by the post office. I write to them more to my satisfaction, through my poems."[14]

Whitman's personal experiences went into this volume just as they had fleshed out the first edition. In "Broad-Axe Poem" ("Song of the Broad-Axe") he uses almost verbatim the hyperbolized self-description of the phrenologically perfect individual found in "Walt Whitman, A Brooklyn Boy," one of the anonymous reviews of the first *Leaves* that was sewn into the first and second editions. We remember that Whitman had appended his 1849 phrenological reading to that review; now in the second edition it became poetry. Phrenology strikes the modern reader as mildly absurd, and Whitman himself was skeptical, but many people believed in it in the 1850s. Whenever Fowler & Wells sponsored a phrenology lecture series, as they often did at the Columbian Hall in Manhattan or Trenor's Dancing Hall in Brooklyn, thousands attended.[15]

Whitman speaks in "Broad-Axe Poem" of a place "Where women walk in public processions in the streets the same as the men." The phrase no doubt had its origin in Abby Price's statement of the credo of the second women's national rights convention in 1851, to wit: "We assume the position that all human beings in order to fulfill their highest destiny should be usefully and agreeably employed: That the right to liberty of choice with regard to avocation is equally inherent in male and female."[16] The broad-axe, the symbol of American progress westward, also meant progress for women.

> Her shape arises!
> She, less guarded than ever, yet more guarded
> than ever,
> The gross and soiled she moves among do not
> make her gross and soiled.
> . . . .
> She too is a law of nature, there is no law greater
> than she is.

In "Broad-Axe" Whitman describes himself perhaps more egotistically than representatively (he removed the description after the 1860 edition of the poem):

> Arrogant, masculine, naive, rowdyish
> . . . .
> Of pure American breed, of reckless health, his
> body perfect, free from taint from top to toe,
> free forever from headache and dyspepsia,
> clean-breathed,

Ample-limbed, a good feeder, weight a hundred
 and eighty pounds, full-blooded, six feet high,
 forty inches round the breast and back
. . . .
Never offering others, always offering himself,
 corroborating his phrenology,
Voluptuous, inhabitive, combative, conscientious,
 alimentive, intuitive, of copious friendship,
 sublimity, firmness, self-esteem, comparison,
 individuality, form, locality, eventuality.

Generally, the first edition, appendices included, inseminated the second. By the time the reader came to "Poem of Procreation" ("A Woman Waits for Me"), it must have seemed a "dirty book" indeed. Here this voluptuous, inhabitive, combative lover of the flesh and spirit announces that "A woman waits for me" who contains everything. "I draw you close to me," he says.

I do not hurt you any more than is necessary for
 you
. . . . .
I dare not withdraw till I deposite [*sic*] what has so
 long accumulated within me.

By poem No. 28, "Bunch Poem" (the title refers to semen), Whitman speaks of "The poems of the privacy of the night, and of men like me." He even envisions his own penis as a poem—"This poem, drooping shy and unseen, that I always carry, and that all men carry." Entitled "Spontaneous Me" in 1867, this poem must have shocked even the poet's own family, who later vaguely disapproved of the "Children of Adam" series, which it clearly anticipates. George Whitman once referred to the latter as being of "the whore-house order."[17]

Pulling more energy from the first edition, this time from his 1855 Preface, he insists in "Poem of Many in One" ("By Blue Ontario's Shore") that "By great bards only can series of peoples and States be fused into the compact organism of one nation."[18] In "Poem of the Road" ("Song of the Open Road"), the theme is friendship, or "adhesiveness" (the phrenological term), orchestrated in anticipation of the more personal "Calamus" poems of the third edition.

It is "Sun-Down Poem" ("Crossing Brooklyn Ferry"), however, that is Whitman's greatest celebration of the transcendentalist unity of existence and certainly the crown jewel of the 1856 edition. Here is a poem Whitman had been preparing all his life. He had found the idea for its first title as far back as 1839 in the "Sun-Down Papers, From the Desk of a Schoolmaster." The idea of "crossing" (symbolizing not a passage but the eternal ebb and flow of life) is already in the 1856 version of the poem, if not yet its title. Read in its original position in the second edition, following "Poem of You, Whoever You Are" ("To You") with its second-person frankness and intimacy, "Sun-Down Poem" gives up its meaning almost immediately. The poet focuses on what it is to be alive in Brooklyn and New York and at the same time part of the greater life of humanity across the ages.

> I too lived,
> I too walked the streets of Manhattan Island, and
> bathed in the waters around it;
> I too felt the curious abrupt questionings stir with-
> in me,
> . . . . . .
> I too had been struck from the float forever held
> in solution,
> I too had received identity by my body.

Two audiences are addressed here: not merely Whitman's contemporaries but more emphatically readers "scores or hundreds of years later" (who today note that it is as if the poet is reading the poem over their shoulder).[19]

In what is now famous as "Crossing Brooklyn Ferry," Whitman celebrates and underscores with parallel lines and repeated phrases the unity of life that cannot be denied or defeated.

It avails not, neither time or place—distance
avails not,
I am with you, you men and women of a generation, or ever so many generations hence,
I project myself, also I return—I am with you,
and know how it is.

Just as you feel when you look on the river and
sky, so I felt,
Just as any of you is one of living crowd, I was
one of crowd,
Just as you are refreshed by the gladness
of the river, and the bright flow, I was
refreshed,
Just as you stand and lean on the rail, yet hurry
with the swift current, I stood, yet was hurried,
Just as you look on the numberless masts of ships,
and the thick-stemmed pipes of steamboats, I
looked.

Later, in the "Brooklyniana" essays, he would debate the merits of Manhattan and Brooklyn, but here he describes the spiritual commerce between the two competing cities (where he had almost equally divided his residence over the past twenty years). There is the possibility of crossing and re-crossing until the two become one like everything else in the universe. Death is not the end, merely compost for the next life—the theme of another new poem in the second edition, "Poem of Wonder at The Resurrection of The Wheat" ("This Compost").

❋ ❋ ❋

John Burroughs maintained—and the poet himself may have thought as he wrote his second edition—that Whitman's acceptance as a great poet would happen only when the criteria for poetry changed. In the open letter to Emerson in the 1856 edition, one of Whitman's biographers has noted, Whitman tried to redefine American poetry and the

American poet.[20] Whitman's brand of poetry would be in high demand in the future he foresaw, when it would be based on the emerging American imagination as it was brought forth by the emerging print technology and book distribution. "Of the twenty-four modern mammoth two-double, three-double, and four double-cylinder presses now in the world, printing by steam," he told the unmechanically minded Emerson in his letter, "twenty-one of them are in These States." The country's 12,000 bookshops, large and small, he said, were prophetic. "What a progress popular reading and writing has made in fifty years! What a progress fifty years hence." As in "Sun-Down Poem," the present glistened in the reflection of its future image. "The time is at hand when inherent literature will be a main part of These States, as general and real as steam-power, iron, corn, beef, fish."

Emerson was now irrevocably linked to this language (and printing) experiment, but he wasn't quite prepared to sell literature in the open market of the popular press or at its subterranean, pornographic level. There were parts of the "book" (probably the second edition, which he had *not* praised in writing) he told Moncure Conway, his recent emissary to Whitman in Brooklyn, "where I hold my nose as I read." He thought the examples of the beauty of nature Whitman chose could sometimes have been more sanitary. Emerson was never prepared to go as far as Whitman on what he termed the American "infidelism about sex." We don't have Emerson's reaction to seeing his words emblazoned on the spine of the 1856 edition or the full text of his letter in its appendix, but Whitman's misuse of the letter in this fashion must have given him at least slight pangs of regret. In a letter about Whitman to Thomas Carlyle, he hedged his bet slightly. "I thought to send you," he wrote on May 6, 1856, a "nondescript monster" of a book with "terrible eyes and buffalo strength." But he didn't mail it, he said, because the book "throve so badly with the few to whom I showed it." On second thought, however, he decided to send Carlyle a copy, with the admonition that if the English writer thought it "only an auctioneer's inventory of a warehouse," he could "light [his] pipe with it." To Caroline Sturgis, an old friend whose poetry he admired, Emerson referred to *Leaves of Grass* as "one strange book" with an "unpromising portrait on the frontispiece," but he insisted that it was "the best piece of American philosophy that any one has had the strength to write, American to the bone." The book, he admitted, was also characterized by "some crudeness" and "weary catalogues of things like a warehouse inventory."[21]

On October 12, 1856, another New England literary aristocrat, James Russell Lowell, wrote to Charles Eliot Norton, a Harvard lecturer and an anonymous but favorable reviewer of the first *Leaves of Grass:* "Whitman—I remember him of old; he used to write for the *Democratic Review* under O'Sullivan. He used to do stories then, à la Hawthorne. No, no the kind of thing you describe won't do. When a man aims at originality he acknowledges himself consciously unoriginal, a want of self-respect which does not often go along with the capacity for great things. The great fellows have always let the stream of their activity flow quietly—if one splashes in it he may make a sparkle, but he muddies it too, and the good folks down below (I mean posterity) will have none of it." Later, as editor of the *Atlantic Monthly,* Lowell published Whitman's "Bardic Symbols" ("As I Ebb'd with the Ocean of Life"), but he insisted that two lines graphically describing a corpse be removed. Lowell was enforcing Emerson's "better judgment"—a reflection of his New England Brahmin environment and mind-set—which ultimately, in 1874, excluded Whitman's poems from *Parnassus,* Emerson's all-time best-selling book and anthology of "favorite" poems. But the Emerson who threw caution to the winds in his Divinity School Address also recognized that *Leaves of Grass* contained "fine stories of genius & unforgettable things."[22] He suspected that the "folks" down posterity's stream would treasure the book.

Whitman's literary reputation grew significantly in the late 1860s and 1870s with the English edition of *Leaves of Grass* and the approving essays by Moncure Conway, William Michael Rossetti, Edward Dowden, and Anne Gilchrist. Whitman's earliest English sympathizer, however, was Richard Moncton Milnes, or Lord Houghton. Houghton told Nathaniel Hawthorne on June 30, 1856, that a new American book had just fallen into his hands. "It is called 'Leaves of Grass,' and the author calls himself Walt Whitman. Do you know anything about him? I will not call it *poetry,* because I am unwilling to apply that word to a work totally destitute of art; but, whatever we call it, it is a most notable and true book. It is not written *virginibus puerisque;* but as I am neither the one nor the other, I may express my admiration of its vigorous virility and bold natural truth. There are things in it that read like the old Greek plays."[23] Hawthorne's response, if any, is lost.

Two other New Englanders, Amos Bronson Alcott and Henry David Thoreau, visited Whitman in the mid-1850s. Whereas Emerson had made his visit to Whitman before the appearance of the second edition, these two came afterward. Since he had encouraged their visits, Emerson may not have been as annoyed by Whitman's misuse of his letter as contemporaries and subsequent literary historians have thought. Alcott was spending the late fall and winter in New York City, and Thoreau was staying across the river at the former Raritan Bay Union in Perth Amboy. Ironically, the author of *Walden* (1854)—an account of his two years, two months, and two days in a one-man Utopia—was surveying the property of the failed New Jersey commune for its conversion into a community of small private estates called "Eagleswood."[24] Alcott, whom Emerson once called "an intellectual *torso,* without hands or feet," was slightly less egocentric than Thoreau and certainly had less to lose in confronting the strange genius from Brooklyn whom Emerson had been promoting to his friends. But Whitman's open letter in the 1856 edition, where he called Emerson "Master," may have threatened Thoreau's sense of territoriality with the "Master." Ultimately both Thoreau and Whitman denied or understated the importance of Emerson's influence on their work.

Although Emerson left only the scantest record of his visit to Brooklyn in December 1855, Alcott left one of the fullest accounts we have of the poet's demeanor and personality at the height of his poetic creativity. When he and later Thoreau and others visited the Whitman house, now at 91 1/2 Classon Avenue, in the newly rising suburbs of Brooklyn—even farther out on Myrtle Avenue than Ryerson—the poet was writing or about to write some of his greatest "pomes" (as he pronounced the word to Alcott), which would not make their debut until the 1860 edition of *Leaves of Grass.* Alcott first met Whitman on the afternoon of October 4, 1856, and spent a couple of hours with the newly announced poet. Whitman recalled that Alcott stayed for a dinner involving "a fine bit of beef," prepared by Mrs. Whitman, and revealed himself a vegetarian.[25] The tall, slim New Englander found Whitman "to be an extraordinary person, full of brute power, certainly of genius and audacity, and likely to make his mark on Young America"—a nationalistic literary movement spearheaded by Melville's anonymous praise of Hawthorne's genius in 1850 and the promotional writings of Everet Duyckinck (Melville's editor at Harpers) and Cornelius Mathews, a literary wild man popular at the time.

Whitman gave Alcott a complimentary copy of the second *Leaves of Grass* and asked him to write back his impressions as well as any news he had of Emerson. Alcott thought Whitman "not so easily described." "Broad-shouldered, rouge-fleshed, Bacchus-browed, bearded like a satyr, and rank," Alcott recorded in his journal, "he wears his man-Bloomer [baggy trousers] in defiance of everybody." His open collar revealed a red-flannel night shirt, at once covering and exposing the poet's "brawny neck." Over this Whitman wore a "striped calico jacket" with a "Byroneal" collar, finished off with coarse cloth overalls, cowhide boots, and "a slouched hat, for house and street alike." The poet was inquisitive yet shy with Alcott, "as if fearing to come short of the sharp, full, concrete meaning of his thought" (as if that would have bothered the dreamy Alcott). "Has never been sick," Alcott concluded that day's record, "nor taken medicine, nor sinned; and so is quite innocent of repentance and man's fall."

The father of the future author of *Little Women* was much taken with Whitman and quietly encouraged his literary efforts both during the war and afterward, when he purchased a later edition of *Leaves of Grass* from the poet in Camden.[26] Slightly more than a month after his first visit to Whitman, Alcott returned to Classon Avenue, bringing along Thoreau, only to find the poet not at home. They found his mother Louisa instead, who spoke of what a good and wise boy her son had been and how "his four [*sic*] brothers and two sisters loved him, and how they take counsel of the great man he is grown to be now." Walt, she said, had always stood up—as we know from his *Eagle* and *Freeman* days—"for the weaker against the stronger." She urged them to return early the next day when they "should be sure of finding him at home and glad to see us."

✻ ✻ ✻

The following day, November 10, the two came back as promised in the company of Sarah Tyndale, described irreverently by Alcott as a "solid walrus of a woman." This time the visitors were escorted up two narrow flights of stairs and crowded into an attic bedroom occupied by the poet and his youngest brother, Eddy. The first thing they saw was an unmade bed in one corner, showing still the impression of its recent occupants, "and the vessel scarcely hidden underneath. A few books were piled disorderly over the mantel-piece, and some characteristic pictures—a Hercules, a Bacchus, and a satyr—were pasted, unframed upon the rude walls." In the company of the recently famous Concord saunterer and the voluminous Mrs. Tyndale, Whitman was even more hesitant and shy than before with Alcott alone. Looking at the unframed pictures, Alcott asked which one best represented the new poet. Whitman begged him with a mixture of modesty and egotism not to put his questions "too close," but Alcott merely took that to mean Whitman thought he was a combination of all three mythical personae. He added in his journal: "I think he might fairly, being himself the modern Pantheon—satyr, Silenus, and him of the twelve labours—combined."

Whitman loosened up and told them of visiting the public baths daily even in midwinter, riding atop omnibuses up and down Broadway "from morning till night beside the driver," dining afterward with "whipsters," attending the opera, and living to write poetry and "nothing else particularly." But when Alcott tried to put Whitman in more direct communication with Thoreau, once the party had come downstairs and seated themselves in the parlor, Whitman tightened up again and his entrenchment was matched by Thoreau's lockjaw unsociability. "Each seemed planted fast in reserves, surveying the other curiously," Alcott recorded, "like two beasts, each wondering what the other would do, whether to snap or run, and it came to no more than cold compliments between the two." He wondered whether each threatened the other's sense of superiority—"Whether Thoreau was meditating the possibility of Walt's stealing away his 'out-of-doors' for some sinister ends, poetic or pecuniary . . . , or whether Walt suspected or not that he had here, for once, and the first time, found his match, . . . a sagacity potent, penetrating and peerless as his own, if indeed not more piercing and profound, finer and more formidable."

Thoreau also received a signed copy of Whitman's second edition, perhaps in exchange for one of the 706 copies of the remaindered *A Week on the Concord and Merrimack Rivers* (1849), and his impression of the poems shows that he was more objective about Whitman than Whitman would be about him—later Whitman remembered that he found Thoreau personally likable but also a tad morbid and undemocratic.[27] Thoreau had read the poems of the first edition of *Leaves of Grass* before visiting Whitman, and that impression, combined with his reading of the second, apparently led him to tell his close friend Harrison Blake that Whitman was "the greatest democrat the world has seen. Kings and aristocracy go by the board at once." During his meeting with Whitman, he asked him, "Do you have any idea that you are rather bigger and outside the average—may perhaps have immense significance?"

Thoreau admired the poem later called "Song of Myself," and he liked the best poems in the 1856 volume, including "Sun-Down Poem" ("Crossing Brooklyn Ferry"), but he was less happy with the sexual poems, "2 or 3 pieces in the book" that, he said, "are disagreeable to say the least, simply sensual." He who had courted the beautiful Ellen Sewell (until her father rejected both Thoreau and his brother John as suitors) said Whitman "does not celebrate love at all. It is as if the beasts spoke," adding that men were not ashamed of their libidinous urges without reason. Yet even here he thought the poet spoke "more truth than any American." He found the poems "exhilarating" and "encouraging" and thought the book might ultimately be less sensual than it initially appeared. "I do not so much wish that those parts were not written," he told Blake, "as that men & women were so pure that they could read them without harm." And he thought *Leaves of Grass* worth more than "the sermons so-called that have been preached in this land."[28] This last observation would have delighted the would-be orator.

In *Leaves of Grass,* Whitman had challenged the current standards of decency in literature. Following Emerson the transcendentalist, who said that nature was an emblem of the Oversoul, or God, and that everyone therefore was divine, Whitman reasoned that everyone was not only spiritually but also politically equal. This idea eventually gave the self-proclaimed Poet of Democracy license to celebrate all aspects of nature, including human sexuality. With Whitman's *Leaves*, even the body and its "disagreeable" parts figured into the celebration of life, which had been previously marked by poems that hastily transcended the flesh for the sentimental. In the days before electricity, when it was unsafe to leave open-flame lights burning throughout the house, a family typically gathered round one central lamp, while the father or the mother read a story or a poem aloud—Bryant's "Thanatopsis," for example, or even Longfellow's "A Psalm of Life," which exalted the spirit over the flesh. As brilliant and original and sincere as *Leaves of Grass* was, it couldn't be read in such company. This was the problem Emerson and Thoreau came up against whenever they were "exhilarated" by reading Whitman's book. They were finally aloof from its sexual parts. Emerson, Thoreau, and Alcott, Whitman remembered, "all had the same manner. . . . they meant me to see they were willing to come only so far: that coming an inch beyond that would mean disaster to us all."[29]

⁂ ⁂ ⁂

Sometime in the spring of 1857, and possibly until the spring of 1859, Whitman started contributing to the *Brooklyn Daily Times* (formerly the *Williamsburgh Daily Times* until the borough of Williamsburgh, near Brooklyn Heights, was absorbed by the city of Brooklyn). Since the publication of *I Sit and Look Out: Editorials from the Brooklyn Daily Times* (1932), edited by Emory Holloway and his graduate student Vernolian Schwarz, biographers have accepted their claim that Whitman was the editor of the paper, while generally ignoring the facts that (1) the empirical evidence for such a claim is almost nonexistent, and (2) most of the editorials are politically conservative at a time when Whitman was radicalizing American poetry in theme as well as manner.

The argument that Whitman was the editor instead of a frequent or even occasional contributor is based on the following evidence. First is

Whitman's reply of January 19, 1885, to Charles M. Skinner, one of his successors as editor of the *Brooklyn Eagle,* about his duties on the *Times.* Whitman said that he "worked as an editorial writer . . . along in 1856, or just before"—not between 1857 and 1859 as the editors of *I Sit* allege. Whitman remembered arguing, as he had in Bryant's *Evening Post,* for a waterworks in Brooklyn.[30] Holloway and Schwarz assert that Whitman was fired from his position at the *Times* by founding owner George C. Bennett in 1859 for "articles which were very unfavorably criticized by ministers and church people" and also by Bennett himself.[31] However, in his letter to Skinner, Whitman remembered Bennett as "a good, generous, honorable man"—hardly the words of a dismissed employee, regardless of the lapse of time since the firing. There was, as we shall see, an article on female sexuality that might have offended the community's more delicate sensitivities, but its author may not have been Whitman.

The second supporting document is an article in the *Atlantic Monthly* in 1903 entitled "Whitman as an Editor,"[32] in which Skinner asserts that Whitman's tenure on the *Times* was not long because ("It is said") certain orthodox clergymen objected to his editorials. The most casual perusal of Skinner's article reveals he knew little or nothing about Whitman's association with the *Times.* The *Atlantic Monthly* piece simply echoes Brooklyn gossip handed down from local legend and focuses mostly on Whitman's editorship of the *Brooklyn Eagle,* where such information was readily available to then editor Skinner. Third, when the *Times* celebrated its sixtieth anniversary on February 28, 1908, it featured the reminiscences of a German immigrant and poet named Frederick Huene, who had worked in the composing room of the *Times* when Whitman supposedly edited it. He remembered Whitman rather accurately as "a tall, well-built man [who] wore high boots over his pants, a jacket of heavy dark blue cloth, always left open to show a woolen undershirt, and a red handkerchief tied around his brawny neck." He also recalled Whitman's having trouble with the local deacons and resigning "his place in consequence of articles which were unfavorably criticized." Nowhere in his reminiscence, however, does Huene state that Whitman was more than a contributing editor or freelancer—only that he "often came upstairs and walked up and down on the part of the floor where the job office was located." He did similar pacing as editor of the *Aurora* in 1842, but Huene says that Whitman was pacing near "where the job office was located," not the editor's office, suggesting that Whitman's contributions were piecework.

This is the only way to explain how Whitman could have been connected with the paper when it was publishing editorials that were so diametrically opposed to what he was writing in the first and second editions of *Leaves of Grass*—as well as previously in the *Star, Eagle,* and *Freeman.* As one critic has astutely observed, there is "less of Whitman in the [*Brooklyn Times*] than there had been of him in his previous papers—less of his personality; fewer of his personal convictions, activities, and stylistic idiosyncrasies."[33] The *Times* editorials are generally conservative on social questions, whereas the pre-*Leaves of Grass* journalism often called for some kind of change in the status quo. In the 1840s on the question of capital punishment, for example, Whitman came close to the radical positions that the editor of the *Times* deplored in the mid-1850s. As editor of the *Eagle,* he bemoaned the death penalty in general and the execution of the condemned Wyatt in particular. A decade later, on November 13, 1858, he—or at least the editorial (not included in *I Sit*)—thought that if New York was to have the death penalty, it should be carried out swiftly so that the "romantic penny-a-liner and sympathetic old ladies" would not have time to argue for executive clemency. And the poet who had so recently, in the first edition of *Leaves of Grass,* alluded to the forbidden subject of female sexual desire in what is now Section 11 of "Song of Myself" and who in the second edition celebrated the same subject in "Poem of Procreation" supposedly came out against female education in an editorial entitled "Our Daughters" on September 25, 1857, which stated that it was wrong, "as the records will show, to expose these impressible intellects—to the miscellaneous associations of one of those caravanseras [*sic*] denominated boarding schools. . . . Educate them at home. In that way they will keep clear of many temptations."

"Can All Marry?" of June 22, 1859, was probably the editorial that got Whitman fired, if he was fired or if he even wrote the piece. Like the "twenty-ninth bather" in Whitman's poem, "ugly women" in "Can All Marry?" contemplate sexual intercourse, even if it is out of wedlock. Yet this radical idea is clothed in the misogynistic concept of women as mere social and sexual commodities for whom crocheting and crossword puzzles are inadequate releases from the libidinous urge. It is difficult to imagine that an author who speaks in the same essay of "hard-featured visages" of old maids would have been comfortable in the company of middle-aged feminists and overweight abolitionists at the Abby Price gatherings.[34]

Comparison of the editorials selected for *I Sit* with their originals in the *Times* reveals inaccurate transcriptions as well as silent omissions. In explaining Whitman's sudden conservatism in the mid-1850s, the editors suggest that he had matured and "at last found himself."[35] The implication here, made in the wake of the successful Bolshevik Revolution in Russia and in the midst of the Great Depression in the United States (when reforms tainted with socialism were about to be attempted by the Roosevelt administration), is that Whitman was reversing himself, or at least backpedaling, on social issues. As the editor of the *Eagle,* for example, Whitman averred that African slaves bled and wept just like white people. Yet in correctly attributing the editorial entitled "Prohibition of Colored Persons," *I Sit* silently omits three paragraphs that, when restored, reduce the editorial from the racial bigotry it has foisted upon Whitman's reputation to the level of casual racism shared by opponents of slavery, including Lincoln, who though he "freed the slaves" considered blacks inferior to whites.[36] Published in the *Times* on May 6, 1858, the *I Sit* version of the editorial supporting the proposed Oregon constitution forbidding "colored persons, either slave or free, from entering the State" presents the following paragraph as the third instead of the sixth:

> Who believes that the Whites and Blacks can ever amalgamate in America? Or who wishes it to happen? Nature has set and [*sic*] impassable seal against it. Besides, is not America for the Whites? And is it not better so? As long as Blacks remain here, how can they become anything like an independent or heroic race? There is no chance for it.[37]

There is little doubt that Whitman is the writer of this editorial. And there is no question that this statement, with or without further context, is racist, but the objection to blacks is primarily based upon the free-soil notion that—as Whitman wrote in the *Eagle* of September 1, 1847—"the *workingmen* of the free United States . . . are not willing to be put on the level of negro slaves."[38] Without the missing paragraphs in "Prohibition of Colored Persons," however, the statement about the amalgamation of "Whites and Blacks" presents the objection as the personal belief of a writer opposed to blacks on any basis whatsoever within the United States. But in fact—true to the epiphany he experienced when he heard the abolitionist speaker at the end of 1847 (see Chapter 4)—Whitman finds the Oregon proposal necessary not because he believes blacks inferior or distasteful but because the *American people* will never accept their full integration on any basis.

Following the paragraph quoted above (and included in the *I Sit* version), Whitman writes: "Yet we believe there is enough in the colored race, if they were in some secure and ample part of the earth, where they would have a chance to develope [*sic*] themselves, to gradually form a race, a nation, that would take no mean rank among the peoples of the world. They would have the good will of all the civilized powers and they would be compelled to learn to look upon themselves as freemen, capable, self-reliant, mighty." But he also concludes that "all this, or any thing toward it, can never be attained in the United States."

Whitman believed that only blacks would help blacks, never whites, because of their ingrained prejudice that extended beyond the free-soil issue. "Can any person of moral and benevolent feelings, then," he asks in one of the paragraphs missing from the *I Sit* version of "Prohibition of Colored Persons," "countenance such a plan as the total exclusion of an unfortunate race, merely on account of their color, or because there is a prejudice against them? No, not if there were a shadow of a hope that battling against this prejudice will ever succeed in rooting it out in America. But taking a deep and wide view of the whole question, the answer might perhaps be Yes—strange as it sounds at first." Then follows the question, no longer so rhetorical, "Who believes that the Whites and Blacks can ever amalgamate in America?" Unfortunately, he also speaks about "impassable seal against it," ordained by "Nature." It appears that he believes that white prejudice is *natural* as well as unavoidable. Thus: "As long as

Blacks remain here, how can they become anything like an independent and heroic race? There is no chance for it."

There is a distinction to be made, therefore, between the narrator of "Song of Myself" who assists a runaway slave and the free-soil editorialist who is a reluctant advocate of segregation. Whitman apparently hated slavery more than he loved black slaves. And in this conflicted state of mind, he resembled most other white nineteenth-century Americans, who opposed slavery but were not convinced that blacks were equal to whites. During the first two years of the war, Lincoln dared not allow the Radical Republicans to declare the Civil War a war on slavery, lest he alarm the majority of northern whites whose military support he needed to restore the integrity of the Union.

❊ ❊ ❊

In 1858, however, the poet was still conflicted somewhat between poetry and oratory. We don't know the facts, but only their poetic results. Although he had been ebullient about *Leaves of Grass,* he soon began to think again of oratory and of "founding a *new school* of Declamation/Composition." He determined to "practice and experiment" until he found a more "flowing, *appropriate speaking, composition style,* which requires many different things from the written style." Having written "America's Mightiest Inheritance" for *Life Illustrated* in 1856, he began to gather notes on language, posthumously published as *An American Primer* (1904).[39] About the same time he may have tried to sell his political tract, *The Eighteenth Presidency!* For some reason, the pages of *Life Illustrated* became unavailable to him (the piece would have been too long for Bennett's *Times,* which did not publish separate supplements), but the 7,000-word screed in support of Republican presidential candidate John C. Fremont got only as far as proof sheets—somewhere, perhaps in Rome's print shop.

Whitman had also been embarrassed the previous year by a bad debt of $200 owed James Parton, a journalist and biographer who had recently married Fanny Fern. According to his own testimony, Whitman paid the debt, or most of it, with cash and art possessions, including a painting by Jesse Talbot, the now deceased artist from Whitman's circle of artist-friends in 1850. Parton settled for these goods and apparently a few more, charging no interest (but $16 for legal fees). It is doubtful, then, that Whitman wrote the editorial, often attributed to him, of July 9, 1857, which denounced the kind of education that would enable women to become "authoresses and poets" by saying, "One genuine woman is worth a thousand Fanny Ferns." Moreover, Fern (Sara Payson Parton) had written one of the earliest favorable reviews of the first *Leaves of Grass.*[40]

Finding himself out of steady work in the economic depression of 1857, Whitman may have started drinking again—regularly—something he apparently had not done since 1840. Despite (or perhaps because of) the use of Emerson's letter in the second edition, it had not sold any better than the first. Many copies were either given away or lost. He began to spend more time in New York City, riding up and down Broadway alongside his teamster friends, visiting them in the old New York Hospital at the foot of Broadway facing Pearl Street, or sitting alone with a glass of beer against the back wall of Pfaff's cellar restaurant and saloon, which was partially nestled under Broadway just north of Bleecker Street.[41]

Leaves of Grass had not only been excoriated in the press but had been made the butt of friendly jokes among his newspaper acquaintances at the *New York Press,* near Pfaff's. Often the regulars made light of the book in the poet's presence. Whitman went along with and even enjoyed (so he said) the amusement at his expense, as when he was greeted with a quote from a critical review of his book: "Here comes the unclean cub of the wilderness!" But he also remembered his deeper, adverse reaction to the book's hostile reception by the literary establishment. "I don't know," he told Traubel, "if you have ever realized it—ever realized what it means to be a horror in the sight of people about you: but there was a time when I felt it to the full—when the enemy—and nearly all were the enemy then—wanted for nothing better or more than simply, without remorse, to crush me, to brush me, without compunction or mercy, out of sight, out of hearing: to do anything, everything, to rid themselves of me."[42]

It is difficult to understand how the poet could have felt so put upon, or paranoid, at the same time he was making the following bold plans with regard to his next book of poems. He jotted down the following notation to himself in June, 1857:

> *The Great Construction of the New Bible.* Not to be diverted from the principal object—the main life work—the Three Hundred & Sixty five [poems].—it ought to be ready in 1859.[43]

He who had proclaimed in 1855 that "there will soon be no more priests" now thought to fulfill his prophecy. Such ups and downs of the spirit indicate that Whitman's late-1850s "slough" was probably episodical. If we accept the probability that he was not regularly employed by the *Times* between 1857 and 1859 (Whitman's only signed contribution, and that identified only with his initials, is a letter to the editor dated March 14, 1857), we can better understand the poet's state of mind. Indeed, it was partly his depression that produced the finest poems of the 1860 edition of *Leaves of Grass,* poems that he probably wouldn't have had the time to write if he had been busy as a full-time newspaper editor. Rather, he probably worked mainly as a copyist and freelance journalist, occupations that had served his literary ambition in the past and would again during the war.[44]

The hospital work, for which the poet became famous in his lifetime, began during this period with the care of disabled stage drivers. At that time Broadway, originally an Indian trail, had been developed as far north as Union Square, but there were no cable or horse-drawn trolley cars, only stagecoaches driven by skillful teamsters generally, like Whitman, from the countryside of Long Island. Whitman was always drawn to this brawny type of American innocence, and as one eyewitness to the poet's Broadway and Pfaff's days noted, they were "a set of men by themselves."[45] Typically, a driver worked winter and summer on grueling shifts of twenty hours, six days a week, carried, as one contemporary remembered, "all kinds of passengers, and [was] always in imminent danger of collision at certain parts of his trip" on the congested routes. Whitman was "constantly" seen perched atop the box alongside such men as they maneuvered their wagons up and down the cobblestoned and granite avenue. He helped them collect fares, for there were no conductors in those days. One of the doctors in the hospital where the whipsters frequently ended up without anything like medical insurance or compensation for missed days remembered Whitman dressed in garb matching that in Alcott's description. Evidently, the "Good Gray Poet" was gray before the war. "His hair was iron gray, and he had a full beard and mustache of the same color. His face and neck were bronzed by exposure to the sun and air. He was large, and gave the impression of being a vigorous man." Vigorous or not, Whitman probably did not—as some have suggested—take disabled drivers' places at work because the poet, though country-bred, lacked the technical skills required of the Broadway drivers.

The same doctor accompanied Whitman to Pfaff's, where bohemian writers gathered around Henry Clapp, the editor of the influential *Saturday Press* (powerful mainly because it shared most of the literary market with the equally new *Atlantic Monthly*—the publications being only two and three years old in 1860). Such restaurants (Raffelty's at 20 Church Street was another he frequented) were quite common along Broadway in those days—cramped subterranean vaults, with white walls highlighting a bar, an oyster stand, and several stalls filled usually with men only. Whitman later compared Pfaff's in size to his Mickle Street bedroom. Perhaps because it lacked white walls, it didn't look as spic-and-span as most of the other establishments, and it had tables instead of stalls. At one of these tables William Dean Howells, fresh from Ohio and his first encounters with the literary Brahmins of New England, allegedly met Whitman, who "reached out his great hand to me, as if he were going to give it me for good and all."[46] But William Winter, one of the regulars at Pfaff's, later challenged Howells's recollection, insisting Howells never once visited the dusky establishment. Howells, who published a number of short poems in the *Saturday Press,* claimed to have seen some of the Pfaffians (and perhaps Clappians, for Clapp was a heavy drinker who died in the gutter of alcoholism in 1875) "just recovered from a fearful debauch," their "locks still damp from the wet towels used to restore them," but Winter, who shared Howells's dislike of *Leaves of Grass,* replied that his comrades from the literary saloon weren't sots—they were so poorly paid as writers that they couldn't afford to get drunk.[47]

Winter's remark supports the assertion that the only literary set Whitman was ever truly comfortable with was one made up of writers with humble backgrounds, like those anthologized by Brenton in *Voices from the Press* in 1850.

The bar frequently filled with such figures as Ada Clare ("the Queen of Bohemia"), E. C. Stedman, Fitz-James O'Brien, George Arnold, William Winter, John Swinton, Artemus Ward, Ned Wilkins, Adah Issacs Menken, Thomas Bailey Aldrich, and of course Henry Clapp ("the King of Bohemia"). Apparently, Pfaff's was one of the few saloons in the city that welcomed women, or at least women like Ada Clare, a liberated beauty from Charleston, South Carolina, who was unabashedly proud of her illegitimate son by the composer and pianist Louis Moreau Gottschalk.[48] Many of the Pfaffians, or the *Saturday Press* set, died early of complications stemming from their hedonistic lifestyles, which included opium use—though Clare (née Jane McElheney) succumbed to a freak accident, and the brawling, loudmouthed O'Brien fell victim, ironically, to lockjaw resulting from a hastily bandaged wound during service in the Civil War.[49] One of the bohemians who did become well known, or "respectable," after he left New York for New England was Aldrich, whom Whitman later remembered as "the dainty book man." Swinton went on to distinguish himself as managing editor of the *New York Times.*

Whitman was never seen "tipsy," according to one hearsay source, but it is the same one that identified Whitman as the editor of the *Brooklyn Times.* His brother George, however, testified that he never saw Walt under the influence.[50] Even though he indulged, he may have been chastened enough by his experience in 1840 to know when to stop or how to do it moderately. About this time, he drafted (but never published) a poem about the Pfaff's cave and its inmates, entitled "The Two Vaults." The second vault is the drinker's early grave.

> The vault at Pfaffs where the drinkers and laughers meet to eat and
>   drink and carouse
> While on the walk immediately overhead pass the myriad feet of
>   Broadway
> As the dead in their graves are underfoot hidden

And the living pass over them, recking not of them,

. . . .

The lights beam in the first vault—but the other is entirely dark.

If Whitman was not altogether comfortable as a drinker, he was probably never completely at home either as a bohemian (said to "keep his boots and his cheese in the same drawer," quipped Ada Clare in her weekly column for the *Press*). As one literary historian put it, "Walt was a vagabond, but never a Bohemian . . . closer to the earth than the sidewalk."[51]

One of his best friends from the Pfaff's crowd was Swinton, but the Pfaffian Whitman valued most during that time was Clapp. After hearing the poet read "Out of the Cradle Endlessly Rocking," the *Saturday Press* editor published the poem as "A Child's Reminiscence" on December 24, 1859; he later worked tirelessly with the publishers of the third edition of *Leaves of Grass* to distribute review copies and to promote the book generally. Whitman emphatically told Traubel that one must know about Clapp to comprehend fully the history of *Leaves of Grass.* Like Emerson, Thoreau, and Alcott, Clapp did not accept *Leaves of Grass* "wholesale," but he wanted Whitman's poetry to receive a fair hearing. When Whitman's "Bardic Symbols" (later "As I Ebb'd with the Ocean of Life") appeared in the *Atlantic Monthly* in early 1860, Clapp congratulated him, saying that "papers all over the land have noticed your poem."[52]

Clapp followed up his publication of "A Child's Reminiscence" in the January 7, 1860, issue with a celebratory piece entitled "All About a Mocking-Bird," which answered an attack on the poem in the *Cincinnati Commercial* (reprinted in the same issue of the *Press*). "All About a Mocking-Bird" may have been written by Whitman. It shows the same intimate regard for *Leaves of Grass* as the poet's 1855 anonymous self-reviews, denigrating Old World themes and methods while at the same time suggesting a likeness with Homer. Rather than writing according to convention, it said, Whitman's "method in the construction of his songs is strictly the method of the Italian Opera." It also observed that *Leaves of Grass* thus far "has not yet been really published at all." By 1857 Whitman had counted a total of one hundred poems for the next *Leaves of Grass.* He began his search for a publisher by having Rome Brothers set up his new edition in type, creating what eventually became much of the printer's copy for the 1860 edition. Indeed, there is evidence that Whitman had composed some of the 1860 edition poems even before the publication of the second edition, suggesting that most of the poems of the first three editions of *Leaves of Grass* were born of the same mood or mystical spirit and were, with notable exceptions in the third, of a piece.[53]

Clapp also prepublished several of the other poems that went into the 1860 edition, before Whitman knew exactly how or when the third edition would be published. Besides "A Child's Reminiscence," the *Saturday Press* published "Chants Democratic No. 7" ("You and Me and To-Day") on January 14; "Calamus No. 17" ("Of Him I Love Day and Night") on January 28; and "Calamus No. 36" ("Earth! My Likeness!") on February 4. Each time a poem was published, it was followed relentlessly (in the *Saturday Press,* for Clapp felt even bad publicity was better than no publicity) by pseudonymous parodies now well known to students of Whitman—the most stinging of which was "Your and Mine, and Any-Day (A Yawp, After Walt Whitman)."[54]

Unknown until now, Clapp also published other poems from the 1860 edition-to-be in the *Press* of February 11. Entitled simply "Leaves," the three numbered verses combined two future "Calamus" poems (Nos. 21 and 37, "That Music Always Round Me" and "A Leaf in Hand") with No. 15 of the future "Enfans d'Adam" series ("As Adam Early in the Morning"). Today, the "Calamus" poems are thought by many to be homosexual chants, whereas the "Enfans d'Adam" ("Children of Adam" after 1860) are considered celebrations of heterosexual love (albeit from a strictly male point of view), but no one in Whitman's day ever publicly suspected homosexuality in the "Calamus" poems; it was the "Adam" poems that brought outrage. Whitman apparently, initially at least, drew no distinction between the kinds of love celebrated in each series, suggesting today either bisexuality or a view of heterosexuality comfortably allied with a degree of male bonding possibly not suspect as homosexuality in the nineteenth century.

❋ ❋ ❋

Clapp's publication of Whitman's poetry may have led directly to its Boston publication. The edition became a reality only a few months later, after Whitman received a letter from William R. Thayer and Charles W. Eldridge, a pair of upstart Boston publishers with abolitionist sympathies. The two progressives were cut from the same ideological cloth as the others who from the beginning admired *Leaves of Grass*—for example, the women's rights activist Abby Price and the abolitionist Sarah Tyndale. The same year that Thayer and Eldridge published *Leaves of Grass,* they also published an anti-slavery novel by William O'Connor and several works by James Redpath in defense of the recently executed John Brown.

"We want to be the publishers of Walt. Whitman's poems—Leaves of Grass," the two Bostonians proudly wrote on February 10. "When the book was first issued we were clerks in the establishment we now own. We read the book with profit and pleasure. It is a true poem and writ by a *true* man." They promised that they would sell "a large number of copies," which turned out to be true—or was becoming so until the war caused the firm's bankruptcy—for the first printing of one thousand copies sold out quickly that summer. A second issue was quickly printed, along with *Leaves of Grass Imprints,* a separately published pamphlet with sixty-four pages of reviews. A paperback edition and the little book of poems, *Banner at Daybreak* (perhaps the embryo for *Drum-Taps*), were on the drawing board.[55] Yet eager though they initially were, Thayer and Eldridge were cautious enough to promise only to publish works contained in the plates of the 1855 and 1856 editions. They were willing to consider new poems as well, but they wanted to read them first. Yet they were equally prepared to be thrilled with whatever Whitman sent them, and author and publisher quickly agreed on a contract giving Whitman 10 percent of net sales.[56]

Whitman went to Boston for the first time in his life around March 15, where he worked three hours a day reading proof for his book at his new publishers' offices at 114 and 116 Washington Street, near Boston Common. Part of the reason for Thayer and Eldridge's confidence is that the publishing company was also a wholesale bookseller, so that they could better control the distribution of their products.[57] They expected *Leaves of Grass* to be a "valuable investment," Walt told his brother Jeff near the end of his stay, "increasing by months and years—not going off in a rocket way, (like 'Uncle Tom's Cabin')." He told Jeff, who had just helped his mother and wife move into the latest Whitman family quarters, at Portland Street near Myrtle Avenue (the spot today absorbed by the thirty-eight-acre "Walt Whitman" low-income housing project), that he had had "a very fair time" in Boston, finding its citizens "friendly" and "generous." But the "great *cramper* of the Bostonian," he said, was "to be kept on the rack by the old idea of *respectability,* how the rest do, and what they will say." "Of course," he added with pride, "*I* cannot walk through Washington street, (the Broadway here,) without creating an immense sensation."

Whitman took in the sights of the city. He noticed and admired the way African Americans mingled freely with whites. There were fewer blacks in Boston than in New York or Philadelphia, he noted in his diary, and their status was different. "At the eating-houses," for example, "a black, when he wants his dinner, comes in and takes a vacant seat wherever he finds one—and nobody minds it." Whitman added that he himself as "much a citizen of the world" did not mind either. He attended an afternoon of the trial of abolitionist (and later literary gadfly) Frank Sanborn, suspected of aiding some of John Brown's followers in his ill-fated raid on the Federal arsenal in Harper's Ferry, Virginia. One day he came upon a painting by his brother-in-law Heyde hanging in a local gallery. On another, in April, he watched young men playing football in their shirtsleeves and pronounced it "a noble and manly game."[58]

During the very first week of his stay, in his humble $2/week room, the greatest Bostonian (certainly in Whitman's opinion), Emerson, came in from nearby Concord to see him. His ulterior motive was making sure neither his name nor his words were to be emblazoned on the cover of *this* edition of *Leaves of Grass.* But that little scandal had been more important to Emerson's "respectable" Bostonian friends than to the "Brahmin" who had grown up in reduced economic circumstances. "Emerson called upon me immediately," Whitman told Abby Price back in Brooklyn on March 29, "treated me with the greatest courtesy—

kept possession of me all day—gave me a bully dinner, &c."[59] Part of that "possession" involved a two-hour walk on the Common during which Emerson, who had apparently been allowed to read all or part of the next *Leaves of Grass,* tried in vain to get the poet to perform a little expurgative surgery. He wanted Whitman to excise the "Children of Adam" poems, the logical development of the poems in the 1856 edition that had discomfited Thoreau. Emerson quite rightly feared that Whitman was "in danger of being tangled up with the unfortunate heresy" of free love. He hoped Whitman would give his book an opportunity to sell instead of being condemned outright by the moralists of their day. Whitman responded that such a denunciation had already occurred—that indeed "worse heresies" had been charged against him.[60] We don't know what Whitman meant here, but he was probably alluding to Rufus Wilmot Griswold's contemptuous review of the first edition, where he had coyly raised the possibility of the poetry's homosexual subtheme. There is no record that the "Calamus" poems about the "adhesive" nature of male friendship ever came up for discussion that day.

The two did discuss the "Adam" poems, and Whitman held his ground, saying that to excise them from the book would be like a literary castration. "What does a man come to with his virility gone?" he asked. Emerson did not respond directly but took Thoreau's approach to the use of sexuality in the book by saying that he didn't think "anything in Leaves was bad," but that "people would insist on thinking some things bad." In spite of Emerson's repeated urgings ("he was the talker and I the listener," Whitman recalled), the poet gave Emerson essentially the same passive argument he (Emerson) had given to Henry Ware, Jr., following the alleged blasphemy in his Divinity School Address twenty-two years earlier. When pressed for a final response to the points against including "Calamus," Whitman told his former "Master," "Only that while I can't answer them at all, I feel more settled than ever to adhere to my own theory and exemplify it."[61] With this now famous discussion thus ended, the two poets dined at the American House.

Anonymously, either Clapp or Whitman reviewed the third edition of *Leaves of Grass* in the *Saturday Press* of May 19. As noted, Clapp was fully committed to the promotion of the book, even acting as book review distributor, because he hoped that Whitman's publishers might eventually underwrite his journal, which was always on the financial edge. The review made a clear distinction between poetry that rhymed "kisses" with "blisses" and persistently mourned dead infants and poetry that wasn't ashamed of its private parts or bored with the routine miracles of nature.

Clapp expected to follow up this support with a favorable review by Juliette H. Beach of Albion, New York, who had contributed at least one poem to the *Saturday Press* before the appearance of the third *Leaves* and one afterward.[62] But Mrs. Beach's husband apparently read the book first and sent in his own review, which the sometimes boozy Clapp mistook for hers and (without reading) sent to the printer.[63] "The suspense is ended," wrote the irate and perhaps jealous Mr. Beach in the *Press* of June 2. "The 'Distinctive American Poem'—the only one (God be thanked!) the country has yet produced—has appeared." The reviewer said that he had liked with a "degree of admiration" the first edition of *Leaves of Grass* but had read this one no further than the "Enfans d'Adam" poems without throwing the book down with disgust and incredulity. "Until such time as the novels of [Charles] de Kock find place upon parlor-tables, and the obscene pictures, which boys in your city slyly offer for sale upon the wharves, are admitted to albums, or grace drawing-room walls," the reviewer gasped, "quotations from the 'Enfans d'Adam' poems would be an offence against decency too gross to be tolerated."[64]

Clapp retaliated in the next issue by publishing "Manahatta" (ignoring Whitman's spelling with two *n*'s) and "Longings for Home." In response, as it were, to Mr. Beach's Victorian condescension and middle-class snobbishness about poetry and people, "Mannahatta" spoke of a city "solid-founded" with "Immigrants arriving, fifteen or twenty thousand in a week" to a "free city! no slaves! no owners of slaves"—

The city of such women, I am mad to be with them!
  I will return after death to be with them!
The city of such young men, I swear I cannot live
  happy, without I often go talk, walk, eat, drink,
  sleep with them![65]

Clapp included a note in the same issue (June 9) telling his readers that the offended reviewer was Mr. Beach.

Denied her publication, Juliette Beach reviewed *Leaves of Grass* privately in a letter to Clapp of June 7, until now unknown. The *Tribune* of June 5 had quoted part of her husband's review, and she now felt put in a "false position": "I like Leaves of Grass! I have the greatest faith in the book. Its egotism delights me—that defiant ever recurring *I,* is so irresistably strong and good." She thought that "No one can read the book earnestly . . . and fail to receive from it new life and strength." And she was disappointed that no "man of candor and ability" had come forth to defend the book. One should not try to say that one part of the book was good and the other offensive. "One can no more take the different parts and reconcile and arrange them to his satisfaction than he can reconcile and arrange to his satisfaction the puzzling yet harmonious laws of nature and the universe." Juliette Beach's praise anticipates Anne Gilchrist's epistolary review of the 1867 edition of *Leaves of Grass.* It also foreshadows the efforts of the "man of candor," William O'Connor, in suggesting the Christ parallel. "The king is here," she announced in her letter, "but his crown is withheld. It is not the first time such an event has occurred." She thought, however, and this was also Emerson's argument, that Whitman should have "sublimated" his profound thought so that it might stand a chance of general acceptance. Instead, "the majority of men will look at it in a personal light, and shallow women will giggle over it or hold up their hands in horror."

As Juliette Beach admitted in her next letter to Clapp, dated August 13, she fully intended for Whitman to read her praise. The letter was nevertheless confidential, and Whitman respected the caveat. If he had published it, as he did Emerson's encomium in the fall of 1855, Mrs. Beach would have found herself in roiling marital waters. The reason for her second (and promised last) letter to Clapp on the matter was her fear that Clapp and Whitman would not preserve the confidentiality of her interest. But then she went back to *Leaves of Grass* and its brave author. "I understand you to say," she inquired, "that neither you nor Walt Whitman believe in love." This was possibly the case with Clapp, who she felt had "two natures," but "with Walt's book before me, I should not believe it of *him* if he were to swear to it forever. I know he put his soul in that book, and the book *is* Walt Whitman; and if the man you know and see every day is not like that, then he is not the Walt Whitman I love, and alas! there is *no* Walt Whitman anywhere." Finally, she explained that she had not addressed her original praise directly to Whitman because she had promised her husband not to write to him. "Otherwise," she told Clapp, "I would have written him all I wrote you, and perhaps more. Believe me there is nothing which I so passionately and bitterly regret, (all the more passionately and bitterly because the regard is useless,) as the fact that I am a woman and therefore obliged to deny myself the happiness of Walt Whitman's friendship."[66]

Whitman later told Traubel that "the girls have been my sturdiest defenders, upholders" and that *Leaves of Grass* was "essentially a woman's book."[67] Earlier Ada Clare had dismissed William Winter's "much eulogized" "Song of the Ruined Man" as written by "a practiced versifier [who] might go on rhyming until the seas were dry." On the other hand, "Walt Whitman's 'Child's Reminiscence' could only have been written by a poet, and versifying would not help it. I love the poem." Another woman who came to Whitman's defense in the issue of June 9, Mary A. Chilton of Islip, Long Island, boldly signed her name to a letter that described Whitman as the "apostle of purity." In the *Saturday Press* issue of June 23, "A Woman" (perhaps the abused Mrs. Beach but more likely the wife of William Thayer, one of Whitman's publishers) declared: "All hail then to Walt Whitman, and to this grand result of creative genius, 'Leaves of Grass.'"[68]

Encouraged by the controversy, Whitman's publishers placed a column-long advertisement in the *Press* of June 30, listing the book's table of contents and printing (without either sources or quotations) more than a dozen endorsements. In the same issue the anonymous "Walt Whitman and American Art" appeared, probably intended to be taken as the paper's editorial but very possibly written by the editor's favorite poet at the time, Walt Whitman. A poet among poetasters, it said, Whitman had given the first extended picture of "life as we live it in America, where thought is not scholastic, where the influence of books is very little, of Nature very great." Whoever wrote the review had perhaps read Emerson's "Phi Beta Kappa Address," where it is observed that "books are for the scholar's idle times." When the American could read God directly in nature and experience, the hour was "too precious to be wasted in other men's transcripts of their readings."

Another person who showered praise on Whitman was William O'Connor, whose *Harrington* appeared that summer. O'Connor had admired *Leaves of Grass* from its first edition and found "astonishing beauty" in "A Child's Reminiscence" when he first read the poem in the *Saturday Press.* The future champion of Whitman and arch-enemy of his would-be censors first met the poet in Boston at Thayer and Eldridge's. "The great Walt is very grand & it is health & happiness to be near him," he told the Providence poet Sarah Helen Whitman (no relation to the poet). "He is so large & strong—so pure, proud & tender, with such an ineffable *bon-hommie* & wholesome sweetness of presence; all the young men & women are in love with him."[69] This was Whitman's effect on many, it appears. William Thayer and Charles Eldridge had known Whitman hardly a month before they were waxing in the same direction.[70]

With the third edition, Whitman determined to avoid the built-in publicity of the previous two. He no longer wanted anything to obscure "the *true* Leaves of Grass": "no other matter (no letters to or from Emerson—no notices, or any thing of that sort)."[71] But now with a publisher and a literary magazine behind him, the publicity campaign shifted out of the author's direct and complete control. Thayer and Eldridge took out at least two large advertisements for *Leaves of Grass* in the *Saturday Press* and published *Leaves of Grass Imprints.* Days after publication, they also sent Clapp more than a dozen copies for distribution to "the Editorial Fraternity," including Ada Clare and the consumptive Ned Wilkins, who having, as Whitman remembered, "the weakest voice I ever knew in a man," had courageously defended *Leaves of Grass* when it was attacked or parodied at Pfaff's one evening.[72] Hardly an issue of Clapp's weekly magazine did not carry an item, usually more than one, about the 1860 *Leaves,* not only positive reviews but at least two negative ones as well as parodies. Whitman apparently felt he had found in Clapp the person who could take over his promotion efforts. (This would be a pattern repeated with Burroughs, O'Connor, Bucke, and Traubel.)

Clapp, who had once studied French and lived in Paris, even published what were alleged to be excerpts from a French translation of the 1860 *Leaves.* Obviously cut from whole cloth, the "translation" suggests that Clapp was possessed by either a perverse sense of humor or a declining knowledge of the French language. When he printed excerpts from the "forthcoming" volume, the line from "Calamus No. 17" "And now I am willing to disregard burial-places" became "Et maintenant je suis disposé à me ficher de cimetières" (roughly the equivalent of "I don't give a shit about churchyards").[73]

When translated into the American fear of the body and sexuality, *Leaves of Grass*—and especially the section of fifteen poems entitled "Enfans d'Adam"—was, of course, "obscene" for its time. Yet the issue of obscenity has perhaps numbed our perception of the actual book and poems Whitman finally brought together. He called his "Adam" poems part of a "programme" against the Victorian "infidelism about sex," but he intended a broader "programme" in the 1860 edition—a "New Bible," which offered a "third religion." The 1855 and 1856 editions have been unfairly described as mere "collections of poems," whereas the 1860 *Leaves of Grass* is—perhaps equally unfairly—called "an articulated whole, with an argument."[74] It is true that Whitman was better prepared for this edition in that he now had time to think about structure and arrangement. On the other hand, the offer from Thayer and Eldridge came out of the blue, and he—though he had many poems set in type—may have rushed the final presentation (the lapse of time between the publishers' initial offer and publication was a matter of only ninety days).

The first edition talks about freedom, and the second about unity in nature. The third, however, addresses nothing in particular except the notion of the poet as a visionary, anticipating the "religious" poet of the 1870s and 1880s who—in "Passage to India," for example—sees the poet as the "son of God," instead of one with God. At best, the 1860 edition represents the collected works of Walt Whitman in 1860 and is to be distinguished not for structure, theme, or invention, but mainly for the addition of some of Whitman's best poems, including the already published "Out of the Cradle Endlessly Rocking," "As I Ebb'd with the Ocean of Life," the "Adam" poems, and the "Calamus" sequence. And these poems represent a departure in Whitman's focus from a celebration based on Transcendentalism to one based on the self in a world of ruthless change and unfulfillment. Whitman attempted autobiography in the third, indeed saw the removal of "Enfans d'Adam" as castration, but the book as a whole is fragmented by the recycling of old poems (and old themes) among new poems (and new themes) with no particular raison d'être.

"Proto-Leaf" (which later became "Starting from Paumanok") replaced "Song of Myself" as the opening poem.

> Born here of parents born here,
> From parents the same, and their parents' parents
> the same,
> I, now thirty-six years old, in perfect health,
> begin,
> Hoping to cease not till death.

Whitman in fact celebrated his fortieth birthday the month the poem containing these lines was published, indicating that he had composed some of the lines of "Premonition" (the title of "Proto-Leaf" in manuscript) during the time of the first and second editions. They are now part of the definitive version of "Song of Myself."

Even before the lines were excised, "Proto-Leaf" is a little stiff compared to "Song of Myself." Yet here at least Whitman holds on to transcendentalist principles.

> Was somebody asking to see the Soul?
> See! your own shape and countenance—persons,
> substances, beasts, the trees, the running rivers,
> the rocks and sands.

Whitman hit his nadir in the 1860 edition, however, with the "apostroph" to "CHANTS DEMOCRATIC and Native American," which follows "Song of Myself" (now cheekily called "Walt Whitman").

> O mater! O fils!
> O brood continental!

O flowers of the prairies!
O space boundless! O hum of mighty products!

O-O-O! for more than sixty lines, this hysterical poem is Whitman's worst catalog. It introduces twenty-one poems, but the best of the lot have been recycled from the 1855 and 1856 editions. "Poets to Come" (No. 14 in "CHANTS DEMOCRATIC") is the most notable new one, hinting at the new theme of the poet as the leader of the people, not simply the most representative of them. Other poets wait in the wings of literary history to be born so they can justify his poems and their celebration of democracy. He looks to the American future and expects to be "realized" in all the states, including Canada, which he thought would eventually become part of the United States. Indeed, if he is not, his message about freedom and democracy will be dead on arrival.

The next major section is, curiously, called "LEAVES OF GRASS." Of its twenty-four poems, only ten are new—and none of these is exactly distinguished. These are followed by five free-standing poems of which only one, "Poem of Joys," is new. Yet one—"A Word Out of the Sea"—is almost new. It is one of the poet's very best. This poem represents Whitman's return to Paumanok, to Long Island and his childhood, for memories necessary to understanding the present. His closest return previously was in 1855 in "There Was a Child Went Forth." The ultimate title of "A Word," "Out of the Cradle Endlessly Rocking," calls up the innocence of childhood; so does its title in the *Saturday Press,* "A Child's Reminiscence." This poem and its thematic companion, "As I Ebb'd with the Ocean of Life" (certified by Whitman when they appeared together under the heading of "Sea-Drift" in the definitive edition), present the poet as a fallen transcendentalist, overwhelmed like Emerson in his crisis-essay "Experience" by the particulars of life, human suffering, and individual death. The man-child cries, "O give me some clew!" Later it was changed to "the clew," indicating the loss of tension and the poet's return to a more traditional worldview of an ordered universe. The narrator of the poem emerges afterward with the knowledge, imparted by the sea of his evolutionary origins, that the only true songs are those of Love and Death. These two poles of existence work together to provide the conditions for freedom. When "A Word Out of the Sea" was published separately in the *Saturday Press,* it was reviewed there as if it were a book of poems. Stranded between the generally old and the new ("Enfans d'Adam" and "Calamus"), it introduces and encapsulates the private poet in the throes of sexuality and desire.

In "Enfans d'Adam" Whitman integrated old and new poems with much more success than he achieved in earlier sections of the book, perhaps because the series has an identifiable storyline or argument. Only three of its poems are old, and these—ultimately "I Sing the Body Electric," "A Woman Waits for Me," and "Spontaneous Me"—help to develop the idea of Adamic man waking up to his sexuality and using it. Perhaps, as "Once I Pass'd Through a Populous City" ("Enfans d'Adam" No. 9) suggests, Whitman was falling back on his New Orleans memories (of either real or imagined events) to celebrate the joys of heterosexual love.

> Once I passed through a populous city, imprinting
> my brain, for future use, with its shows, architec-
> ture, customs, and traditions;
> Yet now, of all that city, I remember only a woman
> I casually met there, who detained me for love
> of me,
> Day by day and night by night we were together,—
> All else has long been forgotten by me,
> I remember I say only that woman who passionately
> clung to me,
> Again we wander—we love—we separate again,
> Again she holds me by the hand—I must not go!
> I see her close beside me, with silent lips, sad and
> tremulous.

There is, however, evidence that the lover in the poem was once designated as male—"one rude and ignorant man who, when I departed, long and long held me by the hand, with silent lip, sad and tremulous."[75] When Emory Holloway first saw this version of the manuscript, he assumed (reluctantly) that the love described in the poem was originally inspired by the "Calamus" feeling and Whitman had revised it to conceal that fact.[76] Holloway did not concede, though, that "Calamus" meant "homosexual," but maintained that it was merely "manly love," permissible before the homophobia of the twentieth century. Today, we are less certain what that romantic convention of male adhesiveness meant. And that uncertainty, whether in the cause of socially suppressing homosexuality or accepting it, animates the twentieth-century reading of the "Calamus" poems in ways that Whitman may—or may not—have intended.

9

CALAMUS AND THE NATIONAL CALAMITY

My book and the war are one.

WALT WHITMAN
"To Thee Old Cause"

"Calamus" may have served as an emancipation proclamation for Whitman as dramatic as the one President Lincoln signed to free southern slaves in 1863. In the poems he speaks softly and lovingly of dear friends, males whose closeness made him absolutely joyous. He wonders who and what he is—admitting shame but declaring acceptance of himself just the same. "I am ashamed—but it is useless—I am what I am," he says in "Calamus" No. 9. Yet in No. 36 ("Earth! my likeness!"), he dares "not tell it in words—not even in these songs." Nevertheless, his "songs" provided a way to express feelings he otherwise concealed. The "one great difference between you and me, temperament and theory," he told John Addington Symonds on August 19, 1890, after Symonds had inquired about a homosexual theme in "Calamus," "is *restraint*—I know that while I have a horror of ranting & bawling I at certain moments let the spirit impulse, (?demon) rage its utmost, its wildest, damnedest." And he added in parentheses that should not underestimate its significance: "I feel to do so in my L of G. & I do so."[1]

What he did not put into *Leaves of Grass,* however, was an original sequence of twelve poems, which were dispersed among the forty-five in the 1860 edition possibly because they were too intimate and suggestive of homoeroticism. Entitled "Live Oak, with Moss" in manuscript, these poems appear in "Calamus" in the following order: 14, 20, 11, 23, 8, 32, 10, 9, 34, 43, 36, and 42. The secret sequence begins with the poet's burning desire for a lifelong lover who is male; he admits that, like the live-oak tree, he cannot live alone ("I Saw in Louisiana a Live-Oak Growing"). He anticipates his lover and hopes that his homoerotic feelings are shared throughout the world. Acknowledging that even poetry is not strong enough to absorb these feelings, he uses his pen to describe love between two males he espies. By "Live Oak" No. 8, he doubts that there is anybody else who, like himself, feels distracted by the need for a male lover. He dreams of a homosexual utopia ("the city of robust friends") and addresses its ideal lover. Such feelings, he now insists, are *natural,* yet there is also "something fierce and terrible" in them. No. 12 addresses the ideal "élève," who shares these homoerotic needs.[2]

Possibly like the unfinished stories of two bachelors (discussed in Chapter 3), this "Calamus" tale could not be completed for publication. Whitman chose to bury it in a broader celebration of Adhesiveness. And—in the nineteenth century—he got away with it. America was still publicly naive about, and not so fearful of, homosexuality. Then (and into the twentieth century) male children were often dressed up as little girls, with their hair grown long. Even the macho Ernest Hemingway, born in 1901, was costumed and coifed this way as a small child.[3] There existed in Whitman's day a romantic or sentimental convention of male friendship (admitting into print "Calamus" but not its "Live Oak, with Moss" sequence), which permitted same-sex touching and common sleeping arrangements. It is significant that William Michael Rossetti included thirteen "Calamus" poems in his selected (Rossetti's method of expurgation) edition of *Leaves of Grass* in 1868. More significant, the list of offensive poems in the Boston district attorney's attempted censorship of the Osgood edition of *Leaves of Grass* in 1881 included none from "Calamus."[4]

Today it seems we cannot read "Calamus" without thinking Whitman a homosexual. But anyone who thought that way in the 1860s held his tongue. Neither William O'Connor nor John Burroughs spoke of it. As late as 1910, Ellen O'Connor, who fell in love with the poet during the war and was perhaps in denial, provided Edward Carpenter, a homosexual, with an ingenious explanation of the poet's sexuality. Carpenter had suggested in *Days with Walt Whitman* (1906) that "Calamus" No. 8 ("Long I thought that knowledge alone would suffice me") was too personal and disturbingly revealing. (Much later—in his "Some Friends of Walt Whitman"—he welcomed the poem as evidence of the poet's homosexuality.) In No. 8 Whitman declares that he can no longer sing for America because "One who loves me is jealous of me, and withdraws me from all but love."

> I heed knowledge, and the grandeur of The States,
> and the example of heroes, no more,
> I am indifferent to my own songs—I will go with
> him I love,
> It is to be enough for us that we are together—We
> never separate again.

Recalling Carpenter's mention of the poem, which Whitman had withdrawn from all editions after 1860 (encouraging a later biographer to say it was "born of a mood, and must not be unduly exaggerated"), Ellen suggested it was the "key": "Change that pronoun for the feminine, and remember what he tells of his early life in New Orleans, and what he told *us*,—William and me,—and it gives a clue to much." She went on to suggest a "girl" who had clung to him, who perhaps followed him north, but whom he could never marry "for many reasons."[5]

According to the lore of Whitman scholarship, the only one of the poet's literary acquaintances to broach the question of the homosexual meaning of "Calamus" to the poet directly was the English critic John Addington Symonds, in a letter of August 3, 1890. Whitman answered with what seems a denial. Symonds was one of the very few, apparently, in the 1860s to admit that he thought he found a homosexual thesis, after first hearing "Calamus" No. 8 read aloud by a classmate at Trinity College, Cambridge. From that day forward, he considered *Leaves of Grass* his "Bible" because it ennobled his "abnormal inclinations" with the bracing concept of male comradeship. "I imbibed a strong democratic enthusiasm, a sense of the dignity and beauty and glory of simply healthy men."[6] Yet—as he confessed in the moonlight of an autobiography that would not see publication for almost another century—he could not finally exclude his physical desire for male lovers. In his copy of the 1860 edition, which he no doubt kept close to his side as he poured forth his lamentations for posterity, he wrote opposite Whitman's line in "Calamus" No. 41 ("I meant that you should discover me so, by my faint indirections") the following: "This is the true method wh[ich] I have failed in."[7]

Symonds, who never met the poet in person, first contacted him in Washington in a letter dated October 7, 1871, telling Whitman his poems had been his "constant companions" for the past six years. He enclosed his "Love and Death: A Symphony"—"which you may perchance detect some echo, faint & feeble, of your Calamus." Symonds, who described himself cautiously as "an Englishman, married, with 3 children," compared his poem with "Calamus" No. 2 ("Scented herbage of my breast. . . ."). Whitman's poem speaks of the torment of not being understood or appreciated and of the determination "to unbare this broad breast of mine—I have long enough stifled and choked." To Symonds, the poem spoke volumes on the torment he himself felt and would continue to feel throughout his fifty-three years on earth. The first of his three children was probably not conceived on his wedding night, when, he painfully recalled, "nature refused to show me how the act should be accomplished." Still an uninitiate before marriage both heterosexually and homosexually, he loved his wife for her gentle spirit but found the sexual touch of her body absolutely "nauseous."[8]

"Love and Death" suggested a new way of looking at male bonding, due no doubt to Symonds's immersion in Greek literature. Long before Oscar Wilde became fatally fascinated with the Greek fondness for boys, Symonds was quietly promoting Greek literature and life as a means of dignifying homosexuality—the way chivalry of the Middle Ages had canonized Petrarchan love conventions. For otherwise, he committed to his memoir, "Plato is injurious to a certain number of predisposed young men." Whitman's celebration in "Calamus" of what was ostensibly the romantic concept of male friendship gave this homosexual a comfort zone in the heterosexual world, he said, "even while I sinned against law and conventional morality."[9]

Whitman first wrote to Symonds on January 27, 1872. He placed "Love and Death" among "the loftiest, strongest, & tenderest"—saying he wanted to know Symonds better and promising to send him a copy of the 1871 edition of *Leaves of Grass.*[10] Symonds must have brooded a little when his favorite "Calamus" poem turned up missing from the new, 1871, edition of *Leaves of Grass* Whitman sent him, but the two kept up an intermittent correspondence till the end of the poet's life. Even afterward Symonds wrote to Traubel, though here he was mainly concerned that the poet's disciples were getting up an edition of letters *to* the poet. He had heard, no doubt, of Whitman's unauthorized publication of the Emerson letter, which would have served well enough as a precedent for such a book (which was in fact never undertaken). Fearful of English laws against pederasty and homosexuality in general, much tougher in England and America—as he once told Whitman—than in France and Italy, Symonds conceded to Traubel that he had told Whitman "things about my own past life (with the object of [showing] how he had helped me), wh[ich] were not meant for the eyes of the public, & the diffusion of which would not only cause me great pain, but would also provoke me to a violent attack on Whitman's literary executors."[11]

Although what Symonds was referring to in his Whitman correspondence seems at first readily apparent, in the absence of the entire correspondence between the two, it is ultimately simply puzzling. In his most notorious extant letter to Whitman, Symonds dances around the issue of homosexuality for himself personally as he begs Whitman to say something definite regarding whether "Calamus" allows for "the possible intrusion of those semi-sexual emotions & actions which no doubt do occur between men." Addressing Whitman as "My dear Master," he did not ask for his approval of homosexual relationships but merely whether the poet was "*prepared to leave them to the inclinations & the conscience of the individuals concerned.*" His need to know was not personal, he insisted in what the poet must have interpreted as a transparent lie. It was academic, vital to him as one of Whitman's disciples, because he had heard English colleagues object to "Calamus" "as praising & propagating a passionate affection between men, which (in the language of the objectors) has 'a very dangerous side,' and might bring people into criminality." As Whitman's disciple "& as one also who wants soon or later to diffuse a further knowledge of your life-philosophy by criticism," Symonds urged, "it is most important to me to know what you really think about all this."[12]

Symonds wrote his book on Whitman in record time during the last year of his life. There, properly admonished by Whitman's apparent rejection of the sexual side of the "Calamus" feeling, he conceded that the poet had intended a love that was "ethereal" and "disembodied."[13] Even in his privately and posthumously published *Studies in Sexual Inversion,* which included a chapter on Whitman, he quickly exonerated the poet of having anything "to do with anomalous, abnormal, vicious, or diseased forms of the emotion which males entertain for males."[14] The vehemence of Whitman's denial (he at first thought to answer with silence) and the extract from Symonds's response of September 5 (reprinted in the standard edition of the poet's letters) have perhaps misled us, however, as to exactly what Symonds got from Whitman with his bold questioning. While saying in *Studies in Sexual Inversion* that Whitman's concept of Adhesiveness was "purer" than the Amativeness of medieval chivalry, he insisted that Whitman "recognizes among the sacred emotions and social virtues, destined to regenerate political life and to cement nations [suggested in the poet's dream of "the new City of Friends" in "Calamus" No. 34], an intense, jealous, throbbing, sensitive, expectant love of man for man." This is no sexless love but "a love which yearns in absence, droops under the sense of neglect, revives at the return of the beloved; a love that finds honest delight in hand-touch, meeting lips, hours of privacy, close personal contact."[15]

In his letter of September 5, Symonds expresses "great relief" to know precisely what the poet thought about the question of homosexual love in "Calamus." "Your phrases, 'gratuitous & quite at the time undreamed and unrecked possibility of morbid inferences—which are disavowed by me & seem damnable,' set the matter as straight as can be, [and] base this doctrine of Calamus upon a foundation of granite." Yet he was only mildly apologetic and admonished his "Master" for thinking that such "morbid references" were gratuitous, "or outside the range of possibility. Frankly speaking, the emotional language of Calamus is such as hitherto has not been used in the modern world about the relation between friends."

If Whitman answered Symonds, his reply has not survived. But one wasn't necessary because Whitman had in his letter of August 19 already given what Symonds regarded as license to insist on a deeper, physical Calamus feeling: "you have answered clearly," he said, "that a great potential factor lies latent in comradeship, ready to leap forth & take a prominent part in the energy of the human race."[16] Symonds was referring to the sentence in Whitman's letter in which he sanctioned a vicarious homosexual reading of parts of his book. It sheds a bright light on the actual meaning the poet gave to Adhesiveness in "Calamus," if not his actual practice.

Nevertheless, these feelings may have occupied a place in Whitman's psychological make-up that had almost the strength of *Leaves of Grass* itself, whose impulse Whitman thought, as already noted, was "as total and irresistible as those which make the sea flow, or the globe revolve."[17] In August 1890, at the same time that Symonds was writing to Whitman, the Englishman was probably compiling his own memoir, in which he bristled at the idea—soon to be popularized by such psychological scientists as Cesare Lombroso and John Ferguson Nesbit[18]—that homosexual temperaments were evidence of a "neurotic malady." In fact, Symonds believed that a "high degree of nervous sensibility" was mainly responsible for his literary achievement. "Morally and intellectually," he wrote, ". . . I am more masculine than many men I know who adore women. I have no feminine feeling for the males who rouse my desire. The anomaly of my position is that I admire the physical beauty of men more than women, derive more pleasure from their contact and society, and am stirred to sexual sensations exclusively by persons of the male sex."[19]

Clearly, this seems to describe Whitman's attraction to men, too. Yet—unlike Symonds—he also seemed to derive pleasure from the sight and sex of women. Otherwise, "Enfans d'Adam" (renamed "Children of Adam" in the 1867 edition) is a lie—or, possibly, an emphatic act of the imagination, as could be "Calamus"—in terms of what it suggests. Unlike "Calamus," however, they are more about lust than about love—"The love, the life of their bodies, meaning and being." "This is the female form," he wrote in "Enfans d'Adam" No. 3,

> A divine nimbus exhales from it from head to foot,
> It attracts with fierce undeniable attraction,
> I am drawn by its breath as I were no more than
> a helpless vapor—all falls aside but myself
> and it,
> Books, art, religion, time, the visible and solid earth,
> the atmosphere and the clouds, and what was
> expected of heaven or feared of hell, are now
> consumed,
> Mad filaments, ungovernable shoots play out of it, the
> response likewise ungovernable,
> Hair, bosom, hips, bend of legs, negligent falling
> hands, all diffused—mine too diffused,
> Ebb stung by the flow, and flow stung by the ebb—
> love-flesh swelling and deliciously aching,
> Limitless limpid jets of love hot and enormous,
> quivering jelly of love, white-blow and delirious
> juice,
> Bridegroom-night of love, working surely and softly
> into the prostrate dawn,
> Undulating into the willing and yielding day,
> Lost in the cleave of the clasping and sweet-fleshed
> day.

In the thrall of such (heterosexual) "libidinous joys," the poet abandons the world of "Books, art, religion, time" with the same ecstatic haste that he drops "knowledge" and the poetic celebration of America for the jealous lover who threatens to withhold his love in "Calamus" No. 8. The first lines, just quoted from "Enfans d'Adam" No. 3, appeared in all successive editions of *Leaves of Grass;* "Calamus" No. 8 disappeared after its first and only appearance in the third edition—suggesting perhaps the poet's sense of "*restraint.*"

Whitman probably never sustained an ongoing sexual relationship with a woman. He of course never married. He treated women, perhaps even prostitutes, like sisters—and in fact one of his sisters-in-law, Andrew's widow, was a prostitute with whom he kept up occasional contact until the year preceding his death. In a note to a Miss Gregg, a nurse in Ward A of the Armory-Square Hospital, thanking her for her "labor of love & disinterestedness here in Hospital," he addressed her in the same tone in which he asks the woman in "To a Common Prostitute" to become worthy of her appointment with him ("Not till the sun excludes you do I exclude you"). "As I am poor I cannot make you a present," he told the nurse in the autumn of 1863, "but I write you this note, dear girl, knowing you will receive it in the same candor & good faith it is written."[20]

Women were attracted to Whitman. Fanny Fern expressed more than literary admiration of him in 1855; Susan Garnet Smith, possibly the first groupie in American letters, announced in 1860 that her womb was "clean and pure . . . and ready for thy child," guarded by a "vestibule of angels until thou comest to deposit our and the world's precious treasure"; and in 1871 the Englishwoman Anne Gilchrist first proposed marriage after knowing Whitman only by his book and photograph.[21] The closest we have come to finding evidence of a female sexual partner, however, is in a mysterious letter from "Ellen Eyre." In a diary entry in July 1862, Whitman recorded that he had told Frank Sweeney "the whole story to, about Ellen Eyre," probably because he "talks very little." Since there is more than one version (the original was copied out by one of Whitman's disciples from the original in Traubel's possession), we print the original text of the lady's holograph, dated March 25, 1862:

My dear Mr. Whitman

I fear you took me last night for a female privateer. It's true that I was sailing under *false colors.*—But the flag I assure you covered nothing piratical—although I would joyfully have made your heart a captive.

Women have an unequal chance in this world. Men are its monarchs, and "full many a rose is born to blush unseen and waste its sweetness in the desert air."

Such I was resolved should not be the fate of this fancy I had long nourished for you.—A gold mine may be found by the Divining Rod

> but there is no such instrument for detecting in the crowded streets of a great city the [unknown?] mine of latent affection a man may have unconsciously inspired in a woman's heart. I make these explanations in extenuation not by way of apology. My social position enjoins precaution & mystery, and perhaps the enjoyment of my friend's society is heightened which in yielding to its fascination I preserve my incognito; yet mystery lends an ineffable charm to love and when a woman is bent upon the gratification of her inclinations—She is pardonable if she still spreads the veil of decorum over her actions. Hypocrisy is said to be "the homage that sin pays to virtue," and yet *I* can see no vice in that generous sympathy with which we share our caprices with those who have inspired us with tenderness,—
>
> I trust you will think well enough of me soon to renew the pleasure you afforded me last P.M., and I therefore write to remind you that there is a sympathetic heart, both of which would gladly evolve with warmth for your [direction?] & comfort.—You have already my whereabouts & my [hours]—It shall only depend upon you to make them yours and me the happiest of women.
>
> I am always
>
> Yours sincerely,
> *Ellen Eyre.*[22]

By the time of this letter, Whitman was caught up in the period of transition between Poet and Wound Dresser, looking for relief in his past on Long Island. His enthusiasm for Pfaff's and the bohemian life of late-night drinking was probably more than beginning to wane. Not surprising, there is no "Ellen Eyre" listed in the Manhattan directory for that year—because "Ellen Eyre" is no doubt a penname. A reasonable guess for the identity of Eyre is Ada Clare, who had publicly admired "A Child's Reminiscence" when it first appeared in Clapp's *Saturday Press.* The style of the letter and Clare's style in her *Saturday Press* column, "Thoughts and Things," are similarly breezy and allusive. More significant, her mention of being mistaken for a "female privateer" may be an allusion to the fact that *The Female Privateer* was then in rehearsal in the Bowery Theatre, where Ada was in all probability a member of the cast.[23] The letter is obviously written not by a prostitute but an educated person who can allude to Thomas Gray's "Elegy Written in a Country Churchyard" ("full many a rose. . . .") and the duc de La Rochefoucauld ("the homage. . . .") and also give a nod to Charlotte Brontë's *Jane Eyre* in her choice of pseudonym. Moreover, a witty woman with not a little literary talent like Clare would have appreciated the fact that "Ellen Eyre" and "Ada Clare" share the same rhyme and anapestic rhythm.

Clare's acquaintance with Whitman prior to this letter was probably nothing more than a recognition across the crowded and smoky basement at Pfaff's. But she was a dangerous flirt who once, according to Whitman's own account, compelled a young lover, a farmboy off in the city but engaged "to a very fine young lady who wrote him affectionate letters," to go back home and make love (in the twentieth-century sense) to the young woman before she (Clare) would accept him as a lover. "Any woman who writes such letters as that can be seduced," Clare cynically told him. "You will both learn something; and then you may come back to me."[24]

The beautiful Ada Clare hunted amorous conquests, and Whitman in his rustic costume and growing reputation as a radical poet (mainly because of the recent attention in the *Saturday Press*) would have seemed an adventure. As we know, she was daring enough to own publicly that her child was illicit, and—like Whitman—she dressed flamboyantly. Like the poet's "twenty-ninth bather" filled with sexual longing in "Song of Myself," who "hides handsome and richly drest aft the blinds of the window," Ellen Eyre (or Ada Clare) also preserves her "incognito" and is bent on "the gratification of her inclinations." She hopes Whitman will soon "renew the pleasure you afforded me last P.M." Whatever the pleasure, it hadn't been consummated—earlier the letter writer states that she "would joyfully have made your heart a captive." This is at least part of the story Whitman told his New York comrade Sweeney, and if the man was simply another B'hoy of Broadway, there may have been some manly laughter about a woman who had come on too strongly. But whoever she was, Ellen Eyre was not important to Whitman, who insisted that he was no longer interested in anyone who could think of something besides the war. It was probably not until he met Peter Doyle that his great love became "personal" again.

❖ ❖ ❖

In January 1863 Whitman settled into Washington, D.C., where his "Adhesiveness"—whatever it was—was largely absorbed by his wide sympathy for the sick and wounded soldiers who lay in various stages of misery at military hospitals all over the city, including the insane asylum at St. Elizabeth's. Whitman considered the three years he spent in the hospitals to have provided the most profound lesson of his life. "People used to say to me," he later recalled, "Walt, you are doing miracles for those fellows in the hospitals. I wasn't. I was . . . doing miracles for myself." "It may have been odd," he confessed in *Specimen Days,* "but I never before so realized the majesty and reality of the American people *en masse.*" Elsewhere in the book he wrote that he doubted anyone could get a fair idea of "what genuine America is, and her character, without some such experience as this I am having."[25] He came to view his role as a "hospital missionary" as a sacred undertaking. "I cannot give up my Hospitals yet," he told his brother Jeff in March, when he still thought this new career was temporary. "I never before had my feelings so thoroughly and (so far) permanently absorbed, to the very roots, as by these huge swarms of dear, wounded, sick, dying boys—I get very much attached to some of them, and many of them have come to depend on seeing me, and having me sit by them a few minutes, as if for their lives."[26]

Whitman had traveled to Washington in charge of the worst of the wounded from Burnside's defeat at Fredericksburg. There are no actual notebook entries from the journey back to the capital, but his retrospections in *Specimen Days* reveal that he witnessed horrendous scenes of death and dying as the medical party endured the fifty-mile trip by rail and river. The sick and wounded were first transported on open platform cars ("such as hogs are transported [on]," Whitman noted in an article to the *New York Times*), exposed to either blazing sun or wind-swept rain. At Aquia Creek they were crowded onto a government steamer that took them up the Potomac River to Washington. Upon their arrival at the Seventh Street wharves in the southwest section of the city, the evacuated sick and wounded often waited for hours before rickety, two-wheel ambulance wagons could take them to hospitals made up in many cases of rows of tents or large sheds.

When the streets of Washington weren't mud, they gave off immense amounts of dust. The city's foul-smelling canal (which followed what is today the course of Wisconsin Avenue south of the White House) hosted malaria, and hospitals contended with typhoid poisoning and diarrhea because of an irregularly clean water supply. In an era when microbes were unknown, hospital sanitation was inadequate (a surgeon might wet stitching thread with his tongue or sharpen a scalpel on his shoe). More patients died from disease than from battle wounds, and it may be said that the hospitals killed more patients than they saved.

Whitman had visited sick soldiers sent to Fort Hamilton in New York in May 1862; and we already know of his activities at the New York Hospital on Broadway. He was thus well prepared for his role as "Wound Dresser," but the experience in Washington nevertheless took its toll. Although there were officially recognized agencies such as the Sanitary and the Christian commissions, Whitman operated independently so that he could follow his own schedule. He also had no respect for the Sanitary Commission "& the like" because of their slapdash treatment of the sick soldiers. He told his mother, "You ought to see the way the men as they lie helpless in bed turn away their faces from the sight of these Agents, Chaplains &c." He thought better of the Christian Commission, because "they go everywhere & receive no pay."

Actually, Whitman (and several biographers as well, because of his remarks) was unfair to the United States Sanitary Commission, organized in June 1861 to ensure that the latest medical science, such as it was, was applied to the wartime hospitals. Its purpose was "neither humanity nor charity" but "to economize . . . the life and strength of the National soldier." This organization supposedly provided the political clout to see that the relief efforts were supplied with adequate nursing and hospital services, as well as providing lodging for troops who needed shelter but were ineligible for hospitalization. The commission's members provided these services free but paid their field agents, whose behavior probably gave Whitman and others the idea that they lacked humanity if not efficiency. The Christian Commission, organized by the YMCA the same year as the Sanitary Commission, gave "Spiritual good" and "intellectual improvement as well as physical comfort and reading material."[27] Like Whitman, it also provided items like writing paper, but not tobacco (which Whitman distributed). Despite the work of these organizations, conditions in Washington were chaotic.

One of the poet's recently recovered notebooks in the Library of Congress (missing from the notebooks and manuscripts edited by Edward F. Grier in 1984 because of a World War II theft) reveals a newspaper list of wartime hospitals in Washington. Most of these facilities had been hastily established around the Union capital after the chilling defeats at First Bull Run and elsewhere, when the Confederacy still had the talents of General Stonewall Jackson. Whitman, it seems, visited them all—the Ascension on H Street between 9th and 10th, the Armory-Square at 7th Street, the Carver near Boundary (today Florida Avenue) between 13th and 14th Streets, the Patent Office (today the National Portrait Gallery) at the corner of 7th and F Streets (closed at the end of 1863), the Columbian, the Cliffburne, the Douglas, the Emory, the Methodist, the Presbyterian Church, Stanton, Trinity, Union—the list approaches forty such sanctuaries for seriously wounded and dying soldiers. He recorded that Washington and its environs of Alexandria and Arlington supported more than fifty military hospitals for varying types of medical treatment. Some of the temporary hospitals were churches whose congregations had laid plank floors over pews and stored church furniture underneath.[28] Whitman's attention to his "boys" in these hospitals and the meaning of the war overshadowed almost every other interest now. No one who reads the poet's wartime notebooks and letters, or the moving commentary in *Memoranda During the War* and *Specimen Days* as well as his newspaper articles, will be surprised at the post–Civil War line in *Leaves of Grass,* "My book and the war are one."

Later in *The Good Gray Poet,* William O'Connor tried to record what Whitman did during the war:

> For his daily occupation, he goes from ward to ward, doing all he can to hearten and revive the spirits of the sufferers, and keep the balance in

> favor of their recovery. Usually, his plan is to pass, with haversack [today preserved in the Library of Congress] strapped across his shoulder, from cot to cot, distributing small gifts; his theory is that these men, far from home, lonely, sick at heart, need more than any thing some practical token that they are not forsaken, that some one feels a fatherly or brotherly interest in them; hence, he gives them what he can; to particular cases, entirely penniless, he distributes small sums of money, fifteen cents, twenty cents, thirty cents, fifty cents, not much to each, for there are many, but under the circumstances these little sums are and mean a great deal. He also distributes and directs envelopes, gives letter-paper, postage-stamps, tobacco, apples, figs, sweet biscuit, preserves, blackberries; gets delicate food for special cases; sometimes a dish of oysters or a dainty piece of meat, or some savory morsel for some poor creature who loathes the hospital fare, but whose appetite may be tempted. In the hot weather he buys boxes of oranges and distributes them, grateful to lips baked with fever; he buys boxes of lemons, he buys sugar, to make lemonade for those parched throats of sick soldiers; he buys canned peaches, strawberries, pears; he buys in the market fresh fruit; he buys ice-cream and treats the whole hospital; he buys whatever delicacies and luxuries his limited resources will allow, and he makes them go as far as he can.[29]

All this has been verified by the poet's own letters and the observations of others, including D. Willard Bliss, the heroic surgeon at the Armory-Square Hospital, who averred that "no one person who assisted in the hospitals during the war accomplished so much good to the soldiers and for the Government as Mr. Whitman." Dr. Bliss—who attended President (and Whitman's future friend) James A. Garfield following his assassination—testified in a deposition before Congress when it was considering a pension for Whitman in return for his hospital work. The pension was not granted (indeed, the idea was ridiculed in print by Thomas Wentworth Higginson), and Whitman said that he would not have accepted it anyhow.[30]

At least one earlier biographer has suggested that at forty-three when the war began Whitman was too old to fight as a soldier and also lacked any inclination toward military violence. Yet Whitman claimed that he was ready to see his name on any conscription list and may have even criticized the Quakers for claiming the status of conscientious objectors, saying they should at least be taxed more to compensate for their absence on a battlefield. He may, of course, have been slyly arguing for the substitute system, which benefited Jeff later that year. Furthermore, he suspected that the earliest talk of conscripts was simply Lincoln's attempt to ward off any thought of interference from "Louis Napoleon, or any other foreign meddler."[31]

One look at Whitman by an army recruiter, however, would probably have disqualified him for military service. Although still enjoying excellent health (never ill in his life, he boasted), he had taken on all the appearances of advanced middle age. He little resembled the figure in the frontispiece to the 1855 and 1856 editions of *Leaves of Grass.* Nor did he remind one very much of the Byronesque figure that is the frontispiece to the 1860 edition. He had grayed to some extent before the war, and now with his casual costume he more resembled an old sea captain or a frontier scout than he did a poet. There was a rugged look to his appearance. "My health, strength, personal beauty, &c.," he told friends from Pfaff's self-mockingly but also self-adoringly, "are, I am happy to inform you, without diminution, but on the contrary quite the reverse. I weigh full 220 pounds avoirdupois, yet still retain my usual perfect shape—a regular model. My beard, neck, &c. are woolier, fleecier, whiteyer than ever. I wear army boots, with magnificent black morrocco tops, the trousers put in, wherein shod and legged confront I Virginia's deepest mud with supercilious eyes."[32]

⁂

To support himself at his one-room quarters at 394 L Street, northeast of the White House, Whitman found a job as a part-time copyist in the Army Paymaster's Office, housed in the Corcoran Building, a five-story structure near the Treasury Building at 15th and F Streets. He spent much of his time here during off hours, seated by a window overlooking the Potomac and the Virginia shore, writing letters home. Here he also began to memorialize his work in Washington with a series of articles in the *New York Times* (where his friend from the Pfaffian days, John Swinton, was now editor) and the Brooklyn papers. His ostensible purpose was to call attention to the needy soldiers and their courage in the face of amputation or death, but he was also reviewing his hospital work—and not anonymously as he had his work in the first edition of *Leaves of Grass.* He published "The Great Army of the Sick" in the *Times* of February 26, 1863. Earlier, he rehearsed the article in a letter to Emerson, saying he would write a book about "America, already brought to Hospital in her fair youth." He spoke in both his letter and the *Times* of the 50,000 sick and wounded already in Washington. "Our own New York," he told his Manhattan readers, "in the form of hundreds and thousands of her young men, may consider herself here—Pennsylvania, Ohio, Indiana and all the West and Northwest the same—and all the New-England states the same."[33]

Whitman emphasized the "great tact" needed for success in the hospitals. He didn't say it, but he was referring to their general pandemonium. Hospital doors were open to all, not simply relatives (lucky enough to find the names of their wounded on incomplete newspaper lists) and representatives of relief agencies. Peddlers tried to sell items to the penniless sick, and religious zealots made themselves a painful nuisance to the helpless. As one historian describes the scene, some visitors "fed improper food to the sick. Others wearied them with impertinent questions. Even desperately ill men were not protected from the intrusions of the tactless and the curious. The haphazard distribution of gifts resulted in much inequality. Some would give only to those from a favorite State. Others selected pets, whom they gorged with delicacies, leaving their neighbors quite neglected."[34]

Whitman stressed that these were not ordinary hospitals or havens for the sick and needy, like the New York Hospital on Broadway. These patients were America's best—"American young men, intelligent, of independent spirit, tender feelings, used to a hardy and healthy life; largely the farmers are represented by their sons—largely the mechanics and workingmen of the cities. Then they are *soldiers.*" He believed, as William O'Connor noted, that what these men needed first, before medical aid, was a kindly glance and a friendly gesture or inquiry. In *Specimen Days* Whitman speaks of a soldier of the 154th New York Volunteers, dying of a bad wound complicated by chronic diarrhea, who asked him to read from the Bible. Whitman chose "the first books of the evangelists, and read the chapters describing the latter hours of Christ, and the scenes at the crucifixion. The poor wasted young man ask'd me to read the following chapter also, how Christ rose again." The soldier died a few days later, and Whitman had yet another example of what he had seen at Fredericksburg and would record in "A Sight in Camp in the Daybreak Gray and Dim"—a young man whom he thought he knew intuitively, "this face of the Christ himself, / Dead and divine and brother of all, and here again he lies."

At first, before people from Brooklyn to Boston began to respond to his need for monetary contributions, a kindly glance and a friendly gesture were all he could give. Afterward, they were still his greatest gift. He went to the hospitals twice a day, six or seven days a week, usually in the afternoon from noon to four during the work week, after his part-time duties at the Paymaster's Office, and then again for another three or four hours in the evening. Frequently, he sat up all night with a particularly distressing case or slept in an adjacent room near the wardmaster's office. With the exception of the Judiciary-Square Hospital—the oldest of the military hospitals, where Whitman deplored the excessive military ceremony—he was welcomed everywhere and generally admired for his work. At least one senior nurse felt scandalized by having the author of *Leaves of Grass* in her hospital. While not the only regular "visitor" to the hospitals, he soon became the best known. The soldiers, he said, loved him. He told his mother, "I fancy the reason I am able to do some good in the hospitals, among the poor languishing & wounded boys, is that I am so large and well—indeed like a great wild buffalo, with much hair—many of the soldiers are from the west, and far north—and they take to a man that has not the bleached shiny & shaved cut of the cities and the east." This last remark seems misleading until we remember from our reading of the first two editions of *Leaves of Grass* that Whitman is talking about an average, not particularly a westerner or a farmer, but the common man or American with the *spirit* of the West. He disliked the northeastern cities for their "obedient reflex of European customs, standards, costumes, &c." and thought the nation's capital would eventually be removed to some more geographically representative place farther west. "How," he asked, "can the prairie America, the boundless and teeming West, the region of the Mississippi, the California, Idaho and Colorado regions (two-thirds of our territory lies west of the Mississippi River) be content to have its Government lop-sided over on the Atlantic, far, far from itself—the trunk, the real genuine America?"[35] To the last, Whitman was a Wilmot Proviso idealist who saw the West and western ways as fulfilling the promise of America.

He gave in "The Great Army of the Sick" an example of the love that the hospitals required. He told of a Massachusetts soldier who had been evacuated after First Fredericksburg. The wounded soldier was so enfeebled by the time he boarded a boat going up the Potomac to Washington that he could not untie his blankets from his haversack or get anyone to assist him. When he told one of the crew that he could not help himself, the man rejoined, Whitman wrote, "that he might then go without them, and walked off." "Poor boy!" Whitman exclaimed, "the long train of exhaustion, deprivation, rudeness, no food, no friendly word or deed, but all kinds of upstart airs, and impudent, unfeeling speeches and deeds, from all kinds of small officials (and some big ones,) cutting like razors into that sensitive heart, had at last done the job. . . . He felt the struggle to keep up any longer to be useless. God, the world, humanity—all had abandoned him. It would feel so good to shut his eyes forever on the cruel things around him and toward him." The next sentence said everything of the kind of care Whitman gave his precious soldiers: "As luck would have it, at this time, I found him."

Sometimes Whitman's love for his soldiers overwhelmed him. The consequent overflow of affection may have embarrassed some soldiers into silence or elicited an awkward response. This was apparently the case with Sergeant Thomas P. Sawyer of the Eleventh Massachusetts Infantry. Sawyer had been a patient in the Armory-Square, which received the worst cases and more of Whitman's attention than any other hospital. Sawyer was a friend of Lewis ("Lewy") Kirk Brown, of the same regiment. He went back to camp in April and fought in the Battle of Gettysburg that summer. Whitman sent him repeated vows of deep affection, which went unanswered for a long time. Like

Brown, Sawyer was semi-literate; his only response was an apology that he had not lived up "to my Prommice because I came away so soon that it sliped my mind"—this not even directly addressed to Whitman but sent through Lewy. It is hard to know Whitman's intentions here because he apparently envisioned a situation in which he would live with both Tom and Lewy. Generally in his letters (and also in his newspaper articles and in the letters he wrote to parents of dead soldiers, where he shows no hesitation to articulate his emotional involvement) Whitman expressed an avuncular or paternal affection for his soldiers. His feeling might also be described as fraternal, although he was never this affectionate with his soldier brother George, a strong silent type who loved Walt but didn't think *Leaves of Grass* worth reading when it first appeared in 1855.[36]

There were exceptions, and the letters to Sawyer provide the best examples. In one, Whitman envisions the soldier wearing "something from *me*" around his body. In another he admits that the affection he expresses in letters may "sound strange & unusual." In a third, he writes that he told Lewy Brown that when he wrote to Sawyer he should never send the poet's "respects" but "always my love." To Brown he wrote, "when you write to Tom Sawyer you know what to say from me—he is one I love in my heart, & always shall till death, & afterwards too."[37]

His longest wartime notebook contains two entries from the New York period in which Whitman writes that he "slept with" a male acquaintance. Both entries were made in 1862, before Whitman went to Washington, and both refer to apparently unlettered youths like his Washington soldiers. David S. Reynolds argues that—because of close urban accommodations in the mid-nineteenth century and more open shows of male friendship—the phrase "slept with" did not necessarily have the sexual connotation it took on in the 1890s (the word "homosexual" apparently came into the English language in 1892). But in fact, the phrase did imply sexual intimacy or cohabitation long before the nineteenth century. There is nothing in the context of the two notebook entries, however, to suggest that the phrase refers to anything more than a contingency sleeping arrangement in a working-class neighborhood. In John Burroughs's earliest recorded impression of Whitman, whom he met in 1863, he wrote his wife: "I have been much with Walt. Have even slept with him. I love him very much. The more I see and talk with him, the greater he becomes to me."[38] Interestingly, Whitman never uses "slept with" in the letters or notes he wrote about his soldiers.

❋ ❋ ❋

On March 19, 1863, Whitman published "The Great Washington Hospital" in the *Brooklyn Eagle.* This was essentially a hometown version of the piece on the hospitals he had written for the *Times.* After only two months of visiting the hospitals, he was already beginning to feel the strain and to complain, for the first time in his life, of poor health. He told Jeff, "The Hospitals still engross a large part of my time and feelings—only I don't remain so long and make such exhausting-like visits, the last week—as I have had a bad humming feeling and deafness, stupor-like at times, in my head."[39] Whitman was still ten years away from his first and most severe paralytic stroke, but already preparing for it. He got a great deal of exercise, walking all over Washington, up and down broad Pennsylvania Avenue between the Federal offices near the White House, to the troop hospitals northwest of the Capitol, and over the Long Bridge to Alexandria County, but the city was not a healthy place, with dust in the air and miasmas wafting from the swampy area in the unseasonably hot summers. Once or twice Whitman thought he had suffered sunstroke, which had afflicted him in the summer of 1858, and he now armed himself with an umbrella and a fan for his treks to the hospitals on steamy afternoons. Once there, he endangered himself by holding and kissing sick soldiers—exposing himself to pneumonia, typhoid, malaria, and patients pallid with diarrhea. When he was finally struck down in the autumn of 1863, he was diagnosed as having "hospital malaria."[40]

Things were relatively quiet after the Union defeat at Fredericksburg. In January 1863 Burnside was replaced by General "Fighting Joe" Hooker as commanding general of the Army of the Potomac, and Burnside took his Ninth Army to Newport News, Virginia, where in March Whitman's soldier brother received his first furlough since joining up. George spent ten days in Brooklyn with the Whitman family but did not see Walt in Washington. A few weeks after he returned to his regiment, the Ninth Army was assigned to the Department of Ohio. It ultimately joined the western campaign under Grant and was present at the siege of Vicksburg in July.[41]

With brother George in the West, Walt was spared from worry about him in May when the wounded cascaded in from Chancellorsville. The battle there climaxed a military campaign of movements and countermovements by the opposing armies under Hooker and Robert E. Lee (still camped in Fredericksburg). Dangerously low on supplies, Lee reduced the force of the Army of Northern Virginia by dispatching troops south to forage under General James Longstreet.[42] Hooker gained the upper hand at one point by outflanking Lee's army, but he failed to follow through, ultimately doubting his military judgment, and fell into a defensive position at Chancellorsville, about twelve miles west of Fredericksburg. There approximately 13 percent of his troops, whose morale had only recently been restored after the Fredericksburg defeat, were killed or wounded. One part of Hooker's force, under General O. O. Howard, was completely surprised and routed by troops under Lee's "right arm," Stonewall Jackson. This was Jackson's last battle, however. Riding out beyond his lines, he was mistaken for a Federal officer and shot by his own men. He died on May 10, 1863.[43]

The next day Walt told Moses Lane, Jeff's boss at the Brooklyn waterworks and a regular contributor to his hospital fund, of the "heart-rendings cases . . . coming up in one long bloody string from Chancellorsville." By June the hospitals were bulging with agonized patients, and Whitman told his mother that he had not missed "a day at Hospital" for three weeks. He noted for a newspaper article on the history of the war during the previous two years (and repeated in *Specimen Days*) that many of the casualties from Chancellorsville had been "fearfully burnt from explosions of artillery caissons. . . . Yesterday was perhaps worse than usual. Amputations are going on—the attendants are dressing wounds. As you pass by, you must be on your guard where you look." The other day, he added, someone watching one of the dreadful operations out of mere curiosity saw "the awful wound they were probing," and fainted dead away.[44]

By the end of the month Whitman was feeling sick himself. "Mother," he wrote, "I have had quite an attack of sore throat & distress in my head for some days past," though that particular day he was feeling better. He had been told by doctors, he said, "that I hover too much over the beds of the hospitals, with fever & putrid wounds." Also distressing to him were the contraband camps, which incarcerated former slaves of rebel masters, jailed supposedly as an act of charity because of their destitution. After one or two visits, he couldn't bring himself to go again, this errand of mercy apparently too much even for Whitman. "When I meet black men or boys among my own hospitals," he wrote, "I use them kindly, give them something"; he did the same for wounded rebels. His "own hospitals" included the Armory-Square, which was located near the filthy Washington Canal (on what is now the Mall near the Smithsonian Air and Space Museum).[45]

The next "bloody string" of casualties came from Gettysburg, the bloodiest battle of the war, during the first three days of July. Lincoln had removed Hooker on the eve of the first day of battle, and the Union army was now under the command of General George G. Meade. Lee had invaded Pennsylvania with the ultimate intention of once more threatening Washington, which had already been vulnerable to Confederate attack several times. Union forces intercepted Lee's forces at Gettysburg, but this time, in contrast to Fredericksburg, they had the advantage of being in the fortress. Meade's fishhook formation resisted Confederate attacks, including General George E. Pickett's suicidal charge on the Union center on the last day of the battle. In spite of the heavy Union losses, Gettysburg was viewed as a victory, and, as it turned out, it was the turning point in the war. But Meade, like every other general Lincoln appointed before stumbling upon Grant, turned success into disappointment by losing his nerve. He failed to pursue Lee's beaten army as it waited before the rain-swollen Potomac, which stood between the Confederate troops and their retreat into the South.[46]

Four days after the battle, Walt told his mother that the casualties—killed and wounded—on both sides numbered "as many as eighteen or twenty thousand—in one place, four or five acres, there were a thousand dead, at daybreak on Saturday morning," American Independence Day. "Mother, one's own heart grows sick of war, after all, when you see what it really is." He later exclaimed to Traubel: "O God! that whole damned war business is about nine hundred and ninety nine parts diarrhea to one part glory." At the end of July he heard from Lewy Brown, who was home on medical furlough in Elkton, Maryland, and whose battle wound would require his leg to be amputated later in the year. Brown obviously delighted Whitman with news of his beloved Tom Sawyer, but the message was far from cheerful. "He has bin in that Gettysburg Battle," he wrote. "He sais that it was awful, and that he never wants to see the like of it again."[47]

In August, when the influx of casualties had slowed, Whitman began to feel restless, no doubt exhausted from his relentless hospital work. In a letter that month to one of his fellow Pfaffians, he reminisced about the good times they had enjoyed on Broadway. He was responding to the untimely death of another Pfaffian, Charles Chauncey, and remembered the merry meetings at Pfaff's—"our drinks & groups so friendly, our suppers." Caught between the deaths of his soldiers and that of an old acquaintance, Whitman seemed depressed and even homesick, now not for Long Island and times long ago but for Brooklyn and his Manhattan haunts in the late afternoons and evenings. A week or so later, he asked: "Mother, don't you miss *Walt*—loafing around, & carting himself off to New York, toward the latter part of every afternoon?"[48]

Walt was also worried about brother Andrew, who at thirty-five was suffering from a mysterious throat ailment. "Bunkum" was an alcoholic with a wife and two children. To avoid an unstable life at home, he had been spending most of the time at his mother's house on Portland Avenue, but she feared that his continued presence would bring in Nancy and the children as well. The house was already crowded with Jeff's family, the twenty-eight-year-old Eddy, and a family of renters and regularly threatened with permanent occupancy by the often unemployed Jesse Whitman. Earlier Walt had given Andrew (through his mother) a long phrenologically inspired lecture about good health, advising that medicine was of little account except to pacify the person, "and the way to make a *real cure* is by gentle and steady means to recuperate the whole system." Feeling guilty perhaps about not being home to help shoulder the family burden (at one point Jeff urged him to return immediately), Whitman lamented that ("if I had the means") he would give anything to purchase Andrew's recovery. Living hand-to-mouth before landing a $1,200-a-year clerkship in the Department of the Interior in 1865, Whitman had nothing to give his nearly indigent mother except an occasional dollar. More often he advised her to spend George's army pay carefully.[49]

It was about this time—probably only a few days before Whitman went home to Brooklyn (after two weeks' delay) on November 2—that he commenced one of the most enduring friendships of his life. He made the acquaintance of the twenty-six-year-old "Jack" Burroughs, who had abandoned his teaching job at Marlboro-on-the-Hudson and gone to Washington with the precise ambition of meeting Whitman, whom he had shadowed through a Washington friend's letters and press accounts since 1861.[50] Burroughs had been a reader of the *Saturday Press* during its heyday, when it was publishing and promoting Whitman and essays of the other Pfaffians, including the provocative Ada Clare, who fascinated Burroughs and his friend Myron Benton almost as much as Whitman. When he heard from E. M. Allen, who owned an army supply store in Washington, that Whitman frequently visited his establishment, Burroughs left for Washington and the hope of a government job, which he soon found in the Treasury Department. When the former country schoolmaster (Burroughs was too "feeble" and "pale" for the army) finally cast eyes on the infamous poet in the rear of Allen's store, leaning back in a large canvas lounging chair, he wrote his wife Ursula, still in New York: "I have seen Walt and think him glorious."[51]

Whitman returned to Brooklyn. But instead of standing watch at Andrew's bedside, he spent most of his time in Manhattan, out on the town with his former friends or at the opera with his sister-in-law Mattie. In a long letter to Lewy Brown, he described his activities at the opera and the New York Academy of Music. He seemed to revel in the almost peaceful contrast between New York and Washington. "It looks so different here in all this mighty city," he said, "every thing going with a big rush & so gay, as if there was neither war nor hospitals in the land." Here he lost himself in old habits, crossing on the

Fulton or South Ferry, talking to the pilots and deckhands, taking in the shipping scenes along the wharves that he had already commemorated in "Crossing Brooklyn Ferry." He told his Washington soldiers, "As I sit up there in the pilot house, I can see every thing, & the distant scenery, & away down toward the sea, & Fort Lafayette &c. The ferry boat has to pick its way through the crowd. Often they hit each other, then there is a time." He told Ellen O'Connor a week later that he found his friends "the same gay-hearted, joyous fellows, full of friendship & determined to have pleasure. We have been together quite a good deal. They have given me supper parties, men only, with drinking &c." Most of these friends, however, were in their twenties, while Whitman was in his mid-forties. When in Washington, Whitman had shown Allen some of their letters, which he thought that "by reading you would judge [Whitman] to be a young fellow, and indeed, he is young, with perfect health and youthful tastes."[52]

Writing Tom Sawyer, once again without answer, Walt feared Andrew would die; yet he left New York for Washington two days before his brother's death on December 3, 1863. It was almost as if he considered it more important to be with his soldier "brothers" than to be present at the pitiful death of an actual brother. Justin Kaplan has hinted that Whitman may have had more than a brotherly affection for Jeff, who accompanied him to New Orleans in 1848 and shared his delight in Italian opera. But other than Jeff, Walt was not that close to his brothers, including George, whose career he celebrated in a series of journalistic essays.[53] Indeed, his closest "sibling" during the war was Jeff's wife, Mattie. He was slightly paternalistic toward his male siblings and more affectionate toward his two sisters. At least two of his brothers had repeated their father's apparent fondness for drink and the kind of domestic violence that Whitman recorded in his early fiction. Jesse, the eldest at forty-six and, if we are to believe Whitman's early fiction, the favorite son of his father, was by 1863 so unstable that he threatened Jeff's wife and daughter while Andrew still lay in state on the first floor of the Whitman residence. The most we know Walt ever did for Jesse, who was apparently homeless and often laid off as a laborer at the Brooklyn shipyard, was to commit him involuntarily to the Kings County Lunatic Asylum on December 5, 1864.[54]

Walt finally heard from Tom Sawyer directly on January 21, 1864. The battle-weary soldier was encamped with the Army of the Potomac in northern Virginia, where the Union force lay in preparation for the final assaults of the war, the battles of the Wilderness and the long marches on Petersburg and Richmond. It was possibly the last time Whitman ever heard directly from Sawyer, formerly a soapmaker from Cambridge, Massachusetts. He had enjoyed the same luck as Whitman's brother George, who, though he missed Gettysburg, fought in most of the war's worst battles. Indeed, Sawyer was luckier, for while George went off to the bloody Wilderness campaign, he was detailed to New Orleans. He mustered out of service on June 12, 1864. After the war, he married, fathered eight children, and died of old age in Indiana in 1928.[55] Sawyer was last heard from by Whitman's circle of soldier friends in 1867.

Without an appreciation of Whitman's blue-collar, poverty-ridden background and the poetry it produced, it is difficult to understand what he saw in somebody like Sawyer, assuming it wasn't simply a sexual interest (for which there is little or no evidence). To Whitman these soldiers, and earlier the mechanics of Brooklyn and New York, were his brothers in a working-class democracy. They seemed like extensions of his own family. He treated them as brothers and sons, and they often addressed each other as "comrade." When Whitman, for example, wrote to Elijiah Fox, a wounded combatant from the Third Wisconsin in Armory-Square Hospital, he addressed the married veteran as "son & comrade;" and in the letter Whitman was apparently answering, Fox addressed him as "Dear Father," adding, "Walt, you will be a second Father to me won't you, for my love for you is hardly less than my love for my natural parent." Later, in the summer of 1864, he told Whitman: "I'm afraid I shall never be able to recompense you for your kind care and the trouble I made you while I was sick in the hospital."[56] In his letter of January 21, Sawyer addressed Whitman as "Dear Brother Walter." (For all the informality the public "Walt" was supposed to convey, Whitman's most intimate address—the one his mother and most of his soldier friends used—was "Walter.") Sawyer made no effusive declarations but merely apologized for not writing, saying that he was "buisy" fixing his tent for the winter. The letter

Whitman had looked for, had pleaded for in several letters, turned out to be a farewell letter, possibly because the soldier doubted that his luck in battle would hold. "I hope we may meet again in this world," he wrote and signed it "Your Brother, Sergt Thomas P. Sawyer."[57]

⁂ ⁂ ⁂

During the spring of 1863, Whitman also received a series of letters of a different order. Lacking the pathos and reverent tone of the soldiers' letters, their tone recalls that of Abraham Leech, the addressee of young Whitman's sarcastic epistles when he taught on Long Island in 1840. The correspondent was Will W. Wallace, a hospital steward whom Whitman probably met in Campbell Hospital. Wallace had been transferred to a Union hospital in Nashville, Tennessee, a border state that remained neutral throughout the war. He gave Whitman details about the hospital that the poet, as we know from his detailed journalistic reports, would have appreciated (especially now that his brother was fighting in that area). Wallace also told Whitman, "I have five young ladies who act in the capacity of nurses," adding with emphasis that "*one of them is French,* young and beautiful to set your eyes upon. Can you not visit us and note for yourself?"

We don't have Whitman's answer, but Wallace's next letter suggests that the poet begged off on the grounds that he had contracted a sexually transmitted disease. "I am surprised at your frenchy leaving you in such a deplorable state," he told Whitman, "but you are not alone. I had to dismiss mine to save the reputation of the Hospital and your humble servant." When Emory Holloway first found these letters in 1915, he was disappointed to learn that Whitman had gone with prostitutes but relieved to think the letters proved Whitman was not a homosexual. Another biographer, Roger Asselineau, published the letters in 1949 and saw them as evidence of the poet's homosexuality. In his 1954 biography, he argues that Whitman's literary gift came partly from the psychological conflict involved in resisting or reconciling his homosexual identity. Asselineau speculates that Whitman's boast about having his own "frenchy," or prostitute, and acquiring a venereal disease from her, was "a white lie" to get out of accepting the invitation to Nashville and to hide his homosexual nature. But Wallace's expectation of Whitman's (heterosexual) interest in the female nurses is evidence of Whitman's own heterosexual experience, or at least his "manly" expression of it to the hospital steward.[58] In any case, without a hospital stewardship with regular pay and government connections, Whitman could not have afforded to travel as far away as Nashville for any reason.

In July soldiers of the Union army were called to New York City to quell an Irish riot over Lincoln's introduction of military conscription. Not wanting to fight to free slaves who would compete with them for the lowliest jobs, Irish mobs stormed through the city for three days in July, burning down a Negro orphanage and generally threatening banks and other symbols of economic power before federal troops arrived. George wrote from camp near Covington, Kentucky, that it was "almost enough to make a fellow ashamed of being a Yorker." Just one social notch above the black freedman, most of the Irish, who earned no more than $500 a year, could not afford military substitutes. Jeff, who somehow could afford the $400 fee (usually $300), was furious at the culprits. The only feeling he had for them, he told Walt on July 19, was "that they did not kill enough of 'em. . . . I am perfectly rabid on an irishman. I hate them worse than I thought I could hate anything. Their conduct for the past week has made me do it."[59] Jeff was excitable (often for a good reason) and sometimes unreasonable (though seldom in the eyes of his family, including Walt).

As the war reached a fever pitch in 1864 and 1865, Whitman began to assess his place in what he called the "quicksand years." He told his mother that the next time he came home, "I shall not go off gallivanting with my companions half as much, nor a quarter as much as I used to, but shall spend the time quietly at home with you." While still back in Brooklyn in 1864, he told Charlie Eldridge, his former publisher and Major Hapgood's clerk in the Army Paymaster's Office, that he had to get back to his literary work and bring out a collection of war poems, to be called *Drum-Taps.* "I shall range along the high plateau of my life & capacity for a few years now," he told him, "& then swiftly descend."[60] He thought life in New York City "flippant & shallow" compared to what he had seen in the Washington hospitals.

George was home for another furlough in January 1864, but Walt again missed him. The poet visited the "front" for the second time in his life in February, at Culpepper, Virginia, where the Army of the Potomac was regrouping under Grant. The poet stayed about ten days in camp at Culpepper, helping Eldridge and Paymaster Hapgood pay the troops and visiting the remaining sick, though most of them were now in Washington. Walt had to leave the bedside of Lewy Brown, who finally had his left leg amputated five inches below the knee and was just beginning to get around on crutches. The operation, which Whitman had observed from the doorway to the operating room, was nearly botched. The poet's favorite army surgeon, Willard Bliss, was called away for an emergency while they were stitching up the stump. Thinking an artery had opened, his assistants thought (the poet recorded in his diary) "to cut the stitches again & make a search but after some time concluded it was only surface bleeding. Then they stitched it up again & Lew felt every one of these stitches, though yet partially under the influence of ether."[61] Like other amputees Whitman had comforted, Lewy could still feel his lost leg and foot; his imagined toes got hopelessly tangled.

By 1864 Grant, because of his western victories culminating with Vicksburg on July 4, 1863, commanded the Union armies. On May 4, 1864, his great force began to cross the Rapidan River, intending to get through the dense thicket near Chancellorsville and Fredericksburg in order to move into clear country for battle.[62] Before Grant could get his supply wagons through the wood, however, he encountered the enemy. The ensuing Battle of the Wilderness (May 5–6) initiated the first stage of the last long campaign of the war. George was in the middle of its first two-day engagement, which cost the Union a total of eighteen thousand killed, wounded, and maimed troops and almost a thousand from Burnside's Ninth Army alone. Walt learned later that the canteen hanging at George's side had been struck "& half of it wrenched off."[63] Next came the Battle of Spotsylvania (May 8–20), where three of George's compatriots were shot dead close by him. The charmed life of Major Whitman continued, and he lost only a coat, which was mysteriously riddled with "grape."[64]

The fighting, some of the worst of the war, went on all that month and the next as Grant pushed through battle after battle—North

Anna, Cold Harbor, and finally the siege of Petersburg on June 15. During its ten months, George's regiment was in various skirmishes around Petersburg. It was present for the notorious Battle of the Crater, where Union forces tunneled under enemy lines on July 30 and set up an explosion. They had positioned themselves too close to Confederate lines and were stunned by the blast. They hesitated in their charge, giving the enemy troops time to reorganize. The fighting was soon reduced to hand-to-hand combat, which cost both sides dearly. But George continued to survive unscathed until September 30, 1864, when almost his entire regiment was surrounded and captured at Poplar Grove Church, Virginia. Several of his close friends from Brooklyn were killed. Shortly after the capture, George wrote: "Here I am perfectly well and unhurt, but a prisoner." By the end of the month, he was languishing in the infamous Libby Prison.[65]

Even before his brother's capture, Walt was growing discouraged at the increasing number of casualties. He was also feeling unwell again, telling his mother that "if this campaign was not in progress," he would come home. He was experiencing painful headaches and dizziness, and the trouble got worse when he left for home on June 22. Bedridden in Brooklyn for a couple of weeks, he finally went out for a carriage ride around the neighborhood with Jeff on July 8. By September he reported that his health was "quite re-established," but he added here and again subsequently that he would never be able again to enjoy "the same unconscious state of health as formerly."[66] He never did.

The Whitman family was disheartened by the fate of George, especially when it became clear that Grant wasn't in any hurry to exchange well-fed Confederate prisoners for emaciated Union troops. George, always hearty, spent the month of December in the Confederate Military Hospital in Danville with "lung fever."[67] Walt published a long retrospective on the war and his part in it entitled "Our Wounded and Sick Soldiers; Visits Among Army Hospitals" in the *New York Times* of December 11. This article tried to enlist the public's sympathy by appealing to its interest in the workings of the hospitals, but in the *Times* as well as the *Eagle* of December 27, he spoke for the public directly as he vented his outrage over the way the Union was dragging its feet on a general prisoner exchange. "The public mind," he wrote, "is deeply excited, and most righteously so, at the starvation of the United States prisoners of war in the hands of the Secessionists." He asked pointedly, "Whose fault is it at bottom that our men have not been exchanged?" He blamed the bigwigs and especially Edwin Stanton, the secretary of war, who was reported in the press to have said it was not in the military interest of the Union to carry out an exchange. This was one of Whitman's angriest letters ever, and he also assailed another top official for saying that "none but cowards are ever taken prisoners in war." Surely, this description did not fit George or the countless other heroes Whitman had come to know in the last two years of war. He observed sarcastically that the only exchange that had taken place thus far was one in which one-fourth of "those helpless and most wretched men . . . have been exchanged by deaths of starvation."[68]

Whitman had already placed a piece specifically on the Fifty-First New York Regiment in the *New York Times* of October 29, but nothing seemed to move the Federal authorities to act on behalf of the prisoners, an issue Whitman had not concerned himself about until George's capture.[69] The day after Christmas 1864 George's trunk arrived in Brooklyn, and Walt recorded that he, his mother, and Eddy stared at it for "some hours" in the Portland Avenue basement parlor before venturing to open it. "One could not help feeling depressed. There were his uniform coat, pants, sash, &c. There were many things reminded us of him. Papers, memoranda, books, nick-nacks, a revolver, a small diary, roll of his company, a case of photographs of his comrades (several of them I knew as killed in battle) with other stuff such as a soldier accumulates." Whitman read the small pocket diary, which he called a "perfect poem of the war," but it wasn't very poetic except in its stark and emotionless listing of dates and places and routines (with no mention of Walt's arrival at Fredericksburg back in December 1862). Walt brought to it the emotion that George apparently never felt or displayed. In spite of its skeletal nature, he wrote in his own diary, "I can realize clearly that by calling upon even a tithe of myriads of living & actual facts," it would "outvie all the romances in the world, & the most famous histories & biographies to boot." The family hadn't heard from George since his capture, Whitman said, apparently forgetting his brother's letter from Danville on October 23, telling their mother *not* to worry about him and to arrange for an officer in the regiment who had not been captured to send his trunk to Brooklyn by express.[70]

George almost died in prison. He managed once more to survive, however, and became part of a general prisoner exchange on February 22, 1865. Arriving in Annapolis from "the Hotel De Libby" (a tobacco warehouse) on the following day, he wrote his mother that "if ever a poor devil was glad to get in a Christian Country it was me." At first the Whitmans didn't think he was included in the exchange, but George was indeed among the Union prisoners now freed. He was given a thirty-day, much deserved furlough and arrived home in Brooklyn in less than fair health on March 5. By April 5, when his furlough came to an end, George was still feeling ill. Reluctantly, at the insistence of his mother and Walt, he applied for an extension. He was suffering from rheumatism, the result apparently of a long running fever he had contracted in prison.[71]

❋ ❋ ❋

In January 1865, just a month before the excitement of the general prisoner exchange, Walt himself had received a long-awaited stroke of luck in his search for a better-paying government post. He was hired as a first-class (lowest grade) clerk in the Bureau of Indian Affairs, Department of the Interior. While he was still in Brooklyn on December 30, William O'Connor had written him an affectionate letter instructing him to make an application, which also served as a writing sample to determine whether he would make a good scrivener. Already Whitman's ardent admirer and soon to be his outspoken champion, O'Connor had arranged for the poet's interview through William T. Otto, assistant secretary of the interior, who had promised "to put you in." "Now, dear Walt," O'Connor wrote, "do this without delay. . . . I have every confidence that you will get a good and an easy berth, a regular income, &c., leaving you time to attend to the soldiers, to your poems, &c—in a word, what Archimedes wanted, a place on which to rest the lever."

O'Connor added that all was well in Washington but that their circle of friends dearly missed his company.[72] And probably Whitman missed theirs, as he had missed his companions at Pfaff's after moving to Washington. The O'Connors, along with Eldridge and two or three others including Burroughs, had been his family away from home ever since he had taken up residence in Washington. At first Whitman lived in a room in the O'Connor residence, then nearby at 394 L Street and 456 6th Street. He took his daily meal with the O'Connors until he moved over by the Capitol (at 502 Pennsylvania Avenue), when his visits were usually limited to Sundays and holidays. When he returned to Washington in January 1865, he took up residence at 468 M Street, near the O'Connors again and adjacent to the Bureau of Indian Affairs, located in the northeast corner basement of the Patent Office.[73]

No one has done a thorough and systematic search of the Indian Affairs records during Whitman's short tenure. A limited investigation in the National Archives has revealed that Whitman kept a low-key presence in the department, while he also worked on his poetry, mostly in the evenings when not in the hospitals. We know from our examination of "Arrow-Tip" in the 1840s that Whitman had, like most citizens of nineteenth-century America before the war, mixed feelings about the American Indian. It appears that he did not take his new situation all that seriously but saw the position in the terms O'Connor had suggested in his letter. Hardly a week on the job, Walt told Jeff that it was "easy enough—I take things very easy—the rule is to come at 9 and go at 4, but I don't come at 9, and only stay till 4 when I want, as at present to finish a letter for the mail." He described the "Indian office" as a bureau of the Interior Department, "which has charge of quite a large mass of business relating to the numerous Indian tribes in West & Northwest, large numbers of whom are under annuities, supplies, &c for the government." The work was easy enough but apparently only as engaging as his passing interest in the Indian at this time. "All I have hitherto employed myself about," he said, "has been making copies of reports & Bids, &c for the office to send up to the Congressional Committee on Indian Affairs."[74] Indian Affairs was hardly a hot topic for either Congress or Whitman in January 1865.

One of the books he was working on was *Drum-Taps,* perhaps inspired by Louisa May Alcott's reminiscence of her nursing experiences (before she too fell ill, from typhus) in *Hospital Sketches* (1863). Whitman had been putting together *Drum-Taps,* first with poems upbeat for war after the firing on Fort Sumter and then after Fredericksburg with compositions full of pathos at the horror of the contest. Like *Leaves of Grass,* these poems were written on the go. *Drum-Traps,* Whitman told Traubel, "was all written in this manner—all of it—all put together by fits and starts, on the field, in the hospitals, as I worked with the soldier boys."[75] By March 1865 he had gone back to Brooklyn to have the book printed.[76]

It was nearly printed when one of the worst events of the war occurred—the assassination of Abraham Lincoln. While watching the play *Our American Cousin* at Ford's Theatre on April 14, Good Friday evening, he was mortally wounded by John Wilkes Booth, an actor and southern sympathizer. The president died the next day in a residence across the street. Whitman had deeply admired Lincoln and steadfastly believed in him politically, although members of his family, including George and Jeff, did not, at least not as consistently. It has been said that Lincoln read aloud passages from *Leaves of Grass* in his law offices in Illinois. There is also the story, possibly apocryphal, that once from the East Room Lincoln asked the identity of a figure who regularly passed the White House to or from one of the hospitals. Hearing it was Whitman, Lincoln allegedly remarked, "Well, *he* looks like a *man.*"[77]

We know from the entries in *Specimen Days* what Whitman thought of Lincoln, but most of the evidence arguing for Lincoln's awareness of Whitman is based on sketchy evidence. We do know, however, that Lincoln was aware of Whitman and of the poet's admiration for him. Much of what Whitman said about the president in *Specimen Days* appeared in his journalism before the assassination, and much of that was in the *New York Times,* which Lincoln undoubtedly read. "I see the President almost every day," Whitman had written in the *Times* of August 16, 1863. Whitman did indeed see him almost daily that summer as Lincoln rode into town from the Soldier's Home in the northern part of the city, where he spent the nights to escape the heat. "The party makes no great show in uniforms or horses," Whitman noted appreciatively. "Mr. Lincoln generally rides a good-sized easy-going gray horse, is dressed in plain black, somewhat rusty and dusty; wears a black stiff hat, and looks about as ordinary in attire, &c., as the commonest man." He came close to addressing Lincoln as a "Calamus" lover in his fond descriptions. "I saw very plainly the President's dark brown face, with the deep cut lines, the eyes, &c., always to me with a deep latent sadness in the expression." He went on: "I saw the President in the face fully, as they were moving slow, and his look, though abstracted, happened to be directed steadily in my eye. [He bow'd and smiled, but far beneath his smile] I noticed well the expression I have alluded to. None of the artists or pictures have caught the deep though subtle and indirect expression of this man's face. They have only caught the surface. There is something else there. One of the great portrait painters of two or three centuries ago is needed." In subsequent versions of this article, after Lincoln's death, he added the part in brackets. Later, in his Lincoln lectures, Whitman would continue slyly to exaggerate his relationship with the fallen president.[78]

His new position at the Indian Bureau, with its improved salary, allowed him to pay for the printing of his war poems. The first edition appeared in late May and contained fifty-three new poems, including the hastily composed "Hush'd be the camps to-day," responding to the assassination. The "second edition," or "Sequel to *Drum-Taps*," was printed in October 1865. Sewn into the first issue (or "edition"), whose copies were mostly held back from distribution over the summer, the sequel contained eighteen new poems, including two written for Lincoln. Copies of the original *Drum-Taps* are extremely rare, while the combined edition of *Drum-Taps* and the "Sequel" is easier to find and also available in facsimile.[79] The original *Drum-Taps* poems were dispersed throughout the final (1881) arrangement of *Leaves of Grass* so that, of the seventy-one contained in the first issue of *Drum-Taps* and the "Sequel," only thirty-eight are retained in the definitive groupings "Drum-Taps" and "Memories of President Lincoln."[80]

Many of the original *Drum-Taps* poems were short fillers, written to avoid the sea of white on the page when another poem ended in the middle. This was a practice Whitman must have adopted as a printer.

Many of these poems were removed to obscure sections of the definitive edition or discarded entirely. Three of the "fillers," however, have come down to us as part of Whitman's more memorable compositions—"When I heard the learn'd Astronomer," "A Broadway pageant," and the poet's closest thing to a traditional love poem, "Out of the rolling ocean, the crowd." They clearly have nothing to do with the war, but neither do some of the other poems in the first issue, including "Beginning my studies," which was transferred to the "Inscriptions" section of the definitive edition. "Shut not your doors to me, proud libraries" was also placed there in 1881, but as Gay Wilson Allen remarks, the poem in its initial version was appropriate to the war theme: contrary to the impression created by the poem's placement in the 1881 edition, what the poet brings is not poems that might be refused by the censor but verses about the war and the national sacrifice for democracy.[81]

> Shut not your doors to me, proud libraries,
> For that which was lacking among you all, yet needed
> most, I bring;
> A book I have made for your dear sake, O soldiers,
> And for you, O soul of man, and you, love of comrades;
> The words of my book nothing, the life of it everything.
> A book separate, not link'd with the rest, nor felt by
> the intellect;
> But you will feel every word, O Libertad! arm'd
> Libertad!
> It shall pass by the intellect to swim the sea, the air,
> With joy with you, O soul of man.

By far, the most important poem of the eighteen in the "Sequel" (and one of Whitman's finest) is "When Lilacs Last in the Door-yard Bloom'd." It came out of one of the great accidents of history, a book that was initially completed before the assassination. Another poem about Lincoln in the series—"O Captain! My Captain!"—has been mocked by serious Whitman critics for its sing-song quality and its near-conventional meter and rhyme, internal as well as external. It became the poet's best-known poem during his lifetime (brother George's favorite), but Whitman once complained to Traubel, "I'm almost sorry I ever wrote the poem."[82] What is finally wrong with it is the tone; it could possibly—and this may have been the reason for its popularity, not only then but today—have served as the lyrics to a song by the Hutchinson or Cheney family singers, whose patriotic songs had warmed Whitman's heart before he fully discovered opera in the late 1840s or early 1850s. The poem has a sing-along allure that undercuts the solemnity and symbolism of what Whitman considered a landmark in American history. One of its three stanzas should suffice for an illustration of its tinpan quality:

> O CAPTAIN! my captain! our fearful trip is done;
> The ship has weather'd every rack, the prize we sought is
>   won;
> The port is near, the bells I hear, the people all exulting,
> While follow eyes the steady keel, the vessel grim and daring:
>   But O heart! heart! heart!
>   Leave you not the little spot,
>   Where on the deck my captain lies,
>   Fallen cold and dead.

"When Lilacs Last in the Dooryard Bloom'd" certainly established the proper tone, but today the poem's original greatness has perhaps been obscured by critics and teachers who overemphasize its trinity of symbols in the lilacs (the poet's perennial love for Lincoln), the fallen star (Lincoln), and the hermit thrush (death, or its chant). Whitman himself did not consider it his best poem.[83] Like Milton, Shelley, Tennyson, and his other predecessors in the art of the elegy, this poet does not mention the name of the deceased in his poem. In Whitman's case, he did not know the subject of the elegy personally. But as his remarks in his wartime journalism and *Specimen Days* suggest, he knew Lincoln intuitively—"I love the President personally," he committed to his diary of October 31, 1863. It was Whitman's passion for the president as the redeemer of the Union and its democracy that makes the poem so successful as a national elegy, turning a monologue into a dialogue with the American reader. Also at work is Whitman's mourning for Lincoln as the commander-in-chief of his beloved soldiers, who suffered and died as Lincoln now has. It was probably the poet's intense involvement in the hospitals that made Lincoln's death so monumental to him. The poet of "Lilacs" claims that he saw "as in noiseless dreams, hundreds of battle-flags," but the "Wound Dresser" actually saw "battle corpses, myriads of them" in the hospitals. For him, Lincoln's death symbolized the war's most profound loss.

The drama of the war was no less disturbing to Whitman because it was presented indirectly. He saw the war through its medical consequences, and he knew the president from a distance that only a vicarious exchange of looks could overcome. He most likely missed the showing of Lincoln's coffin in the East Room of the White House on April 19 (the date in the original subtitle to "Hush'd be the camps today") because he was probably still in Brooklyn, and he probably just missed the ceremonies in New York City on April 24 because he left Brooklyn for Washington on April 21. This would suggest that his descriptions of the president's coffin passing through the "crape-veil'd" cities were based on second-hand information. His route, however, went inland through Harrisburg, so that his train may well have passed the one carrying Lincoln. It may have even stopped in Harrisburg at the same time as the Lincoln train ("With the waiting depot, the arriving coffin, and the sombre faces"). In any event, Whitman had already absorbed the funereal mood of the country while he was in Brooklyn, where the *Eagle* of April 20 reported that "nearly every home was draped in the habiliments of woe."[84]

Despite the overemphasis of the critics, the poem's trinity of symbols is brilliant. Overstressed, the symbols tend to reduce this dynamic threnody to a paradigm like "O Captain! My Captain!" with the image of a ship coming into the port of democracy, its captain "fallen cold and dead." But Whitman does not allow them the reductionist effect they can acquire in a classroom. "Lilacs" is a song of lamentation. Making good use of notes on the habits of the hermit-thrush that he took in conversation with Burroughs,[85] Whitman sings both from the heart of his own experience (as he had in the first and second editions of *Leaves of Grass*) and as Emerson's representative poet, weeping for all Americans. Most in the country were dumbfounded by the president's murder, since Lincoln had ended the war and favored a rapprochement with the South. The *Eagle* of April 17 noted that Booth, according to his neighbor in London for several years, "was afflicted with a temporary aberration of mind one day in every month, and that in the Spring of the year the attacks were the severest." The article suggested hereditary insanity by alluding to the erratic behavior of Junius Brutus Booth, a flamboyant actor and the assassin's father.[86] Whitman saw that the only way to accept Lincoln's death was to understand death itself as the ultimate soother of life's ills and the divine midwife deserving of its own apostrophe.

> Come, lovely and soothing Death,
> Undulate round the world, serenely arriving, arriving,
> In the day, in the night, to all, to each,
> Soon or later, delicate Death.
> . . . .
> Approach, encompassing Death—strong Deliveress!
> When it is so—when thou hast taken them, I joyously sing
> the dead,
> Lost in the loving, floating ocean of thee,
> Laved in the flood of thy bliss, O Death.[87]

With the "knowledge of death" on one side and the "thought of death" on the other, the mourner loosens his hands from both companions, resolving that the death of Lincoln is symbolically good for America. As Whitman wrote in *Specimen Days,* from a notebook entry the day after Lincoln died, "He was assassinated—but the Union is not assassinated—*ça ira!* One falls, and another falls. The soldier drops, sinks like a wave—but the ranks of the ocean eternally press on. Death does its work, obliterates a hundred, a thousand—President, general, captain, private—but the Nation is immortal."[88]

Within weeks of Lincoln's assassination and the publication of *Drum-Taps,* Whitman was dismissed from his Indian Affairs position effective June 30, 1865. He may or may not have been fired because the new secretary of the interior, James Harlan, a former professor of mental and moral science from Iowa, considered *Leaves of Grass* obscene. Whitman later claimed that Harlan had found a copy of the 1860 edition of *Leaves of Grass* (which was being revised for the 1867 edition) in the poet's office desk.[89] In a defense of his actions twenty-nine years after the fact, Harlan stated that Whitman was dismissed solely "*on the grounds that his services were not needed.* And no other reason was ever assigned by my authority." As he noted in his letter, when he took over the department his payroll included "a considerable number of useless incumbents who were seldom at their respective desks," and no doubt this included Whitman, who told Jeff that he came and went as he pleased.[90]

Harlan notified his various bureaus to weed out "needless and worthless material." Although he does not acknowledge it in his letter, the order to fire Whitman actually came directly from him, however, because William P. Dole, chief of Indian Affairs, resisted the secretary's directive. Dole denied that any of his subordinates in the Indian Bureau were guilty of conduct that (in Harlan's words) did "not come within the rules of decorum & propriety prescribed by a Christian Civilization." (This last phrase may be evidence that Whitman was fired for his book.) Dole himself was dismissed by Harlan for insubordination on June 10.[91] Harlan, it appears, was combining a bureaucratic housecleaning with an effort to get a writer whose work he despised out of government service.

Harlan was not the first official who had tried to prevent Whitman's employment in Washington. As a United States senator who had given up his position to become Lincoln's interior secretary and a politician who strongly supported the president's war policy, Harlan was in a cabinet circle that included Salmon P. Chase, a proper New England dignitary who hoped to succeed Lincoln and was therefore careful not to incite public scandal by hiring any questionable individuals in his Department of the Treasury. Chase, in a sense, had also "fired" Whitman from government work. Although he had preserved the letter he received from Emerson on December 11, 1863, recommending Whitman to him for government service, he could not agree with Emerson's endorsement. He was helped in this decision by John Townsend Trowbridge, a fellow New Englander and Whitman's acquaintance from 1860 who served as an intermediary between the poet and the treasury secretary. Yet Trowbridge was somewhat two-faced when it came to the poet. Trowbridge had come to Washington to write Chase's campaign biography for the 1864 election. He lived at the Chase residence.[92] After presenting Whitman's Emerson letter to Chase he remembered, "I felt that the Secretary, if he was to appoint him, should know just whom he was appointing."[93] In any case, Whitman should have known that he would have no chance with Chase. He had recorded in his notebook in 1862 that the secretary of the treasury had asked a mutual acquaintance who kept a copy of *Leaves of Grass* in his house for guests to see, "How is it possible you can have this nasty book here?"[94]

One New Englander Whitman could count on was the Boston-born O'Connor, who was irate when he heard of the dismissal. An ardent abolitionist, O'Connor must have been just as devastated politically by Lincoln's assassination as Whitman was personally, for during the war the president seemingly had come around to the position that the fiery Irishman had long and vigorously supported. In fact, he shared the concern of Charlie Eldridge that, with the death of Lincoln, the Emancipation Proclamation might somehow be turned around or fatally modified. But in *The Good Gray Poet* O'Connor wrote an eulogy instead of an elegy, for Whitman instead of Lincoln. J. Hubley Ashton, a member of the O'Connor-Whitman circle in Washington and the assistant attorney general who afterward hired Whitman in his own office, remembered the events thirty-seven years later:

> O'Connor came down to my office from his room above in the Treasury Building [he was then working for the Light-House Board, a position he had held since 1861] . . . with Secretary Harlan's letter to Walt in his hand, and his terrific outburst against the Secretary for his act of infamy, as he described it. . . . I fancy that there was never before such an outpouring of impassioned eloquence in the presence of an audience of *one.* The wrong committed, as O'Connor said, was the ignominious dismissal from the public service of the greatest poet America had produced, an offence against the honor and dignity of American letters, and against humanity itself as consecrated in "Leaves of Grass."[95]

Ashton's statement sums up the forty-six-page pamphlet O'Connor produced later that summer and fall, which excoriates Harlan as "Cato the Censor" and celebrates Whitman. This was the first book ever written about Walt Whitman—if not the first formal biography, the first (and most famous) hagiography. O'Connor has been censured himself for the zealotry of *The Good Gray Poet,* some even arguing that Whitman helped write it as he later helped Burroughs write *Notes on Walt Whitman as Poet and Person* (1867). But the outspoken O'Connor was uncannily aware of Harlan's agenda and mostly his own person in writing *The Good Gray Poet.* Whitman's only contribution was to approve of the project and to suggest some specific statements about his poetry in the pamphlet's initial stage of composition, which was outlined as a letter of complaint from Assistant Attorney General Ashton to Secretary Harlan. The holograph was drafted in O'Connor's hand, but there also survive several pages of suggestions ("Something like the following will probably suggest the intention & theory of Leaves of Grass") in the poet's hand.[96] Although Ashton was a close friend, it is doubtful that he would ever have consented to sign such a hostile letter to a fellow officer in the presidential administration. *The Good Gray Poet* appeared to mixed reviews in January 1866, printed by Bunce and Huntington, the same firm that printed the "Sequel to *Drum-Taps.*"

Meanwhile, Whitman settled into the Attorney General's Office, filling a spot just vacated by Edmund Clarence Stedman, who later wrote an important, if not altogether approving, assessment of *Leaves of Grass.*[97] The job was more demanding than his post at Interior, at least at first. The main work, he told several of his soldier friends, was interviewing Confederate officers and others for presidential pardons. Technically, membership in the Confederate Army was treason. But Andrew Johnson, Lincoln's successor, had issued a proclamation in May automatically pardoning all offenders except leading Confederates and those owning $20,000 or more in taxable property. These individuals had to apply for a pardon in person in the Attorney General's Office. "There are some real characters among them," Whitman wrote of the petitioners, "and you know I have a fancy for anything out of the ordinary." Four or five thousand applications had already passed through the office, either in person or represented by their widows, all "dressed in deep black."[98]

Outside, in the streets of Washington, a different kind of procession was taking place. For two entire days in late May 1865 the victorious Union armies of the East and West passed down Pennsylvania Avenue in grand review, afterward to disperse forever. On May 25 Whitman told his beloved mother that "it was too much & too impressive, to be described." He then proceeded to put on record what is probably one of the best contemporary descriptions of the historic reunion and farewell. "Imagine a great wide avenue like Flatbush avenue," he told her, "quite flat, & stretching as far as you can see, with a great white building half as big as fort Greene at the commencement of the avenue, & then through this avenue marching solid ranks of soldiers, 20 or 25 abreast, just marching steady all day long for two days, without intermission, one regiment after another, real war-worn *soldiers,* that have been marching & fighting for years." Two of the generals who passed close by on horseback as Whitman watched were William Tecumseh Sherman ("old Bill, the soldiers all call him") and Grant ("the noblest Roman of them all"), but he told his mother that "the *rank & file* was the greatest sight of all."[99]

One of the marchers who had risen from those ranks was Mrs. Whitman's son George, recently returned from his extended furlough and promoted to major. Before he was discharged from the army later that summer when the Fifty-First Regiment of New York Volunteers finally disbanded, he was promoted once more, to the rank of breveted lieutenant colonel, possibly in consolation for the army's refusal to grant him a regular or permanent commission because he was not a graduate of a military academy.[100]

As "Colonel Whitman" prepared to return to Brooklyn and his former trade as a cabinetmaker, his older brother adjusted to his new job in the Attorney General's Office. Walt also continued his hospital work, as the massive medical effort in Washington attempted to wind itself down. He told the parents of one soldier on June 10 that there were still "hundreds & thousands of [men] here, wounded or sick, in the great army hospitals"—"many of them suffering with amputations & wounds—others with sickness & so faint & weak, this weather—it is enough to make one's heart bleed." There were twice as many sick as there were wounded. In spite of the lingering caseload, the Patent Hospital, activated only after battles with heavy casualties, had closed for the last time over a year before, and the infamous Armory-Square was broken up in late August—"all the sick & wounded . . . taken away, or forwarded home." Nevertheless, the poet noted, even though the "war is over . . . the hospitals are fuller than ever."[101]

10

TRUE LOVE

No single person is the subject of Whitman's song, or can be; the individual suggests a group, and the group a multitude, each unit of which is as interesting as every other unit, and possesses equal claims to recognition.

EDWARD DOWDEN
"The Poetry of Democracy"

In October 1866 the *London Fortnightly Review* published an essay by Moncure Conway in which the old friend of Emerson—and Whitman—trailed after the Brooklyn poet as he mingled with the working people in his neighborhood. Conway asked a man in corduroy work pants whether he knew the identity of the man in the beard and casual attire. "'That be Walt Whitman.' 'What sort of man is he?' 'A fusrate man is Walt. Nobody knows Walt but likes him; nearly everybody knows him, and—*loves* him.' . . . 'He has written a book—hasn't he?' 'Not as ever I hearn on.'" Just as O'Connor remarks in *The Good Gray Poet* that few, or perhaps none, of the soldiers in the hospitals knew of Whitman's publications, Conway notes that few of the poet's ferry pilot and stage driver friends knew that he had ever written a book. He also points out that before the first edition of *Leaves of Grass,* Whitman had almost nothing to do with literary people. Although Whitman and O'Connor were disturbed by some of Conway's exaggerations about the poet's eccentric ways, the piece nevertheless presents a picture that rings true, of someone who was truly at home in public places and in the company of nonliterary laboring folk.

Whitman seldom if ever mentioned his poetry to his mechanic and blue-collar friends, possibly because he got no coherent response or show of interest. Indeed, one wonders just what he talked about with this class of friends. Yet because they were on the same level as most of his siblings, they were extensions of his family, or the Ryerson Street neighborhood that had witnessed the birth of *Leaves of Grass.* Now, in the wake of the war, the "neighborhood" was Washington, its book *Drum-Taps.* The working-class friend of this era became Peter Doyle.

The Irish-born Doyle may or may not have been Whitman's lover, but it is certain he became Walt's dearest friend. Through Walt, he also became the fond acquaintance of Eldridge, Burroughs, and O'Connor. When the Civil War broke out, Doyle was approximately eighteen.[1] He was living with his large family (like Whitman's) in Richmond, Virginia, and working as a cooper. Enlisting in the Richmond Fayette Artillery on April 25, 1861, he fought in the war on the Confederate side in some of the bloodiest early battles. (Doyle's regiment was named for the Marquis de Lafayette, one of Whitman's Revolutionary heroes.) He was wounded at Antietam, as he fought across the line from Lieutenant George Whitman. One of his brothers, later a police officer in Washington who fell in the line of duty, fought for the Union. Pete mustered out on November 7, 1862, shortly before the Battle of Fredericksburg, where his unit also fought and where he would have found himself across the firing line from another Whitman, the noncombatant Walt. After his wounding, Doyle obtained a release from the army by reclaiming his status as a British subject. But instead of returning to Ireland as promised, he remained in Virginia until a crackdown on foreigners falsely claiming exemptions threatened to put him back into a Rebel uniform. He immediately crossed Rebel lines and went to Washington. His imprisonment in the spring of 1863 for attempting to enter from "the insurgent states, without a permit" has led to unfounded speculation that he was also, like the poet's brother, a prisoner of war. Between April 18 and May 11, 1863, he was confined to the Carroll Prison, an annex of the Old Capitol Prison. Upon taking the oath not to aid the Rebellion, he was released.

It is not clear exactly when Whitman met Doyle. Although their extant correspondence does not commence until 1868, the conductor traced their relationship to a stormy Washington night in 1866. And his biographer has gathered evidence to suggest the meeting occurred in the winter of 1865. Whitman boarded Doyle's trolley at the Capitol after visiting John Burroughs, whose house and large garden were on the hill now occupied by one of the Senate office buildings. Doyle told Bucke the story in 1895:

> You ask where I first met him? It is a curious story. We felt to each other at once. I was a conductor. [Doyle's route passed Whitman's office at the Treasury Building, running up and down Pennsylvania Avenue between Georgetown and the navy yard.] The night was very stormy. . . . Walt had his blanket—it was thrown round his shoulders—he seemed like an old sea captain. He was the only passenger, it was a lonely night, so I thought I would go in and talk with him. Something in me made me do it and something in him drew me that way. He used to say there was something in me had the same effect on him. Anyway, I went into the car. We were familiar at once—I put my hand on his knee—we understood. He did not get out at the end of the trip—in fact went all the way back with me. . . . From that time on we were the biggest sort of friends.[2]

Even if we take into consideration the differences between conventional male relationships today and those of more than a century ago, something unusual was going on here. Sometime later, in an encrypted notebook entry that has had its fill of interpretations, Whitman wrote, "TO GIVE UP ABSOLUTELY & *for good, from this present hour,* this FEVERISH, FLUCTUATING, *useless* UNDIGNIFIED PURSUIT *of 164.*" The number allegedly refers to the sixteenth and fourth letters of the alphabet, "P" and "D" for Peter Doyle. The entry identifies "PD" first as a man, then (with "him" apparently erased) as a female: "LET THERE FROM THIS HOUR BE NO FALTERING, NO GETTING—*at all henceforth,* (NOT ONCE, UNDER *any circumstances*)—*avoid seeing her, or meeting her.* . . . "[3] Was the feminine pronoun another example of Whitman's concealing the gender of his male lover, as he may have done in a manuscript version of "Once I Pass'd Through a Populous City"? If so, why didn't he simply destroy the entry? Whitman's pocket notebooks are riddled with evidences of such missing pages.

One thing the entry suggests is that Doyle was not a willing homosexual lover, since the "PURSUIT" is described as "*useless*" and "UNDIGNIFIED." Because he was a willing companion and, as his later testimony confirms, deeply enamored of the poet as a friend and confidant, it seems unlikely that Doyle was homosexual but not interested in Whitman.[4] If the entry is a concealed reference to Doyle, it may also be evidence that Whitman himself was resisting his strong attraction to the streetcar conductor. Doyle confesses in his description of their first meeting that he felt an equally extraordinary attraction for Whitman. In any case, it is impossible to know the intimate details of the relationship. Whitman's letters to Doyle are warm but fatherly, calling him "boy" and "son." Doyle, around twenty-four years younger than the poet, probably became Whitman's last soldier boy, one like Lewy Brown, through whom Whitman sent his regards to the rest of the gang at the hospitals when he was home in Brooklyn. Now it was the conductor gang, and Whitman conveyed witticisms and inside jokes to them through Doyle. He seems to have known the conductor's associates intimately, the same class of fellows as the one who told Conway he had never "hearn" of Walt's writing a book. Their talk included risqué allusions to women and illicit affairs, or the fantasy of one,[5] and it is hard to believe that these men were homosexual. Whitman might have kissed them. He told Pete on September 10, 1869, that he had kissed his New York mates, but then he added significantly, "I am an exception to all their customs with others."[6]

Indeed, what separated this transcendentalist and realist from his literary contemporaries was his intense need for human affection and his endless resources to give it. Emerson and Thoreau were socially "cold," and Melville was perhaps "angry." We can see Whitman's capacity for love not only in his letters to soldiers such as Tom Sawyer, whom Whitman dearly missed after he went back to battle, but also in his correspondence with soldiers toward whom he was not romantically inclined—lads who had gone home after the war and would never see the poet again. Whitman's earliest ancestors had crossed over from England on the *True Love,* the ship's name perhaps a sign of what was to come. Walt was the fellow, as the man told Conway, who was known—and *loved*—by all, at that most democratic of American social levels.

❋ ❋ ❋

During the spring of 1865 and through 1866, the political situation between the president and Congress heated up considerably. In July Henry Stanbery, a staunch ally of President Andrew Johnson's, became attorney general and Whitman's new boss. Johnson, the son of a porter and himself a former tailor, had picked up right where the slain Lincoln left off in his attitude toward the defeated South and how and when it should be reunited with the northern states. Both presidents believed that the rebellious states had never constitutionally left the Union, a position that Congress did not accept and that later set up Johnson for his historic battles. Radical Republicans, members of the very party that had drawn Whitman away from the Democratic Party in the late 1840s with its favorable stand on the Wilmot Proviso, now represented the former "Union" party, which argued that the seceding states had forfeited their constitutional rights and would only be readmitted to the Union as "conquered provinces." The Republicans wanted to make sure the northern victory meant something, that southern aristocrats didn't regain everything, or anything, on the sly. Johnson himself had talked the same tough talk at first, but he more or less reversed himself with the Proclamation of May 29, 1865, which, while it disenfranchised most leading Confederates, permitted other southern whites "loyal" to the union to reorganize state governments. This about-face offended the Republican Congress led by the feisty Thaddeus Stevens of Pennsylvania, who hated the South so much for its slave-holding that he demanded at his dying hour to be buried in a Negro cemetery. In effect, the proclamation appeared to preempt Congress's own will, whose official effect had to wait until December when Congress then regularly met. Everyone, of course, expected the eventual restoration of these governments, but Johnson's idea seemed both premature and wrong-headed, a means by which the rebellious states could erase most of the northern gains of the war and perhaps even reinstate slavery.[7]

The political unity in the North that directly followed Lincoln's assassination was finally shattered on April 6, 1866, when Congress passed the first Civil Rights Act over Johnson's veto. (Just a century later another President Johnson signed the second.) History has proved Andrew Johnson constitutionally correct and generally above politics with his seemingly lenient stand on the South, and it was probably his temperament, rather than his policies, that brought about his downfall. Johnson was no Lincoln. Both presidents had begun their lives in relative poverty, but Johnson was a consummate outsider, whereas Lincoln was one of our shrewdest statesmen and consensus builders. Johnson was tough enough to get up in the world in spectacular fashion, serving at all levels of state government in Tennessee including a prewar governorship, but he strove for social acceptance instead of self-acceptance. He had long resented the southern aristocracy in North Carolina and Tennessee that mocked his humble economic and social beginnings. He even became Lincoln's vice president in 1864 because he was a political outsider. As a senator from Tennessee, he had refused to go along with the state's attempt to secede with the rest of the South and in consequence became its northern military governor during the conflict. And now this former Democrat was fast becoming an outsider in his own—Republican—party.

Essentially, Johnson, always stubborn over principles, clashed with the Radicals. After successive vetoes were overruled by an obdurate Congress, the president was reduced to a partial figurehead.[8] In March 1866 the Republicans (outnumbering the Democrats 128 to 35 in the House and 40 to 12 in the Senate) passed the Civil Rights Act. Johnson's veto was overridden in April, and the legislation was turned into the Fourteenth Amendment, which awarded ex-slaves full U.S. citizenship and required state constitutions to give full suffrage to all male citizens, including former slaves. (One of the reasons for its passage was to discourage blacks from moving north, where even military veterans who had fought to free them strongly opposed the black vote.)[9] The measure was aimed at punishing the South: it made possible the eventual election of black legislators at the height of Reconstruction.

On March 7, 1867, less than a year after passage of the Civil Rights Act, Congress passed the Military Reconstruction Act, which swept away the southern state governments established under Johnson's policy and created five military districts, each commanded by a former

Union general and fortified by 20,000 troops. And to ensure that southern states, once readmitted to the Union, did not rescind Negro suffrage under the Fourteenth Amendment, Congress proposed the Fifteenth Amendment, passed in 1869 and ratified a year later, which gave black males the national right to vote.

❋ ❋ ❋

Whitman himself thought highly of Johnson, noting in the letter to his mother about the grand review of Union troops in 1865 that he found the new president "very plain & substantial . . . just that plain middling-sized ordinary man [who] . . . should be the master of all these myriads of soldiers." For now he took a neutral position on the debate between the Republicans and the president.[10] In July 1866, shortly before the end of the "Civil Rights" Congress, he told his mother, "It is generally expected Congress will adjourn the last of this month, & then there will be some high old times in politics & the Departments—most of us think that AJ is only waiting for that, to lay around him & kick up his heels at a great rate. Well, we shall see what comes to pass—but I guess the Republicans are just every bit as ferocious as he is—they won't back down an inch."[11] A recent biography has suggested that Whitman compromised his former political principles with regard to civil rights because he was dependent on a government job and its influence. Since the late 1840s and his *Eagle* editorship, however, he had stayed above the game, and he continued the pattern in Washington. "There's not much excitement in Washington," he told Broadway Jack, a New York stage driver, after the impeachment trials of Johnson, "at least none that I take any interest in. Politics and politicians carry the day here—but I meddle with them very little."[12]

On the first of May in 1866 ("Moving Day" in Brooklyn and New York), Mrs. Whitman, "Edd," and the Jeff Whitmans moved from Portland Street, the house they had occupied throughout the war, to what was to Walt's mother a less satisfactory rental house at 840 Pacific Avenue, between Washington and Grand avenues. By this time Jeff was frequently away on out-of-town jobs; he would take a permanent one in St. Louis in 1867. Mat and the girls were either living with Mrs. Whitman and Eddy, or close by. There was more fresh air at the new address, which was somewhat elevated, but this turned into cold winds that pierced the poorly insulated walls in winter. George was building houses in Brooklyn, and Walt hoped vaguely to persuade his brother to build their mother one on a lot George owned on Portland Street.[13] Mrs. Whitman had begun to dream of a house of her own, farther away from Jeff's two children, whom she loved but was getting too old to have underfoot. She even urged Walt to build a little house in Washington, but neither house ever materialized. If Walt had purchased the lot from George (at $250, the price he paid), George might have gone ahead with the plan.

In late August Walt came home to Brooklyn on leave, in order to print the fourth edition of *Leaves of Grass*—"that *unkillable* work," he told Abby Price. Because the Pacific Avenue house was too small for guests, he planned to lodge somewhere in the neighborhood. But Mrs. Price, who now lived in Manhattan and had an extra room at 279 East 55th Street, invited him to stay there. Walt was undoubtedly not the easiest houseguest. Though almost obsessed with personal cleanliness, he was otherwise not an orderly person. Helen, Abby's daughter, then a teenager, remembered that the curtains in his room were an "abomination." "I would . . . find them twisted into ropes and drawn back as far as possible." The guest room was strewn with letters, cuttings, and "scraps on which there would be words, lines, and sometimes a page of manuscript."[14] With his edition put swiftly into production, he was back in Washington by the end of September. While still in Brooklyn, he noted that the war and incarceration had "left their mark" on George, who also suffered from periods of brooding apparently common to the Whitmans and apparently attributable to the father. Walt's mother and older sister, Mary, also suffered from the same dizziness "in the head," probably from high blood pressure, that Whitman continued to complain about after the war.[15]

Whitman's postwar plan was primarily literary, to build up the reputation of *Leaves of Grass* (and himself as America's only authentic poet), a recognition effort that had been derailed by the war. He also began, no doubt spurred on by O'Connor's pamphlet, a quiet but relentless campaign to demonstrate that he had been consciously ignored in his own country. A decade later, this campaign may have resulted in an article in the *West Jersey Press* that stated, "Whitman's poems in their public reception have fallen still-born."[16] For three editions before the war, he had withstood criticism, often using himself as an anonymous reviewer for the defense. Others such as Henry Clapp and Ada Clare had helped, but their era had vanished with the war. Whitman was now coming into a new literary age—the age of realism, which defined itself in contradistinction to the romanticism of the previous era, first by factual reports of the war and then by a kind of romanticism of its own, based on nature's opposition to human happiness.

Whitman's previous book, *Drum-Taps,* and its "Sequel," had hardly been published before it came under attack. Most reviewers, like the one in the *Brooklyn Daily Union* of November 23, 1865, praised Whitman's wartime hospital service, but they refused to grant him the title of poet. In the *Round Table* William Dean Howells, fresh from Venice, where he had sat out the war with a consulship for writing Lincoln's campaign biography, thought Whitman was less than a true poet because he gave his readers the process of art rather than the result. "We want its effect, its success," Howells wrote in the issue of November 11, "we do not want to plant corn, to hoe it, to drive the crows away, to gather it, husk it, grind it, sift it, bake it, and butter it, before eating it, and then take the risk of its being at last moldy in our mouths. And this is what you have to do in reading Mr. Whitman's rhythm." The future realist was in effect complaining about Whitman's naturalistic detail, which gave his readers pathos, he thought, but not artistic transcendence. (Burroughs would be right the next year when he said that the criteria for art would have to change before Whitman would be accepted.) In making this claim Howells ignored such poems as "Vigil Strange I Kept on the Field One Night" and "A Sight in Camp in the Daybreak Gray and Dim." Nevertheless, the review is important for the way Howells, who later claimed to have greeted Whitman in Pfaff's, probably goaded the poet into undertaking a lifelong campaign to make *Leaves of Grass* not merely part of the American canon but its new model.

Echoing Emerson's comment to Carlyle (which must have become public knowledge long before the publication of the Emerson-Carlyle correspondence in 1883) about having to hold one's nose to read parts of *Leaves of Grass,* Howells observed that one did not have to do the same while reading *Drum-Taps. Drum-Taps* was simply too abstract—"unspeakably inartistic." Then Howells went for a main artery: "The time to denounce or to ridicule Mr. Whitman for his first book is past. The case of *Leaves of Grass* was long ago taken out of the hands of counsel and referred to the great jury. They have pronounced no audible verdict; but what does their silence mean?" Now, rejected by the public for his indecency, the poet had "cleansed the old channels of their filth" to pour through "a stream of blameless purity, and the public has again to decide . . . on the question of his poethood." The verdict was already in for the future editor of the *Atlantic Monthly.* "Art," he concluded, "cannot greatly employ itself with things in embryo. The instinct of the beast may interest science; but poetry, which is nobler than science, must concern itself with natural instincts only as they can be developed into the sentiments and ideas of the soul of man." The depth of Howells's aversion to Whitman's new brand of poetry, clean or unclean, has never been stated clearly enough. When one of his friends from Columbus, Ohio, asked him to contribute to the purchase of a horse and buggy for Whitman in 1888, he did so on the condition that his gift of $10 not be regarded as "a critical endorsement of [Whitman's] poetry or his theory of poetry . . . and on the condition that I do not appear in the list of subscribers."[17]

Within a week of the Howells review, Henry James, Jr., called *Drum-Taps* "an offense against art" in the *Nation.* Generally, he agreed with Howells's complaint that the wartime poems assaulted the emotions while insulting the intellect and its sense of art as a lofty rendition of experience. "Of course the tumult of a battle is grand, the results of a battle tragic, and the untimely deaths of young men a theme for elegies," he wrote. "But he is not a poet who merely reiterates these plain facts *ore rotundo.* He only sings them worthily who views them from a height."[18] James thought *Drum-Taps* "a melancholy task to read" because its verses "openly pretend to be something better" than the run of wartime poetry in newspapers when they clearly were not.

From a later and more mature perspective—when he referred to his review as "a little atrocity"—James came quite about-face on Whitman's poetry. In the Lamb House library in Rye, England, James's copy of the 1900 issue of *Leaves of Grass* (including the "Drum-Taps" section) has been favorably marked by its owner. Edith Wharton remembered an evening at the Mount, her American retreat in Lenox, Massachusetts, when the two sat up late one night reading *Leaves of Grass.* James's voice, she recalled "filled the hushed room like an organ adagio" as he read from not only "Song of Myself" and "Out of the Cradle Endlessly Rocking" but the best poem of the "Sequel" to *Drum-Taps,* "When Lilacs Last in the Dooryard Bloom'd."[19]

But converts from upper-crust literary America were, like James, long in coming. Since the American average reader, as Howells noted, hadn't spoken out for *Leaves of Grass,* Whitman decided to seek the approval of the English, whose opinion even the American literary Brahmins and Harvard elites still feared. The poet's first foray was arranged by O'Connor, who either persuaded or helped Conway, who was now living in England, to introduce Whitman and his book to the British reading public. Conway, who had been Emerson's first emissary to Brooklyn upon the appearance of the 1855 edition of *Leaves of Grass,* was an impressionable man of the cloth who had subscribed to several denominations during his brief career. Born into a slave-owning Virginia family, Conway began his adult life as an itinerant Methodist preacher out of Rockville, Maryland. He soon came under the influence of Hicksite Quakers and their doctrine of the "inner light." Before he was twenty, he came to the conclusion that slavery was wrong. He enrolled in the Harvard Divinity School and immediately sought out Emerson in Concord. It was his hero-worship of Emerson that made him also Whitman's disciple.[20]

Conway's extravagantly written "Walt Whitman" appeared in October 1866. Walt told his mother the next month: "I sent you day before yesterday a paper with the piece in (or most of it) from the London *Fortnightly Review*—it was meant well, but a good deal of it is most ridiculous." O'Connor in particular rued the essay, mildly chiding Conway for his excesses and privately calling it "a frightful mess of misstatement and fiction."[21] Through O'Connor, Whitman had tried to control what Conway said, hoping the essay would focus more on the originality of *Leaves* and less on Whitman as a literary curiosity. Together they wrote the literary manifesto that Conway included verbatim in his essay, its having been conveyed to him in a letter under O'Connor's signature.[22] The passage is an almost exact copy of a paragraph in the letter O'Connor and Whitman wrote together in 1865 after the poet's dismissal from the Bureau of Indian Affairs, the one to be sent to James Harlan under J. Hubley Ashton's name, which was never used.[23] Both letters mark the beginning of a campaign to attack the current state of American literature as the work of dilettantes. "I assume," Conway said, now openly attributing the words to Whitman, "that Poetry in America needs to be entirely recreated. On examining with anything like deep analysis what now prevails in the United States, the whole mass of current poetical works, long and short, consists either of the poetry of an elegantly weak sentimentalism, at bottom nothing but maudlin puerilities, more or less musical in verbiage, . . . or else that class of poetry, plays, &c, of which the foundation is feudalism, with its ideas of lords and ladies, its imported standards of gentility, and the manners of European high-life-below-stairs in every line and verse." What was needed was a literature as strong as America's "mighty and vital breezes, proportionate to our continent with its powerful races of men, its tremendous historic events, its great oceans, its mountains, and its illimitable prairies."

Conway performed a valuable service for Whitman. In spite of the romantic biographical exaggerations and factual errors in the essay, the tone is not only respectful but devoutly committed to the promotion of its subject. The *Fortnightly Review* essay led directly to William Rossetti's English edition of *Leaves of Grass* in 1868. Conway shows a savvy appreciation of Whitman's work and quotes some of his best and most provocative lines. The essay's strategy was first to admit all the bad that Howells and James had complained about ("there is, too, a startling priapism running through it," Conway conceded) and then to argue that the crudeness of nature is a part of everything great. "One might not unreasonably find in the wild and grotesque forms of Walt Whitman's chants, so instinct with life, the true basis of any shaft, not the duplicate of any raised elsewhere, that American thought is to raise."

Conway capped the argument for a more palatable poet with the authorized statement—given long before it appeared in the preface to *As a Strong Bird on Pinions Free* in 1872—that Whitman was now turning to "the religious nature of man, which he regards as essential to the completion of his task."

⁂ ⁂ ⁂

Whitman returned to Washington in the fall of 1866 to find, to his satisfaction, that his position of third-class clerk in the Attorney General's Office had been changed from "temporary" to "permanent." He also received a pay increase, bringing his monthly take to $127 (minus "a little off, every time they pay, on acc't of gov't tax"). From now until the end of the decade, he made more money than at any other time in his life (except for the landslide of cash he received upon the banning of the sixth edition of *Leaves of Grass* in Boston). He was generous as always with his largess, sending his mother money in every letter and lending Jeff money on at least two occasions.[24]

The poet continued tending his sick soldiers, though now his visits were as infrequent as once a week, usually on Sunday. Several of his soldier friends, often amputees, became alcoholics; others died in the hospitals. One who subsequently died had been a guest at the party Whitman organized during Christmastime in 1866, which the poet described as a "complete success—there was plenty, & good too—turkey & four or five kinds of vegetables, & mince pie, &c.—then I purchased a large quantity of navy plug, & smoking tobacco, & pipes, &c. and after dinner every body that wanted to, had a good smoke." He added on a less charitable note that the hospital chaplain was "a miserable coot, like the rest of his tribe." Whitman may have been moving into a "spiritual" phase in *Leaves of Grass,* but he still disapproved of organized religion (as much as it disapproved of him). He got along "wonderfully well," however, with Roman Catholic priests who visited the hospitals.[25]

Whitman brought food regularly, not merely on special occasions. "I carry a big cake often of Sunday afternoons," he told his mother. "I have it made for me by an old mulatto woman, cook, that keeps a stand in the market [today the site of the National Archives on Pennsylvania Avenue]—it is sort of molasses pound cake, common but good." With such sweet and heavy desserts, it is little wonder that healthy people were described as "fat" in the nineteenth century. Whitman's time was also filled up that winter in the library in the Treasury Department, which he had helped to establish and stock. "We have five or six hundred miscellaneous works," he told his mother, and he went on to describe the comforts of his office and its view of the Potomac, which he seldom forgot to mention.[26] His living quarters were another matter. In February he moved two doors down to 472 M Street, near 12th Street, where he occupied a cramped attic apartment. Jeff visited him there that month and was entertained by the O'Connors. Whitman was happy here; he slept soundly for a change and ate well as usual. He told his mother he had "a pocket full of money—which you can call upon when you want any."[27]

The literary side of his life was also picking up. On December 1, 1866, the *Galaxy* published John Burroughs's "Walt Whitman and His 'Drum-Taps,'" a rehearsal of parts of his future *Notes on Walt Whitman as Poet and Person,* which, like O'Connor's letter to Conway, was partly written by Whitman.[28] The *Galaxy* piece, too, with its litany of complaints about the shabby way the book had been received in the United States, looks like Whitman's work. Perhaps thinking of the Howells and James reviews, Whitman's mouthpiece averred that Whitman "has been sneered at and mocked and ridiculed; he has been cursed and caricatured and persecuted, and instead of retorting in like strain, . . . he has preserved his serenity and good nature under all, and illustrated the doctrine of charity he has preached by acts of the most pure and disinterested benevolence."

The Burroughs article also carried Whitman's first public denial of his having read Emerson before writing the 1855 edition of *Leaves of Grass.* "Considering how the critics have fathered him on Emerson, it is valuable to know that he did not make the acquaintance of Emerson's mind" until 1856, when he allegedly took Emerson's essays to Coney Island to read. Transcendentalism had been in the cultural conversation for decades, and Whitman had heard Emerson lecture between 1842 and 1852 at least five times. This denial was literally insincere, especially in light of the way he had exploited Emerson's letter in the second edition, but besides wanting to get in his own spotlight Whitman also realized that he had been influenced by many things, which Emerson may at most have drawn into focus for him in the early 1850s. "He has been a reader of men and of things, and a student of America, much more than of books," the review said. This was true enough. Whitman, though a wide reader and a former bookstore owner, kept relatively few books among his possessions. He drew his main strength from Long Island, or "Paumanok where I was born," from the city that boasted of Broadway, and from the idea of the West, where democracy had the best chance of flourishing. Yet without Emerson, he would have lacked part of the vision of The Poet, or The Artist, who alone—as Emerson's "Representative Man," as singer—could report back the subconscious conversations that human beings have with nature. As Whitman *may* have told John Townsend Trowbridge, Emerson had brought his poetic "simmering" to "a boil."[29]

No sooner did the Burroughs essay appear than O'Connor burst back into print, refreshed from a year's rest after bringing out *The Good Gray Poet,* to publish a four-column review of the 1867 *Leaves of Grass* in the *New York Times* of December 2. From Whitman's point of view, this must have seemed a one-two punch against his critics: *Drum-Taps* was reviewed by one disciple, and *Leaves of Grass* by the other. ("Disciple," however, is probably too strong a word for these independent-minded individuals.) Henry Raymond, the *Times* managing editor who was interested in hiring O'Connor at one point, had either solicited the review or, more likely, been persuaded by O'Connor to run it.

It had also been because of O'Connor's influence and reputation that the Church brothers, William Conant and Francis Pharcellus, had published Burroughs, then almost totally unknown as a writer. They had originally written to O'Connor for a contribution, when the *Galaxy* was founded in 1866 as a New York rival to Boston's *Atlantic Monthly* (which later absorbed it). He begged off and recommended the Burroughs review. The Churches, perhaps fearful of the effect of Whitman's reputation among the established literati, rejected Burroughs's submission, however, until O'Connor convinced them that

Whitman's reputation among American readers and European critics was growing in spite of the official American rebuke.[30]

Showing the O'Connor mixture of eloquence and thunder, the *Times* review was a miniature of *The Good Gray Poet,* and O'Connor concluded it with the same Homeric parallel he used in his pamphlet. But his praise was somewhat compromised by Raymond's qualified appreciation in the editor's preface. While he praised *Drum-Taps* and particularly "When Lilacs Last in the Dooryard Bloom'd" as "some of the loftiest and most beautifully majestic strains ever sounded by human meditation," he couldn't agree that *Leaves of Grass* alone justified "the great claims" O'Connor put forth in the review. And there was another problem, Raymond added. Whitman sometimes "soars aloft" but sometimes wallows "exultingly in unredeemed and irredeemable indecency and filth." Invoking the standards of the day, Raymond concluded: "Until the social circle, the dinner table and the fireside are deemed fitting theatres for every topic and for every act for which the sanction of Nature can be invoked, this volume cannot be accepted as fit for the audience which it seeks and claims." Privately, he told O'Connor: "I hope you won't think the prefatory note needlessly harsh or unjust."

Even the allies, it appeared, were part of the problem of getting *Leaves of Grass* a national audience. Whitman's own brother-in-law Charles Heyde, a scoundrel domestically in the opinion of the Whitman family for the alleged mistreatment of his wife, Hannah, nevertheless had declared himself a friend (albeit a qualified one) of Whitman's poetry. Yet following the O'Connor piece, Heyde wrote Raymond to demur. Whitman told his mother that Heyde had written that "'Walt was a good fellow *enough—but*'—& then he went on to run down Leaves of Grass, like the rest of 'em."[31] Even Raymond's high praise of the elegy to Lincoln was sullied by the fact that he had recently published *The Life and Public Services of Abraham Lincoln* (1865).

With the exception of Burroughs and O'Connor, most of Whitman's "respectable" or middle-class friends seemed to mentally filter out what they saw as indecency. The successful attorney and assistant attorney general J. Hubley Ashton had found Whitman a job when

James Harlan allegedly wanted him thrown out of government as an outrage to the social standard. Ashton could not have hired him without the support of his superior, James Speed, an almost equally powerful presidential advisor. Yet neither Ashton, who later housed the sick Whitman in his Washington mansion for several weeks, nor Speed, whose legal practice was successful, if not lucrative, would have become involved in any defense of Whitman's perceived indecencies. Like Raymond, they loved Whitman when he soared but ran for cover when he started "plunging his seminal muscle" (as "By Blue Ontario's Shores" describes).

Speed stepped down from his government position on July 17, 1866. Shortly afterward, no doubt prompted by his love for the lofty side of Whitman, he asked the poet through Ashton whether he would revise a speech he was scheduled to give on February 12, 1867, in Louisville, Kentucky. On December 29, 1866, Speed wrote Ashton that he had been asked to preside at the unveiling of a statue of Lincoln, which still stands today on the west side of the Louisville public library. "Will you see our friend Walt Whitman and ask him whether he will take my rough draft . . . and revise & finish it for me—I have a notion that if he has the time & is in the mood he can do it better than any man I know." Evidently, Whitman obliged. The speech shows mostly the lawyer's touches of Speed, but here and there we find undeniable Whitman flashes of pathos enshrined in the transcendentalist view of nature's ability to recycle itself out of the compost of death.

> [Lincoln's] character was the legitimate product of American institutions. Step by step he ascended from the humblest to the highest position. His elevation was not an accident. The student of his life must see that he was the child of progress, as the student of our institutions must acknowledge that they are founded on the law of progress. Not the irregular and revolutionary efforts that would pull down rather than build up, but that progress that would wisely use the debris of the past to fertilize the soil for the coming seasons, the healthy and life-giving progress which comes from a clearer and broader view of human rights . . . ; the progress which makes the lessons and wisdom of our fathers the pedestal upon which brighter and higher hopes are to be realized in the future.

The speech depicted Lincoln the statesman as "the legitimate product of American institutions," just as Whitman the poet saw himself as "born here of parents born here from parents the same, and their parents the same." Both were totally "American." It also expressed optimism about the nation in the wake of war by positioning it in the future instead of the present or past, a theme Whitman developed in "Democracy" and *Democratic Vistas.* The poet is most clearly revealed in the phrase "the debris of the past to fertilize the soil" of the future, with its echoes in not only "This Compost" (originally called "Poem of Wonder at The Resurrection of The Wheat") but also the more recent "When Lilacs Last in the Dooryard Bloom'd." There the slain president's coffin passes "the yellow-spear'd wheat, every grain from its shroud in the dark-brown fields uprisen." "It is this backward looking," said the future author of "A Backward Glance O'er Travel'd Roads" through the former attorney general, "which often gives us brighter visions in the future." The essay also employs compound adjectives (e.g., "large-heartedness of Mr. Lincoln"), which Whitman favored. It emphasizes the simplicity of the president's character—"not a learned man, nor did he pretend to be." And like Whitman, Lincoln was above the sectional fray in the Civil War, even though he, like Whitman, wanted the North to win. Lincoln's patriotism "could never be narrowed and dwarfed by State or sectional lines . . . and when he said country, he meant the United States of America, each and all, as well as those that madly sought to sever the bonds that make us one."[32] The Speed essay constitutes Whitman's first prose effort on Lincoln following his death, an effort that culminated in his Lincoln lectures in 1879 and afterward.

❋ ❋ ❋

The war and Lincoln's assassination had left Whitman artistically if not emotionally exhausted, as the fourth (1867) edition of *Leaves of Grass,* with only six new poems, demonstrates. All he could do (and this actually turned out to be an important juncture in the evolution of his book) was to start the rearrangement that culminated in the sixth American edition of 1881. Of the six new poems that found their way into the fourth edition, only three were in any sense significant additions—"Inscription," "When I Read the Book," and "The City Dead-House." The first became, in a shortened version, the first poem in the "Inscriptions" section that opens the 1871 and 1881 editions of *Leaves of Grass.* The second and third lines read:

> *Man's physiology complete, from top to toe, I sing. Not*
> *physiognomy alone, nor brain alone, is worthy for*
> *the muse;—I say the Form complete is worthier*
> *far. The female equally with the male I sing.*
> *Nor cease at the theme of One's-self. I speak the word*
> *of the modern, the word* EN-MASSE.

Perhaps Whitman set these lines in italics because they encapsulate the major themes of *Leaves of Grass.*

"When I Read the Book" is almost identical to its final form in subsequent editions. It asks, "Will some one, when I am dead and gone, write my life?" suggesting that Whitman was actively worrying about the permanence of his reputation as a poet. He also seems troubled and perhaps frightened by death, or at least a premature death as result of the strains of the war. "The City Dead-House," a poem that shares the theme and language of "To a Common Prostitute," speaks of "an outcast form, a poor dead prostitute brought," whose body, though it lies "unclaim'd" on the pavement, is nevertheless that of "The divine woman." Such scenes were common enough on the streets of Washington and New York, but Whitman may have also been thinking—perhaps worrying—about his own sister-in-law, Nancy McClure. Mrs. Whitman had written him that Nancy was wandering the streets as a prostitute and leaving her children to beg when she drank up her profits. She had been pregnant when Andrew died in 1863; that child would be run over by a brewery wagon in 1868. Earlier, in 1865, an older son, Jimmie, was, in the words of his paternal grandmother, "certainly going to destruction."[33]

Walt thought the 1867 *Leaves of Grass* was possibly his last edition (he thought the same thing about his new edition in 1871). But no sooner was it out than he decided to add more poems, though not new ones, to a second issue in the winter of 1867. Just as he had sewn the "Sequel" into *Drum-Taps,* he now sewed the 1865 texts of *Drum-Taps* with its "Sequel" into the new *Leaves;* then in a third issue he added a newly paginated section of previously composed poems under the heading of "Songs Before Parting." The fourth edition is therefore known as "The Workshop Edition" because of its heavy revisions. Its printer's copy is known as the "Blue Book Edition" because Whitman revised directly on the pages of an 1860 edition that he kept in blue covers. It was this book that James Harlan allegedly took from Whitman's desk in Indian Affairs without permission and read. He then dismissed the poet for writing indecent literature.[34]

❋ ❋ ❋

Sometime that spring Burroughs brought out *Notes on Walt Whitman as Poet and Person,* a small slender volume of 108 pages. The book, financed perhaps by Whitman, was printed by the American Book Company in New York. It was intended primarily to advertise the 1867 edition of *Leaves of Grass* and secondarily to continue the campaign to challenge the standard of the evening lamp in literature. Burroughs (or Whitman) asserted "the theory that the standard by which to measure the work of a poet of the very first class, is neither the standard of the parlor, of society, nor even of aesthetics or erudition, but the standard of the actual World, with humanity as its choicest fruition." With Whitman and his eradication of sexual taboos, democracy was "embodied" in poetry for the first time. Not since Poe had any American poet so entwined himself with a literary theory. The poetry itself may not have been coming out of a laborer's house on Ryerson Street in Brooklyn any longer, as it had in the first edition, but the poetic theory was. Even the New England Brahmin influence of Emerson had to be jettisoned from this ship of freedom from the past, whether political or poetical, and so Whitman's denial of having read Emerson was repeated from the *Galaxy* review.[35] Burroughs proposed the "Standard of the Natural Universal"—or nature—instead of society or satire as the basis for art. "We have swarms of little poetlings, producing swarms of soft and sickly little rhymelets, on a par with the feeble calibre and vague and puerile inward melancholy, and outward affectation and small talk, of that genteel mob called 'society.'" The language here resembles that of the letter to Ashton in 1865, following Whitman's dismissal from the Interior Department, and the one to Conway for his *Fortnightly* essay.

Notes also set in print for the first time some of the autobiographical notations that later appeared in *Specimen Days* and in Bucke's biography of the poet. O'Connor had spoken of the mythological Whitman in *The Good Gray Poet;* now the effort was to get more particulars on record. Burroughs was used for cooler defenses, and later in his life he distanced himself from the more fanatical disciples. A year later, when the O'Connors occupied an attic apartment in the Burroughses' home on Capitol Hill, the two men apparently quarreled—perhaps because O'Connor, for reasons unknown, initially disapproved of Burroughs's book.[36] But these potential rivals were close allies in 1867 and apparently patched things up later. O'Connor reviewed *Notes* in the *New York Times* of June 30. In the process, he may have picked up the main idea for his next attempt at Whitman myth in his short story "The Carpenter," for Burroughs suggests that Whitman was like "a visitant from another and distant clime. . . . from that atmosphere of far-back time when God descended and walked as a brother among men."[37]

In "Walt Whitman," O'Connor reviewed not only Burroughs's book but Whitman's entire life as it was now on record, quoting heavily from *Notes* and adding his own appreciation of the bard whose greatness he compared to Michelangelo's. In fact, he mildly chided Burroughs for resisting "language similar" to that of the painter's two hagiographers (who wrote while Michelangelo was still living). Otherwise, the review was naturally positive and laudatory, with O'Connor audaciously comparing *Notes* to Emerson's "first essays." Such hyperbole was a hopeful assertion that the euphoria over Whitman and his book, however concocted and orchestrated by the bard himself through his two younger friends, was catching on. Burroughs, though in a slightly lower register, had used similar superlatives in his book. And together they had made a convert of someone in England far more influential than Moncure Conway.

William Michael Rossetti, brother of the poets Christina and Dante Gabriel and a critic of high standing in Great Britain, had quietly admired *Leaves of Grass* ever since he received the first edition, a remaindered copy purchased from an itinerant book peddler, as a Christmas present in 1856.[38] Rossetti had been exposed to the high praise of Whitman in both *The Good Gray Poet* and *Notes* (the latter in proofs provided by Conway), and he had also read Whitman's latest productions in *Drum-Taps* and the 1867 edition of *Leaves of Grass.* The result, in an article on Whitman appearing just a week after O'Connor's (*London Chronicle* of July 6), was his characterization of Whitman's poetry as "the largest poetic work of our period"—this from the countryman of Tennyson and Arnold. Rossetti went even further and placed *Leaves of Grass* among the classics of Homer, Dante, and Shakespeare.

By the summer of 1867, things were picking up all around. Mrs. Whitman finally moved from her drafty cottage on Pacific Avenue to 1194 Atlantic Street, and Whitman sold "A Carol of Harvest for 1867" to the *Galaxy* for $60.[39] As in the case of Burroughs's essay, the poem had been commissioned through O'Connor, to whom William Conant Church wrote on August 1: "It seems to me that this glorious harvest of 1867, sown & reaped by the returned soldiers, ought to be sung in verse. . . . Walt Whitman is the man to chaunt the song. Will you not ask him to do it for The Galaxy?" As Burroughs told Conway ten days later, Whitman readily accepted the proposition; "and a few mornings afterward he fell to work, and in a couple of days had finished the piece."[40] Whitman was quick to write the poem because it was a direct invitation to develop the agricultural metaphor he had used in "Lilacs" and in the revision of Speed's dedication of the Lincoln statue. The subject also brought back to him the grand spectacle of the two Union armies meeting for the last time in the streets of Washington. In republishing the poem in *Two Rivulets* (1876), he considered the return of the veterans greater than the Union victory itself: "The grandest achievement yet for political Humanity . . . was the return, disbanding, and peaceful disintegration from compact military organization, back into agricultural and civil employments, of the vast Armies."

Grander yet was the return of the fallen veterans as spiritual compost for the American soil and soul. "A Carol of Harvest for 1867" (ultimately "The Return of the Heroes") was, as Whitman stated in a subsequently dropped line, "A Song of the grass and fields." This poem served as Whitman's catharsis from the shock and sadness he had carried away from the war and the hospitals. "When late I sang sad was my voice," the poem said. "But now I sing not War." Now he hears "another gathering army!" following the one that returned alive.

> Swarming, trailing on the rear—O you dread, accruing army!
> O you regiments so piteous, with your mortal diarrhea! with your fever!
> O my land's maimed darlings! with the plenteous bloody bandage and the crutch!
> Lo! your pallid army follow'd!

The dead were not dead, or gone forever, because "they fit well in Nature; / They fit very well in the landscape, under the trees and grass, / And along the edge of the sky, in the horizon's far margin." Just as they toiled in war, which was surely one cycle of nature, they now acted in another to fertilize blood-drenched fields in the minds of those who would never forget them.

> Toil on, Heroes! harvest the products!
> Not alone on those warlike fields, the Mother of All,
> With dilated form and lambent eyes, watch'd you.

❋ ❋ ❋

Whitman took his annual leave in September and returned to Brooklyn. By this time he had given up his pattern of carousing (in his own particular fashion) in New York and on Broadway until the early morning hours, but he still went about. He went to Pfaff's and drank lager with his old friend Henry Clapp, now replaced as champion of *Leaves of Grass* by Burroughs and O'Connor. Clapp said that Ada Clare had been on the stage in Memphis and was about to perform in

Albany. They may have spoken of her recent novel, *Only a Woman's Heart* (1866), an ably written romance about a feisty young woman who is ruined by her compatriots' persistent suspicion that she was seduced by an actor. The heroine (innocent of the charges) is as noble and fearless as the protagonist in O'Connor's *The Good Gray Poet,* which Clapp thought, as he told Whitman at their meeting, "absolutely one of the most vital productions in Literature."[41]

Whitman tried to look up the Church brothers, and he finally found them. That meeting led to more contributions to the *Galaxy,* including two important essays in Whitman's construction of his "programme" for an "autochthonous" American literature. As in his days with the *Democratic Review* back in the early 1840s, he once again found himself in respectable literary company, which included such names as Richard White Grant, Rebecca Harding Davis, Horace Greeley, and, yes, that upstart reviewer of *Drum-Taps,* Henry James, Jr.

After Thomas Carlyle published "Shooting Niagara: and After?"—a condemnation of the excesses of democracy in the wake of the expansion of English suffrage in 1867—and Greeley reprinted the entire essay in the *Tribune* of August 16, Whitman was urged by the Churches or, more likely, by O'Connor, to write a response in the *Galaxy.* The result was "Democracy," published in December 1867. It has been said repeatedly in biographies and criticism that Whitman started *Democratic Vistas* with the intent of rebutting Carlyle but that he had come at least partially around to Carlyle's fear of the leveling tendency of democracy by the time the monograph was completed. It was actually "Democracy" that formed his response to Carlyle, and *Democratic Vistas* was involved only in the sense that "Democracy" makes up one-third of its pages.

"Democracy" comes fresh from the poet's experience in the war and its aftermath. His faith in democracy rests—now even more squarely than before—on the shoulders of the people, native-, not foreign-, born Americans (a refrain in his wartime newspaper pieces). "We have seen the alacrity with which the American-born populace, the peaceablest and most good-natured race in the world, . . . and the least fitted to submit to the irksomeness and exasperation of regimental discipline, sprang, at the first tap of the drum, to arms—not for gain, nor even glory, nor to repel invasion—but for an emblem, a mere abstraction—for the life, *the safety of the Flag*." These people had fought for independence *and* brotherhood and sisterhood—Whitman's "Adhesiveness." Perhaps in this essay more than anywhere else, the Poet of Democracy preempts the claim often made in the post–Vietnam War era that American individualism (which Whitman defined further in the essay "Personalism") is imperialistic by nature. One of his bases for democracy is the transcendentalist belief that all men and women are divine, and thus politically equal. But Whitman, this lover of public places, also realizes that democracy isn't merely another name for individualism, which he says can also isolate citizens instead of uniting them. There is "another half—Adhesiveness, or Love—which fuses, ties, and aggregates, making the races comrades, and fraternizing all."[42]

Whitman quarreled with O'Connor in 1872 about the fitness of black Americans for the ballot, but five years earlier he had more faith in the egalitarian process. The best apology for democracy, he argues, is that it mirrors nature's laws. Though never mentioning Carlyle by name (only that "eminent and venerable person abroad"), he alludes to the essayist's anti-democratic concepts by saying, "The only course eligible, it is plain, is to plumply confront, embrace, absorb, swallow (O, big and bitter pill!) the entire British 'swarmery,' demon, 'loud roughs' and all. . . . Nature's stomach is fully strong enough not only to digest the morbific matter . . . but even to change such contributions into nutriment for highest use and life—so American Democracy's." In light of Carlyle's prediction that in the end democracy will be deadly to the idea of civilization, he thinks that "no community furnished throughout with homes, and substantial, however moderate, incomes, commits suicide, or 'shoots Niagara.'"[43]

If Whitman had not been so optimistic, O'Connor might never have created a Radical Republican hero for "The Carpenter," which he published in *Putnam's* in January 1868. The Irishman had always been for the underdog, ever since he was thrown out of his father's house at the age of eight and had to grow up on his own in Boston. His several short stories exemplify this attitude. "The Ghost," a Dickensian meditation published in *Putnam's* in 1856, takes place on Christmas Eve, also the day of the action that opens "The Carpenter." Though O'Connor may have gotten the idea for Whitman as a Christ figure from Burroughs's *Notes,* it is just as likely that Burroughs got the idea from O'Connor, whose "Good Gray Poet" resembles Christ in his altruistic ways.

The protagonist in "The Carpenter" is a Whitmanesque individual who loves freedom because it mirrors the rhythm of nature; he is a "mechanic" who "walks the hospitals." Both "The Ghost" and "The Carpenter" introduce central characters who, like Thoreau's "livestock" in *Walden,* are miserable because they are materialistic. In "The Ghost" the Scrooge-like figure of Dr. Charles Renton falls asleep on Christmas Eve to have the ghost of Fevel, a poor poet dead fifteen years ago to the night, say to him, "In the name of the Savior, I charge you, be true and tender to all men." In "The Carpenter" George Dyzer, a spendthrift, finds himself on Christmas Eve in 1864 ("when the armies of Grant and Lee were locked in the death-grapple for Richmond") beset by both financial and domestic problems. Not only has he squandered his inheritance from an uncle, but his daughter-in-law is about to commit adultery and two of his three sons are missing in the war. (Even worse, one of them is fighting for the South.) Just as Fevel, the good man alive with Christian principles, brings moral order into Renton's existence, the carpenter arrives to set the Dyzer house in order. The story seems unnecessarily contrived—the occasion for his visit to the farmhouse is to return a carpenter's plane found at its front gate. But this bit of business would have fit with Whitman's moonlight hikes around Washington, almost always with Doyle, on the hard-packed military roads connecting the forts and barracks that protected the capital during the war. O'Connor also may have had the Doyle family in mind when he plotted two of the Dyzer brothers as fighting, as had Pete and brother Francis M. Doyle, on opposite sides of the war. And before the wandering carpenter appears, there is a discussion between Dyzer and his youngest child about the true identity of Christ. Dyzer recalls his uncle's theory that the Savior is a mechanic and a carpenter who is not dead but still walks the earth doing good. The only difference was that "he'd grown old and gray walking in the world so many hundred years."[44]

The Christ-Whitman parallel was obvious to anyone who had heard about the hospital reputation of Walt Whitman. From as far away as Vienna, John Hay, Lincoln's former private secretary and an old Providence friend of O'Connor's, wrote: "I do not know why, but the instant he came into the firelighted room I knew it was Whitman, before one word of description followed."[45] Others were not so delighted as Hay with the hagiographic extension of Whitman, who was depicted by O'Connor as walking first the hospitals and now the world since the Crucifixion—what we might term, after Whitman's *Galaxy* poem, the "return" of the Hero. Although the *Nation* of December 12, 1867, found the story "powerful," it thought the character's "holiness" disgusting and an affront to Christian belief.[46] O'Connor complained that he was after something more subtle—not Christ but the example of Christ. But in the heat of his artistic effort, he crossed the line from Christianity into the transcendentalist belief that all who see themselves as a microcosm of nature, or the emblem of God, are as divine as Christ. To Emerson and to Whitman there was not one Christ but thousands, potentially millions, to be recognized by their self-reliance and love of democracy.[47]

❋ ❋ ❋

No doubt the favorable reference to him in Swinburne's *William Blake* (1868) lifted Whitman's self-reliant spirits even higher than O'Connor's thinly disguised hagiography had. (Three years later in *Songs Before Sunrise,* Swinburne included "To Walt Whitman," an ode that seemingly conveyed complete approval of *Leaves of Grass.* Later still, he attacked Whitman for what he considered the poet's naive political theory.)[48] The English were continuing to appreciate him. The London publisher John Camden Hotten was bringing out Rossetti's English edition of *Leaves of Grass,* promising Whitman "a fee" on every copy. (As it turned out, he received no royalties from the book—merely three complimentary copies, for which he had to pay $3 in duty.)

Washington was heating up politically. Congress was moving steadily toward the impeachment of President Johnson, stopping only after two unsuccessful attempts at a conviction. Whitman, who sometimes spoke of the president less than approvingly, didn't know what the outcome would be but considered it "serious business" with both sides determined to win. He and O'Connor thought the impeachment proceedings a mistake. For her part, Mother Whitman wavered, moving in and out of thinking Johnson deserved removal from office.[49]

Whitman found himself highly appreciated by his superiors at the Attorney General's Office, not only James Speed, who had resigned in the summer of 1866 because he disagreed with Johnson's Reconstruction policies, but Speed's successor, Henry Stanbery, who looked like Emerson and bowed to the poet when they met. "I have had the good luck to be treated with 'distinguished consideration,'" he told Abby Price that spring. Yet he added, as Stanbery resigned in March 1868 to help defend Johnson in his impeachment trial, there was always the possibility of the eventual appointment, after Johnson's removal by impeachment or political succession, of a "Harlan, or some pious & modest Radical of similar stripe . . . —in which case, doubtless, I should have to tumble out."[50] Whitman was uneasy perhaps because Stanbery's successor and the interim head of the Attorney General's Office, Orville Hickman Browning, had been Harlan's successor as secretary of the interior.

In May 1868 Whitman published "Personalism" in the *Galaxy,* where he defines individuality as the "compensating balance-wheel and *sine qua non* of the successful working machinery" of democracy. Echoing the argument in Emerson's essay "History," he adds, "if we think of it, what does civilization rest upon—and what object has it, with its religions, arts, schools, etc., but Personalism?" Yet this is no mere echo of the man who reduced history to biography. A serious student of democracy since his days at the *Eagle* in the 1840s, he had watched the people of his country go through its toughest test, a civil war. His faith in the goodness and selflessness of the average working American had been strengthened by watching the American soldier in agony and triumph, in the bloody scenes of Armory-Square Hospital and in the last parade of the triumphant Union armies down Pennsylvania Avenue. His view included women as well. The service of female nurses, far outnumbered by male aides, confirmed his prediction that "the day is coming" when "woman's full entrance" into American life "will be put to decision and real experiment."

Curiously, his emphasis on the future as the crowning moment of American democracy led him into the first stages of his interest in eugenics, which turned out to be more spiritual than practical. Though he saw a time when parenthood "shall become a science," he was more interested in the metaphysical side of personality—where the American average "dilates to the idea of the Infinite." True Personalism is accomplished in "the noiseless operation of one's isolated Self."[51] In the last analysis he thought "programmes" less useful than "personality." Individualism for Whitman, it seems, became not merely a political concept but almost a mystical one.

When Rossetti's selected edition was finally published that spring, the editor sent Whitman some early English reviews. In his Prefatory Notice Rossetti nervously hoped that the English public was "prepared" for the book, and that it would eventually whet the popular appetite for a complete edition. He had been careful to avoid offensive poems, though he printed an almost uncut version of the Preface to the first edition (leaving out, or substituting for, such words as "womb" and "prostitute"). Mainly, he kept to his principle of omitting an entire poem if it carried an offensive term, leading to the omission of Whitman's greatest poem, "Walt Whitman" ("Song of Myself"), and all the "Children of Adam" poems. (Rossetti followed the same policy when he included thirty-two of Whitman's poems in his 1872 anthology of *American Poems,* which was dedicated to the poet.) "Starting from Paumanok" had to stand in for "Song of Myself," and the closest the book came to treating sexuality was in its printing of several "Calamus" poems. Even here, he changed many of the titles. For example, "As I Lay with My Head in Your Lap Camerado" became "Questionable." "Walt Whitman" was reduced to a "cluster," or series, heading, but that cluster featured two of Whitman's masterpieces, "A Word Out of the Sea" ("Out of the Cradle Endlessly Rocking") and "Crossing Brooklyn Ferry."

This new edition, though certainly inferior to the one published in 1867 (which had a second and third issue in 1868), did much more for Whitman's reputation.[52] It brought the British—indeed, the Europeans—to the rescue. This was a strange development for the New World poet who scorned the meters and contrived passions of conventional poetry. In Cologne a formerly exiled German revolutionary, Ferdinand Freiligrath, spoke wildly of Whitman's "rhapsodic utterances" and how they threatened to overwhelm "our whole *Ars poetica,*" "our games with ding and dong, our syllable counting and syllable measuring, our sonneteering and building of strophes and stanzas [which] will seem almost childish to us." Freiligrath, who became a friend of Karl Marx during his exile in England, had been involved in the 1848 European revolutions and no doubt would have appreciated Whitman's anti-slavery poems of 1850, had he read them.[53]

Perhaps as another consequence of the Rossetti edition, Whitman placed a number of new poems in the October issue of *Broadway Magazine* in London. "Whispers of Heavenly Death" was one of several moving poems about death to go into the 1871 edition. Whitman was almost fifty, and death seemed to be particularly on his mind for some reason. Death is a mystery to be solved by conceding that it *existed* as much as life existed. The whispers the poet hears are the "labial gossip" of nature, which suggests "some solemn immortal birth" at life's supposed end. Likewise, "A Noiseless, Patient Spider" neither denigrates the flesh nor denies its permanence in its focus on the spiritual correlation with the natural. Rather, it poeticizes Whitman's point in "Personalism" about the "noiseless operation of one's isolated Self":

A noiseless, patient spider,
I mark'd, where, on the little promontory it stood isolated,
Mark'd how, to explore the vacant, vast surrounding,
It launch'd forth filament, filament, filament, out of itself;
Ever unreeling them—ever tirelessly speeding them.

And you, O my Soul, where you stand,
Surrounded, surrounded, in measureless oceans of space,
Ceaselessly musing, venturing, throwing,—seeking the spheres, to
connect them,
Till the bridge you will need, be form'd—till the ductile anchor
hold,
Till the gossamer thread you fling, catch somewhere, O my Soul.

More noiselessly than in earlier communications, Whitman sent his old and perhaps reluctant mentor Emerson "Proud Music of the Sea-Storm," hoping that he would get James T. Fields to publish it in the *Atlantic Monthly,* which he did in February 1869. This poem has been rightly noted for its direct use of the poet's experience with opera, another "whisper" of nature. It mentions particular operas and singers, including Whitman's favorites, *Lucia di Lammermoor* and the Italian contralto Marietta Alboni. Foreshadowing the theme of universal brotherhood and sisterhood in "Passage to India" in 1871, "Proud Music" celebrates the way music blends "all the tongues of nations" so that its harmony reflects a spiritual harmony. The poem records a dream come true: the poet awakes to find that the world's music is not from nature alone but of "a new rhythmus . . . bridging the way from Life to Death."

It was odd for Whitman to fall back on Emerson for his professional advancement—after denying in Burroughs's *Notes* he had read the bard before 1856 and paying him only a left-handed compliment in "Personalism" by including him with "the rich pages of old-world Plutarch and Shakespeare"—a body of literature soon to be outdone by the "cheapest vulgar life" of the American people. But just as there was an adolescence about Whitman in private life, a quirkiness that his Washington circle often remarked on, there was a similar (perhaps feigned) naïveté in his professional life. When Traubel asked him why he had gone to Emerson, Whitman answered: "For several reasons, I may say. But the best reason I had was in his own suggestion that I should permit him to do such things for me when the moment seemed ripe for it."[54]

❊ ❊ ❊

Whitman may have thought of Emerson because of a visit he made to New England in the fall of 1868. While taking his annual vacation and staying again in Manhattan with Abby Price, he was invited to Providence as the guest of the suffragette Paulina Wright Davis and her husband, a wealthy industrialist. Possibly, Whitman had met Wright at Abby Price's home in Brooklyn in the 1850s. Halfway through his visit he shifted his quarters to the home of Dr. William F. Channing and his wife, Mary Jane. The latter was Nellie O'Connor's sister, and William O'Connor joined Whitman in Providence for a few days during his visit. The poet was in good company, respectable yet unconventional enough in its literary taste to appreciate *Leaves of Grass.* Dr. Channing, the son of William Ellery Channing the Elder, was a medical doctor who devoted most of his life to scientific research, mainly of electricity, which led to his co-development of the nation's first fire alarm system. The Channings were also contributors to Whitman's hospital fund.[55]

At the height of his New England visit, Walt told Nellie back in Washington that he had seen—and liked—the poet Sarah Helen Whitman, one-time fiancée of Poe and former mentor to O'Connor. Mrs. Whitman praised Whitman while reviewing a new book by Bronson Alcott in the *Providence Journal* of October 30, 1868. Mentioning America's best writers, a list that included Emerson, Margaret Fuller, Hawthorne, and Thoreau, she wrote: "Nor to these should we forget to add . . . a man whose serene and stately presence we have lately seen looming above the crowd of our own city, and known everywhere by his well-won title of the 'Good Grey Poet,' conferred upon him in William D. O'Connor's gorgeous and powerful pamphlet of vindication." She may in fact have inspired O'Connor with her own pamphlet of vindication, *Edgar Poe and His Critics* (1860). Perhaps in gratitude for the *Journal* mention, the Brooklyn Whitman sent his "cousin" an autographed copy of the 1867 *Leaves.*

Sarah Helen Whitman lamented to O'Connor that she had not come to appreciate *Leaves of Grass* earlier,[56] but one person who responded to the very first call was the Englishwoman Anne Gilchrist. The widow of Blake biographer Alexander Gilchrist and the mother of four children, this accomplished woman of "early middle age," as Rossetti described her to O'Connor, had finished her late husband's biography of William Blake in 1866 and also established herself as an accomplished essayist on domestic and women's issues. She was on a familiar footing with the British literati, including not only William Michael Rossetti but his sibling poets. She knew Tennyson, and Carlyle had been her next-door neighbor on Cheyne Row in London when her husband was still living.[57]

In June 1869 Anne Gilchrist read Rossetti's selected edition of Whitman's poems, and her life changed forever. Her first letters in 1871 to the poet confirm the statement in a recent biography that she, like many married women of the Victorian era (and beyond), had not been in love with her husband. Even in Rossetti's "expurgated" edition, Whitman had aroused the passion she had long thought extinguished by the drudgery of caring for the wrong man. She wrote to Rossetti that the volume had held her "entirely spell-bound." She found—oddly, in the "Calamus" poems Rossetti had included—the spirit of passionate friendship she had missed in her marriage. Rossetti was delighted that his book was indeed introducing Whitman. Hoping, as he had written in his introduction, that a full edition of *Leaves of Grass* might eventually be published in England, he loaned her the unbound pages of the 1867 edition, where, of course, she may have been further excited by the depiction of the "twenty-ninth bather" in "Walt Whitman." Whitman sent the pages to Rossetti, who was supposed to present them to Hotten to consider for an unexpurgated edition.

Reading the full "Walt" apparently completed her romantic conversion. She literally fell in love with the author of *Leaves of Grass*—not only with his brave thought about human passion and sexuality but with the flesh-and-blood person behind the mask. After publishing an epistolary essay about *Leaves of Grass* in the *Radical* in 1870, she wrote Whitman three letters (the first two went unanswered). She acknowledged in the first of these that life with her husband had been fulfilling—she had done her duty and raised her children—but now, she told the initially astonished poet, "I understand the divineness & sacredness of the Body."[58]

Whitman had by this time read the passages of praise about *Leaves of Grass* in her letters to Rossetti as well as their published form in the *Radical.* He very much appreciated the benefit of having a *woman* declare herself, even anonymously (Rossetti had advised her that a woman championing *Leaves of Grass* "wd. not be treated with *more* chivalry & rectitude than a man, but with less").[59] Although "An English Woman's Estimate of Walt Whitman" was anything but emotionally detached, it made ringing points about Whitman's originality, reinforcing Burroughs's and O'Connor's arguments that *Leaves of Grass* not only defied literary conventions but possibly vanquished them. "I know that poetry must do one of two things," she wrote in "An English Woman's Estimate," "either own this man as equal with her highest, completest manifestors [even Rossetti thought Whitman second only to Shakespeare], or stand aside, and admit that there is something come into the world nobler, diviner than herself, one that is free of the universe, and can tell its secrets as none before." We might criticize a palace or a cathedral, she declared, "but what is the good of criticizing a forest?"[60]

Not since Juliette Beach's two letters to Henry Clapp in 1860, in the wake of her husband's negative review of *Leaves of Grass* in the *Saturday Press,* had a woman been so positive in her assessment, and Gilchrist's remarks were euphoric as well as public. The Beach letters, now in the Library of Congress, were never published, but Clapp no doubt showed them to Whitman. Ellen O'Connor insisted that "Out of the Rolling Ocean, the Crowd" was written for Beach,[61] though the poem (another seashore poem written, in fact, before Anne came into the poet's life) better describes his relationship with Gilchrist.

Out of the rolling ocean, the crowd, came a drop gently
 to me,
Whispering, *I love you, before long I die,*
I have travel'd a long way, merely to look on you, to touch you,
For I could not die till I once look'd on you,
For I fear'd I might afterward lose you.

(Now we have met, we have look'd, we are safe;
Return in peace to the ocean, my love;
I too am part of that ocean, my love—we are not so
 much separated;
Behold the great rondure—the cohesion of all, how perfect!
But as for me, for you, the irresistible sea is to separate us,
As for an hour carrying us diverse—yet cannot carry
 us diverse for ever;
Be not impatient—a little space—know you, I salute
 the air, the ocean and the land,
Every day, at sundown, for your dear sake, my love.)

In her first letter to the poet, Anne Gilchrist expropriated the imagery of this poem to propose marriage. "In May 1869 came the voice over the Atlantic to me," she announced on September 3, 1871. It was the voice of her "Mate," the author of the unexpurgated *Leaves of Grass.* ". . . Come, my darling: look into these eyes and see the loving ardent aspiring soul in them. Easily, easily will you learn to love all the rest of me . . . and take me to your breasts for ever and ever."

Gilchrist was possibly so lovesick that she fell ill late in 1870 of what sounds like "neurasthenia," a nervous disorder Victorian-era women frequently experienced. When the 1871 edition of *Leaves of Grass* followed on the heels of her essay and Whitman sent her a copy through Rossetti, she was profoundly disappointed that there was "no word for me alone." After checking with Rossetti that he hadn't left anything out of the "package" Whitman sent for her, she unleashed her free-flowing passion.[62] It was clearly a case of infatuation in which the critic confused the author with his book.

This was Whitman's inference when he finally wrote her, apologizing for the delay and claiming that his "book is my best letter." He did not, Gilchrist's recent biographer has noted, treat the English widow's letters with the disdain he had Susan Garnet Smith's 1860 letter, which he had labeled in the margin "insane asylum."[63] In fact, in his letter of November 3, 1871, he treated his newest champion with dignity and compassion, saying he had been "waiting quite a long while for time & the right mood to answer your letter in a spirit as serious as its own, & in the same unmitigated trust & affection." He said, in what in its modest terms is a love letter, too, that he "wished to give to it a day, a sort of Sabbath or holy day apart to itself," adding, "I am not insensible to your love. I too send my love." Gilchrist wrote back immediately on November 27 that "the tie between us would not grow less but more beautiful . . . if you knew me *better,*" but this and other more passionate declarations earned only a brief response from Whitman, declaring nothing more than his acknowledgment of her affection.[64] If he didn't already love her then, he would learn to in the coming years, but probably only as a sister and friend, after she moved to Philadelphia with her grown children.

Recently Whitman had also received a letter of love from someone closer to home—the wife of a close friend. On November 20, 1870,

Nellie O'Connor, perhaps experiencing the marital problems that would soon dissolve her marriage, wrote that she felt she already possessed Whitman's love. "It is good to feel so assured of one's love as not to need to express it," she wrote him. But then she, like Anne Gilchrist, fell to groveling: "I always know that you know that I love you all the time, even though we should never meet again. . . . and I am *sure* that you know it as well as I do. I do flatter myself too, that *you* care for *me,*—not as I love you, because you are great and strong, and more sufficient unto yourself than any woman can be." She continued, writing from Providence: "It is only when I am away from you that I am conscious of how deeply you have influenced my life, my thoughts, my feelings, my views, *myself* in fact, in every way, you seem to have permeated my whole being."[65] Her affection, which went well beyond the platonic, would contribute to the quarrel that erupted between Whitman and her husband sometime in 1872.

❋ ❋ ❋

More and more, Whitman's poetic subject became death. Perhaps the false reports of his death in a railroad accident in March 1871 had something to do with his mood. As Whitman concluded the Civil War decade, his health got no better and indeed somewhat worse, as his blood pressure undoubtedly continued to trouble him. "About one third of the time I feel pretty well," he told Doyle. His beloved sister-in-law Mattie, now in St. Louis with Jeff and the girls, developed tuberculosis, and she would be unwell till her early death at the age of thirty-seven. Jesse, Walt's only older brother, died in the insane asylum on March 21, 1870, at the age of fifty-two, from the "rupture of an aneurism."[66] When Whitman published "The Mystic Trumpeter" in the *Kansas Magazine* of February 1872, it merely continued the death poems that he had been writing since the war, most of which would go into the 1871 edition of *Leaves of Grass*—or editions, since *Passage to India* was a separate volume containing seventy-three poems, twenty-three of them new.

Whitman published three books in 1871—the fifth edition of *Leaves of Grass, Passage to India,* and *Democratic Vistas*—or actually, one book of 384 pages and two pamphlets of 120 and 84 pages, respectively. Whitman's second and third issues of the fifth edition absorbed *Passage to India* whole, without any change in pagination.

Democratic Vistas remained separate from Whitman's collected works for some time to come. It did not sell as well as the other two; in fact, it was generally ignored and perhaps for good reasons. Although Gay Wilson Allen promoted it as Whitman's first "serious contribution to prose literature," critics have generally been at a loss to explain exactly why.[67] The pamphlet, which was advertised in 1871 with the fifth edition of *Leaves of Grass* and *Passage to India*, is the literal sum of three essays—"Democracy" and "Personalism," both of which the *Galaxy* had already published, and "Orbic Literature," which the magazine had rejected—plus a short introduction. This scissors-and-paste organization partly explains why *Democratic Vistas* is so unsatisfactory for anyone looking for a coherent thesis. Prose was too linear for Whitman's imagination; his syntax is often interrupted by long parenthetical ideas, giving him—right or wrong—a reputation as an awkward prose stylist. "Orbic Literature" reargues issues found in "Democracy" and "Personalism" with no discernible advance. Forcing the two earlier essays into the pamphlet format, apparently only to compile something long enough for separate publication, was a mistake, and Whitman seems to confess it in the preface. He calls the work "in fact, a collection of memoranda . . . [and possibly] open to the charge of one part contradicting another," and excuses himself by saying that "there are opposite sides to the great question of Democracy."

This language reflects Whitman's concern that things were falling apart in the American democracy. In the preface, which he wrote in September 1870 while on leave again in Brooklyn, he speaks out against "the appalling dangers of universal suffrage in the United States." This essay, like "Orbic Literature," tends to be preachy. Its didactic eugenics, which talk about "new races of Teachers, and of perfect Women," reveal Whitman's frustration with his country (along with its failure to recognize his genius) instead of the confidence similar remarks conveyed in the 1855 Preface. America now needs "a religious and moral character" to go along with the privilege to vote. "For you know not, earnest reader, that the people of our land may know all how to read and write, and may all possess the right to vote—and yet the main things may be entirely lacking."[68] The answer is a "divine Literatus" to replace the priest. This is also the subject of the "Orbic Literature" part of *Democratic Vistas* where, in a continuation of his attack on conventional literature, he calls for a literature that is Hegelian and transcendental.

The companion piece to this pronouncement is "Passage to India," which has been shown to have been as haphazardly constructed (or contrived) as *Democratic Vistas.*[69] Whitman, the transcendentalist poet of the present, has now become the poet of the future. The Civil War shook his confidence, almost irrevocably—not in the people themselves but in the idea that representatives of the "divine average" would ever come into their own political kingdom. Things had not worked out as he hoped. The economy was weak, and several of Whitman's stage driver and railroad-worker comrades were out of work. Also, his country had *not* yet "absorb[ed] him as affectionately as he [had] absorbed it."[70]

Democracy, he said in "Personalism," would have to dilate to "the idea of the Infinite"—or, in the new book of poems, the idea of a "passage to more than India!" Later, in "Prayer of Columbus," a continuation of the imagery of exploration described "A batter'd, wreck'd old man, / Thrown on this savage shore far, far from home"—perhaps more transparently biographical than the poet, who had by then suffered his first and worst paralytic stroke, intended. In "Passage to India" the focus is on democracy, which must and will transcend its shortcomings but probably only (for now at least) by going beyond the material and mortal. Citing recent milestones in world communication (the opening of the Suez Canal, the completion of the American continental railroad, and the laying of the Atlantic telegraph cable), the poet envisions an even greater accomplishment.

> After the seas are all cross'd, (as they seem already cross'd,)
> After the great captains and engineers have accomplish'd their work,
> After the noble inventors—after the scientists, the chemist, the
>   geologist, ethnologist,

Finally shall come the Poet worthy that name,
The true Son of God shall come, singing his songs.

Whitman lowercased "Poet" and "Son" in the definitive version of "Passage to India," playing down a poetic ego worthy of the ecstatic praise in Anne Gilchrist's love letters. The poem obliquely extends his complaint about American indifference to *Leaves of Grass,* veiled, of course, like the complaint in *Democratic Vistas.* It continues the brooding poet's claim for postwar literary attention, only to become more bitter, as we shall see, in "Prayer of Columbus" and the anonymous *West Jersey Press* article in 1876.

Most of the "new" poems in *Passage to India* had been published in magazines after the 1867 edition of *Leaves of Grass.* They either looked to the future (e.g., "Proud Music of the Storm," slightly renamed here), or they sang of death. One not previously published that sang of death was "This Dust Was Once a Man," Whitman's last poem to Lincoln. And in this volume Whitman began to break up and disperse some of the poems from *Drum-Taps* and the "Sequel." Two sections featuring them were called "Ashes of Soldiers" and "President Lincoln's Burial Hymn." The second brought together all four of Whitman's poems about Lincoln—"When Lilacs Last in the Dooryard Bloom'd," "O Captain! My Captain!" "Hush'd Be the Camps To-day," and "This Dust Was Once a Man." The transfer of poems from *Leaves of Grass* to *Passage to India* freed up the book for its ultimate arrangement. With the fourth edition, the book had become a literary barge, trolling for loose poems as it drifted slightly off course. Whitman would require another decade to come up with his final arrangement, but for now at least his ship of state rode a little higher in the water.

As if to signal the change of course that was beginning in the fifth edition, Whitman inserted the *Drum-Taps* poem "The Ship Starting" after "Starting from Paumanok." This edition is longer than the last, but Whitman was now thinking of jettisoning poems from *Leaves of Grass* instead of just adding them. There is a difference in theme: the new poems about the sea, such as "In Cabin'd Ships at Sea," take place at sea instead of on the land's edge. And only eight poems are new to the 1871 *Leaves of Grass* (as opposed to twenty-three in *Passage to India*).

Most of the poems had not been published elsewhere; the *Galaxy* had rejected "Ethiopia Saluting the Colors" ("Ethiopia Commenting" when offered to the Church brothers) in 1867. This poem came out of Whitman's mixed emotions about blacks after their emancipation. On the one hand, he thought that Radical Republicans were exploiting the freed slaves, but on the other he was repulsed by blacks' behavior in the massive demonstrations in Washington that celebrated the anniversary of the Emancipation Proclamation.[71] In the poem, which asks who this "ancient hardly human" creature is who salutes the colors of victorious Union soldiers, Whitman may have been thinking of the black woman who sold him molasses cakes in the Washington market. But this is also another of Whitman's poems to a woman, or to women, which celebrated the way women—who represented the "moral affections" in Victorian America—will save society from the aggressiveness of men. They, or at least mothers, will save democracy somehow. Even though this particular woman was "*from [her] parents sunder'd*" a hundred years ago, she maintains an elusive dignity:

> Her high-borne turban'd head she wags, and rolls her darkling eye,
> And curtseys to the regiments, the guidons moving by.

This "fateful woman" is either utterly confused by recent events, or, more likely, she uncannily sees their significance.

❋ ❋ ❋

To help promote the 1871 edition of *Leaves of Grass,* John Burroughs brought out a second edition of his *Notes on Walt Whitman as Poet and Person,* just as his first edition had tried to advertise Whitman's fourth edition. "I have the author's express authority," he announced in the "Supplementary Notes" to the second edition (consisting of 17 newly numbered pages added to the original 108), "for averring that this, the fifth edition of Leaves of Grass, is the final one." America had not yet absorbed its poet and now, Burroughs seemed to say, the fifth edition was its last chance. He made every effort to see that the opportunity wasn't missed. He quoted the Emerson letter. He cited Gilchrist on "Calamus." He even put into publication for the first time the possibly apocryphal story about Lincoln watching Whitman from the White House and remarking on his appearance.[72] And Burroughs's second edition picked up the baton about the public's love of Whitman in spite of the supercilious critics, admitting that "Passage to India" was refused by "the monthly magazines successively in New York, Boston, San Francisco, and London."

This was finally Whitman's work more than Burroughs's—just as the first edition of *Notes* had been. It has all the earmarks of Whitman's near paranoia about his literary reputation. There is even a cryptic reference to Whitman's almost leaving the Attorney General's Office by the same door he left Indian Affairs: "and afterward, (1869,) he is subjected, in another Department, to trains of dastardly official insolence by a dignitary of equal rank [to Harlan's], from whom he narrowly escapes the same fate."[73] The incident in the Attorney General's Office occurred during the last half of 1869 when, as a reward for successfully heading up Johnson's impeachment defense team, the brilliant attorney William Maxwell Evarts was appointed to succeed Henry Stanbery as attorney general. Whitman told his mother he hoped his new boss would be "agreeable. . . . but somehow I don't believe he will." Just why Whitman felt threatened by Evarts is not clear. Government clerkships in those days, before the reform of the Civil Service, were generally destabilized when there was a change in the party affiliation of the president. There was at this time, however, a minor reshuffling of clerkships in the treasury, war, and other departments, which may have threatened Whitman's position in the Attorney General's Office. The crisis evidently passed when Ebenezer Rockwood Hoar was appointed attorney general in the spring of 1869. Walt told his mother, "The new Attorney General, Mr. Hoar, treats me very kindly—He is from Concord, Mass. & is personally intimate with Emerson."[74] The poet's new boss was the father of Elizabeth Hoar, one of Emerson's fellow transcendentalists and the one-time fiancée of his late brother Charles.

One of the first returns from the 1871 campaign promoting *Leaves of Grass* came on August 1, in a letter from the Committee of the

American Institute of New York, an organization promoting technology in the city. It asked Whitman to open the institute's fortieth annual exhibition with an original poem written especially for the occasion. He would receive travel expenses from Washington, collect an honorarium of $100, and be entertained "hospitably." Whitman was "rather staggered" to receive the offer. "I was everywhere, practically everywhere, disavowed—hated, ridiculed, lampooned, parodied," he told Traubel.[75] He delivered "After All, Not to Create Only" on September 7, 1871. Dressed in gray with a white vest, no necktie, and beard aflowing, he read his poem in what was described by a reporter as a strong voice, in a huge, barnlike structure crowded with the displays of the latest goods and machinery. On September 11 the *Washington Chronicle,* always friendly to Whitman, printed the following remarks, which were probably penned by the poet himself:

> In the middle of this [exhibit hall], to an audience of perhaps two or three thousand people, with a fringe on the outside of five or six hundred partially-hushed workmen, carpenters, machinists, and the like, with saws, wrenches, or hammers in their hands, Walt Whitman, last Thursday, gave his already celebrated [?] poem before the American Institute. . . . His voice is magnificent, and is to be mentioned with Nature's oceans and the music of forests and hills.[76]

This was another "Passage to more than India!"—the carpenter-poet reading his poetry before mechanics.

The press reaction was extensive and generally favorable, but the poem is not rated very high in the Whitman canon today.[77] It repeats, with less effect, ideas from "Passage to India"; in addition, Whitman, in his defense mode, felt that the occasion called for a "speech" instead of a poem. Here was a chance for one of those "barrels" of lectures he allegedly wrote back in the early 1850s, updated by five editions of *Leaves of Grass* and one civil war. As the original title of the poem suggests (it became "Song of the Exposition" in 1876), he set out to honor not only the inventors of technology but its users. The people, he suggests, can make something of the inventor's genius that will enrich their lives. But for them to do so—and here comes again the argument of *Democratic Vistas*—the muse of great poetry must migrate to the New World, "a better, fresher, busier sphere." Unfortunately, the muse would despair at the American literary scene she found: "a terrible aesthetical commotion, / With howling desperate gulp of 'flower and bower.'" The true source of poetry, that muse would discover, lies in the *occupations;* there she will be

By thud of machinery and shrill steam-whistle undismay'd,
Bluff'd not a bit by drain-pipe, gasometers, artificial fertilizers,
Smiling and pleased, with palpable intent to stay,
She's here, install'd amid the kitchen ware!

In the peroration, the poet-speaker calls for "far superber themes for poets and for art." This was a practical poem for a practical occasion, effective in getting its message across, and Whitman did as much as he could to publicize the event. With the help of Bronson Alcott he had the poem published separately by Roberts Brothers of Boston, later the publisher of Emily Dickinson's earliest posthumous editions in the 1890s.

Shortly before his reading before the American Institute, Whitman was delighted by the attention of Edward Dowden, Professor of English Literature at Trinity College, Dublin, in a long article on American poets in the *Westminster Review* of July. Both Dowden and Rossetti sent the poet copies. In his first letter to Whitman, on July 23, Dowden told him that he had written his praise more "coolly than I feel because I wanted those, who being ignorant of your writings are perhaps prejudiced against them, to say: 'Here is a cool judicious impartial critic who finds a great deal in Whitman—perhaps after all we are mistaken.'"[78] Certainly, Dowden's head was cool, compared to O'Connor's or Freiligrath's, for example. Whitman years later said the article was written with restraint. In another letter Dowden described himself as a young man (he was twenty-eight). In the article, he is much taken by the poet's Calamus idea, which he claims to find sexless. "He deliberately appropriates a portion of his writings to the subject of the feeling of sex [Dowden wrote in the section on Whitman, entitled "The Poet of Democracy: Walt Whitman"] as he appropriates another, 'Calamus,' to that of the love of man for man, 'adhesiveness' as contrasted with 'amativeness,' in the nomenclature of Whitman, comradeship apart from all feelings of sex."[79]

Either Dowden, like most of his nineteenth-century contemporaries, did not find any homosexual allusions in "Calamus," or the Irish professor was encoding his true feelings in the same way that John Addington Symonds did. When Symonds sent his first letter to the poet that fall, on the heels of Dowden's first two letters, he boasted that he had read (the 1860) *Leaves of Grass* "in Italy by the shores of the Mediterranean, under pine trees or caverns washed by the sea—& in Switzerland among the alpine pastures & beside the glaciers." His own poem that he enclosed, "Love and Death: A Symphony," began "Too long have I refrained" and asked, "How shall I dare in this ephemeral rhyme / To tell what thou hast taught me."[80] By contrast, Dowden was more indirect but not much less enraptured with Whitman's thought. He readily accepted Whitman's role as "the true Son of God," a phrase he used in his article. Furthermore, in describing the variety of Whitman's "friends on this side of the water whom I know myself," he listed a clergyman whom he called "the most sterling piece of manhood I know" and added: "he has I daresay taken you in more thoroughly than any of us." Whitman may have found out more about the handsome clergyman. He sent his reply to Dowden's last letter by John Burroughs, who was visiting Europe that fall.[81]

Dowden, who shows keen insight into Whitman's sense of the diversity in his democracy, probably believed with Whitman that nature was a great leveler, and that democracy reflected this phenomenon.[82] If there was any one place where Whitman got that sense of multiplicity, it was on Broadway, which he had so aptly and comprehensively described in "Broadway, the Magnificent!" in 1856. He told Doyle that in his ride atop the stagecoach from 23rd Street to Bowling Green, "You see everything as you pass, a sort of living, endless panorama—shops, & splendid buildings, & great windows, & on the broad sidewalks crowds of women, richly-dressed, continually passing. . . . Then about the Broadway drivers, nearly all of them are my personal friends."

These men were his most immediate examples of the "divine average." He had been riding with them for years and was doing so in the summer of 1871 when he was saddened, but perhaps not altogether shocked, to learn that one of them, William Foster, had become known to all of Manhattan as the "car assassin."[83] "Shocking Murder. The Story of an Unparalleled Crime in This City" read the headline in the *New York Times* on April 28, 1871. While intoxicated and riding with a fellow driver who was on duty, Foster, a laid-off streetcar conductor, fatally struck a passenger with a carhook. The man lay helpless and ignored in the street, treated like a drunk by passersby, until his female companion managed to summon the police. He died of a fractured skull days later. Foster, Whitman told Doyle, "the 'car assassin,' is an old driver & conductor that I knew quite well—he was a very good man, very respectable, only a fool when drunk—it is the saddest case I know, he has three fine children—the public is down upon him savage—& I suppose no hope for him." Foster was hanged in the Tombs Prison on lower Broadway just one month short of the second anniversary of his crime. Some of Whitman's "roughs" were dangerous.[84]

❋ ❋ ❋

Whitman continued his correspondence with Anne Gilchrist in early 1872, trying to level the new relationship into a friendship. He told her of receiving an invitation from Tennyson, with whom he had recently begun a correspondence, to visit him in England. "Sometimes I dream of journeying to Old England, on such visit," he wrote, "& then of seeing you & your children—but it is a dream only."[85] He was still fending off her infatuation. "You must not construct such an unauthorized & imaginary ideal Figure, & call it W. W. and so devotedly invest your loving nature in it," he protested with a touch of false humility. "The actual W. W. is a very plain personage, & entirely unworthy such devotion." Whitman was not trying to discourage Gilchrist to the point of killing the relationship. He felt the tenderness beneath her exhortations. He responded in kind, letting her into his private cares and anxieties; he spoke about his mother, who was "towards eighty," and even recalled his father, who had died seventeen years earlier. This letter was sent from Brooklyn in March, where Whitman had been since February 10, visiting his mother in her last Brooklyn rental on Portland Avenue, not far again from Myrtle Avenue and the Arsenal on Fort Greene. It was a bitter cold winter that year, and Walt stayed home "more than usual."[86]

More evidence of his growing literary reputation came that month with Danish scholar Rudolph Schmidt's article about *Leaves of Grass* in *For Ide og Virkelighed.* In thanking Schmidt in May, he said the article was being translated for him.[87] It was thought "magnificent" by his friends, and after the poet's death his literary executors featured the full translation in *In Re Walt Whitman* (1893), a collection of reminiscences and other memorabilia. Whitman included excerpts of it in an appendix to *As a Strong Bird on Pinions Free* (1872), which also featured six poems besides the title poem and a preface suggesting the new spiritual or religious bent hinted at in the recent poems and essays. Actually, he did even better and quoted excerpts and paraphrases from Schmidt's lengthy encomium in the *New York Commercial Advertiser,* another paper friendly to him. In his essay, for which he probably received help from Whitman, Schmidt supported the general ideas of Dowden in the *Westminster Review* and Gilchrist (here openly named for the first time as the author of "An English Woman's Estimate") in the *Radical,* seeing Whitman as "the first literary *esthetik* in America who has deliberately based a lyrical utterance for the American States squarely on their own present political, social, industrial, and even military conditions and character, and who has undertaken to root their verse on their own soil and give it hues and flavors of its own."[88]

Whitman was happy to tell Schmidt of yet another indication of his success: he was to deliver the commencement poem at the conservative Dartmouth College in New Hampshire. He read "As a Strong Bird on Pinions Free" ("Thou Mother with Thy Equal Brood" in 1881) there on June 26, 1872.[89] In its own way this was another encomium in the tradition of Dowden, Gilchrist, and Schmidt.

The conceits of the poets of other lands I bring thee not,
Nor the compliments that have served their turn so long,
Nor rhyme—nor the classics—nor the perfume of foreign court, or
    indoor library.

Instead of these, America's truly autochthonous poet would bring the odor "from forests of pine in the North, in Maine," the "breath of the Illinois prairie," the "open airs of Virginia, or Georgia, or Tennessee," and so forth. The theme of the poem, which the later title more clearly indicates, is a celebration of the "equal brood" of the mother democracy.

Whitman had been invited by the Dartmouth senior class without the explicit approval of the faculty or administration. If the editorials of the six months preceding the poet's visit in *The Dartmouth,* the college magazine, are any indication, the students and the alumni believed that the board of trustees and the faculty had fallen behind the times (best defined for them by Harvard and Yale). The aging trustees had lifetime appointments, a system perpetuated by the rule that they appointed their successors without the full consent of alumni. Only one-third of the board could consist of alumni from out of state, but according to *The Dartmouth,* four-fifths "if not nine-tenths of the wealth, professional ability and culture of the graduates lie outside the state."[90]

As Bliss Perry suggests, Whitman was not the ideal commencement poet in the eyes of the Dartmouth faculty, but his speculation that Whitman's invitation was a prank may not be accurate. When Perry wrote to Professor Charles F. Richardson of Dartmouth in 1905 for information about Whitman's selection as a commencement speaker, he begged the question by saying that the "choice, under all the circumstances, seems to have been an unusual one." Caught between chagrin at his college's having hosted what was then considered an obscene poet and pride that Dartmouth in spite of itself had given "an early hearing to an 'advanced man'" (underscored by the fact that Perry, a Harvard man, was writing his biography), Richardson responded in kind, suggesting the invitation was a hoax and Whitman an embarrassment to most of the faculty.[91] But the Class of 1872, from whose ranks of sixty-nine students came the editorial writers of *The Dartmouth,* was also at odds with the faculty over the curriculum and the college's general state of inefficiency. There were, for example, three student-run, unheated libraries, one owned by the college and two established by student societies, which duplicated what few titles they possessed. The students demanded a professional librarian to oversee one consolidated library whose hours of operation would exceed the hour per week that the three libraries then offered. They also complained about having to take botany in the New Hampshire winter. They demanded more than one semester of a modern language, in light of the fact that the "Atlantic Bridge" (the Atlantic Cable) now put the United States on an international footing. Most significant, these seniors complained of the college's "very bad way of hurrying over the classics." Instead of surveying a large number of Greek and Roman writers, they wanted to study Homer and Horace intensively; they wanted to know the "power" that had made these writers "the admiration of the ages." Furthermore, the magazine's review of a recent volume of Tennyson's poetry suggests that the students subscribed to a progressive theory of literary creation; they complained that Tennyson was a "poet of construction rather than conception."[92]

The reports of Whitman's performance are contradictory, one saying, for example, that he read in a monotone and could not be heard, and another describing his "clearness of enunciation."[93] Commencement day was rainy and the ceremony was long. Whitman may well have missed the morning services but surely had to endure the afternoon orations. First Professor Charles Aiken of the Princeton Divinity School delivered "a philosophical address" on "The Right of Doubt." This was followed by a long eulogy for Nathan Lord, Dartmouth's president for the past thirty-five years. Probably the perceived highlight was the Rev. Edward Everett Hale's hour-long meditation on Milton and the merits of self-denial. Then, as the *Daily Monitor* of Concord, New Hampshire, reported the following day, "Walt Whitman, of Washington, D.C., came forward and delivered something which the audience (and evidently the speaker) did not understand. We pass him by." *The People,* another Concord paper, was more generous, describing Whitman's delivery as "enthusiastically received" but the poem as "one of Mr. Whitman's peculiar productions." Hale received an honorarium of $125 for his address; Whitman got a total of $35.[94]

Even at this bargain rate, the faculty probably thought the poet was overpaid. In welcoming the new world of democracy, whose light was lighting and whose shadow was shadowing "the entire globe," Whitman declared:

> . . . I do not undertake to define thee—hardly to comprehend thee;
> I but thee name—thee prophesy—as now!
> I merely thee ejaculate!

Nor would the faculty's "strictly orthodox Congregationalism" have necessarily embraced Whitman's definition of America as a "Land tolerating all—accepting all—not for the good alone, all good for thee." This kind of welcome did not yet apply to Irish immigrants, nor would it have applied to the freed slaves ("*not an African to be seen all day,*" the poet said in a letter describing Hanover),[95] who the North hoped would stay (and vote) in the South. But in any case, it is not clear that Whitman's "equal brood" included blacks either—certainly not immediately.

Whitman's first appearance before a college audience no doubt caught the attention of his brother-in-law Heyde, whom he subsequently visited along with his sister Hannah in Burlington, Vermont. The cigar-smoking Heyde had always thought himself Whitman's artistic better, at least in the sense of knowing the limits of artistic license.[96] Heyde also dabbled in poetry, and he may have suspected that his brother-in-law had silently borrowed something from one of his old poems for the Dartmouth performance. Heyde's "To the Swallows" begins with birds on "pinions light."[97] Whitman made sure his brother-in-law was impressed with his new level of acceptance by somehow having a *New York Herald* account of the Dartmouth reading, which he obviously penned, published in the *Burlington Free Press* of July 5. Edward Bernays, the "Father of Public Relations" in this century, had nothing on Whitman. Noting that the "'good gray' poet, as he is styled by his admirers," was visiting his relatives in Burlington, Whitman wrote:

> The principal meeting was about three o'clock in the church. Punctual to the time the tall figure of Walt Whitman made its appearance, walking slowly, yet not without a certain alertness, up the aisle. It is the same figure, well-known in New York and Washington. Athletic enough, now becoming aged, yet still smacking of the open air, with sunburn features, open neck and shaggy beard. Whitman alternates in

> his costume between an entire dress of gray, and one of summer hue. This time it was the latter, with white vest, low and wide shirt collar without any necktie. . . . He was very easy in his manner of delivery and evinced an unusual degree of what might be called inward emphasis, but outwardly he shows perfect nonchalance. His vitality and electricity are in the voice, which, although not startling and loud, is impressive and animating, almost beyond example. There is no doubt that the man is devoutly in earnest and believes fully in his own poems, written or spoken. He is patriotic, too.

Hannah, a hypochondriac who outlived all her siblings, adored Walt for his self-constructed fame as much as his brotherly allegiance. For his part, Walt was relieved to see that his sister's connubial storms had recently subsided. Apparently, the couple often led a near hand-to-mouth existence, changing residences in Burlington frequently or moving to other villages as Heyde continued to paint the same rural scenes. The best part of Walt's visit was time spent around Lake Champlain, the Adirondacks, and the Green Mountains.[98]

As was his custom with new poems, Whitman had "As a Strong Bird" set up in print to read at Dartmouth, and after his return to Washington he sent copies to friends and admirers, including Tennyson and possibly Carlyle. (He might well have sent one to Emerson, who had delivered a similarly revolutionary message in "Literary Ethics" at Dartmouth thirty-four years earlier.) Washington was unseasonably hot in August of 1872, and Whitman complained about his health. That month his mother and Eddy moved to Camden, New Jersey, to live with George and his new wife, Lou. George himself had been living in Camden and working as a pipe inspector since 1869. Mrs. Whitman would never be very happy there, and Eddy missed his Brooklyn church. Whitman visited them in Camden in September. While there he crossed the Camden ferry to Philadelphia and was delighted with the city's "*middling classes[:]* mechanics, laborers, operatives in factories (both sexes), traders, &c."[99] Back in Washington, he found the city filled with excitement over the presidential election, in which Horace Greeley unsuccessfully opposed Grant and died shortly after Grant's second inauguration. More frequent dizzy spells apparently prompted the poet to make out his first will, in which he left his mother everything, including more than $1,000 he had in the bank.[100]

Sometime that fall, Whitman's increasing displeasure with the Radical Republicans—whose latest measure had just become the Fifteenth Amendment, giving male ex-slaves the national right to vote—led to a bitter quarrel with his friend William O'Connor. Whitman's conviction that freedmen should be educated before they were given the vote clashed with O'Connor's unequivocal dedication to freedom at any price. The O'Connor circle had experienced heated debates before, but this time Walt and William crossed swords once too often. Burroughs, who would soon move out of Washington permanently, was present and recalled it was the poet more than his champion who was at fault. "O'Connor," he said, "became enraged at what Walt said. . . . They were in the habit of goring each other in argument like two bulls, and that time Walt was, I guess, rather brutal and insulting. . . . O'Connor fired up and turned on him. Walt took his hat and went home in a pet."[101] Eldridge, who was also present that evening, agreed with Burroughs's assessment. Later, after Whitman's death, when he was planning a personal memoir of the poet, he worried over how to describe Whitman's questionable behavior that evening.[102] Whitman, who had confessed to Nellie during the war that the abolition of slavery was clearly secondary to stopping the wartime slaughter,[103] had angered his best friend and literary champion in his own parlor. O'Connor was as dedicated to abolition and full black citizenship as he was to Whitman and *Leaves of Grass,* which he defended with the zeal of an abolitionist.

Whitman later described his friend as "warrior-like for the anti-slavery idea." And he confessed his resentment of such unqualified dedication. "I can easily see now," he told Traubel, "that I was a good deal more repelled by that sentiment—by that devotion in William (for with him it was the profoundest moral devotion)—than was justified." By then he regretted his position, calling it first "extreme," then "lethargic in [his] withdrawals from William's magnificent enthusiasm. . . . After all I may have been tainted a bit, just a bit, with the New York feeling with regard to anti-slavery."[104] Whitman had insulted the man who almost single-handedly engineered the postwar campaign for the acceptance of *Leaves of Grass,* sending letters of support to British and European advocates, arranging for the publication of Burroughs's essay in the *Galaxy* and Gilchrist's article in the *Radical* after its rejection by the *Galaxy*—overall shoving aside his own literary ambitions in the holy crusade for his "Good Gray Poet." Whitman realized his error the very next day, and when the two met on the street he extended his hand in apology. "But William," Burroughs remembered, "shied around and went on past. The iron had entered his soul."[105] They did not speak to each other for the next decade.

The year 1872, which had started out so well, ended tragically. Not only had Whitman concluded, seemingly forever, one of his closest friendships, but he also witnessed the breakup of William and Nellie's marriage. Nellie, who had consuming feelings about the poet, may have taken his side. Or William, who may not have been faithful to his wife, may have been angered by her devotion to the poet, at least on that evening. O'Connor moved out and sent his wife most of his paycheck every month. They never got completely back together as man and wife, but after their daughter Jeannie died in 1883, O'Connor "yielded to [Nellie's] wish and dined daily with her."[106]

But if 1872 ended badly for the poet, 1873 was the worst year of his active life. He suffered a crippling stroke in January. His beloved sister-in-law Mattie died in St. Louis in February. And his mother, his truest love, died in May. Whitman was almost completely immobile in the weeks after his paralytic attack. He had been at his desk in the Treasury Department when its first signs appeared and barely made the hundred-yard walk back to his rooming house. He woke the next morning to find his left side paralyzed.[107] With electric shock treatments, he was finally ambulatory enough to travel to Camden when his mother began to fail. He arrived three days before her death. Her funeral in the front room of George's house on Stevens Street in Camden had about thirty mourners, some from as far away as Brooklyn, including Abby Price and her daughter. Helen recalled in 1919 that upon taking her seat for the services she was distracted by a thumping that faintly vibrated the parlor. It came from the adjoining room, which contained Mrs. Whitman's coffin. Peering through the partially opened doorway, she glimpsed the poet sitting by its side. "He was bent over his cane, both hands clasped upon it, and from time to time he would lift it and bring it down with a heavy thud on the floor." George's wife, Lou, told her that Walt had been there all the previous night. In acknowledging the Prices' condolences, he described his mother's passing as a "staggering, staying blow. . . . My physical sickness, bad as it is, is nothing to it."[108]

11

THE GOOD OLD CAUSE

❈ ❈ ❈

Instead of making you feel (as many do) that the Present
is a kind of squalid necessity to be got over as best may be,
in view of something always in the future, [Whitman] gave
that good sense of *nowness,* that faith that the present is enjoyable,
which imparts colour and life to the thousand
and one dry details of existence.

EDWARD CARPENTER
Days with Walt Whitman

Down in health and spirit, Whitman remained in Camden two weeks after losing his mother. Since his stroke in January, he had been improving slowly, but the traumatic blow of his mother's death set him back, the hypertension bringing back the dizzy spells.[1] When he returned to Washington on June 2, he apparently couldn't bear the solitude of his rented room and became a guest of Ashton and his family. The change was helpful at first, as it was a large, well-appointed house, and there were women and a baby, but he was no better physically after two weeks' stay. Charlie Eldridge told Burroughs that Walt had returned to Washington "in a very depressed condition and complaining more in regard to himself than I have ever heard him do since he got sick."[2] He feared the poet was about to suffer another stroke.

Around the middle of June, Whitman moved to Camden to live with his brother George and wife, Lou, at 322 Stevens Street. This was a working-class neighborhood near the ferry to Philadelphia, which lay across the Delaware River, and the great depot of the Camden and Amboy Railroad. The trains rumbled past the row house day and night, as close as a football field away, and the neighborhood was filled with railroad men and their families. "If I only felt just a little better," he wrote Doyle later that summer, "I should get acquainted with many of the men." He was situated on the second floor in rooms his mother had occupied. He had windows both north and south and was happy to be living with the "emotional history" of his mother's furnishings. At first he kept the room exactly as she had left it, not even removing a favorite dress that hung in the wardrobe.[3]

But despite the domestic support of his brother and sister-in-law, Whitman was intellectually and emotionally isolated in Camden. He always felt slightly ill at ease at George's, and eventually—once his health began to improve—he spent large blocks of time visiting friends. In the beginning, he clung to Doyle and the memory of their times together as he sank further into the melancholy that had enveloped him since his mother's death. It has been suggested that the poet's relationship with his mother was "unhealthy," asserting as an example that he slept on his mother's pillow for two years after her death. But the idea that Whitman's reaction to his mother's death was excessive ignores nineteenth-century ways of griefwork, which involved strong physical encounters with the loved one's remains. Emerson, for example, opened the coffins of both his first wife and his first son. And in any case, the pillow in question was not his mother's, but one his mother had made for him and slept on occasionally.[4]

Whitman seemed to be at loose ends. He wrote to Doyle of returning to Washington and getting a place near Pete's car route, "a couple of unfurnished rooms, or top floor somewhere." And in a curious turnabout in his cautious approach to Anne Gilchrist, he sent her a ring that had possibly belonged to his mother.[5] He thought of taking in the salt air of Atlantic City, fifty miles away by rail, but he was too sick to venture beyond the nearby streets of George's house. By the middle of August, he hired a substitute, Walter Godey, to perform his clerk's tasks in Washington. (Before the reform of the Civil Service, a person could sublet his position and turn a profit.) Every payday, Whitman sent Godey's "salary" to Eldridge.

Walt's grief apparently led him to think of his lost friend, William O'Connor, and to ask Doyle whether he had seen the author of *The Good Gray Poet* recently. O'Connor had been promoted to chief clerk of the Light-House Board, located in the Treasury Department; he eventually became librarian of its collection, which Whitman had helped to establish in the 1860s. Perhaps because he had supposedly perished in a railroad accident in 1871, the poet also followed the railroad news and worried about Doyle, who had moved from streetcars to trains, to work on the Baltimore and Potomac Railroad as a baggage man on its Boston-to-Washington line. Before the advent of automatic signaling in 1880 and the use of different tracks for trains traveling in opposite directions, head-on collisions were common. Derailments were the other main cause of railroad wrecks. These tragedies were often exacerbated by fires from hot coals in the potbelly stoves used to heat passenger coaches.[6] Whitman sent Doyle a clipping from *Harper's* that reported "probably the narrowest escape in the history of railroading from a total wreck." He also relayed reports of a huge smashup in a tunnel outside Washington, telling Doyle that he had run his eyes over the news account "with fear & trembling—& only on reading it over a second time, was I satisfied that you were not in it. . . . The papers here publish full, & I guess very good accounts of the whole affair—I liked what the [*Washington*] *Star* said so plainly—that *the cause below all others,* of such accidents, is because they run such a route, *over a single track.*"[7]

Another tragedy struck closer to home. The once beautiful Ada Clare was dead at 166 Bleecker Street, not far from Pfaff's, at the age of thirty-eight. "Poor, poor, Ada Clare," Whitman bemoaned to Ellen O'Connor. "I have been inexpressibly shocked by the horrible & sudden close of her gay, easy, sunny free, loose, but *not ungood* life."[8] The case was especially gruesome. The woman who may have tried to entice Whitman with the "Ellen Eyre" letter in 1862 died of rabies, having been bitten in the face weeks before by a pet dog. Not long after publishing her only novel, *Only a Woman's Heart* (described as a "failure" in one of the obituaries), she had married an actor of some note named Noyes, according to one news account of her death, and returned to the stage. Following the dogbite and its cauterization by a physician, she went to Rochester for an acting engagement. "While on stage in Rochester," said the *New York Times* of March 6, 1874, "she was seized with hydrophobia, and at once brought to this City. The symptoms grew in intensity, until on Wednesday evening her agony became so great that she implored her husband to shoot her, and begged Dr. Carnochan to bleed her to death. Opiates were administered, which, to some extent, relieved her sufferings, and she died calmly." Henry Clapp died an alcoholic the next year. The Pfaff's era was gone forever.

Also gone, for now at least, was the poet's campaign to make *Leaves of Grass* the latest model for American literature. But that effort—which Whitman would pursue to his grave—soon resumed. Shortly after his stroke, he began to publish a number of poems, many of them mediocre for Whitman, in the *New York Daily Graphic.*[9] And there would be more because the paper had a new editor, an iconoclast and a reformer named David Goodman Croly. One of Croly's interests was the thought of Auguste Comte, which he helped to popularize in America with *A Primer of Positivism* (1871); Comte's philosophy was congenial to Whitman's ideas in *Democratic Vistas* regarding the logocentric underpinnings of democracy and the value of personalism, or independent character. Born in Ireland and about the same age as O'Connor, Croly was one of the anonymous authors of *Miscegenation,* a pamphlet issued during the presidential election of 1864. It argued that when President Lincoln issued the Emancipation Proclamation, he had proclaimed the mingling of the races. Since Croly was a Democrat, this screed—which called for a national blending of the "Races"—may have been a spoof intended to smear the Republican, or Union, Party.[10]

Croly's ideas were not strange to Whitman, who, like the early Emerson,[11] entertained the wisdom of many reformers. With the exception perhaps of the *Galaxy* and a few nods from New England, the poet's support came from people whose political opinions ranged from the fringe of conventionality to immoderate progressivism. Often he found something in their radicalism that was not at all political or practical. Whitman took from the women's suffrage movement, for example, not primarily the argument that women deserved the vote but the idea that "there is nothing greater than the mother of men." Yet he supported women politically with all his body and soul and, unlike many of his progressive friends, would have disagreed with the misogynistic sentiments that appear in *Miscegenation.* Arguing that breeding exclusively within one racial group is leading even the "English race" to decay, the pamphlet cites the "excessive number" of females born in Great Britain as evidence. This statement would not have shocked the average citizen of the era, who held the opinion popularized by Sylvester Graham's eugenic theories, that a female birth was possibly the result of an unimpassioned coupling. Nor would the average reader have minded the comparison of Great Britain with the "effete races of Northern Mexico," where "it is remarked that six or seven females are born to one male."[12]

Whitman's tolerance of Croly's views would have stopped short of Grahamism—though in Section 24 of "Song of Myself" he echoes Graham's popular notion equating the loss of semen to the loss of blood ("You my rich blood! your milky stream pale strippings of my life!"). After publishing ten of Whitman's poems, three essays including "A Christmas Garland, in Prose and Verse," and a series of Civil War reminiscences entitled "'Tis But Ten Years Since," Croly asked the poet to write about spiritualism, in its way another reform movement. (In the 1840s Congress had even considered an Illinois petition to establish a commission to study its validity and possible uses.) Whitman flatly refused. "I am neither disposed nor able to write anything about this so-called Spiritualism," he wrote the editor of the *Daily Graphic* on December 16, 1874. "It seems to me nearly altogether a poor, cheap, crude humbug."[13]

❋ ❋ ❋

Written at a time when the Grant administration in Washington was besmirched by scandal, many of Whitman's poems in the *Daily Graphic* deal with current events. "Nay, Tell Me Not To-Day the Publish'd Shame" expresses dismay and disappointment over the main topic of the day, the Crédit Mobilier scandal. The Union Pacific Railroad had formed a construction company of insiders who, for example, paid themselves almost twice as much to lay a mile of track as it ordinarily cost. Even though the worst excesses had taken place in 1867 and 1868, before Grant became president, the revelation of the company's practices in 1873 severely blemished his reputation. The poem looks to "honest farms," "untold manly healthy lives," and "noiseless mothers, sisters, wives, unconscious of their good" to provide salvation. In "The Singing Thrush" (called "Wandering at Morn" in *Two Rivulets*), he finds the hermit thrush of "When Lilacs Last in the Dooryard Bloom'd" fame "coil'd in evil times." But even here—as in the "Democracy" and "Personalism" sections of *Democratic Vistas,* he prophesies relief and recovery with the old compost idea.

> If worms, snakes, loathsome grubs, may to sweet spiritual songs
> be turn'd,
> If vermin so transposed, so used and bless'd may be,
> Then may I trust in you, your fortunes, days, my country;
> —Who knows but these may be the lessons fit for you?
> From these your future Song may rise, with joyous trills,
> Destin'd to fill the world.

The other poems Croly published treat less political subjects. "Warble for Lilac-Time" had appeared in the *Galaxy* in 1870, and "Song of the Universal," the poet's invited poem recited in absentia at Tufts College (an invitation he could not, because of his stroke, accept), appeared in many other papers on the same day, June 17, 1874. "The Ox-Tamer," though first published in the *Daily Graphic,* was not a new poem; it is listed as part of the never-published *Banner at Daybreak,* compiled in 1860.

In "A Christmas Garland," published in the December 1874 issue of the *Daily Graphic*, Whitman used the magazine as he had the *Galaxy,* as a vehicle for political theorizing. But even here he borrowed from the past, taking lines almost verbatim from another unpublished work, *The Eighteenth Presidency!* In the subsection entitled "Rulers Strictly Out of the Masses," he wrote that he "would be much pleased to see some heroic, shrewd, fully-inform'd, healthy-bodied, middle-aged, beard-faced American blacksmith or boatman come down from the West across the Alleghanies [*sic*], and walk into the Presidency, dress'd in a clean suit of working attire, and with the tan all over his face, breast and arms."[14] One Lincoln was not enough.

He took up again the theme of his response in "Democracy" (and *Democratic Vistas*) to Carlyle's derision of the leveling aspects of democracy. There he had applied the concept of cultural digestion to argue that democracy's stomach could handle just about anything.[15] In "A Christmas Garland" he wrote, with a casual racism (and xenophobia) typical of northern whites at the time, "As if we had not strained the voting and digestive calibre of American Democracy to the utmost for the last fifty years with the millions of ignorant foreigners, we have now infused a powerful percentage of blacks, with about as much intellect and calibre (in the mass) as so many baboons." Yet he then characterized the freedmen as yet another potential example of the miraculous might of democracy. "We stood the former trial," the next sentence reads, "solved it—and, though this is much harder, will, I doubt not, triumphantly solve this."[16]

The belligerence in the essay may reflect Whitman's poor physical condition and the parallel feeling that he was out of the loop with his friends and literary activity. But the poet had other fish to fry here. In the opening section of "A Christmas Garland," in which he briefly defines literary genius, he plays Scrooge to two of the three writers he discusses—Victor Hugo (one of O'Connor's favorite writers), George Sand, and Emerson. Although Madame Dudevant's "stories are like good air, good associations in real life, and healthy emotional stimuli," Hugo fails to prune his plots of their "blotches and excesses."

He saves the worst for Emerson, however, who not so many years before assisted Whitman in placing "Proud Music of the Sea-Storm" in the *Atlantic Monthly.* Evidently, word of Emerson's occasional doubts about Whitman was filtering back to him. Emerson had spoken "very amusingly" about the poet to the Englishman James Bryce in 1870—"from whom he [Emerson] evidently does not expect much more now, thinking he has not improved in his later productions."[17] Soon Burroughs attacked Emerson on Whitman's behalf, although he might have tempered his remarks if he had known of the New Englander's approaching loss of short-term memory. He also could not have suspected that Emerson's declining enthusiasm toward *Leaves of Grass,* most recently indicated by the snub of Whitman's poetry in *Parnassus* (an anthology of Emerson family favorites), was perhaps intertwined with the state of Emerson's health. Whitman missed the mark as widely as Burroughs when he asked rhetorically in "A Christmas Garland" whether Emerson's "fault" was not finally "too great prudence, too rigid a caution." His criticism targeted the old man now increasingly influenced by conventional taste and "managed" on the lecture circuit by his daughter Edith (the actual editor of *Parnassus*), not the daring essayist "with no Past at [his] back" who wrote "Self-Reliance."

By 1874 Whitman had moved with George and Lou down Stevens Street to the corner of West, where his brother built an attractive three-story house. George was prospering as an inspector of pipework in both Philadelphia and Camden. At 431 Stevens Walt could watch the trains, "20 a day in full view from here."[18] His health began to improve enough to write that year. In addition to "A Christmas Garland," he published a series of six articles entitled "'Tis But Ten Years Since" in the *Daily Graphic* between January 27 and March 7 and two major poems back to back in *Harper's Magazine* of February and March, "Song of the Redwood-Tree" and "Prayer of Columbus." Nostalgia and self-pity pervade these works. "Already," he grumbled in his first attempt at a prose rendering of the Civil War since his dispatches to the New York papers during the war, "the events of 1863 and '4, and the seasons that immediately preceded, as well as those that closely followed them, have quite lost their direct personal impression, and the living heat and excitement of their own time, are being marshalled for casting . . . into the cold and bloodless electrotype plates of History."

As he completed the first installment of "'Tis But Ten Years Since," he complained of his paralyzed left leg, his dizzy spells, and his intense loneliness in Camden. "I am told," he wrote to Doyle shortly before the appearance of "Prayer of Columbus," "that I have colored it with thoughts of myself—very likely." He told Ellen O'Connor almost the same thing. Urging her to "write oftener," he now realized that he had "unconsciously put a sort of autobiographical dash" in the voice of Columbus, described in the poem as abandoned, sick, and dying.[19] He missed the camaraderie of his wartime buddies and his postbellum walks with Peter Doyle in and around Washington. He looked to the nation's first centennial as somehow rekindling the best of that past. "'Tis But Ten Years Since" was a rehearsal for *Memoranda During the War* (1876), which was itself a precursor to the wartime sections of

Specimen Days (1882). All three wartime reminiscences consist generally of random selections from his mass of notebook jottings—a dreamy recycling of a time he had once described as "quicksand years."

Whitman may have done some of this writing in the Mercantile Library on 10th Street in Philadelphia. Ferry accommodations from Camden were accessible, even for a semi-invalid. The streetcar stopped only a block from George's house, and it was less than half a mile to the ferry at the end of Federal Street and a short glide across the Delaware, where another streetcar waited at the foot of Market Street. But perhaps a library, with its volumes of conventional literature, was too confining for the poet who wrote best out of doors. "Song of the Redwood-Tree," despite its theme of western, democratic progress, contained—however faintly—the autobiographical complaint of "Prayer of Columbus." As the giant in the literary forest, Whitman accepts his fate—to be the "Voice of a mighty dying tree in the redwood forest dense." His spirits were possibly dampened when the poem, as he told Mrs. O'Connor, was "abused & sneered at in the newspaper criticisms." Whitman even feared he might die, and by February 11, 1874, had already "twice hurriedly destroyed a large mass of letters & MSS.—to be ready for what might happen."[20]

❋ ❋ ❋

Shortly afterward Whitman lost his government job when a new solicitor of the treasury was appointed and Congress abolished one of his department's senior clerkships. He managed, however, to win two months' severance pay. He had tried to prevent the discharge by appealing to President Grant directly. That winter he had sent the president clippings from "'Tis But Ten Years Since," hoping that he would remember him, "or my occasional salute to you in Washington." When Congress approved a bill in June reducing the staff in the Department of Justice, he wrote again to Grant, asking directly that "I not be disturbed in my position as clerk."[21] Grant answered the first letter through his secretary, assuring Whitman of the president's "polite attention" and sending "his best wishes for your speedy recovery."

The second was answered by George H. Williams, the current attorney general, in announcing Whitman's discharge. Whitman may have gone to Washington in November 1875 to look for another job. Sixteen of his Washington friends sent a petition to the secretary of the treasury, but no job ever materialized. Whitman was never well enough to work again anyway.[22]

In 1874 and 1875 the poet teetered on the brink of complete defeat, but somehow found the health and spirit to go forward. "I am still holding out here—don't get well yet—& don't go under yet," he wrote to William J. Linton, a New Englander who did the woodblock print of Whitman that, along with the 1855 engraving by Gabriel Harrison, became the basis for the portraits in the Author's Edition of *Leaves of Grass* in 1876.[23] The first illustration catches Whitman at the apex of his career, artistically and physically upright; it faces the poem "Walt Whitman." The second shows him after the war, looking serenely fatigued; it faces "The Wound Dresser." This picture was made from an 1871 photograph by George C. Potter. The poet was very likely carrying latent tuberculosis, contracted either from his brother Andrew, who died of the disease in 1863, or from his sick soldiers in the hospitals. It would contribute to his death twenty-one years later.[24] In their portrait, Potter and Linton captured the inner as well as the outer image of Whitman at the time. Their depiction of the war-worn poet contrasts curiously with the photograph he posed for in Camden or Philadelphia in 1873. There the Good Gray Poet, as if in need of a prop to convey his oneness with nature, holds aloft a fake butterfly. In mid-February 1875 Whitman suffered a second stroke, which stunned his right side but was not severe or life-threatening. The same week he ordered a thousand impressions of the Linton woodcut, "my head, to go in book."[25]

The following fall Whitman was well enough to travel possibly first to Washington and then on to Baltimore for the reburial of Edgar Allan Poe. Perhaps feeling almost buried alive himself, Whitman was honoring a literary genius whose premature death at the age of forty, in 1849, had deprived the canon of contemporary American literature of a major contributor. Poe's physical remains were removed from his nearly pauper's grave and reburied on the same lot, now accommodating a church, on November 17 under a monument constructed especially for the purpose. Some of the newspapers made light of the occasion, but obliquely, so as not to offend the ladies of the Western Female Academy in Baltimore who had raised the funds for the reinterment. One report mocked the Raven's final resting place as his "Westminster burial ground" and recounted how the gravediggers held up the skull of the crumbling remains and rattled what was left of the brain inside.[26]

Whitman wasted no time in capitalizing on the occasion. He published an anonymously written piece about himself in the *Washington Evening Star* the next day entitled "Walt Whitman at the Poe Funeral" and subtitled "Conspicuous Absence of the Popular Poets." "About the most significant part of the Poe re-burial," he said (not forgetting to mention that it was attended by "the very best class of young people, women preponderating"), "was the marked absence from the spot of every popular poet and author, American and foreign. Only Walt Whitman was present." When the piece was later reprinted in *Specimen Days,* this observation was left out. Especially when linked to the lines that followed—which pictured the "Old Gray," who, "though ill from paralysis, consented to hobble up and silently take a seat on the platform"—it smacked of more self-pity, albeit through Poe this time.

William O'Connor also attended the ceremony. A worshiper of Poe before he worshiped Whitman, he tried in his contribution to a collection of essays (intended by its Western Female Academy sponsors simply to mark the occasion) to lash out at the establishment for treating Poe shabbily when he was alive and for scorning his reburial ceremony. But the editor, Sara Sigourney Rice, overruled the polemic. Nor would Rice, a professor of elocution at the academy, allow a similar plaint on Whitman's behalf. Borrowing perhaps from Whitman's self-description in the *Star,* O'Connor tried to evoke the image of his old friend slowly limping up to the speaker's platform (where Whitman declined to speak), "broken with his hospital service to the wounded and dying of both sides in the war, and grand in his age and infirmity, like a crippled eagle."[27] It took five more years before the author of the *Good Gray Poet* could bring himself to speak directly to Whitman in person. Nevertheless, O'Connor's pen was soon called back into service, along with Burroughs's.

Still recovering from his stroke, Whitman managed that previous April to critique two essays on Emerson that Burroughs would place in the *Galaxy*.[28] This was not the first time, of course, that Whitman had coached Burroughs in his writings, and the Emerson essays, published in the February and April 1876 issues of the *Galaxy*, pertained as much to Whitman as they did to Emerson. When the *Nation* printed harsh words about Whitman to praise Joaquin Miller's *Songs of the Sunlands* (1873), he sent Burroughs a rebuttal that he could either sign or use as a basis for his own response to the criticism. It was Whitman's usual method, adopted since the end of the war, though Whitman added a new wrinkle to the argument when he wrote that the "author's theory" from the outset had evidently been based on the "deep axiom 'it is reserved for first-rate poems never immediately to gratify.'"[29] That essay never appeared in the *Galaxy* or anywhere else as far as is known.

Burroughs apparently declined to act on this occasion as a Whitman scribe. He was now established in the field of "nature writing," a genre popular in the face of the onrushing technology that followed the Civil War. *Wake Robin,* his first book, properly speaking, had appeared in 1871 along with the second edition of *Notes on Walt Whitman as Poet and Person,* and *Birds and Poets,* even more successful than *Wake Robin,* would appear in 1877. Yet even though he was beginning to chart his own course as a professional writer, in the Emerson essays Burroughs continued to echo the old Whitman argument. In his response to Burroughs, however, Whitman found himself of two minds. On the one hand, he was as angry as Burroughs about the exclusion from *Parnassus,*[30] yet on the other he may have had some misgivings at seeing his younger friend wax as negative as he himself had in "A Christmas Garland" in criticizing Emerson for backing away from his endorsement in 1855. He saw that his literary campaign was possibly corrupting someone who before the *Leaves of Grass* flap had adored Emerson as much as he had. Perhaps he feared losing Burroughs through some sort of misunderstanding the way he had O'Connor. At any rate, he wrote Burroughs on April 1, 1875, to say that his essays, "A Word or Two on Emerson" and "A Final Word on Emerson," produced "a not agreeable notion of being written by one who has been largely grown & ripened & gristled by Emerson, but has at last become dissatisfied & finicky about him, & would pitch into him but cannot . . . [original ellipses] and so keeps running around in a sort of circle of praises & half praises, like a horse tied by a tether."[31] In the first essay shown to Whitman in draft, Burroughs wrote that Emerson's "power of statement is enormous," but that "his scope of being is not enormous."[32] This was obviously an oblique complaint that Emerson had not lived up to his works when he apparently abandoned Whitman—either by the omission from *Parnassus* or by his relative silence on *Leaves of Grass* in the wake of the first edition.

Whitman advised Burroughs to tone down his criticism of Emerson ("My name might be brought in, in one or two places as a foil or suggestive comparison—but *my name only,* without any praises or comments"), but Burroughs published both essays much as they were drafted. Curiously, Whitman was delighted with the published results, saying the "late pieces" showed a marked vitality—"leaves the impression now upon me (after two readings) of the noblest piece of criticism on these things yet in America." Now he apparently could not resist Burroughs's observation in the second essay that Emerson's transcendentalism, or his exclusive focus on "spiritual law," possibly showed a lack of "the passions and the springs of action, as in Shakespeare," "the awful hobgoblins of hell and Satan, as in Dante," or the "vast masses and spaces and the abysms of aboriginal man, as in Walt Whitman."[33] This had been Whitman's very point in "A Christmas Garland."

Yet like Burroughs, who practically worshiped at Emerson's feet when he first met him at West Point in the early 1860s, Whitman could not completely reject or denounce the "Master." The enemy wasn't Emerson, but the literary establishment, which had tried—and succeeded to some extent—to dilute the teachings of "the arch radical of the world," as Burroughs characterized him after reading "Circles."[34] But Burroughs's criticism of Emerson was only the latest low blow delivered in Whitman's campaign against the establishment. In the anonymous "Walt Whitman's Actual American Position," published in the *West Jersey Press* in Camden on January 26, 1876, he wrote, "All the established American poets studiously ignore Whitman. The *omnium gatherums* of poetry, by Emerson, Bryant, Whittier, and by lesser authorities, professing to include everybody of any note, carefully leave him out."[35]

❋ ❋ ❋

Parnassus may have been the primary stimulus for the newspaper article. But when Whitman placed "Walt Whitman's Actual American Position" in the *West Jersey Press,* he may also have been angry at *Scribner's* for rejecting "Eidólons" (which he subsequently printed in *Two Rivulets*). Whitman had sent the poem to Josiah P. Holland, editor of the magazine; it was "rejected—not rejected mildly, noncommittedly, in the customary way, but with a note of the most offensive character." "Sick and blue at the time," he was sufficiently provoked, he later recalled, to toss the rejection letter into the fire.[36] Holland considered it his ethical duty to silence Whitman whenever he could, having never forgiven him for the "obscene" early editions of *Leaves of Grass.* Echoing Salmon P. Chase's earlier revulsion, he once asked Edmund Clarence Stedman, "How can you touch the wretched old fraud?"[37]

Whitman would have still written the *West Jersey Press* article without Holland, but he would possibly have been more circumspect in his denunciations. As it turned out, his condemnation of the opposition included individuals and magazines that had been receptive to his work, such as Emerson and the *Galaxy.* According to the essay, the reputation of Whitman's poetry required, quite literally, a future: "Still he stands alone," after twenty years. "No established publishing house will yet print his books. Most of the stores will not even sell them. In fact, his works have never been really published at all." This had been Whitman's refrain since the war, but now, half-crippled and needing money, he had finally become visibly annoyed with all the resistance and was in no way hesitant to complain, all the way down to particulars. "Worst still; for the past three years having left [his publications] in charge of book agents in New York City, who, taking advantage of the author's illness and helplessness, have, three of them, one after another, successively thievishly embezzled every dollar of the proceeds!"

Not only had he been ignored by all the leading anthologists, but the American literary establishment had disregarded the high praise of his works in the *Westminster Review, Revue des Deux Mondes,* and *Gentleman's Magazine,* "while the scolding and cheap abuse of Peter Bayne is copied and circulated at once in the Boston [*Littell's*] *Living Age.*" Whitman's point drew blood here. Generally, the national literary press *had* ignored the growing European interest in *Leaves of Grass* (perhaps without even knowing most of it came almost exclusively from literary or political radicals). He followed up the point with the remark that during the previous year he had prepared a centennial edition of his book, "which he himself sells, partly 'to keep the wolf from the door' in old age—and partly to give before he dies, as absolute expression as may be to his ideas."[38]

Whitman was, on the whole, treated much better than he thought, or claimed. Even during his sickest days of 1873 and 1874, he published poems in several places, sometimes collecting handsome fees.[39] Yet he wanted more, much more. He believed himself to be the greatest American poet, and he believed more fervently than ever that his kind of poetry was the poetry of the future—that it had to be as democracy spread around the world. The day "Walt Whitman's Actual American Position" appeared, he sent a copy to Rossetti, suggesting he publish it in the *Academy* and saying that his situation was "even worse *than* described in the article."[40] Rossetti failed to place the article there, but found a home for excerpts (including the two sentences quoted from Whitman's letter) in the *Athenaeum* of March 11. Whitman also sent copies to Schmidt in Denmark and Dowden in Ireland. Then he arranged for another anonymous article to be printed in the *Tribune* of February 19, this time a straightforward review, or preview, of his 1876 volumes.[41]

The result was a transatlantic debate over the merits of Whitman's oeuvre, in which one of the stickier issues turned out to be the early behavior and later opinion of Emerson with regard to *Leaves of Grass.* Although news of the *West Jersey Press* article in England triggered the contest, the battlefield was being prepared as early as December 1875, when one of Dowden's colleagues, Standish O'Grady, praised Whitman as the "Poet of Joy" in *Gentleman's Magazine.* In the same month, Peter Bayne, a Scottish journalist, attacked Whitman's poetry in the *Contemporary Review* primarily because of its transcendentalism, or what he saw as the reduction of art to the mere cataloging of nature as microcosmic symbols. Though the review (essentially of the poems in the first and second editions of *Leaves of Grass,* ignoring the later, more spiritual pieces) was full of insults, characterizing Whitman's verse as "spurts and gushes," Bayne also made a perceptive argument against modernism and its inversion of logocentrism—and ultimately, although he didn't know it, against all artistic doctrines from imagism to postmodernism that celebrate the fragmentary, or minor, aspects of life as central and equal in magnificence to heroes and sunsets. This kind of poetry flattered the mob into thinking that they as transcendentalists were as good as their betters, Bayne insisted, and thus Whitman's poetry, as insane, silly, untutored, and obscene as it was, was not as much harmless as it was worthless. In fact, it was "poisonously immoral and pestilent."[42]

What Bayne missed, what many critics today miss in adapting Whitman's democratic poetry to modern expectations, is the insistence throughout *Leaves of Grass,* especially in the postwar poems, on the *potential* of the equality celebrated. Just as in *Democratic Vistas*—or "To a Common Prostitute," where a woman's divinity is yet to be realized—so Whitman's celebration of democracy requires a future as much as a present—possibly more so. This is an important difference between him and Emerson. For Emerson, the nature of things, if we would only see it, is perfect; if spared the trivial pursuits of society, humans will fulfill their vocation and destiny. For Whitman, the nature of things includes urban squalor, drunkenness, domestic horrors, and early death by crime or industrial accidents; nature requires a future to appreciate the present.[43]

The debate remained relatively calm until Robert Buchanan entered it, through the English *Daily News* of March 13, with a flaming endorsement of Whitman as, variously, a "golden eagle, sick to death . . . pursued by a crowd of prosperous rooks and crows"; as Christ with "His crown of thorns"; and as Socrates with "his hemlock cup." Buchanan's decision to compare Whitman to Christ was a strange choice for someone who had been raised as an agnostic and a socialist. The marriage of his parents in 1840 had been presided over by none other than the Scottish socialist Robert Owen. Buchanan, born a year later, grew up comfortably in Glasgow, where his socialist father owned three newspapers, but when he was eighteen, his father lost all his money in careless investments, and then all his fair-weather friends.

Young Buchanan eventually made his way into the London literary world, first by reviewing other people's books and then by publishing one of his own, *London Poems,* in 1860. He achieved instant notoriety in 1871 for an article he published in the *Contemporary Review* under the pseudonym of Thomas Maitland. This article, "The Fleshly School of Poetry," made Buchanan a strange bedfellow in the 1876 Anglo-American debate because it attacked the Pre-Raphaelites, of which the most prominent was Rossetti's brother, Dante Gabriel.[44] The Pre-Raphaelite campaign, begun in 1848, was doubtless the basis of William Michael Rossetti's admiration for *Leaves of Grass:* like Whitman, the Pre-Raphaelites turned away from the traditions and rules of art to treat experience "naturalistically." And this move led in turn to dithyrambs by the painter-poet Dante Gabriel and his sister Christina—both with poems almost as sensual as those found in Whitman's "Children of Adam." What Whitman did not share with the Pre-Raphaelites, however, was their retreat from everyday reality into a kind of romantic medievalism. Dante Gabriel Rossetti, who buried a manuscript containing a number of new poems with his dead wife in 1862 only to disinter and publish them eight years later, went into a rage over Buchanan's criticism of him and the Pre-Raphaelite movement in "The Fleshly School of Poetry."

The poet is linked to this attack on the movement because Buchanan lauded Whitman in the article at the expense of Dante Gabriel Rossetti, and Algernon Swinburne, Rossetti's friend and literary compatriot, took offense, which led to his attacks on Whitman in 1887. Swinburne claimed that it was the poet's awkward and bloated statements about democracy that changed his mind about Whitman's greatness, but the truth was that he could not abide anybody, even Whitman, who received the ecstatic praise of the noisy and disrespectful Buchanan.[45] Buchanan's attack on the Pre-Raphaelites was personal as well as literary. Not long before he published the article (which today has its own entry in literary encyclopedias), Swinburne had provoked him by making an insulting remark in print regarding a book by one of Buchanan's boyhood friends, recently deceased. And Dante Gabriel Rossetti entered the fray as well. Following a lukewarm review by Buchanan of Swinburne's *Poems and Ballads,* he attacked Buchanan as "a poor and pretentious poetaster." "From that instant," Buchanan recalled in his memoirs, "I considered myself free to strike at the whole Coterie, which I finally did, at the moment when all the journals were sounding extravagant paeans over the poems of Dante Gabriel Rossetti."[46]

The reaction to "The Fleshly School of Poetry" was so fierce that Buchanan had to publish under yet another pseudonym for several years afterward. He was the perfect literary outlaw to defend the American literary outlaw, perfect, that is, for raising the roofbeams of Anglo-American literary criticism. Harold Blodgett has called him the British O'Connor, but O'Connor, whose invective also backfired occasionally, was perhaps timid in comparison. Furthermore, without Buchanan's participation in the British discussion of Whitman's shabby treatment in his own country, it is probable that the debate, which ultimately boosted Whitman's reputation in the United States, might have never crossed the Atlantic.

Like O'Connor on the subject of Whitman and blacks, Buchanan was caught up in a slight contradiction when it came to Whitman and the body. In 1868, when he published his first critique of Whitman in the London *Broadway Magazine,* he had deplored the bad taste of "Children of Adam" while extolling Whitman's celebration of democracy. Since Buchanan cited the poet as one of the great moral teachers in his attack on Pre-Raphaelite sensualism, Swinburne asked the embarrassing question in the *Examiner* of how he could deplore the "ulcerous inroads of Sensualism" at home and admire "so much the poetry which is widely considered unclean and animal in America." As Whitman later remarked, Buchanan, who was afraid of nothing, was "afraid of Children of Adam."[47]

❋ ❋ ❋

Bayard Taylor, who picked up the fight in America, had more in common with the poet than his condescending *Tribune* editorials suggest.

Both Whitman and Taylor came from Quaker stock that had largely dissipated by their generation, they worked as journalists in New York in the 1840s, and they passed through New Orleans in almost the same year, again working as journalists. In 1876 Taylor was at the height of his fame. Though—also like Whitman—he was without a university education, he had become internationally renowned as a poet, travel writer, and journalist. He had translated Goethe's *Faust* and was the author of almost fifty books and more than seven hundred newspaper and magazine articles. The first poem he ever published, "The Soliloquy of a Young Poet," in the *Saturday Evening Post,* expressed with youthful bravado a wish for fame, which—though he enjoyed it in life—has since evaporated into history.

> High hopes spring up within;
> Hopes of the future—thoughts of glory—fame
> Which prompt my mind to toil and bid me win
> That dream—a deathless name.[48]

A lifelong correspondent for Greeley's *Tribune,* he had reported on the California gold rush, acted as minister to Russia during the Civil War, and delivered more than a thousand lectures about his travels on the lyceum circuits. In the spring of 1876, at a time when he was defending the New England and New York literary establishments (where his tone made him sound like their official representative) and publishing demure denunciations of Whitman's art in the *Tribune,* he was selected by the Centennial Commission in Philadelphia to write the national hymn. (The honor had first been offered to Longfellow, then to Lowell, Holmes, Whittier, and Bryant, who all apparently felt too old or too busy for the task.)[49] Taylor was only fifty-two and as eager for the task as he was up to defending the kind of American literature that flourished before the age of Whitman and Pound. His reward was an ambassadorship to Germany the following year, also the year before his early death.

In "In Re Walt Whitman," published in the *Tribune* of March 28, Taylor first attacked the poet indirectly through Buchanan, whom he assailed as a third-rate poet trying to gratify "his restless passion for personal notoriety." He then chided Whitman for publishing Emerson's letter in and (part of it) *on* the second edition of *Leaves of Grass.* Emerson's letter was not an endorsement of the book but an "impulsive, extravagant *private* letter to Walt Whitman." Taylor acknowledged the "humanity" and "integrity" of Whitman's wartime service but nevertheless insisted that the poet's book was not fit to "be read aloud under the evening lamp." He expressed his resentment at a statement made by Rossetti in publishing excerpts of the *West Jersey Press* article that the American literati should be ashamed of their refusal to accept anything but conventional poetry. He then quoted an abusive article from the English *Daily Times* of March 16 comparing Whitman to a lump of dough instead of a block of marble—out of which might be carved the statue of a true poet. To demonstrate that New York critics were not personally hostile to the poet, he argued that it was members of the literary class who had rallied to get Whitman his job in the Attorney General's Office after he was fired by Harlan (whom, interestingly, he condemned for the same censorship Whitman was now effectively receiving in the United States).

Under the current editorship of Whitlaw Reid, the *Tribune* had been friendly to Whitman, but the English assault apparently carried the day in the editorial department that spring. The same day that Taylor's editorial appeared, a letter from "G.W.S." ("G. W. Smalley, appropriate name!" O'Connor wrote in the margin of his copy) complained that "Mr. Buchanan thinks Mr. Whitman's merits can best be urged by denying those of everybody else." Letters pro (John Swinton in the *New York Herald* of April 1) and con (an anonymous writer in the *Boston Transcript* of the same day, suggesting Whitman was not "condemned" in America, simply not "mentioned") shot back and forth in a variety of publications. The editor of *Appleton's* astutely suspected that the entire brouhaha was an "advertising trick" on the part of Whitman and his disciples to sell his latest works.[50]

Soon Burroughs and O'Connor jumped in. Burroughs brought the weight of his recently won reputation as a nature writer to bear on the *Tribune's* belittlement of Whitman's literary achievement. "As a young man," his letter printed in the April 13 issue of the *Tribune* said, "I have obtained no such moral and intellectual lifts, as some one has aptly

Top: John Burroughs in the 1860s. Library of Congress.

Bottom: Whitman and Peter Doyle in 1869. Duke University.

Opposite, top: William Douglas O'Connor, circa 1865. Library of Congress.

Opposite, bottom: Ellen O'Connor, circa 1870. Library of Congress.

Above: Whitman in 1871. Courtesy of Ohio Wesleyan University.

Above: Whitman around 1872. Library of Congress.

Opposite, top: Thomas Jefferson Whitman, the poet's favorite brother, about 1872. Missouri Historical Society.

Opposite, bottom: Martha Mitchell Whitman ("Mattie"), Jeff's wife, about 1872. Missouri Historical Society.

Opposite, top: The Corcoran Building, which housed the Army Paymaster's Office, where Whitman first worked in Washington. The poet lived on the top floor of the next building in the foreground, suffering his first paralytic stroke there in 1873. The Treasury Building, which housed the Attorney General's Office, was across the street to the left. Department of the Treasury.

Opposite, bottom: The Treasury Building, where Whitman worked in the Attorney General's Office on the first floor of the front-right corner (center). To the right can be seen the Army Paymaster's Office, where Whitman found his first government job, and immediately below it the building in which Whitman rented a room. Department of the Treasury.

Above: Anne Gilchrist, painted by Herbert Gilchrist, 1882–84. Department of Special Collections, Van Pelt Library, University of Pennsylvania.

Beatrice Gilchrist, circa 1881. Private collection.

The Tea Party, painted by Herbert Gilchrist, 1884. Department of Special Collections, Van Pelt Library, University of Pennsylvania.

Walt Whitman
1877

Opposite: Whitman holding a fake butterfly in 1877. Library of Congress.

Above: Harry Stafford and Whitman in the late 1870s. Metropolitan Library, Sheffield, England.

Main Street, Kansas City, about 1879. Kansas City Public Library.

American House, Denver, about 1879. Denver Public Library.

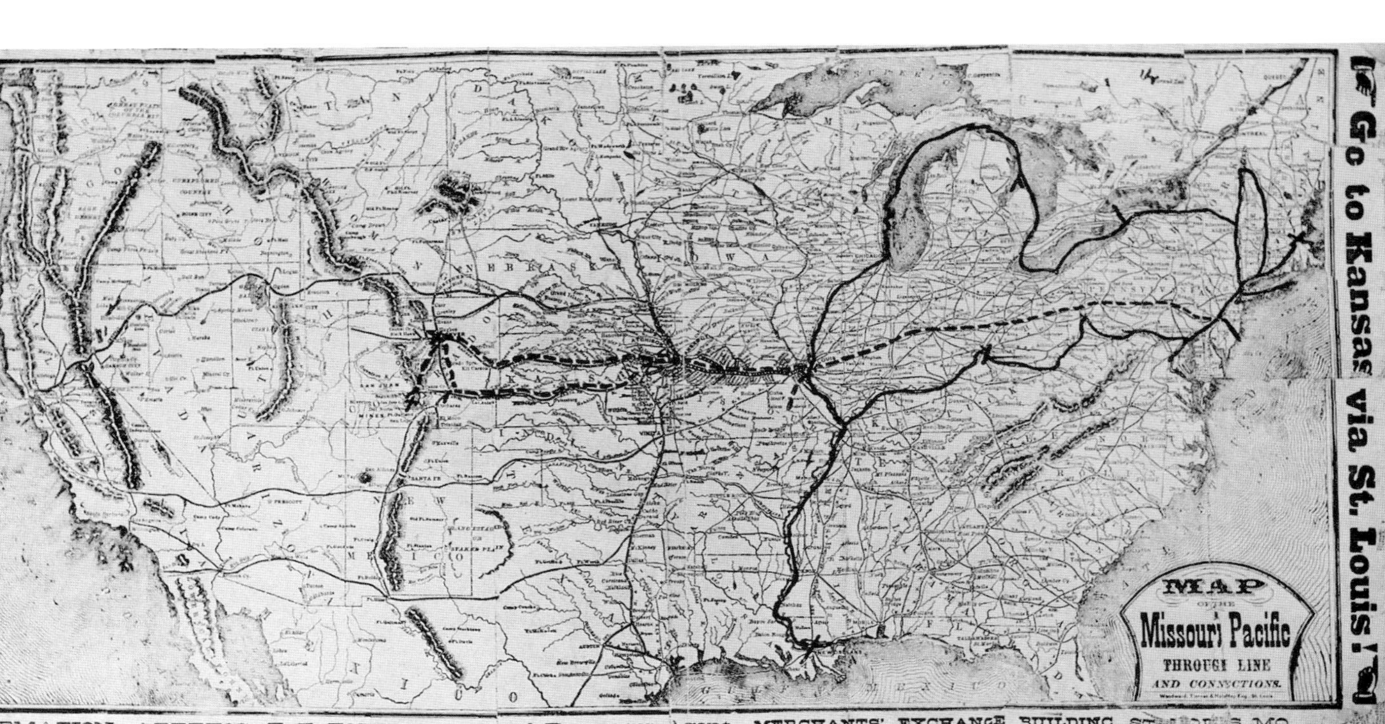

Go to Kansas via St. Louis!
MAP OF THE Missouri Pacific THROUGH LINE AND CONNECTIONS.
NEBRASKA
KANSAS
IOWA
NEW MEXICO
MERCHANTS' EXCHANGE BUILDING

Opposite: Map Whitman sent to Burroughs on November 23, 1879, showing his lifetime travel. Library of Congress.

Above: Oscar Wilde in 1882.

Whitman and Bill Duckett in the 1880s. Ohio Wesleyan University.

The poet's home on Mickle Street. Library of Congress.

Above: Warren Fritzinger ("Warry") and Whitman in the 1890s.

Opposite: Hemingwayesque photograph of Whitman in 1863, given to Traubel in 1888. University of Virginia.

Walt Whitman
taken from life 1863
war time Washington
D C

to Horace L Traubel
from his friend W W
June 1888

Opposite: Anne Montgomerie Traubel circa 1891. Library of Congress.

Above: Anne Montgomerie Traubel with Whitman collector Oscar Lion in the 1930s. Library of Congress.

Whitman in 1891. Library of Congress.

Whitman's funeral. Library of Congress.

Traubel next to Whitman's tomb in Camden, New Jersey. Courtesy of the New York Public Library.

named this kind of service, from any other source as from [Whitman's] poems and his contact and conversation." He also argued that the opinions of the *Daily News* against Whitman were not indicative of "the opinion of a majority of the rising men in the fields of English poetry and criticism," and he named William Michael Rossetti, Dowden, Swinburne, and Symonds as among Whitman's admirers in Europe. "The truth is," Burroughs wrote, directing his remarks point-blank at Taylor and his kind of poetry, "sweet poets, elegant poets, learned, correct, beautiful poets, are not rare, in our age, but powerful poets, poets who can confront and compel the gigantic materialism of our times and land, and who by dint of inward native force can rise above the poetic and literary consciousness with which the very atmosphere is rotten, are rare, and it seems misunderstood when they come."

O'Connor's letter to the *Tribune* on April 22 served Whitman less well. It was long and windy, resembling the worst aspects of *The Good Gray Poet.* Apparently O'Connor, still estranged from his friend, was overcompensating. His letter went on and on (certainly evidence of the *Tribune*'s belated attempt to be fair to Whitman), reviewing the debate as if no such summary had already appeared. He did get in two salvoes, however. If it had been in such bad taste to publish Emerson's letter of July 21, 1855, he asked, why then did the *Tribune* print it? And catching Taylor in the same corner Swinburne had found Buchanan, he asked him ("fresh from his fine translation" of Goethe) "whether 'Faust' was written to be read aloud under the Argand [lamp]." (The next day Whitman quietly sent his ex-friend copies of the newly published *Memoranda During the War* and *Two Rivulets.*)[51] Taylor lashed back at both O'Connor and Burroughs in the same issue that carried O'Connor's letter, claiming that the influence of the Pre-Raphaelites, who championed Whitman in England, had corrupted them into praising Whitman's sensuality. "Both of these gentlemen," he said, "sufficiently illustrate their dependence upon that English criticism, the phenomena of which, as we have recently explained, spring partly from ignorance of all distinctively American material and partly from a strong craving for new and piquant literary sensations."

Rossetti had organized a subscription sale of the centennial volumes of *Leaves of Grass* in England, and Swinton in his letter of April 1 had suggested a similar movement in the United States. A problem arose, however. It began to look as though these sales campaigns were based exclusively on Buchanan's claim for Whitman's poverty and not the literary value of *Leave of Grass.* Whitman had shrewdly waffled on the question of his finances, saying, yes, he needed income, but no, he was not starving. On April 4 he expressed his appreciation to Buchanan for every aspect of all three of his public letters.[52] One wonders what George Whitman and his wife thought of all this, if they indeed knew of the Anglo-American controversy or its specific points. Their household was prosperous (George's estate in 1902 contained bank accounts totaling almost $60,000),[53] and Jeff was thriving out in St. Louis, well beyond his initial expectations. Yet when Taylor printed in the *Tribune* a paragraph by Conway from the *Daily News,* saying that the report that "Walt Whitman is in want, or dependent on his relatives, is unfounded," Whitman immediately wrote Rossetti on April 7, "I do not approve his letter." A month later, he was even more upset and (perhaps recalling the inaccurate *Fortnightly Review* article of 1866) told Rossetti that Conway lacked "delicacy & insight."[54]

Whitman must have been in the dark regarding the ongoing quarrel between Buchanan and the Pre-Raphaelites because of his essay on "The Fleshly School of Poetry" and ignorant of the fact that Conway's note to the *Daily News* was probably intended to take the English (Pre-Raphaelite) support out of Buchanan's hands. Conway learned from Rossetti that Whitman was annoyed at his denial of the poet's financial need. He wrote from the Kensington section of London, where as a sometime clergyman he was now preaching, to say that he had merely been trying to save "those of your countrymen who would share their last loaf with you; and to free you from the charge of getting aid on false pretences of which you were in danger, and myself from equal peril of abetting what I knew to be a lie by silence." Conway's effort had been particularly inspired by a letter from Alfred Austin in the *Daily News* of March 16 (paraphrased in the *Tribune* by Smalley on March 28) to the effect that Whitman deserved financial help not because he was a true poet but because of his hospital work. In other words, Buchanan's campaign for Whitman's book may have devolved to the level of "alms for Whitman."[55]

Whitman never quite agreed with this estimate but hemmed and hawed when he told Buchanan in May that he would not have instigated the English plan to sell his books, "& if I had been consulted, should have peremptorily stopt it—but now that it has started, & grown, . . . I am determined to respond to it in the same spirit in which it has risen." In the draft version of this letter, he conceded, "There is doubtless a point of view from which Mr. Conway's statement of April 4th might hold, technically—but." He was responding to a letter from Buchanan, marked "Private," which expressed bewilderment and frustration over Conway's remark and Whitman's apparent failure to deny it. By January of the next year, Buchanan dropped out as one of the English distributors of the centennial editions—because of "the [unpleasant] tone adopted by certain of your friends here."[56]

❋ ❋ ❋

Whitman, who once described the American flag as "beautiful and spiritual" and "floating lovely as a dream,"[57] probably wanted to be designated the official centennial poet, a completely unrealistic aspiration given the controversial state of his literary reputation. That honor went to Bayard Taylor, and Whitman's disappointment may have been another of the reasons for his *West Jersey Press* article. Yet it not only launched the Anglo-American debate over *Leaves of Grass,* but it also publicized his 1876 edition (technically an issue from 1871) of his lifelong book as well as its companion volume that year, *Two Rivulets.* The publicizing process followed the pattern that began with his publication of the Emerson letter in 1855 and his inclusion of anonymous articles about the first *Leaves of Grass,* sewn into the second issue and included under "Leaves-Droppings" in the 1856 edition. In 1860 with the third edition, he got Clapp and the *Saturday Press* to start a commotion, and Burroughs promoted the 1867 and 1871 *Leaves* with the first and second editions of his *Notes on Walt Whitman.*

When Whitman returned from Washington and began to prepare, or complete, work on his centennial books, he had been unemployed since 1874 (actually 1873 if we factor in the wages he had to pay his government substitute in 1874). He maintained to his English friends that his status as a paying boarder at George and Lou's house had depleted his savings. This was probably something of an exaggeration since he had earned a salary of $1,600 per year, an income sufficient for a family of four in those days. Nevertheless, he must have been getting low on whatever he had saved, a creeping development that threatened his independence from the conventional living conditions in Camden. (George, whom Walt much admired, showed little or no interest in his brother's literary life.) Whitman had also lost money with three of the distributors of the 1871 *Leaves of Grass, Passage to India,* and *Democratic Vistas.* He told a friend from his Pfaff's days who had heard rumors of the poet's poverty and offered help, "I have come to the end of my rope, & am in fact ridiculously poor."[58] But when English supporters inquired about his finances, he told them that he was not truly worried about basic necessities, merely fearful of spending too much of what he had left in the bank on printing the centennial editions.

This printing was done at the local print shop of the *Camden New Republic,* where *Memoranda During the War* was also printed. *Memoranda* along with the centennial edition of *Leaves of Grass* (also called the "Author's Edition") and *Two Rivulets* made up a trio of publications in 1876 just as *Democratic Vistas* made up a trinity with the fifth edition of *Leaves of Grass* and *Passage to India* in 1871. At first Whitman printed only a hundred copies of each centennial volume, which he sold out of George's house by mail-order subscription. (In one sense, he was reopening his Brooklyn bookstore of 1850, but selling only his own titles.) After the first printing of *Memoranda During the War,* the text was sewn into *Two Rivulets;* consequently, the book is extremely rare as a separate publication. The combined version and the 1876 *Leaves of Grass* each went through one more printing of 600 copies.[59]

Memoranda is a strange, haunting revisiting of the war, in which Whitman dramatizes his memoir by quoting directly from his hospital notebooks and pretending to have been present at memorable events when he wasn't—for example, at Ford's Theatre during the assassination (an exaggeration that later leaked into his Lincoln lectures). Here he borrows from news accounts and from Doyle, who actually was in Ford's Theatre that night. He also gives the vague impression that he visited more than the two battle sites of Fredericksburg and Chancellorsville during the war and witnessed actual battles. (Studies of *Drum-Taps* have not sufficiently emphasized that its poems are based primarily on what the "Wound Dresser" saw and heard in the hospitals.)

In *Memoranda* Whitman reminisces not only about his experiences in the hospitals but also about the "perfection of physical health" he so confidently enjoyed. Now gone, it hadn't actually been that robust during the war either. He speaks for the first time in print of his preparation for the hospital visits. "My habit, when practicable, was to prepare for starting out on one of those daily or nightly tours, of from a couple to four or five hours, by fortifying myself with previous rest, the bath, clean clothes, a good meal, and as cheerful an appearance as possible."[60] He also attended Lincoln's second inauguration, he said, and most profoundly records his impressions during the inaugural ball in the Patent Office: "I could not help thinking of those rooms, where the music will sound and the dancers' feet presently tread—what a different scene they presented to my view a while since, fill'd with a crowded mass of the worst wounded of the war. . . . To-night, beautiful women, perfumes, the violins' sweetness, the polka and the waltz; but then, the amputation, the blue face, the groan, the glassy eye of the dying, the clotted rag, the odor of wounds and blood, and many a mother's son amid strangers, passing away untended there."[61]

The 1876 *Leaves of Grass* is identical to the 1871 edition except for the addition of the poem "Come, Said My Soul" (which also serves as the epigraph to the 1881 edition) and four filler poems, crudely pasted in and called "Intercalations."[62] *Two Rivulets* is far more curious, because of its gimmicky arrangement and its attempt to gather up not only the contents of *Passage to India* but every other work written since the war. The title indicates the parallel streams of poetry and prose, a mixing first tried in "A Christmas Garland" (1874).

> Two Rivulets side by side,
> Two blended, parallel, strolling tides,
> Companions, travelers, gossiping as they journey.

Both reader and poet contain both—the "Real" in prose, the "Ideal" in poetry, "Object and Subject hurrying, whirling by."

Whitman very well may have considered this volume and the 1876 issue of *Leaves of Grass* as "death-bed" editions. "At the eleventh hour, under grave illness," he writes in the preface, "I gather up the pieces of Prose and Poetry left over since publishing, a while since, my first and main Volume, LEAVES OF GRASS—pieces, here, some new, some old—nearly all of them (sombre as many are, making this almost Death's book) composed in by-gone atmospheres of perfect health—and, preceded by the freshest collection, the little TWO RIVULETS, and by this rambling Prefatory gossip." He adds in a footnote here (hardly distinguishable in print size from "Thoughts for the Centennial," a series of short, paragraph-length essays that run along the bottom half of the page beneath poems written since the 1871 edition) that this preface is "not only for the present collection, but, in a sort, for all my writings." Like the burning of letters, this preface was an insurance policy against sudden death.

Almost as long as the 1876 *Leaves of Grass, Two Rivulets* contains fourteen poems (many of which had appeared in newspapers and magazines since 1871) under the subheading of the same name, "TWO RIVULETS." In all, the volume has five general headings: the subterranean "Thoughts for the Centennial"; "CENTENNIAL SONGS," which presents "Song of the Exposition" ("After All Not to Create Only"), "Song of the Redwood-Tree," "Song of the Universal," and "Song for All Seas, All Ships"; "AS A STRONG BIRD ON PINIONS FREE," containing the poems in the 1872 *As a Strong Bird on Pinions Free;* "MEMORANDA DURING THE WAR," incorporating the original text of the book; and "PASSAGE TO INDIA," reprinting the poetry in that 1871 collection. The volume, as the poet later acknowledged, was expensively priced for its day, five dollars apiece or ten for the two-volume set of *Leaves of Grass* and *Two Rivulets,* postage and packaging included.

❋ ❋ ❋

That summer Hattie and Jessie, Jeff's daughters, had been visiting their uncles in Camden, and Jeff joined them on September 26.[63] One reason for the visit, or its extension, was that young Walter Orr Whitman, George's only child, had died in July of water on the brain. He was only eight months old, and Whitman had doted on the infant. He told folks that "little Walt" liked it best when the poet took care of him and once spoke of "young Walt raising *his* song" over the rooftops of the world.[64] When the child passed away, Whitman was moved to write a sentimental account of the funeral held in the front parlor of the Stevens Street house. Like Mrs. Whitman's funeral, this one was marked by Quaker simplicity. There was no sermon or ceremony, just a white coffin containing the dead baby, surrounded by fresh geranium leaves and tuberoses. Neighborhood parents and their children streamed noiselessly through the parlor. Whitman described himself—in the "Personal" column of the *Tribune,* the very paper that had attacked him—as sitting in a "great chair" near the tiny corpse, "enveloped by children, holding one encircled by either arm, and a beautiful little girl on his lap. The little one looked curiously at the spectacle of death and then inquiringly in the old man's face. 'You don't know what it is, do you, my dear?' said he, adding, 'We don't either.' Many of the children surrounding the coffin were mere babes, and had to be lifted up to take a look."[65] Whitman, ever the manipulating journalist for the "good old cause" (not only of American democracy but of *Leaves of Grass*), exploited this funeral the same way he had Poe's.

It was at the print shop on Federal Street where the "Author's Edition" of *Leaves of Grass* was prepared that Whitman met another young man who would occupy an important place in his life. Harry Stafford was an eighteen-year-old, emotionally troubled lad whose "blue spells" may indicate he suffered from a mild case of manic depression.[66] Working then as an errand boy, he—like Doyle and Whitman—came from a large family. He was boarding in Camden, ten miles from his parents' tenant farm at "White Horse" (Whitman's term for Kirkwood, now Laurel Springs, New Jersey), the third or fourth stop on the Camden and Atlantic Railroad Line, on what is today known as the White Horse Pike to Atlantic City. The Stafford residence, one of a half-dozen houses and stores in the scattered farming community, stood a mile and a half from the station. It consisted of a six-room house, a barn, a few fruit trees, and undulating fields running down to Timber Creek, which the poet once described as a "very secluded beautiful druidic creek." There he frequently sun-bathed nude or sat for hours in an old chair, taking in the essence of the place. (Within Whitman's lifetime, the farm was sold, sliced up into building lots, and turned into a resort visited by hundreds of people at a time.)[67]

George Stafford, a part-time Methodist preacher, farmed the place with the occasional help of his two sons, though Harry, like the younger Walt, disliked farm work. The Stafford family also included a grown-up daughter. Today our view of Whitman's relationship with the young man may reflect the theories of Freud and the current interest in Whitman's possible homosexual tendencies more than the actual facts.[68] The poet "adopted" Harry as his "nephew" and tried to get him a printer's apprenticeship—as he had previously sought to get Doyle employment opportunities. He came to know Harry's parents and siblings almost as well as he knew Harry, having spent much time recuperating at their country retreat. Apparently, no one in the Stafford family thought Walt's attention to Harry unusual. Harry's mother, Susan, who worried about her son's future, very much appreciated Whitman's attention. "He *is* a good man," she told Edward Carpenter in 1877 when he visited Kirkwood with the poet. "I think he is the best man I ever knew." That spring, after Harry had bolted from his job at the *New Republic* with no immediate prospects, she told Whitman that she thought it "better still for him to be with you but I fear he is to [*sic*] much trouble to you all ready."[69]

At about this time, Whitman was also acquiring a new English admirer—George Eliot—although he didn't learn about it for more than a decade. H. Buxton Forman, whose *Our Living Poets* (1871) employed two quotations from Whitman in its epigraphs, later revealed that he had recommended *Leaves of Grass* to the novelist. George Henry Lewes came into the room at that point and remarked flippantly, "Let me see, the author wrote Heel-taps, didn't he?" At that time Eliot was also unenthusiastic about Whitman's poetry, saying it had "no message for her soul." But Forman got her to look again, and weeks later she sent a message, through Lewes, that Whitman did indeed have a message for her.[70] She was at the time just beginning to serialize her famous novel *Middlemarch* (1872). By the time Whitman learned of Eliot's opinion, they had both been published by the Boston firm of James Osgood, and Mary Ann Evans, born the same year as Whitman, had died at the age of sixty.

Another admiring English woman crossed the Atlantic with three of her four children and settled in America to be near the poet. Anne Gilchrist arrived in Philadelphia on September 10, 1876. Whitman's fear of this aggressive woman has been exaggerated. In fact, his gift of a ring when his mother died belies the assumption that he did not encourage her affections—at least on a close platonic basis. Anne Gilchrist was another perfect mother-woman to Whitman. Although from the beginning of their relationship he had fended off her romantic overtures with either rational talk or silence and in his avuncular way often turned their epistolary conversations to the subject of her children, he clearly welcomed her company in Philadelphia. He also gave a ring to young Harry Stafford that September, which went back and forth between the two of them until February of the next year as the old man tried to stabilize the younger one with friendship and perhaps too much love.[71]

When Anne Gilchrist and her family arrived, Philadelphia was well into its Centennial Exhibit, officially opened back in May. Possibly because he was completely left out of the official celebration, Whitman had visited the festivities, centered initially in Fairmont Park on the Schuylkill River, only once. Displayed among other novelties and engineering marvels were Edison's telegraph, Westinghouse's airbrakes, Pullman's palace car, and Bell's telephone; but Whitman's centennial entry, *Leaves of Grass,* remained in Camden. Another possible reason for Whitman's apathy was a heat wave in July, which reduced the attendance until September, when hotel accommodations became scarce again.

The Gilchrists checked into the Montgomery House until they found a house on the west side of the city, in the general neighborhood of the University of Pennsylvania. Whitman, who knew only of their general arrival time, had written to Rossetti expressing his impatience on the first of September. As soon as he learned they had reached Philadelphia safely, he visited them, on September 13. John Burroughs happened to be visiting the exposition at the time and staying at the Montgomery House, so he actually met Anne Gilchrist before Whitman did. He described her as a "rosy woman without a gray hair in her head." Burroughs may have prepared Gilchrist for her first meeting with the semi-paralyzed bard, for she soon realized, if she had not discerned so before, that the kind of romantic bonding she had envisioned in her letters over the last six years was hopeless. What she found instead was a great friend and a frequent boarder for the next eighteen months. He also became "uncle" to her children who had accompanied her to the United States (Percy, the oldest, remained in England), especially Herbert, who studied painting in Philadelphia. "Walt came over every evening from Camden," Burroughs recalled while the Gilchrists were still in their boardinghouse, "and took supper with us and we had much talk. He likes Mrs. Gilchrist and her family, and they like him." The other two children, Beatrice and Grace, he described as "fresh and comely, like soft, light-skinned peaches." He thought the Gilchrists would be a "god-send to Walt," who was now showing definite signs of semi-recovery from his long illness, something he would never put completely behind him.[72]

Once the household was established at 1929 North Twenty-Second Street, Anne Gilchrist prepared a permanent guest room for the poet equipped with a sheet-iron wood stove and a rocking chair. Not only did Whitman stay there at will, but he also invited relatives and friends to visit. Hattie and Jessie stopped there for five days before they went back to St. Louis in the fall of 1876. The next year Joaquin Miller came. In the January issue of the *Galaxy*, he had published a poem to Whitman written in iambic pentameter, which praised his "roughly set" songs. Another literary guest was Edward Carpenter, on his first visit to the United States in 1877. He described Walt's home away from home as "a kind of prophet's chamber." The summer evening he arrived, he found the entire family sitting out front by their white marble "stoop," or doorstep, a Philadelphia custom entirely new to people such as Gilchrist and Carpenter. The poet, whom Carpenter was meeting after a frequent exchange of letters, was seated in the family's midst, in a large rattan rocking chair, "his white beard and hair glistening in the young moonlight, looking like some old god."

Whitman's magnetism was immediate and long lasting with the Gilchrists. No "great talker," Carpenter recalled how he communicated with people about ideas on the "basis of personal affection." While Carpenter was there, they spoke of art, politics, history, foreign countries, slavery, and Lincoln. The poet even recited poetry on occasion, though seldom his own. One exception was "The Mystic Trumpeter," whose theme is the presence of music in nature, life, and memory. One night, while Carpenter was still a guest, Whitman read Tennyson's "Ulysses"—"in a clear, strong, and rugged tone." "Whitman had a knack of making ordinary life enjoyable, redeeming it from commonplaceness," Carpenter remembered.[73]

In 1898 Grace Gilchrist recalled "the long, hot dewless" summer evenings when the family would sit outside with the poet. She compared "formal, prim, Quaker Philadelphia" with "the somewhat dreary suburb of Camden"—from which the poet ferried in the late afternoon in time "for tea-supper." His presence was "majestic" despite the fact that "he walked lame, dragging the left leg, and leaning heavily on a stick. He was dressed always in a complete suit of grey clothes with a large and spotless white linen collar, his flowing white beard filling in the gap at his strong sunburnt throat." She remembered his voice as "a full-toned, rather high [and] baritone," which she thought was "a little harsh and lacking in the finer modulations for sustained recitations." The frequent overnight guest, who sometimes stayed for weeks, liked to sing in the bath, and Grace remembered that although he had an excellent memory and could quote from Shakespeare and Tennyson and the "Star Spangled Banner," he knew simply fragments of things, for example, "the opening bars of many songs." She also recalled the frightful way Whitman destroyed books as he read them: "He would tear a book to pieces—literally shed its leaves, putting the loose sheets into the breast pocket of his coat—that he might pursue his reading in less weighty fashion under the favorite branches at Timber Creek." He thought American formal education "bookish." "Among the young boys and girls," he told Herbert, "there is a tendency to dyspepsia, to wear glasses, and look interesting." This may have been a particular reaction to the students at Swarthmore college, where he gave a reading of his poems in 1877 that was no more—or less—successful than his Dartmouth performance.[74]

The Gilchrists came to know Lou and George in Camden and the Stafford family out at its farm. Herbert sketched the poet in the seclusion of Timber Creek several times. Whitman was apparently comfortable mixing the blue-collar Staffords and the educated Gilchrists, who took to each other fondly. The exception was Harry, who seems to have resented Walt's closeness to Herbert. After a Gilchrist family visit in August 1877, Harry told Walt back in Camden: "Herbert cut me prety [*sic*] hard last night at the supper table. . . . he called me a 'dam fool.'" The subject of the altercation has been forever muffled by the then nineteen-year-old's crude diction, but he told Walt in clearer terms that if he "had been near enough to [have] smacked [Herbert] in the 'Jaw' I would have done it." Walt, accustomed to Harry's mood swings and outbursts, barely touched on the matter in his letter to him on August 7 and then seemed to take Herbert's side. "I don't know the particulars about the Herbert scrape," he told Harry, "but you must let up on him—I suspect you said something pretty tantalizing before he call'd you that."[75]

Except for Horace Traubel, Harry was Whitman's last regular "son"—though at the same time, but more briefly, there was a hired hand about the same age by the name of Edward Catell as well as others, sailors and male nurses, who knew the poet for briefer periods. He apparently competed for Walt's attention until the poet told him to stay away from the Stafford farmhouse while he was visiting, possibly to keep Harry from another fit of jealousy. Harry was the poet's best company for almost two years (his "foil or refuge from the intellectual bores," according to Burroughs)[76] and a loyal friend even after he married in the 1880s.

"Mr. Whitman and I are sitting in the room togeather [*sic*]; he is reading the New York Herald, and I am writing these lines for exercise," Harry wrote in April 1877.[77] This sentence may indeed capture the essence of their association when Harry was not in the midst of one of his temper tantrums or frequent migraine headaches. Together they whiled away the hours at one of Whitman's favorite pastimes, keeping track of his fame in the press. Sometimes they wrestled, with Harry getting the better of the old man, he proudly remembered. When they visited Burroughs at Esopus-on-the-Hudson in March 1877, Burroughs was slightly annoyed by such shenanigans. He was also bothered—or his wife, Ursula, was—by their not getting down to breakfast on time. Ursula Burroughs had also been piqued when Whitman came late to weekly breakfasts in their Washington days.[78]

The poet encouraged the boy's attention; according to Harry, they also shared an interest in young women. But Whitman slowly backed away from his young friend as time went on and the tenant farming was taken over by George Stafford's brother, Montgomery. Soon after that the property was sold off for commercial use. In the spring of 1881, shortly before Whitman packed Harry off to a job as an attendant at Bucke's Asylum for the Insane in Ontario, Canada, the young man told Walt, "Well I have a new *gal* and a mighty nice little thing she is too; Just such a one as you would like, and I [k]now if you were to see these pretty rosy lips you would be charmed beyond measure with them." Whitman also talked to Harry of young women. In 1881 he wrote of a neighbor on Stevens Street: "I think she is the handsomest woman & pleasantest ways for young, I ever knew—full figure, blonde, good hair, teeth, complexion, ab't 19, a worker too, cooks & scrubs, but when she dresses up, she takes the shine off of all—(O that I was young again)—always feel better the whole day, when I can see & talk with her."[79]

❋ ❋ ❋

In the spring of 1876, the Civil War and postwar "boy general," George A. Custer, and his 264 officers and men were cut down at Little Big Horn in the Black Hills of Dakota (the present-day Montana) by Sitting Bull and a rifle-armed contingent of 2,500 warriors. Whitman wrote a poem of consolation. Appearing in the *Tribune* of July 18, "A Death-Sonnet for Custer" ("From Far Dakota's Cañons") spoke of Custer's cavalry as "fighting to the last in sternest heroism." One of Whitman's longtime poetic themes, arising from his days as a Wilmot

Proviso activist in the late 1840s, was the American West and its promise of democracy without slavery. Whitman saw the vanquished soldiers as the latest symbol of the westward movement, which could not be stopped by the Indians of the Great Plains—grand legions of men and women who, since the end of the war, had found themselves directly in the path of "American progress." Overlooking the government's long history of broken treaties with Native Americans as well as its exploitation of them by corrupt Indian agents, Whitman contributed to the myth of the general who died with "tawny flowing hair in battle" as an innocent target of "an Indian ambuscade." (Custer was actually a lieutenant colonel, and his hair was unfashionably short at the time of his death.) He hailed Custer as a noble victim in a "most desperate, most glorious" defeat, "ending well in death the splendid fever of thy deeds."

The poem and its sentiment were something of a contradiction for the poet who had since his newspaper days stood up for the victims of capitalism. Burroughs had just praised Whitman in "The Flight of the American Eagle" (the title came from Buchanan's defense in the *London Daily News*) as being "in entire sympathy with actual nature" and opposed to literature of the "soda-fountain" with its "many gassy and sugared drinks." (Whitman had helped Burroughs sharpen the article.) Whitman's early fiction had included a somewhat sympathetic picture of American Indians, and his attitudes in the Office of Indian Affairs suggest that he thought the prewar Policy of Removal deprived America of something of its "native" quality. But here the former "Paumanok" came down on the side of "civilization," just as earlier he had opted for the integrity of the Union over the immediate abolition of black slavery when *that* minority seemed to threaten the growth of "These States." Meanwhile much of New England, having "neutralized" its Indian problem long ago, opposed the majority opinion articulated by Whitman. The best poet of the "soda fountain" convention, Henry Wadsworth Longfellow, published "The Revenge of Rain-in-the-Face," implying the defeat was due to the flagrant mistreatment of the Indians.[80]

The shocked nation had thought the "Indian Problem" was under control, and the resounding defeat at Little Big Horn led directly to the Final Removal and the establishment of human zoos known as "reservations." John Hay, Lincoln's former secretary and Theodore Roosevelt's future secretary of state, wrote Whitman on July 22, calling the Custer poem "full of a noble motive" and asking how he could subscribe to the latest edition of *Leaves of Grass.* On August 1 Whitman sent Hay a centennial volume with "A Death-Sonnet for Custer" hastily pasted in as the latest "intercalation."[81]

Burroughs had been right when he foresaw an upswing in Whitman's health and spirit with the arrival of Anne Gilchrist and her children. The poet, who had kept writing since his stroke but stayed pretty close to home in Camden, embarked on a new pattern of activity. In January 1877 he delivered "The Memory of Thomas Paine" at Lincoln Hall in Philadelphia, possibly with the Gilchrists in the audience, their enthusiasm for the old man (he looked more and more aged in spite of his social energy) warming him to the occasion. Custer—whose personal demeanor as a military officer of field rank had not been above criticism—was not unlike Paine, who languished during his last days in the depths of delirium and poor personal hygiene, made more grotesque by overgrown toenails that encircled his feet. But Whitman saw the Revolutionary patriot as a "noble personality . . . especially [in] the later years of his life." "I am sure of it," he insisted, denouncing the actual circumstances of the patriot's demise as "foul and foolish fictions."[82] Paine, like Custer, was saved from his failures by Whitman's determined sense of patriotism.

By 1877 Walt knew many people in Camden and Philadelphia and had made a new friend in New York City whose palatial residences came to replace the comforts of Abby Price's New York apartment. This was John H. Johnston ("J.H.," one of several Johnstons who peopled Whitman's old age), a Manhattan jeweler, whom Whitman met through Joaquin Miller. Whitman thought Johnston "a splendid *champagny* fellow, of the American type," and came to count him as part of the inner circle of his disciples. Johnston had purchased a copy of the 1860 edition of *Leaves of Grass* on his twenty-third birthday and thought little of the poetry until one day in 1872, when he read it aloud to his wife. The next day he wrote the poet a letter, which may or may not have been answered.[83] Whitman first visited the jeweler and his wife at 113 East 10th Street on March 2, 1877, and stayed for two weeks. He brought along Harry Stafford, whom he described as a traveling companion who "occasionally transacts my business affairs," asking that they share a room.

This request, as well as a similar one to Burroughs, whom they visited at Esopus-on-the-Hudson immediately afterward, has recently been viewed with suspicion by critics, but apparently the Johnstons—if not the Burroughses—thought nothing unusual of the arrangement.[84] Perhaps they were simply overawed by the poet's presence and the host of visitors he attracted during his stay. Later Johnston's second wife, Alma (the first Mrs. Johnston died of Bright's disease while giving birth to a son ten days after Whitman's first visit)[85] remembered that the poet became "Uncle Walt" to the Johnston children, two of whom are pictured with him in extant photographs.

Back in Camden, almost a year to the day of her first son's death, Lou suffered a miscarriage. Other bad family news that plagued the poet upon his return home that spring was word that Jeff had lost his job as superintendent of the St. Louis waterworks in a political upheaval; the wily engineer, however, ultimately prevailed and became water commissioner of St. Louis when the abolished state board of water management was replaced by a city board.[86] Jeff and George were the most successful Whitmans in the material sense. Walt continued his visits to Timber Creek and 1929 North Twenty-Second Street, and these sojourns were supplemented by Sunday brunches and dinners at the Camden homes of James Matlack Scovel, a lawyer, and John R. ("Jack") Johnston, a Philadelphia artist. Both men, Civil War veterans like George Whitman, went by the title of "Colonel." In September that year, Jeff's two daughters passed through Camden again on their way to Mrs. Archer's Patapsco Seminary in Elliott City, Maryland. They were annual visitors to Camden for the next several years.

More "family" troubles materialized from a "somewhat severe operation" Anne Gilchrist underwent in September to cure an injury she had sustained in giving birth. Whitman ceased his regular visits while she was hospitalized but was back to dinner within two weeks of her surgery. The next month the poet's old nemesis Charlie Heyde wrote from Burlington to say that his wife, Walt's sister Hannah, was haunted by sexual fantasies and smelled his clothes when he returned from his studio each day, declaring "that I have been abed somewhere."[87]

By now, Heyde's career as a landscape artist had crested. For the first few years after leaving Brooklyn in 1852, the couple had led a nomadic life, moving from hotel to hotel as Heyde bartered paintings for room and board, wandering throughout New England in search of more scenes to paint. By 1856 he had found his first patron and settled in Burlington, Vermont, where he led a respectable life as an artist, culminating in his appointment to paint Vermont's state seal (which he merely made over, adding nothing original or distinctive). By 1864 the couple had stopped renting and purchased a cottage at 21 Pearl Street, close to the battery overlooking Lake Champlain. Once the war was over and the market for his paintings of the same mountain or lake had dwindled, Heyde began to exhibit the delusional behavior that finally landed him in the Vermont State Asylum at Waterbury, only months after Whitman's death. At the time he wrote Whitman in Camden, he was just entering his long decline. The rest of his life was punctuated by throes of connubial agony—and epistolary reports to Walt. Today Heyde is considered a noteworthy regional painter, whose productions are eagerly sought. But in his last days, both patrons and neighbors turned away from his work and his embarrassing behavior in public, which included urinating and walking naked in the streets.[88]

Another tragedy, closer at hand, lay ahead. His friend Charlie Eldridge paid him a Christmas visit in 1877 and told him the story of a young woman, the daughter of a mutual friend, "who too overwhelmingly swamped herself" as a medical student and suffered "terrible brain troubles." Whitman was reminded of Beatrice Gilchrist, who was a student at the same medical school in Philadelphia. He feared that Bee, about the same age as the other young woman and his favorite of the two Gilchrist daughters, was overworking and in danger of an emotional breakdown. The poet added that perhaps the same high stress level had been somehow responsible for his own stroke and paralysis. Edwin Haviland Miller notes in his edition of Whitman's correspondence that Whitman was almost prescient in his concern for

Bee.[89] Following her graduation from Women's Medical College, an internship at the New England Hospital for Women in Boston, and further study in Berne, Switzerland, she suddenly gave up medicine in 1881 and then as quickly returned to it. According to Anne Gilchrist's latest biographer, a photograph taken that year of this sad-faced young woman, who favored her father but possessed her mother's clear hazel eyes, suggests depression and perhaps the stress of pursuing what was a man's career in the nineteenth century. She took her life in Scotland on July 20, 1881, at the age of twenty-six, with an overdose of hydrocyanic acid. Her badly decomposed body was discovered three weeks later on the outskirts of Edinburgh.[90]

❖ ❖ ❖

The Paine lecture may have revived Whitman's prewar appetite for lecturing. On February 3, 1878, Burroughs planted the seed for the first of Whitman's Lincoln lectures by telling the poet that Richard Watson Gilder, then assistant editor of *Scribner's,* hoped he would deliver an address on the thirteenth anniversary of the president's assassination. This lecture had to wait for more than a year, however, because Whitman's health worsened, this time with a painful attack of rheumatism in his right shoulder and wrist in the early months of 1878. About the time the lecture was originally scheduled, the Gilchrists broke up their household in Philadelphia after eighteen months in America. As Bee had at least until June to complete her Boston internship, Anne planned to remain in the country, traveling and doing what she could for her children. Grace traveled with her, and Herbert moved to Brooklyn to study with Wyatt Eaton and other prominent American painters and sculptors.[91]

In June Whitman was well enough to attend the funeral of William Cullen Bryant, his longtime favorite American poet. He stayed again with his friend "J.H.," but the accommodations of the New York jeweler were even more lavish than before. Johnston had moved uptown to a four- or five-story house on Fifth Avenue, one door down from 86th Street. He had also remarried, within a year of his first wife's death, and Whitman liked the "new Mrs. Johnston." Alma Johnston remarked later that he kept his room in chaos; his habits in her house were just as Helen Price remembered when he inhabited the guest quarters in her mother's house—even down to the curtains being twisted into a rope to let in as much sunlight as possible. "The floor of his room," his new hostess recalled, "was strewn with scraps of paper,—turned envelopes, the blank spaces of erased manuscript, the backs of old letters,—all bore his patient scribblings." Like many of Whitman's supporters, she tried to overlook the seemingly blatant sexual references in his poems and once was even bold enough to suggest changing the title of "A Woman Waits for Me" to "Woman Waits for Me," making the poem more philosophical, she said. Whitman agreed but didn't change the title.[92]

Again, like a visiting pope, the poet received literary visitors during his stay. One of them was Richard Maurice Bucke, who had admired deeply Whitman's poetry since 1867 and met Whitman for the first time in Camden on October 18, 1877.[93] They attended Bryant's funeral together, along with Gilder and Edmund Clarence Stedman. There Whitman met John Bigelow, former minister to France and Bryant's co-editor at the *Post,* and his wife. Mrs. Bigelow was so charmed by the poet in his flowing beard and gray suit that the couple invited Whitman on a cruise up the Hudson. Afterward, he followed the same routine as in 1877, going to Burroughs's home on the Hudson for a few days (bringing along Johnston's teenaged son) and then returning to Johnston's mansion, where he was welcome to stay even when the family was absent.

After a month away from Camden, Whitman returned to fight off his fatigue from overactivity, a reaction that was part of his life pattern from now on. His Philadelphia refuge gone, he divided the rest of his time in 1878 almost equally between Camden and Timber Creek. He kept track of Anne Gilchrist and her family through her letters. That fall she visited Concord and met the Emersons, or at least Ellen Emerson, since by this time the poet and philosopher may have limited his visitors. By December Anne and Grace were back in New York City, where they spent the winter at 325 West 19th Street. Whitman did not visit them there; he was possibly not invited because of their cramped accommodations.

The Stafford haven also disappeared about this time, with George Stafford subletting Timber Creek to his older brother. At first the Staffords were supposed to open a store in nearby Glendale, but eventually they rented another, smaller farm. Whitman tried to resume his visits, but by August 1878 he was lamenting to Anne that he had recently spent "a while with the Staffords at their new farm, but I missed my main attraction & comfort, *the Creek,* & did not make a long visit." The "Creek" had been his best medicine, and he dearly missed its sylvan charm and solitude. He thought of collecting his newspaper pieces, including those describing his recent travels, in what would become *Specimen Days,* but at the time the best title he could conjure up in the wake of lost havens and the numbing routine of Camden was "Idle Days & Nights of a Half Paralytic."[94]

Whitman finally delivered his first Lincoln lecture in Steck Hall on 14th Street in New York City on April 14, 1879, the fourteenth anniversary of the president's assassination. He furnished Whitelaw Reid of the *Tribune* and other members of the press advance copies of his speech, "The Death of Abraham Lincoln." The *Tribune* printed the entire speech and described Whitman as seated in a chair, reading from notes. Whitman had published a piece on Lincoln in the *New York Sun* of February 12, 1876, and he built upon it to suggest the irony that the powerful drama of Lincoln's murder had interrupted a puny drawing-room comedy about an American in English society—"a Yankee, certainly such a one as was never seen, or the least like it ever seen, in North America." Pretending or at least allowing, as he did in "'Tis But Ten Years Since," that he was present at the assassination, Whitman recalled the scene in *Our American Cousin* "in which two unprecedented English ladies are inform'd by the impossible Yankee that he is not a man of fortune, and therefore undesirable for marriage-catching purposes; after which, the comments being finish'd, the dramatic trio make exit, leaving the stage clear for the moment. At this period came the murder of Abraham Lincoln." He went on to tell how Booth, after mortally wounding Lincoln, jumped from the president's box and caught his foot in the bunting below, which included the American flag. Continuing his juxtaposition of the two dramas, Whitman then asked whether Booth had practiced for his performance as carefully as the other actors on the boards that night. "Had not all this terrible scene—making the mimic ones preposterous—had it not all been rehears'd, in blank, by Booth, beforehand?"[95]

Without either the Staffords or the Gilchrists, Whitman needed something new in his life. He told Reid that he hoped to make a small living as a lecturer and a reader of poetry (presumably his own). If the audio recording of his voice first played on National Public Radio and at the Whitman centennial conference at the University of Iowa in 1992 is any indication, Whitman may not have had the high-pitched voice claimed by biographers and specialists, but perhaps a deeper, resounding one, somewhat even below the baritone Grace Gilchrist remembered. Since the tape itself has not been entirely authenticated, it is hard to know whether a weak voice or a racy reputation kept him off the lecturer's circuit.[96]

Soon after Whitman's lecture on Lincoln, John W. Forney reported in the *Philadelphia Progress* that he had accepted an invitation from the Old Settlers of Kansas to speak on the silver anniversary of the territory's organization in 1854.[97] He asked other former Free-Soilers to accompany him. Forney had been the conduit for much of Whitman's self-publicizing over the past decade because he had been until recently the editor of both the *Washington Chronicle* and the *Progress.* Previously a Democrat like the poet, he too broke with the party and became a Republican in 1856. During the Kansas bloodshed, he had been clerk of the House of Representatives when after a long struggle it elected Nathaniel P. Banks, later a general in the Union army, as Speaker. One of the people Forney invited was Banks, who had to decline, but another was Whitman, who jumped at the opportunity—it gave him a way both to visit Jeff and his nieces in St. Louis and to see—finally—the Great Plains and other parts of the America he had already celebrated in *Leaves of Grass.*

Whitman boarded the train at the West Philadelphia Station on Wednesday morning, September 10, with Forney and three other journalists. Almost exactly forty-eight hours later, the party arrived in St. Louis, after being delayed by a train collision at Urbana, Ohio. Thirty-one years earlier, Whitman and Jeff, then just fourteen, had briefly toured St. Louis as they returned from New Orleans. Now Water

Commissioner Whitman could show the poet quite a different city, decked out with handsome five- and six-thousand-dollar homes surrounded by beautiful gardens but also sullied by pollution from nearby coal mines. Jeff and his daughters met Walt at the St. Louis station and went immediately to the Planter's Hotel, where they all breakfasted on "perfect beefsteak, broiled chicken, oysters, good coffee &c." That evening he was interviewed by the St. Louis press—a reporter for the *Missouri Republican* described him as "well advanced in years" and having "snow-white" hair and beard, giving him "a decidedly venerable appearance." After a tour of the city, Walt spent the night at Jeff's house, which he described to Lou as "very nicely fixed."[98] His visit lasted hardly twenty-four hours, however; the train for Kansas departed early the next morning.

The party arrived in Kansas City the same day after midnight, when Whitman, now further west than he had ever been, was reported to remark, "Well, gentlemen, I see you do not wear pistols." The poet and Forney were then taken to the home of John P. Usher in nearby Lawrence. Usher, now mayor of Lawrence, had been Whitman's first boss in the Department of the Interior before Harlan took over the secretaryship. On Sunday morning Whitman passed up an opportunity to hear Edward Everett Hale preach at the Congregational Church, but he would hear him speak on Monday, the official Settlers' Day. He had also heard the Reverend Mr. Hale speak at Dartmouth—on Milton for an hour—before he delivered "As a Strong Bird on Pinions Free." Instead, Whitman went sightseeing around Kansas City and Lawrence and possibly out to Bismarck Grove, where the "Silver Wedding" anniversary was to be held on Monday and Tuesday, September 15–16, 1879.

The Old Settlers' Committee was under the misapprehension that Whitman would deliver a poem on the second day of the festivities, but the poet considered himself merely the personal guest of Forney—with whom he had arranged only to show himself, not to speak or eat any public dinners. After being asked to recite a poem, he half agreed, but, apparently either deciding against it later or fatigued by Monday's excitement, he skipped the second day altogether. Instead, he delivered a short speech in *Specimen Days,* where he said a poem would have been "almost an impertinence" before "these interminable and stately prairies."[99] Generally, what Whitman did see of the two-day program of speeches, poetry, and music ("Old John Brown") delighted him. The Free-Soil movement had been the political fire from which the first poetry of *Leaves of Grass* emerged; yet by 1879 he had seen the excesses perpetrated in its name by the postwar Radical Republicans.

The next stop on the western tour was Topeka. That city—much larger than Lawrence, which had around 9,000 residents—impressed Whitman with its combination of the rural and the urban. Busy but clean with wide streets, its churches resembled "small cathedrals." While in Topeka, Whitman accompanied Forney and the local sheriff to the town jail holding twenty Indians. According to sculptor Sidney Morse, to whom Whitman told the story, the sheriff informed his prisoners that their visitors were distinguished personages. The Indians paid little heed to their guests, except for Whitman whose garb and flowing beard apparently caught their attention.

> The old chief looked at him steadily, then extended his hand and said his "how." All the other Indians followed, surrounded Whitman, shaking hands, making the air melodious with their "hows." The sheriff could not understand it. "I confess," said W. W. [to Morse], . . . "that I was not a little set up to find that the critters knew the difference and didn't confound me with the big guns of officialism."[100]

It will never be known, of course, whether this anecdote was yet another newspaper puff, this one for posterity, from the writer who three years earlier had celebrated Custer as a tragic innocent victim of an "Indian ambuscade."

By this time Forney had turned back east, but in Whitman's recollections of the entire trip in *Specimen Days* he pretended he was traveling alone, making no mention of his old "free-soil" ally and the editor who had published his anonymous reports over the previous years. After a brief stop at Fort Wallace, Whitman and the remaining members of his party went on to Denver, which was then a boomtown. There Whitman stayed at the American House, built as one of the finest hotels in America when the railroad reached the city in 1868. A glittering barroom and lavish lobby led guests inside spacious suites of walnut and silk. The beds had feather mattresses, and rooms had their own baths (whose tubs were filled from pitchers).[101] While in Denver, Whitman praised the West as having given the nation two of its most important leaders, Lincoln and Grant. He was awestruck and left almost speechless by the rugged beauty he saw on a visit to Platte Canyon, and, in a poem written afterward, he described nature's rough artistry as a confirmation of his own poetic experiments.[102] He expressed an interest in seeing the silver-mining town of Leadville, southwest of the city, but the railroad did not yet extend that far and the stagecoach trip was rocky and long.

Whitman began his trip back east by traveling south to Pueblo on September 23, where he caught the Atchinson, Topeka and Santa Fe Railroad to Sterling, Kansas. There he heard the term "cow-boys" for the first time and had a reunion with one of his Civil War soldiers, Ed Lindsay. He stayed with Lindsay two nights. Lindsay was "married & running the hotel" in Sterling, Whitman wrote Peter Doyle from St. Louis. "I had hard work to get away from him—he wanted me to stay all winter."[103]

When the party reached St. Louis on September 27, Whitman got off for a planned two or three weeks with his brother and nieces. Because of illness, however, and possibly because of a lack of travel funds (he was probably compelled to give up his train pass when he left the Old Settlers' party in St. Louis), he remained in the city until just after New Year's. A two-and-a-half-week trip by rail would have fatigued even a healthy sixty-year-old, and this one, like other recent journeys, had worn him down. On October 11 he wrote his sister-in-law in Camden to ask George to send him whatever mail had accumulated. He also instructed the Camden post office to forward his future letters. He was experiencing "head spells" again but thought he would return home in two weeks. On November 5 he was still at Jeff's; he told Doyle of his illness and thought he would leave for the East in yet another two or three weeks. While in St. Louis—as was his habit anywhere—he got to know Jeff's neighbors and associates. He even visited a kindergarten regularly, where he told the children stories, including the fable of "The Two Cats." (The feline protagonists take the same trip but report back different experiences: one discovers wonders; the other encounters disappointment.)[104]

By New Year's, his health had improved. So had his money problems, thanks to a hundred-dollar gift secretly contributed by the publisher James T. Fields and sent through Burroughs.[105] Whitman said good-bye to Jeff and the girls on January 4, 1880, and boarded the 8:00 A.M. train to Philadelphia. His return was faster than the trip to St. Louis, getting him into Philadelphia late the next day and home to Camden just after nightfall. He told Doyle shortly before he left St. Louis, "This is a wonderful country out here, & no one knows how big it is till he launches out in the midst of it."[106]

12

DALLIANCES OF EAGLES

There was something of poetic justice, too, in thinking of the reception of this man who had been scorned as a barbarian rhymester, whose burning lines, surcharged with the future, had long fallen unheeded upon the indifferent ears of his countrymen, and whose very presence was now felt almost as a benediction.

BOSTON EVENING TRAVELER
April 15, 1881

Whitman liked to tell his soldiers that life was like the weather: you had to take what comes. His literary life in fact created storms during the heyday of his early compositions in *Leaves of Grass,* but after the war, and especially after the poet turned sixty in the spring of 1879, his ship simply followed the gales and the calms. He had worked—and plotted—hard the previous decade to get his kind of literature accepted, and as a result, a growing number of adherents had begun to gather, both in the United States and abroad. Now events took over. He learned upon his return from St. Louis in January 1880 that a biography was being written about him. He discovered that Professor Frederic Louis Ritter of Vassar College had arranged one of his poems, "Dirge for Two Veterans," as a "Piano accompaniment for recitation" after Ritter's wife rhapsodized about the "musical interior" of *Leaves of Grass.*[1] And on April 15, 1880, he gave his second Lincoln lecture, a well-attended and well-received performance in Philadelphia's Association Hall, where Harry Stafford served as an usher.[2] From now on, the course of this self-described "half-paralytic" would be largely guided by his literary fame.

Whitman must have felt that his literary life had crested. He continued to write poems—and many good ones—till the last, but he was now ready to take stock not only of himself but of others, especially the competitors who still held sway. When the *Boston Literary World* celebrated Emerson's seventy-sixth birthday in 1880 with a special issue, Whitman was among the contributors, along with such editors and sages as George W. Cooke, George William Curtis, and Frederick Henry Hedge. Revisiting his complaint in "A Christmas Garland," he said that Emerson was clearly one of the American writers who shied away from depicting real nature with warts as well as wonders. Whitman charged that Emerson had never really captured the rugged beauty and originality of American democracy and its mighty masses, which was equal to that of Europe's Old World culture. In "Emerson's Books, (The Shadows of Them)," published on May 27, he conceded that Emerson had partly succeeded where the others had failed completely, but he compared the entire lot of established poets to "some little fleet of boats, hugging the shores of a boundless sea, and never venturing, exploring the unmapp'd—never Columbus-like, sailing out for New Worlds." The Columbus of this composition had fully recovered from the dreary figure depicted in "Prayer of Columbus."

Whitman could not forget Emerson's "deepest lessons" or the fact that he himself had once contracted "a touch of Emerson-on-the-brain," prompting him to salute Emerson as "Master" in the second edition of *Leaves of Grass*. Nevertheless, he opined that even though Emerson had "much to say of freedom and wildness and simplicity and spontaneity," his literary performances were based on "artificial scholarships and decorums at third or fourth removes (he calls it culture,) and built up from them." Because his celebrations of nature ignored "unconscious *growth*," they produced not nature but porcelain statuettes of nature. This was grossly and unconscionably unfair criticism of the author of "The Poet," who had had the courage long before the beginning of Whitman's "great career" to say that "the vocabulary of an omniscient man would embrace words and images excluded from polite conversation." It overlooked the essayist of "Experience," who said that "the mid-world is best. Nature, as we know her, is no saint. . . . She comes eating and drinking and sinning." It also ignored the Emerson who responded to "Children of Adam" in 1860 by saying that it was not Whitman's candor about human sexuality that was ill-advised but its inclusion in the third edition of *Leaves of Grass,* which (in an age when not only the classics but even Shakespeare and the Bible were expurgated) would blind readers to the book's true worth.

Whitman continued to be vexed at his exclusion from *Parnassus.* He quipped that Emerson preferred the "verbal polish" of Richard Lovelace and Edmund Waller to the poetic thunder of Homer and Shakespeare, or even the Bible. The anthology included poems by these seventeenth-century artists, whose work exemplified the highly abstract and contrived paeans to beautiful women. But one of Whitman's main objectives in the essay was to establish his literary identity outside the shadow of Emerson's books, or beyond Transcendentalism, which subordinates nature to the spirit. "The best part of Emersonianism is," he announced, "it breeds the giant that destroys itself. . . . No teacher ever taught, that has so provided for his pupil's setting up independently."[3] Indeed, Emerson had said as much himself. He wanted self-reliant followers, not disciples. He would not, however, have appreciated Whitman's other objective, had he been aware of the article or able to defend himself by this time. Whitman was apparently trying to tar Emerson with the same brush he had used in the 1860s to criticize other poets whose "maudlin puerilities" could be read in the drawing room. Although he later regretted and rescinded the indictment,[4] Whitman exploited Emerson to rebut the argument that good poetry, like nature, hides the ugly parts—or the process, which, according to Howells and James when they had reviewed *Drum-Taps* in the 1860s, did not belong in poetry.

❋ ❋ ❋

In May 1880 an old admirer of *Leaves of Grass* and a newly won friend of its author, Dr. Richard Maurice Bucke, arrived from London, Ontario, to pay a visit to the poet. Bucke and his wife, Jessie, had lived most of their married life in Sarnia, Ontario, west of London, on the United States-Canadian border, where Bucke practiced psychiatry. They moved east to Hamilton, on Lake Ontario, in 1876, when he became superintendent of a newly opened mental hospital, but within a year they moved west again to London, where the doctor lived and worked for the rest of his life, earning a reputation for his "moral treatment of the insane." His methods allegedly included the abolition of physical restraints and the use of distilled alcohol as a sedative. Possibly the only blemish on his professional reputation was a complaint late in his career about "meddlesome gynecology," possibly the performance of ovariectomies or abortions.

Bucke had been an enthusiast of *Leaves of Grass* since 1867. Three years later he got up the nerve to write the poet, enclosing money to purchase the earlier editions, but received neither an answer nor his money back. The two men met for the first time in 1877, shortly before they attended William Cullen Bryant's funeral together. By then Bucke was fast at work on his first book, *Man's Moral Nature* (1879), which was loosely based on his thesis written in 1858 at McGill University, where he received his medical degree. Bucke believed in the direct relationship between the physical and the spiritual, or moral, leading him to study theosophy and mysticism. In his book he argues that the source of knowledge is both intellectual and moral (or "emotional"). Whereas the rational element, which originates in the cerebrospinal system, has kept pace with evolutionary change, the "moral nature," which is grounded in the sympathetic nervous system, has not. This element has failed to develop into an adequate aesthetic appreciation of nature, thereby also failing to reveal the true essence of the universe, which is love—or the comradeship that Whitman had promoted in "Calamus." Bucke dedicated the book "to the man who of all men past and present that I have known has the most exalted moral nature—TO WALT WHITMAN."[5]

The next logical step was to write a biography of Whitman himself. Bucke had come to Camden hoping to persuade the poet to return with him for a couple of months so that he could interview him in detail. Whitman quickly accepted. He needed something to do, anything to get out of George's house for a time. As much as he loved Lou and George, he was never altogether comfortable in their home. Lou doted on him as much as his mother had—or Susan Stafford and Anne Gilchrist. But he was bored there. The first leg of the trip to Canada ended on June 3 at Niagara Falls, which Whitman hadn't seen since he and Jeff were returning from New Orleans, more than thirty years ago. The two men reached London late the next day, arriving at the sprawling grounds of the 1,000-inmate asylum where Bucke was superintendent. The very next morning Whitman was busy giving interviews to the local press.[6]

Whitman enjoyed his stay in Canada and at the asylum, where he made friends with the attendants and mingled with the inmates. He went out late in the evenings to look at the stars and ramble around the grounds with their "gravel walks and velvety grass." He observed recitations in pantomime by "deaf and dumb" patients, including a young woman who, he recorded in his diary, "rendered *Christ stilling the tempest.*" He raptured over the haymaking ("a sweet, poetic, practical, busy sight") and relished the variety of birds ("no gunning here, and no dogs or cats allowed").[7] One Sunday he attended an Episcopal ceremony on the grounds, where he sat in an armchair next to the pulpit. There he faced a "motley, eager, pitiful, huddled, yet perfectly well-behaved and orderly congregation." On another occasion he enjoyed a "frolic" at the asylum. "Some one had sent in some wine: Mrs. Bucke, the children—all of them I think—were in bed: the bottles were appropriated—emptied. . . . the night wore on: by and by someone proposed that we bury the bottles . . . we marched in procession out, across the lawn, chanting, chanting: here and there an invocation." Bucke, who subsequently became a teetotaler, "took very little if anything."[8]

Bucke was thrilled to have Whitman as his guest, but his wife was not so pleased. In a 1992 video entitled "Beautiful Dreamers," Whitman wins over Jessie Bucke, but in real life Mrs. Bucke was less affectionate. We should not forget why Whitman was a cause célèbre as late as the 1880s. James Redpath once chided him sarcastically, "It is believed that you are not ashamed of your reproductive organs."[9] His verse was generally considered obscene, and Jessie felt her neighbors' rebukes for having Whitman as a houseguest. The situation may have come to a boiling point when Bucke took the poet to visit Sarnia and the couple's closest, perhaps conservative acquaintances.

Jessie Bucke may have been relieved when Whitman later went in the other direction of Sarnia and traveled with her husband to Montreal and Quebec. They set out by train for Toronto on July 26 and from there steamed out upon Lake Ontario, across to Kingston and then up the St. Lawrence, stopping for two nights in Montreal and briefly in Quebec, before reaching the Saguenay River on August 6. Their boat ventured up and down the Saguenay for two days, and Whitman soaked up the pristine roughness of it all. "Up these black waters," he recalled in one of his characteristic sentence fragments, "over a hundred miles—always strong, deep, (hundreds of feet, sometimes thousands,) ever with high rocky hills for banks, green and gray—no flowers or fruits (plenty of delicious wild blue-berries and raspberries though)."

He compared the river to the Hudson but found the Canadian river more "defiant." It was also an ideal place for echoes. While moored at Tadousac, at the mouth of the Saguenay, "I was sure I heard a band at the hotel up in the rocks—could even make out some of the tunes. Only when our pipes stopped, I knew what caused it. Then at Cape Eternity and Trinity Rock, the pilot with his whistle producing similar marvelous results, echoes indescribably weird, as we lay off in the still bay under their shadows." Whitman had been sick briefly in London before the trip, but the sometimes arduous steamboat journey served only to invigorate him. He told Edward Carpenter that he was "feeling heartier physically than for years."[10] Once back in London on August 14, Whitman remained in Canada until the end of September—spending four months in the only foreign country he ever visited.

Although Whitman hoped afterward to return to Canada, even planned to do so, he was never invited back. When he hinted of traveling to London the next summer, Bucke told his wife: "I have written to Walt Whitman and have done my best to stop him from coming here without being absolutely rude to him." Jessie Bucke must have kept her misgivings to herself until the poet departed for Camden, for Bucke was under the impression that "you liked him." He blamed her caution on their longtime Sarnia friends. Apparently, she wrote the poet a frank letter about her feelings, but Bucke would not permit its mailing. "I have taken a different course," he told her on June 19, 1881, "and one that I hope will prevent his coming without letting him see that we don't want him for I want him as little as you do now." But he added that his wife could never allow herself "to imagine for a moment that you or any of you can shake my affection for Walt Whitman."[11]

It was probably on the Saguenay that Whitman got the inspiration for one of his most popular poems today. There he may have witnessed the mating of eagles high above the river's rocky terrain. Clara Barrus claims that "The Dalliance of the Eagles" arose from Burroughs's description of such a spectacle at Marlboro-on-the-Hudson in the early 1860s, before he met the poet. But the fact that the poem was published shortly after Whitman's return from his steamboat adventure suggests otherwise. The lifelong nonsmoker's poem first appeared in a British journal, *Cope's Tobacco Plant* ("I am *not* an anti-tobacconist. . . . my brothers & all my near friends are smokers," he told the editor), in November 1880.[12] Just as a year earlier he had viewed the austerity of Platte Canyon in Colorado as confirmation of his poetic experiments in depicting real nature (and wrote there "Spirit That Form'd This Scene"), he was probably inspired to pen "The Dalliance of the Eagles" in Canada. Few places other than a wilderness river provide the opportunity to see such "miracles" of nature.

> Skirting the river road, (my forenoon walk, my rest,)
> Skyward in air a sudden muffled sound, the dalliance of the eagles,
> The rushing amorous contact high in space together,
> The clinching interlocking claws, a living, fierce, gyrating wheel,
> Four beating wings, two beaks, a swirling mass tight grappling,
> In tumbling turning clustering loops, straight downward falling,
> Till o'er the river pois'd, the twain yet one, a moment's lull,
> A motionless still balance in the air, then parting, talons loosing,
> Upward again on slow-firm pinions slanting, their separate diverse
>   flight,
> She hers, he his, pursuing.

Jessie Bucke would not have been surprised that Whitman, at the age of sixty-one, was still sexually involved enough to write an "obscene" poem—"Dalliance" was placed on the Boston district attorney's list in 1882.

❋ ❋ ❋

By the time Walt returned to Camden, Harry Stafford was working in a telegraph office in Atlantic City. The poet spent five days there in early October, and then another ten in November with Harry's family in Glendale, where they now ran a general store. He had second thoughts about nearby Timber Creek, saying it was as exhilarating as ever, but it is doubtful that he ever returned there again.[13] He continued to sell the centennial editions of *Leaves of Grass* by mail, but an earlier edition was more on his mind. In 1879 a printer named Richard Worthington told the poet that he had purchased the Thayer and Eldridge plates to the 1860 edition, wanted to print copies for sale, and offered Whitman a royalty of 10 percent, the same percentage his Boston publishers had given him. Whitman had later editions to sell and declined the offer, hoping Worthington would simply go away. But Bucke, during his trip to the United States to escort Whitman to Canada in 1880, found numerous copies of the bogus edition for sale in Boston and New York, apparently struck off by Worthington.[14] This information probably enraged the poet at first and then gave him pause. Because sales of the centennial edition were pretty flat by this time, he may have welcomed the possibility of additional income.

While in Canada, Whitman wrote to Worthington again to ask whether the offer was still good. Getting no response by the time he returned, he asked the Camden lawyer James Scovel, whose friendship extended to storing unsold copies of the 1876 issues in his law offices, to proceed to New York and confront the printer. Scovel returned with a "royalty" check of $50, which Whitman acknowledged. This action he came to regret, for Worthington now felt he had the poet's implied permission to print further issues of the edition, which he did off and on throughout Whitman's life.[15] The existence of Worthington's copies was galling. Bookstores in Boston and New York (even in Philadelphia, where the poet spotted a copy in November 1881 in a store on Chestnut Street) were willing to sell a "counterfeit" *Leaves* at a lower price than the latest edition.

By this time, Whitman was using the Philadelphia-Camden ferry as productively as he had the Brooklyn Ferry in his days as editor of the

Brooklyn Eagle. It was his ticket to another neighboring metropolis and another "Broadway"—Philadelphia and Market Street, where the bearded poet (his beard was now totally white) was familiar to trolley conductors, shopkeepers, and even bartenders. He never tired of being out on the Delaware River, and once in the winter, he claimed, he even hobbled with his cane halfway across it—until the ice looked unreliable. He watched the return of the seagulls in the spring, the crows on the winter ice, the steamboats in the summer, and the chiaroscuro of the heavens at night. He knew "intimately" all the ferrymen and the various skippers. "Little they know," he wrote in Forney's newspaper, "how much they have been to me, day and night—how many spells of listlessness, ennui, debility, they and their hardy ways have dispell'd. . . . And the ferry itself, with its queer scenes—sometimes children suddenly born in the waiting-houses (an actual fact—more than once)—sometimes a masquerade party, going over at night, with a band of music, dancing and whirling like mad on the broad deck, in their fantastic dresses." Frequently, he boarded the ferry at ten in the evening and crossed over and back until midnight, concluding the night out with a repast of oysters "& a drink" in a restaurant at the foot of Market Street.[16]

Thus began the era of the "Old Gray," whose observations on anything and everything often seemed more a blessing than a critique. On New Year's Eve 1880 he told Jeannette L. Gilder that he would supply her with "some out-door sketches" for the *Critic,* a new magazine she was launching with her husband, Joseph B. Gilder. This became the series of six essays entitled "How I Get Around at 60, and Take Notes." The publishing venture helped to keep him in the national eye and brought other invitations. Richard Watson Gilder, Joseph's brother (an assistant editor at *Scribner's* and then, in 1881, the editor of its successor, the *Century*), had helped to organize Whitman's first Lincoln lecture in 1879. Jeannette adored Whitman from the moment she met him at the lecture and once promised to write the old man's biography (but ultimately wrote only a brief reminiscence). By the end of the decade, Whitman thought her enthusiasm had cooled somewhat. Yet he never forgot the fact that she had accepted him when other editors had not.[17]

In February of the new year the *North American Review* paid $100 to print his essay entitled "The Poetry of the Future," where Whitman wound up his long campaign for an original American poetry that looked like his own. The mark of an "entire and finish'd" national greatness, he said, came only "in the blossom of original, first-class poems. No imitations will do."[18] In April *Harper's* published "Patroling Barnegat," the result of a visit in the company of Harry Stafford or his folks to Barnegat, overlooking a salt inlet above Atlantic City. Stylistically, the poem bears a remarkable resemblance to "The Dalliance of the Eagles." Both commence with present participial phrases describing raw nature. The second lines turn to a distinctive sound—"the roar of the gale" in "Patroling Barnegat" and the sexual "air of the sudden muffled sound" in "The Dalliance of the Eagles." "Patroling Barnegat" is a sonnet with lines ending in present participles to suggest the steady motion of the sea-scene's elements—"running," "muttering," "lashing," "careering," "slanting." This is the sea at midnight, the "savage trinity" of waves, wind, and darkness.[19] After his own fashion, Whitman was becoming a "nature writer" like his friend Burroughs; the late essays collected into *Specimen Days* dwell on nature with no human beings present and come up with the same romantic adorations that Thoreau made popular in *Walden.* The pieces in "How I Get Around at 60, and Take Notes" are also mainly of this genre.

But the third essay in the series, published in the *Critic* of May 7, was devoted to a visit to Boston between April 13 and 19, where Whitman gave his third Lincoln lecture. George Parsons Lathrop, Hawthorne's son-in-law and a journalist, had extended the invitation. Three years earlier, Lathrop had tried to get Whitman to contribute to an anthology he was preparing for Roberts Brothers but lost out when he insisted that "owing to the general character of the collection . . . your contribution would have to conform to the more usual rhythms at least as far as Captain, my Captain!"[20] Whitman may have been flattered to receive what was essentially an obsequious letter from an in-law of the man whose short fiction he had imitated in the 1840s. Like many, Lathrop respected Whitman primarily for his work in the hospitals and for the poems in *Drum-Taps.* He had requested something with "a patriotic tune." The next best thing was the bard's Lincoln lecture. He invited Whitman to give it in the Hawthorne Room of St. Botolph's Club, which Whitman did on April 15, 1881—the sixteenth anniversary of the assassination.

John Boyle O'Reilly, a poet who had once been imprisoned for radical activities and was now editor of a Roman Catholic paper called the *Pilot,* arranged for Whitman to stay free of charge, board included, at the Revere House, and Mrs. John T. Sargent arranged a reception for Whitman on the afternoon of his lecture.[21] We can hardly imagine the poetic "barbarian" in such society, perhaps shaking hands with writers and readers whose idea of American literature he deplored. Sylvester Baxter, one of Whitman's recent journalist friends, wrote in the *Boston Herald* the next day, "Many of the leading *literati* were at his lecture, and among them Mr. Howells was most cordial in his greeting." Special cards of invitation had been printed, but Lathrop may have feared Whitman would bolt. He advised the poet as graciously as he could to attend the reception and stick around after the lecture, adding, "We have sold a fine lot of tickets."[22] Evidently, the whole affair went swimmingly. Baxter reported, "Old and young, old friends and new, have gathered around him." As usual, Whitman's delivery was informal—perhaps in slight imitation of Emerson's "supremely natural" platform style, which he later admitted to Traubel he may have assumed in all his Lincoln lectures. Baxter likened it to reading "to a few personal friends—but with none of the tricks of the elocutionizing trade."[23] Another journalist, for the *Boston Evening Traveler* of the same day, viewed Whitman's appearance before the high-browed audience more solemnly: "In the audience before him were many eminent in art and letters, who had come to pay homage to one who is already fast being regarded as the typical citizen of the Republic." Sitting in the audience and also impressed with the moment and the man was James R. Osgood, one of America's leading American publishers, whose offices were in Boston.[24]

❋ ❋ ❋

Beginning as a clerk in 1855, Osgood had loyally worked his way to the top in Ticknor and Fields. That year the firm published Longfellow's

Hiawatha, while in New York the phrenologists Fowler & Wells "published" the first edition of *Leaves of Grass.* Ticknor and Fields became Fields, Osgood and Company in 1868, and James R. Osgood and Company in 1871.[25] In most Whitman biographies, Osgood is described as a leading figure in the business at the time Whitman's next edition appeared, but he owed much of his success as a publisher to the reputation of James T. Fields, whose list of authors included Emerson, Hawthorne, Longfellow, Whittier, and other current household names of American literature. Whitman's Boston publishers in 1860, Thayer and Eldridge, had been radicals in literature for their time (though Thayer was more devoted to the financial end of the publishing operation); Osgood lived off the fat of the literary establishment. It is remarkable that he agreed to publish Whitman's controversial book. He was certainly aware of the poet's failure in the past to meet standards of public acceptance, but he was apparently willing to take a chance in view of the generous reception Whitman received at his Lincoln lecture. Also, he needed authors with name recognition, and he no longer had the advice of Fields, his longtime friend and mentor, who had died in the spring of 1881. He managed to publish Twain, Howells, and Harriet Beecher Stowe, but like Thayer and Eldridge his firm went belly up. In 1885 he was unable to pay creditors more than $100,000.[26]

The idea of publishing Whitman was probably suggested to Osgood by O'Reilly. A week after Whitman returned to Camden, O'Reilly wrote that Osgood wished to see "the material for your complete book." Whitman replied on May 8 that he wanted to bring all his poems under one title again. There would be twenty-two new poems, many published in recent magazine issues, but he warned Osgood clearly on one point: "the old pieces, the *sexuality* ones, about which the original row was started & kept up so long, are all retained, & must go in the same as ever."[27] What is known as the "definitive" edition of *Leaves of Grass* went to press that August, but Whitman had only a couple of weeks to prepare a new manuscript—so little time, in fact, that the 1881 arrangement was probably no more "final" than those of 1867 and 1871. His main task was integrating the poems then published in *Two Rivulets* (although the title poem didn't make it into the Osgood edition). The edition is "definitive" because Whitman was finally too old to make any further changes. Furthermore, the subsequent controversy surrounding it rendered the Osgood arrangement final because otherwise Whitman could have been perceived as giving in to the censors. Only "annexes" were allowed in later "editions."

During the week that the first run of 1,000 copies went to press, Whitman likened the composition of *Leaves of Grass* to the construction of a carefully planned "cathedral." Critics and biographers of the last generation have wisely doubted the claim and argued instead for an evolutionary growth. But they have never explained exactly why the poet came up with the cathedral argument in the first place.[28] It was a preemptive strike against his censors, and it first appeared in the *Boston Daily Globe* of August 24, obviously planted or contrived through a friendly (or naive) journalist.[29] This argument for *Leaves of Grass,* made twenty-five years after the book's first appearance, was the very same Emerson had made about nature—that nothing is ugly or evil when seen in its full context, where all is harmony. In the first editions Whitman was reported by the *Globe* to say, "The plan of his book involved the unflinching expression of the elements which lie at the foundation of man's being." When this portion of the "cathedral" appeared "alone, without a suggestion as to its subordination to the whole, it had made a great hubbub. People supposed that was the whole building." Now, years later, the structure was complete. But, Whitman added, perhaps without blinking, "All the objectionable passages which were the cause of so much complaint at the time of their appearance will remain. Not a word is to be changed. . . . The great difference . . . is that whereas in the original volume they made a main portion of the book here they occupy but five or six pages out of 400."

Perhaps envisioning a triumphant return, Whitman had returned to Boston to see his book through the press as he had in 1860, although it wasn't necessary this time because the actual proofreading was performed mainly by Osgood's staff. Had he stayed away, the book might have gotten off more quietly. But the Boston newspapers reported his presence and the fact that the new book had not been expurgated. O'Reilly's *Pilot* of August 27, 1881, a week after Whitman arrived, noted that "the author [had] made that a condition of his contract." But it also alluded to the "completeness and relative proportion" of the latest edition. In the *Herald* of October 30, about a week after Whitman returned to Camden and the book was about to appear, Sylvester Baxter tried to keep the focus on more positive things, like Emerson's endorsement twenty-five years ago. Yet he, like O'Reilly, may have opened a Pandora's box for the reception of the sixth edition of *Leaves of Grass,* because in restating Whitman's cathedral argument about the offensive poems, he criticized Edmund Clarence Stedman, the first advocate for Whitman's poetry who was a member of the mainstream literati.

A year earlier Stedman had published in *Scribner's* what is today considered the first nonpartisan defense of *Leaves of Grass* as art. Although Baxter's action was impolitic at the time, he was correct in his appraisal. For an essay that has been hailed in this century as marking the beginning of Whitman's "public critical acceptance," it has a surprisingly large number of negative things to say about Whitman as a poet.[30] Its harshest criticism is that Whitman fails to describe nature "in a clean way,—that he was too anatomical and malodorous withal." There may be nothing in nature that is at bottom "mean or base," Stedman concedes, but "there is much that is ugly and disagreeable. . . . Even Mother Earth takes note of this, and resolves, or disguises and beautifies, what is repulsive upon her surface." When Whitman read the critique, he thought it was as good "as could be expected" of someone from Stedman's school of literature. Later he forgave Stedman almost completely and counted him among his strongest admirers for his warm reception of *November Boughs* and his *Complete Poetry and Prose* in 1888.[31] But when the *Scribner's* article appeared, he was simply pleased that the businessman who doubled as a critic was dispelling the old idea that Whitman was to be honored only for his hospital work. "To me," Stedman announced, "it seems that his song is more noteworthy than his life." Otherwise, the essay suggests that Emerson's letter of 1855 was impulsive; thinks that Whitman's brand of transcendentalism, or belief in man's divinity, is limited largely to the working class; criticizes his supporters for making acceptance of Whitman a condition of their respect for other critics and authors; and finds parts of what will be called "Song of Myself" for the first time in the Osgood edition "wearied by pages cheap in wisdom and invective or—intolerably dull." Numbering Whitman "among the foremost lyric and idyllic poets" at the opening of the essay, Stedman concludes with the guess that "Of our living poets, I should think him most sure of an intermittent remembrance hereafter, if not a general reading." *Leaves of Grass* will at best "be revived from time to time by dilettants [*sic*] on the hunt for curious treasures in the literature of the past."[32]

Baxter concluded his article in the *Herald,* "'Leaves of Grass' is a kosmos, and the leaving out of that which Mr. Stedman, in common with many, finds objectionable, would make it like an imperfect body." It didn't help the cause, however, when a nasty review in the *New York Tribune* of November 19, probably by William Winter, a Pfaffian of old, referred to the new *Leaves* as a "slop-bucket." Some Boston papers followed suit with equally disparaging comments, and by December Trubner and Company in London had declined to act as agents for the edition.[33]

❋ ❋ ❋

While Whitman was in Boston, Frank Sanborn—who had known him since his first visit to Boston in 1860 (when the New England transcendentalist was on trial for violating the Fugitive Slave Act)—invited the poet out to Concord, where he dined on successive days at the Sanborn residence and the Emerson homestead. Given the controversy over his literary relationship with Emerson and his latest essay on Emerson in a Boston publication, it is remarkable that he gained entrance to the latter home at all. Yet there he was, seated before his "Master" of old, in both Concord residences. Unfortunately, the only record of Whitman's visit—and this may tell the true tale of his actual welcome—was by the poet himself. In a letter to Lou on September 18, he mentioned his first of two visits, which became the basis for No. 5 of "How I Get Around" in the *Critic* of December 3, 1881.[34]

"Long and blessed evening with Emerson," he recalled, noting that things couldn't have been "better or different." Emerson, who had less than a year to live, may have exhibited behavior resembling Alzheimer's disease. The New Englander sat almost silently across from his old literary protégé after the meal at the Sanborn house. The other guests included Louisa May Alcott and her father, an admirer of Whitman's since his Ryerson Street days. They talked of Thoreau and Margaret Fuller, but Whitman's attention was focused mainly on Emerson. "My seat and the relative arrangement were such that, without being rude," he said in the *Critic,* "I could just look squarely at E., which I did a good part of two hours." More of the same the next afternoon at Emerson's, where Whitman found his old adviser with "healthy color" in his cheeks and "good light in the eyes." This was Whitman's last meeting with the man who had entered *Leaves of Grass* into the annals of American literary history in 1855. Everything was nearing the end, a fact prophetically underscored the next day when Whitman learned of Beatrice Gilchrist's suicide.

Death was part of the "weather" of life. The day after his second visit with Emerson, President Garfield—a casual friend from his Washington days—died from an assassin's bullet after lingering in and out of a coma for six weeks. A new congressman fresh from Ohio in the late 1860s, James A. Garfield had known Whitman when he was working in the Attorney General's Office. After Whitman's poem delivered before the American Institute Exhibition in New York in 1871 was quoted in a number of newspapers, Garfield never failed to greet the poet with a phrase from it, "after all not to create only." At midnight on September 19, the night of Whitman's second visit with Emerson, the Concord church bells rang out to announce the president's death. The next day, Whitman wrote "The Sobbing of the Bells." It was published in the *Boston Globe* a week later and hastily included in the Osgood edition. Later, O'Connor mildly chastised Whitman for taking as his first half line (and title) one of Poe's best-known lines from "The Bells." He also regretted that the poem memorialized a president whom he himself considered "personally and politically base."[35]

Shortly before his departure from Boston in October, Whitman—perhaps inspired by his reception following his Boston Lincoln lecture—hosted an affair for his Boston friends, "especially the printers" at Rand, Avery and Company, where his 1860 edition had also been stereotyped. "We had a jolly time too," he told Lou; "there were three hundred came & went—at ten o'clock we had a supper—but one such affair will answer for a life time."[36] Just who paid for the celebration is history's guess. Possibly, Baxter, who doted on Whitman and wrote him up in the *Herald* several times, arranged for it (and took up a collection to pay for it).

Back in Camden, Whitman spent possibly the happiest of Christmases in 1881. His book had finally been accepted by an established publisher, and it was already in the second or third printing, the first having been exhausted by mid-November. In mid-January he received a card from the co-owner of the *Philadelphia Ledger,* or actually from his wife, Mrs. George W. Childs, inviting him to a dinner in honor of Oscar Wilde. The twenty-seven-year-old writer was touring America, having just issued his *Poems* (1881), which mixed Christian and pagan images, to the revulsion of many of his reviewers. His trip had been arranged by the producer of Gilbert and Sullivan's operetta *Patience,* which parodied the aesthetic movement. Not yet that famous as a writer, Wilde was valued as a well-known aesthete; his lectures on "the Beautiful," it was hoped, would boost attendance at the operetta, which began its American performances in New York City in the fall of 1881.

Before reaching Philadelphia, Wilde hobnobbed in New York City with actresses Clara Morris and Mary Anderson, both currently on stage in other plays. He also attended a reception for Louisa May Alcott at the home of David Croly, Whitman's editorial connection at the *New York Daily Graphic* in the 1870s. The young Wilde outrivaled even the Old Gray Poet when it came to costume. Speaking at Chickering Hall, he wore a dark purple sack coat, knee-breeches, black hose, shoes with shiny buckles, and a coat lined with lavender satin and a frill of lace at the wrists. His message, fresh from the influence of the Pre-Raphaelites' "Fleshly School of Poetry" and Walter Pater's *Studies in the Renaissance* (1873), was exaltedly "art for art's sake." Wilde concluded with Pater's "Conclusion"—that since existence was a dream of isolated acts, one should cultivate each moment fully, seeking "not the fruit of experience, but experience itself." In his New York performances, he was unsure of his reception, the sharpest wit in the world perhaps feeling outgunned by *Patience,* in which he was the purported model for Bunthorne. "You have listened to *Patience* for a hundred nights," he told one audience with a hint of exasperation, "and have listened to me for only one." When he spoke in Philadelphia at Horticultural Hall, his performance provoked amusement and mild disapproval.[37]

Whitman declined the invitation to the Childses' residence but then sent a card to Wilde's other Philadelphia host, Joseph M. Stoddart, saying, "Walt Whitman will be in from 2 till 3 1/2 this afternoon, & will be most happy to see Mr Wilde and Mr Stoddart." At first the Camden poet had not been particularly interested in meeting the man who he later concluded wrote lucidly but artificially about life, but he apparently changed his mind after reading in the Philadelphia press that Wilde had named Whitman and Emerson as the greatest American writers.[38] Wilde didn't add that, as an aesthete who valued form over content in art, he actually thought Poe was the strongest American poet; he said only that Longfellow wasn't because he imitated European models too closely.

Accompanied by Stoddart, Wilde took the ferry over to "Camden Town" and a carriage up to 431 Stevens on January 18. It is not clear whether Stoddart was present for the entire two-hour conversation. If so, he said little, as the two worthies first assessed each other and then got on like old friends. Whitman later recalled that Stoddart left the two alone during most of the visit.[39] Wilde had first read *Leaves of Grass* with his Irish mother and later purchased the Rossetti edition. He thought Whitman the most Greek of the American or modern poets. He was curious to know what Whitman thought of the new aesthetic school, and the American bard replied that anyone "who makes a dead set at beauty by itself is in a bad way. My idea is that beauty is a result, not an abstraction." Flushed with the mere joy of being in the old man's company, the younger poet feebly accepted Whitman's admonition, saying, "Yes, I remember you have said, 'All beauty comes from beautiful blood and a beautiful brain,' and after all, I think so too."[40]

At the outset of their meeting, the two poets downed a bottle of Lou's elderberry wine. (Stoddart, who declined the homemade beverage, remarked to Wilde on their return to Philadelphia that evening that it must have been hard to get down. Wilde declared, "If it had been vinegar I should have drunk it all the same.") According to the *Philadelphia Press* of the next day, Whitman expressed the thought that Oscar was "a fine handsome youngster" and suggested they shift to a first-name basis. Wilde, allegedly sitting on a stool at Whitman's feet and laying his hand on his knee, replied, "I like that so much." At the end of the interview, Whitman gave his new friend "a big glass of milk punch." The American also presented the Irishman with two photographs of himself, one for Swinburne, and Wilde promised to send one of himself to Whitman, which he subsequently did. In March he also wrote to Whitman, closely paraphrasing a letter from Swinburne to himself in which Swinburne tried to distinguish his pleasure at Whitman's early poems from his displeasure at his political ramblings in *Democratic Vistas* and elsewhere. In closing, Wilde told Whitman: "Before I leave America I must see you again. There is no one in this wide great world of America whom I love and honor so much."[41]

Earlier biographers and students of Whitman have doubted that Wilde ever made a second visit to Camden in May. But Wilde's latest biographer, Richard Ellmann, suggests that he did, on the basis of what Wilde later allegedly told George Ives, a young proselytizer for homosexuality at Oxford in the 1890s. In his journal for January 6, 1901, Ives wrote: "I had better put down while I think of it what Oscar said of Whitman. He was discussing his answer to Symonds' enquiry and asking whether Whitman was not one of the Greek Lovers. Of course said Oscar, but he restrained Symonds' curiosity. 'I have the kiss of Walt Whitman's still on my lips.' So far as I can remember all those years ago, the last sentence was in his words." Ellmann quotes directly from Ives only Wilde's statement about the kiss, implying that it was bestowed when Stoddart was not present.

The kiss could have been planted during a second visit by Wilde, at a time that can now be ascertained. He lectured again in Philadelphia, this time at Association Hall, on May 10, 1882. The *Philadelphia Press* of the next day reported that the visit was only for the afternoon and that Wilde "dined with friends and left for New York on the 8 o'clock train." This would have given him little time to see Whitman in Camden, but apparently he found it. Charles Godfrey Leland, evidently one of Wilde's dinner companions that evening, recalled in his diary for May 10 that Wilde had made his visit to Whitman "got up as a far-away imitation of a cowboy, whom he thought the most picturesque product of America." Just how Whitman reacted to the costume is not known, but he may have been put off by the Englishman's widely reported remarks about American taste ("I have never seen so many badly made things in my life—so many glaring, hideous wall papers, furniture not joined but glued, and wretchedly woven carpets"). In fact, it was rumored in the press that Whitman had called him "a damned fool." Yet Whitman was clearly flattered by Wilde's attention. He told Harry that his visitor "had the *good sense* to take a great fancy to *me!*"

Wilde later visited Burroughs at Riverby, New York, but the naturalist could not appreciate his aestheticism. He later complained to Clara Barrus that Wilde thought of all things in terms of art. "Christ is to him the great artist." After Wilde's scandals and death, Burroughs thought that the distinguished playwright and wit had destroyed his genius. He thought him "a voluptuary. As he walked from you," he recalled from the Riverby visit, "there was something in the motion of his hips and back that was disagreeable." During Wilde's time in New York City, a less committed champion of *Leaves of Grass,* E. C. Stedman, carefully avoided social events that the Irish wit might attend, having been warned of his poetic obscenities.[42]

❋ ❋ ❋

Closer to home, Harry Stafford had been experiencing bouts of depression again. Walt admonished him on January 31, 1882, "I don't have any such spells—& seems to me it is time you grew out of them." He gave Harry the Thoreauvian advice to live from within rather than from without, but it was probably the interior landscape that made the young man "blue." And in March, when Whitman first heard that attempts were being made to suppress the Osgood edition of *Leaves of Grass,* he must have been a little "blue" himself, considering how well the book had been selling under the auspices of an established press.

On March 1, 1882, the Boston district attorney, Oliver Stevens, notified Osgood that its edition of *Leaves of Grass* violated the statutes of "obscene literature" and insisted on excisions (not yet specifically identified) of the offensive poems or parts.[43] Osgood sent the letter to Whitman on March 4, saying, "We are given to understand that if certain parts of the book should be withdrawn its further circulation would not be objectionable." To this Whitman immediately responded, on March 7, that he was not afraid of the challenge and wanted Osgood "to be satisfied, to continue as publishers of the book." He tentatively agreed to make some "revision & cancellation," thinking the changes wouldn't amount to "more than half a dozen" pages. Admitting to Osgood that he had "already thought favorably of some such brief cancellation," he eventually agreed to limited censorship (affecting "I Sing the Body Electric," "A Woman Waits for Me," and "Spontaneous Me"). In stating his acceptance of some cutting, however, he advised Osgood, "Let this whole matter be kept quiet in the house—no talk or information that may lead to newspaper items—the change[s] to be silently made—the book, & at casual view all its pages, to look just the same—only those minutely looking detecting the difference."[44]

Whitman had dearly wanted to have *Leaves of Grass* published by a mainstream, top-of-the-line publisher, and he was making more concessions than he probably ever wished to be remembered for. But when he saw the district attorney's full list of excisions, he told Osgood he saw "no other way" than to break with the firm and retrieve the plates and unbound sheets. Whitman should have read between the lines of Osgood's letter of March 4, which stated in conveying the district attorney's complaint that he was "naturally reluctant to be identified with any legal proceedings in a matter of this nature."[45] Osgood was no Thayer and Eldridge, his young, idealistic publishers in 1860 who undoubtedly would have fought any such attempt at censorship.

The list of poems and lines turned out to be extensive, as indicated by the copy marked by Stevens now at the University of Texas. In one sense, it supported Whitman's cathedral theory regarding the "obscene" poems: according to O'Connor's count, thirteen of the twenty-two offending passages or poems belonged to the first edition.[46] In one case, however, a previously revised passage actually caused a problem. In Section 3 of "Song of Myself," the "hugging and loving bedfellow" became potentially offensive once He was no longer identified by name ("As God, comes a loving bedfellow" in 1855). The mystical/physical/sexual union of Body and Soul in Section 5 also had to go. The "unseen hand" of the "twenty-ninth bather" caressing the bodies of the nude swimmers in Section 11 offended. Also a number of lines in Section 24: "And of the threads that connect the stars, and of wombs and of the father-stuff"; "I keep as delicate around the bowels as around the head and heart, / Copulation is no more rank to me than death is"; "You my rich blood! your milky stream pale strippings of my life!"; "Winds whose soft-tickling genitals rub against me it shall be you!" The last eleven lines of Section 28, which celebrate touch, were ruled out. The line about turning the bridegroom out of bed and tightening the bride "all night to my thighs and lips" clearly threatened Boston family values. Likewise, the eugenic lines in Section 40 that read, "On women fit for conception I start bigger and nimbler babes, / (This day I am jetting the stuff of far more arrogant republics)." The list called for half of "From Pent-Up Aching Rivers" to disappear, essentially leaving pent-up Adam in the Garden without his Eve. Chunks of "I Sing the Body Electric" (from Sections 5 and 9), describing a close-up tour of the body, were also marked. Whole poems included "A Woman Waits for Me," "To a Common Prostitute," and the recently composed "The Dalliance of the Eagles." Apparently, birds weren't allowed to copulate in poetry either.

Whitman had been hoping that Osgood would also publish *Specimen Days* ("*It* at least will not be liable to any District Att'y episodes," he told the publisher on March 21) and Bucke's biography, but the game was up when he realized the district attorney's list of excisions was not negotiable. The entire list, he had already warned Osgood, would be "rejected by me, & will not be thought of under any circumstances."[47] By May Whitman had received free from Osgood and Company the 1855 steel engraving (the only illustration in the Osgood edition) and 225 unbound copies of the edition. He also got a check for $100, which brought his total royalties (12 percent, or 25 cents from each $2 copy) to $405. Osgood had been generous in this defeat and a gentleman all along, but he couldn't help observing Whitman's seeming rigidity in the face of litigation. "It is perhaps not an important matter," he told Whitman on April 13, "but as your letter seems to imply that this possible change is the result of a 'settled decision' on our part, we feel it right to say that it is not we who have fixed inflexible conditions under which this matter could be decided. These conditions have been fixed by yourself and they appear to be such as to obviate the possibility of compromise."[48] Whitman had tried to compromise, but not hard enough for the district attorney or the standards of decency in nineteenth-century America. Later he, O'Connor, Traubel, and others liked to think that it was Osgood's failure to fight censorship and not his unwise business transactions that caused the financial ruin of his publishing house.[49] (As it turned out, Osgood should have stood his ground—the obscenity charges came to nothing.)

Osgood may have thought this was the end of it. Whitman, too, may have thought so, though he quickly rallied O'Connor, who, completely ignoring their ten years' quarrel, joined the subsequent fray with his old vehemence. In fact, O'Connor had been moving toward a reconciliation for the past year by consulting with Bucke on the biography, to which he had agreed to contribute. That spring, all hell broke loose, as it had in the Anglo-American contest of 1876, but this time—in the words of Edwin Haviland Miller—the censorship and the ensuing debate in the newspapers immortalized Boston's "dubious morality by making it a national joke."[50] The label "Banned in Boston" was dramatically bestowed on one of America's national literary treasures, *Leaves of Grass.*

Whitman told O'Connor on May 25 that he thought the controversy might actually increase interest in the book.[51] He was right. Once the plates were received by Whitman and given first to Rees, Welsh of Philadelphia, and then to David McKay, as their publishing successor and also the owner of a bookstore on the premises, this edition of *Leaves of Grass* (banned from Wanamaker's, Philadelphia's most famous department store) went rapidly through five editions, or issues of 1,000 copies each. By the end of 1882 it had earned Whitman royalties of more than $1,500, or a total of almost $2,000, counting the Osgood royalties. The first Philadelphia issue, published on July 18, sold out in twenty-four hours. The second issue, published on August 6, sold out in a week.[52]

Yet the exchange in the press was bruising, started by the book's hostile reviewers and matched by Whitman's advocates and disciples. He was defended by almost as many as attacked him, even (though without his consent) by the New England Free Love League and other fringe elements.[53] It would have been difficult for such a group to ignore Whitman, since he had been discovered in England by the Pre-Raphaelites. The effort, it seems, having developed from the resentment of the American literary establishment in 1876, was to condemn much of Victorian literature along with Whitman. And here the defenders tried to defend Whitman against the association. The *Springfield Republican,* for example, always moderately friendly to the poet, tried to impress on its readers the literary consequences of the Comstockery that was attacking *Leaves of Grass.* Why worry anyway, it asked in an article on May 26, about a book that had been published long ago in Boston and was now being "issued at a high price above the popular figures, so that a popular circulation is not to be expected"? *Leaves of Grass,* it vaguely implied, was nothing compared to the "fleshly poets," "the dirty poems" of Swinburne, the "'fleshly' sonnets of Philip Bourke Marston," or "such productions as that long poem ["Humanitad"] the modern aesthete Wilde has put in his book."[54]

Bucke had sounded a similar note in the *Springfield Republican* on May 22. It might be understandable, although still unacceptable, he wrote, if *Leaves of Grass* "were, for instance, comparable to Byron's 'Don Juan,' Sterne's 'Tristram Shandy,' Fielding's 'Tom Jones,'" and other books "in which sensual pleasures were pictured and praised for their own sake." O'Connor first spoke out in the *New York Tribune* of May 25, resorting to the old defense that the book had received the enthusiastic support of writers in England and on the Continent as well as of Emerson. The mere mention of the Emerson letter of 1855—especially since Emerson had died only weeks before—once again turned the debate away from the merits and demerits of *Leaves of Grass* and toward Emerson's opinion of it. This tack infuriated Anne Gilchrist, who thought it didn't matter what Emerson thought—that if he had thought well of the volume, it would have assisted his reputation more than Whitman's.[55] But Emerson had been one of O'Connor's earliest literary heroes—he had praised the Concord philosopher in *Harrington*—and he argued the case as much for Emerson's sake as for Whitman's.

O'Connor's letter elicited a response from John W. Chadwick, a Unitarian minister in Brooklyn, who outfoxed both O'Connor and Whitman. Citing Whitman's own testimony of his talk with Emerson on Boston Common in 1860, paraphrased in O'Connor's letter of May 25, he argued logically that Emerson's advice to excise the "Children of Adam" poems, "which contain the greater part of all that with which Mr. Oliver Stevens is offended," was proof that he had changed his mind about *Leaves of Grass* since 1855. O'Connor answered in the *Tribune* of June 18 that Emerson's advice about "Children of Adam" sprang exclusively from "conventional and technical literary considerations" regarding marketability.[56]

Whitlaw Reid, still editor of the *Tribune,* treated Whitman about as fairly as he had in 1876, giving O'Connor most of his shots but also meting out opposing views in order to keep the controversy going for the benefit of newspaper sales. The same day O'Connor's answer to Chadwick appeared, the *Tribune* carried what O'Connor, quoting from Reid's note, described to Whitman as "a savage article on the other side!" This was an anonymous attack, signed only "Sigma" (who was either Librarian of Congress Ainsworth Rand Spofford or Richard Henry Stoddard). It matched the viciousness of an attack in the *Tribune* the previous fall declaring that "the chief question raised [by the Osgood publication] is whether anybody—even a poet—ought to take off his trousers in the market-place."[57] Sigma condemned Whitman's poems as "a glorification of the animal man, who is exhibited to us—regardless of sex—*in puris naturalibus.*" As to Emerson, he never sanctioned the indecent parts of Whitman's work; in fact, he had been relieved upon first meeting the Brooklyn bard in 1855 to find in his conversation "none of that disgusting Priapism which appears to some parts of his book."

Before O'Connor thought to answer this letter (he never quite knew when to quit), various free thinkers rose up to defend *Leaves of Grass,* specifically to challenge the Comstock law against sending obscene materials through the mail. At least three individuals challenged the restriction by printing poems from *Leaves of Grass* or advertising the book by mail order. George Chainey, a Boston minister-turned-reformer published excerpts of several poems and the full text of "To a Common Prostitute" in his weekly journal, *This World.* They were accompanied by a sermon entitled "Keep Off the Grass." Benjamin R. Tucker, one of the principal advocates of "free love," printed an advertisement in his journal, *Liberty,* for "The Suppressed Book!" Worse yet in the view of Whitman, who oddly never supported the Free Love movement, Ezra H. Heywood, president of the New England Free Love League and old foe of Anthony Comstock (who had had him imprisoned for sending graphic medical texts through the mail in 1877), also published the texts of "To a Common Prostitute" and "A Woman Waits for Me" in his magazine, *The Word.* The issue of Whitman's poetry and the U.S. mail was decided in the poet's favor by the postmaster general in July;[58] the decision protected only "To a Common Prostitute," published by Chainey. "A Woman Waits for Me" was cleared at Heywood's obscenity trial a year later.

Whitman jumped into the fray himself this time. "A Memorandum at a Venture" appeared in the *North American Review* in June. Whitman told Burroughs in April that in it he was attempting to "ventilate my theory of sexual matters, treatment & allusion in *Children of Adam.*"[59] It was not a success. All the old points were there, with an epigraph from Millet, whose paintings Whitman to his delight had recently viewed in Boston—"All is proper to be express'd, provided our aim is only high enough." He brought up the cathedral defense, but he also, perhaps daunted by the recent threat to keep *Leaves of Grass* out of the mails, fell into legalistic jargon, which wreaked havoc with his sentence structure and meaning when wedded to his normally serpentine prose syntax. It was indeed a "venture." Yet he did bring up a vitally needed social point, at least in the minds of his feminist friends of the 1850s (the best of whom, Abby Price, had died the previous year). He said that "current prurient, conventional treatment of sex is the main formidable obstacle" to women's entrance into the spheres of business, politics, "and the suffrage."[60]

❋ ❋ ❋

As this storm gathered in the fall of 1881 and the spring of 1882, Whitman was also busy reading, critiquing, and rewriting Bucke's manuscript, which was published as *Walt Whitman* (a subtitle, "A Study," was dropped) the following year. Sending it back by Adams Express, possibly for the second time, on February 7, Whitman told the alienist, "You will be surprised, probably enraged, at the manner in which I have gone through it."[61] The book, not a biography properly speaking but a critical study (and defense) anchored in biographical methods, would be Whitman's as much as Bucke's. Whitman essentially ghost-wrote Part 1, or "Biographical Sketch," in his conversations with Bucke while in Canada. In Part 2, Bucke tried to continue the thesis he proposed in *Man's Moral Nature,* making the case more for a prophet or savior than a poet. At one point he considered the epigraph: "Walt Whitman Is the Savior, the Redeemer of the Modern World."[62] But Whitman replaced most of his argument with a more focused discussion of the major poems of *Leaves of Grass* and analyses and praises of the book by others, mainly the writers and critics in England and on the Continent who had defended his poetry since the late 1860s. As we lack the manuscript Whitman first edited and much of Bucke's correspondence during the period, it is impossible to know all the specific changes.

By the time the book was ready for the press in the summer of 1882, they had lost Osgood as a publisher, and Putnam's, which had published *Man's Moral Nature,* declined. David McKay was willing, but Whitman urged Bucke to hold back his book till 1883 so that *Specimen Days* could appear in the fall of 1882. This Whitman considered a twin, though clearly inferior, volume to *Leaves of Grass.* He described it repeatedly in letters to friends as "a *prose* jumble."[63] It was ultimately called *Specimen Days & collect.* The "collect" allowed him to throw in some of his early fiction, essays written over the years (including "Emerson's Books"), *Democratic Vistas,* prefaces to the 1855 and 1872 editions and the centennial issue, his Lincoln lecture—making it a motley collection somewhat like *Two Rivulets. Specimen Days* was also published in 1882 in Scotland under the imprimatur of Wilson and McCormick (using unbound pages from McKay) along with the firm's edition of *Leaves of Grass.* The main section consists of short biographical and genealogical pieces, but these soon give way to contemporaneous accounts of the war, which had already appeared in slightly different form in his newspaper articles, "'Tis But Ten Years Since," and *Memoranda During the War.* Like Emerson's essays, some of Whitman's ideas in this section can be traced back to diary accounts. The book then moves through Whitman's nature writing, picks up his incidental essays, or versions of them in the *Philadelphia Press,* and then his impressions of his trip out west in 1879 and to Canada in 1880 (e.g., "The Women of the West" and "The Savage Saguenay"). By Whitman's (perhaps exaggerated) account, the book sold well at the outset, approximately 1,100 of the run of 1,500 by November, and then slacked off.[64]

One essay Whitman did not include in the "collect" part of the volume was "Robert Burns; A Modern Poet on the Scotch Bard," which had appeared in Croly's *Daily Graphic* for January 25, 1875. In the article, which Whitman revised and republished in the *Critic* December 16, 1882, he is both loving and judgmental of Scotland's most famous poet. Primarily, he admires the fact that Burns "poetizes work-a-day agricultural labor and life." On the other hand, he has "little or no spirituality." This is a harsh judgment, but the 1875 version is rougher, calling Burns "a poet of the third, perhaps fourth class."[65]

❋ ❋ ❋

Two days after Christmas 1882, Whitman sent a card to his recently reconciled friend O'Connor, saying he had been out to Germantown, northeast of "center city" Philadelphia, beyond Fairmount Park and next to the Wissahickon Woods, where he rode in an expensive horse and buggy. In February he was scheduled to go back to Germantown for a few days. In another note to O'Connor, he described the surroundings there as a "big family & big house, wife, son, two splendid daughters of a Quaker friend, whose carriage comes for me presently. The eldest daughter, age 20, an admirer of L. of G. who comes up even to you." This was the family of Robert Pearsall Smith, then a wealthy sales executive for a prosperous glass factory in Millville, New Jersey. He and his wife, Hannah, had been devout Quakers when they married in 1851 but eventually broke away from the fold to explore more experimental routes to salvation. Robert turned out to be a first-rate evangelist, preaching at huge revivals first in America and then in England and (through translators) on the Continent. By the early 1870s he had become famous in Europe, but he fell from his high pulpit when he got the idea that a shortcut to redemption lay in knowing Jesus carnally through another person, not necessarily one's spouse. Rumors and then accusations that he was having an affair with one of the female members of his congregation caused his disgrace and a quick retreat to America, where he reluctantly but successfully took up the glass business owned by his rich father-in-law.[66]

By the early 1880s the Smiths were the parents of three surviving children, Mary, Logan, and Alys. Mary, the eldest, born in 1864, was the one with the burning enthusiasm for *Leaves of Grass.* Although strictly raised as a Quaker, she was a spirited, flirtatious girl who had no intention of acquiring either the Quaker distrust of art and music or her mother's now deep-seated distrust of men and their libidinal needs. While a student at Smith College in the spring and fall of 1882, she fell in love with *Leaves of Grass* despite its reputation for being a smutty book. At first she found it "an insufferable mass of conceit and nonsense. . . . with perfectly *disgusting* parts," but she soon concluded that there was "something almost sublime in it, it is so fearfully reckless and courageous and honest."[67] When she returned home to Germantown for Christmas vacation, she insisted on meeting Walt Whitman, who, she was delighted to learn, lived so near Philadelphia. Her father at first forbade her to search out such a questionable character, but when Mary threatened to go to Camden herself, Robert desisted and, bringing along his son, accompanied her there in his fashionable carriage. Once at the Stevens Street address, they were announced to the poet by Lou, who shouted up the stairs: "Walt, here's carriage folk come to see you!"[68]

After an hour's conversation, the former evangelist found himself quite converted to the poet and invited him to return to his palatial home on Arch Street in Germantown as a weekend guest. According to Logan's reminiscence, Whitman initially declined, "but when he had hobbled to the window and seen, waiting in the street outside, my father's equipage, he said that he thought he might as well come after all and, hastily putting a nightshirt and a few other objects in a little bag, he hobbled downstairs and we all drove off together."[69] Logan added that Whitman stayed a month, but the poet's letters of the period do not support this statement. During future visits, and there were many, he did stay for weekends and weeks or more at a time, arriving and leaving when he pleased, at least once combining the trip with a visit to his other recently acquired palace away from home, the comparable mansion of his friend Johnston in New York City.

He told Traubel that the Smith house with its servants ever at the ready "could not have been more mine if I had owned it—the overflowing table, which contained about everything but a tipple (you know the Smiths were opposed to all tippling)—yes, everything but the tipple, which, by the way, some of us would now and then slip out and get round the corner."[70] The only Smith Whitman didn't hit it off with completely was the mother, Hannah, who accepted the poet reluctantly but would not permit a copy of *Leaves of Grass* in her house. When the poet gave Alys an inscribed copy, this mother's daughter, though she came to love Whitman's work and reminisce about it on the BBC after World War II, cut out all the offensive passages.

All three children shared their father's enthusiasm for the Gray Poet. Mary brought her friends over to Camden to meet Whitman, including, in 1884, an Irish barrister named Frank Costelloe. She had met him while studying at the Harvard Annex (later Radcliffe), after she left Smith College without graduating. In November Mary told Whitman, who once compared her independent spirit to Anne Gilchrist's, that Costelloe had read *Leaves of Grass* to his fellow passengers on his voyage back to England, where he eventually became a Fabian politician arguing for Home Rule in Ireland.[71] That December Costelloe proposed marriage to Mary by cable; she accepted, and the entire family moved to London the following summer. Mary, Alys, and later Logan kept up a correspondence with Whitman, who wrote Mary a letter of introduction to Lord Houghton and recommended her to Anne Gilchrist (who most likely died before a meeting could take place).[72] In July Mary wrote to tell Whitman of a movement of Oxford fellows enamored of social reform who had established a settlement house and named it for Arnold Toynbee, a friend of Frank Costelloe. It was, he heard through either Eldridge or O'Connor, a priesthood of sorts in which Whitman was its "Master" and great exemplar. The poet welcomed the idea of helping others, he told Mary, if not the canonization of himself as "Master." "I think much of all genuine efforts of the human emotions . . . to exploit themselves for humanity's good—the *efforts in themselves,* I mean . . . without stopping to calculate whether the investment is tip-top in a business or statistical point of view." He thought it "the theory & practice of the beautiful God Christ."[73]

Whitman the democrat despised aristocratic societies, but not earned wealth. From time to time he enjoyed its fruits, but he was also satisfied to return to his working-class surroundings. He noted that the elder Smith especially liked the English brand of living high—"service, servants, finger bowls, a big fellow back of your chair attending every beck and call." It helped, of course, when the rich host minimized the true value of his fortune, as Smith did. Perhaps because of his son-in-law Costelloe, he dabbled in socialist concepts and became an acquaintance of Henry George, the proponent of the Single Tax.[74]

His son, Logan, worshiped wealth in the same reluctant manner, ultimately shielding himself from the family business. He also worshiped Whitman the same way that Herbert Gilchrist did—as an artist–father figure; Whitman initially preferred Mary and Alys, as he had at first preferred the Gilchrist daughters, or at least Beatrice. Both young men had "*the fever called literature,*" the same passion that Whitman attributed to another, American proponent of *Leaves of Grass,* William Sloane Kennedy, who was just out of college and working for a Philadelphia newspaper in the early 1880s.[75] Logan, who attended Oxford after Haverford and Harvard, was influenced by the Oxford- and Cambridge-bred infatuation with art and literature that had begun in the 1860s when Symonds and Carpenter were students. He subscribed to the cult of Beauty as Oscar Wilde did, but without the latter's complete artistic and social commitment. For Logan, and for Herbert, the commitment was first to society—where one might safely rhapsodize about fossilized literature and art. While at Harvard, he and his sister Mary had heard the English essayist and literary biographer Edmund Gosse give the Lowell Lectures. "Of these lectures I have forgotten everything except one pregnant sentence, in which the name of Botticelli first echoed in our ears. 'Botticelli,' the lecturer said, in that cultivated 'English accent' which was music to us. . . . 'Botticelli,' that name which is an open sesame to the most select, the most distinguished, the most exclusive circles of European culture."[76] Strange bedfellows for the salty, sanguine author of *Leaves of Grass.* Yet just as Mary had found something "sublime" in the allegedly pornographic poems, the Logans of the world found something in his democratic themes that assuaged their guilt about wealth and made them feel like freedom fighters of the soul.

Back in Europe after so many years, Robert Pearsall Smith felt oddly misplaced and gradually atrophied into a ghostlike lord in a rented country mansion at Friday's Hill in Sussex, a 180-acre estate consisting mostly of woods. One of his problems was manic-depression, which his children, especially Logan, later shared. In a letter to Whitman dated August 13, 1889, he wrote: "My old enemy 'melancholia' spreads its vampire wings still over my life." A year later he told Whitman of having a lease on his mansion for twenty-one years ("longer than a lease on life") and confessed tinges of guilt "in occupying so much space for private pleasures."[77] There the senior Smiths entertained the artistic, literary, and political leaders of London society, beginning a complex network of connections that extended well into the twentieth century.

In 1889 Mary suffered an emotional breakdown. At Friday's Hill in 1890 she met and fell in love with the future art critic Bernard Berenson, with whom she went off to Florence, abandoning her two daughters to the care of her mother. She eventually divorced Costelloe and married Berenson, helping him to create the mansion and grounds of I Tatti. Its art treasures, paintings, and library brought in connoisseurs, aesthetes, and museum curators, and also Edith Wharton, who visited and worked there annually beginning in 1910.[78] Indeed, the great affection Henry James and Edith Wharton held for *Leaves of Grass* at the turn of the century seems less of an isolated response when we realize how far the Smith connection extended Whitman's English reach into the twentieth century.

Logan Smith went on to write a number of literary studies, most notably *Trivia* (1903), a collection of aphorisms that was revived with a 1918 reprinting and finally brought its author fame. Best known for the company he kept, his friendship with Henry James certainly did not hurt his literary stature in London. Nor did the Bloomsbury marriages of his nieces (Mary's daughters by Costelloe). Rachel Costelloe married Oliver Strachey, Lytton's elder brother. And Karin, who eventually committed suicide at the age of 64, married Adrian Stephen, the son of Sir Leslie Stephen and brother of Virginia Woolf.

Their aunt Alys became Bertrand Russell's first wife in 1894. Two years later she took the future sage to the Whitman shrine on Mickle Street. Russell, who was co-author with Alfred North Whitehead of what is arguably the most important philosophical work of the twentieth century, *Principia Mathematica* (1910), went on to marry three more women and to earn the scorn of many of his countrymen after World War I for his doctrine of pacifism. He moved to the United States, where he spent many years avoiding incarceration (he had been jailed twice in England) for the legal consequences of his pacifist beliefs. During the Vietnam War he became an icon to people who opposed American participation in the conflict.

❋ ❋ ❋

In September 1883, between sojourns in Germantown and New York, Whitman stayed two weeks at the Sheldon House in Ocean Grove, on the upper New Jersey coast. Burroughs joined him, and the two spent some precious days together. "Am on the beach quite all day & the surf sings me to sleep every night. John Burroughs is here," he told O'Connor. In his journal, Burroughs wrote that Whitman's presence was like a grand tonic that "loosens my tongue." "There is something grainy and saline in him," he declared, "as in the voice of the sea. Sometimes his talk is choppy and confused, or elliptical and unfinished; again there comes a long splendid roll of thought that bathes one from head to foot, or swings you quite free from your moorings."[79] While at Ocean Grove, Whitman wrote "With Husky-Haughty Lips, O Sea!" Born a seashore poet, "Paumanok" was now beyond the emotional crises of the late 1850s that he had recorded in his two greatest poems of the genre, "Out of the Cradle Endlessly Rocking" and "As I Ebb'd with the Ocean of Life." Now the sea was simply "The first and last confession of the globe."[80]

Back at the Smith mansion in late October, he wrote Harry Stafford about the poem. While there he read the Sermon on the Mount to the family and their guests, perhaps consoling the Smith matriarch, Hannah, somewhat for his allegiance to the rebel Quaker Elias Hicks.[81] Harry was getting ready to travel to Bucke's asylum in Ontario for a temporary job as a "turnkey," where he would not like the work, also complaining of the "many unearthly noises" that kept him awake at night. As he had done in the past, he asked Whitman for letters of recommendation to help him (this time) land a job in a telegraph office. He thought of looking in Detroit and Chicago. "I am *determined* to make a hit somewhere and dont forget it," he told Whitman, adding perhaps in response to an earlier admonition that he hadn't had a "blue spell" for some time.[82]

In December Peter Doyle made one of his infrequent visits to Camden, and Whitman promised to write in support of one of Pete's several brothers, also a streetcar conductor, in search of work in Washington.[83] The visit must have heightened Whitman's nostalgia for his Washington days, including the brief time spent in Indian Affairs, because the man who salutes the "friendly and flowing savage" in "Song of Myself" wrote "An Indian Bureau Reminiscence," published twice in the winter and spring of 1884. Offsetting his tribute to Custer, he delights in his memory of heroic-looking chiefs—"Omahas, Poncas, Winnebagoes, Cheyennes, Navahos, Apaches, and many others." There is something about "these aboriginal Americans, in their highest characteristic representations, essential traits, and the ensemble of their physique and physiognomy . . . that our literature, portrait painting, etc., have never caught, and that will almost certainly never be transmitted to the future, even as a reminiscence."[84]

Whitman spent Christmas 1883 back in Germantown, this time with the family of Francis Howard Williams, a poet and dramatist whom he probably met through the gregarious Smiths. Over the years Walt had spent a great deal of time away from Stevens Street, visiting others—a total of almost three years out of the nearly eleven he lived there.[85] He had been bored with George's rigid routine, which tended to override Lou's domestic kindnesses. But now something else was wrong. George was building a farmhouse in Burlington, New Jersey, fifty miles north of Camden and out of the loop for foreign and most domestic visitors whose presence was becoming more and more a tonic to the poet. By February or March the crisis had elevated. George was first baffled and then angered that Walt would not accompany them to Burlington, where the house—George's last—had been built to accommodate his brother. "Bad as the weather is," Walt told George and Susan Stafford, "I must up & go out & across the river, or I shall have the horrors."[86]

At first he thought of living with John and Ursula Burroughs, but Riverby, eighty miles up the Hudson from New York City, was more isolated than Burlington. Then came a real estate tip and the quick purchase of a "shanty," from Rebecca Jane Hare, a widow and dressmaker, around the corner at 328 Mickle Street. The two-story row house had six small rooms but no furnace, and Whitman had no furniture for it at first. It had been rented by Alfred Lay, a laborer and the grandfather of one of Whitman's Camden "roughs" who had recently died. Lay couldn't afford to pay the rent for March, and Whitman lent him the $16 he needed. After Whitman moved into the house on March 26, Lay and his wife cooked for their accommodations. Whitman paid $1,750 cash for the house and had to borrow $500 from George W. Childs to complete the payment. Mickle Street was possibly even noisier than George's corner location on Stevens, but as the poet exaggerated to Burroughs it was "half way nearer" to his beloved ferry.[87]

In June Whitman attended the marriage of Harry Stafford and Eva Wescott, which was performed by the mayor of Camden. Relations with Harry kept up just the same, but now Walt had Eva as a new Lou Whitman or Susan Stafford. "Eva, my dear friend," he wrote later that year, "it would be a true comfort for me if it was so I could come in every few days, and you and Harry and I could be together."[88] Sales on his books by this time were down dramatically, and he started selling the McKay volume by mail directly from Mickle Street—sometimes for more than McKay charged.[89] His publication rate had not exactly slowed, but the poetic products were sometimes thinner—as though the muse was wearing down. Whitman became more sedentary, if not yet "house-tied," as he later described himself. He told Susan Stafford, "My walking power gives out more this year, & I am afraid is destined to be worse, instead of better." To Harry and Eva, the prognosis was even worse—"it probably wont be long before I shall be unable to get around at all."[90] The latent tuberculosis he had been carrying since the war began to assert itself as age and lack of physical activity weakened his immune system.

Whitman continued to publish in the *Critic.* "A Fabulous Episode" in the issue of March 31, 1884, was a third-person dismissal of a statement published in the *Lynn [Massachusetts] Saturday Union* that Whitman had asked Longfellow if he could dedicate the first edition of *Leaves of Grass* to him. According to the report, Longfellow—who had died in the spring of 1882, a month before Emerson—had agreed but only if the book were purged of its indecencies. On September 27 Whitman published "What Lurks Behind Shakespeare's Historical Plays," an article influenced by O'Connor's support of the theory that Francis Bacon wrote Shakespeare's plays. Whitman never completely gave himself over to the idea and was probably writing to humor his old friend—to whom it seemed at times that the theory was second in cosmic importance only to the campaign for *Leaves of Grass.* In November the *Critic* carried "The Dead Tenor," a poem written on the occasion of Pasquale Brignole's death—the funeral took place in New York City on November 3. Whitman had heard Brignole sing his favorite Italian operas in the 1860s. Another poem, commemorating the reburial of a famous old Iroquois warrior, appeared as "Red Jacket (from Aloft)" in the *Philadelphia Press* of October 10. The ceremony had honored the chieftain Red Jacket for leading his nation in support of the American side in the War of 1812.

Whitman's fame now extended to presidents, including Grover Cleveland, who became the Democratic nominee for president in

1884. The previous year, when the future candidate publicly endorsed Whitman's book, the *Boston Weekly Transcript* of July 10 predicted that the New York governor's "chances for the presidency have reached the vanishing point." While staying at the Smith residence in 1883, Whitman declined an invitation from the Johnstons to meet Cleveland, answering after the opportunity had already passed. But on October 26, 1884, just before Cleveland won his first term in the White House, Whitman published a poem in the *Philadelphia Press* that was ultimately entitled "Election Day, November, 1884." It prized America's day at the polls over all her natural wonders.

> If I should need to name, O Western World, your powerfulest
> scene and show,
> 'Twould not be you, Niagara—nor you, ye limitless prairies—nor
> your huge rifts of canyons, Colorado,
> Nor you, Yosemite—nor Yellowstone, with all its spasmic geyser-
> loops ascending to the skies, appearing and disappearing,
> Nor Oregon's white cones—nor Huron's belt of mighty lakes—
> nor Mississippi's streams:
> —This seething hemisphere's humanity, as now, I'd name—*the*
> *still small voice* vibrating—America's choosing day.

Whitman did not vote in the 1884 presidential election. He told Traubel, "I always refrain—yet advise everybody else not to forget." He was probably speaking of his later years, not the 1840s and 1850s when, as a journalist, he was actively involved in politics.[91]

Right after New Year's in 1885, Edmund Gosse—who had so dazzled Logan Smith at Harvard—visited Whitman on Mickle Street. Mary Smith happened to be on the same ferry as Gosse, crossing the Delaware from Philadelphia to visit Whitman. Guessing that such a distinguished-looking chap could only be going to the working-class city of Camden to see Whitman, she introduced herself. The pair proceeded to Whitman's house but received no answer when they rang. According to the story retold by her brother, Mary—who was sure that the poet was at home—boosted Gosse up through the window so that he could unlock the door from the inside. Gosse later denied this detail,[92] but then he also lied about how he came to be invited to Whitman's house in the first place. In *Critical Kit-Kats* (1903) he claimed that Whitman had invited him while Gosse was in Boston, beseeching him "not to leave America without coming to see him." "My first instinct," he added, "was promptly to decline the invitation." In fact, it was Gosse who wrote Whitman for permission to visit him. On December 29 he told the poet, "I am very anxious not to leave this country without paying my respects to you, and bearing to you in person messages which I bring from Mr. Swinburne and other common friends in England."[93] It seems that everyone who came from England brought Whitman messages from Swinburne, who by this time could hardly suppress his soured opinion of the Camden poet. Whitman later described Gosse to Traubel as "very largely a formal craftsman but he has little disposition our way." Whitman was right: in *Critical Kit-Kats,* Gosse called *Leaves of Grass* "literature in the condition of protoplasm."[94]

Not only was Whitman still writing regularly for the *Critic,* but he was being written up there as well. On February 28, 1885, editor Jeanette Gilder gives us this snapshot:

> Of late years the poet, who will be sixty-six years old on the last day of May ensuing, has been in a state of half-paralysis. He gets out of doors regularly in fair weather, much enjoys the Delaware River, is a great frequenter of the Camden and Philadelphia Ferry, and may occasionally be seen sauntering along Chestnut or Market Street in the latter city. He has a curious sort of public sociability, talking with black and white, high and low, male and female, old and young, of all grades. He gives a word or two of friendly recognition, or a nod or smile, to each. Yet he is by no means a marked talker or logician anywhere. I know an old book-stand man who always speaks of him as Socrates. But in one respect the likeness is entirely deficient. Whitman never argues, disputes, or holds or invites a cross-questioning bout with any human being.[95]

The style and tone of the piece suggest that Whitman had a hand in this contribution, too. And later, on June 16, he sent the world another update, this time through Camden attorney James Scovel in the

Springfield Republican. "Though venerable looking from his white hair and beard, his paralysis and extra lameness, he really ages slowly in body, and in mind not at all. He still keeps throwing out little poems or prose articles every week or two, which not only indicate no failure, but show an increase of power and dexterity over former years."

❋ ❋ ❋

Whitman was totally without family now. Eddy had been boarded out in the country years before Walt made his move to Mickle Street. George and Lou were in Burlington, and generally Walt saw only Lou, who visited him regularly. He was now totally responsible for his room and board—though George may have assisted in later years. Walt sent occasional small sums to Hannah and Mary, and even to Heyde. He could still afford this generosity—though affordability was never much of an issue with him. Beginning in 1885 with a bank balance of approximately $1,200, Whitman took in at least $1,296.75—of which only $20.71 came from royalties from McKay's editions of *Leaves of Grass* and *Specimen Days.* He earned $350.20 for poems and articles he sold to magazines and newspapers. He received another $925.84 from England, where Herbert Gilchrist and Rossetti had arranged a "free will offering" from well wishers, and Edward Carpenter and another person contributed individually. Along with volumes of *Leaves of Grass* and *Specimen Days,* he sold copies of Bucke's biography and the second edition of Burroughs's *Notes* through the mail—books that he had written most of anyway.[96]

Whitman's arrangement with the Lays apparently deteriorated, and he started dining at friends' homes as often as possible. "Evening Jan 6," one diary entry reads, "Oyster and champagne supper at Bart Bonsall's—good time." Bonsall, an old Camden friend, was co-editor of the *Camden Daily Post,* another newspaper Whitman could count upon for squibs and notices about himself. The Lays, who had paid Whitman two dollars a week for their room in addition to cooking, finally moved out on January 20, and Whitman started eating breakfast around the corner at 412 West Street, the home of Mary O. Davis, a sailor's widow. Mrs. Davis, according to Whitman's initial descriptions a youngish woman, took care of elderly people in the neighborhood. On February 24, 1885, she moved into 328 Mickle as Whitman's housekeeper.

More and more, once he had Mary Davis to serve him, he kept to his house. "I have no idea of going abroad," he told the jeweler Johnston, "couldn't do it anyhow—as I am very lame & find it difficult to get about here, even small distances." In June he sprained his ankle, and the next month he began to suffer attacks of vertigo, perhaps because of sunstroke, which had bothered him briefly during the war. Even with these problems, Mrs. Davis continued to assist—she was "in every respect (handiwork & atmosphere) the very best and most acceptable that could have befallen me," he told Mary Smith, who had recently moved to England with her family.[97]

Public events now became Whitman's muse. On February 22 he had published a sonnet called "Ah, Not This Granite Dead and Cold" ("Washington's Monument, February, 1885") in the *Philadelphia Press* to commemorate the completion of the Washington Monument. During the Civil War, when the monument had only attained a third of its final height of more than 555 feet, Whitman had fantasized that the nation's capital would eventually be moved to the West. But Washington now belonged to the world—"not yours alone, America."

> Wherever sails a ship, or house is built on land, or day or night,
> Through teeming cities' streets, indoors or out, factories or farms,
> Now, or to come, or past—where patriot wills existed or exist,
> Wherever Freedom, pois'd by Toleration, sway'd by Law,
> Stands or is rising thy true monument.

The tone resembles his prewar anti-slavery poems, such as "Resurgemus." Here also democracy is "pois'd" to prevail.

In April *Harper's Weekly* hastily commissioned a poem from Whitman in anticipation of the death of "the sick Chieftain," Ulysses S. Grant. During the war Whitman had resented the commanding general's initial resistance to a prisoner exchange, which ultimately freed his brother George, but now Grant's place in history erased that personal memory. The former president had fallen dangerously ill, and by the end of March, while he was still at work on his memoirs, his doctors thought he was finally dying of cancer.[98] Whitman's poem, "As One by One Withdraw the Lofty Actors" ("Death of General Grant"), was scheduled for publication on May 16, but as Grant then appeared to be rallying, Whitman had to add one more stanza, which Scovell said gave the poem "a graceful turn and reaction, and fits it for whatever might happen."

One of Whitman's better poems of occasion (especially considering that, according to Scovel, it was composed in an hour), it captured the autumnal mood by which both the poet and his era were now defined.

As one by one withdraw the lofty actors,
From that great play on history's stage eterne,
That lurid, partial act of war and peace—of old and new contending,
Fought out through wrath, fears, dark dismays, and many a long suspense;
All past—and since, in countless graves receding, mellowing,
Victor's and vanquish'd—Lincoln's and Lee's—now thou with them,
Man of the mighty days—and equal to the days!
Thou from the prairies!—tangled and many-vein'd and hard has been thy part,
To admiration has it been enacted!

The new stanza, added because of Grant's sudden refusal to die on schedule, read:

And still shall be:—resume thou hero heart!
Strengthen to firmest day, O rosy dawn of hope!
Tho dirge I started first, to joyful shout reverse—and thou O grave,
Wait long and long!

Grant, whose earliest of "superstitions," as he wrote in his *Memoirs,* "had always been . . . not to turn back, or stop until the thing intended was accomplished," finished his book and died on July 23, 1885.[99]

In May Whitman had heard from his newest English disciple, Ernest Rhys, a twenty-six-year-old romantic who wrote excitedly from London on the poet's sixty-sixth birthday to ask if he could prepare a selected edition of his poems for a series "called (foolishly & without reason) *the Canterbury Poets,*" to be published by Walter Scott. Rhys, who later became the principal editor for J. M. Dent's Everyman's Library, had met Bucke at a party in London, England.[100] The young editor had started a letter to Whitman two years earlier to the day (he enclosed that day's journal entry to prove it), "when living among the miners of the north." Apparently because the letter gave no details about royalties and failed to mention Bucke's name, Whitman ignored it. Rhys wrote again in July 1885, dripping with apologies for not stating the proposal in full. He still received no answer. What was wanted in England, Rhys now said, was an edition affordable by the "hue and caste" celebrated in *Leaves of Grass.* "The price of Wilson & McCormick [Whitman's publisher in Scotland in 1883]—half a guinea—practically damns the popular circulation of the book, & gives colour to the notion of its being a luxury only for the rich. What we want then is an edition for the poor, & this proposed one at only a shilling would be within reach of every man." Perhaps this edition had more political than poetic purposes (later Rhys briefly became involved in the Fabian movement), for the former coal miner, or "mining engineer," went on to say he had "a great love & desire to help the struggling mass of men, to be a true soldier in 'the War of Liberation of Humanity.'"

Finally, Whitman sent his permission after Rhys sent him an advance of ten pounds and further described himself as one "of the people, not academics; not mere University Students, but a healthy, determined, hearty band of comrades, seeking amid all their errors & foolishness to help the average, everyday men about them." This letter, strikingly similar to the invitation of Thayer and Eldridge, the young publishers of Whitman's third edition, spoke of the comradeship Whitman had long promoted—civil love or civil reform, rather than civil war. The poet's only stipulation was that the edition not be made available for sale in the United States. According to a note scrawled by Whitman over the top of Rhys's third letter, the shilling edition of 10,000 copies was a box office success, eventually selling out completely. But he told Traubel that 20,000 copies had been sold, for which he received a poor return of only $50.[101]

When *Leaves of Grass. The Poems of Walt Whitman [Selected]* was published in 1886, it resembled Rossetti's in the sense that the "selection" effectively expurgated the selection. The book followed the Osgood arrangement, but Rhys's version would have pleased the Boston district attorney. Among the many poems omitted were "Song of Myself," "From Pent-Up Aching Rivers," "I Sing the Body Electric," "A Woman Waits for Me," and "To a Common Prostitute." Although Stevens had not objected to the "Calamus" poems, Rhys, perhaps sensitive to eyebrows raised at the love of Greek life found among students and ex-students at Oxford and Cambridge, apparently did, omitting such as "Whoever You Are Holding Me Now in Hand," "City of Orgies," and "We Two Boys Together Clinging." "The dirtiest book in all the world," the poet later growled, "is the expurgated book. Rossetti expurgated, . . . and it was much the same with Rhys." But in both cases, Whitman knew in advance and acquiesced.[102]

In August Whitman's old friend James Redpath, now editor of the *North American Review,* used his connections with the *New York Tribune* to get the poet $60 for "Booth and 'The Bowery,'" a reminiscence of forty years earlier. He also paid Whitman $50 for "Slang in America," published in the *North American Review.* In the latter, Whitman defined slang as "the lawless germinal element, below all words and sentences, and behind all poetry." Slang, in a word, was indirection, the attempt to escape "bald literalism" and express oneself "illimitably." Then he stole almost directly from Emerson's statement in the "Language" section of *Nature* to argue that the mythological nature of slang brings us close to the time when things were originally named: "Thus the term *right* means literally only straight. *Wrong* primarily meant twisted, distorted. *Integrity* meant oneness. *Spirit* meant breath, or flame. A *supercilious* person was one who rais'd his eyebrows."[103] The piece is also remarkable for its many illustrations—for example, nicknames for states during the war. While it is better organized and more original than "Booth and 'The Bowery,'" Whitman later condemned it as "quite insignificant." Both essays reveal the forced rhythm of somebody writing primarily for money. And evidently Whitman had originally asked for more. When Redpath sent him the check for $50, he emphasized, "This is the very highest rate that is paid for contributions, and exactly double what is paid for nine-tenths of the articles that appear [in the *North American Review*]."[104]

That fall, on November 29, Anne Gilchrist died, apparently from breast cancer. Walt learned of the approaching end from Herbert in September but had not actually heard the news from England by December 8, when he wrote his final letter to the woman who probably loved him more than any other, except his mother. As with Grant at death's door, there was evidently no telling what the future might bring. "I know I have myself felt convinced several times during the last twelve or thirteen years of serious conditions & finales that endurance has tided over—& O I so hope that you will surmount all—& that we may yet meet each other face to face." But another of Whitman's "lofty actors" crossed the stage. When he finally heard the tragic news, his response was to say little, just as after Beatrice's death he could not write to Anne for months. "Nothing now remains but a sweet & rich memory—none more beautiful, all time, all life, all the earth," he told Herbert. "I cannot write any thing of a letter to-day. I must sit alone & think."[105]

Another dear old friend also began to show signs of life's early exhaustion. O'Connor had been in dubious health since 1883, when his daughter died suddenly at the age of twenty-five. He broke out in rheumatic sores and had trouble walking. By the end of 1885 he was still walking on "gelatine legs."

On the Sunday before Christmas, Whitman journeyed the ten miles down the snow-wet White Horse Pike to the Staffords, driven by then Mickle Street neighbor William H. Duckett in the poet's rig, a simple two-seater pulled by a sorrel pony named "Frank." The horse-and-buggy outfit was a gift of thirty-two fellow writers (including Mark Twain), organized by Thomas Donaldson, one of the earliest of the poet's Camden disciples. The poet's Sunday dinners at either the

Staffords or the Scovels had become of late almost his sole occasions for leaving 328 Mickle Street. There were three reasons for staying home, he told Burroughs: "my natural sluggishness & the paralysis of late years, the weather, & my old, stiff, slow horse, with a lurking propensity to stumble down."[106]

13

GOOD-BYE MY FANCY

Ah, whispering, something again, unseen,
Where late this heated day thou enterest at my window, door,
Thou, laving, tempering all, cool-freshing, gently vitalizing
Me, old, alone, sick, weak-down, melted-worn with sweat;
Thou, nestling, folding close and firm yet soft, companion
better than talk, book, art.

WALT WHITMAN
"To the Sun-Set Breeze"

Now established in his own home, Whitman tried to take life as it came. "The fire goes out, the clock stops, & the water-pipe bursts in the bath room," he told Susan Stafford, "but the sun shines, the bird [a canary] sings away, & Mrs. Davis is in jovial humor."[1] He looked to Camden and 328 Mickle Street as pretty much his universe now.

Shortly before the close of 1885, Burroughs wrote him what the poet termed a "Dutch Uncle" letter offering dietary advice. All his life, Whitman had dined regularly on a high-fat, low-fiber diet, including even at breakfast such high-cholesterol foods as red meat and oysters. He was usually red-faced (a sign of good health then) and heavy (by today's standards) for his height of just under six feet in old age. Impressed by an article on diet he had read in the *Fortnightly Review,* Burroughs wrote: "I am almost certain you eat too heartily and make too much blood and fat." He urged Whitman to eat only "a little meat once a day" and substitute cereals and fruits for his meat and oysters at breakfast time.[2] These days Whitman was often congested and quickly fatigued. Yet he fairly dismissed the advice, saying that he had been "very abstemious the past three years." He took a stoic's view of his unsteady health and told Traubel it was simply a matter of the looming fact that his time had come—or was steadily approaching.

Increased paralysis prevented him from walking the neighborhood or down to the ferry any longer. Later, during his first serious grapple with death in 1888, he told Traubel, "Give my love to all the boys at the ferry—tell them I dream of the ferry. . . . It all belongs to me."[3] Now his outings were by horse and buggy, though he failed to leave the house for the first two months of 1886, complaining of lameness and the "tainted" air of Camden during the winter months. Breathing complaints, increasing as his activity lessened, sparked a "summer cottage fund" drive in Boston led by O'Reilly, Kennedy, and Baxter. Whitman said he wanted to build a shack out at Timber Creek, but it is doubtful that he ever intended to so invest the sum ultimately collected ($800), which quietly disappeared into his dwindling bank account.[4]

More and more he was becoming dependent on the charitable contributions of his friends and admirers. In January 1885 the "English Offering" fund made another payment of approximately $160.[5] His income from newspaper pieces decreased, but his magazine publications continued at about the same rate as before 1885. He also continued to give his Lincoln lectures. He had already given three, in 1879, 1880, and 1881; the best estimate is that he gave a total of ten such lectures, the last one in Philadelphia in 1890.[6]

The fourth lecture took place on February 2, 1886, in Elkton, Maryland. It was arranged by Folger McKinsey, a young journalist from Philadelphia, who had recently become a reporter for the *Cecil Whig* in Elkton. McKinsey had met Whitman in 1884 through Edward Carpenter during his second visit to America. Whitman lectured to a full house, but his performance, or at least its reception, was somewhat marred by the fact that the Elkton lyceum members were used to more lively, less laid-back lecturers. The *Elkton Appeal* also increased expectations perhaps by stating that the subject of Whitman's lecture was to be "Horace Greeley." Some in Elkton thought the lecture an outright failure, unfavorably contrasting Whitman with an energetic Philadelphia clergyman who had immediately preceded him in the lyceum series. The *Whig* of February 6 endeavored to put the whole performance in perspective, saying that the lecture was a success to "those who were capable of understanding and appreciating [Whitman's] peculiar though by no means eloquent style, as eloquence is now generally understood. . . . He is 66 years of age, and so infirm from paralysis that he is unable to stand upon his feet while delivering the lecture." Whitman himself may have felt the need to compensate for his relative passivity on the platform by planting in the *Whig* of January 30 the palpably false statement that he had been "upon terms of close intimacy with Mr. Lincoln and occupied a seat by his side when the fatal shot that killed the martyred President was fired."[7] He received $25 for this reading of "The Death of Abraham Lincoln."

Despite his recurring illnesses, Whitman managed to give the lecture three more times that spring. On March 1, during a bitter "norther," he delivered it in Morgan's Hall in Camden for $30. The *Philadelphia Press* of the following day commented that "Camden's prophet is by no means without honor in his own country at the other end of Market Street Ferry." The hall was filled, and long applause broke out when the white-haired poet limped to center stage aided by "a stout stick." His voice was described as having "none of the quaver or falsetto tendency of age." Just before turning to his text, he stopped his introduction to move closer to the light and "moved the heavy chair with difficulty." Whitman concluded this lecture, as he did the others, with a reading of "O Captain! My Captain!"

On April 15, the twenty-first anniversary of the assassination, he gave the lecture again, at the Opera House on Chestnut Street in Philadelphia, receiving a whopping sum of almost $700. The event was organized and funded by Tom Donaldson and journalist Talcott Williams, who together contributed most of the amount. The audience included a number of Whitman's old and influential friends, Richard Watson Gilder, Horace Howard Furness, George W. Childs, and Dr. S. Weir Mitchell, who specialized in nervous diseases and later was consulted on Whitman's medical condition. The performance was preceded by a twenty-minute concert featuring Suppe's "Poet's Dream," Schubert's "Serenade," and Misserd's "La Paloma." The *Press* described Whitman's voice as strong. Before he began, he noted objections to reviving bitter memories of the war and said he hoped to his dying day to gather with friends every April 15 to remember Lincoln. Afterward, during an informal reception backstage, an impulsive young woman gave the bard "a rousing smack on the lips."[8]

Evidently, there was no charge to the audience in Philadelphia, but in Haddonfield, New Jersey, where the seventh lecture was delivered on May 18, the ticket proceeds were devoted to a church building fund Whitman had promised to assist. Never as an adult a supporter of organized religion, he was actually helping out a friend. The lecture netted only $22, even though it was described as "a grand success" by the *Camden Democrat.* Whitman gave it in a decrepit World's Fair building, brought over from Philadelphia years earlier and now dark and dank with rickety steps up to its stage. Yet as one witness remembered, Whitman's arrival and presence set the place aglow. "He recited as though there was no audience before him and often without looking at the paper he held. The dingy auditorium was forgotten; he took us all into his own poetic realm."[9]

From Washington O'Connor sent the poet a copy of his new book. The first two, *Harrington* and *The Good Gray Poet,* had sounded political notes, striking out against slavery and literary censorship, but *Hamlet's Notebook* attacked Shakespeare as a fraud and named Bacon as the author of the plays and sonnets. In acknowledging the gift, Whitman told his friend that he had been "looking it over,"[10] suggesting that he never read it. He had little patience for the tedious arguments illustrated with graphs and charts and the rigidly enforced rules of logic that characterized such polemics, but he admired O'Connor for even this fool's errand. "I wonder what Leaves of Grass would have been," he asked Traubel, "if I had been born of some other mother and had never met William O'Connor?" O'Connor stood higher than any other friend, even Burroughs, whom Whitman (and O'Connor) suspected at times of being slightly corrupted by the New York literary crowd.[11]

That summer a first edition of *Leaves of Grass*—Bucke's favorite of all the editions—sold for $18, and a signed Whitman letter went at auction for $80 (as more and more requests for his autograph came in by mail). In June he granted permission to Charles Morris to include "Song of the Redwood-Tree" in his four-volume *Half-Hours with the Best American Authors* (1886–87). Morris may have chosen the poem for its anti-ecological theme of man over nature, the giant sequoias giving way to westward expansion. His next book was entitled *The*

Aryan Race: Its Origins and Achievements (1888).[12] All sorts were drawn to Whitman's poetry and patriotism, from the grand capitalist Andrew Carnegie to the socialist Horace Traubel. Whitman was even "mainstream" enough to have an essay included in Allen Thorndike Rice's portly volume entitled *Reminiscences of Abraham Lincoln by Distinguished Men of His Time* (1886). Other contributors included Frederick Douglass, Henry Ward Beecher, Robert G. Ingersoll, Charles A. Dana (one of the first reviewers of *Leaves of Grass* in 1855), and southwestern humorist David Ross Locke ("Petroleum V. Nasby"). Never comfortable in literary circles, Whitman considered his essay "unworthy the theme."[13]

Much of what he was writing these days recycled earlier material. In Rice's volume he quoted himself from a Civil War notebook (also incorporated in *Memoranda During the War* and *Specimen Days*) about seeing Lincoln almost daily and even occasionally "pass[ing] a word" with him. He contrasted Lincoln with the still beloved Washington, presciently hinting that the Civil War president, "far less European, far more Western, original, essentially non-conventional," would soon replace the first president as the democratic father of his country—"one raised through the commonest average of life—a rail splitter and a flat-boatman!"[14]

One essay that grew almost exponentially with revision, "How I Made a Book," appeared in Talcott Williams's *Philadelphia Press* on July 11, 1886. Ultimately, it became the second half of "A Backward Glance O'er Travel'd Roads," which was first the opening piece in *November Boughs* (1888) and then, as Whitman's "last word" on *Leaves of Grass,* appropriately included at the end of the 1888 issue. The first half of "A Backward Glance" comes from "My Book and I," which would appear in *Lippincott's Monthly Magazine* for January 1887.[15]

It is perhaps unfortunate that Whitman did not make "A Backward Glance" a preface instead of an afterword to the 1888 edition and the others that followed before his death. In its present placement readers usually ignore it, and when they do read it they are often put off by the awkward prose that makes up its first half, which is somewhat chatty and anecdotal. In the last half of the essay, however, the old metaphors about the foreground of *Leaves of Grass* are recycled: its "practical and general plowing, planting, seeding, and occupation of the ground, till everything was fertilized, rooted, and ready to start its own way, for good or bad." Here the poet names the classical literary sources—the Old and New Testament, Shakespeare, Ossian, the Hindu poems, Homer, Dante—and wonders why he did not succumb to the anxiety of authorship. He was not overwhelmed and intimidated by these literary masters, he writes, because he read them outdoors, in the woods and on the beaches of Long Island ("probably to better advantage for me than in any library or indoor room—it makes such difference *where* you read"). He also credits the influence of Poe, not the poems that employed conventional meter and rhyme or the stories, many of which he considered morbid, but the Raven's theory that there can be no such thing as a long poem. This admission may strike us as odd when we consider "Song of Myself" the first American epic of world-class achievement, but "Song of Myself" is in fact a series of short poems. It is a rhapsody of the self that critics have generally failed to fit into any one recognizable structure.[16] It was the accident of Ryerson Street. There are patterns, of course, but just when one seems to be satisfactory, something seemingly out of place appears. The poem is sheer music, a symphony in the opinion of Gay Wilson Allen, but when he revised his *Walt Whitman Handbook,* he removed his attempt at explaining the detailed structure of the poem.[17]

"A Backward Glance" also anticipates the school of criticism in this century known as Reader Response. "I round and finish little, if anything" he announces in the second half of "A Backward Glance." "The reader will always have his or her part to do, just as much as I have had mine." This philosophy reflects the theory behind his hospital work that he gave his soldiers only what he got in return. The best thing Whitman brought to the wounded and lonely soldiers, far from home, was—as O'Connor put it in *The Good Gray Poet*—"some practical token that they are not forsaken." Today that role has been dubbed "psychological nurse," but the term possibly misses the point because Whitman was in no way clinical or distanced from his soldiers anymore than he is distanced from his readers in "Song of Myself," where he puts his arm around the reader or blows him—or *her*—full of "grit." "Behold," he insists in what became Section 40 of the poem, "I do not give lectures or a little charity, / When I give I give myself." The war years enhanced the poet's appreciation of his earlier celebration of democracy. They were "the real parturition years (more than 1776–83) of this henceforth homogeneous nation. Without those three or four years and the experiences they gave," he insisted, "'Leaves of Grass' would not now be existing."[18] Whitman's "I" in "Song of Myself" could not exist without its "you": the soldiers peopled the apparitions in the original poem. Yet Whitman's fraternalism, his love of society in the rough, is balanced by his love of American individualism. He had stressed this point in "Democracy" in the late 1860s (and then in *Democratic Vistas*). "While the ambitious thought of my song is to help the forming of a great aggregate Nation," he says in "How I Made a Book" (and later in "A Backward Glance"), "it is, perhaps, altogether through the forming of myriads of fully develop'd and enclosing individuals."[19]

As he revised his old essays and published them, Whitman also revised his past by destroying more manuscripts and letters. Nevertheless, vast amounts of primary material survived to be collected in the Library of Congress and university libraries. Whitman had trunks of material in Camden. When he bought the Mickle Street house, he had them shipped from Washington, where they had been stored, possibly at the residence of J. Hubley Ashton. When Mary Costelloe came to see him during her visits back to Philadelphia, she noted that his uncarpeted bedroom, which ran almost the entire half of the upstairs area, contained "a collection of trunks, never more than half unpacked since he came from Washington, in which you may see bundles of old letters, souvenirs of his mother, and a sea of manuscript."[20] And though he owned only one copy of the 1855 *Leaves,* he hoarded multiple copies of his other books—he possessed at least fifty copies of *As a Strong Bird on Pinions Free*—which he gave out to visiting friends and admirers. One of the recipients was the Irishman Bram Stoker, who later used Whitman as the model for the murderous count in *Dracula* (1897).[21]

Personal sorrow arrived on September 3, 1886, when Jeff's elder daughter, Mannahatta, died of enteritis at the age of twenty-six. Hattie and her younger sister, Jessie, had done well since their mother's death in 1873, going to a finishing school in the East and visiting the poet in Camden yearly. At the poet's suggestion, Jeff and Mattie had named her Mannahatta, as he had once named himself Paumanok. Unlike Jessie, who lived until 1957 and was initially called California, Hattie retained her symbolic name. In a way, her death took away something of his dear mother as well, for it was Louisa Whitman who had helped Mattie care for the two girls during and after the war. The day after the burial Walt told Jeff, "I think every hour of the day, (& night too when awake) of Hattie—& of how it must be there with you & Jess." To mark the mournful event, Walt enclosed a newspaper clipping containing the final lines of a poem by Longfellow, even to Whitman still America's premier poet of home and hearth.[22]

In spite of the loss, Whitman's health was relatively good during the fall and the winter of 1886–87. He continued his habit of planting news items about himself. In the *Philadelphia Press* of February 1 he—or perhaps editor Talcott Williams—wrote: "Yesterday was Walt Whitman's best day for a long time. He went out phaeton-riding in the mid-day. . . . Yesterday, too, he received a warm letter from Alfred Tennyson commencing 'Dear Old Man.'"

Whitman had been something of a regional celebrity since the publication of the first *Leaves of Grass*, but now his fame was spreading. William Sloane Kennedy, who had moved to the Belmont section of Boston and was working for the *Boston Herald*, was writing a book about him, which Kennedy felt would be superior to Bucke's biographical account. Apparently, the journalist did not know of Whitman's role in the Bucke book. Ironically, he fell into the same trap when he let Whitman read his manuscript and suggest revisions. But in Kennedy's case, the book, *Reminiscences of Walt Whitman*, was not published until 1896, so he had time to recover from some of Whitman's changes. He later edited *Walt Whitman's Diary in Canada* (1904) and wrote an impassioned study entitled *The Fight of a Book for the World* (1926).

In *Reminiscences* he would respond passionately to what he perceived as Symonds's implications about Whitman's sexual orientation in his 1893 book, *Walt Whitman: A Study*. Most of the Camden poet's intimates were shocked and disgusted at the suggestions of homosexuality that—with one exception (the Griswold review of 1855)—were just beginning to emerge. Eldridge scoffed at the idea in a letter to Burroughs.[23] Kennedy's remarks in his preface characterized the general response: "We here in America were astounded that it seemed to [Symonds] necessary in his work on Walt Whitman to relieve the Calamus poems of the vilest of all possible interpretations. It was a sad revelation to us of the state of European morals, that even the ethical perfume of those noblest utterances on friendship could not save them from such a fate."[24]

Whitman continued to speak publicly, appearing on the evening of February 22 at the Philadelphia Contemporary Club. The *Philadelphia Press* reported the event, but its garbled facts demonstrate that Whitman had nothing to do with the story this time. The poems he read—"The Mystic Trumpeter" and the section of "Out of the Cradle Endlessly Rocking" introducing the "Two feather'd guests from Alabama"—were renamed in the article as "The Mysterious Trumpeter" and "Two Birds." The article also reported, perhaps accurately, that the poet had to be coaxed to read "Out of the Cradle," which he still regarded privately as "A Word Out of the Sea." Two in attendance that night were Daniel G. Brinton, a professor of anthropology at the University of Pennsylvania, and Horace L. Traubel.[25]

This is the first evidence of Traubel's active role in Whitman's literary life. Before long he would become the aging poet's amanuensis, errand boy, and lifeline to the world. He began simply as another of those young men in the neighborhood Whitman took a liking to. The difference was Traubel's intelligence and his deep conviction that everything the poet did and everything he touched would be of the greatest importance someday.

Horace Logo Traubel was born in 1858. The son of Jewish immigrants from Germany, he grew up in Whitman's Camden neighborhood, where his parents moved after first settling in Germantown. The Traubel family had been neighbors of George and Lou Whitman before Walt moved to Camden. Walt was well acquainted with Horace's parents, Maurice and Katherine, and also his sister, Agnes, who married Thomas B. Harned, a Camden lawyer. Whitman and Traubel fondly recalled years later that the two had first met on the day George's only son died. Horace, who was eighteen, attended the funeral with his parents. They talked afterward and chanced to meet again on the ferry an hour later. Traubel remembered the details better than Whitman, but the poet did recall, as he told Traubel, "that on the boat you bought some wild flowers from an old nigger mammy who had been all day trying to sell them in the city and was going home dispirited: you bought the flowers and handed them to me. Do you remember that?"[26]

Horace trained as a printer. After he left school, he became a typesetter at the *Camden Evening Visitor* printing office—attaining the rank of foreman at the age of sixteen. Afterward he worked in his father's lithographic shop in Philadelphia and became a paymaster in a factory. By the time of his daily visits to Whitman in March 1888, or soon afterward, he was working as a clerk in the Philadelphia Farmers and Mechanics' Bank, a job he lost in 1902 because of his socialist leanings and publications. Traubel subsequently corresponded with countless leftists and reformers, including Eugene Debs, Emma Goldman, and Upton Sinclair, but at the time he met Whitman, he was a follower of Felix Adler, founder of the Society for Ethical Culture in 1876. Adler had forsaken orthodox religion (and a career as a rabbi) because of his belief, like Kant's, that the deity could not be demonstrated and that morality or "practical reason" could be established without relying on theology. Today, he is remembered mainly by educational theorists, who tend to dismiss him because his Victorian views conflict with their more psychologically based pedagogy.[27] Even though Traubel was an officer in the Philadelphia branch of the Society for Ethical Culture, it was Adler who was more attuned to Whitman's thought. Though he supported women's rights, Adler stopped at outright equality for fear that motherhood as a vocation would decline.

In 1890 Traubel founded the *Conservator,* which after Whitman's death and until his own in 1919, served primarily as an organ of Whitman worship and as a rebuke to anyone who (in Traubel's opinion) was unfair to the poet's memory or his poems. Most of its contributors belonged to the Whitman Fellowship, which Traubel also founded; several of its members were homosexual or bisexual, including

Traubel, who carried on an affair with Gustave Wiksell, a Boston dentist.[28] Three books have been written about Traubel (by sympathetic socialists), and he wrote three monographs containing political chants.[29] But his greatest contribution to world literature is *With Walt Whitman in Camden,* a day-to-day summary, with quotations, of his generally half-hour meetings with the aging poet. Its first volume was published in 1906, and two more appeared during his lifetime. Six more have since been published, the final two appearing in 1996.[30]

Traubel was thirty when he started keeping notes on their daily conversations, but Whitman often talked to him as if he were younger. Traubel fancied himself at times as the next poet of the masses. He rode the ferry and loitered about Philadelphia as Whitman had enjoyed the Brooklyn Ferry and "loafed" in New York. When the poet was largely confined to Mickle Street, he frequently invited Traubel to become his eyes and ears, and the younger man seems to have responded with remarks he thought the old man might appreciate. On election night 1888 he described "the bands playing: the singing and whistling: the drunken gentlemen and the respectable toughs," adding that Whitman "was all ears for it. Especially for 'the drunken gentlemen and respectable toughs.'"

Whitman often flattered Traubel as a Whitmanesque observer (while largely undercutting his socialist views). Once when Traubel was praising factory life, Whitman advised him to "jot down" these incidents of human worth, saying he had the "considerable faculty for telling a story." But he added significantly, "I'm afraid sometimes you're a little too much inclined to the didactic." He thought Traubel's moral earnestness pressed him too far in the direction of the reformer. "You will probably worm out of it," he told the thirty-year-old, "but that's how you seem to be at this stage." Sometimes they quarreled, but as Whitman became more and more dependent on Traubel, he usually withdrew. On this occasion, he ended by predicting that the younger man would find the right road and "travel it with distinction."[31] *With Walt Whitman in Camden* reflects Traubel's effort to report the last four years of Whitman's life as accurately as possible, and it is to his credit that he included these less-than-flattering accounts of himself.

Whitman delivered two Lincoln lectures, his eighth and ninth, in 1887. The first was at the Unitarian Church in Camden on April 6, where one auditor took offense when Whitman referred to Lincoln's death as a "murder."[32] It is not known how much this lecture paid, if anything, but the next one, at the Madison Square Theater in New York on the afternoon of April 14, was one of the most lucrative of all. The jeweler J. H. Johnston organized it, as he had the first one in 1879, ensuring the best accommodations and advertising. Escorted to New York by his old Quaker friend Robert Pearsall Smith, who was back on a visit from England, Whitman received $600 for the lecture, including $350 from Andrew Carnegie for the rent of a theater box he did not occupy that evening. The balance came from the sale of reserved-seat tickets at $1.50 and general admission at $1.00.[33] Whitman stayed at the Westminster Hotel, where he was visited by Burroughs and other old friends on April 13. In fact, more than 250 callers paid homage to the poet, in the same suite Charles Dickens occupied when Whitman wrote about him in the 1840s.[34] The next day Whitman gave his speech before a sparsely filled auditorium. The Gilders and the Stedmans were on hand, of course. And there Burroughs met James Russell Lowell for the first time. He joined him in a box also occupied by Charles Eliot Norton, one of the earliest admirers of *Leaves of Grass.*

The curtain rose at four o'clock sharp on a stage set to suggest a drawing room. The enfeebled poet, his famous gray hair turned white, entered from the right, escorted by Bill Duckett, a sailor who was an acquaintance of Mrs. Davis's. According to a report in the *New York Times* of April 15, the old poet "leaned on the arm of a young man, supporting himself with a cane. He came slowly to the table, sat in the chair beside it, and laid his cane on the floor. The audience gave him the greeting of friends to a friend. He fumbled a little as his hand sought his glasses and adjusted them. Then he took up his manuscript and read." Whitman once again suggested he was present, perhaps at Lincoln's side, at the assassination, according to one auditor writing down his recollections in 1922. Stuart Merrill described Whitman's address as "as gripping as the reports of the tragedies of Eschylus." Applause broke out from the audience, which also included Mark Twain, Moncure Conway, Edward Eggleston, John Hay, and the sculptor Augustus Saint-Gaudens.[35] Following the lecture, Stedman's six-year-old daughter ran onto the stage and gave the poet a huge bouquet of lilacs. Whitman hoisted her to his lap and kissed her.[36]

Exhilarated by the experience, Whitman returned to Camden to discover that, more than ever, he was the subject of wildly disapproving articles in the press. He was attacked by Thomas Wentworth Higginson in several pieces published by *Harper's Bazaar*, apparently triggered by Sylvester Baxter's effort to secure Whitman a government pension for his hospital work.[37] Higginson had been antagonistic to Whitman throughout his literary career. When the 1860 *Leaves of Grass* was going through the press in Boston, he occasionally visited the offices of Thayer and Eldridge. Once, Eldridge later told Burroughs, Higginson "saw a copy of L of G on my desk and said that the book always made him sea-sick having first become acquainted with it on a voyage to the West Indies. . . . He further showed his disgust by saying that if Walt's book represented health then he (Hig.) was diseased."[38] Higginson, a wounded Civil War veteran who led one of the first black regiments into battle, not only castigated Whitman for his failure to fight in the war but—in a piece of March 26 entitled "Women and Men. The Victory of the Weak"—reiterated earlier attacks made by Sidney Lanier that characterized Whitman as a "dandy" for his depiction of roughs.[39]

Lanier's criticisms of Whitman's poetry had appeared in *The English Novel and the Principle of Its Development* (1883), a book based on lectures that Lanier had given at Johns Hopkins University in the winter of 1881. A Civil War veteran, but from the Confederate side, Lanier died in September of that year, never healthy after his near-death experiences as a prisoner-of-war. He in turn was responding to Whitman's 1881 essay "The Poetry of the Future," which attacked the manners of conventional poetry as a form of "dandyism." Lanier felt that Whitman's idealization of the rough was the true dandyism—"the dandyism of the roustabout," who in no way represented the accomplishments of American democracy. "What would our courtly and philosophic Thomas Jefferson look like, if you should put this slouch hat on him, and open his shirt-front at the bosom, and set him to presiding over a ruffianly nomination?" he asked pointedly.

For Lanier, freedom in poetry was no better than anarchy in politics. "This poetry is free, it is asserted, because it is independent of form. But this claim is also too late. It should have been made at least before the French Revolution." Citing the primitivistic Section 32 of "Song of Myself," where the poet announces that he "could turn and live with animals, they are so placid and self-contain'd," Lanier suggested that the becalmed animals must be cows; for it would be otherwise if Whitman "were taking one of his favorite night-strolls in the woods of Bengal rather than of New Jersey."[40] The poetry of the future, Lanier asserted, lay not in the abandonment of forms but in their extension. Lanier was an accomplished flutist whose theory of poetry paralleled his respect for mathematical precision in music. Only three years before, he had written Whitman praising *Leaves of Grass* as a "modern song" about "the absolute personality of the person, the sufficiency of the man's manhood *to* the man, which you have propounded in such strong and beautiful rhythms." Though he admitted that they would never agree "in all points connected with artistic form," he felt his dissent insignificant in "the presence of that unbounded delight which I take in all the bigness and bravery of all your ways and thoughts." When Traubel later read the letter aloud to Whitman, the poet retorted: "He first tells me he disagrees with me in all points connected with artistic form and then speaks of me as the master of strong and beautiful rhythms. That hardly seems to [agree]: I don't say I am one or t'other but I know I ain't both."[41]

What Lanier may have intended with his phrase "strong and beautiful rhythms" was Whitman's celebration of his own personality, which was a law unto itself. He told Bayard Taylor, who introduced him to Whitman's work, that *Leaves of Grass* "was a real refreshment to me—like rude salt spray in your face—in spite of its enormous fundamental error that a thing is good because it is natural."[42] Burroughs had said something very similar about Whitman's conversation after spending time with him in Ocean Grove in 1884. There was a quality about Whitman's verse that attracted the conventionally minded in spite of themselves—and Burroughs is included here, in the sense that he wrote nature books respected by the literati who hated Whitman. It may have been—and here Burroughs is an exception—the same thing that attracted Symonds, Whitman's possibly homosexual celebration of male friendship.

Bayard Taylor, who had lashed out at Whitman and his supporters during the Anglo-American debate of 1876, was an even more surprising crypto-convert. He and Lanier were no doubt brought together when they shared centennial poet honors, with Lanier assigned the task of writing the cantata. Earlier Taylor had written Whitman two letters in the vein of Lanier's letter. On November 12, 1866, he admired Whitman's "remarkable powers of expression, your broad, vital reverence for humanity." A month later he claimed to have read *Leaves of Grass* "many times" and praised Whitman's "awe and wonder and reverence and beauty of Life, as expressed in the human body, with the physical attraction and delight of mere contact which it inspires, and that tender and noble love of man for man which once certainly existed, but now almost seems to have gone out of the experience of the race."[43] Whitman saved these letters along with Lanier's and gave them to Traubel, knowing that some day they would see the light of publication.

During the spring of 1887 Herbert Gilchrist's *Anne Gilchrist: Her Life and Writings* appeared, and Whitman told Herbert he thought it was "making quite a ripple" in America. He had gone back to England for a short time and would return there periodically. Herbert was possessive of Whitman, and when Bucke asked him for the poet's letters to his mother, he refused. Likewise, when Herbert asked Whitman for permission to publish extracts of those letters in his book, the poet demurred. "I do not know," he told Herbert, "that I can furnish any good reason, but I feel to keep these utterances exclusively to myself." Later Harned published the correspondence between Anne Gilchrist and the poet.[44] That June Herbert arrived back in Camden and began a portrait of Whitman. The original picture was eventually exhibited in England to much applause; today it remains there in a private collection. Herbert also painted a copy, which now hangs in the Van Pelt Library at the University of Pennsylvania.

Herbert vied with Traubel for Whitman's attention, just as he had with Harry Stafford. The poet loved Herbert as a son and tried to put his work (both the Gilchrist biography and the portrait) in the kindest light. But like Logan Smith, Herbert was one of those Whitman disciples who sought acceptance in the very artistic establishments that were threatened by Whitman's disavowal of conventional art and literature. He hobnobbed with British artists but was profoundly disappointed at never gaining admission to the Royal Academy of Art. Shortly before Whitman's death, he settled on Long Island, but never totally succeeded as an artist. Like his sister Beatrice, he took his own life, in 1914 at the age of fifty-nine. Herbert may have suspected that he had not been accepted into Whitman's academy of art either. He never cut the pages in his autographed copy of *November Boughs*.[45]

During the summer of 1887, when Gilchrist was completing Whitman's portrait, another artist was also competing for the poet's time. While Herbert painted from one angle in the Mickle Street parlor, Sidney Morse sculpted a bust of the poet from another. Morse, whose artistic career had, like Whitman's, begun in midlife, was a better writer than a sculptor and had been the editor of the *Radical* when Anne Gilchrist's essay on Whitman was published there. Before that he had been a Unitarian minister with short stints in Cincinnati (succeeding Moncure Conway) and Haverhill, Massachusetts. He knew most of the transcendentalists and had sculpted Emerson (his best work) before moving to Washington to make a bust of President Cleveland in 1887. Afterward, Morse stopped in Camden to work on Whitman. He had first known the poet during the World's Fair eleven years earlier, when Whitman sat for him in his Philadelphia studio. Sometimes, according to Morse, he read from his own poetry as Morse sculpted—a passage from "Song of Myself" or "The Singer in the Prison."

On his arrival at Mickle Street, Morse could see that the past decade had wrought its changes. "I found Whitman," he recalled, "much more crippled, and quieter in manner than we met before. . . . He was, however, in a less perturbed frame of mind." He said Whitman recalled that their first meeting had taken place during "the darkest period of my life, but before the summer had gone there came that burst of sunlight over the sea." He was referring to his displeasure at being ignored by the American centennial authorities and his delight at being supported by English readers who were purchasing the centennial edition of *Leaves of Grass.* (At the same time, the arrival of Anne Gilchrist and her family also lifted his spirits.) "Forevermore I shall love old England," he told Morse. "With no discounting of friends at home, I must say that English business stands apart in my thought from all else."[46]

The busts Morse cast in 1876 were failures, but Whitman liked the ones he did in 1887. They were eventually exhibited in New England, but their reception there was unenthusiastic. At Whitman's behest, Kennedy struggled to get one positioned in "some appropriate permanent gallery" in Boston. A year later it had been "refused everywhere there in high quarters." It was finally accepted, Whitman noted, by the Concord School of Philosophy, where it remained as long as that institution, one of Alcott's last noble projects, existed. Mary Costelloe tried unsuccessfully to find a home for another Morse Whitman in London. The success of Morse's busts (and Herbert's painting), it seems, paralleled the course that Whitman's reputation had taken in the past. They were accepted where friends resided—by the Pre-Raphaelites and their successors in London and by Alcott, always friendly to Whitman, in Concord.[47]

In December 1887 the painter Thomas Eakins took the ferry over from Philadelphia, where he was an art teacher at the Pennsylvania Academy of Fine Arts, and began a painting of Whitman. He had first been introduced to the poet in November by Talcott Williams. According to Traubel, Whitman "'remembered well' his first meeting with Eakins," who simply showed up two or three weeks later with his canvas and "painted like a fury."[48] As Whitman told Traubel a year later, "The two pictures [Gilchrist's and Eakins's] sort of bark at each other, they are so unalike." Whitman preferred the Eakins portrait because it depicted him "without feathers." Eakins himself was thought by many in Philadelphia to be "uncouth" and lacking social graces. He painted Whitman in his own (and Whitman's) image—austere and primitively realistic. Herbert, more attuned to mainstream art of the day, painted a romantic, pre-Raphaelite poet, quietly adding "Italian curls" when the portrait was exhibited in London.[49]

Whitman was becoming a commodity by 1887. That spring and summer an admirer named Carl Sadakichi Hartmann visited and soon afterward attempted to found a Walt Whitman Society in Boston, soliciting funds apparently without Whitman's permission. Whitman seemed annoyed and announced that he had gotten Baxter to squelch the movement. Another intruder that summer was a "philosopher-farmer" from Alabama named John Newton Johnson. He arrived in Camden on May 18 and remained exactly thirty-nine days, visiting the poet almost daily. A Confederate war veteran, he had memorized nearly all of Whitman's poems. Whitman had corresponded with Johnson for the last thirteen years and thought of the cotton planter as his ideal reader, but when that reader talked back by offering criticisms of some of the changes Whitman made from one edition to the next, the fantasy was over. The poet became bored and occasionally feigned other business when Johnson showed up.[50] A third admirer, Grace Channing, was more difficult to discourage because she was O'Connor's niece. In June 1887 she proposed a calendar of quotations from *Leaves of Grass.* When O'Connor visited Whitman in Camden for the last time in October, he was enthusiastic about the project. As with the Whitman Society, Whitman was at first passive and then alternately for and against the idea, but he was finally relieved when Stedman failed, after repeated attempts, to find a publisher for the enterprise. *Leaves of Grass,* the poet noted (and subsequent books of quotations have verified), could not be quoted piecemeal.

But there was another reason for the project's failure: it came with a startling design created by the portrait painter Charles Walter Stetson. Stetson's wife, Charlotte Perkins Gilman, was a close friend of Grace Channing. Stetson himself had come a long, if not enlightened, way in his admiration of Whitman. In an 1883 diary entry, he was struck after bathing by the contrast between "the softness of my skin" and the brute sexuality found in *Leaves of Grass,* which he hoped his wife would not read. "I did not want her to think all men such animals as Whitman described them." The design that Stetson envisioned for the calendar featured the poet's head, painted in a warm tint and surrounded by "a sort of wreath of lilac leaves and pine (with cones and needles of course)." He also wanted the "leaves of grass" to be depicted as growing out of "a half-buried inoffensive skull," to suggest the idea that change, even death, pointed toward life.[51]

Although Boston was still rejecting Whitman—or at least Morse's bust—the rest of America was coming around. The country was about to celebrate another centennial, this time of the Constitution, and Whitman was formally invited to participate in the festivities in Philadelphia, to compose and read a "patriotic poem commemorative of the triumph of popular institutions." But this time America was too late. "I have been pressingly invited," he told Kennedy, "but cannot go—(A crowd & hubbub are no place for me)." The Constitutional Centennial Commission never got its poem either, even though Tennyson wrote Whitman that fall, praising "the great founders of the American Constitution, whose work you are to celebrate."[52]

Instead Whitman wrote "As the Greek's Signal Flame," saluting John Greenleaf Whittier on his eightieth birthday. It appeared in the *New York Herald* and the *Boston Advertizer* on December 17.

> As the Greek's signal flame, by antique records told,
> Rose from the hill-top, like applause and glory,
> Welcoming in fame some special veteran, hero,
> With rosy tinge reddening the land he'd served,
> So I aloft from Mannahatta's ship-fringed shore,
> Lift high a kindled brand for thee, Old Poet.

For at least one reason, this was an odd poem for Whitman to write. He was under the false impression that Whittier, who never publicly committed himself on *Leaves of Grass,* had pitched his copy of the first edition into the fire after encountering an indelicacy. Whittier thanked Whitman on January 13, saying that his "brother writers" had been very generous to him. This particular phrasing must have struck Whitman as awkward, for many of Whitman's brother writers had not been generous. The two poets never met.[53]

❈ ❈ ❈

The year 1887 was a good one for Whitman. He published more than a dozen essays or poems, given his most memorable Lincoln lecture, and earned through lecture fees, publications, and donations

$2,575.98, an income far in excess of the average of that of most households in his working-class neighborhood of Camden.[54] In 1888 this literary activity also brought the poet another articulate admirer. Charles T. Sempers, a student at Harvard, wrote to convey an invitation to lecture at the college and be a guest at the home of Professor William James. Sempers called Whitman's attention to an essay that he had published on the poet in the *Harvard Monthly* earlier that year.[55] A native of Philadelphia and, he said, familiar "with the quiet streets of Camden," in 1880 he had attended Whitman's second Lincoln lecture with Kennedy, then still a journalist in Philadelphia. "After the lecture," he wrote, "my friend the reporter went up to Whitman to speak with him about some matter, when the venerable, patriarchal-looking poet put his arms around my friend's neck and kissed him,—a stripling he had never seen before that night." Later that summer Sempers purchased a copy of *Leaves of Grass* at McKay's bookstore, and a year later came across Whitman's work in Stedman's 1885 anthology of American poets. From that time on he became a serious reader and admirer of *Leaves of Grass.*

The *Harvard Monthly* article, "Walt Whitman and His Philosophy," is one of the earliest attempts by someone outside Whitman's various circles of support to identify what is most admired about *Leaves of Grass.* Whitman was a poet, Sempers declared, whom the American people could no longer afford to ignore. "He has spiritualized trade, commerce, the toils of lowly men. The city with its belching furnaces and foundries, its rattling factories, its noise and whir and roar, is the incarnation of a human energy which is divine. A lover of nature in all her moods, he loves the city with its streaming multitudes. . . . Other poets have denounced the materialism of our age. He has found a soul in its materialism."[56]

Ironically, Sempers, who was first attracted to Whitman by his Lincoln lecture, charged that Whitman "deserves nothing from the world as a writer of prose," alluding to the "wild and thorny maze of words" of *Democratic Vistas.* He was more on target in his despair that later poems introduced or preceded earlier, truly great poems in the later editions of *Leaves of Grass.* After praising "When Lilacs Last in the Dooryard Bloom'd" and "Out of the Cradle Endlessly Rocking," he advised the new reader of Whitman to "avoid the inscriptions which are placed first in the edition of 1882 and subsequent editions." Most important, Sempers joined Lanier in arguing against Whitman's seemingly Jacksonian brand of literary democracy, which—as Lanier suggested—brought Jefferson down to the level of a disheveled Brother Jonathan, the character that today represents "Uncle Sam." Whitman ("like Wordsworth") was most successful when he violated this theory of democracy in his poetry and made distinctions based on merit. "We saw that in theory he held all deeds to be of equal worth, but in the main he denies this both in his writings and in his life, which has been one of the noblest and most humane lives that ever honored our land."[57]

Whitman probably read the essay, because he sent it to O'Connor, though without comment. He gave Sempers's letter to Traubel later that year—dismissing it as "from Harvard University: some one's avowal." There is no evidence that he responded to the invitation that it contained, but in any case he was too weak by then to accept it. It is doubtful he knew anything about William James in 1888, except his relationship to Henry, whose philosopher father Whitman did admire. As for the "junior" Henry, Whitman told Traubel that year, apparently never forgiving the novelist for his review of *Drum-Taps,* "I don't see anything above the common in him: he has a vogue—but surely his vogue won't last: he don't stand permanently for anything."[58]

Almost immediately after 1888 commenced the poet complained of more severe problems—"inveterate constipation, & bad kidney tribulation," he told Bucke, who from then on kept an almost daily correspondence with the poet about his medical problems. Ernest Rhys arrived that December for his first visit to Camden and then proceeded to New York and Boston after New Year's, where he lectured on Whitman and related subjects, stirring up the old controversy about the literary worth of *Leaves of Grass.* When he first crossed the ice-clogged Delaware from Philadelphia, he found Mickle Street dark and deserted, reminding him of "a thoroughfare in some small French town." By then Whitman was moving with more difficulty because of his paralysis. He also complained of weakness in his limbs, eyesight, and breathing. Eakins had returned to finish his portrait, which Whitman hyperbolized as the picture of a "poor, old, blind, despised & dying King." As Traubel started his daily record of conversations on March 28, we know that he steadily complained and declined.[59]

A study of the poet's temperament from 1873, when his health crises began, and even earlier, during the war, when he faced occasional problems of serious proportion, suggests that he had a remarkable capacity to look beyond his medical situation. He managed to find the same poetic rhythms in life he had come to celebrate first in *Leaves of Grass.* That he kept on writing poems, making "Sands at Seventy" an annex to his life's work, goes a long way to reinforce this impression. Furthermore, Whitman's tone in making literary judgments on conventional poets as well as modestly asserting his own position remained full of calm confidence. Traubel records occasional states of depression over health problems in 1888 and afterward, but they give way on almost every visit to lively discussions of subjects well beyond the "caged" location of the second-story bedroom.

On June 2 Whitman suffered a series of paralytic strokes that almost killed him.[60] He had just celebrated his sixty-ninth birthday at the Harneds' house at 556 Federal Street. All the Camden regulars were on hand, including Traubel and his girlfriend, Anne Montgomerie. Jeff had visited Walt on May 29 but did not stay for the party. Kennedy came down from Boston. It seemed almost like a family event, and Whitman looked "animated." He returned to the Harneds' the following Sunday. Bucke was on a surprise visit to Camden that day and joined the party for the midday dinner. Afterward Whitman drove him to the ferry in his buggy. Instead of returning directly to Mickle Street, he drove north into the country and finally to the banks of the Delaware River at Pea Shore. There he caught a chill while gazing at the sun as it disappeared over the horizon. That night in bed he suffered the first of three strokes, the other two coming in the next two days.

At first Whitman tried to weather out the attacks by himself, but Mrs. Davis, Harned, Bucke, and Traubel soon hovered over him. By this time he had suffered six strokes since 1873. His friends were particularly worried because he slept that week with his bedroom door locked. On the following Saturday he suffered another "spell" and seemed to be on the edge, spending the day delirious and hallucinating that O'Connor and Burroughs were downstairs. Fearing the worst, Bucke recommended that literary executors be named and suggested himself, Harned, and Donaldson. When Whitman rallied on June 12, he substituted Traubel for Donaldson, perhaps because he astutely sensed that, in spite of his practical assistance, Donaldson was insincere in his praise of *Leaves of Grass.*[61]

Whitman was unable to leave his bedroom for almost the next year. He had a series of nurses—first Nathan Baker, an intern under S. Weir Mitchell, and later W. A. Musgrove and Ed Wilkins—paid by not-so-secret contributions from Bucke, Harned, and others. Warren Fritzinger, an adopted son of Mrs. Davis, was on the scene but not yet on the job as nurse. Bucke also sent over Dr. William Osler from Philadelphia, who was somewhat distracted by the clutter of Whitman's bedroom ("The magazines and newspapers, piled higher than the desk, covered the floor so completely that I had to pick my way by the side of the wall of the room to get to the desk") and brought him wine and cocoa for his "feebleness." As in the past, Whitman blamed his sickness on the war but had no regrets when he remembered the soldiers he had aided. He told Traubel from his sickbed, with proof sheets of *November Boughs* scattered about, "I suppose I should have been free of all this today—free at least in part—if in those last years 63–4–5 I had gone off to a place of safety, avoided the hospitals—kept away from them—taken special care of my own person: but here I am, sick, nearly gone, and I do not regret what I did. That was no time for doubt."[62]

Whitman credited Bucke with saving his life. The other thing that probably saved him was the putting to press of *November Boughs,* which he couldn't have completed without Traubel. The new book should have been called "December Boughs," Traubel joked in frustration while waiting for a piece Whitman had sold to appear before the book could be published.[63] Mainly, it contained the essays and poems published since *Specimen Days,* including poems written in an open contract for the *New York Herald* between January 27 and May 27, 1888. Like *Two Rivulets,* it was a potpourri of prose and poetry. The poems, published under the heading of "Sands at Seventy" became the first annex to the final issues of *Leaves of Grass.*

By the time of his strokes, Whitman had finished all but the last prose piece, an essay on Elias Hicks. It seemed almost a miracle (to both Whitman and Traubel) that he managed to complete it that summer in the shadow of both a severe illness and a prolonged convalescence. He felt a stern duty to write about this early influence, as he had felt when he wrote his essay on Paine, and writing it brought Whitman back from death's door to recall two fathers: Walter Whitman, Sr., and Emerson. Hicks, born like Whitman on Paumanok, or Long Island, had helped to shape the poet of *Leaves of Grass.* His nostalgia for the old Quaker took him back to his boyhood days when Walter Whitman came home from work as a carpenter one day and announced to his wife, "Come, mother, Elias preaches to-night." Whitman accompanied his parents to the sermon, and he never forgot the experience—or Hicks. The Quaker preacher was probably the first to introduce Whitman to the transcendentalist view of Christ as no more godly than any other part of nature—clearly Emerson's view.[64] The poet remembered how he had dreamed, after hearing Hicks speak, of writing a piece about him. Now for all he knew, after the scare of June 2, this might be his last composition. What Hicks taught him, which Emerson later refined, he acknowledged, was "naked theology." "Others talk of Bibles, saints, churches, exhortations, vicarious atonements," he wrote; "E.H. [spoke] to the religion inside of man's very own nature."[65]

There were other, more pressing reasons to recall Hicks from the grave. He had been a carpenter. Like Whitman, he had suffered and survived a stroke. And like Whitman, he had become something of a pariah for his outspoken beliefs. Furthermore, he was deeply religious without believing in churches. This Quaker—like his predecessor George Fox—had stood up for these positions. After Emerson left the ministry, he wrote a lecture on George Fox.[66] Whitman, at the other end of his literary career, wrote one on Fox, too, as a postscript to the Hicks essay.

This essay brings the book full circle to the themes of "Mannahatta" and "Paumanok," the first poems in which the New York and Long Island of the poet's youth are recalled and celebrated. These poems gave way to poems of defeat ("To Those Who've Fail'd") and ones describing his current position at three score and ten ("A Carol Closing Sixty-nine"). In "As I Sit Writing Here," he fears that the gloom of his sick room might filter into his poems, and in "My Canary Bird" it threatens at first to do just that—the poet sings of a caged bird like himself. But the warble heard is "joyous," "filling the air, the lonesome room, the long forenoon."

November Boughs was reviewed in most of the New York and Philadelphia newspapers and magazines, and the judgments were generally favorable, or at least charitable. The few objections focused on Whitman's work as a whole and its deviation from the rules of conventional poetry.[67] But Whitman's acknowledgment in "A Backward Glance" that he had probably not gained acceptance in his own time brought Jerome Buck, a Philadelphia lawyer, to the conclusion that the essay was the work of "a disappointed man." That assessment sent the Whitman circle into a small turmoil. John H. Clifford, a Unitarian clergyman from Germantown who often quoted *Leaves of Grass* in his sermons, declared, "A man who can say at the end of a career like his that he can afford to wait a hundred years for confirmation is in no way or measure a disappointed man." Whitman concurred: "Whatever may be the truth of what Clifford says about me I hope there may never stray out of my work anywhere a note of dissatisfaction, disappointment, despair: indeed, I may say I am sure there does not—sure of it."[68]

November Boughs was in fact Whitman's "backward glance" on a life he had always insisted was not literary but literal in its love of the people and places he enshrined in his poetry. But in the end, it was the sea that inspired some of his best poems. In "Had I the Choice," he would willingly trade the greatest poets and their works ("Metre or wit the best, or choice conceit to wield in perfect rhyme, delight of singers") for one wave upon the shore.

> These, these, O sea, all these I'd gladly barter,
> Would you the undulation of one wave, its trick to me transfer,
> Or breathe one breath of yours upon my verse,
> And leave its odor there.

As he wrote in "A Backward Glance," "It makes such difference *where* you read." First and last, he was the poet of Paumanok. He had grown up around sailors and would have one—Warren Fritzinger—as his last nurse. His conversations in Traubel's *With Walt Whitman in Camden* sparkle with ship metaphors—for example, likening his bedroom to a ship's cabin. The sea and sailors were also in his ancestry, celebrated in "Old Salt Kossabone."

Whitman considered *November Boughs* his "last, my final, my conclusive, message."[69] But no sooner was it in press than he undertook the first collection of his works, entitled *Complete Poems & Prose of Walt Whitman,* a 900-page, wide-margined volume bringing together in original pagination the texts of *Leaves of Grass, Specimen Days & collect,* and *November Boughs.* To his disappointment, McKay could not publish it, because of Whitman's rather desperate cost-cutting measures; instead, as with the centennial volumes, he simply had Ferguson Brothers in Philadelphia print the book, subtitling it with the phrase, "Authenticated & Personal Book (handled by W.W.)." Short notes at the beginning and end of the stout volume offered biographical glimpses (including the story of his being held by Lafayette as a baby) and the biographical theory that his writings in *Leaves of Grass* were the truest record of—indeed, an incarnation of—himself. He personally signed all 600 copies of what became a "limited" edition (numbered by Traubel) so that McKay, the book's distributor, could be assured of better sales. The volume was dated "1888–'9," and copies arrived at Mickle Street after the first of the year. Whitman, always generous, sent the "big book" to his supporters, including a copy to each of the O'Connors, at no little cost to himself in postage.

❋ ❋ ❋

By then William O'Connor was paralyzed from the waist down. Still drawing his government salary, he stayed in his two-story brick home on O Street in Washington, nursed only by his wife, who had gradually returned to him after the death of their only daughter in 1884. In March Bucke traveled to Washington, trying to patent a water meter that he hoped (in vain) would make him a millionaire. He took Traubel with him, and the two men called on O'Connor. As a result, we have not only the vivid details of the visit but also a sense of

O'Connor's impressive aura that afternoon. The dying champion of *Leaves of Grass* now considered himself practically one with Whitman, part of an almost divine duo that had courageously challenged the world's prejudices in both literature and life.

The two disciples took the morning train from Philadelphia to Washington. Ushered by Nellie into O'Connor's upstairs sitting room, they found him looking "mighty, but ill. . . . He was stout, even thick—almost fat. When aroused, animated, the color would mount to his cheeks and his eyes would flash." O'Connor had been waiting eagerly for them, treating their upcoming visit almost like one from the poet himself. When Bucke went downstairs to confer with the doctor, O'Connor suddenly stared at Traubel and reached out his arms. "'Come!' he said. I went to him: he took both my hands: he drew me to himself—kissed my lips and eyes and brow: he pressed my body against his. His eyes filled with tears." Traubel was deeply touched by the scene and close to tears himself. "When you get back to Walt," ordered O'Connor in his husky voice deepened by a cold, "tell him you are mine as well as his—tell him that in our brotherhood you don't belong to one of us but to all of us!" He pronounced Traubel "the next to come" in the fight for the "good cause" of liberty. Hugging both Bucke and Traubel as they left, he sobbed: "Horace, you must return as my delegate to Walt . . . so that he may know I have survived whole and entire and complete in the old faith." All the time, Nellie—"restrained and composed"—stood outside the little parlor filled by the three men. When Bucke and Traubel finally departed, both now reduced to tears, she said that their meeting had been beautiful and that her husband would "carry it with him into the next world."[70]

Back in Camden, Whitman waited for the reports but almost serenely as if he knew everything before it was told him. He was nevertheless delighted with the details, praising O'Connor's "fraternal quality" ("that is William: the sympathetic is the center of his being") and reveling in the fact that in spite of the illness, his appearance still expressed his inner personal beauty.[71] Between the time of Bucke and Traubel's return from Washington and May 9, 1889, the day of O'Connor's death, Whitman wrote his best friend a postcard almost every day. It was his last chore before turning in—his prayer, he said, for O'Connor, for both of them. He would ask a futile question about O'Connor's health and then give a brief report on his own.

One topic that constituted real news was the work being done on the seventieth birthday issue of *Leaves of Grass,* to be published in time for what became known as "Camden's Compliment," a birthday party in Morgan's Hall on May 31. This was a limited or "Special Ed'n," of 300 copies priced at $5 each. It used the Osgood plates for the main text, as had every Philadelphia edition, though this time, as with the "big book," McKay was merely the distributor. Whitman referred to the volume, which annexed "Sands at Seventy" and "A Backward Glance," as a pocketbook. With a Morocco binding equipped with a clasp to latch the book shut, it resembled a Catholic missal. He signed every title page as he had with the *Complete Poetry & Prose* so as to personalize what *now* looked like his last book. "The volume," he wrote in the preface, "is more A PERSON than a book." It carried five photographs, including the now famous butterfly picture. Ironically, this personal touch was the work of a poet who regularly tore up autograph requests after carefully removing the return postage.

The day after O'Connor died, Whitman left his Mickle Street abode for the first time since his strokes of the previous June. The excursion was made possible by a wheelchair purchased on Harned's credit at Wanamaker's department store and "propell'd" by his faithful nurse, Ed Wilkins.[72] The poet went out hesitantly at first but then regularly, for two hours a day on most days. Permanently weakened from the strokes and still suffering occasionally from dizziness caused by high blood pressure, he was also often bloated because of an enlarged prostate and constipation. But once outdoors again and in sight of the Delaware River, he came back almost miraculously to a sense of good health.

These outings continued till the last year of his life, when the out-of-doors tended to disorient him. Often, following one of the jaunts, he would be found in the chair in front of his residence, with children on his lap and friends sitting on the front stoop. One day he went next door to the home of Mrs. Button, who was seriously ill and confined to her bedroom. As the door opened, Whitman stood there somewhat unsteadily with a bouquet of flowers (just given to him by an admirer). "Give them to Mrs. Button," he told the person who opened the door. "Tell her they are from Walt Whitman—that he left them at the door himself."[73] Though now white with age and infirm himself, he remained to the end the Good Gray Nurse.

As plans for the seventieth birthday party mounted, Whitman feared its excesses but finally worked up almost the same enthusiasm as his disciples. The original idea was to exclude women, but Traubel strongly objected (with Whitman's assent), and some were invited. The Morgan's Hall banquet was planned for 200 people at $5 a head. More than 150 came. It was a local affair with out-of-town invited dignitaries sending letters of praise for the newly minted septuagenarian. Whitman even fantasized that ex-president Cleveland, known to like *Leaves of Grass,* might accept an invitation.[74]

The dinner went as planned. Those who attended or spoke included Julian Hawthorne, Hamlin Garland, and Herbert Gilchrist. Whitman skipped the entrée, accompanied by Appollinaris water, and arrived in time for the dessert and speeches. Though the occasion was "dry," the honored guest enjoyed an icy mug of champagne brought over from Harned's house. It was almost his first taste of intoxicants in nearly a year, since Bucke had discouraged Whitman in his condition from drinking alcohol. Whitman told Bucke, who couldn't attend, "I felt better & more something like myself, and nearer chipper, than for a year."[75]

At the very height of these festivities, as Whitman noted mournfully a few days later, the city of Johnstown—a thriving coal and steel center in western Pennsylvania, sixty-five miles southeast of Pittsburgh—was literally drowning. An earthen dam, hastily constructed to provide an exclusive summer resort lake for Pittsburgh's industrialists, including Whitman's benefactor Andrew Carnegie, had burst at three o'clock that afternoon in the mountains above the city. The torrent of water sped through the meandering valley, wiping out small villages and bridges along the way, and reached Johnstown almost without warning an hour later. It was the equivalent, later estimates claimed, of receiving the brunt of Niagara Falls. In ten minutes Johnstown, which stood on a nearly level flood plain at the confluence of two rivers, was almost completely erased by the thirty-six-foot-high wave. Only a stone Methodist church and two or three other structures withstood the thunderous inundation and the fire that subsequently cremated hundreds of victims.[76] The total dead exceeded 2,200.

Newspaper reports of the Johnstown Flood were vivid and sometimes distorted, one paper estimating 10,000 deaths. The first paper to have a correspondent on hand was Joseph Pulitzer's *New York World.* Three days after the cataclysm, it offered Whitman $25 through its Philadelphia agent for "a threnody on the Johnstown dead." Whitman promised only to consider the task, not knowing if after his last year's illness he could do the tragedy justice. The next evening, he told Traubel he had "got it off" in an hour and a half at noon, while Wilkins barred all visitors.[77] Whitman was much moved by the slaughter of the working-class metropolis, like Camden in its growth and potential economic development. He may also have been inspired by a grizzly account in the *Philadelphia Press* on the day he composed his poem. It described how the undertakers, too busy for meal breaks, had to snatch a bite as they washed the legions of corpses.[78] The clammy presence of death no doubt suggested Whitman's title, "A Voice from Death," which best summed up the effect of the flood. The poem appeared on the front page of the *World* on June 7 and was copied by other newspapers around the country.

> A voice from Death, solemn and strange, in all his sweep and
> power,
> With sudden, indescribable blow—towns drown'd—humanity by
> thousands slain,
> The vaunted work of thrift, goods, dwellings, forge, street, iron
> bridge,
> Dash'd pell-mell by the blow—yet usher'd life continuing on,
> (Amid the rest, amid the rushing, whirling, wild debris,
> A suffering woman saved—a baby safely born!)

The poem's broadest message is the inescapable balance of nature, which civilization ever tries in vain to overcome and forget.

For I too have forgotten,
(Wrapt in these little potencies of progress, politics, culture,
 wealth, inventions, civilization,)
Have lost my recognition of your silent ever-swaying power,
 ye mighty, elemental throes,
In which and upon which we float, and every one of us is
 buoy'd.

This is almost vintage Whitman, the old magic stirred up perhaps by the outdoor jaunts and the affair at Morgan's Hall. He combines the common with the cosmic, even weaving in the newspaper report of Rose Clark who, leg pinned down, was trapped in the path of oncoming floodwaters carrying timbers and other debris until a last-second rescue.[79] Whitman, whose reading of the stoic philosopher Epictetus ("What is good for thee, O nature, is good for me!" he more than once recited to Traubel)[80] kept him from utter despair even in the face of such catastrophe, saw "the same old law," as he had written in Section 14 of "Song of Myself." In "A Voice from Death," he continues,

E'en as I chant, lo! out of death, and out of ooze and slime,
The blossoms rapidly blooming, sympathy, help, love,
From West and East, from South and North and over sea,
Its hot-spurr'd hearts and hands humanity to human aid moves on;
And from within a thought and lesson yet.

He is also referring here to the outpouring of contributions, both from America and from abroad, to help the people of Johnstown. By the time Whitman wrote his poem, Pittsburgh alone had raised more than $100,000, not only in hefty donations from the rich but in nickels and dimes from laborers, schoolchildren, and even convicts. Camden's blue-collar community added to its big-sister city Philadelphia's contribution of $600,000.[81]

❖ ❖ ❖

The year 1889 also brought personal distress—or at least annoyance—to the poet. Shortly before his birthday, Edward Emerson, the Concord essayist's surviving son, published *Emerson in Concord,* which included the following note:

> When Leaves of Grass appeared at a later period than that of which I speak, the healthy vigor and freedom of this work of a young mechanic seemed to promise so much that Mr. Emerson overlooked the occasional coarseness which offended him, and wrote a letter of commendation to the author, a sentence of which was, to his annoyance, printed in gold letters on the covers of the next edition. But the first work led him to expect better in future, and in this he was disappointed. He used to say, this 'Catalogue-style of poetry is easy and leads nowhere,' or words to that effect.[82]

Having been forewarned of the statement by friends, Whitman was willing at first to ignore the slight as he looked forward to reading an intimate portrait of Emerson. He relished anything about the man who had allegedly brought him to a boil, recently enjoying Oliver Wendell Holmes's biography of Emerson (although he thought the picture dry). But Edward's comment gnawed at him, and he soon lashed out at the Emerson family. He hinted to Traubel that "there should be something uttered counter to Edward" at the birthday party (there was). He even thought of responding himself in print—to defend not only himself but Emerson, against the sin of respectability. "Think of his wife, alone: think of Emerson,—the great, the free, the pure—united in marriage to a conventional woman." Actually, as Robert D. Richardson, Jr., has shown, Lidian Emerson, an abolitionist, was hardly a conventional woman.[83]

He knew that Mrs. Emerson and her two daughters were particularly "inimical" to him, but he remembered Edward as being genial in welcoming him when he visited Emerson for the last time in 1881. Defensive in his hurt, he ignored the truth of Edward's footnote. Emerson *had* tired of Whitman's catalogs, saying so in a letter to Carlyle, which Whitman had read in the recent edition of the letters of Emerson and Carlyle. But then Emerson tired of almost every poet he embraced, including Thoreau. What Whitman apparently refused to consider was the likelihood that Edward was avenging the poet's portrayal of his father in "A Christmas Garland" and "Emerson's Books, (The Shadows of Them)." There Whitman had presented Emerson as overcultivated. Whitman, described as "a young mechanic" in Edward's note, was clearly undercultivated.

Whitman had already come to regret his unfair criticism of Emerson without Edward's help, but after the book appeared, he began somewhat to reconsider.[84] Later that year he received some consolation from Frank Sanborn, who wrote Traubel on November 6 to say that while Emerson had expressed annoyance with the publication of his private letter and objected to the "too frequent mention of the organs of generation," his 1855 letter to Whitman "was his more constant way of looking at Whitman's genius." Sanborn added that Emerson would never have referred to the poet condescendingly as little more than a "young mechanic." Hearing this, Whitman concluded that Edward was "constitutionally my enemy" and a "determined liar."[85]

Edward Emerson's assault began the second-generation endeavor to separate the New England saint from the Brooklyn sinner. Less than a year later, Charles J. Woodbury published "Emerson's Talks with a College Boy" in *Century Magazine.* It was incorporated in his *Talks with Ralph Waldo Emerson* (1890), quoting Emerson as lamenting that Whitman became a "bohemian" after his first edition and complaining that the poet had met him for dinner at the Astor House "without a coat." Whitman suspected a touch of Edward in the Woodbury affair. He privately denied the coat story, finally printing, anonymously, his response in the *Camden Post* on August 12 and in *Lippincott's Magazine* of March 1891. In the meantime Woodbury wrote the poet, promising to expunge the anecdote from his book. Nevertheless, it appeared—perhaps because Traubel had subsequently written him back a spiteful letter about the incident.[86] Woodbury's letter to the poet was not his first. Like Lanier and Taylor, he had earlier written a letter asserting his passionate approval of the poet. Not long after Whitman's dismissal from the Department of the Interior in 1865, which was widely reported in the press, Woodbury wrote from Williamstown, Massachusetts, in praise of *Leaves of Grass* and in damnation of its critics.[87]

Whitman was also assaulted from within, by his own disciples. While Traubel and others were ever ready to respond to attacks on their "Walt," they were also social radicals (in theory, at least) who looked for the master radical in Whitman. The literary naturalist Hamlin Garland, for example, was enamored of Henry George and his Single Tax plan. Whitman told Traubel one day in June 1889 that he would never oppose "the Anarchists, Socialists, Communists, Henry George men" in theory because their reforms were needed in "a country like Russia—or in crowded England." He did not, however, see the "pertinency" of such reform in the United States. Like Emerson and Melville, he ran from what he called panaceas and reformers with tunnel vision. "Look at Wendell Phillips—great and grand as he was . . . he was one-eyed, saw nothing, absolutely nothing, but that single blot of slavery. And if Phillips of old, others today." Phillips had been one of O'Connor's heroes, praised in his novel *Harrington* as second only to Emerson.

All his life, Whitman *favored* social radicals—Frank Sanborn, Abby Price, Sylvester Baxter, Horace Traubel—but he was never completely one himself. He was too much a stoic to be a reformer. (Edward Bellamy's utopian novel *Looking Backward* [1888], which envisioned Americans a hundred years hence living contentedly in dormitories and overall sameness, bored him immediately.)[88] If true reform were to come about, it had to have an Emersonian stamp, to lift "the Whole Man" and not merely one of his—or her—social parts.

Disciples also became a problem on the subject of "Calamus." Symonds's letter of confrontation on the subject (see Chapter 9) was right around the corner. From Berlin Whitman received an obsequious letter from the sexologist Eduard Bertz. Bertz had read Freiligrath's translation of *Leaves of Grass,* but having spent several years in the United States he wrote perfect English. He sent an article that he had published in the *Deutsche Press* of June 2, adding in a letter that Whitman received in June 1889 that he hoped later to write an essay "better suited to do justice to your genius." In a letter of July 20–22, in which he thanked Whitman for books he had sent, he mentioned his own book, *The French Prisoners* (1884), which told "the story of a friendship between a German boy and a young French soldier." One of the chapters had a motto from *Leaves of Grass.* In 1905 Bertz published his "Whitman: Ein Charakterbild" ("A Character Sketch"—it has never been fully translated into English). This oversized article of some 125 pages was the first direct, published assertion of Whitman's possible homosexuality. By this time, Bertz was more interested in homosexuality and its social acceptance than he was in Whitman.[89]

In October 1889 Whitman's latest nurse, Ed Wilkins, returned to Canada to finish his studies in veterinary science, and Warren Fritzinger took over. Warry, as he was called, gave Whitman regular rubdowns, or "curryings."[90] That month Traubel's "little dinner book" (*Camden's Compliment*) was printed, memorializing the seventieth birthday party speeches. Nellie O'Connor visited that fall, not having seen Whitman in fifteen years. Earlier Bucke suggested that she might become Whitman's nurse and housekeeper, but this idea went nowhere. Now going partially deaf, with eyesight failing, and so paralyzed that he had to "wriggle" from bed to chair, Whitman needed a strong sailor type such as Warry. He was also perfectly contented with Mrs. Davis's services. But Nellie sorely needed a job. O'Connor had left her almost penniless; when she saw Walt, he gave her $10. She eventually found a job in the pension bureau in Washington and then remarried.[91]

A new cemetery—Harleigh, on the edge of Camden—opened up. Perhaps as a publicity stunt, its director offered Whitman a free plot anywhere in the cemetery in exchange for "a poem on it." Whitman readily accepted, but never wrote the poem. Just before Christmas 1889 he went out cheerfully in a borrowed carriage to choose his last residence. He told Traubel that the cemetery officials hoped he would pick a prominent place (there were already fifty or so graves at Harleigh), but he went off into the woods and chose a hillside that sloped down to Cooper's Creek. He urged Horace to go down and see it. Some were surprised that Whitman wished to be buried in Camden instead of New York. "What comes then," he told his friend, "is not to be worried over."[92]

The new year opened with Whitman regularly imbibing champagne at Harned's Sunday dinners and getting his jug filled weekly with stronger spirits at the lawyer's house. Now aided by an electric light in his parlor, he took to reading James Fenimore Cooper, whom he found more wholesome than Hawthorne (or Poe). Thanks to Warry and perhaps the "toddies," he began to feel a little stronger—to the extent that he volunteered to give another Lincoln lecture, this one to be on the silver anniversary of the president's murder. Whitman believed this would be number thirteen, but it was probably the tenth—and his last. As the event approached, however, he came down with influenza and the lecture was almost canceled.

But he recovered in time. The lecture was held on April 15 in the Contemporary Club, where Whitman had performed before. Traubel succinctly notes that Whitman "read preliminarily a few written paragraphs of introduction, then the lecture as known in print." He told his audience, estimated to exceed three hundred, "My subject this evening for forty or fifty minutes' talk is the death of this man, and how that death will really filter into America." Dressed in a suit of Canadian gray wool, with his customary open shirt-collar, he compared Lincoln, "familiar, our own," with Moses, Joshua, Ulysses, and Cromwell.[93]

Weaker now, he predicted that this would be his "last public appearance," but there was another birthday party in the offing, first planned to take place at Harned's when Whitman was still ill, and then, as he rallied, moved to the large upstairs room of Reisser's, a German beer hall in Philadelphia. Again he insisted on the presence of women and was particularly disappointed when Alys Smith, now in the United States for college, backed out at the last minute. In fact, the Smiths (with the exception of Logan and perhaps Alys) had begun to grow away from Whitman—perhaps because he did not wholly approve of Mary Costelloe's impassioned socialism.[94]

The featured speaker of the seventy-first birthday party was Colonel Robert G. Ingersoll, a notorious New York attorney and reformer known to Americans as "the Great Agnostic." He and Whitman resembled each other in their disapproval of organized religion, but there was also something "spiritual" Whitman found in Ingersoll, who for his part liked *Leaves of Grass* because it treated the "miracle" of the material world. Whitman much admired Ingersoll for his great gift for oratory, which he himself lacked. At the dinner Ingersoll, sitting to the poet's left, spoke off the cuff for forty-five minutes, turning to Whitman as he talked. The guest of honor occasionally responded to the words of praise with "Do you say so, Colonel?"—to which the speaker replied: "I do, and I say further." Whitman was delighted with the speech, as indeed were all in attendance. The *Camden Post,* not always friendly to Whitman, called it a "flattering summary! The Whitmanites for the first time in their lives were fully satisfied." As a result of Ingersoll's success, another lecture ("Liberty in Literature") was gotten up that fall, netting $869.45 for Whitman. This time "Colonel Bob," armed with a prepared text, spoke for an hour and forty-five minutes, and the poet, though afterward enthusiastic, was mostly silent and pale.[95]

Whitman's "grippe" of April had not entirely left him. Bucke, fearing the poet was near his end, began sending down books by Whitman from Canada for signing. Bucke and Traubel were already envisioning themselves as beacons of their poet's memory after his death.[96] But instead of Whitman, it was Walt's favorite brother, Jeff, who died, of typhoid pneumonia on November 26. The poet recalled in a letter to Bucke that he had been fifteen when Jeff was born. George went out to St. Louis to help with the burial arrangements, and Walt broke the news to the institutionalized Eddy in his only extant letter to his brother. He also got sicker himself, mainly with his prostate problem, and showed signs of confusion on at least one occasion immediately following the news of Jeff's demise.[97]

❋ ❋ ❋

Medically speaking, Whitman probably should have been dead by now. His weakened condition prompted one disciple, William Sloane Kennedy, to speculate on the posthumous fame of his poet. "Do you suppose a thousand years fr. now," he asked, "people will be celebrating the birth of Walt Whitman as they are now the birth of Christ?"[98] Whitman's ego, and the need to write, probably kept him going. His functioning body was reduced to a clear head most of the time and a "strong right arm."

The spring of 1891 saw the publication of his last book, the poems of which eventually formed the "2d Annex" to *Leaves of Grass. Good-Bye My Fancy,* a sixty-six-page pamphlet, was another mixture of recently published poetry and prose. Here Whitman is packing his literary bags for eternity. The pamphlet is filled with Whitman's anticipation of his own impending death; yet its tone is wonderment instead of fear. Ever the observer of life—especially his own, which he could now examine with perhaps greater distance than in the heyday of his talent—Whitman did not want to miss any details of its final act. In "The Pallid Wreath," he likens his own lingering to a Christmas wreath in January. "Somehow I cannot let it go yet. . . . / So let the wreath hang still awhile within my eye-reach, / It is not yet dead to me, nor even pallid." A few of the pieces are poems of occasion. Just as he celebrated the completion of the Washington Monument with a poem in *November Boughs,* he now greets the French on the construction of the Eiffel Tower in 1889 with "Bravo, Paris Exposition!" Many are chants on old themes. Several hostile critics condemned the quality of Whitman's last turn at poetry,[99] but there were at least two gems in this death-bed collection, "A Voice from Death" (discussed above) and "To the Sun-Set Breeze."

When Ezra Pound read the latter in 1909, he complained that American criticism had not yet come to appreciate Whitman's "deliberate artistry."[100] But Whitman's art was seldom "deliberate" (at least in the sense of Poe's claim of planning everything out beforehand). All his life he was "stubborn": he would never write until moved to do so. Like the Quaker he fancied himself in part to be, he waited for an "inner light" to click on. Little in his immediate environment, it seems, was lost on him, and when the lens of that "eye-reach" zoomed in on one thing in particular, or one combination of things, a poem emerged.

Like "A Voice from Death," "To the Sun-Set Breeze" responds to a link with nature and its cycle of life and death. Here it is a faint West Jersey breeze on Mickle Street. The poem contains one of the very few enjambed lines in *Leaves of Grass* ("Thou, laving, tempering all, cool-freshing, gently vitalizing / Me, old, alone, sick, weak-down, melted-worn with sweat;"). To the very end, Whitman was experimenting with form.

The breeze, like the muted sounds in "Whispers of Heavenly Death," offers a clue to the ensemble of creation. The breeze offers this physically "wreck'd" old poet an "occult" medicine, which dilates him with the universal vastness it symbolizes, indeed personalizes.

I feel the sky, the prairies vast—I feel the mighty northern lakes,
I feel the ocean and the forest—somehow I feel the globe
  itself swift-swimming in space;
Thou blown from lips so loved, now gone—haply from
  endless store, God-sent,
(For thou art spiritual, Godly, most of all known to my sense,)

Whitman concludes by asking this "Minister" for a further clue. Now much nearer to death than when he begged for "some clew" in "Out of the Cradle Endlessly Rocking," he is no less curious, merely becalmed.

The poem was first published in *Lippincott's Magazine* in 1890, after being rejected by *Harper's*—as he told his readers in *Good-Bye My Fancy*—for "being 'an improvisation' only."[101] Yet almost everything he wrote, beginning with the printing experiment in 1855, was an improvisation. The best prose piece of *Good-Bye,* prose-poetry really, is "Gathering the Corn." Unlike the other pieces, it was written almost fifteen years earlier, in 1878. The journalist-turned-poet offers "news" about the beauty of the "average West Jersey farm," obviously modeled on the Stafford place. He describes scenes worthy of Blake and "Shakspere" (Whitman's favored "shortened" spelling of the name). How the "half-mad vision of William Blake . . . [and the] far freer, far firmer fantasy that wrote 'Midsummer Night's Dream'—would have revell'd night or day, and beyond stint, in one of our American corn fields!"

The imaginative energy of "Gathering the Corn" was perhaps transferred to the next piece, "A Death Bouquet, Pick'd Noontime, Early January, 1890," where Whitman the improviser claims to give only "a few random lines" on death—"as one writes hurriedly the last part of a letter to catch the closing mail." Harking back to "To the Sun-Set Breeze" and earlier yet to "Whispers of Heavenly Death," he writes: "Like an invisible breeze after a long sultry day, death sometimes sets in at last, soothingly and refreshingly, almost vitally." Whitman chose the word "Good-Bye" in his title because behind it—like "So long!"—"there lurks much of the salutation of another beginning." Though he probably had his spiritual crises, this poet was an essentialist to the last. In a short give-and-take with Ingersoll during his seventy-second birthday dinner ("Ingersoll's Speech," in *Good-Bye My Fancy*), he asked the Colonel: "If the spiritual is not behind the material, to what purpose is the material? What is this world without a further Divine purpose in it all?"[102]

Like *November Boughs, Good-Bye My Fancy* was expedited by Traubel, who also continued his daily note-taking on the sick poet's now grinding routine of taking medications and looking (usually in vain) for the slightest signs of improvement. He was always welcome, even when Whitman was gravely sick. The poet often took Traubel's hand just to get the feel of the outdoors. Another visitor who occasionally brightened his day was Anne Montgomerie, Horace's future wife. She first met the poet in the spring of 1885 or 1886, and it was she who suggested to Horace that he keep a journal on Whitman. She recalled for her daughter, Gertrude, born in the year of Whitman's death, the magnetism she felt on the day of their meeting. "As I stood beside his chair, I felt a strange power radiating from him with so much force that I felt pushed away." Anne came again and then regularly until she felt "that this man was as lovely as my father."[103]

On rather short notice, she and Horace decided to marry on May 28, 1891. The ceremony was held in Whitman's bedroom, the poet welcoming all the witnesses from his bed, including Warry, Mrs. Davis, the Harneds, and the Rev. Mr. Clifford, who presided over the ritual. Three days later, "ab't 40 people, choice friends mostly," the poet wrote Dr. John Johnston, celebrated the poet's last birthday. Along with J. W. Wallace, Johnston headed up a group of working-class enthusiasts from Bolton, England, who held regular readings and discussions of *Leaves of Grass*. Whitman had graced their shrine with signed books and other souvenirs, which also shortly included his canary, now dead and stuffed for posterity. Both men made pilgrimages to Camden. At the birthday party, Traubel presented Whitman with "a big goblet of first-rate champagne." The affair allowed the sick poet to forget his troubles and thoroughly enjoy himself. "I suppose I swigg'd it off at once," he told Johnston, and in all consumed, he supposed "near two bottles champagne" during the evening.[104]

By December, racked by hiccups and tormented by a pain in his left side, Whitman was ready psychologically and practically for death—or almost.[105] Though he owned a cemetery plot, the cost of the granite, house-shaped tomb he had commissioned came to $4,000, almost twice what he had paid for the house at 328 Mickle Street. Accompanying the poet on one of several visits to Harleigh to inspect the tomb when it was under construction, Mrs. Davis predicted that "Mr. Whitman won't be paler when he is dead than he was when he had alighted from the carriage and gone into the tomb. He leaned up against the wall—yet seemed to want to get away from the subject—spoke of the trees outside."[106] Whitman had already paid $1,500 in two installments and he had more than $8,000 in the bank, but he worried fretfully that there would be too little left of his estate to care for Eddy. The matter was finally settled when Harned—days before Walt's death—paid the remaining $1,000 himself and silently placed a lien for this amount against the poet's estate.[107] The plan was to have the poet's parents and dead siblings reburied there but not—as he told Bucke ten months earlier, because of the "fuss" it would cause "down south" (presumably New Orleans)—his "two deceased children (young man & woman—illegitimate of course)."[108]

At 6:43 P.M. on March 26, just two months and a few days short of his seventy-third birthday, Whitman died of bronchial pneumonia, the culmination and final complication of miliary tuberculosis contracted during the war. The autopsy, performed at Mickle Street over the objections of George Whitman, revealed a collapsed left lung and a right lung with only one-eighth of its breathing capacity. Daniel Longaker, Whitman's attending physician for the past year and a member of Philadelphia's Society for Ethical Culture, noted that the postmortem revealed no trace of alcoholism or venereal disease; this was to "silence forever the slanderous accusations that debauchery and excesses of various kinds caused or contributed to his break-down." The poet's heart, the *New York Times* of March 28 recorded, "was surrounded by a large number of small abscesses and about two and half quarts of water." Only the brain, "abnormally large," was in a fairly healthy condition. And that, Justin Kaplan has claimed, was subsequently dropped and destroyed by a laboratory assistant at the American Anthropometric Society, founded to study "high-type brains."[109]

Whitman entered his new house at Harleigh on March 30, 1892, four days after his death. A public viewing of the body was held first at the Mickle Street house, from eleven until two in the afternoon. Old neighborhood friends along with the curious—at least a thousand including laborers on their lunch hour—lined Mickle Street and quietly streamed through the parlor to see the poet in his oak coffin. The mourners included the poet's "tenderest lover," Peter Doyle, who because he was late for the viewing, was almost turned away by a police officer stationed at the door to regulate traffic. Later Burroughs spotted Doyle at the burial site, but off by himself—"up the hill, twirling a switch in his hand, his tall figure and big soft hat impressively set against the white-blue sky."[110] Thousands lined Haddonfield Pike as the bier was taken by carriage to the cemetery. They filled the hillsides around the tomb, which was fronted by an open-flapped tent for the speakers and special guests. The gravesite was far off to the left as the funeral procession entered the memorial grounds. Today Camden's pre-adolescent youths, mainly working-class blacks and Hispanics, frolic and bike in the cemetery, and every one of them seems to know where the poet is buried. It is not unusual to find a wilted rose and a note attached to the bars that guard the entrance to the little granite house.

The day of the funeral was sunny and mild, but the dignitaries perspired under the heavy tent.[111] Harned spoke for the city and for Whitman, who had urged him to say "thanks, thanks, thanks." He spoke of Whitman's utter faith in immortality ("that man is as indestructible as his Creator") and his complete lack of fear in the face of imminent death. Bucke, known even then for the hyperbole of his devotion, complained that it was difficult to speak about his poet because he was "so great . . . so far above other men"; when anyone who actually knew the poet tried to describe him, it sounded like "extravagant exaggeration." Others spoke, including Ingersoll, whose agnostic message was toned down for the occasion.[112] Burroughs, a pre-disciple, did not speak. Traubel, the junior member of the triad of literary executors, did not speak either. Perhaps he was still choked up with grief, having kissed the cold face of his poet for the last time four hours after death.[113] Whitman's youngest brother, Eddy, was absent. So was Whitman's niece Jessie, who had made the trip from St. Louis to Camden in December when the end looked certain. This left brother George as the only blood relative in attendance. The Civil War hero whose wounding at Fredericksburg had drawn Whitman to Washington and his dearly remembered hospital work, and whose residence in Camden had drawn the poet there, belonged to the "divine average" of mechanics Whitman celebrated in his poetry. But George made no speech to the mourners, not being in the same intellectual class with the other speakers. George, who loved Walt but seemed "incredulous as to the great applause greeting his brother" that day, had never understood *Leaves of Grass*.[114] No matter now. Paumanok was dead.

ABBREVIATIONS

The text of the sixth American edition of Leaves of Grass *(1881) is used for all quotations unless the poem is discussed chronologically; then the earliest or other relevant version of the poem is quoted.*

Berg Henry W. and Albert A. Berg Collection, New York Public Library.

Bucke Richard Maurice Bucke. *Walt Whitman.* Philadelphia: David McKay, 1883.

C *Walt Whitman: The Correspondence,* ed. Edwin Haviland Miller. 6 vols. New York: New York University Press, 1961–77.

DN *Daybooks and Notebooks of Walt Whitman,* ed. William White. 3 vols. New York: New York University Press, 1978.

EPF *Early Poems and the Fiction,* ed. Thomas L. Brasher. New York: New York University Press, 1963.

GF *The Gathering of the Forces,* ed. Cleveland Rodgers and John Black. 2 vols. New York: G. P. Putnam's Sons, 1920.

Glicksberg — *Walt Whitman and the Civil War,* ed. Charles I. Glicksberg. Philadelphia: University of Pennsylvania Press, 1933.

GWW — *Civil War Letters of George Washington Whitman,* ed. Jerome M. Loving. Durham: Duke University Press, 1975.

HW — Joseph Jay Rubin. *The Historic Whitman.* University Park: Pennsylvania State University, 1973.

In Re — *In Re Walt Whitman,* ed. Horace L. Traubel, Richard Maurice Bucke, and Thomas B. Harned. Philadelphia: David McKay, 1893.

LC — Charles E. Feinberg, Thomas H. Harned, or Horace L. and Anne Montgomerie Traubel Collections of Walt Whitman at the Library of Congress.

LG — *Leaves of Grass: Reproduced from the First* (1855) *Edition,* ed. Clifton Joseph Furness. New York: Columbia University Press, 1939.

LGCRE — *Leaves of Grass: Comprehensive Reader's Edition,* ed. Harold W. Blodgett and Sculley Bradley. New York: W. W. Norton, 1965.

LVVW — Louisa Van Velsor Whitman (the poet's mother).

NUPM — *Walt Whitman: Notebooks and Unpublished Prose Manuscripts,* ed. Edward F. Grier. 6 vols. New York: New York University Press, 1984.

NYD — *New York Dissected: A Sheaf of Recently Discovered Newspaper Articles by the Author of Leaves of Grass,* ed. Emory Holloway and

Ralph Adimari. New York: Rufus Rockwell Wilson, 1936.

PW — *Walt Whitman: Prose Works 1892,* ed. Floyd Stovall. 2 vols. New York: New York University Press, 1963–64.

SD — *Specimen Days.* Philadelphia: David McKay, 1882.

Sit — *I Sit and Look Out: Editorials from the Brooklyn Daily Times,* ed. Emory Holloway and Vernolian Schwarz. New York: Columbia University Press, 1932.

Solitary Singer — Gay Wilson Allen. *The Solitary Singer: A Critical Biography of Walt Whitman.* New York: New York University Press, 1955.

Trent — Josiah P. Trent Collection of Walt Whitman, Duke University.

UPP — *The Uncollected Poetry and Prose of Walt Whitman,* ed. Emory Holloway. 2 vols. New York: Peter Smith, 1932.

WBC — Clara Barrus. *Whitman and Burroughs, Comrades.* Boston: Houghton Mifflin, 1931.

WEBDA — Thomas L. Brasher. *Whitman as Editor of the Brooklyn Daily Eagle.* Detroit: Wayne State University Press, 1970.

WNYA — *Walt Whitman of the New York Aurora,* ed. Joseph Jay Rubin and Charles H. Brown. State College, Pa.: Bald Eagle Press, 1950.

WWC — *With Walt Whitman in Camden,* ed. Horace Traubel. 9 vols. (1906–96).

WWJ *Walt Whitman: The Journalism,* I, ed. Herbert Bergman, Douglas A. Noverr, and Edward J. Recchia. New York: Peter Lang, 1998.

WWQR *Walt Whitman Quarterly Review.*

WWR *Walt Whitman Review.*

NOTES

❈ ❈ ❈

CHAPTER I. CARESSER OF LIFE

1. *C,* I, 59. See also "Our Wounded and Sick Soldiers," *New York Times,* December 11, 1864.

2. *PW,* I, 32–33, 43; and *C,* I, 81.

3. *GWW,* 164–67. See Martin G. Murray, "Bunkum *Did* Go Sogering," *WWQR* 10 (Winter 1993): 142–47. Another brother, Thomas Jefferson Whitman, paid $400 for a military substitute in 1864. *GWW,* 14, 130.

4. *C,* I, 54–60.

5. Bucke, 26.

6. Elizabeth Robins Pennell, *Charles Godfrey Leland: A Biography* (Boston: Houghton Mifflin, 1906), II, 110–11.

7. *The Complete Works of Ralph Waldo Emerson,* ed. Edward Waldo Emerson (Boston: Houghton Mifflin, 1903–4), III, 340. See also Jerome Loving, *Emerson, Whitman, and the American Muse* (Chapel Hill: University of North Carolina Press, 1982), 139–42.

8. *Solitary Singer,* 260–62; see also *C,* I, 55.

9. *UPP,* I, 180–81.

10. *UPP,* II, 224.

11. *UPP,* I, 180; and *UPP,* II, 274–75.

12. Jerome Loving, "'Broadway, the Magnificent!': A Newly Discovered Whitman Essay," *WWQR* 12 (Spring 1995): 209–16.

13. *UPP,* II, 313–14; compare *UPP,* II, 317–20, with "Letters from a Travelling Bachelor," No. 9, in *HW,* 341–47.

14. *GWW,* 71.

15. Frank E. Vandiver, *Blood Brothers: A Short History of the Civil War* (College Station: Texas A&M University Press, 1992), 14.

16. Glicksberg, 17–18.

17. *GWW,* 29.

18. Glicksberg, 42.

19. *GWW,* 45–50.

20. Higginson wrote anonymous criticisms of Whitman and his hospital work in lieu of soldiering in *Harper's Bazaar* of March 5 and 26, 1887, and in the *New York Evening Post* of March 28, 1892, two days after the poet's death. See William Sloane Kennedy, *The Fight of a Book for the World* (West Yarmouth, Mass., 1926), 70–71. In another attempt to tarnish Whitman's character, in 1897, Higginson was behind James Parton's threat to sue the Whitman estate for an allegedly unpaid loan made in 1857 (Horace L. and Anne Montgomerie Traubel Whitman Collection, LC). Higginson was also one of the first critics to suggest the possibility of a homosexual theme in *Leaves of Grass.* In "Recent Poetry," *Nation* 55 (July 7, 1892): 10–12, he wrote: "There is the same curious deficiency shown in him, almost alone among poets, of anything like personal and romantic love. Whenever we come upon anything that suggests a glimpse of it, the object always turns out to be a man and not a woman."

21. Jerome Loving, "'Our Veterans Mustering Out'—Another Newspaper Article by Whitman About His Soldier-Brother," *Yale University Library Gazette* 49 (October 1974): 223; and Chapter 9.

22. J. G. Randall and David Herbert Donald, *The Civil War and Reconstruction* (Lexington, Mass.: D. C. Heath, 1969), 191, 223.

23. *GWW,* 78. Whitman's letters, obtained before he got Emerson's similar endorsement, were written by George Hall, "Late Mayor of Brooklyn," and by New York congressman Moses Fowler Odell; the first is undated; the second is dated December 16, 1862 (Horace L. and Anne Montgomerie Traubel Whitman Collection, LC).

24. Louisa Van Velsor Whitman to Walt Whitman, May 3, 1860 (Trent).

25. *GWW,* 9–10.

26. *Letters of Martha Mitchell Whitman,* ed. Randall H. Waldron (New York: New York University Press, 1977), 22.

27. *U.S. Army War College Guide to the Battles of Chancellorsville and Fredericksburg,* ed. Jay Luvaas and Harold W. Nelson (Carlisle, Pa.: South Mountain Press, 1988), 3.

28. *C,* I, 58–59.

29. *Battles and Leaders of the Civil War* (New York: Appleton, Century, Croft, 1956), III, 129.

30. *GWW,* 78–79; and *WWC,* VIII, 44.

31. *The War of the Rebellion: A Compilation of the Official Records of the Union and Confederate Armies* (Washington: Government Printing Office, 1880–1901), XXI, 311–12, 66.

32. Major General Darius N. Couch, "Sumner's 'Right Grand Division,'" in *Battles and Leaders,* III, 116–17; and *NUPM,* II, 503.

33. *WWC,* IV, 260.

34. *NUPM,* II, 502; and *C,* I, 62.

35. *Dear Brother Walt: The Letters of Thomas Jefferson Whitman,* ed. Dennis Berthold and Kenneth M. Price (Kent, Ohio: Kent State University Press, 1984), 22–24.

36. *C,* I, 61–68, 73–74. The source of the story about Chase's keeping the Emerson letter can be found in John Townsend Trowbridge, *My Own Story: With Recollections of Noted Persons* (New York: Houghton Mifflin, 1903), 388.

37. Emory Holloway, *Whitman: An Interpretation in Narrative* (New York: Alfred A. Knopf, 1926), 198.

38. *C,* I, 81–82.

39. *SD* in *PW,* I, 32–33.

40. *NUPM,* II, 508–9.

41. *NUPM,* II, 513.

42. *LGCRE,* 306n.

43. *C,* I, 69.

44. Gay Wilson Allen, *Solitary Singer* (1955).

CHAPTER 2. A THOUSAND SINGERS, A THOUSAND SONGS

1. *PW,* I, 12.

2. *PW,* I, 10.

3. *PW,* I, 12.

4. "Walt Whitman in Huntington," *Long-Islander,* August 5, 1881; reprinted in Bucke, 223.

5. *PW,* I, 4–6.

6. *PW,* I, 7–8.

7. *Faint Clews and Indirection: Manuscripts of Walt Whitman and His Family,* ed. Clarence Gohdes and Rollo G. Silver (Durham: Duke University Press, 1949), 47; *NUPM,* I, 23–24; Bucke, 18n; and *WWC,* IV, 298. The quotation comes from Justin Kaplan, *Walt Whitman: A Life* (New York: Simon and Schuster, 1980), 56–57.

8. *PW,* I, 13; *PW,* II, 687–88.

9. *In Re,* 33–34. See *HW,* 32–33, for the claim that the poet's father sold the family farm in West Hills for $2,250.

10. For the variants for the Lafayette story, see *PW,* I, 13n.

11. Florence B. Freedman, *Walt Whitman Looks at the Schools* (New York: King's Crown Press, 1950), 14.

12. Ralph Foster Weld, *Brooklyn Village, 1816–1834* (New York: Columbia University Press, 1938), 220–23.

13. Weld, *Brooklyn Village,* 187, 223; and *HW,* 16.

14. Freedman, *Walt Whitman Looks at the Schools,* 16.

15. Freedman, *Walt Whitman Looks at the Schools,* 19.

16. *Brooklyn Daily Eagle,* June 12, 1846.

17. *EPF,* 56.

18. Bucke, 15.

19. *WWC,* II, 98; *PW,* I, 13; *Solitary Singer,* 16–17; and *HW,* 22–23. In an editorial protesting the removal of trees to make way for new construction in Brooklyn, Whitman wrote in the *Eagle* of July 11, 1846, of the "beautiful large trees that stood so long on Dr. Hunt's old place," which he remembered from "our childhood up," and "of the towering elms on the opposite of Fulton street, from James B. Clarke's old place up to Clinton street" (*WEBDA,* 62).

20. *UPP,* II, 4.

21. *Solitary Singer,* 18.

22. See Shelley Fisher Fishkin, *From Fact to Fiction: Journalism and Imaginative Writing in America* (Baltimore: Johns Hopkins University Press, 1985).

23. *Solitary Singer,* 18; Roger Asselineau, *The Evolution of Walt Whitman: The Creation of a Personality* (Cambridge: Harvard University Press, 1960), 20; and *WWC,* II, 471.

24. *UPP,* II, 3–4; and Weld, *Brooklyn Village,* 168–69.

25. *UPP,* II, 247–48.

26. William White, "A Tribute to William Hartshorne: Unrecorded Whitman," *American Literature* 42 (January 1971): 554–58.

27. *Solitary Singer,* 21; and *WWC,* IV, 505–6.

28. Whitman may not have finished his apprenticeship at Spooner's. In the *Brooklyn Evening Star* (formerly the *Long Island Star*) E. B. Spooner, son of Alden Spooner, attacked Whitman after a political speech, adding: "Come back, young man, and finish your apprenticeship." See *UPP,* I, 32–33n. For the *Mirror,* see *PW,* I, 287; in *SD* Whitman wrote: "I had a piece or two in George P. Morris's then celebrated and fashionable 'Mirror.' . . . I remember with what half-suppress'd excitement I used to watch for the big, fat, red-faced, slow-moving, very old English carrier who distributed the 'Mirror' in Brooklyn. . . . How it made my heart double-beat to see *my piece* on the pretty white paper, in nice type." One of his pieces, signed "W.W.," may have been "The Olden Time" (*WWJ,* I, xliv–xlv).

29. Katherine Molinoff, *Whitman's Teaching at Smithtown, 1837–38* (Brooklyn: Privately printed, 1942), 11–20. Later Molinoff implied that Whitman taught at a ninth school, the Locust Grove School in Southold, on the northeastern prong of Long Island near Greenport; see *Walt Whitman at Southold* (Privately printed, 1966). The pamphlet presents materials purported to support the story of Whitman's being denounced in the pulpit and tarred and feathered for sodomy with one of his students. See also David S. Reynolds, *Walt Whitman's America: A Cultural Biography* (New York: Alfred A. Knopf, 1995), 69–73. This myth is discussed further in Chapter 9, n. 4.

30. Freedman, *Walt Whitman Looks at the Schools,* 67–68.

31. Freedman, *Walt Whitman Looks at the Schools,* 27; and Molinoff, *Whitman's Teaching at Smithtown,* 23.

32. In an 1855 notebook Whitman listed out of order and with omissions the Long Island towns where he taught (*UPP,* II, 86–87). See also Thomas Farel Heffernan, "Walt Whitman in Trimming Square," *WWQR* 11 (Summer 1993): 32–34.

33. *In Re,* 39.

34. Freedman, *Walt Whitman Looks at the Schools,* 28–30.

35. See, for example, the reminiscence of Mrs. Orvetta Hall Brenton, *UPP,* I, xxxiii n. For Whitman's debating activity, see Molinoff, *Whitman's Teaching at Smithtown.*

36. *PW,* I, 287.

37. *UPP,* I, xxxiii n.

38. *EPF,* 327–30.

39. Arthur Golden, ed., "Nine Early Whitman Letters, 1840–1841," *American Literature* 58 (October 1986): 342–60, reprinted by Edwin Haviland Miller in the *WWQR* 8 (Winter/Spring 1991): 9–17.

40. *EPF,* 328–29; and Golden, ed., "Nine Early Whitman Letters," 356.

41. Abraham P. Leech to Walt Whitman, June 27 and August 10, 1840 (LC). For Leech's temperance activities, see his autograph notebook in the Library of Congress (Accession number 19, 188). See also my further development of this information in Chapter 3, in the discussion of *Franklin Evans.*

42. William White, "The Very Earliest Whitman," *American Book Collector* 19 (October 1968): 20; and *UPP,* I, 32.

43. *EPF,* 27–28 (where quotations from the early pieces are taken unless otherwise indicated); and *UPP,* I, 1.

44. *The Early Lectures of Ralph Waldo Emerson,* ed. Robert E. Spiller and Wallace E. Williams (Cambridge: Harvard University Press, 1972), III, 348.

45. *WNYA,* 105.

46. *HW,* 47.

47. Golden, ed., "Nine Early Whitman Letters," 348.

48. The first three appeared in the *Hempstead Inquirer* of February 29, March 14 and 28, 1840; see Herbert Bergman and William White, "Walt Whitman's Lost Sun-Down Papers," *American Book Collector* 20 (January 1970): 17–20. The next six installments appeared in the *Long Island Democrat* of April 28, August 11, September 29, October 20, November 28, 1840, and July 6, 1841. The final essay was published in the *Long Island Farmer* of July 20, 1841; see *UPP,* I, 32–51. These essays are now conveniently collected in *WWJ,* I, 13–30.

49. Horace L. Traubel, "Walt Whitman, Schoolmaster: Notes of a Conversation with Charles A. Roe, 1894," *Walt Whitman Fellowship Papers,* no. 14 (April 1895), 81–87.

50. *Solitary Singer,* 39.

51. Leech to Whitman, June 27, 1840 (LC).

52. *UPP,* I, 51.

CHAPTER 3. SOME LITERARY PERSON

1. *UPP,* II, 87. "Each Has His Grief" and "The Child's Champion" appeared in the *New World* of November 20, 1841.

2. Edward K. Spann, *Ideals and Politics: New York Intellectuals and Liberal Democracy* (Albany: State University of New York Press, 1972), 54; Merle M. Hoover, *Park Benjamin: Poet and Editor* (New York: Columbia University Press, 1948), 104–18; and *WWC,* II, 531–32.

3. Hawthorne, who contributed two dozen stories to the *Democratic Review* between 1838 and 1845, received $3 to $5 a page (Arlin Turner, *Nathaniel Hawthorne: A Biography* [New York: Oxford University Press, 1980], 95).

4. *EPF,* 16n, 18–19n.

5. Katherine Molinoff, *Monographs on Unpublished Whitman Material* (New York: Comet Press, 1941), 19–22; see also *GWW,* 9–10.

6. *EPF,* 83.

7. *EPF,* 88n.

8. "On my left, through an opening in the trees," Whitman wrote in "The Tomb Blossoms," "I could see at some distance the ripples of our beautiful bay." Internal evidence in "The Last Loyalist" also suggests Whitestone as the place of composition: "On a large and fertile neck of land that juts out in the Sound, stretching to the east of New York City" (*EPF,* 89, 101).

9. *EPF,* 99, 222.

10. *Brooklyn Daily Eagle,* March 30, 1842.

11. *WNYA,* 2.

12. *WNYA,* 12.

13. William Cauldwell, "Walt Whitman as a Young Man," *New York Times,* January 26, 1901.

14. James Robinson Newhall, *The Legacy of an Octogenarian* (Lynn: Nichols Press, 1897), 130–31; and *WNYA,* 12.

15. *New York Aurora,* August 29, 1842. For one of Whitman's attacks on Park Benjamin, see *WNYA,* 110–11.

16. *WNYA,* 13.

17. *The Conservator* 12 (1901): 76.

18. Cauldwell, "Walt Whitman as a Young Man."

19. Lydia Maria Child, *Letters from New York* (New York: C. S. Francis, 1843), 68.

20. *WNYA,* 19.

21. *Early Lectures of Ralph Waldo Emerson,* ed. Robert E. Spiller and Wallace E. Williams (Cambridge: Harvard University Press, 1972), III, 352–53.

22. *WNYA,* 20–21.

23. *WNYA,* 23.

24. Diary of Abraham Paul Leech, LC, Accession number 19, 188.

25. *WNYA,* 29.

26. *WWC,* II, 383; and *WNYA,* 114–16.

27. *The Diary of Philip Hone* (New York: Dodd, Mead, 1889), II, 140–41.

28. *WNYA,* 47, 139 n. 26.

29. *WNYA,* 57.

30. Cauldwell, "Walt Whitman as a Young Man."

31. Jerome Mushkat, *Tammany: The Evolution of a Political Machine, 1789–1865* (Syracuse, N.Y.: Syracuse University Press, 1971), 185–86, 192–98.

32. *WNYA,* 141n.

33. *Dear Brother Walt: The Letters of Thomas Jefferson Whitman,* ed. Dennis Berthold and Kenneth M. Price (Kent, Ohio: Kent State University Press, 1984), 65–66.

34. *GWW,* 14, 130.

35. *C,* I, 117.

36. *WNYA,* 6–8.

37. *WWC,* III, 439.

38. *WNYA,* 112–13.

39. *WNYA,* 82–83; *WEBDA,* 125–29; and *WWC,* III, 59.

40. "Heaven save the mark," wrote Edwin Spooner. "Shall not we have some more scraps from the desk of a school-master? We feel ourselves bound to look after Long Islanders, and this is a great joke! . . . Teaching very small children [, Whitman,] may be an easy life, but teaching those big children of Tammany Hall may look big but it seems very ferocious" (*UPP,* I, 33n).

41. *Letters from New-York,* 101–10.

42. *WNYA,* 105–9, 135; *WEBDA,* 58, and *WWJ,* I, 190–91.

43. *WNYA,* 49–52.

44. *Early Lectures of Ralph Waldo Emerson,* III, 352.

45. *Benjamin Franklin's Autobiography,* ed. J. A. Leo Lemay and P. M. Zall (New York: W. W. Norton, 1986), 36; and Jack S. Blocker, *American Temperance Movements: Cycles of Reform* (Boston: Twayne, 1989), 3.

46. Blocker, *American Temperance Movements,* 4.

47. *WWC,* I, 79.

48. Whitman-Feinberg Collection (Accession number 19, 188), LC.

49. Lincoln addressed the Washingtonians of Springfield, Illinois, on Washington's birthday, 1842; see *Abraham Lincoln: His Speeches and Writings,* ed. Roy P. Basler (Cleveland: World, 1946), 131–41.

50. *EPF,* 121.

51. *WNYA,* 35–36.

52. *EPF,* 130.

53. Emory Holloway, "Portrait of a Poet: A Life of Walt Whitman," unpublished manuscript in the Berg Collection of the New York Public Library, 504 n. 60.

54. *Sit,* 184.

55. *WWC,* I, 93.

56. *WBC,* 322.

57. Holloway, "Portrait of a Poet," II, 504 n. 60.

58. *EPF,* 124n, where the background to the novel is summed up, giving all the original sources. *Franklin Evans* was advertised as *Franklin Evans; or the Merchant's Clerk* in the *New World* of August 19, 1843; an abridged edition of the novel appeared under a pseudonym in the *Brooklyn Daily Eagle* of November 16–30, 1846, while Whitman was its editor.

59. *EPF,* 213; see also p. 206.

60. *EPF,* 204, 209. See my argument on *Pudd'nhead Wilson* in *Lost in the Custom-house: Authorship in the American Renaissance* (Iowa City: University of Iowa Press, 1993), 125–40.

61. *EPF,* 236–37, 239.

62. The discovery of this second temperance novel, or its fragment, was made by Emory Holloway; see *American Literature* 27 (January 1956): 577–78. *The Madman* can be found in *EPF,* 240–43.

63. *WWJ,* I, 183–88.

CHAPTER 4. HEART-SONGS IN BROOKLYN

1. Esther Shephard, "Walt Whitman's Whereabouts in the Winter of 1842–1843," *American Literature* 29 (November 1957): 289–96.

2. Shephard, "Walt Whitman's Whereabouts," 292–96.

3. *WWJ,* I, 164–65. See *WWJ,* I, 159–98, for the latest collection of Whitman's publications between late 1842 and 1845.

4. "New England Reformers," in *Essays: Second Series* (1844); quoted from the Riverside Edition (1891), 241.

5. For the full text of "A Sketch," see Jerome Loving, "A Newly Discovered Whitman Poem," *WWQR* 11 (Winter 1994): 117–22. "Stanzas," published in the *New World* of October 22, 1842, and signed "W," may also be Whitman's. See *WWJ,* I, 153–54.

6. Park Benjamin Collection, Columbia University Library. See also Merle M. Hoover, *Park Benjamin: Poet and Editor* (New York: Columbia University Press, 1948); and *Poems of Park Benjamin* (New York: Columbia University Press, 1948).

7. Park Benjamin Collection.

8. In "Our Future Lot" we get the same affirmation of the afterlife found in the conclusion to "A Sketch." In the first poem we find the statement that "The flickering taper's glow shall change / To bright and starlike majesty, / Radiant with pure and piercing light / From the Eternal's eye." The second concludes with the "sweet star, whose golden gleam, / Pierces the tempest's gathering gloom, / In the rich radiance of its beam [to tell] of light beyond the tomb!"

9. For the story of Holloway's discovery of the manuscript and its biographical results, see Jerome Loving, "Emory Holloway and the Quest for Whitman's 'Manhood,'" *WWQR* 11 (Summer 1993): 1–17. In his 1926 biography, Holloway ignored his discovery of the male lover in "Once I Pass'd Through a Populous City."

10. See Holloway, *UPP,* I, lviii n. 15, where it is stated that the original draft of Ellen O'Connor Calder's "Personal Recollections of Walt Whitman" (Berg Collection, New York Public Library), *Atlantic Monthly* 99 (June 1907): 825–34, included this claim.

11. Justin Kaplan, *Walt Whitman: A Life* (New York: Simon and Schuster, 1980), 96.

12. *Early Lectures of Ralph Waldo Emerson,* ed. Robert E. Spiller and Wallace E. Williams (Cambridge: Harvard University Press, 1972), III, 364.

13. *EPF,* 244–47.

14. *EPF,* 251–56.

15. Shephard, "Walt Whitman's Whereabouts," 294.

16. *EPF,* 248–50. The consensus is that Whitman wrote "My Boys and Girls" as early as 1835 because he alludes to one of his sisters, "a beautiful girl in her fourteenth year." Mary Elizabeth, the poet's older sister, would have been fourteen that year. Yet it is unlikely that Whitman wrote this piece at age sixteen or that he would have taken so paternalistic an attitude toward a sister only two years his junior and possibly ahead of him in her passage through adolescence. Not only is the style similar to other writings in the mid-1840s, but there is a retrospective tone about the essay that may project, especially in the case of Mary, her future problems (by 1840 she had run off and married a man who became an alcoholic). Furthermore, the narrator in "My Boys and Girls" writes of Andrew that "at this moment I question whether, in a wrestle, he would not get the better of me, and put me flat." Unless this is simply a case of brotherly hyperbole, it is unlikely that the eight-year-old Andrew would have bested his sixteen-year-old brother in 1835, though it might have been possible in 1844, when Andrew was around seventeen and Walt twenty-four. There are also allusions to other children not necessarily related to the narrator, listed by initials in the fashion Whitman later listed his male comrades in his daybooks. For these reasons, it seems unlikely that "My Boys and Girls" was written in 1835; its theme and style match too well with what he was writing in 1844.

17. Edwin Haviland Miller, *Walt Whitman's "Song of Myself": A Mosaic of Interpretations* (Iowa City: University of Iowa Press, 1989), 118. For more recent analyses of Whitman and American Indians, see William J. Scheick, *The Half-Blood: A Cultural Symbol in Nineteenth-Century American Fiction* (Knoxville: University of Tennessee Press, 1979), 36–38; and Ed Folsom, *Walt Whitman's Native Representations* (Cambridge: Cambridge University Press, 1994), 55–98.

18. Roy Harvey Pearce, *Savagism and Civilization: A Study of the Indian and the American Mind* (Berkeley and Los Angeles: University of California Press, 1988 [1953]), 194.

19. *Brooklyn Daily Eagle,* June 1–6, 8, 9, 1846.

20. *The Confidence-Man,* ed. H. Bruce Franklin (New York: Bobbs-Merrill, 1967), 206.

21. George M. Frederickson, *The Black Image in the White Mind: The Debate on Afro-American Character and Destiny* (New York: Harper and Row, 1971), 172.

22. *EPF,* 287, 291.

23. Emory Holloway, "More Light on Whitman," *American Mercury* 1 (February 1924): 183–84.

24. *EPF,* 292.

25. *Brooklyn Daily Eagle,* April 24, 1846.

26. See also "An Incident of Life in New York Beneath the Surface" and "The Cause and the Man," *Brooklyn Evening Star,* September 30 and October 2, 1845.

27. "Tear Down and Build Over Again," *American Review* 2 (November 1845): 536–38, reprinted in *UPP,* I, 92–97; and *Brooklyn Evening Star,* October 4, 1845.

28. *WWJ,* I, 160–63; *Brooklyn Evening Star,* March 24, 1846; and *WWC,* VIII, 308 ("I have wondered today why people should so object to electrical execution. If there must be execution, this is very *clean!*").

29. "A Dialogue," *Democratic Review,* November 1845, and *Brooklyn Evening Star,* November 28–29, 1845.

30. *Narrative of the Life of Frederick Douglass, An American Slave, Written by Himself,* ed. Houston A. Baker, Jr. (New York: Penguin, 1986), 83.

31. "Hurrah for Hanging!" in *GF,* I, 97–101.

32. "Wyatt's Execution and Dying Speech," *Brooklyn Daily Eagle,* August 20, 1846; and "Execution of Wyatt," *Brooklyn Evening Star,* August 19, 1846.

33. *Brooklyn Evening Star,* October 10, 11, 1845, and January 7, 8, February 16, March 6, 1846.

34. See Florence Bernstein Freeman, "Educating the Young," *Whitman Looks at the Schools* (New York: Kings County Press, 1950), 82–85.

35. "Art-Singing and Heart-Singing" (see *UPP,* I, 104–6). Whitman slightly revised the essay under the caption "Music That *Is* Music" and printed it in the *Brooklyn Daily Eagle* on December 4, 1846 (see *GF,* II, 346–49).

36. Robert D. Faner, *Walt Whitman and Opera* (Carbondale: Southern Illinois University Press, 1951), 37. See also Floyd Stovall, *The Foreground of Leaves of Grass* (Charlottesville: University of Virginia Press, 1974), 79–100.

37. *UPP,* I, 104n.

38. *PW,* 17, 231, 723.

39. *GF,* I, xxi; see also *WEBDA,* 19.

40. *PW,* 16.

41. *GF,* I, xxiii; and *WEBDA,* 77; see also his "Conversion to Phrenology," *Walt Whitman Newsletter* 4 (June 1958): 95–97; and Edward Hungerford, "Walt Whitman and His Chart of Bumps," *American Literature* 2 (January 1931): 350–84, which includes Lorenzo N. Fowler's phrenological analysis of Whitman's character.

42. *WNYA,* 105.

43. *GF,* II, 91–96; *GF,* I, 59–65; and "Women's Property," *Brooklyn Daily Eagle,* October 3, 7, 1846.

44. "The Little Minstrel Girl," *Brooklyn Daily Eagle,* July 13, 1847.

45. *Brooklyn Daily Eagle,* May 7, August 31, 1847; July 10, 1847.

46. *Brooklyn Daily Eagle,* August 17, 1847.

47. "Atrocious Practice of Publishing Private Letters," *Brooklyn Daily Eagle,* April 17, 1846.

48. *GF,* I, 187–91.

49. *Brooklyn Daily Eagle,* March 24 and November 5, 1847.

50. See my discussion of this famous quarrel, which kept the two apart for ten years, in *Walt Whitman's Champion: William Douglas O'Connor* (College Station: Texas A&M University Press, 1978), 95–102.

51. W. E. B. Du Bois, *The Souls of Black Folk* (New York: American Library, 1969), 45–46.

52. *GF,* I, 222, and *WWJ,* I, lxviii.

53. See William S. McFeely, *Frederick Douglass* (New York: W. W. Norton, 1991), 62. Since Whitman had essentially made this argument as early as 1847 in the *Eagle* (see *GF,* I, 208–14), his similar argument in the 1850s may not be evidence of his reading Douglass. On the other hand, it is perhaps difficult to believe that the man who edited the *Brooklyn Freeman* in 1849 did not read Douglass in 1855.

54. *WWC,* IV, 473.

55. *GF,* I, 227–28.

56. *Brooklyn Daily Eagle,* December 10, 1847.

57. McFeely, *Frederick Douglass,* 115, 147–51.

58. The best study of Emerson on this subject is Len Gougeon, *Virtue's Hero: Emerson, Antislavery, and Reform* (Athens: University of Georgia Press, 1990).

59. *GF,* II, 270–71.

CHAPTER 5. CRESCENT CITY SOJOURN

1. Henry Bryan Binns's enhancements are discussed later in this chapter; in *Walt Whitman: His Life and Work* (Boston: Houghton Mifflin, 1906), Bliss Perry writes: "Each man [Rousseau and Whitman] wrote superbly about paternity and each deserted his own children" (p. 278).

2. "Starting Newspapers," in *PW,* 288.

3. The *Crescent* was owned by the A. A. Hayes Company, with Hayes and McClure listed as the "Founders and Owners" and Hayes owning a majority of the stock; see Charles F. Youngman, *Historic Sketch of the Daily Crescent and New Orleans Daily, from March 5, 1848, to April 20, 1869* (New Orleans: City Archives, 1938), iii.

4. J. E. McClure to William F. McClure, December 25, 1848 (Hill Memorial Library, Louisiana State University).

5. *UPP,* II, 78; see also *NUPM,* I, 86–87.

6. *PW,* 605.

7. *C,* I, 31, 29.

8. *UPP,* I, 181–89.

9. *C,* I, 27.

10. *C,* I, 29; and *WWC,* II, 559. In "A Walk About Town," *Crescent,* April 26, and credibly credited to Whitman by Holloway (*UPP,* I, 223–24), the author describes his residence as "near Lafayette" Street, which intersected St. Charles Avenue two blocks south of Poydras. See also Charles E. Feinberg, "A Whitman Collector Destroys a Whitman Myth," *Papers of the Bibliographical Society of America* 52 (Second Quarter 1958): 78.

11. Lyle Saxon, *A Walk Through the Vieux Carre and a Short History of the St. Charles Hotel* (New Orleans: Dinkler Hotels, 1941), 45; and *UPP,* II, 77.

12. *C,* I, 30.

13. *UPP,* I, 199.

14. *GF,* II, 210–11.

15. *UPP,* I, 78.

16. *UPP,* I, 204n; and *PW,* 606.

17. Holloway is also the biographer who printed without explanation the "heterosexual" version of "Once I Pass'd Through a Populous City," when he knew of—indeed had discovered and printed earlier—the "homosexual" version; see Jerome Loving, "Emory Holloway and the Quest for Whitman's 'Manhood,'" *WWQR* 11 (Summer 1993): 4; and Emory Holloway, *Whitman: An Interpretation in Narrative* (New York: Alfred A. Knopf, 1926), 66.

18. *UPP,* I, 204; "Mrs. Giddy Gay Butterfly" is reprinted in William White, "Sketches of the Sidewalks and Levees; With Glimpses into the New Orleans Bar (Rooms): Mrs. Giddy Gay Butterfly,'" *Walt Whitman Newsletter* 4 (September 1958): 87–90.

19. Henry Bryan Binns, *A Life of Walt Whitman* (London: Methuen, 1905), 51.

20. *C,* V, 73.

21. Leon Bazalgette, *Walt Whitman: L'homme et son oeuvre* (Paris: Société de Mercure de France, 1908), 59–95.

22. *Solitary Singer,* 96–97.

23. Bennet Dowler, M.D., in *Tableaux of New Orleans* (New Orleans: Daily Delta Office, 1852); quoted in *C,* I, 31n, the same page where, in the text, the source of Jeff's remarks is located.

24. *UPP,* I, 193.

25. Echoed in the *Brooklyn Daily Eagle* of February 4, 1848.

26. *UPP,* I, 191.

27. *HW,* 194.

28. *New Orleans Daily Crescent,* March 22, 23, 1848; and *New Orleans Picayune,* March 16, 1848.

29. *UPP,* I, 225.

30. "Annexation" (June 6, 1846) and "More Stars for the Spangled Banner" (June 29, 1846), *GF,* I, 242–46.

31. In the *New Orleans Delta* of March 16, 1848, Larue advertised his part-time services as "Attorney and Counselor at Law" with an office at 99 Gravier Street: "Claims prosecuted and Collections made for Northern and Western Merchants in any part of the State." Larue is also listed among the co-owners of the *Crescent* after September 9, 1848.

32. *UPP,* II, 78.

33. *New Orleans Daily Crescent,* March 16, 1848.

34. *New Orleans Daily Crescent,* March 23 and May 17, 1848.

35. *New Orleans Daily Crescent,* April 14, 1848.

36. *New Orleans Daily Crescent,* April 22, 28, and May 20, 1848.

37. During the Civil War, Whitman—according to Ellen O'Connor (Calder)—lamented the carnage, saying: "I dont [*sic*] care for the niggers in comparison with this slaughter"; see Jerome Loving, *Walt Whitman's Champion: William Douglas O'Connor* (College Station: Texas A&M University Press, 1978), 86–87; and William Sloane Kennedy, *Reminiscences of Walt Whitman* (London: Alexander Gardener, 1896), 35. In a letter to Thomas H. Johnston, May 29, 1902, Charles W. Eldridge, Whitman's close friend and former publisher, recalled: "Of the Negro as a race [Whitman] had a poor opinion. He said that there was in the constitution of the negro's mind an irredeemable trifling or volatile element, and that he would never amount to much in the scale of civilization. I never knew him to have a friend among the negroes while he was in Washington, and he never seemed to care for them or they for him, although he never manifested any particular aversion to them" (Berg Collection, New York Public Library). In an entry for March 8, 1890, Horace Traubel records Whitman as saying that "one reason why I never went full on the nigger question [is that]—the nigger would not turn—would not do anything for himself—he would only act when prompted to act. No! no! I

should not like to see the nigger in the saddle—it seems unnatural; for he is only there when propped there, and propping don't civilize. I have always had a latent sympathy for the Southerner—and even for those in Europe—the Cavalier-folk—hateful as they are to me abstractly—un-democratic—from putting myself in a way in their shoes. Till the nigger can do something for himself, little can be done for him" (*WWC,* VI, 323). See, however, an important addition to our knowledge of Whitman's racial attitudes in Chapter 8.

38. *GF,* I, 29–30, 47–50.

39. *UPP,* II, 78: "a young fellow named Da Poute, officiated as translator of Mexican and foreign n[ews]-items, factotum in general." This last phrase seems to reinforce the possibility that Da Poute did all the foreign news.

40. *HW,* 198; and Larry J. Reynolds, *European Revolutions and the American Literary Renaissance* (New Haven: Yale University Press, 1987), 134. Unfortunately, Rubin (*HW*) does not date precisely the quotations he ascribes to Whitman, but Reynolds (pp. 134–35) follows up with more scholarly care, citing Whitman editorials—in addition to the March 31 article—for April 7, 8, 21, 27, May 3 and 18. Of these (excluding March 31), all but one are general editorials, very likely written by Larue or in combination with the editorial staff that included Whitman; the article of April 8 is a one-sentence filler entitled "A Fact."

41. *New Orleans Daily Crescent,* April 1, 1846.

42. *GF,* I, 242–43; Preface to 1855 *LGCRE,* 709.

43. "Resurgamus," *Providence Journal,* September 23, 1853; O'Connor also rejected the 1848 revolutions because of their excesses in "Storm," apparently never published. See Loving, *Walt Whitman's Champion,* 4–7.

44. *WWC,* III, 43.

45. Youngman, *Historic Sketch,* 25.

46. *C,* I, 34.

47. *UPP,* II, 77–78.

48. Eric Foner, *Politics and Ideology in the Age of the Civil War* (New York: Oxford University Press, 1980), 79–82; and George M. Frederickson, *The Black Image in the White Mind: The Debate on Afro-American Character and Destiny* (New York: Harper and Row, 1971), 131, 140. The distinction between the free-soil and the abolitionist position is carefully analyzed with reference to Whitman in Martin Klammer, *Whitman, Slavery, and the Emergence of Leaves of Grass* (University Park: Penn State University Press, 1995), 27–43. For Whitman's subsequent relationship with the *Eagle,* see the *Crescent* for March 28, 1848, which carried the following message from the *Brooklyn Eagle*: "Cousin of the Brooklyn Eagle, we reciprocate your good wishes—for 'auld lang syne.'" The *Eagle* had also praised the first issue of the *Crescent* on March 14, 1848; see *GF,* I, xxxvi.

49. *UPP,* II, 77; in *HW* (201), the date of departure is stated as Friday, May 26.

50. "The Mississippi at Midnight" became "Sailing the Mississippi at Midnight" (an inferior version, which manifests Whitman's later propensity to overstate his descriptions in an

effort to seem more "religious") in *SD;* see *EPF,* 42–43. Unlike "The New World," "The Mississippi at Midnight" is signed "WW." "Crossing the Alleghenies," which includes the lines about converting infidels, is reprinted in *UPP,* I, 181–86.

51. The ellipses are Whitman's—following the usage of the rhetorics of the day, which employed them to indicate pauses in a speech.

52. Denise B. Bethel, "Notes on an Early Daguerreotype of Walt Whitman," *WWQR* 9 (Winter 1992): 148–53; see also Margaret Denton Smith and Mary Louise Tucker, *Photography in New Orleans: The Early Years, 1840–1865* (Baton Rouge: Louisiana State University Press, 1982), 49.

53. J. E. McClure to William F. McClure, December 25, 1848 (Louisiana State University).

54. "New Orleans in 1848," *PW,* 604–10; and *UPP,* II, 78–79. See also *WWC,* III, 43. The manuscript of "New Orleans in 1848," unknown until now, is deposited in the Louisiana State Museum and Historical Center in New Orleans; my thanks to its librarian, Kathryn Page, for calling it to my attention.

55. This sentence is crossed out in the copy of "Whitman in New Orleans" he sent to the *Picayune,* most likely by Whitman himself.

56. Fragment of 1848 notebook (whose verso Whitman used for another memorandum), Duke University Library.

57. *NUPM,* I, 41, where the document is possibly misdated as 1890. The manuscript in the Van Sindern Collection, Yale University Library, is catalogued as "May, 1891."

CHAPTER 6. SIMMERING, SIMMERING, SIMMERING

1. See *Solitary Singer,* 100–101, for the implied misplacement of the *Eagle* attack. "The Shadow and the Light of a Young Man's Soul" has been reprinted in *EPF,* 327–30; and *UPP,* I, 229–34; see Chapter 2 for its discussion.

2. "A Legend of Life and Love" was published in the *Long Island Democrat* on August 7, 1849; for Brenton's interest, see *UPP,* I, xxxii n. 6; see Chapter 2 for Whitman's performance on the *Democrat.*

3. *Voices from the Press; A Collection of Sketches, Essays, and Poems,* ed. James J. Brenton (New York: Charles B. Norton, 1850), iii–iv. "Tomb-Blossoms" originally appeared in the *Democratic Review* of January 1842. Whitman refers to Brenton as "Dr. Franklin" in "Letters of a Travelling Bachelor" No. 4 (*HW,* 326).

4. The *New York Tribune* of January 21, 1848, reported "that the Barnburners of Brooklyn are about starting a new daily paper, as, it is said, The Eagle has returned to Old Hunkerism again. Mr. Walter Whitman, late of the Eagle, is to have charge of the new enterprise." The *Eagle* responded to this report the next day: "This will be news to our friends in Brooklyn. The Tribune need not console itself with any such nonsense. The democracy of Kings county will continue to present a solid front to the old bank, high tariff, federal and

anti war party, and we promise that they shall have the benefit of all *raging and bitterness* which exists among us."

5. "Good-Bye My Fancy," in *PW,* II, 697; and *HW,* 208.

6. *HW,* 210.

7. *Brooklyn Freeman,* September 9, 1848; a facsimile of the only known copy of the *Freeman* is packaged with a *Catalogue of the Whitman Collection in the Duke University Library Being Part of the Trent Collection,* ed. Ellen Frances Frey (Durham: Duke University Press, 1945).

8. *Brooklyn Daily Eagle,* September 11, 1848. It has been suggested that fires were deliberately set in Brooklyn, and that the *Freeman* office may have been torched by pro-slavery advocates (see Gay Wilson Allen, "Whitman Biography in 1992," *Centennial Essays: Walt Whitman,* ed. Ed Folsom [Iowa City: University of Iowa Press, 1994], 5, but Whitman's paper was primarily arguing for the provisions of the Wilmot Proviso, which forbade slavery in the new territories, not the abolition of slavery in the southern states, where its status was protected by the Constitution. Furthermore, New Yorkers were mainly neutral about slavery, and this neutrality extended to the Whitman family. See, for example, army lieutenant George Whitman's remarks after the Battle of Antietam, on September 30, 1862, quoted in Chapter 1.

9. *UPP,* I, lii–liii; the quote comes from the *Brooklyn Evening Star* of November 1, 1848. See also *UPP,* II, 88 (for Whitman's purchase of the house at 106 Myrtle) and *GF,* II, following p. 242, for a photograph of 106 Myrtle, where the *Freeman* was published.

10. "One or Two Index Items," *PW,* 360.

11. *UPP,* I, liii n. 2.

12. This editorial is reprinted in *Sit,* 5.

13. *Brooklyn Daily Eagle,* November 13, 1848; *In Re,* 33; for details about the *Salesman,* see *HW,* 268. See Chapter 8 for the erroneous notion, entertained by previous biographers, that Whitman was editor of the *Brooklyn Daily Times.*

14. See Chapter 1.

15. *HW,* 323.

16. *HW,* 337, 347–48; "Philosophy of Ferries" (August 13, 1847), in *GF,* II, 159–66, and *UPP,* I, 168–71; "My Passion for Ferries," *PW,* 16.

17. Bucke, 24.

18. *HW,* 350.

19. For the fullest discussion of this notebook, see *NUPM,* I, 53–55; "[T]albot Wilson" refers to Jesse Talbot, a Brooklyn painter who lived on Wilson Street; Whitman wrote about him in 1850 (*HW,* 379 n. 11). Holloway dated this notebook as early as 1847 on the basis of two entries, but Whitman—as the curators of the Trent Collection at Duke discovered—often reused paper, sometimes pasting the used sides of two sheets of paper together to make a clean one on both sides. Since Whitman stated through Bucke (p. 24) that he did not begin writing out the actual poems for the first edition until 1854, the jottings that anticipate "Song of My-

self" and other poems rather directly were probably written long after 1847. Because this notebook was one of ten stolen from the LC during World War II, the edition of it in *NUPM* had to be based on a partial photocopy (which, as it turned out when four of the originals were recovered in 1994, reproduced all but the inside front and back covers). See *The Notebooks and a Cardboard Butterfly Missing from the Whitman Papers* (Washington, D.C.: Library of Congress, 1954); and Alice Birney, "Missing Whitman Notebooks Returned to the Library of Congress," *WWQR* 12 (Spring 1995): 217–29.

20. The results of the examination are dated July 16, 1849, but the fact that Whitman gave his age as twenty-nine suggests that it was done earlier and the report written up in July; see *Faint Clews and Indirections: Manuscripts of Walt Whitman and His Family,* ed. Clarence Gohdes and Rollo G. Silver (Durham: Duke University Press, 1949), 233–36, where Whitman's phrenological analysis is reprinted.

21. For Whitman's criticism, see Chapter 4; and Edward Hungerford, "Walt Whitman and His Chart of Bumps," *American Literature* 2 (January 1931): 358.

22. Hungerford, "Walt Whitman," 363; Whitman published his phrenological review in several places, including the second printing of the first *Leaves of Grass,* its second (1856) edition under "Leaves-Droppings," and *Leaves of Grass Imprints: American and European Criticisms on 'Leaves of Grass'* (1860).

23. Arthur Wrobel, "Whitman and the Phrenologists: The Divine Body and the Sensuous Soul," *Publications of the Modern Language Association* 89 (January 1974): 17–23.

24. Hungerford, "Walt Whitman," 364.

25. Paul I. Wellman, *The House Divides: The Age of Jackson and Lincoln, from the War of 1812 to the Civil War* (New York: Doubleday, 1966), 323–24.

26. *EPF,* 46, where Brasher fails to note the change from the 1850 version: "Douglas, Cass, and Walker" for "Webster, Cooper, Walker."

27. Edgar Lee Masters, *Whitman* (New York: Charles Scribner's Sons, 1937), 87. Greeley's paper had also praised Whitman's efforts as editor of the *Brooklyn Freeman;* see *Sit,* 6. See also *WWC,* V, 207–8, for a curious discussion of "Blood-Money." For his part, Whitman recalled that "Greeley was not a first-classer—never got beyond outer walls" (*WWC,* VIII, 295–96).

28. Gay Wilson Allen, *The New Walt Whitman Handbook* (New York: New York University Press, 1975), 219. "Blood-Money" is reprinted in *EPF,* 47–48, where the text varies slightly from that printed in the *Evening Post* of April 30, 1850.

29. *EPF,* 36–37; and *UPP,* I, 25 n. 2.

30. Wellmann, *The House Divides,* 331–32.

31. See Jerome Loving, *Emerson, Whitman, and the American Muse* (Chapel Hill: University of North Carolina Press, 1982).

32. Wesley T. Mott, *"The Strains of Eloquence: Emerson and His Sermons* (University Park: Pennsylvania State University Press, 1989). See also Susan Roberson, *Emerson in His Sermons: A Man-Made Self* (Columbia: University of Missouri Press, 1995).

33. Albert J. von Frank, *An Emerson Chronology* (Boston: G. K. Hall, 1994), 254–55; and William Charvat, *Emerson's American Lecture Engagements: A Chronological List* (New York: New York Public Library, 1961), 24–25.

34. Emerson to Marcus Spring, March 22, 1850; *Letters of Ralph Waldo Emerson,* ed. Ralph L. Rusk (New York: Columbia University Press, 1939), IV, 186.

35. *Letters of Ralph Waldo Emerson,* IV, 86n.

36. *New York Evening Post,* March 15, 1850.

37. *WWC,* IV, 161, 165–67.

38. Quotations from "Natural Aristocracy" are based on a conflation of the manuscript at the Houghton Library, Harvard University (bMs Am 1280.200 1) and "Aristocracy," in *Lectures and Biographical Sketches* (Boston: Houghton Mifflin, 1890), 33–67. For Cabot's role in *The Complete Works of Ralph Waldo Emerson,* see Nancy Craig Simmons, "Arranging the Sibylline Leaves: James Elliot Cabot's Work as Emerson's Literary Executor," in *Studies in the American Renaissance 1983,* ed. Joel Myerson (Charlottesville: University Press of Virginia, 1983), 335–89.

39. *In Re,* 35.

40. See, for example, C. Carroll Hollis, *Language and Style in Leaves of Grass* (Chapel Hill: University of North Carolina Press, 1983), chap. 1 ("The Oratorical Impulse").

41. "Eloquence," in *Society and Solitude* (Boston: Houghton Mifflin, 1883), 63–98.

42. *Walt Whitman's Workshop: A Collection of Unpublished Manuscripts,* ed. Clifton Joseph Furness (Cambridge: Harvard University Press, 1928), 37; and *In Re,* 38.

43. "Books," in *Society and Solitude,* 186–210.

44. *In Re,* 39.

45. The French title of *The Journeyman Joiner* is *Le compagnon du tour de France,* and the English translation is called *The Journeyman Joiner; or The Companion of the Tower of France.*

46. Esther Shephard, *Walt Whitman's Pose* (New York: Harcourt, Brace, 1936); and *UPP,* I, 135.

47. Roger Asselineau, *The Evolution of Walt Whitman* (Cambridge: Harvard University Press, 1960), I, 58–60. Another French writer whose thought parallels Whitman's is Jules Michelet, whose *History of France* (1847) Whitman reviewed in the *Brooklyn Eagle.* See Gay Wilson Allen, *The New Walt Whitman Handbook* (New York: New York University Press, 1975), 268–70.

48. *WWC,* III, 422–23; and *PW,* 759.

49. George Sand, *Consuelo; A Romance of Venice* (New York: Da Capo Press, 1979), 3; and Bucke, 29, 148.

50. *PW,* 759.

51. See, for example, P. M. Mitchell, *A History of Danish Literature* (New York: Kraus-Thomson, 1971), 118.

52. Bernhard S. Ingemann, *The Childhood of King Eric Menved,* trans. J. Kesson (London: Bruce and Wyld, 1846), 139–40.

53. *C,* V, 282–83; this letter chronologically belongs in *C,* I, and appears in *C,* V, under "Addenda."

54. William White, "Whitman's First 'Literary' Letter," *American Literature* 35 (March 1963): 84–85.

55. *C,* I, 39.

56. Bernhard S. Ingemann, *King Eric and the Outlaws; or The Throne, the Church, and the People in the Thirteenth Century,* trans. Jane Frances Chapman (London: Longman, Brown, Green, and Longmans, 1843), I, 208.

57. Ingemann, *The Childhood of King Eric Menved,* 140.

58. *UPP,* I, 234 n. 1; *Walt Whitman: A Descriptive Bibliography,* ed. Joel Myerson (Pittsburgh: University of Pittsburgh Press, 1993), 659; and *C,* I, 38.

59. See also John Dizikes, *Opera in America: A Cultural History* (New Haven: Yale University Press, 1993), 126–27.

60. *WEBDA,* 41–42.

61. *Brooklyn Daily Eagle,* September 2 and 4, 1850.

62. *UPP,* I, 257; *PW,* 21; and Dizikes, *Opera in America,* 134, 127.

63. *PW,* 696.

64. Robert D. Faner, *Walt Whitman and Opera* (Carbondale: Southern Illinois University Press, 1951), 10, 30. See also Gary Schmidgall, *Walt Whitman: A Gay Life* (New York: Dutton, 1997), 1–3, 13–68; and Floyd Stovall, *The Foreground of Leaves of Grass* (Charlottesville: University Press of Virginia, 1974), 79–100, where it is argued—somewhat unpersuasively—that Italian opera was not necessarily superior in influence to British and French opera.

65. Rev. M. Owen Lee, "Walt Whitman and Opera," First Intermission Feature, Texaco-Metropolitan Opera Broadcast of *Lucia di Lammermoor,* January 29, 1994, p. 3; and John Townsend Trowbridge, *My Own Story, With Recollections of Noted Persons* (Boston: Houghton Mifflin, 1903), 369.

66. Lee, "Walt Whitman and Opera," 4.

67. *PW,* 235n; Whitman confessed a similar indebtedness to the singing of Bettini in 1851 ("I have often wished to know this man, for a minute, that I might tell him how much of the highest order of pleasure he has conferred upon me. His voice has often affected me to tears"). See also *PW,* 694; and *WWC,* II, 173.

68. *Faint Clews and Indirections,* 19.

69. Dizikes, *Opera in America,* 140; and *Faint Clews and Indirections,* 19.

70. Faner, *Walt Whitman and Opera,* 45, 47.

71. Trowbridge, *My Own Story,* 367.

72. *Dictionary of American Biography,* I, 496–97.

73. Rollo G. Silver, "Whitman in 1850: Three Uncollected Articles," *American Literature* 19 (January 1948): 304–5.

74. "Something About Art and Brooklyn Artists," *New York Evening Post,* February 1, 1851, reprinted in *UPP,* I, 236–38. See also Whitman's "Brooklyn Art Union—Walter Libby—A Hint or Two on the Philosophy of Painting," *Brooklyn Daily Advertizer,* December 21, 1850; and *WWC,* II, 506.

75. Silver, "Whitman in 1850," 306–8.

76. Alice Cook Brown, "Charles Louis Heyde, Painter of Vermont Scenery," *Antiques* 101 (June 1972): 1027–30.

77. Barbara Knapp Hamblett, "Charles Louis Heyde, Painter of Vermont Scenery" (M.A. thesis; Oneonta: State University of New York Press, 1976), 12–13; see also Katherine Molinoff, *Some Notes on Whitman's Family* (New York: Comet Press, 1941), 37.

78. Ruth Bohan, "'The Gathering of the Forces': Walt Whitman and the Visual Arts, 1845–55," *The Mickle Street Review,* no. 12 (1990): 26; reprinted in *Walt Whitman and the Visual Arts,* ed. Geoffrey M. Sill and Robert K. Tarbell (New Brunswick: Rutgers University Press, 1992), 1–27.

79. "Art and Artists," in *UPP,* I, 241–47.

80. *Complete Works of Ralph Waldo Emerson,* ed. Edward Waldo Emerson (Boston: Houghton Mifflin, 1903–4), III, 27.

81. "Letters from Paumanok" and "A Plea for Water" are printed in *UPP,* I, 247–59.

82. *PW,* 681.

83. Floyd Stovall, *The Foreground of Leaves of Grass,* 238–39; a list of Whitman's readings and clippings can be found in *Complete Writings of Walt Whitman,* ed. Richard Maurice Bucke, Thomas B. Harned, and Horace L. Traubel (New York: G. P. Putnam's Sons, 1902), IX, 47–206; and some of the actual marginalia are in the Trent Collection, Duke University Library. See also Kenneth M. Price, *Whitman and Tradition* (New Haven: Yale University Press, 1990), 8–34.

84. *Solitary Singer,* 111; Asselineau, *The Evolution of Walt Whitman,* I, 63; Betsy Erkkila, *Whitman the Political Poet* (New York: Oxford University Press, 1989); Martin Klammer, *Whitman, Slavery and the Emergence of Leaves of Grass* (University Park: Pennsylvania State University Press, 1995); and M. Wynn Thomas, *The Lunar Light of Whitman's Poetry* (Cambridge: Harvard University Press, 1987). Asselineau is less sure of Whitman's conversion than Allen.

85. Daniel Hoffman, "'Hankering, Gross, Mystical, Nude': Whitman's 'Self' and the American Tradition," in *Walt Whitman of Mickle Street: A Centennial Collection,* ed. Geoffrey M. Sill (Knoxville: University of Tennessee Press, 1994), 1.

86. Bucke, 24; Whitman read and reviewed Bucke's manuscript, making many changes; see Chapter 12.

87. Richard Maurice Bucke, *Cosmic Consciousness: A Study in the Evolution of the Human Mind* (New York: E. P. Dutton, 1923), 227–28; and Charles W. Eldridge to John Burroughs, March 7, 1896 (Berg).

88. *NUPM,* I, 56.

89. *NUPM,* I, 57, 59.

90. *NUPM,* I, 70. See Henry S. Saunders, *Parodies on Walt Whitman* (New York: American Library Service, 1923).

91. *NUPM,* I, 75; and Justin Kaplan, *Walt Whitman: A Life* (New York: Simon and Schuster, 1980), 147.

92. *WWC,* II, 471.

CHAPTER 7. THE BEGINNING OF A GREAT CAREER

1. *As a Strong Bird on Pinions Free* (*LGCRE,* 739–44); and "A Backward Glance O'er Travel'd Roads," in *PW,* 714.

2. *LG,* v–vii, x–xi.

3. *Walt Whitman's Leaves of Grass: The First (1855) Edition,* ed. Malcolm Cowley (New York: Penguin, 1959), vii.

4. *LG,* x.

5. "Walt Whitman's Leaves of Grass," *Putnam's Magazine,* September 1855, one of the reviews Whitman bound into the second issue of the first edition of *Leaves of Grass;* and *In Re,* 35.

6. *UPP,* II, 88 n. 8; see also Charles Feinberg, "A Whitman Collector Destroys a Whitman Myth," *Papers of the Bibliographical Society of America* 52 (Second Quarter 1958): 73–92; and *Solitary Singer,* 600.

7. E. L. Doctorow, *The Waterworks* (New York: Random House, 1994), 16; and "The Transcendentalist," in *Nature, Addresses, and Lectures* (Boston: Houghton Mifflin, 1890), 313.

8. For Whitman's comment on the various forms of the first *Leaves,* see *WWC,* VIII, 351. The manuscript suggesting "Song of Myself" with only five divisions is in the Humanities Research Center, University of Texas at Austin. I am indebted to Professor Ed Folsom for calling it to my attention.

9. *WWC,* III, 375; and C. Carroll Hollis, *Language and Style in Leaves of Grass* (Baton Rouge: Louisiana State University Press, 1983), 4.

10. *C,* II, 99–100; quoted in Ivan Marki, *The Trial of the Poet: An Interpretation of the First Edition of Leaves of Grass* (New York: Columbia University Press, 1976), 13–14.

11. These words, in the poet's hand, are found in a paperbound copy of *Leaves of Grass* in the Oscar Lion Collection, New York Public Library.

12. Whitman's anonymous book reviews, in addition to "Walt Whitman, A Brooklyn Boy," were entitled "Walt Whitman and His Poems," *Democratic Review,* September 1855, pp. 2–4, and "An English [Alfred Lord Tennyson] and an American Poet," *American Phrenological Journal,* October 1855, pp. 5–7. The other reviews bound into the second issue of

Leaves of Grass (1855) were E. P. Whipple's review of Rufus Wilmot Griswold's *The Poets and Poetry of America* (*North American Review*, January 1844, p. 1); Charles Eliot Norton's review of *Leaves of Grass* (*Putnam's Monthly Magazine*, September 1855, pp. 4–5); "Have Great Poets Become Impossible?" (*London Eclectic Review*, July 1850, pp. 7–8); and "Extracts from Letters and Reviews." Most of these reviews are reprinted in *Walt Whitman: The Contemporary Reviews*, ed. Kenneth M. Price (Cambridge: Cambridge University Press, 1996).

13. Roy Harvey Pearce, *The Continuity of American Poetry* (Princeton: Princeton University Press, 1961), 165; and Nancy Craig Simmons, "Coleridge's American Reputation, 1800–1853," *Journal of English and Germanic Philology* 87 (July 1988): 359–81.

14. "Whitman's Leaves of Grass," *Putnam's Monthly* 6 (September 1855): 321–23, in *Walt Whitman: The Contemporary Reviews*, 15. The author was Charles Eliot Norton, who kept secret the fact that his admiration of Whitman's gift included the composition of a poem in the style of *Leaves of Grass*. See *A Leaf from Shady Hill*, ed. Kenneth B. Murdock (Cambridge: Harvard University Press, 1928).

15. *Letters of Ralph Waldo Emerson*, ed. Eleanor M. Tilton (New York: Columbia University Press, 1990), VII, 323.

16. *NYD*, 240 n. 28; see also *In Re*, 13–21.

17. *NYD*, 154.

18. Moncure Conway, "Walt Whitman," *Fortnightly Review* 6 (October 15, 1866): 538–48 (see in particular p. 545, where Conway states, "I found him on the appointed morning setting in type . . . a paper from the *Democratic Review* ["An English and an American Poet"], urging the superiority of Walt Whitman's poetry over that of Tennyson"); and *Autobiography: Memories and Experiences* (Boston: Houghton Mifflin, 1904), I, 215–16.

19. Gay Wilson Allen, *New Walt Whitman Handbook* (New York: New York University Press, 1975), 82; "Quit house-building in the spring of 1855 to print and publish the first edition. Then, 'when the book aroused such a tempest of anger and condemnation everywhere [Whitman told Bucke] . . . I went off to the east end of Long Island, and spent the late summer and all the fall . . . around Shelter Island and Peconic Bay,'" Bucke, 26; see also *In Re*, 35.

20. *LG*, xvi–xvii. The Emerson letter is quoted from the original in the LC. Unfortunately, in its text in *Letters of Ralph Waldo Emerson*, ed. Eleanor M. Tilton (New York: Columbia University Press, 1991), VIII, 446, a line was dropped by the printer.

21. *Journals and Miscellaneous Notebooks of Ralph Waldo Emerson*, ed. Ralph A. Orth and Glenn M. Johnson (Cambridge: Harvard University Press, 1983), XIII, 510.

22. Eleanor M. Tilton, "*Leaves of Grass:* Four Letters to Emerson," *Harvard Library Bulletin* 27 (July 1979): 337–39; and William M. Moss, "'So Many Promising Youths': Emerson's Disappointing Discoveries of New England Poet-Seers," *New England Quarterly* 49 (March 1976): 46–64.

23. *HW*, 336–38.

24. "The Eighteenth Presidency!" in *Walt Whitman's Workshop: A Collection of Unpublished Manuscripts*, ed. Clifton J. Furness (Cambridge: Harvard University Press, 1928), 108.

25. James E. Miller, Jr., "'Song of Myself' as Inverted Mystical Experience," *PMLA* 70 (September 1955): 636–61; reprinted in *A Critical Guide to Leaves of Grass* (Chicago: University of Chicago Press, 1957), 6–35.

26. Bryant's interest in prosody led him to some experimentation, too. "Thanatopsis," for example, was written in blank verse. Emerson's irregularity of rhythm also suggested a rebellion from regularly versified lines.

27. See Edwin Haviland Miller, *Walt Whitman's 'Song of Myself': A Mosaic of Interpretations* (Iowa City: University of Iowa Press, 1989), xxiii–xxix.

28. Allen, *American Prosody*, 217–43; and Bliss Perry, *Walt Whitman: His Life and Work* (Boston: Houghton Mifflin, 1906), 96.

29. See n. 8, above.

30. John Burroughs, *Whitman: A Study* (Boston: Houghton Mifflin, 1896), 7 (Burroughs's first book, published in 1867, was called *Notes on Walt Whitman as Poet and Person*); and Bucke, 171–72.

31. Emory Holloway, *Free and Lonesome Heart: The Secret of Walt Whitman* (New York: Vantage, 1960), 22. Holloway claims to have documents indicating that Van Velsor married at seventy-eight; yet according to *Solitary Singer*, 596, he died in 1837 at the age of sixty-nine. Since his first wife, Naomi, died eleven years before him, it is possible that he remarried.

32. "Whitman to Emerson, 1856," in *LGCRE*, 737; the earlier echo of this open letter is also from this page.

33. Gay Wilson Allen, *Walt Whitman Handbook* (Chicago: Packard, 1946), 24; this section on "Song of the Answerer" is not in the *New Walt Whitman Handbook*.

34. See Chapter 2.

35. *NYD*, 162–65; and William White, "Fanny Fern to Walt Whitman," *American Book Collector* 11 (May 1961): 9.

CHAPTER 8. THE NEW AMERICAN BIBLE

1. When Alcott first met Whitman in 1856, he found the poet "inviting criticisms on himself, on his poems"; *The Journals of Bronson Alcott*, ed. Odell Shepard (Boston: Little, Brown, 1938), 287. Whitman told Traubel, "I think I first thrived on 'opposition': the allies came later" (*WWC*, I, 237); *Notes and Fragments* (London, Ontario: A. Talbot, 1899), 84 (also cited in *NYD*, pp. 9–10); *Critic* 15 (April 1, 1856): 170–71.

2. It is not known for sure who received a complimentary copy of the first *Leaves of Grass*, except for Emerson and John Greenleaf Whittier, who allegedly pitched his copy into the fire in disgust; this legend, however, is challenged by Lewis E. Weeks, Jr., "Did Whittier Really Burn Whitman's *Leaves of Grass*?" *WWR* 22 (March 1976): 22–30.

3. Ralph L. Rusk, *Life of Ralph Waldo Emerson* (New York: Columbia University Press, 1949), 374; *Journals and Miscellaneous Notebooks of Ralph Waldo Emerson*, XIII, 510; see also

Edward Carpenter, *Days with Walt Whitman, With Some Notes of His Life and Work* (London: George Allen and Unwin, 1906), 166–67.

4. *WWC,* II, 130, 504; and *WWC,* III, 388.

5. *C,* II, 100; and Eleanor M. Tilton, "*Leaves of Grass:* Four Letters to Emerson," *Harvard Library Bulletin* 27 (July 1979): 337–39.

6. *Walt Whitman's Workshop: A Collection of Unpublished Manuscripts,* ed. Clifton Joseph Furness (Cambridge: Harvard University Press, 1928), 123. Whitman does, however, provide an interesting preface to *Two Rivulets* (discussed in Chapter 11).

7. *The Eighteenth Presidency!* ed. Edward F. Grier (Lawrence: University of Kansas Press, 1956), 43.

8. *UPP,* II, 88n; *In Re,* 35–36; *WWC,* I, 227; and John Burroughs, *Notes of Walt Whitman as Poet and Person* (New York: American Book Company, 1867, 1871), 19. On *Life Illustrated* stationery, Samuel R. Wells wrote Whitman on June 7, 1856: "After 'duly considering,' we have concluded that it is best for us to insist on the omission of certain objectionable passages in Leaves of Grass, or, decline publishing it. We could give twenty reasons for this, but, the *fact* will be enough for *you* to know" (LC).

9. *C,* VI, 30; *Walt Whitman: A Descriptive Bibliography,* ed. Joel Myerson (Pittsburgh: University of Pittsburgh Press, 1993), 19; and William White, "The First (1855) 'Leaves of Grass': How Many Copies?" *Papers of the Bibliographical Society of America* 57 (Third Quarter 1963): 352–54.

10. The advertisement ran between September 12 and October 4, 1856; Fowler & Wells had placed a similarly paced notice in the *Tribune* for the first edition in 1855 (*NYD,* 242 n. 49). For the circulation of *Life Illustrated,* see *NYD,* 200 n. 25.

11. "Greenwood Cemetery," *Life Illustrated,* September 6, 1856; the other essays (mentioned above) are reprinted in *NYD.* See *WWJ,* I, 9–10, 190–91, and 421–23, for earlier Whitman essays on Greenwood Cemetery.

12. See Jerome Loving, "'Broadway, the Magnificent!': A Newly Discovered Essay," *WWQR* 12 (Spring 1996): 215.

13. Sherry Ceniza, "Walt Whitman and Abby Price," *WWQR* 7 (Fall 1989): 49–67; and Bucke, 30.

14. *C,* I, 42.

15. *Brooklyn Daily Times,* November 16, 1857.

16. *New York Herald Tribune,* October 17, 1851.

17. *WWC,* IV, 473.

18. Whitman also drew from the Preface for "Liberty Poem for Asia, Africa, Europe, America, Australia, Cuba, and The Archipelagoes of the Sea" ("To a Foil'd European Revolutionaire").

19. James E. Miller, Jr., *A Critical Guide to Leaves of Grass* (Chicago: University of Chicago Press, 1957), 80.

20. Roger Asselineau, *The Evolution of Walt Whitman* (Cambridge: Harvard University Press, 1960), I, 85.

21. Moncure Conway, *Autobiography: Memories and Experiences* (Boston: Houghton Mifflin, 1904), 215–16; *Correspondence of Carlyle and Emerson,* ed. Charles Eliot Norton (Boston: James E. Osgood, 1883), II, 251; and *Letters of Ralph Waldo Emerson,* ed. Eleanor M. Tilton (New York: Columbia University Press, 1991), VIII, 445. See also Steven Olsen-Smith, "Two Views of Whitman in 1856: Uncollected Reviews of *Leaves of Grass* from the New York *Daily News* and *Frank Leslie's Illustrated Newspaper,*" *WWQR* 13 (Spring 1996): 210–16.

22. For Norton's secret admiration, see *A Leaf of Grass from Shady Hill,* ed. Kenneth B. Murdock (Cambridge: Harvard University Press, 1928); for Lowell's letter to Norton, see *Letters of James Russell Lowell,* ed. Charles Eliot Norton (New York: Harper and Brothers, 1894), I, 242; for Emerson's remarks, see his *Letters,* VIII, 445.

23. Rose Hawthorne Lathrop, *Memories of Hawthorne* (Boston: Houghton Mifflin, 1897), 311; the original is in the M. T. H. Howe Papers (Berg).

24. Walter Harding, *Days of Henry David Thoreau* (New York: Alfred A. Knopf, 1970), 370.

25. *WWC,* V, 103. The account of Whitman in 1856 by Alcott is found in *The Journals of Bronson Alcott,* 278–94; Emerson's description of Alcott is in James Elliot Cabot, *A Memoir of Ralph Waldo Emerson* (Boston: Houghton Mifflin, 1887), I, 280–81; see "Thoreau's Quarrel with Emerson," in Jerome Loving, *Lost in the Customhouse: Authorship in the American Renaissance* (Iowa City: University of Iowa Press, 1993), 88–105, for Thoreau's independence of Emerson; and Chapter 12 for Whitman's retractions.

26. *Letters of A. Bronson Alcott,* ed. Richard L. Herrnstadt (Ames: Iowa State University Press, 1969), 435, 669.

27. See Harding, *The Days of Henry David Thoreau,* 254, for the story of Thoreau's returned copies of his book. Whitman once said this of Thoreau: "I liked Thoreau, though he was morbid. I do not think it was so much a love of woods, streams, and hills that made him live in the country, as from a morbid dislike of humanity"; Herbert Gilchrist, *Anne Gilchrist: Her Life and Writings* (London: Unwin, 1887), 294. Yet on another occasion, he thought the "outdoor man" possibly "bigger" than Emerson for his "lawlessness—his dissent" (*WWC,* III, 375).

28. *WWC,* III, 403; and *Correspondence of Henry David Thoreau,* ed. Walter Harding and Carl Bode (New York: New York University Press, 1958), 441–42, 444–45.

29. *WWC,* III, 403.

30. *C,* III, 385–86.

31. *Sit,* 13; and *NYD,* 182, where Holloway claims that Whitman left his *Brooklyn Times* post "because he was expected to read proof for advertisements."

32. Charles M. Skinner, "Whitman as an Editor," *Atlantic Monthly* 92 (November 1903): 679–86.

33. Ezra Greenspan, *Walt Whitman and the American Reader* (Cambridge: Cambridge University Press, 1990), 184.

34. *Sit,* 120–55; "Our Daughters" appears on pp. 55–56.

35. *Sit,* 3.

36. See Chapter 4.

37. *Sit,* 89–90; the full text of the editorial appears in *Race and the American Romantics,* ed. Vincent Freimarck and Bernard Rosenthal (New York: Schocken, 1971), 46–48, but the editors make no allusion to the earlier, most often cited, misprinting in *Sit.*

38. "American Workingmen, Versus Slavery," *UPP,* I, 171–74.

39. *Walt Whitman's Workshop,* 34–35; for *An American Primer,* see *DN,* III, 728–58.

40. *Sit,* 53–54; for Fanny Fern's review, see Chapter 7. See also *WWC,* III, 237–39; and *C,* II, 89–90, for Whitman's recollection of the loan and its repayment.

41. The most recent and comprehensive study of Whitman's Pfaffian days (1858–61 according to most sources, though the exact dates are arbitrary) is Christine Stansel, "Whitman at Pfaff's: Commercial Culture, Literary Life, and New York Bohemia at Mid-Century," *WWQR* 10 (Winter 1993): 107–26.

42. Helen E. Price, "Reminiscences of Walt Whitman," *New York Evening Post Book Review,* May 31, 1919, quoted in *Whitman in His Own Time,* ed. Joel Myerson (Detroit: Omnigraphics, 1991), 279; and *WWC,* III, 116–18.

43. *NUPM,* I, 353.

44. *Solitary Singer,* 216; Whitman is listed as a copyist in *Lain's Brooklyn Directory* for 1859–60.

45. Richard Henry Stoddard, "The World of Letters," *New York Mail and Express,* June 20, 1893; reprinted in *NUPM,* II, 525–28, to which I am also indebted for the following description of Broadway.

46. Raffelty's is mentioned in *NUPM,* II, 487n. See *WWC,* III, 116, for Whitman's description of the size of Pfaff's. William Dean Howells, *Literary Friends and Acquaintances,* ed. David F. Hiatt and Edwin H. Cady (Bloomington: Indiana University Press, 1968), 67.

47. Howells, *Literary Friends and Acquaintances,* 65–66; and William Winter, *Old Friends, Being a Recollection of Other Days* (New York: Moffat, Yard, 1914), 91–92.

48. Justin Kaplan, *Walt Whitman: A Life* (New York: Simon and Schuster, 1980), 243. According to the *Saturday Press* of February 5, 1859, Aldrich was a co-editor of Clapp's paper.

49. Albert Parry, *Garrets and Pretenders: A History of Bohemia in America* (New York: Dover, 1930), 52–54.

50. *WWC,* V, 112; Skinner, "Whitman as Editor," 680; and *In Re,* 37.

51. Parry, *Garrets and Pretenders,* 42. Clare's comment appears in her "Thoughts and Things" column in the *Saturday Press* of February 11, 1860.

52. *WWC,* IV, 195–96; and *WWC,* I, 236–37.

53. *Saturday Press,* January 7, 1860; the review from the *Cincinnati Commercial* is entitled "Walt Whitman's New Poem," written possibly by William Dean Howells. *C,* I, 44; and

Whitman's Manuscripts: Leaves of Grass (1860), A Parallel Text, ed. Fredson Bowers (Chicago: University of Chicago Press, 1955), xxvi, xxxiii.

54. "Your and Mine, and Any-Day (A Yawp, After Walt Whitman)," January 14; "Poemet.—(After Walt Whitman)," February 11; and "Autopatheia; Dedicated to Walt Whitman," March 17. All three poems were by "Saerasmid" of Philadelphia.

55. Thayer and Eldridge to Whitman, June 14, July 27, and October 11, 1860 (LC).

56. Thayer and Eldridge to Whitman, February 10, 27, 1860 (LC).

57. The publishers' calling card in the Feinberg Collection (LC) describes the firm as "CONSTANTLY ISSUING BOOKS FOR THE PEOPLE" and asks for canvassers and agents to hawk their books.

58. Letter dated May 10 [1860], in *C,* I, 53–54; *NUPM,* I, 422, 427–28; and *Solitary Singer,* 242.

59. *C,* I, 49.

60. *WWC,* III, 439.

61. *PW,* 281–82.

62. See "A Sketch" (same title as one of Whitman's very early poems), in the *Saturday Press* of June 18 and August 4, 1860.

63. "Correction," *Saturday Press,* June 9, 1860; the review appeared on June 2.

64. For the possibility of Whitman's emotional involvement with Juliette Beach, see *UPP,* I, lviii n. 15. DeKock's *Guide to Harems* (1855) depicted carefree, financially independent women who participated in the sexual freedom of the city without threatening society or its norms.

65. "Manahatta," *Saturday Press,* June 9, 1860.

66. Juliette Beach to Henry Clapp, June 7 and August 13, 1860 (LC).

67. *WWC,* III, 117; and *WWC,* II, 331; see also "Whitman's Idea of Women," in Loving, *Lost in the Customhouse,* 109–24.

68. *Saturday Press,* January 14, 1860. In a letter to Whitman dated June 5, 1860, Thayer wrote: "I think that Miss Beach's criticism is just about the damnest piece of scolding ever written by a woman, who does not know what she is talking about. My wife was *indignant,* and I should not wonder if she wrote a reply to it" (LC).

69. See Jerome Loving, *Walt Whitman's Champion: William Douglas O'Connor* (College Station: Texas A&M University Press, 1978), 36–37 nn. 74–75.

70. Thayer and Eldridge to Walt Whitman, March 9, 1860 (LC). Later, when the firm approached bankruptcy, Thayer wrote: "Yes, Walt. Whitman; though men of the world and arch-critics do not *understand* thee, yet some there be among men and women who *love* thee and hold thy spirit close by their own" (August 6, 1860, LC).

71. *C,* I, 44.

72. Thayer and Eldridge to Henry Clapp, May 24, 1860 (LC); and *WWC,* III, 116–18.

73. *Saturday Press,* November 17, 1860. See also Ezra Greenspan, "The Earliest French Review of Walt Whitman," *WWQR* 6 (Winter 1989): 109–16, and "More Light on the Earliest French Review of Whitman," *WWQR* 8 (Summer 1990): 45–46; as well as Roger Asselineau, "The Earliest French Review of Whitman (Continued)," *WWQR* 8 (Summer 1990): 47–48. The first French translation of *Leaves of Grass,* by Jules Laforgue, was not published until 1886. The one alluded to in the *Press* was a hoax perpetrated by Clapp.

74. Roy Harvey Pearce, Introduction to *Leaves of Grass: Facsimile Edition of the 1860 Text* (Ithaca: Cornell University Press, 1961), xxv.

75. This version of the manuscript was originally purchased from Rome Brothers by W. E. Benjamin, the son of Park Benjamin, who published some of Whitman's earliest poetry in the 1840s. *Whitman's Manuscripts: Leaves of Grass (1860), A Parallel Text,* 64.

76. See Jerome Loving, "Emory Holloway and the Quest for Whitman's 'Manhood,'" *WWQR* 11 (Summer 1993): 1–17; see also Emory Holloway to Henry S. Saunders, February 20, 1917 (Brooklyn Public Library), where Holloway talks of first seeing the "male" version of "Once I Pass'd Through a Populous City."

CHAPTER 9. CALAMUS AND THE NATIONAL CALAMITY

1. *C,* V, 73. For recent studies arguing for, or assuming, the poet's homosexuality, see Robert Leigh Davis, *Whitman and the Romance of Medicine* (Berkeley and Los Angeles: University of California Press, 1997); Byrne Fone, *Masculine Landscapes: Walt Whitman and the Homoerotic Text* (Carbondale: Southern Illinois University Press, 1992); M. Jimmie Killingsworth, *Whitman's Poetry of the Body: Sexuality, Politics, and the Text* (Chapel Hill: University of North Carolina Press, 1989); Robert K. Martin, *The Homosexual Tradition in American Poetry* (Austin: University of Texas Press, 1979, 1998); Michael Moon, *Disseminating Whitman: Revision and Corporeality in Leaves of Grass* (Cambridge: Harvard University Press, 1991); and Gary Schmidgall, *Walt Whitman: A Gay Life* (New York: Dutton, 1997). See also Gavin Arthur, *The Circle of Sex* (Heyde Park, N.Y.: University Press, 1966), pp. 136–37.

2. Fredson Bowers, "Whitman's Manuscripts for the Original 'Calamus' Poems," *Studies in Bibliography* 6 (1953): 257–65; and *Whitman's Manuscripts: Leaves of Grass (1860), a Parallel Text* (Chicago: University of Chicago Press, 1955). See also Hershel Parker, "The Real 'Live Oak, with Moss': Straight Talk about Whitman's 'Gay Manifesto,'" *Nineteenth-Century Literature* 51 (September 1996): 145–60.

3. Kenneth S. Lynn, *Hemingway* (New York: Simon and Schuster, 1987), 38.

4. Boston district attorney Oliver Stevens to Whitman's 1881 publisher of *Leaves of Grass,* James R. Osgood, March 1, 1882 (University of Pennsylvania Library). The twentieth-century interest in Whitman's sexual orientation reached its boiling point in the Southold, Long Island, myth of schoolteacher Whitman's being tarred and feathered in 1840 for sodomy with one of his students. See Katherine Molinoff, *Walt Whitman at Southold* (Privately published, 1966); and David S. Reynolds, *Walt Whitman's America: A Cultural Biography* (New York: Al-

fred A. Knopf, 1995), 69–79. See Jerome Loving's argument against the possibility of the story's validity in *WWQR* 12 (Spring 1995): 257–61.

5. Jerome Loving, *Walt Whitman's Champion: William Douglas O'Connor* (College Station: Texas A&M University Press, 1978), 101–2; Gay Wilson Allen, *Walt Whitman as Man, Poet, and Legend* (Carbondale: University of Southern Illinois Press, 1961), 174–75; Edward Carpenter, *Days with Walt Whitman* (London: George Allen, Ruskin House, 1906), 56n, and "Some Friends of Walt Whitman: A Study in Sex Psychology," *British Society for the Study of Sex Psychology,* no. 13 (1924): n.p.; and Holloway, *Whitman: An Interpretation in Narrative* (New York: Alfred A. Knopf, 1926), 172–73.

6. *Memoirs of John Addington Symonds,* ed. Phyllis Grosskurth (New York: Random House, 1984), 189. If Symonds was preceded in his candor with Whitman, it was by Charles Warren Stoddard, who—though he asked no directions about the "Calamus" poems—alluded to them as if they were about "inverted" affections in his several letters to Whitman; see *C,* II, 81–82, 97; and *WWC,* III, 444–45.

7. *Memoirs of John Addington Symonds,* 151n.

8. *Memoirs of John Addington Symonds,* 157.

9. *Memoirs of John Addington Symonds,* 100, 189.

10. *C,* II, 158–59.

11. John Addington Symonds to Horace Traubel, November 13 and December 12, 1892 (LC).

12. Symonds to Whitman, August 3, 1890 (LC); partially quoted in *C,* II, 72n.

13. Whitman's answer to Symonds's letter of August 2 came on August 19; its draft copy in the LC is reprinted in *C,* V, 72–73; John Addington Symonds, *A Study of Walt Whitman* (London: John C. Nimmo, 1893), 68.

14. John Addington Symonds, *Studies in Sexual Inversion, Embodying: "A Study of Greek Ethics" and "A Study in Modern Ethics"* (Privately printed, 1928), 185.

15. *C,* V, 75; and Symonds, *Studies in Sexual Inversion,* 191–92.

16. Symonds to Whitman, September 5, 1890 (LC).

17. *LGCRE,* 739.

18. Lombroso fostered theories of innate criminality and the idea, in his *Man of Genius* (1891), that genius is a form of neurosis; Nisbit also equated genius with insanity in *Insanity of Genius* (1891).

19. *Memoirs of John Addington Symonds,* 64–65.

20. *C,* I, 143.

21. "Peeps from a Parasol," in *Ruth Hall and Other Writings,* ed. Joyce W. Warren (New Brunswick: Rutgers University Press, 1986), 272; and *WWC,* IV, 312–13.

22. The original autograph version of this letter is in the LC, along with a handwritten copy by Gustav Percival Wiksell, a Boston dentist and a member of Traubel's Walt Whitman

Fellowship, which flourished between Whitman's death and Traubel's in 1919. There is also an accurate typescript of Wiksell's copy (given to John Clopton Farley) in Lion / New York Public Library Manuscript Division (see *Solitary Singer*, 279). A third copy, only slightly different and apparently the result of sloppy transcription, appears in Emory Holloway, "Whitman Pursued," *American Literature* 27 (March 1955): 6.

23. George Odell, *Annals of the New York Stage* (New York: Columbia University Press, 1931), VII, 403. I am indebted to Martin G. Murray in helping me make this identification.

24. *WBC*, 3.

25. *WWC*, I, 332–33; and *PW*, 63, 70, 113.

26. *C*, I, 77.

27. *C*, I, 110–11; and Stephen M. Forman, *A Guide to Civil War Washington* (Washington, D.C.: Elliott and Clark, 1995), 53–55.

28. The pasted list of hospitals in Whitman's notebook (LC no. 94; "Return my book," in *NUPM*) is mentioned by Charles I. Glicksberg, who examined the notebook before it was stolen (during World War II) for *Walt Whitman and the Civil War* (Philadelphia: University of Pennsylvania Press, 1933), 152n. See also Forman, *A Guide to Civil War Washington*, 51; and Martin G. Murray, "Traveling with the Wounded: Walt Whitman's Civil War Hospitals," *Washington History* 8 (Fall/Winter 1996–97): 59–73.

29. Loving, *Walt Whitman's Champion*, 198.

30. *C*, I, 91n. The request was attached to H.R. 10707 proposed on February 1, 1887, by the Committee on Invalid Pensions:

> Walt Whitman dedicated himself during the period of the civil war to the unceasing care, as a volunteer nurse, of our sick and wounded soldiers. The almost devotional ministrations of the 'Good Gray Poet' are well known to the citizens of Washington and of the nation.
>
> Beginning his services in 1862, at the front, whither he had gone to attend a brother who had been wounded, he staid on after Fredericksburg through the depth of winter [an exaggeration since Whitman left for Washington on January 2, 1863], in the flimsy tents and in the impromptu hospitals, where thousands lay wounded, helpless, dying.
>
> Returning to Washington with the convalescent wounded, and at the time having no definite plans, but interested in the good work, he continued his visits to the hospitals and staid on, and on, gradually falling into the labor and occupation of nursing. Any place he could be of most good or render most service seemed most satisfactory to him.

The request concluded with testimonials from the *Philadelphia Progress* of November 11, 1882; William Douglas O'Connor; John Swinton; Richard Maurice Bucke; and Dr. Bliss. The report concluded that Whitman never recovered fully from the "hospital malaria" that struck him down in 1864; "He is now a permanent paralytic, and with the greatest difficulty gets from one room to another, in his humble little dwelling on Mickle street, Camden, N.J. He is 68 years old and poor, and were it not for small contributions from time to time, from friends who sympathize with him in his poverty, age, and helplessness, would actually suffer for the bare necessities of life."

A newspaper clipping dated "July 1884" in Whitman's hand states, "There are now about 325,000 pensioners of all classes, and of those 225,000 are soldiers themselves. The remainder are widows, minor children, and dependent parents, including 1200 survivors of the war of 1812, and nearly 3000 widows who served in the war."

These materials can be found in the Harry Ransom Humanities Research Center, University of Texas at Austin. For Higginson's attacks, see Chapter 1, n. 20.

31. See *C,* I, 76; and *Solitary Singer,* 275. In the *New York Times* of May 1, 1931, Charles I. Glicksberg printed a letter allegedly written by Whitman in the *Times* of March 15, 1863 (if true, the date is evidently in error) assailing the Quakers for their pacifism. The style is stiff compared to Whitman's other wartime journalistic contributions, but the content appears to match his sentiments in a letter to Jeff of March 6, 1863.

32. *C,* I, 83.

33. *C,* I, 68–70; this article was reprinted as "The Great Army of the Wounded" in Richard Maurice Bucke's *The Wound Dresser: A Series of Letters Written in Washington During the War of Rebellion* (Boston: Small, Maynard, 1898), 1–10. It was scattered into *Memoranda During the War* (1875) and *Specimen Days* (1883).

34. Margaret Leech, *Reveille in Washington* (New York: Harper and Row, 1941 [Carroll and Graf, 1991]), 206.

35. *C,* I, 89; "Letter from Washington," *New York Times,* October 4, 1863—reprinted in *UPP,* II, 30, 35.

36. For the dying soldier in the 154th NYV, see *PW,* 56–57. Whitman's attempts at communication with Thomas Sawyer are in *C,* I, 90–94, 106–7, 139, 185–86; and Lewis K. Brown to Whitman, July 17, 1863 (University of Texas at Austin); printed in *Drum Beats: Walt Whitman's Civil War Boy Lovers,* ed. Charley Shively (San Francisco: Gay Sunshine Press, 1989), 118. See *In Re,* 35, for George's initial reaction to *Leaves of Grass.*

37. *C,* I, 181.

38. "*David Wilson*—night of Oct. 11, '62, walking up from Middagh—slept with me—works in blacksmith shop in Navy Yard—lives in Hampden st.—walks together Sunday afternoon & night—is about 19"; "Horace Ostrander . . . slept with him Dec. 4th '62"; see *NUPM,* II, 496–97. For the speculation on "slept with," see Reynolds, *Walt Whitman's America,* 393–94. Burroughs's letter of December 19, 1863, to Myron Benton is printed in Clara Barrus, *Life and Letters of John Burroughs* (Boston: Houghton Mifflin, 1925), I, 109.

39. *C,* I, 79.

40. *C,* I, 120–21, 254; and *PW,* 61.

41. *GWW,* 90–110.

42. *Battle Chronicles of the Civil War 1863,* ed. James M. McPherson (New York: Macmillan, 1989), 16.

43. J. G. Randall and David Donald, *Civil War and Reconstruction* (Lexington, Mass.: D. C. Heath, 1969), 400.

44. *C,* I, 98, 110; "Our Wounded and Sick Soldiers," *New York Times,* December 11, 1864; and *PW,* 52–53.

45. *C,* I, 111, 115, 141; Leech, *Reveille in Washington,* 141, 205.

46. Randall and Donald, *Civil War and Reconstruction,* 401–5.

47. *C,* I, 114; *WWC,* III, 293; and Brown to Whitman, July 27, 1863 (University of Texas at Austin), reprinted in Shively, *Drum Beats,* 118.

48. *C,* I, 123–24, 136.

49. *C,* I, 87–90, 143–46; *Dear Brother Walt: Letters of Thomas Jefferson Whitman,* ed. Dennis Berthold and Kenneth M. Price (Kent, Ohio: Kent State University Press, 1984), 79.

50. *WBC,* 1–7; Clara Barrus, *Life and Letters of John Burroughs* (Boston: Houghton Mifflin, 1925), I, 107–10; and *Solitary Singer,* 300.

51. *WWC,* IV, 318 (letter dated November 8, 1863); and *WBC,* 7.

52. *C,* I, 175–83; and *WBC,* 4.

53. Justin Kaplan, *Walt Whitman: A Life* (New York: Simon and Schuster, 1980), 236. Whitman published the following essays about George and the adventures of the Fifty-First New York Volunteers: "From Washington. Military Anxieties . . . The Fifty-First New York," *Brooklyn Daily Union,* September 22, 1863, reprinted in *UPP,* II, 26–29; "Fifty-First New York City Veterans," *New York Times,* October 29, 1864, reprinted in *UPP,* II, 37–41; "A Brooklyn Soldier, and a Noble One," *Brooklyn Daily Union,* January 19, 1865, reprinted in *WWR* 20 (March 1974): 27–30; "Return of a Brooklyn Veteran. Campaigning for Four Years," *Brooklyn Daily Union,* March 16, 1865, reprinted in Glicksberg, *Walt Whitman and the Civil War,* 86–89; and "Our Veterans Mustering Out. Major George W. Whitman, Fifty-First N.Y.V.V.," *Brooklyn Daily Union,* August 5, 1865, reprinted in *Yale University Library Gazette* 49 (October 1974): 217–24.

54. After describing the disturbance to Walt, Jeff wrote: "To think that the wretch should go off and live with an irish whore, get in the condition he is by her act and then come and be a source of shortening his mothers life by years" (*Dear Brother Walt,* 85). Jesse had threatened Mattie after her daughter Hattie annoyed him. Apparently, Jesse Whitman was in a constant state of high nervousness. He usually spent his days in the basement of the house, the Whitman "living room" since the Brown family occupied part of the first floor and second, rocking Mattie's newborn child, California, later named Jessie. See Mattie's letter to Walt of December 21, 1863, reprinted in *Letters of Martha Mitchell Whitman,* ed. Randall H. Waldron (New York: New York University Press, 1977), 32–36.

55. Pension record for Thomas P. Sawyer, National Archives.

56. *C,* I, 186–88; and Charley Shively, *Calamus Lovers: Walt Whitman's Working-Class Camerados* (San Francisco: Gay Sunshine Press, 1987), 79, 84.

57. Thomas P. Sawyer to Whitman, January 21, 1864 (Berg); reprinted in Shively, *Calamus Lovers,* 82–83.

58. See Roger Asselineau, "Walt Whitman, Child of Adam? Three Unpublished Letters to Whitman," *Modern Language Quarterly* 10 (March 1949): 91–95; and Jerome Loving, "Emory Holloway and the Quest for Whitman's 'Manhood,'" *WWQR* 11 (Summer 1993): 5–8.

59. *GWW,* 102; and *Dear Brother Walt,* 65–66.

60. *NUPM,* II, 518 (this line became the basis for "Quicksand years that whirl me I know not" in *Drum-Taps*); and C, I, 185, 193.

61. *NUPM,* 669; and the military service record of Lewis Kirk Brown (National Archives).

62. Randall and Donald, *Civil War and Reconstruction,* 419.

63. Diary entry for May 9, 1865 (Yale University Library).

64. *GWW,* 119n.

65. *GWW,* 125–33.

66. *C,* I, 229, 236–37, 241, 254.

67. *GWW,* 133n.

68. Reprinted in Glicksberg, *Walt Whitman and the Civil War,* 178–80.

69. *UPP,* II, 37–41.

70. Yale University Library; reprinted in *Solitary Singer,* 318–19; see also *GWW,* 133 and 137–60, where George Whitman's Civil War diary is printed.

71. *C,* I, 256–57 n. 34; and *NUPM,* II, 747–48.

72. O'Connor to Whitman, December 30, 1864 (LC); reprinted in *WWC,* II, 400–403.

73. *C,* I, 252.

74. *C,* I, 250.

75. *WWC,* II, 137.

76. *C,* I, 257.

77. Henry B. Rankin, *Intimate Character Sketches of Abraham Lincoln* (Philadelphia: J. B. Lippincott Company, 1924), 54–57, where Rankin's version of Lincoln's exclamation is "There, see Walt Whitman, see his figure and swinging arms as he walks! There goes A MAN!" Rankin also claims that "Lincoln had given Whitman, by special executive order, the fullest hospital privileges at all hours" (p. 85). See also *WWC,* III, 178–79, where the source of Rankin's quoting of Lincoln is printed. The letter may have been a hoax; its author, "A. Van Rensellaer," has never been identified.

78. Cf. *PW,* 59–61.

79. *Walt Whitman's Drum-Taps and Sequel to Drum-Taps,* ed. F. DeWolfe Miller (Gainesville, Fla.: Scholars' Facsimiles and Reprints, 1959).

80. *Walt Whitman: A Descriptive Bibliography,* ed. Joel Myerson (Pittsburgh: University of Pittsburgh Press, 1993), 145–49; *LGCRE,* 278n; and Gay Wilson Allen, *The New Walt Whitman Handbook* (New York: New York University Press, 1975), 111–18.

81. Allen, *The New Walt Whitman Handbook,* 113.

82. *WWC,* II, 304; for an early manuscript version of the poem in the Feinberg Collection (LC), see *WWC,* II, 332–34. See also *Walt Whitman's Drum-Taps,* xxxiv–xxxvii. On April 1, 1865, Whitman signed a contract with Peter Eckler of Manhattan to stereotype 500 copies for $254.

83. *WWC,* I, 156.

84. *Walt Whitman's Drum-Taps,* xl. It is not clear in this account how Whitman might have missed the Lincoln train.

85. Burroughs told Myron Benton that Whitman "is deeply interested in what I tell him of the hermit thrush, and says he has used largely the information in one of his principal poems" (*WBC,* 24).

86. For a profile of Junius Brutus Booth, see Reynolds, *Walt Whitman's America,* 157–61.

87. "Sequel," in *Walt Whitman's Drum-Taps,* 9–10

88. *PW,* 98–99.

89. *WWC,* III, 472.

90. James Harlan to Dewitt Miller, July 18, 1894, in *WBC,* 25–26; *WWC,* III, 471–72; and *C,* I, 250–51.

91. Loving, *Walt Whitman's Champion,* 54–59.

92. *WWC,* V, 287–88.

93. John Townsend Trowbridge, *My Own Story* (Boston: Houghton Mifflin, 1903), 385. Trowbridge was biased and perhaps also unreliable on the subject of Whitman and Emerson; see Jerome Loving, *Emerson, Whitman, and the American Muse* (Chapel Hill: University of North Carolina Press, 1982), 96.

94. *NUPM,* II, 488. See also Whitman's old age memory of this story in *WWC,* II, 397.

95. *WBC,* 28.

96. Loving, *Walt Whitman's Champion,* 61–62, 149–56.

97. *WWC,* VI, 42.

98. *C,* I, 266–71; see also Eric L. McKitrick, *Andrew Johnson and Reconstruction* (Chicago: University of Chicago Press, 1960), 143–44.

99. *C,* I, 260–63; and *WWC,* I, 257.

100. *GWW,* 25–27, 135.

101. *PW,* 97; and *C,* I, 264–65.

CHAPTER 10. TRUE LOVE

1. This is the estimate of Martin G. Murray, who has written the most up-to-date and comprehensive study of Doyle and his relationship to Whitman, "'Pete the Great': A Biogra-

phy of Peter Doyle," *WWQR* 12 (Summer 1994): 1–51. Unless otherwise indicated, I have drawn my information from this monograph.

2. Murray, 13–14; and *Complete Writings of Walt Whitman,* ed. Richard Maurice Bucke, Thomas B. Harned, and Horace L. Traubel (New York: G. P. Putnam's Sons, 1902), V, 5–6. Allen claims that Whitman first mentions Doyle in his diary in December 1865 (*Solitary Singer,* 579 n. 115), citing *Complete Writings,* IV, 133, but there is no such entry there. Nor have I found such an entry in the *Complete Writings.*

3. LC; printed in *UPP,* I, 96; and *NUPM,* II, 888–89.

4. See *NUPM,* II, 891–94, for a brief biography of Doyle.

5. In one letter, Doyle writes on September 27, 1868, echoing Whitman's letter, "Jim Sorrill Sends his love & best respects & says he is alive & kicking but the most thing that he dont understand is that young Lady that said you make such a good bed fellow" (Pierpont Morgan Library; quoted in *C,* II, 51n).

6. *C,* II, 88.

7. Eric L. McKitrick, *Andrew Johnson and Reconstruction* (Chicago: University of Chicago Press, 1960), 48–51.

8. Thomas A. Bailey, *The American Pageant: A History of the Republic* (Lexington, Mass.: D. C. Heath, 1975), 496–97.

9. McKitrick, *Andrew Johnson and Reconstruction,* 57–58; the Radical Republicans realized the color prejudice in the North and wanted the Negro vote to work only in the South. At the time only six northern states allowed blacks to vote, including New York. Whitman's home state was the only one of the six to require the ownership of property.

10. *C,* I, 261.

11. *C,* I, 280–81.

12. David S. Reynolds, *Walt Whitman's America: A Cultural Biography* (New York: Alfred A. Knopf, 1995), 463–94; and *C,* II, 70.

13. *C,* I, 282, 307; and LVVW to Walt Whitman [May 31, 1866], and LVVW to Walt Whitman, June 7 [1866] (Trent).

14. *C,* I, 282–83; and Helen E. Price, "Reminiscences of Walt Whitman," *New York Post,* May 31, 1919; reprinted in *Whitman in His Own Time,* ed. Joel Myerson (Detroit: Omnigraphics, 1991), 274–82.

15. LVVW to WW [December 10, 1865]; and LVVW to WW, April 7 [1868] (Trent).

16. "Walt Whitman's Actual American Position," in *Walt Whitman's Workshop,* ed. Clifton Joseph Furness (Cambridge: Harvard University Press, 1928), 245–46 n. 220. There is slight evidence that "Walt Whitman's Actual Position" may not have been written by the poet (since its attacks on journals included the *Galaxy,* which had published a number of Whitman's pieces in the late 1860s), but its sentiment otherwise caps the campaign begun in 1865 and 1866. Edward F. Grier, "Walt Whitman, the *Galaxy,* and *Democratic Vistas,*" *American Literature* 23 (November 1951): 349.

17. Howells's review in *Critical Essays on Walt Whitman,* ed. James Woodress (Boston: G. K. Hall, 1983), 56–58; and William Dean Howells to Thomas H. Donaldson, September 11, 1888 (LC).

18. *Nation,* November 16, 1865; reprinted in *Critical Essays on Walt Whitman,* 59–63.

19. Edith Wharton, *A Backward Glance* (New York: Charles Scribner's Sons, 1934), 186; Leon Edel, *Henry James: The Untried Years* (Philadelphia: J. B. Lippincott, 1953), 224n; and Leon Edel, *Henry James, the Master* (Philadelphia: J. B. Lippincott, 1972), 255.

20. Mary Elizabeth Burtis, *Moncure Conway, 1832–1907* (New Brunswick, N.J.: Rutgers University Press, 1952), 27.

21. *C,* I, 294n.

22. A fragment of this letter is printed in *C,* I, 287–88.

23. Jerome Loving, *Walt Whitman's Champion: William Douglas O'Connor* (College Station: Texas A&M University Press, 1978), 153–54.

24. *C,* I, 294.

25. *C,* I, 305; and *WWC,* III, 535.

26. *C,* I, 307, 309, 318.

27. *C,* I, 313–14, 316–17.

28. Frederick P. Hier, Jr., "The End of a Literary Mystery," *American Mercury* 1 (1924): 471–78. Burroughs did not include *Notes* in his Collected Works, which contained its own book on Whitman.

29. "Walt Whitman and His 'Drum Taps,'" *Galaxy* 2 (December 1866): 606–15; and John Townsend Trowbridge, "Reminiscences of Walt Whitman," *Atlantic Monthly* 89 (February 1902): 166. Since Trowbridge was devoted to the memory of Emerson and the literary establishment he seemed to represent, we may doubt the veracity of this confession—especially since it was reported ten years after Whitman's death. On the other hand, the workplace imagery suggests that Whitman uttered it.

30. Yet they rejected works he submitted in 1867 but published "The Ballad of Sir Ball" in their March 1868 issue; see *C,* I, 343n; Henry Raymond to O'Connor, April 2, 1866 (Berg); Grier, "Walt Whitman, the *Galaxy,* and *Democratic Vistas,*" 333; and O'Connor to William Conant Church, September 30, 1867 (William Conant Church Collection, Manuscript Division, New York Public Library).

31. Henry Raymond to William Douglas O'Connor, December 3, 1866 (William Conant Church Collection, Manuscript Division, New York Public Library); and *C,* I, 303.

32. James Speed to J. Hubley Ashton, December 29, 1866 (LC); partially quoted in *Solitary Singer,* 377; and *Oration of James Speed upon the Inauguration of the Bust of Abraham Lincoln at Louisville, Ky., February 12, 1867* (Louisville: Bradley and Gilbert, 1867). See also "Walt Whitman: Ghostwriter for James Speed? or 'None Goes His Way Alone,'" *Filson Club History Quarterly* 37 (October 1963): 305–24; and M. Lynda Ely, "Memorializing Lincoln: Whitman's 'Revision' of James Speed's *Oration of James Speed . . .*" *WWQR* 14 (Spring 1997): 176–81.

Shortly before his death in 1887, Speed gave another speech about Lincoln, to the Society of the Loyal Legion at Cincinnati, Ohio. It is recorded in his grandson's reminiscence, James Speed, *James Speed, A Personality* (Louisville: John P. Morton, 1914), 128–36, which fails to mention Whitman or his assistance with the first speech.

33. LVVW to Walt Whitman [May 14, 1868], and December 15 [1865] (Trent); see also *GWW,* 13–14.

34. Gay Wilson Allen, *The New Walt Whitman Handbook* (New York: New York University Press, 1975), 118; Arthur Golden, *Walt Whitman's Blue Book* (New York: New York Public Library, 1968); *WWC,* III, 472–73; and Loving, *Walt Whitman's Champion,* 59.

35. Another reason for playing down the Emerson influence was that Whitman began to hear rumors of Emerson's declining opinion of the subsequent editions of *Leaves of Grass.* In the second edition of *Notes,* published in 1871, Emerson is quoted as stating during a lecture in Detroit: "WW in his first efforts gave very high promise, but he has not fulfilled it since" (p. 112n).

36. On two occasions in 1889 and 1890, Whitman told Traubel about O'Connor's disapproval—also his own: (1) "John published *Notes* against my persuasions—O'Connor's too: our strong objections: but now I know, we both know, we were mistaken: John was right" (*WWC,* IV, 46); and (2) "O'Connor . . . warned me in those early years in Washington, to put my foot down on John's book—to have nothing to do with it—even allow it" (*WWC,* VI, 395).

37. John Burroughs, *Notes on Walt Whitman as Poet and Person* (New York: American Book Company, 1867), 67, 4, 39, 36.

38. *Solitary Singer,* 382–83.

39. *C,* I, 335–36.

40. W. C. Church to W. D. O'Connor, August 1, 1867 (LC); quoted in *C,* I, 336n; and John Burroughs to M. D. Conway, August 10, 1867 (William Conant Church Collection, Manuscript Division, New York Public Library); quoted in Grier, "Walt Whitman, the *Galaxy,* and *Democratic Vistas,*" 335.

41. Jane McElhinney, *Only a Woman's Heart* (New York: M. Doolady, 1866); and *C,* I, 339–40.

42. "Democracy," *Galaxy* 4 (December 1867): 921, 924.

43. "Democracy," 925–28.

44. *WWC,* II, 511–12; "The Ghost," *Putnam's Monthly Magazine* 7 (January 1856): 20–40; and "The Carpenter," *Putnam's Monthly Magazine,* n.s., 1 (January 1868): 55–90.

45. John Hay to W. D. O'Connor, January 8, 1868 (Brown University Library).

46. *Nation* 4 (December 12, 1867): 472.

47. "I do not wonder that there was a Christ; I wonder that there were not a thousand," *Journals and Miscellaneous Notebooks of Ralph Waldo Emerson,* ed. William H. Gilman, et al. (Cambridge: Harvard University Press, 1962–82), VII, 458.

48. For the fullest story of Swinburne's deteriorating view of Whitman, see Terry L. Meyers, "Swinburne and Whitman: Further Evidence," *WWQR* 14 (Summer 1996): 1–11; M. Wynn Thomas, "Whitman in the British Isles," in *Walt Whitman and the World,* ed. Gay Wilson Allen and Ed Folsom (Iowa City: University of Iowa Press, 1995), 12, 29–30; and William J. Goede, "Swinburne and the Whitmaniacs," *Victorian Review* 33 (Spring 1968): 16–21. See Chapter 11, n. 45.

49. *WWC,* III, 157; and LVWW to Walt Whitman (March 13, 1868) (Trent).

50. *C,* II, 20, 26; *WWC,* I, 151; and J. Hubley Ashton to Charles W. Eldridge [1902] (Berg); see also *WBC,* 29; and Dixon Wecter, "Walt Whitman as Civil Servant," *PMLA* 58 (December 1943): 1101.

51. "Personalism," *Galaxy* 5 (May 1868): 540–47.

52. Allen, *New Walt Whitman Handbook,* 10–13.

53. *Critical Essays on Walt Whitman,* 65. The essay originally appeared in German in the *Augsburg Allegemeine Zeitung* of May 10, 1868; its English translation appeared in the *New Eclectic Magazine* 2 (July 1868): 325–29. See also Walter Grunzweig, *Constructing the German Walt Whitman* (Iowa City: University of Iowa Press, 1995), 11–17.

54. See Trowbridge to Burroughs, June 12, 1896 (Berg), where he talks about Whitman's "*naive* characteristics"; and *WWC,* II, 22.

55. Alvin H. Rosenfeld, "Whitman and the Providence Literati," *Books at Brown* 24 (1971): 84.

56. Rosenfeld, "Whitman and the Providence Literati," 89–90; this copy of *Leaves of Grass* is in the Brown University Library; Sarah Helen Whitman's letter to O'Connor of November 23, 1868, is in *WWC,* III, 505.

57. Marian Walker Alcaro, *Walt Whitman's Mrs. G: A Biography of Anne Gilchrist* (Rutherford, N.J.: Fairleigh Dickinson University Press, 1991), 73–75.

58. *Letters of Anne Gilchrist and Walt Whitman,* ed. Thomas B. Harned (New York: Doubleday, Page, 1918), 60.

59. *Letters of William Michael Rossetti: Concerning Whitman, Blake, and Shelly; to Anne Gilchrist and Her Son Herbert Gilchrist,* ed. Clarence Gohdes and Paull Franklin Baum (Durham: Duke University Press, 1934), 34.

60. "An English Woman's Estimate of Walt Whitman," in *Anne Gilchrist: Her Life and Writings,* ed. Herbert Gilchrist (London: T. D. Fisher Unwin, 1887), 292, 290.

61. *UPP,* I, lviii–lix.

62. *Letters of Anne Gilchrist and Walt Whitman,* 60, 63, 68–71.

63. *C,* II, 140; Alcaro, *Walt Whitman's Mrs. G,* 118–22; and *WWC,* IV, 313.

64. *C,* II, 140–43; and *Letters of Anne Gilchrist and Walt Whitman,* 70.

65. LC; partially quoted in Loving, *Walt Whitman's Champion,* 100–101.

66. For the news coverage of the poet's "death" and subsequent corrections, see Todd Richardson, "Walt Whitman's 'Lively Corpse' in 1871: The American Press on the Rumor of

Whitman's Death," *WWQR* 15 (Summer 1991): 1–22; and *C*, II, 123. For his health comment to Doyle and Mattie's death, see *C*, II, 86, 68; and *WWC*, I, 294. Jesse was buried in a "potter's field" near the Kings County Lunatic Asylum on March 23, 1870.

67. Gay Wilson Allen, *The Walt Whitman Handbook* (Chicago: Packard, 1946), 186–87.

68. Walt Whitman, *Democratic VISTAS* (New York: J. S. Redfield, 1871), 4–6.

69. See Arthur Golden, "Passage to Less than India: Structure and Meaning in Whitman's 'Passage to India,'" *PMLA* 88 (October 1973): 1095–1103.

70. 1855 Preface to *Leaves of Grass*, *LGCRE*, 729.

71. *C*, II, 15, 35.

72. The full identity of the letter writer has never been discovered. See *WWC*, III, 178–79; and Chapter 9, n. 77.

73. John Burroughs, *Notes on Walt Whitman as Poet and Person*, 2d ed. (New York: American Book Company, 1871), 109, 112–13, 122–23.

74. *C*, II, 37–38, 80.

75. *WWC*, I, 324–27.

76. *Washington Chronicle*, September 11, 1871; reprinted in Walt Whitman, *After All, Not to Create Only* (Boston: Roberts Brothers, 1871).

77. See *C*, II, 132n, for the press coverage of Whitman's delivery of "After All, Not to Create Only"; see also Allen, *New Walt Whitman Handbook*, 140.

78. LC; reprinted in *WWC*, I, 133–35.

79. *A Century of Whitman Criticism*, ed. Edwin Haviland Miller (Bloomington: Indiana University Press, 1969), 45.

80. Symonds to Whitman, October 7, 1871 (LC); the poem is reprinted in *In Re*, 1–12.

81. Dowden to Whitman, September 5, 1871; reprinted in *WWC*, I, 224–25; and *C*, II, 139–40.

82. *A Century of Whitman Criticism*, 43.

83. *C*, II, 57, 122–23.

84. *C*, II, 123; "Shocking Murder," *New York Times*, April 28, 1871; and "The Death of Foster," *New York Times*, March 22, 1873. John J. Barker, of the Second Tennessee Infantry, was another "rough" prone to violence, though it was due to mental derangement instead of alcohol abuse. In his lucid moments, Barker apparently reminded Whitman of his father—"a large, slow, good natured man (somehow made me often think of father), shrewd, very little to say," he told his mother on September 15, 1863 (*C*, I, 147). After the war, Barker tried to hang his eight-year-old daughter, terrified his wife and children with threats of violence, and killed a woman with a hunting knife in a bar after she first attacked him with a hatchet (Pension record of John J. Barker, National Archives).

85. *C*, II, 164.

86. *C*, II, 170, 165.

87. *C,* II, 175.

88. *C,* II, 142; and, *As a Strong Bird on Pinions Free* (New York: J. S. Redfield, 1872), Appendix, 7–8.

89. *C,* II, 178n. See also Harold W. Blodgett, "Walt Whitman's Dartmouth Visit," *Dartmouth Alumni Magazine* 25 (February 1933): 13–15; *WBC,* 73; and Bliss Perry, *Walt Whitman* (Boston: Houghton Mifflin, 1906), 203–5.

90. *The Dartmouth* 6 (January 1872): 10.

91. Perry to Charles F. Richardson, September 22, 1905 (Dartmouth Archives); Perry, *Walt Whitman,* 203–9.

92. George Goodhue, "Dartmouth College in 1872" (Unpublished memoir, Dartmouth Archives), 1–5; and *The Dartmouth* 6 (February 1872): 82, 85.

93. *C,* II, 178n; and Perry, *Walt Whitman,* 204.

94. *The [Concord, N.H.] People* 5, no. 2 (July 4, 1872): n.p. The "United Fraternity" of Dartmouth paid half of these expenses (Dartmouth Archives).

95. *C,* II, 180.

96. When Burroughs's *Galaxy* article on Whitman appeared, Heyde sent Whitman a copy of it along with a copy of Richard Grant White on Swinburne. He praised Swinburne effusively and had the following to say about Whitman's work: "There is enough beauty in your 'Leaves' to make a rare book, and not cast out sensuous extravagance either. But you are wonderfully, woefully, mistaken in the privileage [*sic*] you take of being merely savagely material, and consequently offensively vulgar" (March 1867, printed in *Faint Clews and Indirections: Manuscripts of Walt Whitman and His Family,* ed. Clarence Gohdes and Rollo G. Silver (Durham: Duke University Press, 1949), 223–24. For Heyde's cigar smoking, see Hannah Louisa Whitman Heyde to Thomas Jefferson Whitman, n.d. (Berg).

97. C. L. Heyde, "To the Swallows," *Burlington Free Press,* April 26, 1856.

98. *C,* II, 182

99. *C,* II, 185.

100. *C,* II, 186n. After his mother's death in May 1873 he drew up another will, dated June 29, 1888; see *WWC,* I, 310–12.

101. *WBC,* 96.

102. Charles W. Eldridge to John Burroughs, March 7 and April 4, 1896 (Berg).

103. Diary note of Ellen O'Connor, October 5, 1889 (University of Pennsylvania Library). See also Chapter 5, n. 37.

104. *WWC,* III, 75–76.

105. *WBC,* 96.

106. Florence B. Freedman, "New Light on an Old Quarrel: Walt Whitman and William Douglas O'Connor," *WWR* 11 (June 1965): 29; see also Freedman, *William Douglas O'Connor: Walt Whitman's Chosen Knight* (Athens: Ohio University Press, 1985), 144–62. For the possi-

bility of O'Connor's unfaithfulness to his wife and the possibility of his having contracted a venereal disease, see Loving, *Walt Whitman's Champion,* 143n.

107. Bucke, 45–46.

108. Price, "Reminiscences of Walt Whitman," *Whitman in His Own Time,* 282; and *C,* II, 242.

CHAPTER 11. THE GOOD OLD CAUSE

1. *C,* II, 285.

2. Eldridge to Burroughs, June 26, 1873 (Berg); partially reprinted in *WBC,* 83.

3. *C,* II, 223, 231, 235.

4. Edwin Haviland Miller, *Walt Whitman's Poetry: A Psychological Journey* (Boston: Houghton Mifflin, 1968), 56; the pillow passage occurs in *C,* III, 145, in an 1878 letter to Susan Stafford. Whitman wrote about the belongings in his "room" in the Stafford household: "I wish Debby [one of the Stafford daughters] to take charge of my big pillow, as it was made by & given me by my mother, & she slept on it & I shall want it again." For Emerson, see *Journals and Miscellaneous Notebooks of Ralph Waldo Emerson,* ed. William H. Gilman et al. (Cambridge: Harvard University Press, 1960–82), IV, 7, and XIV, 154.

5. *C,* II, 235.

6. See Chapter 10, n. 66, for the false report of Whitman's death in 1871; and Edgar A. Haine, *Railroad Wrecks* (New York: Cornwall Books, 1993), 14–15.

7. *C,* II, 329.

8. *C,* II, 285; see also *WWC,* VIII, 312–13.

9. "Nay, Tell Me Not To-Day the Publish'd Shame," March 5; "The Singing Thrush," ("Wandering at Morn"), March 15; "Spain," March 24; "Sea Captains, Young or Old" ("Song for All Seas, All Ships"), April 4; "Warble for Lilac-Time," May 12; "A Kiss to the Bride," May 21; "Halls of Gold and Lilac," November 24; and "Silver and Salmon-Tint," November 29, 1873. See *UPP,* II, 42–52, for the last two items, essays that describe the scenes in the House of Representatives and the Senate in early 1873 and were probably written just before Whitman suffered his first stroke.

10. [David Croly et al.], *Miscegenation: The Theory of the Blending of the Races Applied to the American White Man and Negro* (New York: H. Dexter, Hamilton, 1864), 49–50.

11. See Robert D. Richardson, *Emerson: The Mind on Fire* (Berkeley and Los Angeles: University of California Press, 1995), 363–69, 396, 429.

12. Croly et al., *Miscegenation,* 16.

13. *C,* II, 318.

14. *PW,* 760, 535.

15. "Democracy," *Galaxy* 4 (December 1867): 926–27; see also *PW,* 382.

16. "A Christmas Garland," *PW,* 762.

17. Diary of James Bryce, September 5, 1870, Bodleian Library; and *PW,* 759.

18. *C,* II, 265.

19. "'Tis But Ten Years Since," in *PW,* 310; and *C,* II, 266–67, 272, 278.

20. *C,* II, 272, 276. Whitman also apparently burned letters from Eldridge, Doyle, and Ellen O'Connor from this period.

21. *WWC,* III, 476; and *C,* II, 280–81, 306–7, 313.

22. *C,* II, 342n.

23. *C,* II, 324.

24. Whitman's autopsy in 1892 revealed a collapsed left lung as well as tubercles in the stomach, intestines, kidney, and heart. See *Solitary Singer,* 543.

25. *C,* II, 323.

26. "What Is Left of Edgar A. Poe," *Baltimore Gazette,* October 1, 1875; reprinted in *New York World,* October 3, 1875; and Jerome Loving, "The Good Gray Poe: The Poe Reburial and William Douglas O'Connor's Forgotten Tribute," *Poe Studies* 10 (June 1977): 18–21.

27. Reprinted in Rollo G. Silver, "A Note About Whitman's Essay on Poe," *American Literature* 6 (January 1935): 435–36, and partially in *PW,* 230–33; and Jerome Loving, *Walt Whitman's Champion* (College Station: Texas A&M University Press, 1978), 105–8.

28. The essays, published in the *Galaxy* of February and April 1876, were "A Word or Two on Emerson" and "A Final Word on Emerson."

29. *C,* II, 278; and *WBC,* 107.

30. *WBC,* 134.

31. *C,* II, 327.

32. "A Word or Two on Emerson," *Galaxy* 2 (February 1876): 258.

33. *C,* III, 50, 258; "A Final Word on Emerson," *Galaxy* 21 (April 1876).

34. Clara Barrus, *John Burroughs, Boy and Man* (New York: Doubleday, 1920), 182; and Richardson, *Emerson: The Mind on Fire,* 341.

35. "Walt Whitman's Actual American Position," reprinted in Clifton Joseph Furness, *Walt Whitman's Workshop* (Cambridge: Harvard University Press, 1928), 245–46.

36. See Portia Baker, "Walt Whitman's Relations with Some New York Magazines," *American Literature* 7 (November 1935): 282–83; Robert J. Scholnick, "Whitman and the Magazines: Some Documentary Evidence," *American Literature* 44 (May 1972): 223, 227n; and *WWC,* I, 184. Another provocation for the *West Jersey Press* article may have been a piece in the *Springfield Republican* of January 18, 1876, which attacked the "loose talk" about a neglected literary martyr severely in need of funds; see *C,* III, 20.

37. Holland to Stedman (Columbia University Library), March 22, 1979; quoted in Scholnick, "Whitman and the Magazines," 228.

38. Furness, *Walt Whitman's Workshop,* 246.

39. Scholnick, "Whitman and the Magazines," 222–46; and David S. Reynolds, *Walt Whitman's America: A Cultural Biography* (New York: Alfred A. Knopf, 1995), 516–17.

40. *C,* III, 20.

41. Edwin Haviland Miller, "Walt Whitman's Correspondence with Whitlaw Reid, Editor of the New York *Tribune,*" *Studies in Bibliography* 8 (1956): 242–49; and *C,* III, 23.

42. Peter Bayne, "Walt Whitman's Poems"; the essay was reprinted in *Littell's Living Age* 128 (January 1876): 95.

43. See Terence Martin, *Parables of Possibility: The American Need for Beginnings* (New York: Columbia University Press, 1995), 195–96.

44. Harriet Jay, *Robert Buchanan: Some Account of His Life, His Life's Work, and Literary Friendships* (New York: AMS Press, 1970 [1903]), 159–68.

45. Harold Blodgett, *Walt Whitman in England* (Ithaca: Cornell University Press, 1934), 110. Swinburne turned on a number of associates, and the assault on Whitman may have been caused in part by the uncertain state of Swinburne's health following a severe mental breakdown in 1879, after which he lived under the daily care of his friend Theodore Watts-Dunton. By 1887 Swinburne may have also become uncomfortable with Whitman's "Calamus" idea of male friendship. See Chapter 10, n. 48, for citations on the Whitman-Swinburne relationship.

46. Jay, *Robert Buchanan,* 161–62.

47. Blodgett, *Walt Whitman in England,* 79; and *WWC,* I, 2.

48. Richmond Croom Beatty, *Bayard Taylor: Laureate of the Gilded Age* (Norman: University of Oklahoma Press, 1936), 19–20; see also James C. Austin, *Fields of The Atlantic Monthly* (San Marino, Calif.: Huntington Library, 1953), 327–39.

49. Beatty, *Bayard Taylor,* 322.

50. "Editor's Table," *Appleton's Monthly Magazine* 15 (April 1, 1876): 437. Buchanan's other letters on Whitman in the *Daily News* are "Mr. Walt Whitman" of March 16 and "Walt Whitman" of March 17, 1876; the other *Tribune* editorials identified as Taylor's, using O'Connor's annotated copies, are "American vs. English Criticism," April 12, and ""Intellectual Convexity," April 22, 1876.

51. Loving, *Walt Whitman's Champion,* 207; and *DN,* I, 16.

52. *C,* III, 36–37.

53. *GWW,* 33.

54. *WWC,* I, 345; *C,* III, 38, 44; and Moncure Conway, "Walt Whitman," *Fortnightly Review* 6 (October 15, 1866): 538–48.

55. *WWC,* I, 346.

56. *C,* III, 47–48; and *WWC,* I, 2.

57. "Halls of Gold and Lilac," *New York Daily Graphic,* November 24, 1873; reprinted in *UPP,* II, 43.

58. *WBC,* 114; and *C,* II, 345n. According to one estimate, Whitman paid his brother and sister-in-law only $3.60 a week (*C,* III, 368n).

59. *C,* III, 51.

60. *Memoranda During the War [&] Death of Abraham Lincoln, Reproduced in Facsimile,* ed. Roy P. Basler (Bloomington: Indiana University Press, 1962), 18.

61. *Memoranda,* 44.

62. The four new poems were "As in a Swoon" (p. 207), "The Beauty of the Ship" (p. 247), "When the Full-Grown Poet Came" (p. 359), and "After the Interval" (p. 369).

63. *DN,* I, 45.

64. *C,* II, 344–45; and *C,* III, 45.

65. Miller, "Walt Whitman's Correspondence with Whitlaw Reid," 244–45.

66. Harry Stafford to Whitman, December 17, 1883 (LC).

67. Susan Stafford to Whitman, August 21, 1889 (LC).

68. See Edwin Haviland Miller in his introduction to and annotation of the Stafford material in *C,* III, 3–9. See also his *Walt Whitman's Poetry: A Psychological Journey;* and Stephen A. Black, *Whitman's Journey into Chaos: A Psychoanalytic Study of the Poetic Process* (Princeton: Princeton University Press, 1975).

69. *C,* III, 68. On April 4, 1876, Whitman told a printer in the office of the *Camden New Republic* that he was "anxious Harry should *learn the printer's trade thoroughly* . . . [and] *as fast as possible*" (*C,* III, 37; see also *C,* III, 37 n. 73). Edward Carpenter, "A Visit to Walt Whitman in 1877," *Progressive Review* 1 (February 1897): 407–17; reprinted in Edward Carpenter, *Days with Walt Whitman* (London: George Allen and Unwin, 1906), and quoted here from *Whitman in His Own Time,* ed. Joel Myerson (Detroit: Omnigraphics, 1991), 130–44, 133. Whitman describes his time at Timber Creek in *SD;* see *PW,* 119–36. Mrs. Stafford's letter to Whitman of May 1, 1876, is in the LC; partially quoted in *C,* III, 41n.

70. H. Buxton Forman to Walt Whitman, September 26, 1888; printed in *WWC,* II, 433–34.

71. *DN,* I, 48, 85.

72. *C,* III, 56. An excellent account of the Gilchrists' three years in Philadelphia is Marion Walker Alcaro, *Walt Whitman's Mrs. G: A Biography of Anne Gilchrist* (Rutherford, N.J.: Fairleigh Dickinson University Press, 1991), 158–86. For Burroughs's description of the Gilchrist family, see *WBC,* 138.

73. Edward Carpenter, "A Visit to Walt Whitman in 1877," in *Whitman in His Own Time,* 135–39, 152; and Alcaro, *Walt Whitman's Mrs. G,* 180.

74. Grace Gilchrist, "Chats with Walt Whitman," in *Whitman in His Own Time,* 151–66.

75. *C,* III, 93n.

76. *C,* III, 77; and *WBC,* 164.

77. *Calamus Lovers: Walt Whitman's Working-Class Camerados,* ed. Charley Shively (San Francisco: Gay Sunshine Press, 1987), 151.

78. *Calamus Lovers,* 101; and *WBC,* 20–21, 164.

79. *Calamus Lovers,* 169; and *C,* III, 216.

80. John Burroughs, *Birds and Poets with Other Papers* (Boston: Houghton Mifflin, 1877), 192, 204; and *Works of Henry Wadsworth Longfellow* (Boston: Houghton Mifflin, 1886), 108–9.

81. Thomas A. Bailey, *The American Pageant: A History of the Republic,* 602–5; *WWC,* I, 60; and *C,* III, 53n.

82. This informal talk was absorbed into *SD;* see *PW,* 140–42.

83. *C,* III, 147; *WWC,* II, 423; and Charles N. Eliot, *Walt Whitman as Man, Poet, and Friend* (Boston: Gorham Press, 1915), 149.

84. *C,* III, 67–68, 79.

85. Eliot, *Walt Whitman as Man, Poet, and Friend,* 152.

86. *C,* III, 90; and *Dear Brother Walt: Letters of Thomas Jefferson Whitman,* ed. Dennis Berthold and Kenneth M. Price (Kent, Ohio: Kent State University Press, 1984), 95n.

87. *C,* III, 97n. and 100n.

88. Barbara Knapp Hamblett, "Charles Louis Heyde, Painter of Vermont Scenery" (M.A. thesis, State University of New York at Oneonta, 1976), 26, 44, 65, 85.

89. *C,* III, 104n, 105.

90. Alcaro, *Walt Whitman's Mrs. G,* 208–11.

91. *C,* III, 118n.

92. Alma Calder Johnston, "Personal Memories of Walt Whitman," in *Whitman in His Own Time,* 260–73.

93. Eliot, *Walt Whitman as Man, Poet, and Friend,* 152; *Letters of Dr. Richard Maurice Bucke,* ed. Artem Lozynsky (Detroit: Wayne State University, 1977), 31; and *Walt Whitman's Canada,* ed. Cyril Greenland and Robert Colombo (Ontario, Canada: Hounslow Press, 1992).

94. *C,* III, 147, 161.

95. *PW,* 504–5.

96. For Whitman's voice, see Ed Folsom, "The Whitman Recording," *WWQR* 9 (Spring 1992): 214–16; and Larry Don Griffin, "Walt Whitman's Voice," *WWQR* 9 (Winter 1992): 125–33.

97. The best account of Whitman's western trip, and on which the following account is largely based, is Walter H. Eitner, *Walt Whitman's Western Jaunt* (Lawrence: Regents Press of Kansas, 1981). See also Robert R. Hubach, "Walt Whitman and the West" (Ph.D. diss., Indiana University, 1943).

98. *C,* III, 164.

99. Eitner, *Walt Whitman's Western Jaunt,* 20, 23, 27–35; and *PW,* 207–8.

100. Sidney H. Morse, "My Summer with Walt Whitman, 1887," in *In Re,* 382–83.

101. Eitner, *Walt Whitman's Western Jaunt,* 51.

102. In "Spirit That Form'd This Scene" (1881), he wrote: "I know thee, savage spirit—we have communed together / Mine too such wild arrays, for reasons of their own."

103. *C,* III, 168.

104. *WWC,* III, 412.

105. *C,* III, 172n.

106. *C,* III, 168.

CHAPTER 12. DALLIANCES OF EAGLES

1. *C,* III, 153n; *WBC,* 355; *WWC,* III, 483–84; and *Walt Whitman's Autograph Revision of the Analysis of Leaves of Grass,* ed. Stephen Railton (New York: New York University Press, 1974), 69–70.

2. *C,* III, 176.

3. "Emerson's Books (The Shadows of Them)," *Boston Literary World* 11 (May 27, 1880): 177–78; reprinted largely verbatim in *SD* (*PW,* 514–18). Whitman also printed part of the essay as "A Democratic Criticism. By Walt Whitman," in the *New York Tribune* of May 15, 1882. *Parnassus* (1874) featured Lovelace's "To Althea" and "To Lucasta" and Waller's "On a Girdle" (pp. 63, 73, 445).

4. *WWC,* IV, 440: Forgetting "A Christmas Garland" (1874), Whitman told Traubel, "I used to charge Emerson (it was the one single charge I ever had to make against him) with culture—submitting too many things to the literary measurements: but now . . . I feel half inclined to retract it" (March 28, 1889).

5. See James H. Coyne, *Richard Maurice Bucke: A Sketch* (1923); "The Amazing Dr. Bucke," *London [Ontario] Free Press,* April 9, 1960; Artem Lozynsky, *Richard Maurice Bucke, Medical Mystic* (Detroit: Wayne State University Press, 1977); and *Walt Whitman's Canada,* ed. Cyril Greenland and John Robert Colombo (Ontario: Hounslow Press, 1992). Bucke's first letter to Whitman, December 19, 1870, is found in *WWC,* II, 6–7.

6. *C,* III, 180–81.

7. *DN,* 619–20.

8. Walt Whitman, "Summer Days in Canada," *London [Ontario] Advertiser,* June 22, 1880; reprinted in *Walt Whitman's Canada,* 19–24; absorbed by *SD* (*PW,* 236–41 and 345–46). For the "frolic," see also *WWC,* III, 214.

9. "Beautiful Dreamers," starring Rip Torn and Sheila McCarthy, is the second known video based on the poet's life. The first, also starring Mr. Torn as Whitman, is a CBS docudrama entitled "Song of Myself," released in 1976. For Redpath's comment, see *C,* I, 123n.

10. "Letter from Walt Whitman," *London [Ontario] Advertiser,* August 26, 1880; reprinted in *Walt Whitman's Canada,* 25–28; *SD* (*PW,* 242–43); and *C,* III, 187.

11. Lozynsky, *Richard Maurice Bucke, Medical Mystic,* 77–78.

12. *WBC,* xxiv, 169–70; and *C,* V, 305–6.

13. *C,* III, 190–93.

14. *WBC,* 197–98. The bogus edition lacks the following statement on the verso of the title page: "Electrotyped at the Boston Stereotype Foundry. Printed by George C. Rand and Avery."

15. *C,* III, 186, 196n; and *WWC,* I, 250–51.

16. *WWC,* IV, 82; "Only Crossing the Delaware," *Philadelphia Progress,* April 5, 1879; reprinted as "Delaware River—Days and Nights," in *SD* (*PW,* 181–84); and *C,* III, 201

17. J. L. and J. B. Gilder, *Walt Whitman at Home* (New York: The Critic, 1898); and *WWC,* II, 112, 119.

18. "The Poetry of the Future," *North American Review* 132 (February 1881): 195–210, became with slight revisions "Poetry To-day in America—Shakespere—The Future," in *SD* (*PW,* 474–90).

19. "Patroling Barnegat," *Harper's Monthly* 62 (April 1881): 701, was first published in the *Philadelphia American* in June 1880.

20. George Parsons Lathrop to Walt Whitman, April 20, 1878; printed in *WWC,* II, 315.

21. *WBC,* 204–5; and William Sloane Kennedy, *Reminiscences of Walt Whitman* (London: Alexander Gardiner, 1896), 3.

22. *WBC,* 205.

23. *WWC,* IV, 166; and *Boston Herald,* April 16, 1881; reprinted in *Walt Whitman's Memoranda During the War [&] Death of Abraham Lincoln,* ed. Roy P. Basler (Bloomington: Indiana University Press, 1962), 34–35.

24. *WBC,* 205; and Kennedy, *Reminiscences of Walt Whitman,* 3n.

25. James C. Austin, *Fields of The Atlantic Monthly* (San Marino, Calif.: Huntington Library, 1953), 37–38; and Carl J. Weber, *The Rise and Fall of James Ripley Osgood* (Waterville, Me.: Colby College Press, 1959).

26. Weber, *The Rise and Fall of James Ripley Osgood,* 223.

27. *C,* III, 224n.

28. See Gay Wilson Allen, *The New Walt Whitman Handbook* (New York: New York University Press, 1975), 67–70.

29. The argument was subsequently stated in Richard Maurice Bucke, *Walt Whitman* (Philadelphia: David McKay, 1883), 147; and in Oscar L. Triggs, "The Growth of 'Leaves of Grass,'" *Complete Writings of Walt Whitman,* ed. R. M. Bucke, Thomas B. Harned, and Horace L. Traubel (New York: G. P. Putnam's Sons, 1902), X, 101–3. To make it stick, Whitman insisted on the Osgood arrangement for all future editions. Also thinking perhaps of the Worthington copies of his third edition, Whitman wrote on the copyright page of the 1892 issue of *Leaves of Grass:* "As there are now several editions of L. of G., different texts and dates, I wish to say that I prefer and recommend this present one, complete, for future printing, if there should be any; a copy and fac-simile, indeed, of the text of these 438 pages."

30. See Charles B. Willard, *Whitman's American Fame* (Providence: Brown University Press, 1950), 24–25; and Robert J. Scholnick, *Edmund Clarence Stedman* (Boston: Twayne, 1977), 94. Stedman's essay "Walt Whitman" appeared in *Scribner's Monthly* (over the muted objections of its editor, J. G. Holland, who wrote in the same issue that Whitman's style of poetry had been too eagerly accepted by the English as characteristic of the new American literature, but that it was not imitated in America), 21 (November 1880): 47–64; and with minor revisions in Stedman's *Poets of America* (Boston: Houghton Mifflin, 1885), 349–95. Parts of the *Scribner's* version also appeared in "Walt Whitman," *New York Tribune*, October 17, 1880; and "Walt Whitman's Naturalism" (i.e., his direct treatment of the unpleasant aspects of nature, or human sexuality), November 7, 1860.

31. *C*, III, 198; and *WWC*, V, 35.

32. *Poets of America*, 368, 353, 365, 394–95. Stedman's name comes up repeatedly in *WWC*. Whitman appreciated his humanity ("our most generous man of letters") but doubted his perspicacity as a critic: "You can't put a quart of water into a pint bottle: Stedman holds a good pint, but the pint has is [*sic*] his limit" (*WWC*, I, 188, 222).

33. Weber, *The Rise and Fall of James Ripley Osgood*, 189; see also *C*, III, 255. The *New York Tribune* review of November 19, 1881, began: "After the dilettante indelicacies of William H. Mallock and Oscar Wilde, we are presented with the slop-bucket of Walt Whitman." Whitman later remembered Winter as one of "the New York crowd of scrawlers." He remarked to Traubel, "There's little Willie Winter—miserable cuss!" (*WWC*, I, 61).

34. "How I Get Around at 60, and Take Notes," No. 5, was later absorbed into *SD* (*PW*, 278–80).

35. *WWC*, I, 324–25; and O'Connor to Whitman, July 12, 1883; printed in *WWC*, III, 128–30.

36. *C*, III, 251.

37. Richard Ellmann, *Oscar Wilde* (New York: Alfred A. Knopf, 1988), 47, 151–52, 162–66; and *Solitary Singer*, 502.

38. *C*, III, 263. Whitman later told Traubel, regarding Wilde, "I never completely make Wilde out—out for good or bad. He writes exquisitely—is lucid as a star on a clear night—but there seems to be a little substance lacking at the root." Yet he had "no sympathy with the crowd of scorners who want to crowd him off the earth" (*WWC*, II, 192). Ellmann, *Oscar Wilde*, 167.

39. Lloyd Lewis and Henry Justin Smith, *Oscar Wilde Discovers America* (New York: Benjamin Bloom, 1936), 65, 73–77; and *WWC*, VII, 366: "Years back [Stoddart] came over with Oscar Wilde, when Wilde was here in America and the noise over him was at its height. They came in great style—with a flunky and all that. And what struck me then, instantly, in Stoddart, was his eminent tact. He said to me, 'If you are willing—will excuse me—I will go off for an hour or so—come back again—leaving you together,' etc. I told him, 'We would be glad to have you stay—but do not feel to come back in an hour. Don't come for two or three'—and he did not—I think did not come till nightfall" (*WWC*, VII, 366).

40. Ellmann, *Oscar Wilde,* 169; and Lewis and Smith, *Oscar Wilde Discovers America,* 76.

41. Ellmann, *Oscar Wilde,* 166–72; *WWC,* II, 288; and Lewis and Smith, *Oscar Wilde Discovers America,* 74–78, 343–44.

42. George Ives Diary, January 6, 1901 (University of Texas at Austin); *C,* III, 264; *WBC,* 235; Ellmann, *Oscar Wilde,* 161, 171; and Elizabeth Robins Pennell, *Charles Godfrey Leland* (London: Archibald Constable, 1906), II, 112: "May 10, 1882 . . . Wilde . . . was fresh from Camden, and an hour at the feet of Walt Whitman."

43. "Gentlemen, our attention has been officially directed to a certain book entitled 'Leaves of Grass. Walt Whitman' published by you. We are of the opinion that this book is such a book as brings it within the provisions of the Public Statutes respecting obscene literature and suggests the propriety of withdrawing the same from circulation and suppressing the edition thereof. Otherwise the complaints which are proposed to be made will have to be entertained" (University of Pennsylvania Library; reprinted in *Complete Writings of Walt Whitman,* VIII, 290).

44. *C,* III, 267, 270–71; and Osgood to Whitman, March 4, 1881 (University of Pennsylvania Library; *Complete Writings of Walt Whitman,* VIII, 289).

45. *C,* III, 273, 281; and *Complete Writings of Walt Whitman,* VIII, 289.

46. "22 Specifications," autograph manuscript of William Douglas O'Connor (University of Pennsylvania Library).

47. *C,* III, 269–71.

48. James Ripley Osgood to Walt Whitman, April 13, 1882 (University of Pennsylvania Library; *Complete Writings of Walt Whitman,* VIII, 297).

49. *WWC,* I, 31–32; and *WWC,* IV, 327.

50. *C,* III, 224n.

51. *C,* III, 284.

52. Whitman royalty records and bank accounts are in the LC. See also *C,* III, 277, 294–300; *C,* VI, xi–xxii; and *WWC,* I, 98.

53. *C,* III, 280n; and Jerome Loving, *Walt Whitman's Champion: William Douglas O'Connor* (College Station: Texas A&M University Press, 1978), 132–38.

54. *Springfield Republican,* May 26, 1882.

55. Anne Gilchrist to John Burroughs, July 28, 1882, quoted in *WBC,* 220–22.

56. Chadwick's letter appeared in the *Tribune* of May 28, 1882. O'Connor's second letter, of June 18, was essentially a paraphrase of a letter or statement Whitman sent him on May 30, 1882; see *C,* III, 286–88; and Loving, *Walt Whitman's Champion,* 129–31, 226–32.

57. [William Winter,] *New York Tribune,* November 19, 1881; see *WWC,* III, 49, for speculation as to the identity of "Sigma."

58. At the intercession of the agnostic Robert G. Ingersoll, Postmaster General James H. Marr so ruled on July 1, 1882 (LC); see O'Connor's "Mr. Comstock as Cato the Censor," *New*

York Tribune, August 16, 1882, from whose first sentence Reid scrubbed the material in brackets: "Mr. Anthony Comstock's hostility to the nude [, of which an illustrious example was his famous prosecution of three unfortunate women whom he had hired to dance before him for over an hour, without clothing, in a New York brothel,] appears to extend even to the naked truth" (essay reprinted in Loving, *Walt Whitman's Champion,* 233–36). O'Connor also attacked the Boston postmaster in "Tobey or Not Tobey? That Is the Question," submitted to the *New York Tribune* with a date of September 16, but declined; it was printed in Horace Traubel's *The Conservator* on September 7, 1896.

59. *C,* III, 274. "A Memorandum at a Venture" first appeared in the *North American Review* 124 (June 1882): 546–50; it was later absorbed into *SD* (*PW,* 491–97).

60. *C,* III, 221; and *PW,* 494.

61. *C,* III, 266–67.

62. For the story of Whitman's revisions to *Walt Whitman* (1883), see *Walt Whitman's Autograph Revision of the Analysis of Leaves of Grass,* 63–187; and Harold Jaffe's introduction to the facsimile edition of *Walt Whitman* (New York: Johnson Reprint Corporation, 1970), v–xviii.

63. Jaffee, *Walt Whitman,* xi; and *C,* III, 301.

64. *C,* III, 308n.

65. *PW,* 563, 565; Gary Scharnhorst, "Whitman on Robert Burns: An Early Essay Recovered," *Walt Whitman Quarterly Review* 13 (Spring 1996): 217–20; and Roger Asselineau, "Whitman on Robert Burns: A Footnote," *WWQR* 14 (Summer 1996): 39.

66. *C,* III, 321, 326; and Robert Allerton Parker, *A Family of Friends: The Story of the Transatlantic Smiths* (London: Museum Press, 1959), 48; *Mary Berenson: A Self-Portrait from Her Letters and Diaries,* ed. Barbara Strachey and Jayne Samuels (New York: W. W. Norton, 1983), 13–15; and *WWC,* V, 52–54.

67. *Mary Berenson: A Self-Portrait,* 22–23.

68. Parker, *A Family of Friends,* 57; see also Logan Pearsall Smith, *Unforgotten Years* (Boston: Little, Brown, 1939), 92–108.

69. Smith, *Unforgotten Years,* 96.

70. *WWC,* I, 172.

71. Mary Whitall Smith to Walt Whitman, November 12, 1884 (LC).

72. *C,* III, 392–95.

73. *C,* III, 396–97.

74. *WWC,* III, 195; and *WWC,* V, 45–46.

75. *C,* III, 218.

76. Smith, *Unforgotten Years,* 112–22.

77. Robert Pearsall Smith to Walt Whitman, August 13, 1889, and October 28, 1890 (LC).

78. Edith Wharton, *A Backward Glance* (New York: Charles Scribner's Sons, 1933), 327.

79. *C,* III, 353; and *WBC,* 245.

80. See Jerome Loving, *Emerson, Whitman, and the American Muse* (Chapel Hill: University of North Carolina Press, 1982), 161–71, for speculation on Whitman's "slough" of the 1850s, never adequately explained by any critic or biographer.

81. *C,* III, 355.

82. Harry Stafford to Walt Whitman, November 28 and December 17, 1883 (LC); and *C,* III, 357n.

83. *C,* III, 358.

84. *PW,* 577–80; first published in *Baldwin's Monthly Magazine* in February 1884, and in *To-Day, the Monthly Magazine of Scientific Socialism* in May 1884. Whitman included the essay in *November Boughs* (1888).

85. *Solitary Singer,* 514; and *C,* III, 368n.

86. Amy Haslam Dowe, "A Child's Memories of the Whitmans" (Manuscript Division, New York Public Library), part of which is edited by Edwin Haviland Miller in *WWR* 13 (September 1967): 73–79; and *C,* III, 365.

87. *C,* III, 361, 368n.

88. *C,* III, 371n, 381–82; see also *DN,* II, 337.

89. *C,* III, 372.

90. *C,* III, 381.

91. *C,* III, 348; *WWC,* I, 147; and *WWC,* VI, 113–14.

92. Smith, *Unforgotten Years,* 103–4.

93. Edmund Gosse, *Critical Kit-Kats* (New York: Dodd, Mead, 1903), 100; and *WWC,* I, 40, where the year of the letter is incorrectly given as 1887.

94. *WWC,* I, 40; and *Critical Kit-Kats,* 97. See also *WWC,* VII, 404–5, where Whitman refers to Gosse as "our amiable dude"; and *WWC,* I, 245–46, for an earlier letter (December 12, 1873), in which Gosse is clearly obsequious.

95. Reprinted in Gilder and Gilder, *Walt Whitman at Home,* 13–14.

96. *C,* III, 398–99n, 403n, 409n, 385 (Whitman's bank book [University of Pennsylvania Library] is summarized in *C,* VI, xix); and *DN,* II, 343, 347.

97. *DN,* II, 347, 350, 353; and *C,* III, 387n, 396–98.

98. William S. McFeely, *Grant: A Biography* (New York: W. W. Norton, 1982), 503.

99. *Personal Memoirs of U. S. Grant,* ed. E. B. Long (New York: Da Capo, 1952, 1982), 20. Whitman removed the extra stanza when he printed "Death of General Grant" in *November Boughs* (1888).

100. Ernest Rhys, *Everyman Remembers* (London: Cosmopolitan Book Corporation, 1931), 24; and Frank Arthur Mumby and Ian Norrie, *Publishing and Bookselling* (London: Jonathan Cape, 1974), 323.

101. *WWC,* I, 125.

102. *C,* III, 407; Ernest Rhys to Walt Whitman, May 31, July 7, and September 25, 1885 (LC); *Walt Whitman: A Descriptive Bibliography,* ed. Joel Myerson (Pittsburgh: University of Pittsburgh Press, 1993), 138–39; and *WWC,* I, 124.

103. *WWC,* II, 73–75, 232; LC. These pieces were incorporated into *November Boughs* (*PW,* 572–77 and 591–97). Emerson writes in *Nature* (1836): "*Right* means *straight; wrong* means *twisted. Spirit* primarily means *wind; transgression,* the crossing of a *line; supercilious,* the *raising of the eyebrow.*"

104. *WWC,* I, 461; and James Redpath to Walt Whitman, October 20, 1885 (LC).

105. *C,* III, 411–13.

106. Thomas Donaldson, *Walt Whitman, The Man* (New York: Francis P. Harper, 1896), 172–93; Loving, *Walt Whitman's Champion,* 142; and *C,* III, 34n; *C,* III, 414.

CHAPTER 13. GOOD-BYE MY FANCY

1. *C,* IV, 17.

2. *WWC,* I, 404.

3. *WWC,* I, 359.

4. *C,* IV, 100, 110, 114, 125. The subscribers included William Dean Howells, Mark Twain, Charles N. Eliot, and the actor Edwin Booth (*WWC,* II, 299–300).

5. *C,* IV, 18.

6. For the various estimates concerning the total number of Lincoln lectures, see Henry Bryan Binns, *A Life of Walt Whitman* (London: Methuen, 1905), 332; William E. Barton, *Abraham Lincoln and Walt Whitman* (Indianapolis: Bobbs-Merrill, 1928), 187–216; and *Walt Whitman's Workshop,* ed. Clifton J. Furness (Cambridge: Harvard University Press, 1928), 203.

7. Ernest J. Moyne, "Walt Whitman and Folger McKinsey, or Walt Whitman in Elkton, Maryland: A Study of Public Taste in the 1880s," *Delaware Notes* 29 (1956): 103–17; Rollo G. Silver, "Walt Whitman's Lecture in Elkton," *Notes and Queries* 170 (March 14, 1936): 190–91; and Edward Carpenter, *Days with Walt Whitman* (London: George Allen and Unwin, 1906), 45.

8. *C,* IV, 25n; and *Philadelphia Press,* April 16, 1886.

9. Roy S. Azarnoff, "Walt Whitman's Lecture on Lincoln in Haddonfield," *WWR* 9 (June 1963): 65–66

10. *C,* IV, 26; and *WWC,* II, 2.

11. *WWC,* II, 114; *WWC,* I, 348; and *WWC,* IV, 256, 261.

12. *C,* IV, 32n, 38.

13. *C,* IV, 21, 32.

14. *Reminiscences of Abraham Lincoln by Distinguished Men of His Time,* ed. Allen Thorndike Rice (New York: North American Review, 1886), 469, 473, 475.

15. *Walt Whitman's Backward Glances,* ed. Sculley Bradley and John A. Stevenson (Freeport, N.Y.: Books for Libraries Press, 1947). For Whitman's indecision over a preface for

the definitive edition of *Leaves of Grass,* see *WWC,* II, 311. The only edition that properly carried one was the first, but he felt the need to go on defining his accomplishment. Even earlier precursors to "A Backward Glance" (or "Glimpse," as originally written) are evident in the preface to *As a Strong Bird on Pinions Free* (1872), the preface to the centennial issue of *Leaves of Grass,* and "The Poetry of the Future" in the *North American Review* in 1881 ("Poetry Today in America" in *Specimen Days*). The *Philadelphia Press* essay also appeared posthumously as "How 'Leaves of Grass' Was Made" in *Frank Leslie's Popular Monthly* in June 1892.

16. For a summary of the best theories about structure in "Song of Myself," see *Walt Whitman's "Song of Myself": A Mosaic of Interpretations,* ed. Edwin Haviland Miller (Iowa City: University of Iowa Press, 1989), xviii–xxix; see also Roger Asselineau's structure in *American Literary Masters,* ed. Charles Anderson (New York: Holt, Rinehart and Winston, 1965), 847–48. Whitman described *Leaves of Grass* generally as standing "for something higher than qualities. It is atmosphere, unity: it is never to be set down in traits but as a symphony: is no more to be stated by superficial [i.e., literary] criticism than life itself is to be so stated: is not to be caught up by a smart definition or all given up to any one extreme statement" (*WWC,* II, 373).

17. In the *Walt Whitman Handbook* (Chicago: Packard, 1946), Allen follows a description of Carl F. Strauch's structure with his own theory, on pp. 115–21. In the *New Walt Whitman Handbook* (New York: New York University Press, 1975), this material is replaced by a discussion of other structural theories that followed in the wake of Strauch (see pp. 75–77).

18. "A Backward Glance," in *Walt Whitman's Backward Glances,* 46.

19. *Walt Whitman's Backward Glances,* 47; see also *LGCRE,* 571.

20. *WWC,* II, 413; and Mary Smith Costelloe (Berenson), "Walt Whitman at Camden by One Who Has Been There," *Pall Mall Gazette* 44 (December 23, 1886): 1–2.

21. *WWC,* IV, 152; *C,* IV, 41n; and Barbara Bedford, *Bram Stoker: A Biography of the Author of Dracula* (New York: Knopf, 1996), 46–47. See also *WWC,* IV, 179–86, for two Stoker letters to Whitman in 1872 and 1876.

22. *Dear Brother Walt,* ed. Dennis Berthold and Kenneth M. Price (Kent, Ohio: Kent State University Press, 1984), 184n; and *C,* IV, 47–49. The lines were from the fourth sonnet in a group entitled "Three Friends of Mine." For a recent assessment of Longfellow's reputation, see Eric L. Haralson, "Mars in Petticoats: Longfellow and Sentimental Masculinity," *Nineteenth-Century Literature* 51 (December 1996): 327–55.

23. On February 26, 1894, Eldridge asked Burroughs: "Have you seen Symonds['s] book on Walt . . . part of it is abominable—and contains the very worst things ever said about Walt—It seems that 'Calamus' suggests *Sodomy* to him, and from some remarks he makes I judge he was suspicious about Walt's relations with Peter Doyle. It appears that Walt made an indignant denial of any such construction of his poems but notwithstanding all, Symonds puts it in. Truly I think much learning, or too much study of Greek manner and customs[,] hath made this Englishman *mad.* Was ever such folly or madness shown before by a profound friend?" (Berg).

24. William Sloane Kennedy, *Reminiscences of Walt Whitman* (London: Alexander Gardiner, 1896), vii.

25. *WWC,* IV, 512; and *C,* IV, 67n.

26. The two available stories about Maurice Henry Traubel's background differ slightly. There is a manuscript in the newly acquired Horace L. and Anne Montgomerie Traubel Collection of Whitman at the LC by Gertrude Traubel, their daughter, which maintains that Maurice fell in love with a Christian and had to leave Germantown after the marriage to avoid his angry father. It is labeled "Written by memory July 1954." In *WWC,* II, 252–53, it is stated that Maurice, who also frequently visited Whitman in Camden, "comes of Jewish stock, that he quarreled with his parents about religion when he was a mere boy: left home, weathered out life for himself; came to America with nothing but his brains and faith." The entry is dated September 3, 1888. In Sculley Bradley's introduction to *WWC,* IV, he describes Maurice as "a German by birth" who "came at twenty-one from Frankfurt-am-Main, where he had received a liberal education in the arts" (xi). I am indebted to Ed Folsom's foreword to volume 9 of *WWC* for some of my background on Traubel. See *WWC,* III, 407–8, for the meeting of Whitman and Traubel on the Camden Ferry.

27. Robert S. Guttchen, *Felix Adler* (Boston: Twayne, 1974), 23, 27, 44.

28. See the exchange of letters between Traubel and Wiksell (LC). Ed Folsom is now editing the relevant letters for publication.

29. Books about Traubel are Mildred Bain's *Horace Traubel* (1913), William E. Walling's *Whitman and Traubel* (1916), and David Karsner's *Horace Traubel* (1919); there is also one published in the former Soviet Union in 1980 entitled *Horace Traubel: Fame and Oblivion,* by Alla M. Luibarskaia. Traubel's monograph titles are *Chants Communal* (1904), *Optimos* (1910), and *Collects* (1914).

30. Gertrude Traubel testified that Traubel's notes "were written on small bits of paper to fit into the pocket of his jacket. . . . Within the hour of the words spoken, the material was put into the complete form [as it appears in *WWC*]. . . . There was no vacuum of time or emotion, thus preserving the vitality of the original conversation" (*WWC,* IV, x).

31. *WWC,* III, 44, 357–58.

32. James Hunter; see *WWC,* II, 435–36; and Barton, *Abraham Lincoln and Walt Whitman,* 209–16.

33. *WWC,* IV, 450.

34. *WWC,* II, 431; *C,* IV, 82n; and Barton, *Abraham Lincoln and Walt Whitman,* 209–16.

35. Kennedy, *Reminiscences of Walt Whitman,* 25–29; and *WBC,* 264–65.

36. Barton, *Abraham Lincoln and Walt Whitman,* 211.

37. See Chapter 9, n. 30; and *C,* IV, 56n.

38. Charles W. Eldridge to John Burroughs, April 21, 1892 (Berg).

39. *C,* IV, 87n.

40. Sidney Lanier, *The English Novel and the Principle of Its Development* (New York: Charles Scribner's Sons, 1883), 50, 58–61, 118. See also *WWC,* III, 128, where O'Connor comments on Lanier's attack in a letter to Whitman dated July 12, 1883.

41. Sidney Lanier to Walt Whitman, May 5, 1878; printed with facsimile in *WWC,* I, 208–9; the letter is also printed in *The Conservator* 7 (October 1896): 122.

42. Sidney Lanier to Bayard Taylor, February 3, 1878; reprinted in *Letters of Sidney Lanier: Selected from His Correspondence, 1866–1881,* ed. Henry Wysham Lanier (New York: Charles Scribner's Sons, 1899), 208.

43. Bayard Taylor to Walt Whitman, November 12 and December 2, 1866; printed in *WWC,* II, 148–49, 152–53.

44. *C,* IV, 88; *Anne Gilchrist: Her Life and Writings,* ed. Herbert Harlakenden Gilchrist (London: T. Fisher Unwin, 1887), v; and *Letters of Anne Gilchrist and Walt Whitman,* ed. Thomas B. Harned (New York: Garden City, 1918).

45. Marion Walker Alcaro, *Walt Whitman's Mrs. G: A Biography of Anne Gilchrist* (Rutherford, N.J.: Fairleigh Dickinson University Press, 1991), 229, 256n. Herbert Gilchrist's copy of *November Boughs* is now in the collection of the University of Texas Library.

46. Sidney Morse, "My Summer with Walt Whitman, 1887," in *In Re,* 370, 373–74; and *C,* IV, 92n. Although Whitman liked the bust Morse made of him, he regretted that Morse had not "got a better start in sculpture. . . . he is not quite steady enough at one thing ever to get the best out of it. He writes well—very well—but don't write best: he speaks well—very well—but don't speak best . . . and so with sculpture—his trade" (*WWC,* II, 388). See also Horace Traubel, "Sidney Morse: The Best of Him," *The Conservator* (March 1903): 8–9; and James B. Elliott, "Sidney H. Morse," *Humanitarian Review,* July 1905, 256–58.

47. *C,* IV, 131; *WWC,* I, 284–85. The Morse bust sent to Kennedy may have never actually reached Concord; see *WWC,* II, 466.

48. *C,* IV, 133, 133n; and *WWC,* IV, 155–56. The accuracy of Whitman's memory of his first meeting with Eakins is questioned in Ed Folsom, "Whitman's Calamus Photographs," in *Breaking Bounds: Whitman and American Cultural Studies,* ed. Betsy Erkkila and Jay Grossman (New York: Oxford University Press, 1996), 215–16, which suggests an earlier meeting—one early enough for Whitman to have posed for nude photographs (now in the J. Paul Getty Museum, Malibu, California), taken by Thomas Eakins around 1883. For a challenge to Folsom's argument, not only as to the date of the first Whitman-Eakins meeting but also as to the thesis that Whitman is the person posing for the nude photographs, see William Innes Homer, "Whitman, Eakins, and the Naked Truth," *WWQR* 15 (Summer 1997): 29–30. See also Ed Folsom, "Whitman Naked?: A Response," *WWQR* 15 (Summer 1997): 33–35.

49. *C,* IV, 98–99, 116, 133; *WWC,* II, 295, 458, 475–76; *WWC,* I, 131, 266. For other comments on these paintings, see *WWC,* I, 153–54; WWC, II, 289–90; and WWC, III, 526.

50. For Sadakichi Hartmann, see *C,* IV, 108n; and *WWC,* II, 281–82, 379; Hartmann later wrote the unreliable *Conversations with Walt Whitman,* a fifty-one-page monograph that appeared in 1895. In 1889 Whitman complained to Traubel, referring to Hartmann's "Walt Whitman.

Notes of a Conversation with the Good Gray Poet by a German Poet and Traveller," *New York Herald,* April 14, 1889, which quoted the poet criticizing Stedman: "he wrote down things I never said at all—things entirely alien to me, letter and spirit: things that sounded like anybody else but me: worse than that, he often made me say directly the opposite of what I believed, of what I must have said" (*WWC,* IV, 457). For John Newton Johnson, see Morse, "My Summer with Walt Whitman, 1887," 376–77; Kennedy, *Reminiscences of Walt Whitman,* 18–21; and *C,* IV, 94n.

51. Joann P. Krieg, "Grace Ellery Channing and the Whitman Calendar," *WWQR* 12 (Spring 1995): 252–56; *WWC,* II, 115–16; *C,* IV, 118, 126; *WWC,* III, 10; and *Endure: The Diaries of Charles Walter Stetson,* ed. Mary Armfield Hill (Philadelphia: Temple University Press, 1985), 201.

52. Hampton L. Carson to Walt Whitman, August 3, 1887 (LC); and *C,* IV, 122, 131.

53. *C,* IV, 136; *WWC,* I, 127; *WWC,* II, 8; and Lewis E. Weeks, Jr., "Did Whittier Really Burn Whitman's *Leaves of Grass?*" *WWR* 22 (March 1976): 22–30. "As the Greek's Signal Flame" was also published in *Munyon's Illustrated World* of January 1888.

54. *C,* IV, 138n.

55. Charles T. Sempers to Walt Whitman, March 3–4, 1888 (LC); "Walt Whitman and His Philosophy," *Harvard Monthly* 5 (January 1888): 162.

56. Sempers, "Walt Whitman and His Philosophy," 162. Kennedy, a student at the Harvard Divinity School who left without a degree, was also friends with Sempers in Boston (*WWC,* I, 243).

57. Sempers, "Walt Whitman and His Philosophy," 164, 157.

58. *C,* IV, 143; *WWC,* III, 463; and *WWC,* II, 233.

59. Ernest Rhys, *Everyman Remembers* (New York: Cosmopolitan Book Club, 1931), 121; and *C,* IV, 139, 143, 149n.

60. *WWC,* I, 259ff.

61. Horace Traubel, "Walt Whitman at Date," in *In Re,* 119–20; *WWC,* I, 280, 293–95, 297, 307; and *WWC,* IV, 162–63.

62. *WWC,* I, 464; *WWC,* II, 2–3; Harvey Cushing, *Life of Sir William Osler* (Oxford: Clarendon Press, 1926), I, 264–66; and *WWC,* I, 391, 367. Osler also wrote a long essay on Whitman; see Philip Leon, *Walt Whitman and Sir William Osler: A Poet and His Physician* (Toronto: ECW Press, 1995).

63. *WWC,* I, 439.

64. "Elias Hicks," in *PW,* 636, 645.

65. "Elias Hicks," in *PW,* 627.

66. See *Early Lectures of Ralph Waldo Emerson,* ed. Stephen E. Whicher and Robert E. Spiller (Cambridge: Harvard University Press, 1959), I, 164–82.

67. *Walt Whitman: The Contemporary Reviews,* ed. Kenneth M. Price (Cambridge: Cambridge University Press, 1996), 307–29.

68. *WWC,* II, 503, 506.

69. *WWC*, II, 297.

70. *WWC*, IV, 252–63.

71. *WWC*, IV, 264–65.

72. *WWC*, V, 155, 159, 169–70.

73. *WWC*, V, 191–92.

74. *WWC*, V, 163, 177, 202. Whitman disapproved, sometimes to the point of profanity, of President Benjamin Harrison's person and policies and predicted correctly that Cleveland would be reelected in 1892.

75. *C*, IV, 342–43.

76. David McCullough, *The Johnstown Flood* (New York: Simon and Schuster, 1968), 102–3, 147.

77. *WWC*, V, 266–67.

78. McCullough, *The Johnstown Flood*, 189, 220.

79. McCullough, *The Johnstown Flood*, 173.

80. *WWC*, IV, 452.

81. McCullough, *The Johnstown Flood*, 224.

82. Quoted in *WWC*, V, 172.

83. *WWC*, V, 238; and Robert D. Richardson, Jr., *Emerson: The Mind on Fire* (Berkeley and Los Angeles: University of California Press, 1995), 192, 396–97, 429.

84. *WWC*, V, 233; *WWC*, IV, 440; and *WWC*, V, 322.

85. *WWC*, VI, 121–22; and *C*, IV, 396. See also Jerome Loving, "Emerson's 'Constant Way of Looking at Whitman's Genius,'" *American Literature* 51 (November 1979): 399–401.

86. *WWC*, VIII, 305–6, 324. Woodbury also described Emerson, whose closest acquaintances were Thoreau and Alcott, as disliking "odd people"! He qualified this somewhat by saying that Emerson "enjoyed the unrestrained man and democratic poet, despite the odour his verses perspire [*sic*]." See Charles J. Woodbury, *Talks with Ralph Waldo Emerson* (New York: Baker and Taylor, 1890), 127–28.

87. *WBC*, 36–39.

88. *WWC*, V, 275, 393, 426.

89. *C*, IV, 352n, 362; and *WWC*, V, 330–31, 415. For Bertz, see also Walter Grunzweig, *Constructing the German Walt Whitman* (Iowa City: University of Iowa Press, 1995), 187–98.

90. *C*, IV, 382, 386–87.

91. *C*, IV, 354, 356n, 397, 399; and *WWC*, VI, 124–25.

92. *WWC*, VI, 175, 210, 212; and *C*, IV, 403, 408–9n.

93. *WWC*, VI, 318, 328, 360–69; and *PW*, 684–85.

94. *WWC*, VI, 415; and *C*, V, 26, 50 ("Don't invest thyself too heavily in those reforms or women movements or any other movements over there—attend to *thyself* & take it easy,"

Whitman advised Mary Costelloe on February 10, 1890. A description of Reisser's is found in Harrison S. Morris, *Walt Whitman: A Brief Biography with Reminiscences* (Cambridge: Harvard University Press, 1929), 105.

95. *C*, V, 50n; Horace E. Kittredge, *Ingersoll: A Biographical Appreciation* (New York: Dresden, 1911), 162–72; *WWC*, VI, 435–44, 446; *WWC*, VII, 221–23, 465–98; and *PW*, 686.

96. *WWC*, VII, 239, 300.

97. *C*, V, 122–23; and *WWC*, VII, 341.

98. *WWC*, VII, 397–98.

99. See *Walt Whitman: The Contemporary Reviews*, 347, 353.

100. *LGCRE*, 546n; and Herbert Bergman, "Ezra Pound and Walt Whitman," *American Literature* 27 (March 1955): 60.

101. *PW*, 689.

102. *LGCRE*, 540; and *PW*, 671–73, 687.

103. Jerome Loving and Alice Lotvin Birney, "'A Young Woman Meets Walt Whitman': Anne Montgomerie Traubel's First Impressions of Walt Whitman," *WWQR* 12 (Fall 1994): 104–5; *Solitary Singer*, 538; and John Johnston and J. W. Wallace, *Visits to Walt Whitman in 1890–91 by Two Lancashire Friends* (London: George Allen and Unwin, 1917), 99.

104. *C*, V, 205–6, 223. For the Bolton disciples, see also Joann P. Krieg, "Without Walt Whitman in Camden," *WWQR* 14 (Fall 1996 / Winter 1997): 85–112; and *C*, V, 3–4. See also Paul Salveson, "Loving Comrades: Lancashire's Links to Walt Whitman," *WWQR* 14 (Fall 1996 / Winter 1997): 57–85, where we learn that these late disciples—like the early ones—were socialist in their thinking.

105. Anne Montgomerie Traubel to Ellen O'Connor, December 30, 1891; and February 20, 1892 (LC); and Daniel Longaker, "The Last Sickness and the Death of Walt Whitman," in *In Re*, 403, 409. Besides pneumonia ("pleurisy") and tuberculosis ("consumption"), the cause of death at the autopsy was given as "Parenchymatous nephritis," not a known medical diagnosis today.

106. *WWC*, VIII, 181–82.

107. *WWC*, IX, 164, 167–68, 177, 208, 490–91.

108. *C*, V, 203, 265n. On December 11, 1891, Harned told Traubel: "I went down the other evening and broached that subject of the personal history to him, but he declared, 'I am too sick to give it to you today, Tom: it is a long story.' But I drew from him this much: that there were two women; that they are Southern born and bred; that the families hold their heads very high. He has grandchildren, and they seem to want to come and take care of him. He hears regularly from one young man" (*WWC*, IX, 220, 263).

109. *WWC*, IX, 600; Justin Kaplan, *Walt Whitman: A Life* (New York: Simon and Schuster, 1980), 53, and Longaker, "The Last Sickness and Death of Walt Whitman," in *In Re*, 406, 410. In another section of the issue of March 28, 1892, the *Times* lambasted Whitman for his vulgarity and formlessness. To call him a great poet, it said, "we [must] deny poetry to be an art."

The article concluded that "laziness and self-conceit seem to be at the bottom of Whitman's practice and of his theory." It granted him "a very great poetical sensibility" but faulted him for his catalogs.

110. *WWC,* IX, 619–20.

111. Morris, *Walt Whitman: A Brief Biography with Reminiscences,* 111.

112. Horace Traubel, "At the Graveside of Walt Whitman," in *In Re,* 441, 445; and *WWC,* IX, 607, 629.

113. "10:20 PM: Again at W.'s. W. lay stretched on a stretcher. I went into the room, uncovered and kissed him. . . . The body was already getting rigid. . . . The strange quiet smote me. I leaned over and kissed his forehead (oh! that kiss! and the afternoon's kiss, the life just gone!)" (*WWC,* IX, 601).

114. *WWC,* IX, 626.

INDEX OF WHITMAN'S WORKS

Works no longer attributed to Whitman appear in the General Index.

GENERAL INDEX

❋ ❋ ❋

Designer: Steve Renick
Compositor: Impressions Book and Journal Services, Inc.
Text: 12/14 Adobe Garamond
Display: Adobe Garamond
Printer: Haddon
Binder: Haddon